DISTRIBUTING STATUS

Distributing Status

The Evolution of State Honours
in Western Europe

SAMUEL CLARK

McGill-Queen's University Press
Montreal & Kingston · London · Chicago

ISBN 978-0-7735-4684-4 (cloth)
ISBN 978-0-7735-9856-0 (ePDF)
ISBN 978-0-7735-9857-7 (ePUB)

Legal deposit first quarter 2016
Bibliothèque nationale du Québec

Printed in Canada on acid-free paper that is 100% ancient forest free (100% post-consumer recycled), processed chlorine free

This book has been published with the help of a grant from the Canadian Federation for the Humanities and Social Sciences, through the Awards to Scholarly Publications Program, using funds provided by the Social Sciences and Humanities Research Council of Canada. Funding has also been received from the J.B. Smallman Publication Fund, Faculty of Social Science, Western University.

McGill-Queen's University Press acknowledges the support of the Canada Council for the Arts for our publishing program. We also acknowledge the financial support of the Government of Canada through the Canada Book Fund for our publishing activities.

Library and Archives Canada Cataloguing in Publication

Clark, Samuel, 1945-, author
    Distributing status : the evolution of state honours in western Europe /
Samuel Clark.

Includes bibliographical references and index.
Issued in print and electronic formats.
ISBN 978-0-7735-4684-4 (bound). – ISBN 978-0-7735-9856-0 (ePDF). –
ISBN 978-0-7735-9857-7 (ePUB)

    1. Awards–Social aspects–Europe, Western–History. 2. Decorations of honor--Social aspects–Europe, Western–History. 3. Medals–Social aspects–Europe, Western–History. 4. Social status– Europe, Western–History. 5. Social classes–Europe, Western–History. 6. Awards–Europe, Western–History. 7. Decorations of honor–Europe, Western–History. 8. Medals–Europe, Western–History. I. Title.

AS945.E87C53   2016 001.4'4094   C2015-908462-8
                                       C2015-908463-6

Typeset by New Leaf Publication Design in 10.5/13 Baskerville

To Claudia

Contents

Tables and Figures   ix

Acknowledgments   xi

Illustrations follow page   204

Introduction   3

PART ONE: BOURGEOISIE, ARISTOCRACY, AND
CULTURAL POWER   17

1   Rise of the Bourgeoisie   19
2   Persistence of the Old Order   33
3   Cultural Power   44

PART TWO: STATE, WAR, AND COLLECTIVE POWER   77

4   Theoretical Considerations   79
5   Conditions for Collective Action in Medieval Europe   91
6   Conditions for Collective Action in Early Modern and
    Modern Europe   97
7   Collective-Action Problems and the Honours of States   137

PART THREE: SOCIAL STRUCTURES AND DISCIPLINARY
POWER   195

8   The Middle Ages   198
9   Discipline in Early Modern and Modern Europe   206
10 Disciplinary Functions of State Honours   230

PART FOUR: STATUS STRUCTURES AND STATUS
POWER   255

11   Honours and Existing Status Structures   258
12   Status Struggles   272
13   Status Consequences of State Honours   291

State Honours in Comparative Perspective: A Global
Analysis   341
Conclusion: Toward an Explanation of Modern State
Honours   367
Epilogue: The Endless Spiral of Honours   372

APPENDICES   379

A   Was There a Rise of the Bourgeoisie or Middle Class?   381
B   Characteristics of Members of the Legion of Honour, the
Order of Leopold, and the Order of the British Empire   385
C   Cross-Tabulations of Characteristics of Honours and
Social-Political Characteristics of States and Societies
Sampled in the Comparative Analysis   407

Notes   419
References   451
Index   483

Tables and Figures

TABLES

7.1 Old and new features of the Legion of Honour   146

7.2 Meanings of numismatic and related terms as adopted in this book   170

III.1 Four basic types of disciplinary practices   197

14.1 Cross-cultural sample of twenty states and societies   354

14.2 Social and political processes associated with the evolution of state honours in Western Europe   357

14.3 *Gamma* coefficients between selected variables and honorific rewards   360

FIGURES

6.1 Growth in population of Europe, fourteenth to nineteenth centuries   99

6.2 Growth in population of the British Isles and France, fourteenth to nineteenth centuries   100

6.3 Growth in population of London and Paris, fourteenth to nineteenth centuries   101

6.4 to 6.6 Growth in population of selected European cities, fourteenth to nineteenth centuries   102–4

Acknowledgments

I am only too happy to express my gratitude to the University of Western Ontario, its libraries, and especially the Sociology Department, which have provided me with a wonderful place to teach and do research. I have also benefited from considerable research funding from the Social Sciences and Humanities Research Council and from several grants offered by Western, in particular a publication grant from the J.B. Smallman Research Fund.

Philip Cercone, Ryan Van Huijstee, and others at McGill-Queen's University Press have been immeasurably helpful. Eleanor Gasparik has been far more than a good copy editor and a joy to work with.

A great number of research assistants have contributed to this project over the years. I would most like to thank Laura Godsoe, Zheger Hassan, Aslam Khan, Heather Maddocks, and Nicholas Pettit.

I have exploited the knowledge and collegiality of many academics who have read and critiqued parts of the manuscript. Sociologists and political scientists include Joseph Bryant, Michael Gardiner, Edward Grabb, Helga Hallgrimsdottir, Kevin McQuillan, Murray Milner, Karen Stanbridge, and Richard Vernon. The British and Canadian historians who have been most obliging include Robert Bucholz, Jack Hyatt, Clyve Jones, Brock Millman, Nicholas Rogers, and Mark Towsey. I want to express my gratitude to Christophe Charle, Jonathan Dewald, and Paul Janssens, for their assistance in my research on France and the Low Countries. And I am pleased to convey my sincere gratitude to various historians who study non-European parts of the world. James Flath, Luz Maria Hernández-Sáenz, Timothy May, Kaushik Roy, Charles Ruud, Ian Steele, Michael Szonyi, Carl Young, and Dingxin Zhao helped to broaden my horizons.

I have been extremely fortunate to know two historians who specialize in heraldry and orders of knighthood. The research and publications of D'Arcy Boulton and Peter Galloway have made this project feasible. I have also benefited much from the numismatic expertise of Alan Stahl.

Several people read all or most of the manuscript and gave me both general and specific comments and criticisms: D'Arcy Boulton, Frédéric Caille, Penelope Corfield, Bruce Curtis, Alan Forrest, Peter Galloway, Bruce Morrison, Roger Manning, Eli Nathans, Peter Neary, and Michael Szonyi.

My largest intellectual debt is to my son, Robert Clark, who has been my first go-to person when I want to discuss a point or get a reaction to something I have written.

Peter Neary has been a rock of support through my entire career. My children (Laura, Joey, and Rob) and my nine grandchildren have been an overwhelming source of pleasure. Time and again they have pulled me away from my work on this book to my great benefit.

The book is dedicated to my dearest Claudia, even though one of the many things I admire about her is that she is interested in status less than anyone else I know.

DISTRIBUTING STATUS

Introduction

This book poses some simple questions, the answers to which are not so simple. In many parts of the world, but especially in relatively industrialized countries, vast numbers of honorific or status rewards are bestowed yearly or even monthly, not only by governments but also by churches, businesses, voluntary associations, and educational institutions. Multi-volume directories, such as Gale's *Awards, Honors and Prizes*, despite their massive size, cannot keep up with them all. We live in a world of awards that surpasses any other in human history.

And yet social scientists have given little attention to these recognition practices, and explanations for their rise have been sparse indeed. Nor has there been much interest in explaining the nature of present-day honorific awards. There is, of course, a large literature generated by those responsible for the expansion and by some social scientists that asserts the utility of honorific awards. The reasons given combine psychological, "rational-choice," and organizational conditions.

At the most basic level, psychological reasons for the utility of honorific awards are implicitly or explicitly grounded in behaviourist theory, which says that human behaviour can be understood in terms of positive and negative stimulus-response processes. An award or a prize is simply a positive stimulus. It is functional because it satisfies the need people have to be appreciated and recognized, because there is a basic human drive for status, and because people derive psychological satisfaction from bonding and inclusion, which honorific awards give them in the way that monetary rewards do not.

Rational-choice theory adds to this explanation the notion that it is in the interest of employers and governments to satisfy these basic psychological needs in order to motivate a high level of performance.

The organizational literature calls attention to the organizational advantages of honorific awards over other kinds of rewards. They are low in cost. They do not crowd out intrinsic motivations, but rather reinforce the psychic pleasure that people can derive from doing a good job, or serving the organization or national state to which they belong, an especially important advantage where egalitarian or anti-materialist beliefs are present. Honorific awards are also less subject to diminishing returns than monetary rewards; the more one works, the less time one has to enjoy the benefits of the latter. They also build commitment and loyalty to the organization or the nation. It has even been claimed that they can improve worker morale. And they can be utilized to promote the values of an organization, to provide it with publicity, and (perhaps) to raise its status. In particular, it has been put forth that, where employees must work relatively autonomously, honorific recognition is usually the best way to motivate them. Honorific awards are especially suitable when the performance is difficult to quantify, and for non-profit or volunteer enterprises. And finally, honorific awards can lead to additional rewards, both symbolic and material, and thus provide potential recipients with additional reasons to seek them.

While this literature certainly gives us an idea of why state agents or employers might be persuaded to introduce incentive programs of this kind, it does not answer the questions that most need answering. Why do most societies today have so many honorific rewards? And why did they evolve differently in Europe than in other parts of the world and take the particular form that they do today? The psychological needs that honorific awards allegedly meet are found in all societies, but the quantity and nature of honorific rewards vary. By the same token, if honorific rewards are rational and bestow organizational benefits, this would be the case in many societies, not just in present-day societies. And if they are favoured because they are less expensive than material rewards, this too would be true in other times and places.

Furthermore, this literature does not explain how present-day honorific awards came into being. What is functional does not automatically materialize. This is not to say that the functions served by honorific awards are irrelevant to an explanation of how they have emerged, but simply that recognizing these functions does not, in itself, explain why and how we have come to be blessed (or cursed) with so many honorific awards. Nor does the above literature tell us which of the functions allegedly performed by honorific rewards has been the most instrumental in their evolution. It is unlikely that all of the above functions have been equally important in all historical processes involving state honours. And finally, this literature does not explain differences between present-day recognition institutions and practices and those in earlier periods of history.

This book is based on the fundamental assumption that honorific awards today cannot be understood simply in terms of how they are seen and how they operate at the present time. They are a product of history, and how that product has been created over time must be fully understood if we want to explain current recognition practices. All reward systems are historically specific. Hence, different reward systems require different historical explanations. This does not mean that the psychological/rational-choice/organizational reasons are not helpful nor that there are no common conditions underlying honorific awards in different times and places. But how these multiple forces took effect and how they changed over time will be particular to different historical cases. A comprehensive explanation of all the honorific awards that are being distributed today can be achieved only by different researchers examining the historical evolution of different kinds of honorific awards in different countries.

Obviously, therefore, the question to be answered in this book is not why award systems in general have emerged but rather why a particular award system has emerged. This award system is the state honours system of Western Europe as it has evolved in the past four centuries. Although it is historically specific, this system has, for historical reasons, played a relatively significant role in the evolution of state honours in most countries in the world today.

In answering this question, however, an effort will also be made to advance our understanding of status. Some of the best research on status processes that has been done over the past several decades has used small-group experimental methods.[1] In this research, it is possible to manipulate human interaction to identify the independent effect of status processes. This is nearly impossible to accomplish in the real world, but the study of honorific rewards brings us as close as we can get to it. Honorific awards are all about status. Few other social phenomena elucidate status processes as clearly as honorific rewards do.

HISTORICAL EXPLANATIONS

The explanation I provide for the evolution of state honours in Western Europe can be divided into three broad (though not mutually exclusive) components, which draw on the psychological/rational-choice/organizational explanations but suggest how the conditions for these forces have changed in Western society over time.

Modernization Versus Persistence of the Old Regime

I begin with a way of thinking that attributes the expansion of honours to "modernization." This concept is meant to include a number of processes that presumably have evolved in Western national states and that distinguish them from more "traditional" societies of the past, and from many societies in other parts of the world today. Modernization as a sociological concept refers to changes that include industrialization, higher rates of social mobility, secularization, and democratization. Societies considered to be modern are also assumed to be guided by more universalistic criteria, achievement as opposed to ascriptive orientations, rationality, and flexible social structures organized around the rational utilization of resources. And modernization is almost always thought to entail a displacement of traditional elites by more modern elites.

Whether or not the concept of modernization is used, many references to honours in the historical literature can be placed under this rubric. The expansion of honorific awards has been seen as part of the process of democratization. Rewards formerly limited to a small elite have been extended to a larger segment of the population for many of the same reasons that civil rights, political enfranchisement, et cetera, have been extended to a larger segment of the population. With democracy comes the notion that everyone is now a contributing member of the national state, and so must all be encouraged to do their best and rewarded for doing so.

Another idea that can be placed in the modernization category is the belief that the volume of honorific awards in our midst is a consequence of the displacement of ascriptive orientations by achievement orientations. This distinction refers to the choices people make between treating others in light of who they are versus taking into account what they have done or can do. In some cultures and contexts, people will be guided by norms and role expectations that lead them to place priority on the attributes of others, while in other cultures and contexts people will give priority to performances. It has been suggested that the kinds of honorific awards that are plentiful in modern societies are less often found in societies where ascribed orientations predominate because role expectations are fixed and because rewards for what individuals have done are not seen as appropriate or effective. In contrast, in societies where achievement orientations predominate, it is generally held that achievement is highly contingent and so incentives are necessary to encourage it. It has also been assumed that honorific awards are more useful in modern societies because they provide a public measure of achievement that helps people to judge who is accomplished and who is less so.

Consistent with these assertions, it has also been claimed that the honours system became established in Western Europe during the long nineteenth century – that is, the late eighteenth century to the early twentieth century – as a result of the rise of the "middle class" or "bourgeoisie." In this view, the new rising class forced the state to distribute honorific rewards to non-aristocrats and to expand the number of such rewards to meet growing middle-class demand.

As will be seen in Part I, considerable evidence exists that calls into question the modernization thesis as an explanation of the growth of state honours in Europe. Indeed, there is equal evidence of the opposite – that state honorific rewards had Old-Regime origins and evolved as a result of the survival of Old-Regime beliefs and values. Not a few would contend, as did Arno Mayer many years ago, that Europe was predominantly an Old-Regime society until after the Great War.[2] Others would simply claim that a powerful residue of the Old Regime persisted until then. Whatever purpose they serve today, state honorific rewards, so the argument goes, were constructed by people still tied to this heritage.

Thus, we have two explanations – modernization and the persistence of the old order – that seem to negate one another. Part I seeks to evaluate and dissect them so that they can become part of a larger explanation.

Population Management

The second component of my explanation is what I call the population-management thesis. Some sociologists argue that praise, status, and status awards are employed as a mode of social control.[3] In
a similar vein, several scholars who have studied French decorations
see them as a *technique de gouvernement*.[4] They believe that honorific
rewards affect the behaviour of not only those who aspire to and
receive them but also a larger population, including people ineligible to receive them. This effect can be diffuse and pervasive, sometimes shaping an entire socio-political formation.[5] If we are talking
about state honorific rewards as opposed to honorific rewards in
general, we could argue that they have performed this function for
states and so have evolved with the evolution of centralized states.

The number of writers making assertions of this kind is small and
much of it merely suggestive. The mechanisms by which honorific
rewards have served as a mode of population management have not
been specified. Nor have they sufficiently explained why honorific
rewards have been adopted on such a large scale in Western Europe
during the past several centuries in comparison with other times
and places. In an effort to uncover these mechanisms, I identify two
major ways in which honours serve to manage people. Part II draws
on the large literature on the mobilization and organization of collective action. How can state honours help provide the conditions
that enable states to mobilize collective action? Can one explain the
evolution of state honours in Western Europe as a consequence of
changing conditions for collective action and organization? Part
III draws on the social-science literature on discipline, in which it
is often asserted that a significant transformation has occurred in
the past several centuries in the way in which people have been
socially controlled or disciplined and the part played by the state in
this disciplinization.[6]

Status Competition

The third component of the explanation I offer for the evolution
of state honours in Western Europe builds on the sociological literature on status, in particular the argument that there has been
an increase in status competition in Western societies during the

last two centuries. Greater status competition has emerged as a result of the weakening of traditional status hierarchies, the growth of myths of equal opportunity, higher rates of social mobility, the valuation of achievement and success, the exposure of people to a far larger number of competitors, and a breakdown in cultural monopolies.[7] Several of these changes provide material for the modernization explanation, but here we find less emphasis on ideational processes and more emphasis on structural and conjunctural processes. Honours are sought by individuals and distributed by institutions or groups in order to raise their status in their contest with other individuals, institutions, or groups. Awards lead to more awards as groups compete with one another over who is better than whom in any given social activity.

Some of this literature has been influenced by Pierre Bourdieu. These writers have promoted two particular concepts, "symbolic capital" and "symbolic power," to advance our understanding of status power. Unfortunately, these concepts have become overloaded – taken to refer to a range of social phenomena. In the present discussion, "symbolic capital" denotes the resources that a person possesses by virtue of his or her prestige and by institutional recognitions of that prestige, and "symbolic power" refers to the power that a person is able to exert by virtue of possessing this symbolic capital. (In later chapters, I refer to other meanings adopted by Bourdieu and his followers.)

Awards and prizes, especially literary and artistic prizes, constitute one of the forms of symbolic capital in present-day society. Awards and prizes have evolved, they claim, as a result of a complex process, which I will summarize as follows.[8]

It begins with a decline in traditional cultural monopolies and an increase in the autonomy of cultural spheres. The nineteenth and twentieth centuries have seen a growth in objectified and institutionalized forms of cultural capital in relatively autonomous markets. This has generated greater competition among and within spheres, and has given rise to new techniques of competition, one of which consists of prizes awarded for the best cultural production. Literary and artistic prizes are functional as a means for different protagonists to control the criteria of what is good art, and to have authority over the validation of good art. Prizes are part of a vast apparatus that establishes the authority of some to impose their criteria of appreciation on others; this apparatus includes galleries, museums, academies, salons, art schools, and specialized agents, such as dealers, critics, art historians, and collectors, all of whom are presumably qualified to impose on others a specific measure of value of artistic products. In addition, people struggle over what Bourdieu calls the "exchange rate" between different types of resources or "capital," that is, the extent to which one kind of capital determines another kind of capital. James English puts considerable stress on this exchange of capital and thinks that prizes facilitate the exchange of cultural capital with other kinds of capital. As instruments of cultural exchange, prizes enable symbolic capital to be turned into economic capital in an "economy of prestige." English contends that the evolution of literary prizes can be explained by the increase in cultural production, capital exchange, and the fungibility of capital over the past hundred years.

This kind of analysis has gone a long way toward explaining the evolution of cultural prizes over the past century or more. To contribute to a general explanation of the expansion of status awards, however, it needs to be broadened and incorporated into a more general approach. The expansion in honorific rewarding in Europe began well before the major changes in the nineteenth and twentieth centuries that led to these cultural prizes.

OUTLINE OF THE EXPLANATION
OF WESTERN-EUROPEAN STATE HONOURS

The thesis of the book is that the evolution of state honours in Western Europe is to be explained by a number of causal processes and causal mechanisms. The term "causal process" refers to short or long sequences of events or developments in which one is able to see that one thing leads to another, that events or developments evolve out of one another, et cetera. An increase in prices leads to a decline in consumption, a growth in the size of armies leads to new methods of command, rural-urban migration leads to a breakdown in traditional solidarities – these are all causal processes.

The meaning of the term "causal mechanism" varies in the social sciences. Usually it refers to regularities that enable us understand how causal processes take place. Very simple examples that enable us to explain the above processes include: people make rational choices; collective action requires coordination; and social distance among people reduces their solidarity.

Implicitly or explicitly the analysis of causal processes and causal mechanisms is the dominant mode of explanation among historians. Unfortunately, it is often dismissed as merely descriptive. In fact it is explanatory, and the present work relies mainly on this mode of causal explanation. In Chapter 14, however, I supplement the causal-process and causal-mechanism explanation of the evolution of state honours in Western Europe with a cross-cultural correlation analysis to determine if the kinds of correlations we would expect from the former are borne out by the latter.

Causal Processes

Among the causal processes that brought about the Modern phenomenon of state honours, two categories can be identified.

First are cultural and institutional lineages, that is, the evolution of certain values, beliefs, and practices that have passed from one generation to another. Most obviously, we are interested in lineages of honorific rewards, but other cultural and institutional lineages also played a role in the evolution of state honours in Western Europe. These include Greek and Roman heritages, Medieval Romanticism, heraldry, notions of chivalry, and Early Modern royalty.

Second are significant demographic and structural transformations. These include population growth, the emergence of centralized bureaucratic states, an increase in within- and inter-state competition, an expansion in the scale of war, and changes in the nature of warfare.

Attention to time and place is essential for understanding these causal processes and linking them to state honours.

Causal Mechanisms

A number of causal mechanisms have operated to bring about the evolution of state honours in Western Europe. In my view, two are especially critical.

ADAPTIVE SELECTION

The first causal mechanism is adaptive selection, or more precisely, cultural and social adaptive selection. The theoretical basis for it lies in the large body of literature known as socio-cultural evolutionism (or socio-cultural Darwinism, or cultural and social selectionism), which seeks to understand changes in human society using the

basic principles of Darwinian theory.[9] Cultural and social adaptive
selection refers to the adoption of cultural and social practices that
increase (or do not increase) adaptiveness.

The kinds of adaptive selection that led to the evolution of state
honours in Western Europe becomes apparent over the course
of this book, but I can preview the argument now. State honours
evolved through the efforts of rulers and state officials to meet challenges brought about by the above demographic and structural
processes. It is true that state honours formed a small part of the
practices taken up for this purpose, and it is likely that their contribution was modest in comparison with other practices. If I were
writing a book on how rulers and state officials tried to deal with
the demographic and structural challenges they faced, state honours would not be given much attention. On the other hand, in this
book, which seeks to explain state honours, efforts of rulers and
state officials to cope with these challenges offers, I believe, the best
answer. Parts II and III are devoted to providing this answer.

Adaptive selections do not come out of the blue. They are selected
from cultural and institutional collections that are available to those
who make the selections. Some cultural evolutionists consider these
collections to be analogous to gene pools, but most regard them as
more interconnected than genes in a gene pool. In the case of Western-European state honours, the relevant collections were the product of the cultural and institutional lineages just mentioned. They
are examined mainly in Part I of the book, though some important
cultural and institutional forces are not introduced until Part II.

STATUS COMPETITION

The second causal mechanism that requires special consideration
is status competition. The theoretical basis for understanding it has
already been indicated. In Part IV, its contribution to the expansion
of honorific rewards in Western Europe is examined from a perspective that is not unlike that of Bourdieu and his followers, but is more
Weberian. Status processes will be treated not as capital exchanges
but rather as struggles for power, one type of which is status power.
As well as the adaptive functions that were served – or that rulers
and state officials thought would be served – by honours, status competition had its own dynamic, which drove such practices and ultimately became a major force in the expansion of honours.

Notices

A few things need to be clarified before proceeding.

READERS

This is an interdisciplinary study intended for a varied readership: historians who study European history; historians who do not study European history; academics who take an interest in and know a lot about state honours; academics who know little about state honours; sociologists who know considerable European history; and sociologists who know very little European history, but are interested in the social processes that I discuss. It will be a challenge to please them all.

ORGANIZATION

The book is organized thematically. A consequence is some repetition, as the same empirical phenomena come up more than once when I offer them as evidence in support of different assertions made in different chapters.

TABLES

There are three sets of tables: those in the first set appear within various chapters and are designated according to the number of the chapter and a number assigned to each table; two separate sets comprise Appendices B and C, within which tables are designated numerically.

CONCEPTS, PERIODS, AND PLACES

I define status as positive or negative evaluation. It is derived from the possession of characteristics that people admire or are told they should admire. It is the power to elicit or command respect. In Weber's words, it constitutes "an effective claim to social esteem."[10] It varies in a number of ways, one of which is the degree to which it is institutionalized. When status is well institutionalized it becomes a position in a status hierarchy with certain rights and obligations. Most people hold both non-institutionalized and institutionalized status. And it is possible to lose one more than the other: non-institutionalized status more than institutionalized status (a king who comes to be regarded as a fool) or vice versa (a king who is forced to abdicate but is still highly respected).

There are two types of status power: (1) the possession of high status as defined above and (2) "status-distribution power." Status-distribution power is the power to determine how much status other people have and thus to shape its distribution. Those possessing status-distribution power include what we can call publics or audiences, such as theatre-goers, fans of film stars, sports fans, and so forth. The concern in this book is with a different kind of status distributor, one who is able to raise or lower the position of another in an institutionalized status hierarchy, in this case by deciding what state honours are to be given to whom. This includes rulers and state authorities who create or terminate specific state honours, decide what they should be granted for and on what basis, and sometimes intervene in specific allocations. It also includes the members of committees who decide on the recipients of state honours and the bureaucrats who administer the awards.

When I use the concept "modernization" in lower case, I am referring to the sociological concept as defined above. This is not what European historians mean by Modern, at least when they talk about Early Modern Europe or Modern Europe, which are chronological terms. The Early Modern period runs from the sixteenth to eighteenth centuries. The Modern period consists of the nineteenth and twentieth centuries. When I use "Modern" in upper case, I am employing it in this sense. Similarly, when I refer to the Middle Ages and Medieval Europe, I am using these terms simply to refer to a certain chronological period, roughly from the middle of the first millennium to the end of the fifteenth century.

I use the term "aristocracy" to refer to an elite status group that is considered in some sense to be traditional and whose members, in the majority, inherit the status, though in each generation a large or small number of people may acquire it in some other way. In the British Isles, the aristocracy includes the peerage, the baronetcy, and the landed gentry. In France and the Low Countries, it usually refers to the "nobility," which was sometimes a legal status. By "bourgeoisie," I mean a status group consisting of persons who could not claim to belong to the aristocracy but had sufficient resources to live comfortably. I prefer this term to "middle class" because I do not believe it is useful to conceptualize this group as a "class." My reasons for this view are given in Appendix A.

Most of what is now called Belgium and Luxembourg was known, in the seventeenth century, as the Spanish Low Countries or the

Spanish Netherlands. In the eighteenth century, they came under Austrian rule and were known as the Austrian Low Countries or Austrian Netherlands. Some parts of present-day Belgium were semi-autonomous principalities outside the Spanish/Austrian Low Countries, the largest of which was the Principality of Liège, which was part of the Holy Roman Empire. The Northern Netherlands became the United Provinces after they threw off Spanish rule in the sixteenth century. Conquered by France in 1794, they became the Batavian Republic until 1806 and the Kingdom of Holland until 1810, when they were incorporated into France. After the defeat of Napoleon, the Southern and Northern Low Countries were united as the United Kingdom of the Netherlands, but in 1830, the southern provinces separated and became the Kingdom of Belgium, while the northern provinces remained the Kingdom of the Netherlands.

The United Kingdom of Great Britain refers to the state consisting of England, Scotland, and Wales that was formed in 1707. Ireland was then a separate kingdom. In 1801, these kingdoms were united to form the United Kingdom of Great Britain and Ireland. In 1922, most of Ireland became a separate "Free State," and what remained became the United Kingdom of Great Britain and Northern Ireland. At the risk of offending the Irish, I sometimes use the word "British" or "Britain" to refer to England, Wales, Scotland, and Ireland or to the government that ruled over them.

PART I

Bourgeoisie, Aristocracy, and Cultural Power

Assertions that we can place within the modernization explanation for the evolution of state honours in Europe are to be found most often in literature concerned with relations between the aristocracy and the bourgeoisie. These relations have been a central theme in the historical narrative of Early Modern and Modern Europe. The process of modernization is often seen as a bourgeois project against the traditionalism of the aristocracy, whose displacement was necessary in order for Europe to become modernized. The rise in bourgeois power resulted, it is believed, from a number of forces, but especially from commercialization, industrialization, and political democratization. Many sociologists take the same view, though they usually situate it in a larger theoretical context.

Not surprisingly, among these historians and sociologists, allusions to state honours typically suggest that the expansion stemmed from the rise in the economic, political, and cultural power of the bourgeoisie and the decline of the aristocracy. Thus, though much of it is long-standing, we need to begin our examination of the evolution of state honours with a survey of the historical literature on this subject.

1

Rise of the Bourgeoisie

THE THESIS

Large-scale commercialization evolved earliest in the Northern Low Countries, which became a major centre of world trade in the seventeenth century. Intensive agriculture and proto-industry also developed in these provinces to a greater extent than in most other parts of Western Europe. International trading was also highly developed in the British Isles and in coastal regions of France. The earliest to industrialize was Britain. Not far behind in industrialization was the Southern Low Countries, more specifically Wallonia, their French-speaking provinces. Although industrialization in northeastern France kept pace with Wallonia, other parts of France industrialized more slowly.

Nevertheless, the transfer of economic power from persons holding aristocratic status to persons without aristocratic status came earlier in France than in the British Isles. Various reasons are given for this difference. The most obvious is the French Revolution. Although many members of the French old nobility were able to recover properties confiscated during the Revolution, the bulk of the pre-Revolutionary noble patrimony was lost. Their economic decline has also been attributed to their failure to make the transition from landowning to new types of economic activity. A number of historical conditions in Britain – the early development of capitalist agriculture, the ownership of urban property by aristocrats, the rights of landowners to the minerals under their land, the willingness of aristocrats to engage in non-agricultural business, and rules of inheritance – delayed the decline in economic power of the British aristocracy as compared with the French aristocracy, whose economic prominence fell sharply in the long nineteenth century to the benefit of bourgeois social strata.

It is important to recognize that some of the differences in average wealth between the British and Continental aristocracies were a function of differences in the way in which aristocracy was socially and legally distinguished in each country. In the British aristocracy, landed wealth was the essential criterion of social distinction. It did not determine who was a peer or baronet, but it did determine who was a member of the landed gentry and who was not. In contrast, the French nobility, even before the Revolution, did not include all of France's wealthy landowners, while it did include families with very little land.

Still, when all the similarities and differences are taken into account, it is indisputable that the economic power of the British aristocracy during the nineteenth century was greater than that of the French nobility. It was only with the agricultural depression of the late nineteenth century and the political empowerment of new wealth that the position of the British aristocracy began to decline relative to the wealth of non-aristocratic elites.

The precocious economic development of Belgium provided opportunities for the Belgian nobility in the early nineteenth century, but it too was less wealthy than the British aristocracy. This relative lack of resources prevented Belgian nobles from playing the same role in industrialization that could be played by the British aristocracy. Moreover, in Belgium, economic power became highly concentrated as early as the 1830s as a result of the establishment of major *sociétés anonymes*, most notably the Société générale and the Banque de Belgique. Although nobles were over-represented on their boards, the control of these enterprises was largely in bourgeois hands.[1]

Politically, the pattern is seen as similar. During the eighteenth century, with a few exceptions, the number of appointments to the British and Irish houses of lords was small, an average of two a year. And almost all the new peers were large landowners. In the late eighteenth and early nineteenth centuries, the number of new peerages and the character of those who received them underwent substantial change. According to Michael McCahill, between 1780 and 1830, the number appointed to the British House of Lords for services to the Crown or the government accelerated, representing

50 percent of those elevated after 1801. The majority of the new peers owned property, but not as much as the great landowners of the past. McCahill offers two reasons for the shift. First, the Napoleonic Wars expanded the number of persons whose contributions required some recognition; and second, with the union of the British and Irish parliaments, it was no longer possible for the Crown to use Irish peerages to reward such people.[2]

Nevertheless, the political power of aristocrats persisted longer in the British Isles than did the political power of nobles in France and the Low Countries. Despite the above changes, traditional aristocrats still controlled the House of Lords. Aristocrats also dominated elected representation in Parliament until the late nineteenth century. In 1865, the landed gentry, baronets, Irish peers, and sons of peers or baronets made up 76 per cent of the membership of the House of Commons.[3] In this period, they were never a minority in Cabinets. In the government formed by the Earl of Derby (Edward Smith-Stanley, fourteenth earl of Derby) in 1866, five of ten Cabinet members were not just members of the landed elite but also heirs to long-established peerages or baronetcies.[4]

The persistence of landed power in British politics can be partially explained by the capacity of landowners to influence the votes of those enfranchised by a number of electoral-reform acts during the nineteenth century. This advantage was, however, time limited. The consensus among historians is that the decline in the political power of the British aristocracy was ultimately due to the ability of non-aristocratic factions to mobilize recently enfranchised voters, especially in urban areas.

In the 1885 election, the noble and landed-gentry representation in the House of Commons fell to about one-third; after the 1906 election, it stood at less than one-fifth.[5] Following the Liberal schism in 1885, the Liberals became a largely bourgeois party, but even the Conservative Party came to depend increasingly on bourgeois support. The last mainly aristocratic Cabinet was that of Robert Cecil, third marquess of Salisbury, in the 1890s. But even before then, the British landed elite was drawn into a losing political battle with the Irish tenantry, which culminated in the Wyndham Act of 1903, the provisions of which enabled Irish farmers to buy out their landlords. In 1911, British aristocrats suffered their most serious defeat when the powers of the House of Lords were significantly curtailed.

In Belgium, successive political upheavals – the French conquest, the construction of the Napoleonic regime, the collapse of this regime, the creation of the United Kingdom of the Netherlands, and the Revolution of 1830, which separated Belgium from the Kingdom of the Netherlands – gradually undermined aristocratic political power.[6] Through most of the nineteenth century, the Belgian nobility was still in a strong position in diplomacy and in the Royal Court, and to a lesser extent in the Senate. In the latter, however, their representation fell from 61 per cent in 1840 to 48 per cent in 1850 to one quarter in 1901.[7] From 1831 to 1865, during the reign of Leopold I, twenty-two nobles held Cabinet posts; from 1865 to 1909, during the longer reign of Leopold II, only twelve ministers were nobles. In the Chamber of Representatives, during the years 1870 to 1880, one-fifth of the members were nobles, a marked over-representation, but not enough to challenge the political domination of the bourgeoisie.[8] For the most part, it was the Belgian professional and administrative bourgeoisie, not the commercial and industrial bourgeoisie, that benefited from the political changes of the nineteenth century.[9] Generally speaking, businessmen were not inclined to become involved in politics themselves. Nevertheless, no less than 17 per cent of the representatives of 1870 to 1880 were industrialists.[10]

Accounts of the rising political power of the bourgeoisie in France would begin with the destruction of the political power of the Old-Regime nobility during the French Revolution. Political power under Napoleon was heavily concentrated in the leaders of the new regime, which included some old nobility, but they were a small minority. Otherwise, it was mainly in the hands of the military and what was called the "notability," which consisted mostly of landowners, some of whom claimed noble status. The political power of the old nobility was partially revived under the Restoration (the Bourbon monarchy from 1815 to 1830), though their representation in the Chamber of Deputies declined over the course of Bourbon rule. The Revolution of 1830 further undermined the political power of the old nobility, if only by the refusal of members of the old nobility to participate in the July Monarchy (the Orléanist regime that this revolution brought to power). In 1831, the representation of the old nobility in the Chamber stood at one-quarter. The Second Empire, constructed in 1852 by Napoleon's nephew, Napoleon III, drew the peasantry away from the nobility and notability, whose political power declined in relation to that of the urban elite. This trend continued under the Third Republic, which was established in 1870 after the fall of the Second Empire. As in other Continental countries, the nobility continued to be powerful in local government, the diplomatic corps, and the military, but it enjoyed nothing like the position it had held in the eighteenth century.

Much murkier is the ideological and cultural evolution of Western Europe during the eighteenth and nineteenth centuries. It is difficult to say which countries were more modernized in these terms. Certainly, the French claimed to be the most modernized. From the time of the Enlightenment, members of French educated classes were explicitly committed to greater rationality, tolerance, and reward based on achievement, whether or not we think these goals were attained. France also became, over the course of the nineteenth century, more secularized than British society.

Yet there is considerable disagreement over the relative decline of aristocratic ideology and culture in Western Europe. Many writers would contend that, by the end of the nineteenth century if not earlier, bourgeois interests, values, and standards had seriously undermined the emulation of aristocratic culture in Western Europe. It has long been argued that, as capitalism developed, the bourgeois agenda came to predominate throughout this part of the world, but especially in England, where the "entrepreneurial ideal" of the bourgeoisie triumphed over the course of the nineteenth century.[11] It is purported that bourgeois values acclaiming merit, talent, and achievement gradually displaced aristocratic values of ascription. Jürgen Habermas calls our attention to the contrasting portrayals of the nobility and the bourgeoisie in Wolfgang von Goethe's *Wilhelm Meister*: the noble was what he was, what he seemed, what he represented, while the bourgeois was what he produced.[12] Lenore O'Boyle acknowledged that the bourgeoisie was in many ways divided, but insisted that what held the various fractions together in the nineteenth century was their shared opposition to aristocratic privilege and their common set of values, which included a belief in talent or merit as the basis for advancement.[13] A similar contention has more recently been made by Jürgen Kocka.[14] Harold Perkin, for his part, asserted that during the nineteenth century, the British "middle class" successfully promoted the view that the rewards of wealth, power, and status should go to those who were most successful in a free competition among individuals.[15] Penelope Corfield links the development of meritocracy to the evolution of British professions. She also points out that in Britain the concept of "gentleman" came to refer increasingly, during the seventeenth and eighteenth centuries, to members of the professions as well as the landed gentry, and that in the process, gentility became redefined in less ascriptive terms.[16] And, according to Michael Mann, Napoleon provided proof that "bourgeois birth plus merit could rule."[17]

So powerful was this cultural force that it allegedly penetrated the aristocracy as well as the bourgeoisie in most Western-European countries. Robert Blake suggests that the British "middle class" had so successfully converted British society to their ideals and standards during the first half of the nineteenth century that there was no need to force the aristocracy out of office so long as the latter adapted itself to the new ethic.[18] It has often been pointed out that many British aristocrats were led to adopt policies that were good for business as a result of the general importance attached to economic growth. Christophe Charle has insisted that the French notables who came to hold power after the Revolution were less willing than British landowners to accept and permit a smooth transition to a bourgeois democratic society.[19] Yet the French notability, as a social group, facilitated the eventual assimilation of the aristocracy and the bourgeoisie in France, an assimilation in which the bourgeoisie became the "dominant partner in the alliance."[20]

Whenever the above changes occurred, and however they varied from one country to another, they allegedly broke the monopoly that the aristocracy had enjoyed over state honours. The Legion of Honour, founded by Napoleon Bonaparte in 1802 – the first major state honour instituted during the nineteenth century in Western Europe and the model on which many subsequent state honours were based – was very different from most earlier state honours, the majority of which had taken the form of monarchical "orders of knighthood." The Legion of Honour not only had a much larger membership but also was open to a far larger range of socio-economic groups. Its badge was purposively not a cross, as was the case for most of the Medieval and Early Modern orders of knighthood, but instead had five arms. The grades of the Legion of Honour were very different from those of the earlier orders, even different from those of the Order of Saint Louis, which had inspired it. The Saint Louis had three grades (*grand croix*, *commandeur*, and *chevalier*), while the Legion of Honour was given five by Napoleon (*grand aigle, grand commandeur, commandeur, officier,* and *legionnaire*). Although they were changed under the Restoration to make them closer to those of the older orders (*grand croix* rather than *grand aigle, grand officier* rather than *grand commandeur,* and *chevalier* rather than *legionnaire*), the five grades of the Legion of Honour set a precedent for state honours. And Napoleon chose to call it a "legion" to avoid the term "order," because the latter was associated with the Old Regime. Napoleon also created a decoration known as the Order of the Academic Palms, intended for academics at the University of Paris. And the new nobility Napoleon created in 1808, known as the Imperial nobility, included many men who would not have been regarded as worthy of the status by the pre-Revolutionary nobility.

As the rising bourgeoisie became a force to reckon with, it was only to be expected that the number of persons who might hope to receive state honours rose dramatically, creating pressures that could not be met by traditional state honours.[21] Democratic pressures even led to the view that members of the working class and common soldiers were entitled to recognition for their contributions. The Legion of Honour was awarded not only to members of the bourgeoisie and lower-ranked military officers but also to common soldiers. In 1852, the Military Medal was created in France for soldiers below officer ranks who had drawn attention to themselves for acts of courage or devotion, though it could also be awarded to generals who commanded in a military engagement. Similarly lower-ranked soldiers were prime candidates for the Victoria Cross. In France, especially under the Third Republic, a number of decorations were created for which members of the working class were explicitly eligible. And symbolic rewards for rescuers were intended to reward virtuous acts by ordinary citizens.[22]

A similar sentiment motivated the creation of the Order of the British Empire. It was founded in 1917 to recognize those who had served in the War effort in non-combatant roles and marked a significant expansion in the social range of British state honours. The inclusion of persons of lower or medium socio-economic status in this order incited twenty-five individuals, all privy councillors, all peers or knights, to write a letter to *The Times* in August 1918 denouncing the number of awards and demanding that state honours should be "protected from this sort of cheapening." David Lindsay, a minister in the Coalition government, was equally indignant in his defence

of the Order, and declared that those who had been appointed to
it were "humble people who were receiving well-earned recognition
for work of incalculable value."[23]

Before the French Revolution, membership in most orders was
reserved largely for the aristocracy. Indeed, some orders were
restricted to a small number of aristocrats who were already high in
status or close to the monarch. The prototypical order of this kind
in Britain is the Order of the Garter, which was traditionally limited
to members of the royal family, members of other European royal
families, and those in higher ranks of the peerage, usually men who
held high government office.[24] The French Order of the Holy Spirit
was created in 1578 by France's King Henry III; it was limited to one
hundred state dignitaries who could prove three degrees of nobility.
The Order of the Black Eagle, founded by Frederick I to coincide
with his assumption in 1701 of the title of King of Prussia, was rarely
granted to anyone who was not a member of a German princely family; when bestowed on a commoner, it carried hereditary nobility.[25]

In contrast, during the first twelve years of the Legion of Honour, almost 40,000 persons were made members. At the end of the
Restoration, roughly the same number of legionnaires were in the
Order. In 1848, it was about 47,000, and in 1914, around 50,000.[26]
It has been estimated that on the eve of the Great War no fewer than
1,700,000 French persons held one of sixty-five official honours
then existing.[27] After the War, the numbers increased even further.
By 1923, membership in the Legion of Honour reached roughly
100,000, and by 1938, it was in the neighbourhood of 200,000.[28]

Membership in the Order of Leopold was much smaller. This
state honour was instituted in 1832 shortly after the secession of Belgium from the Kingdom of the Netherlands. The principal reason
for the lower numbers was the smaller size of the Belgian population. However, it was still large compared with earlier state honours
to which Belgians could have aspired. Roughly 15,000 persons were
appointed from the 1830s to the 1880s, and some 18,000 members belonged to the Order in 1932.[29] Even in Britain, there was
an expansion of state honours during the late eighteenth and early
nineteenth centuries, mostly as consequence of an increase in the
awarding of honours that already existed. In 1815, two new grades
were added to the Order of the Bath, which had been founded during the first half of the eighteenth century. By 1833, the number of
members of the Bath had reached almost eight hundred; by 1854,

it was over a thousand; and by 1877, it was over twelve hundred.[30] In Britain, however, the great expansion of state honours came in the late nineteenth and early twentieth centuries. The number of persons made a knight was 448 in 1875–84, a figure that includes both those holding the grade of knight in an order of knighthood and those whose knighthood was independent of an order (the latter known as "knights bachelor"). The number rose to 764 in 1885–94, 1,447 in 1895–1904, 1,794 in 1905–14, and 2,791 in 1915–24. The number of persons made a baronet was only forty-eight in the years 1875 to 1884, but rose to 116 in 1885–94, 136 in 1895–1904, 203 in 1905–14, and 322 in 1915–24.[31] And the Order of the British Empire was supplied with 22,000 members in its first two years. By 1922, it had 25,000 members.

The Liberals were generally more willing than the Conservatives to award a relatively large number of peerages. They did so principally in an effort to overcome their numerical disadvantage in the House of Lords. And they were much less reluctant to include less aristocratic individuals in the House. The Conservatives could afford to be less generous and were also less inclined to increase the number of British peers. Over time, Victoria became more opposed to lavish creations, particularly by William Gladstone, with whom she had a difficult relationship. And the Liberals gradually came to realize that it was hopeless to try to achieve any balance of power in the House of Lords through peerage creations. Nevertheless, the British peerage did experience considerable enlargement in the long nineteenth century. The expansion came in three waves. The number of English peers and peeresses rose from 216 in 1790 to 292 in 1810, mainly as a result of creations by William Pitt the Younger, who was prime minister for most of this period, and then again from 333 in 1830 to 393 in 1840, mainly as a consequence of creations by the Whig prime minister, Viscount Melbourne (William Lamb, second viscount Melbourne). It rose little after that, until the 1880s and 1890s, when the numbers increased sharply once more. By 1900, the number of English peers and peeresses had reached 524.[32]

Significant in the historical literature is the assumption that the shift in wealth from the aristocracy to the bourgeoisie led to a commodification of state honours. In the late nineteenth and early twentieth centuries, several scandals broke out in France and Britain because businessmen were receiving honours in return for donations to worthy causes and to political parties. In some cases, honours were being distributed in return for private payments to persons with influence over the distribution of state honours. More is said about this in Chapter 13, but it should be mentioned here that much has been made of the chronological correlation between (1) the growth in non-aristocratic wealth relative to aristocratic wealth, (2) a sharp increase in the distribution of state honours, and (3) these scandals.

In addition, it is thought that democratization and the rise in the power of the bourgeoisie were responsible for changes in the social composition of recipients of state honours. The powerful position that the bourgeoisie came to enjoy in Belgium after the Revolution of 1830 coincided with an expansion in state honours for economic endeavours. These honours included decorations created in the 1830s and 1840s on the occasion of national industrial exhibitions; an industrial and agricultural decoration created in 1847; and medals to mark the fiftieth anniversaries of certain milestones – the establishment of the first railway, a ferry from Ostend to Dover, and the first telegraph – which were awarded to those who had played an important role.[33]

During the nineteenth century, industrial exhibitions in most parts of Western Europe became the occasion and venue for the distribution of different kinds of honorific rewards – for the organization of exhibitions, for industrial innovations, and for the contributions of some individual industrialists. Enough men were admitted to the Order of the Dutch Lion for their role in the organization of the International Colonial and Export Exhibition of 1883 in Amsterdam that they were sarcastically referred to as "exhibition knights."[34] In France, international exhibitions were often accompanied by the appointment of industrialists to the Legion of Honour.[35]

There was also a transformation in the criteria by which the honours of states were distributed. Many writers distinguish between two types of state honours and two periods in their evolution: (1) Old-Regime "aristocratic orders" based on birth and (2) more recent "orders of merit" based on contributions or achievements. Aristocratic orders and an ascriptive nobility could not survive, it has been argued, in the face of new values of merit promoted by the Enlightenment and dictated by the French Revolution.[36] According to Olivier Ihl, honours became "the basic measure of merit" in the French republic.[37]

Merit has been repeatedly touted, by contemporaries and historians alike, as a distinctive characteristic of the Legion of Honour, and to a lesser extent of Napoleon's Imperial nobility.[38] P.L. Rœderer (a writer and senator of the Revolutionary and Napoleonic periods) defended the creation of the Legion of Honour in the legislature by claiming it would render military and civilian services "the prize of courage that they all merited" and thus would "efface noble distinctions which place hereditary glory above achieved glory and the descendants of great men above great men."[39] Nicholas Harris Nicolas (an influential British specialist in orders and heraldry) declared in his *History of the Orders of Knighthood of the British Empire*, published in 1842, that the purpose of state honours was "to create a lasting Memorial of the distinguished men, by whose talents, conduct, and valour, the country has been raised to the pinnacle of Martial glory, and thus to form, as it were, a general REGISTER OF HONOUR, or LIBRO D'ORO of British Merit."[40] According to Jerome Blum, during the nineteenth century, not only were new "orders of merit" founded but all orders became based on merit, or at least more so, and ennoblement became a "recognition of achievement."[41]

Nicolas, though perhaps ahead of his time in Britain, can be taken to represent the new view on the distribution of state honours. Descendant of a Huguenot refugee, he was the youngest son of a naval captain and himself entered the navy in 1808, but read for the bar after the French wars and was called to the Inner Temple in 1825.[42] He spent his life in antiquarian research and writing, in the reorganization of the Public Records Office, and in an unsuccessful attempt to reform the Order of the Bath, for which he was secretary to the knight commanders and companions. He was possessed of what James C. Risk calls "a curious amalgam of a medieval Crusader with the conscience of a late Victorian Non-Conformist."

These transformations in the character of state honours have been explicitly attributed to the demise of absolute monarchy, the decline of the aristocracy, and the rise in power of bourgeois society.[43] In particular, the advancement of the bourgeoisie under the July Monarchy in France is seen as a triumph of meritocracy. A new class of men received state honours for their intelligence and talent. The Orléanist regime elevated professors, writers, and artists to the House of Peers (established during the previous regime along the same lines as the British House of Lords), even if they did not pay the required level of taxation.

Despite their recognized political function, even appointments to the British House of Lords were seen by some political leaders as rewards for achievement. This was ostensibly the view of Robert

Peel (a British prime minister in the 1830s and 1840s). His father was a wealthy cotton manufacturer. Although certainly raised in elite culture, he was also critical of aristocratic privilege and its assumptions. He granted relatively few peerages, and informed one aspirant not to expect a peerage because he (Peel) believed that they should be used only as rewards for "public service, distinguished either by the length or fidelity of it, or by the eminence of such service." He revealed that he told his own children "to gain distinction, and establish the claim for state honours (if they covet them) by their own personal exertions and public service."[44] Whatever he practised, it is clear what he preached.

PROBLEMS WITH THE THESIS

The most obvious problem with this thesis is the fact that the expansion of state honours began under what were not-so-modern regimes. If measured by the number of orders instituted, the expansion process was earliest in Eastern and Central Europe, where a number of state military honours were created during the seventeenth and eighteenth centuries. Two were especially important as precedents. The first was the Prussian Order of Generosity, created in 1667 and then reinvented in 1740 by Frederick II as the Order for Military and Civil Merit, also known as Pour le Mérite, and subsequently made a strictly military decoration by Frederick William III in 1810. The second was the Austrian Order of Maria Theresa founded in 1757. Others included the Order of Saint Henry, instituted in Saxony in 1736; Duke Charles Eugene of Württemberg's Order of Military Merit, instituted in 1759; and a military order known as Virtuti Militari ("for military virtue"), created by the last Polish king, Stanislaw II, in 1792. In Russia, no less than four such orders were founded, the largest number in any single country. None of these orders excluded commoners.

If the expansion process is instead measured by the number of persons honoured, the most significant institution in the early evolution of European state honours was the Order of Saint Louis, which was founded by Louis XIV in 1693 and awarded to 2,000 military officers between then and the end of his reign in 1715. And the Napoleonic regime, which gave France the Legion of Honour, while modern in certain respects, was a military dictatorship that fancied itself an Empire.

Meanwhile, the most bourgeois Early Modern state, the United Provinces – the only Early Modern state where businessmen were politically dominant – introduced few state honours. Indeed, major state honours were not introduced in the Northern Netherlands until 1815, when the House of Orange, whose members had formerly been governors (*stadhouders*) of most of the Provinces, was officially transformed into a royal house. In Britain, though there was an increase in decorating during the same period – the previously mentioned enlargement of the House of Lords and membership in the Order of the Bath along with establishment of a number of military medals – the British equivalent in size to the Legion of Honour was the Order of the British Empire, created more than a hundred years after the Legion of Honour.

We can also question whether the award of state honours to businessmen is good evidence for the modernization interpretation of these honours. Although it is undeniable that businessmen received honours, they were actually latecomers, and not very great in number among recipients until the late nineteenth and early twentieth centuries. And, as we shall see in Chapter 13, even then their presence was not impressive in comparison with other groups in the population.

It is also hard to argue that the rise of the bourgeoisie in the nineteenth century – or for that matter, anything else that happened in the nineteenth century – commodified state honours in a way that they had never been commodified before. The hereditary title of baronet was introduced in 1611 by James VI/I (James VI of Scotland and I of England and Wales) to raise money for his armed struggle in Ireland. James also sold English and Irish peerages, as did his son Charles, much to the financial benefit of friends or servants of these kings. In the years 1694 to 1715, Louis XIV sold letters of nobility to raise money for the War of the League of Augsburg. Nor was the sale of state honours unique to those parts of Europe where we find the wealthiest bourgeoisie. In the eighteenth century, the dukes of Savoy made available for purchase a large number of fiefs that they had confiscated in Piedmont and sold roughly 1,300 patents of nobility in just over seventy years.[45]

In the seventeenth and eighteenth centuries, common soldiers were frequently rewarded with booty or monetary bonuses. Some of those advocating honorific rewards touted them as more virtuous. Henry Carrion de Nisas (a member of an old noble family,

who managed to negotiate his way through the Revolution and
the Empire) asserted in a speech to the Tribunate that the Legion
of Honour would help overcome the ineffectiveness of pecuniary
recompenses.

> In the last century, French artillery included among its officers a
> man of rare merit, of dazzling courage: the famous Vildepatour,
> covered in wounds and brimming with pecuniary rewards; he
> solicited a decoration … The minister sent him a new pension.
> This brave soldier became indignant. "At one time" he replied
> to the minister, "I had the good fortune to engage in a brilliant
> action, and I received a gratification of so much; another injury,
> another pension; yet another injury, another gratification. In this
> way, by a simple arithmetical calculation, I could know precisely
> the *tariff de prix* of the blood that I spilt. I'd prefer ignominy."[46]

If we also take into consideration that during the seventeenth
and eighteenth centuries, one way of becoming a noble in some
European countries was to purchase an ennobling office, we would
have to conclude that, if anything changed, it was a decline in the
commodification of state honours in the nineteenth and twentieth
centuries, the scandals of the late nineteenth and early twentieth
centuries looking like exceptions to this general trend. Indeed, one
could make a case that what was new in the late nineteenth and early
twentieth centuries was not so much that honours were being purchased but that doing so became scandals, which then led to efforts
to prevent this from happening for reasons of principle. Although
donations to political parties still play a role in the distribution of
British state honours, bargains of this kind can no longer be openly
made without vocal criticism.

2

Persistence of the Old Order

THE THESIS

The inverse of the rise-of-the-bourgeoisie thesis is that state honours in Europe originated in the Old Regime and that, whatever purpose they might serve today, their historical origin and evolution is owed to this cultural tradition. Even today, many people regard state honours as "archaic and irrelevant," an anomaly associated with European states that have strong aristocratic traditions. Irving Kristol, in a debate with Max Beloff over the use of titles in present-day Britain, argued that such titles should be used only for ceremonial occasions and that they are part of a national tradition of "very thin, but tenacious aristocratic pretensions," in which British people are "entrapped."[1]

Bruno Frey has claimed that the demand for state honours is greater in societies with an aristocratic tradition and also where the importance of the market sector in an economy is relatively weaker.[2] He cites the United States and Canada as examples of societies in which the market sector is particularly strong and where, consequently, there are fewer state honours. As he points out, in the United States one finds numerous military state honours, but not a large number of civilian state honours distributed by the federal government. For a long time in Canada some segments of the population were hostile toward state honours because they were associated with the British Empire. In 1917, the Canadian House of Commons adopted several measures that have come to be known (inaccurately) as the Nickle resolution, which restricted the bestowal of foreign honours on Canadians.[3] W.F. Nickle (a Conservative member of Parliament), who proposed the original motion, passionately declared that "titles to-day in England are really only the picturesque effects of the days of feudalism."[4] It is true that, since then, Canada has accumulated a significant number of state awards at the federal and provincial levels, including a comprehensive national order, the Order of Canada. However, some would say that this difference between Canada and the United States reflects the stronger European (or, more precisely, British) institutional tradition in Canada, a tradition that is also reflected in a number of other Canadian institutions – a monarchy, a governor general, and the parliamentary system.

In European historical writing, it is possible to distinguish between two complementary versions of the old-order thesis. The best-known statement of the first version is Mayer's *Persistence of the Old Regime*. He contended that aristocratic domination endured in most of Europe until the end of the Great War, especially in Central and Eastern Europe, but even in France and England. In his view, the honours of states represented one of the traditions of feudalism that persisted into the twentieth century. He maintained that the highest state honours were accorded disproportionately to the aristocracy, while at the same time state honours served as a way of binding the new middle and upper classes to the old order. Ennoblement was the distinction most cherished by all, but commoners were persuaded to value lesser signs of recognition.[5]

I call the second version of the old-order thesis the "aristocratic residue" version. A classic statement is Perry Anderson's interpretation of the survival of aristocratic affectations in England. By the nineteenth century, the English aristocracy had already become capitalist, but it had also preserved items of aristocratic culture, including "a seemingly 'feudal' hierarchy of orders and ranks."[6] Alastair Thompson, in his 1994 article on state honours in Imperial Germany, also sees state honours as an aristocratic residue. His contention is that we should not conclude from German fondness for honours in this period that the old order persisted in Germany longer than elsewhere. Instead he holds that state honours were "widely regarded with bemused contempt" and seen as "part of an outmoded vision of society," contrary to the prevailing bourgeois values in German culture and practice.[7] What he says about Germany is consistent with Lamar Cecil's earlier work on ennoblement in Prussia during the years 1871 to 1918. Ennoblement, Cecil suggested, did not serve to assimilate new men into the elite, as Mayer believed, but rather to provide "a shelter to marginal members of the older noble class" and to fortify eastern elites against the western, more industrial and liberal, parts of the Reich.[8] Karin Kaudelka-Hanisch points out that businessmen were typically awarded the less prestigious honorary title of "commercial councillor" rather than ennoblement, with the exception of a small number of businessmen linked to the court.[9] Indeed, the persistence of princely courts has been offered as part of the explanation for the multitude of orders in Germany in the nineteenth century.[10] Not surprisingly, with the collapse of the old order in central and eastern Europe after the Great War, this aristocratic residue was swept away, but not, so the argument goes, before the Modern state honours system had been largely constructed.

In the 1970s and early '80s, when the academic debate over the European aristocracy and bourgeoisie was at its peak, a large number of scholars, whether or not they agreed with the old-order thesis as a whole, provided evidence of the power of the aristocracy in Western Europe during the nineteenth century. In presenting the rise-of-the-bourgeoisie perspective in the preceding chapter, I referred to evidence indicating the persistence of aristocratic power in Britain, but even many French and Belgian nobles, some historians tried to show, continued to enjoy considerable political power and wealth in this period.[11] It was argued that certain changes once considered damaging to the aristocracy, such as the extension of the franchise, the growth of the state bureaucracy, military reorganization, and even the abolition of seigneurialism and serfdom, yielded gains for many segments of the aristocracy.

The idea that there was a conversion of the British aristocracy to bourgeois values contains an important element of truth, but it is also true that, on both sides of the English Channel, the general population voiced considerable respect for the aristocracy and no small measure of disrespect for the bourgeoisie. In France, the military was a bastion of anti-bourgeois sentiment. There was also noteworthy hostility in the literati toward those who lived off trade, finance, or industry. Bourgeois values were deprecated by many people, including such writers as Émile Augier, Eugène Labiche, and Honoré de Balzac. It has been shown by Sarah Maza, in her review of the social construction of the bourgeoisie from the late eighteenth to the middle of the nineteenth century, that in France during this period "bourgeois" had a negative connotation; the term was associated with money and social climbing.[12] Industry, commerce, and consumption were the target of widespread criticism; and the values usually associated with the bourgeoisie were regarded as a major source of the late eighteenth-century social crisis.[13] This disapproval persisted in the post-Revolutionary period. Even when the bourgeoisie was socially constructed in the 1820s and associated with the July Revolution of 1830, it continued to be the object of criticism, above all for its selfishness and materialism.[14] By contrast, great admiration continued to be felt toward traditional aristocratic values of honour and what was called "chivalry."

In the preceding chapter, I mentioned that Napoleon did not call the Legion of Honour an "order" because he wanted to avoid the association this word would imply between the Legion of Honour and earlier orders of knighthood. What this tells us is that those who established other honours before and after it and called them "orders" were seeking to make such an association. In fact, many honorific orders founded during the Early Modern and Modern periods were cast in the tradition of royal "orders of knighthood" going back to the thirteenth century. Some, such as the Order of the Thistle created in 1687 and the Order of the Bath created in 1725, claimed to be revivals of earlier orders. The Order of the Dutch Lion was originally to be called the Order of the Burgundian Cross, supposedly a re-creation of an order introduced in 1535 by Holy Roman Emperor Charles V.[15]

Under these circumstances, it might be more sensible to explain the expansion in state honours as an evolution of a process that began under the Old Regime. Not only was the first major French honour, the Order of Saint Louis, founded in the seventeenth century but also, by the early nineteenth century, the French system of state honours was well established. Since then, it has been modified and has expanded as the population of the country has grown, but the basic framework was laid before the real decline of the nobility and notability in the late nineteenth century, and certainly before the aristocracy had lost its lustre in European society.

It could be argued that the adoption of the term "legion" rather than "order" was primarily a political decision by Napoleon in an effort to overcome opposition to his new honorific creation. We can be certain that, whatever Napoleon thought, many people, including many of those who were elevated to the Legion of Honour, regarded it as a reworking of the Saint Louis and saw or claimed to see the badges of the two as similar. Proponents of the old-order thesis would also point out that Napoleon restored not a few of the trappings of the Old Regime in the years that he ruled France. The birth of the Legion of Honour was followed by a downpour of Old-Regime symbolism: the crowning of Napoleon as emperor; the revival of the title of marshal for his leading generals; and the formation of an imperial court, grand dignitaries of the Empire, and grand civil officers of the Imperial household.[16] The Old-Regime title of grand chancellor was revived for the Legion of Honour; the grand dignitaries of the Empire took over as the members of the Grand Council of the Legion; and the inauguration of the Legion of Honour was the occasion for the inaugural deployment of the Imperial cortege.[17] And in 1809, Napoleon created the (short-lived) Order of the Three Fleeces in imitation of the orders of earlier dynasties.

If all this were not enough, Napoleon appointed many nobles of the Old Regime to his Imperial nobility, for which he adopted pre-revolutionary titles that were all inheritable. Even membership in the Legion of Honour was inheritable under certain conditions, though few took advantage of the provision. So that his nobility could live in splendour, Napoleon required a certain level of income for each rank. He also required that, for a noble title to be inherited, it was necessary to create a *majorat*, that is, a property attached to the title. Yet this did not mean that wealth became a criterion for ennoblement. Those with insufficient revenue received grants from the Imperial domain or tribute from conquered lands. As D.M.G. Sutherland observes, Napoleon's Imperial Nobility sought to achieve an ideal of the Old Regime: that status should determine wealth, not vice versa.[18]

In monarchical states there was usually a close tie between state honours and monarchs, princes, or dukes. Many state honours were designed or named to evoke particular royal legacies. The main reason for the original plan to use the name "Order of the Burgundian Cross" for what became the Order of the Dutch Lion was to evoke memories of the glorious House of Burgundy.[19] A large number of honours were named after a monarch. During the nineteenth century, in Britain, Belgium, and Imperial France, formal state honours were invariably awarded in the name of the sovereign, who was regarded as the "fount of all honour." Monarchs always took a special interest in the honours of states, and sought to manage them as much as possible. Most had personal honours over which they had control.

In France, under the Restoration, the royal orders of the Old Regime were resurrected and the old nobility was revived. As noted when I discussed the problems faced by the rise-of-the-bourgeoisie thesis, during the same period of time in the Northern Low Countries the mutation of the House of Orange into a royal house led directly to the creation of the first major state honours. The new king also recognized members of the Old-Regime nobility and involved some of them in the creation of these new orders.[20] A similar sequence occurred when Belgium broke away from Dutch rule in 1830. A new monarchy was established. Leopold of Saxe-Cobourg, the widower of Princess Charlotte of Wales (who had been heiress presumptive to the British Crown), was invited to become king. The nobility of the previous regime was then recognized. And the Order of Leopold was founded. In the British Isles, the link between the Crown and state honours was historic; and the expansion of state honours was a significant part of the increase in the Crown's symbolic and ceremonial power during the late nineteenth century, with which it coincided chronologically.

In the aristocratic residue version of the old-order thesis, the honours of states can be seen as an attempt to preserve aristocratic pomp, status, and values in opposition to threats posed by the rising bourgeoisie. In the Early Modern period, the growing authority of monarchies had threatened the power of many members of the aristocracy. In the nineteenth century, however, when new political forces were undermining the power of both the aristocracy and monarchies, the latter felt a greater sense of commonality and increasingly turned to mutual ornamentation to preserve their lustre. Honours constituted one of the realms of state practice over which monarchs continued to have influence at a time when their powers in other areas were declining. The expansion of state honours in the late nineteenth and early twentieth centuries, particularly in Britain, has been attributed at least in part to the need to use traditional symbols to offset the disruption of social change occurring at this time.[21]

In order to accept the old-order thesis, it is not necessary to deny a considerable democratization of honours. In fact, the democratic impulse often came from higher-status social groups. Just as the more sensible of them were not altogether opposed to political democratization, many of those linked to the old order also understood that it was advantageous to acknowledge the contributions of non-aristocrats, even persons at lower socio-economic levels. In France, the first major honour created intentionally to recognize members of the *menu peuple* for virtuous acts such as rescuing – called the "prix de vertu" – was established under the Old Regime.[22] One of the principal architects of the Order of the British Empire was Frederick Ponsonby, son of Queen Victoria's private secretary, and great-grandson of the Third Earl of Bessborough. He was appointed Keeper of the Privy Purse in 1914. In 1915, he strongly believed that British honours needed to be democratized to provide recognition, in his words, for "all classes and indeed for a considerable proportion of the population."[23] And remember the passionate defence of the generous distribution of the Order of the British Empire by David Lindsay, a member of the Coalition government? He was not a Liberal but a Conservative, and not an MP in the House of Commons but a lord in the House of Lords by virtue of being twenty-seventh earl of Crawford and tenth earl of Balcarres.

PROBLEMS WITH THE THESIS

Yet the old-order thesis does not adequately explain the great expansion of state honours any more than the rise-of-the-bourgeoisie thesis. It, too, faces some awkward facts. Let's start with the notion that most of the Western-European population in the nineteenth century associated state honours with an outmoded vision of society and contrary to the prevailing bourgeois values. The reality was that large and growing segments of the population were only too happy to get them. Even those who wanted to bring down a traditional political or social order were not indifferent to them. However much some revolutionaries might huff and puff against them, most revolutionaries in Western Europe did not put an end to the practice of awarding state honours. In this regard, the Irish revolutionaries were exceptional. When they achieved independence, they abolished British state honours and have since created very few. Even the Order of Saint Patrick was rejected by the Irish government. It had been established in the late eighteenth century to provide Ireland with an equivalent to the (English) Order of the Garter and the (Scottish) Order of the Thistle. It lingered as a neglected British decoration until 1974.[24]

In contrast, as will be shown in Chapter 7, during the French Revolution, honorific rewards were abolished, tolerated, and re-created, until the practice of awarding soldiers with their arms became institutionalized in 1799 and known as the Arms of Honour – all this followed by the creation of the Legion of Honour in 1802, and then other Napoleonic rewards. Although Louis-Philippe (the Orléanist king brought to power by the July Revolution of 1830) abolished what he regarded as antiquated orders and decorations, his government did not, by any means, reject state honours. The Legion of Honour was preserved and several new honours were founded. Despite opposition to state honours on the part of some Belgian revolutionaries, their revolution in 1830 was followed by a profusion of state honours, not just the monarchical Order of Leopold. Nor did the French Revolution of 1848 bring forth an immediate abolition of state honours, as many of those who supported it would have preferred. The struggle over this issue was put off, until the question was overtaken by the appointment of more than 600 members of the National Guard to the Legion of Honour as a reward for suppressing uprisings against the new state.[25] Much the same occurred in 1870. Those who favoured the abolition of the Legion of Honour were unable to prevail over the political necessities facing the new republic and the willingness of lesser radicals to make use of state honours for their purposes.

We need to understand the Old-Regime origins of the Napoleonic regime, but we also need to avoid exaggerating them. To repeat a point made in Chapter 1, the Legion of Honour was different in significant respects from the Order of Saint Louis. It was even more different from other Early Modern state orders in the numbers of persons who were appointed, the social range of members, and the number of grades. While all members of the Legion of Honour were entitled to call themselves *chevalier*, the same term was also used to identify the lowest (most massively distributed) grade in the Legion in a manner contrary to the spirit of the royal orders of knighthood of the Medieval and Early Modern periods. And the supposed similarity between the badges of the Saint Louis and the Legion of Honour ignores not only the different number of arms but other dissimilarities as well.[26]

Similarly, there were critical differences between the Imperial nobility set up by Napoleon and the nobility of the Old Regime. His was a nobility of titles to which only titleholders belonged, not other members of their family; and inheritance was not automatic. Consequently, it is considered by some not to have been a genuine nobility.[27] Moreover, it clearly was established to replace, not restore, the old nobility.[28] He appointed members of the old nobility to his new nobility and wanted to assimilate the old and the new elite.[29] But it is reasonable to suggest that he did this in order to co-opt them to his regime and to exploit their prestige. He made sure that legally they enjoyed noble status by virtue of his favour rather than their pedigree.

Of course, the great majority of Old-Regime nobles rejected this assertion. The same had been the case during the Early Modern period when the power of the sovereign to distribute status lacked legitimacy, at least among those who believed themselves to belong to old noble stock. They were obviously less than enthusiastic about the new honours of the eighteenth and nineteenth centuries. To see this expansion as the consequence of the persistence of the Old Regime ignores this unease and opposition in the aristocracy toward the expansion.

As for the greater symbolic and ceremonial power of the British monarchy, it could be argued that it was not so much an attempt to retain power for the Crown and the aristocracy as a reconstruction of the monarchy to strengthen the symbolic power of the British state and to meet public demand for ceremony. In the late nineteenth century, there was a growing taste in the British public for ceremony, and considerable public discontent with the withdrawal from public life of Queen Victoria after the death of her husband. A number of individuals played a key role in this enhancement of the symbolic power of the Crown, one of whom was Liberal leader William Gladstone. The enormous present-day symbolic power of the British monarchy has not been constructed primarily by the royals themselves, and certainly not by the British aristocracy, but has been driven by popular demand and a recognition among politicians and state bureaucrats of the benefits of all this spectacle to the British state, including financial benefits.[30]

Although it is true that the lack of state honours in the United Provinces after independence from Spain is contrary to the modernization thesis, this case does not clearly support the opposite argument either, that is, that state honours were erected in these provinces only when they became less modern under a monarchy during the early nineteenth century. The United Provinces were not as modern in the sociological sense as is sometimes supposed. The merchant elite that dominated the provinces was actually rather traditional in its values and in its social organization, which was based on kinship more than merit.[31] To be sure, it was officially not a monarchical state and the House of Orange had less power than the majority of royal heads of Early Modern European states. Yet they were regarded as royalty. Moreover, it is hard to claim that the creation of the Military Order of William and the Order of the Dutch Lion under the first king, William I, resulted from a regression of the Netherlands to the old order. While admittedly no democrat, William cannot be regarded as anti-modern or anti-bourgeois. He played a critical role in the economic development of the Low Countries and, consequently, an important faction in the business community in the southern provinces supported him in his political struggle against the breakup of the Union.[32]

At the same time, there is no denying the "decline of the aristocracy" in France and its effects on state honours. Ever since the Revolution, state honours in France have been far from the preserve of aristocrats. In contrast, in Britain the aristocracy (that is, the peerage, baronetcy, and landed gentry) continued in the nineteenth century to have enormous influence over state honours and to benefit accordingly. With a few exceptions, the effect was to preserve many state honours for a small number of people until late in the century. This can be seen as evidence of the persistence of the old order, but it kills the thesis as an explanation of the European expansion of state honours.

Whatever its value, this is where the old-order thesis fails us. While it is possible to see manifestations of the persistence of the old order in Western Europe during the nineteenth century, notably in the culture and institutionalization of state honours during this period, this evidence makes it more difficult, not easier, to explain the great proliferation of state honours. Fundamentally, the problem with the old-order thesis is that it provides no explanation for the enormous growth in awards and honours during the nineteenth and twentieth centuries, and especially for the massive increase in the numbers of persons receiving awards. If the honour system that emerged in Europe in the eighteenth and nineteenth centuries had declined – or even not expanded – in the twentieth century, we might have been able to explain it in terms of the persistence of the old order. But this is not what has happened. The European expansion of state honours and the system of honours that today exists in these countries is a current phenomenon, not some relic that has survived from the Old Regime.

It does not make much sense to try to determine which of these two opposing theses – the rise of the bourgeoisie versus the persistence of the old order – provides a better explanation of European honours. Neither of them really does. In the following chapter, however, I propose that they are still helpful in answering our larger questions, primarily because the forces and events that this literature brings to light provided the cultural and institutional context in which the great expansion of honours occurred. This cultural and institutional environment shaped the character of honours and in this way contributed to their evolution.

3

Cultural Power

In order to avoid confusion with the concept of cultural capital, I need to define what I mean by cultural power. It is the power to affect the behaviour of others by shaping their values, beliefs, and perceptions. Like most power, cultural power can be fused with other types of power, including cultural capital or status power, as in the case of pop singers, successful writers, and cult leaders. But this is not always the case. Newspaper reporters and journalists typically have more cultural power than cultural capital or status power.

MERIT AND ACHIEVEMENT

The identification of the bourgeoisie with merit and the aristocracy with birth lineage is the way most members of the bourgeoisie liked to see their differences, and how we today like to see those differences. Yet during the nineteenth century, some members of the aristocracy defended their position in society on the grounds of merit. Many British aristocrats firmly believed that they were more competent to provide superior leadership and thus to fill the leading posts in government. As Dominic Lieven points out, the aristocracy throughout Europe claimed superiority in military leadership and in values such as physical courage, coolness, toughness, endurance, stoicism, and loyalty. The childhood socialization of young aristocrats, directed as it often was at instilling such attributes, could be anything but comfortable. In fact, from the sources that have survived, it would seem that parental love among elites in Early Modern Europe was often more conditional on performance than it is in present-day Europe.[1] In eighteenth and nineteenth-century Europe, armies were the largest and most complicated organizations, as well as the most technologically sophisticated, and they were generally managed by aristocrats or persons with aristocratic connections. The most efficient of them all, the Prussian military, was the most aristocratic in its leadership.[2]

As I indicated in Chapter 1, it is commonly believed that over the past three or four centuries an evolution has taken place from honorific orders based on birth to orders and decorations based on achievement. However, we also saw that, to the extent that such a shift occurred, it was initiated by Old-Regime states. It was most explicit in Frederick II's Pour le Mérite, to which he admitted 924 persons during his reign, 322 of them during the Seven Years' War.[3] He also used ennoblements to reward performance, particularly performance in his state administration. A stress on merit can also be seen in the founding statutes of the Austrian Order of Maria Theresa. Article 3 of the Statutes reads:

> Let us set as an inviolable basic principle, that no one, whoever he might be, because of his high birth, lengthy service, wounds suffered facing the enemy, or because of previous service, still less out of sheer grace, and upon the recommendation of others, but those only and alone shall be admitted into the Order who have excelled in some particularly valiant deed, which is not merely the complete fulfilment of the honour and duties of their post, and those who have not only been present at military councils, but whose clever counsel has been fruitful for our military service. This rule should never be waived nor any exception allowed to it, so that even we are bound by this decision made at our own gracious hands.[4]

The Legion of Honour belongs in many respects to traditions of the Old Regime, but less to the traditions emphasized in the aristocratic/bourgeois framework than to the tradition of aristocratic meritocracy. It was in this tradition that Napoleon – who issued from the lesser nobility not the bourgeoisie – was schooled and in which he remained throughout his reign. The presence of this tradition in the discourse of the Legion of Honour was reflected most visibly in the repeated use of the word "service" ("outstanding services to the state" and "service of the Republic") in the bill creating it.[5] The way Napoleon thought, the enemy of merit was not so much birth as wealth, not so much aristocratic status as a materialist conception of status.[6] Many things he did, including the creation of the Legion of Honour and the Imperial nobility, were designed to combat the ethos of materialism and to reward service to the state, and more particularly to himself. This project was more in the tradition of the French monarchy and nobility than the bourgeoisie.

Aristocrats were frequently at the forefront among those who declared merit to be the proper justification for honours. The generous ennoblement of state bureaucrats in Russia during the late nineteenth century was criticized on the grounds that ennoblement should be for merit, as it supposedly had been in the past.[7] In 1847, British Prime Minister Lord John Russell received a vitriolic letter from Richard Grosvenor (second marquess of Westminster) denouncing Russell's recent elevations to the peerage and comparing his peerage policy unfavourably with the "more dignified" practice adopted by Peel "of conferring peerages for merit only, and not for political subserviency."[8] The aristocratic critique of the inflation and sale of state honours was in the same vein. Aristocratic critics of the inflation of state honours in Britain insisted that democratization led to a decline in standards.[9]

We can, of course, dismiss all this as rhetoric, and indeed I am going to argue that such claims were part of a political struggle in nineteenth-century Europe. Still, a satisfactory understanding of the effect of the rise of the bourgeoisie on the honours of states necessitates a better understanding of the idiom of merit as it was used in earlier periods. A number of historians of French history have suggested that the nineteenth-century European orientation toward merit actually had Old-Regime origins.

Personal Merit

During what we call the Middle Ages, many Western-Europeans talked about personal merit based on an individual's ability and past achievements. In the thirteenth century, a particular culture of achievement, known as "chivalry," evolved in different parts of Western Europe. It was not a precisely defined "moral code." It consisted instead, as D'Arcy Boulton has shown, of a great number of norms of conduct, only some of which would be found in any one text that historians have available to them. Yet the large number and dispersed communication of "chivalric" virtues testifies to the prevalence of this culture. The major literary forms of this era – both the epic and the romance – were stories of individual adventure and accomplishment. One cannot conceive of literature in which individual achievement is more extolled than the construction of heroic figures in the Arthurian tales.

Much Medieval literature was didactic, intended to shape the conduct of readers and listeners. Medieval knighthood, as an exemplar, stood for personal merit, which consisted of honour, prowess, truthfulness, sincerity, courage, purity, humility, duty, loyalty, force of character, generosity, *libéralité*, courtesy, and frankness or plain-speaking. Merit also lay in pity for the suffering and protection of the poor and the weak. In addition, of course, knights were expected to possess certain skills, which were necessary not only for battle but also for the many tournaments and jousts that were held for the distribution of status among knights and for the celebration of their virtues. Erudition was not a top priority, but neither was it irrelevant; ideal knights could be expected to be both wise and learned men. Service to God and to the prince was often mentioned as a requirement of chivalry, along with defence of Christianity and the Church.[10]

Much the same can be said of noble status, for which merit and virtue were also considered essential.[11] The nobility believed themselves to be morally superior, virtuous, and refined.[12] Until the seventeenth century, noble status in France was thought to be based on the military vocation.[13] In the Medieval period, the principal means of spectacular social mobility was military achievement. It could propel an individual into the nobility in one generation. It could also be the basis of mobility over generations. Military service often enabled a family to acquire noble status gradually by prescription. Stress on achievement developed further as princes ennobled men for their valour, competence, and loyalty.[14] Service to the prince became a basis for noble status, and ennoblement could be used to reward such service.[15] As a result of their putative moral superiority, nobles thought of themselves as more qualified to advise the king and to render justice.[16]

Service was a component of lordship as well. The essence of this relationship was contract, which could be, in varying degrees, implicit or explicit. It invariably entailed some kind of performance, by the superordinate, the subordinate, or usually both. Loyal service to one's lord was considered highly meritorious.[17] Royal courtiers vied with one another over who was the most meritorious in his service to the king.

Merit in the Blood

Personal performance was not the only basis for judging merit in the Medieval and Early Modern periods. The other criterion was "merit in the blood." The idea still existed in the nineteenth century, but not to the same extent that it did in the Medieval and Early Modern periods. In these earlier times, it was widely assumed that a man's merit could be judged by his family and lineage. When those of us living in the twenty-first century hear of men being rewarded or claiming reward because of the family to which they belonged, we assume merit was being ignored for other criteria of worth. We are not recognizing that what counted for them was not just personal merit but also collective merit, particularly the achievements of the family into which a person was born. They did not think it strange that the king should appoint someone to a high position because of things his ancestors had done, any more than we would think it strange that a person should be appointed to a position because he had achieved a spectacular sales record over the previous ten years, or had earlier earned a credential of some kind. The way they saw it, merit was both personal and in the blood.

Some historians believe that genealogical thinking became more pronounced in Western Europe during the tenth and eleventh centuries. Groups of kin with vague notions of their ancestry were replaced by patrilineal vertical structures.[18] This change gave rise to – but was also strengthened by – the flowering of genealogy as a literary genre, an evolution that became fully developed by the twelfth century. Genealogical narrative exalted the qualities and accomplishments of one's forbears. History became the collective action of family lineages.[19]

Merit in the blood was also the basis of noble status. Many of the claims of ancestral accomplishments were exaggerated or even fictitious, but this is all the more evidence that the achievement of one's ancestors was seen as fundamental. In this way of thinking, if noble status was based on the military vocation, the pursuit of this vocation by one's ancestors was important in asserting noble status as well as serving in arms oneself.[20] There is no doubt that in the Medieval period, insofar as we can generalize about social groups, the segment of society that was most concerned about merit – that wrote about it and judged people according to this standard – was not the bourgeoisie of the towns, but rather the aristocracy.

It should be acknowledged that in this literature, some people did see a contradiction between personal merit and merit in the blood.

There were debates among savants between those who stressed the one versus the other. However, most people saw no great contradiction because the general assumption was that the capacity for personal merit was inherited and that personal merit and merit in the blood were inseparable. If they acclaimed individual performance – even skill or competence – they were not trying to undermine birth as a standard of evaluation, but rather trying to use personal performance to identify superior birth. As Maurice Keen has pointed out, though Lancelot can be found questioning gentility that is not earned by performance, the romance is abundant in emphasis on the esteem in which family lineage must be held. It is a story about how Lancelot demonstrated that he was worthy of the blood he carried in him.[21]

There was substantial divergence between the ideal and the real. People were appointed to positions or given rewards not as a consequence of either kind of achievement. In France, many state offices were purchased. The venality of offices can be traced to the thirteenth century; it became more common in the fifteenth and sixteenth centuries; and the right to pass a venal office to an offspring became institutionalized in the seventeenth century. The venality of offices was certainly a major impediment to selection by merit, but not one that we can pin on the aristocracy any more than the bourgeoisie. Indeed, members of the nobility repeatedly denounced the sale of offices as non-meritocratic.

Favouritism, prejudices, cronyism, and networks also played a part in the distribution of positions and rewards. Many lords or princes were served by incompetent or wholly self-interested military commanders or state officials. Yet these practices often occur in present-day societies boasting an ideology of achievement and merit. The issue is not how well people lived up to their ideals, but what those ideals were. More precisely, we are concerned with the historical origins of merit as an ideal in Western Europe. While the conception of merit in the Modern period is different in important ways from the conception of merit in the Medieval and Early Modern periods, the latter is nevertheless a genuine type of merit based on respect for achievement. And our present-day conceptions of merit have grown out of it.

Arlette Jouanna laid considerable stress on the need people felt in the early sixteenth century to have public demonstration and recognition of their merit. Like Calvinists who had to demonstrate that they were members of the elect, nobles in the Medieval period and the Early Modern period felt pressure to demonstrate their personal and inherited superiority. Hastiludes, battle heroics, and duels were the most accepted (and deadliest) modes of such demonstration. Ennoblement, either by prescription or by letters patent from the sovereign, was also a form of public recognition of superiority. So were knighthood and orders of knighthood. And just as notions of merit in the Modern period have evolved from earlier notions of merit, honours in the Modern period have evolved from these earlier cultures of recognition.

Military Culture

As implied in the preceding discussion, the most significant culture of achievement in the Medieval period was military culture. Given the place of warfare in my explanation of the evolution of state honours, I want to say a little here about this culture.

Arms were tools of honour, and the achievements of knights were told and retold to provide emulation for others. Among the most striking manifestations of the vitality of this culture were the Crusades. They were not inspired by personal feuds or power contests (though they could be shaped by such struggles), nor by the interest of kings in territorial expansion, nor even by a serious danger to Christianity, but rather by a combination of religious fervour and the military culture.

This military culture came under threat in the late Middle Ages and the Early Modern period. The Renaissance represented an impressive effervescence of non-military culture. So did the evolution of universities and other centres of learning. The Early Modern growth in non-military state personnel also challenged the preeminence of the military culture. As a result, not all noble families encouraged their sons to seek a military career.[22] This was, of course, especially true in those families that we call the *noblesse de robe*, which can be defined narrowly to include only judges or broadly to include all those who held ennobling judicial or administrative positions. Military culture was also negatively affected by a decline in the prestige of those who fought. The reputation of officers was diminished by the incompetence of some of their number and by the practice of selling commissions, while respect for the common soldier was undermined by the participation in the ranks of persons of low status, often non-inheriting sons of poor peasants, but also many vagrants and criminals.

Remarkably, however, in spite of all this, Western-European military culture continued to be powerful during the Early Modern period, especially in Continental countries. If the Renaissance increased the influence of the literati in Western Europe, it did not raise it to the level we find in Ancient India, Imperial China, or Early Modern Korea, where significant anti-militaristic literati cultures were more powerful than any similar cultures were in Early Modern Europe. The European chivalric revival of the fifteenth century gave militarism a boost, particularly in royal courts. A large chivalric/militaristic literature came off the printing presses, consisting of memoirs and accounts of wars and battles. Memorialists were concerned with setting the historical record straight, but they also wanted to defend or celebrate the honour of those who participated in the wars they were describing, particularly their own honour.[23] As a rule, heroic characters were noble warriors in the plays, novels, and poetry of the seventeenth and eighteenth centuries.[24]

Many of those who subscribed to European military culture believed that peace was regrettable because it led to internal strife, effeminacy, and a decline in morals, courage, and mutual respect.[25] War, in contrast, was the pinnacle of merit. It brought out the nobility in man; it corrected vices and excesses; it was the ultimate in human achievement.[26] A philosophical movement that had a profound effect on Western-European military culture was Neo-stoicism, as fashioned by Justus Lipsius (a sixteenth-century native of the Southern Low Countries), combining Ancient Greek and Roman with Christian views, and advocating resistance to the passions. Lipsius directed most of his preaching toward the improvement of military forces. As Gerhard Oestreich points out, Lipsius evoked Cicero's view that military virtue is superior to all others.[27] In England, Neo-stoicism became associated with the militant Protestantism of famous literary courtier Philip Sidney and his circle, and with the Second Earl of Essex, from whom it passed to Henry, eldest son of James VI/I, and to the Third Earl of Essex. Neo-stoicism encouraged army officers to commit to an ideology of constancy, duty, and service.[28]

In all European countries, members of the aristocracy continued to claim pre-eminence in military command and in service to the crown. Although the non-military noble population grew as a proportion of the nobility during the seventeenth and eighteenth centuries, the participation of nobles in the armed forces nevertheless increased as a result of the enormous growth in the size of armies. And all the officers in French armies were nobles. As a consequence, the idealistic identification of noble status with the courage, loyalty, service, et cetera of military heroes persisted through the Early Modern period. For many French kinship groups in what is called the *noblesse d'épée*, war was considered a familial vocation in which at least one member, if not more, in each generation was expected to serve.[29] It is true that new state personnel, most notably provincial *intendants de justice, de police, et de finance*, undermined some of the political power of the *noblesse d'épée*, but they did not undermine its prestige, nor the ideals of the military culture. In fact, the emergence of the *noblesse de robe* gave those who adhered to the military culture a social group from which they could distinguish themselves and over whom they could, in their minds, assert their superiority. This is not to say that robe and sword represented two different antagonistic worlds. Members of the former were often interested in meeting the values of the latter.[30] Many tried to intermarry with the *noblesse d'épée*. And it was not uncommon for a robe family to seek a military office for a member.

The complexities of the subject are revealed even further if we compare countries in Western Europe. Early Modern military culture was weaker in England and less tied to the aristocracy. In comparison with France, England was a "water-based power."[31] In general and speaking relatively, water-based states are less militaristic because they have less need for territorial expansion and less reliance on the manpower of a large army as opposed to a navy. They can also, again relatively speaking, extract resources from a commercialized economy. In addition, England had the geographical advantage of not facing military threats from surrounding land-based states. It is true that water-based states are more likely to acquire interests across seas, but in Europe itself, from the end of the Hundred Years' War, English governments became less interested in Continental territory. In the sixteenth century, and for the better part of the seventeenth century, they were less involved in European wars than they once were and would be in the future. As a consequence, the English population at this time was less militaristic in its culture than most Continental populations. Gradually, Scotland and Ireland were pacified, though the possibility of an invasion through these countries remained a threat. Generally, people thought that a large navy was sufficient to defend Britain and that a large land force would be employed only to entangle Britain in Continental struggles and to strengthen the power of the Crown. Members of the English aristocracy, in particular, were resistant to the establishment of a standing army. Indeed, opposition to the cost of wars was greater among the country gentry than among other social groups. It is hard to imagine the eighteenth-century country nobility in France leading opposition to a standing army.

The United Provinces also formed a water-based state. Unlike the British Isles, they bordered on land-based states and, consequently, were forced to maintain a strong army as well as navy. Still, the Dutch were able to use their commercial wealth to pay for land forces, and those who fought in wars did not have the kind of status that the *noblesse d'épée* enjoyed in France.

These differences were a matter of degree. While the British aristocracy was less enthusiastic than Continental aristocracies about going to war, considerable evidence has been unearthed that it was disproportionately represented in the military, even in the seventeenth and eighteenth centuries.[32] Military culture was also strengthened in Britain by the very large number of men from the British Isles who fought in Continental armies, as Roger Manning has recently shown.[33] The Civil War may have helped to militarize Britain further, but what was more consequential was the involvement of Britain in Continental Wars as a result of (1) the assumption of the Crown by William of Orange, (2) apprehension in Britain about the territorial ambitions of Louis XIV, and (3) efforts of Jacobites to obtain Continental support for their struggle to overthrow the Hanoverian dynasty. As a result, Britain was significantly more militarized in the eighteenth century than it had been previously. And British people came to share the general military culture that characterized Europe.

This military culture remained powerful almost everywhere in Europe until after the Great War. In fact, during the nineteenth century, the common soldier experienced a remarkable rise in status, a subject to which I will return in Chapter 6. And military officers were the single greatest source of national heroes. Horatio Nelson became a superstar. The popularity of the Duke of Wellington was less unanimous, but he was certainly venerated by many members of the British public, including Walter Scott and Charlotte Brontë.[34] Throughout the nineteenth century, Napoleon remained the subject of veneration, the centre of a reverential cult, and a persisting political force.[35] The outrage expressed toward the incompetence of British military officers in the Crimean War and French officers in the Franco-Prussian War did not reflect a disrespect for the military, but rather indignation over the failure of officers in these wars to live up to what people believed were the military traditions of their respective countries.

Changing Conceptions of Merit

The Early Modern period saw a change in the way in which people evaluated merit. Ultimately, this re-conceptualization led to a rejection of merit in the blood. In the Early Modern period, however, merit came to have greater emphasis largely in ways that were consistent with traditional conceptions.

First, the idiom of service became even more central to the definition of merit.[36] It appears in abundance in seventeenth- and eighteenth-century sources. To cite just one study of the subject, an analysis by Monique Cubells of letters of ennoblement in Provence during the eighteenth century found frequent references to services to the crown, the *patrie*, or the state.[37] This emphasis on service was firmly in the tradition of lordship. Indeed, one way of understanding royal service by the aristocracy in the late Medieval and Early Modern period is to think of it as a transfer of lordship from regional lords to rulers of centralized states. This conception of merit was naturally firmest among nobles who were in close proximity to the ruler. A recent study of the French king's *maison militaire du roi* has shown that requests from members of the *maison* for pensions and other favours in the eighteenth century were typically justified by reference to loyal "service."[38]

Nevertheless, as J.M. Smith has argued, the growth of the state and large professional armies during the seventeenth and eighteenth centuries forced monarchs to rely on others to identify meritorious service, which in turn led to a standardization and codification of merit. This mutation had its origins not in bourgeois ideology but rather in the emphasis that the nobility placed on merit as it was played out in a new context in which the presence of the king was realized through the king's agents.[39] Gradually, service to the monarch was emphasized less and less, and service to state administration more and more.

Second, a transformation took place in methods of warfare and the talents that were thought necessary to fight wars. This subject is examined more carefully in Chapters 6 and 7. The point now is that the importance of military training led most states in the eighteenth century, and even more in the nineteenth century, to establish military educational institutions, the purpose of which was to produce military officers who were generally more competent, but specifically more competent in coordinating large armies, utilizing newly developed methods of engaging the enemy, and understanding new forms of military technology. This transition was not so much, if at all, a matter of placing more emphasis on merit – Medieval kings and lords needed competent soldiers just as much as kings and military commanders in the Early Modern period – but rather a gradual change toward new criteria of competency.

A third significant change that occurred was the greater state institutionalization of aristocratic status, especially an increase in state ennoblement from the late Middle Ages. This subject is examined more fully in Chapter 11, but it is relevant here because state ennoblements were routinely, justified by reference to merit. Usually, it was personal merit that was recognized, but not necessarily. In the Duchy of Luxembourg, services "rendered by relatives and ancestors" was still a justification for ennoblements during the eighteenth century.[40] In addition, during the Early Modern period, many families claiming noble status had to prove their nobility by reference to their ancestry. This did not eliminate the importance of personal merit because nobles also had to demonstrate publicly the virtue they presumably inherited. It did lead, however, to a greater emphasis on family lineage, thus reinforcing birth as the defining characteristic of nobility.[41] Family genealogies were drawn up for the same purpose that today we construct personal resumés.[42]

During the fifteenth and sixteenth centuries, most of Europe saw a growth in written genealogy and hagiography of deceased members of families. This is considered the golden age of Welsh genealogy, while in England there was a new craze for pedigrees in the sixteenth century.[43] Elites in Continental countries – Switzerland, the Low Countries, France, and Germany – were also keen on it. France became the leader in genealogical publications.[44] The concern of the nobility with its pedigree was, admittedly, only one of the reasons for the booming interest in genealogy. Genealogy was also a means to secure property rights and may have been stimulated by land transfers. In the United Provinces, merchants laid claim to unbroken lines of honourable descent to secure rights to political and economic privilege.[45] In the British Isles, genealogy determined one's right to sit in the House of Lords. On both sides of the English Channel, non-aristocrats tried to pump up their genealogies in order to rise socially. The result was a spread of genealogies that were, in varying degrees, fraudulent.[46]

In reality, of course, the great majority of members of the bourgeoisie did not think that genealogical research was the best way to climb into the aristocracy. Money worked better. It enabled a non-aristocrat to buy a mansion and a landed estate, and hopefully marry his daughters into the aristocracy. In France, ennoblement through state service could be sought. The professions were also an avenue of upward mobility in Britain and on the Continent.[47] An aristocratic reaction against these and other ways of moving up in the world developed in the eighteenth century. Members of the aristocracy came to place increasing emphasis on the *ancienneté* and *éclat* of their name. This reaction could be found in Britain and in Belgium, but in Western Europe it was again strongest in France. For eighteenth-century aristocrats the struggle over merit was not one of merit versus birth, but rather of birth and merit versus money. It was also a matter of merit versus connections, most notably connections to the Royal Court. Provincial nobles frequently emphasized merit because they wanted to counter the advantages enjoyed by courtiers and others in appointments to the higher ranks of the military and state bureaucracy.[48]

It is in these terms that we need to understand the famous Ségur edict of 1781, which decreed that four quarters of nobility in the patrilineal line were required for promotion to the rank of *sous lieutenant* or above in the French army. This measure was primarily designed to undermine the ability of wealthy new nobility with (presumably) little military background to buy military rank at the expense of those who (presumably) had a long line of ancestors under arms and had been raised in a culture of military service.[49] The loss of the Seven Years' War was traumatic for the pride of the French military and for public confidence in the army and navy. The defeat led to efforts at reform, heated debate, numerous proposals, and a large volume of literature, in which differences in notions of merit were clearly manifested. Much of this literature fell within the traditional conception of merit that included hereditary merit, while some of it reflected a greater unease with the assumption that merit could be in the blood.

Smith has asserted that the eighteenth century also saw the emergence of a larger body of literature that debated two different conceptions of the nobility, as (1) a formally distinct social and legal category or (2) a moral category that could be found outside as well as inside the distinct social and legal category.[50] Those who were willing to accept the latter, to some degree at least, could adapt to different notions of merit. For those who tried to remain committed to the former, however, prevailing discourses on merit were extremely problematic.

In the event, it was not so much military reformers or social pundits who undermined respect for merit in the blood. Rather, it was that merit became the central issue in the political struggle between those for and those against significant social and political change in Western Europe during the eighteenth and nineteenth centuries. A major reason that merit in the blood became discredited was that attacking it was an effective way of attacking the dominant position of the aristocracy in society. Those defending the old order met this offensive in a number of ways, but in many cases by still greater emphasis on merit in the blood.

Conceptions of Culture

It is useful for our purposes to distinguish between two conceptions of culture in academic literature. The first conception is that culture is a world view, a paradigm, a "deep structure," a collective consciousness, or a "dominant ideology." The import of these concepts varies, but they all refer to shared values and perceptions ingrained in people's minds. Although disagreement, confusion, and unanswered questions invariably exist within a paradigm, writers who use these terms typically believe that there are underlying principles and assumptions that are rarely called into question. A cultural paradigm has a logic and consistency. It is internalized in people's minds, "programmed" through socialization.[51] For some students of culture, these paradigms are relatively autonomous of the social structure; for other writers, they are largely a reflection of the underlying social structure. Bourdieu has been influential in furthering such as conception of culture. In his view, "there exists a correspondence between social structures and mental structures, between the objective divisions of the social world ... and the principles of vision and division that agents apply to them." Human agents are "independent, yet objectively orchestrated, cognitive machines," who, even when they seek to change the world or impose their way of seeing things on others, "always do so with points of view, interests, and principles of vision determined by the position they occupy in the very world they intend to transform or preserve."[52]

In contrast, I would argue that the role that aristocratic and bourgeois culture played in the evolution of state honours is much better understood by determining if an adaptive selection mechanism is operating and by conceptualizing culture as a collection of items from which humans select for specific purposes as seems advantageous. This alternative conceptualization of culture is consistent with the assumptions found in a large body of literature in which culture is seen as a fund or stock of knowledge, a "repertoire," or "tool kit" of beliefs and assumptions.[53] While people are certainly influenced and restricted by the prevailing cultural assumptions and the views of others in the society in which they live, they are not necessarily controlled by any particular cultural paradigm. They can pick and choose items from their culture, and what they select is not necessarily what they have been socialized into believing most intensely. Whether or not they can act upon what they pick varies, of course, but over time, if not prevented from doing so, they can develop new ways of doing things and expand their repertoire. They can give new connotations or symbolic significance to existing cultural items. In this literature, ways of thinking can become associated with a certain social group or nation, but not because the members of these groups have been indoctrinated in a given cultural tradition, or have internalized a certain "habitus," to use Bourdieu's very popular term. Rather, these ways of thinking are real to a particular social group in a particular moment of history. In this manner, culture becomes more a set of resources than a paradigm or discourse. This is not to say that items of culture are unconnected. They are interrelated in varying degrees, and as the tool-kit metaphor suggests, some items typically share a certain location in a cultural space and are often selected at the same time to serve the same or a related purpose.

That said, we should recognize that the tool-kit metaphor could be misleading if taken too literally. Tool kits and cultural collections are different in many respects, and noting these differences calls our attention to important features of the latter. Tool kits are intentionally assembled to be ready and used when called for. Cultural values, beliefs, and practices may or may not be consciously and systematically created or utilized. Although tools may wear out over time, they are not substantially altered, or strengthened or weakened, each time they are used. In contrast, cultural values, beliefs, and practices are normally either strengthened or weakened, and often altered, by their use. In addition, cultural items have meaning – frequently multiple meanings – which tools do not usually have. Finally, we form affective attachments to and hold non-instrumental evaluations of items of culture more than we do of the tools in our tool kit.

Yet it is also true that, even when people have strong non-instrumental sentiments in favour of or against an item of culture, their behaviour can still be instrumental. They will pursue their non-instrumental goals in instrumental ways; they even fight wars to advance peace. It is also essential to note that our relationship with our cultural repertoire is not predetermined or permanently fixed. Affective attachments, non-instrumental evaluations, and interpretive meanings can be held by individuals in any number of social groups and social situations, and people can be discriminating in what they like, and what meaning they attach to items of culture, independently – sometimes to a remarkable degree – of the position they occupy in a society. One does not have to have a specific background, or socialization, or cultural tradition to become emotionally attached to a given item of culture, to have a certain value preference, or to perceive a certain meaning in something. And one does not have to accept a whole package (paradigm or discourse) in order to select a specific item of culture.

In the historical literature on nineteenth-century European society, a common view is that of a structure consisting of major classes and their cultures engaged in intense struggles: (1) the aristocracy and the aristocratic culture that determined the behaviour of the majority of the members of the aristocracy, with the exception of deviants or renegades of some kind, of whom the irreverent Lord Byron has been seen as an example; (2) the peasantry, attached to autonomous communities and possessed of deep cultural traditions; (3) the bourgeoisie and its culture, embraced by most members of this social group, with the exception of would-be aristocrats, of whom the stylish Marcel Proust in his youth has been seen as an example; and (4) the working class, which was developing its own culture in this period, famously brought to light in Thompson's *The Making of the English Working Class.*

On the other hand, a researcher adopting a selectionist perspective on culture would point out that items of all four cultures were available for anyone to select, if only in their own imagination, to invoke sometimes but not at other times, to reject when it served them, or to embrace when it served them. It is true that some items of culture were more difficult to take up than others, for financial reasons, or because they required a certain expertise or their adoption by some individuals would be ridiculed. But they were in the culture, and potentially they could be taken up as people saw fit, depending on the circumstances. Thus, every time we see a member of the aristocracy adopting what we consider a bourgeois value or symbol, or a member of the bourgeoisie adopting an aristocratic value or symbol, we should not necessarily seek to understand it as a bourgeoisification of the aristocracy or a gentrification of the bourgeoisie. It may be more a matter of people – regardless of the social group to which they belonged – appropriating for their own (personal or political) purposes a part of the prevailing culture.

This way of thinking about culture can be found in recent literature challenging the conventional notion of the relationship between the aristocracy and the bourgeoisie in Germany. Dolores Augustine proposes that members of the German bourgeoisie did not become "feudalized" in the nineteenth century, though they were superficially and partially "aristocratized," by which she means that they adopted certain status symbols and styles that were associated with the aristocracy because these were part of the language understood in Germany at this time.[54] Similarly, Ute Frevert has effectively contended that the popularity of duels among members of the German bourgeoisie was not the consequence of the persistence of the Old Regime in Germany, nor evidence of it. Members of the bourgeoisie simply took up the practice and made it part of their culture.[55] In France, while almost all radicals were opposed to the advantages and pretensions of the nobility, they were not, in general, opposed to its values. Alexandre Dumas (author of *The Count of Monte Cristo* and *The Three Musketeers*) saw no inconsistency between his Republicanism and his glorification of the ideals of the old nobility.[56]

Some items of culture were attributed by many contemporaries to one group or the other. Love of leisure, antiquarianism, anti-materialism, an explicit concern with status and honour, and a certain measure of sexual promiscuity were associated with the aristocracy; materialism, the pursuit of self-interest, thrift, hard work, a strict moral code, and merit were, for the most part, associated with the bourgeoisie. Yet these associations were great oversimplifications. The reality was a world where values, beliefs, and practices were stirred around and attached to different people, not randomly, but also not according to clearly defined group membership. Honour was a concern of the bourgeoisie and even the working class as well as the aristocracy.

The explicit attribution of certain values, beliefs, or practices to certain social groups usually had political, social, or ideological motives. When aristocrats ran for political office, they frequently appealed to their electorates by trumpeting qualities that members of the aristocracy liked to think were aristocratic, such as honour, gentility, and their sense of duty, even though these electorates were predominantly bourgeois. The attribution of materialism to the bourgeoisie and the denigration of so-called bourgeois values, as documented by Maza, were frequently employed by members of the aristocracy, literati, and socialists to resist what they regarded as the undue and growing power of people engaged in commerce and industry. Meanwhile, others were playing the same game by trumpeting virtues that were claimed by the bourgeoisie. Dror Wahrman has contended that the very notion of a "middle class" in England, and the celebration of its virtues in the early nineteenth century, was politically driven.[57]

Cultural and Institutional Collections

This is not to deny that cultural items come in collections. Although an individual does not have to accept an entire collection, or even most of it, these collections do not consist of a potpourri of values, beliefs, and practices. They usually have a history, often a very long one, during which the collection has been repeatedly modified. It is worthwhile outlining the major cultural and institutional collections on which those who created, legislated, designed, and embellished state honours consciously and unconsciously drew.

ANTIQUITY
The oldest culture on which these status distributors drew was that of Antiquity. The influence of the Ancient cultures of Greece and Rome on the cultural and social evolution of Western Europe is difficult to exaggerate. They were instrumental in the evolution of European military culture. At the same time, they were taken as models of patriotic civic culture.[58] It is, therefore, not surprising that evidence of cultural selection and adaptation from Antiquity

can be found in Early Modern state honours. The link was often made explicitly. "You have learned, my son," Louis XIV wrote in his *Mémoires pour l'instruction du Dauphin*, "what use the Romans, and particularly Augustus, the wisest of their emperors, could make of ... purely honorific distinctions, which were much more common in their time than in ours."[59]

Classical influence was also evident during the French Revolution. The Revolutionaries obviously wanted to avoid any association of the rewards they were distributing with the honours of the Old Regime. It suited them to liken their honours to those of Rome, awarding, for example, civic crowns in imitation of those awarded by the Romans. The "legion" in "Legion of Honour" was adopted from the Romans, though it was never an honour among them. And the image on its insignia was an effigy of Napoleon in a distinctively Roman style.[60]

ORDERS OF KNIGHTHOOD
The cultural and institutional heritage of orders of knighthood is perhaps the most obvious collection of beliefs, values, and practices from which those who have founded and managed honours have drawn. The origins of this heritage can be traced to early Christianity. Beginning in Egypt during the fourth century CE, hundreds of monastic communities – eventually called monasteries or abbeys – were created in the Mediterranean world. Many were organized as formal and quasi-military bodies under the authority of a leader.[61] Their members often came to be seen as *milites Christi*, who defended people from Satan by means of their prayers. From the tenth century through to the early twelfth century, a number of monastic orders, which were federations of monastic communities, were established, with the austere Cistercians (based in the Abbey of Cîteaux, which was instituted in Burgundy in 1098) becoming a model for orders that were both monastic and military.[62] From 1100, Christians were also exposed to the principles attributed to Saint Augustine, which called for them to perform secular good works. The notion of a mighty struggle between good and evil, virtue and vice, became even more pervasive than it had been in earlier centuries.

These passions were not limited to Christians. They coincided with the birth of Islam and a period of increasing militarism in Muslim countries. In addition to armed forces raised by Islamic states to fight with those not sharing their religion, a great number of associations emerged in the ninth century bound together by oaths and secrets, and ready to serve as voluntary fighters in defence of Islam. This was also an era of Islamic schisms (first between Shiites and Sunnis in the seventh century, and subsequently among Shiites), which had the same effect of intensifying militarism among Muslim believers. The best known of the militaristic religious sects was the Nizari Ismailis, a community formed in the late eleventh century. It was a breakaway faction of the Ismailis, who were in turn a faction of Shiites. The Nizari Ismailis practised fierce asceticism. Their notorious mode of struggle with opponents was to murder their leaders. They were called "Assassins" by Europeans. (It has been suggested that this term was a rendering of the word *hashishiyah* (hashish smokers), the name given to them by Arab speakers; however, this derivation of "Assassins" as their name has been contested.)

In the late eleventh century, a major change occurred in Christian attitudes toward war. The papal proclamation of the First Crusade in 1095, which lifted the Christian prohibition of homicide, initiated a new era in which physical force became a legitimate weapon in the defence of Christianity. It was in this context that the first religious orders of knighthood came into existence. The Order of the Hospital of Saint John of Jerusalem was organized just after the First Crusade, when a number of Crusaders were persuaded to remain in Jerusalem to support a hospital that had been founded earlier by some Italian merchants. They became a monastic order in 1103, which initially was devoted to serving the poor and sick, but became increasingly militaristic out of the need to protect Christian pilgrims from Muslim attackers.[63] Another monastic organization that sought to protect Christian pilgrims, the Knights of the Temple of Solomon or Templars, came into being later than the Order of Saint John, but was made a military order earlier, when it was founded in 1120.

The direct influence of monastic communities and orders on those who established the religious orders of knighthood is indisputable. Even the union of religious monasticism with defending religious brethren had precedents in earlier religious communities.[64] The notion of an order that could be both military and religious spread in profusion throughout the Mediterranean and Middle Eastern world. Writing in the 1830s, Austrian Orientalist Joseph von Hammer-Purgstall, in support of his claim that the Assassins were not a dynastic kingdom or principality but rather an order, noted certain similarities between the Assassins and the Templars: political involvement, secret doctrines, certain features of their dress, and their strategy of acquiring castles and strong places.[65] It is true that both the Order of Saint John and the Templars had contact with the Nizari Ismailis, at least in Syria, but most scholars reject the idea of a direct imitation of the Nizari Ismailis by the Christian orders, or vice versa. This is probably not the right way to look at it. It may be more a matter of both movements selecting from a large collection of prevailing practices.

By the end of the thirteenth century, the cultural and institutional accumulation had expanded further to include other bodies of men bound together by a commitment to one another. Some of these new "confraternities" were devoted to the pursuit of secular interests (artisan guilds, for example), while others sought to provide useful services for the society in which members lived. Membership in some of these confraternities was restricted to those of noble birth. Other bodies constituted by nobles were also socially restricted: sworn alliances among knights, brotherhoods formed for mutual assistance, associations organized by aristocrats to encourage chivalrous conduct and to organize local festivities, and the monarchical orders of knighthood in which we are primarily interested.[66]

Moreover, both a product and a contributing part of this cultural accumulation were the accounts of glorious knighthood to which I have already referred. The Arthurian romances were the most influential. Although there is scattered evidence of Arthurian stories in earlier periods, it was Geoffrey Monmouth's *History of the Kings of Britain* – written in the early twelfth century and translated into other languages – that served to spread the Arthurian romantic lore in various parts of Europe. Its popularity reached a peak during the thirteenth and fourteenth centuries when a great number of stories linked to the legend were communicated and fabricated in Europe.

The first monarchical orders of knighthood were established in the early fourteenth century. Politically, they were a consequence of greater royal efforts to centralize power and the need of rulers to secure loyalty to their crown. Culturally and institutionally, however, they were a product of the accumulation I have been describing, reinforced and conditioned by popular celebration of what were seen as knightly values, a growing identification of the nobility with knighthood, and thus the evolution of a status based on both knighthood and nobility. These orders were created and expanded through what we might call a cultural/institutional chain reaction. The first orders were in Hungary in 1325 and in Castile in 1330. These bodies, and in particular the Castilian Order of the Band, influenced the founding by Edward III of the Order of the Garter in 1344, which in turn did much to shape the subsequent evolution of monarchical orders.[67] Every order inspired the formation of additional orders by example and by the dynamics of status competition, processes that continued through the following centuries. To be sure, variations are evident in the number of monarchical orders originating in different time periods and the character of these orders changed greatly over the centuries, but the lineage is unmistakable.

One condition contributing to the emergence of orders of knighthood in Medieval Europe may have been the political fragmentation of the region in conjunction with its religious unity, which contrasted with religious factionalism in most parts of the Mediterranean world. Although there was no shortage of religious sects in Europe, most powerful men remained loyal to the larger church; if they challenged political rulers, it was usually in secular rather than in religious struggles. It was, therefore, an effective option for a ruler to create an order of knighthood that was modelled on religious military orders and to claim to be devoted to the common cause of Christianity, even if the reason for forming the order was principally secular.

In turn, these Medieval orders of knighthood provided the major cultural and institutional collection for the monarchical orders of the Early Modern period. This does not mean that the Medieval orders were replicated in the seventeenth and eighteenth centuries. Rather, the notions of Medieval orders of knighthood that different people held served as templates, if you will, within which those who instituted the later orders selected what they wanted and also introduced new features. The title of "grand master" had long been used by religious orders and was generally adopted for the head of a monarchical order after 1693, when it was assumed by Louis XIV as head of the Order of Saint Louis. Efforts were made to reproduce the confraternal norms and practices of Medieval orders, though it will be seen in Chapter 10 that confraternity was not a simple matter in the orders of the Modern period.[68]

The intersecting tradition of Christianity, the military-religious orders, and secular orders of knighthood made the cross the preferred design of badges and medals in the Early Modern and Modern periods not just for orders of knighthood but even for gallantry medals, such as the Victoria Cross, the Belgian Military Cross, and the French War Cross, to name only three. Especially popular for state honours were crosses similar or identical to the Maltese Cross, an octagonal cross consisting of four arrowheads, with points that meet in the centre and outer ends that look like inverted Vs. Since about 1500, it had been the emblem of the Order of the Hospital of Saint John of Jerusalem, which was forced to transfer its headquarters to the Island of Malta in 1530.

To what extent was this tradition of orders of knighthood invented? Certainly some of it was. The assertion that the Order of the Thistle was a revival of an earlier order has no factual basis. Supposedly, after a battle in the ninth century between the Picts and the English, the victorious Pict commander founded this order in thanks to Saint Andrew, whose vision had emboldened the Picts. Yet there is no evidence of the existence of such an order, either then or in subsequent centuries. This tradition was invented over a long period of time, building on Medieval cultural items that included myths of Saint Andrew and the adoption of the thistle as a Scottish national emblem. The myth of the Order of the Thistle itself was fabricated, mainly during the sixteenth and seventeenth centuries.[69] Thus, we have two sets of inventors for this order: earlier makers of Scottish historical mythology and the architects of 1687.

In contrast, the Medieval origins of the Order of the Bath were invented almost entirely by those who created it in the eighteenth century. It is true that certain knights in the Medieval period were referred to as "Knights of the Bath," owing to the bathing ritual that was performed when this status was awarded, normally at royal coronations or marriages. They did not constitute a corporate order in the sense that the term was meant when the Order of the Bath was instituted in 1725, and the cultural items that the founders of the Bath selected came from a large collection of Medieval practices, not any specific order. Yet the notion that a Medieval order was being revived was useful in the early eighteenth century. It provided a Medieval lustre, which, it was believed, would facilitate the Order's acceptance because it would appeal to pre-Hanoverian traditions in a country that was still much divided over the Hanoverian succession.[70]

ROMANTICISM AND CHIVALRY

State honours of the late eighteenth and nineteenth centuries coincided chronologically with the Romantic movement and with the Gothic and chivalric "revivals" of the late eighteenth and nineteenth centuries. These were not the first cultural movements that sought to emulate what was regarded as admirable in Medieval culture. Earlier in this chapter, I mentioned the chivalric revival of the fifteenth century; then I was referring to a late-Medieval cultural movement that was encouraged by rulers who wanted knights to pursue less particularistic and more lofty ideals. It is especially associated with the Order of the Golden Fleece founded by Philip the Good, duke of Burgundy, in 1430. The British orders of the late seventeenth and early eighteenth centuries were designed during a government-supported rhetorical and antiquarian construction of chivalry, what Antti Matikkala calls a "Chivalric Enlightenment."[71]

The Romantic, Gothic, and chivalric movements of the late eighteenth and nineteenth centuries received less encouragement from rulers, but nevertheless had a cultural influence on nineteenth-century state honours. They shared an interest in the past and reinforced the celebration of Medieval orders of knighthood. The Romantic movement derived its very name from the use of the term "romance" to refer to Medieval tales of chivalry told in a Romance language. All three movements (Romantic, Gothic, and chivalric) engaged in idealization, could be melodramatic, valued heroism and moral seriousness, and scorned materialism, selfishness, and cowardice. Gothic romance portrayed the Middle Ages as the scene of intense struggle between good and evil, in which the former was promoted and the latter denigrated through epics of exemplary (though not necessarily perfect) heroes.

In these cultural movements, a new model of superiority emerged in the public mind. Those who promoted it sought to select items from the cultures of which I have been speaking, to cast them in a new form – that of "gentleman" – and to include within their embrace not just those who could claim a high-status ancestry but anyone who could meet the standard that was supposedly embodied in this status. This chivalric revival was to be found in a wide variety of practices and institutions: painting, schools, gothic castles, home decoration, didactic and fictional literature, collections of armour, re-enactment of Medieval tournaments, sports, celebration of "toughness," moral instruction of the working class, and even workers' movements.[72] The extremes to which it could be carried were often comical, but the movement was also reflected in paintings and novels that are still highly respected. With some exceptions, interest in the Medieval period did not stem from a desire to re-create or re-enact the past, or to adopt the entire package of Medieval chivalry, but rather, at least according to Walter Scott, from a wish merely to preserve or revive certain chivalric values.[73]

Cultural items of the Romantic movement and the chivalric revival were selected and adapted by a large segment of the population in this period because they were useful for the political and personal struggles in which they were engaged. The benefits of the idealization of chivalry to those who could claim aristocratic lineage are obvious, but for those who could not make such a claim, taking on the values and norms of these cultural movements offered a way of denying those with an aristocratic lineage a monopoly over them. The nature of Romanticism and chivalry was such that individuals and groups with quite different political ideologies could take them up. During the 1790s, in the English "pamphlet war" between those sympathetic with and those hostile to the French Revolution, romantic themes and images were employed in abundance on both sides to advance opposing understandings of the events occurring in France. Edmund Burke charged that the fate of Marie Antoinette ensued from the dissolution of the "age of chivalry." Although his political opponents ridiculed the passage, many of them sought to reclaim the notion of chivalry, to which the Revolution, so they argued, was closer than was the Old Regime. A good number of Romantic writers, most notably Leigh Hunt, William Hazlitt, Thomas Love Peacock, and Percy Bysshe Shelley, sought to adapt the theme to their different political purposes.[74]

As was the case with orders of knighthood, all of this cultural activity entailed some invention, but not entirely. Although the notion that there was a Medieval chivalric "code" that all knights were expected to follow was an invention, the chivalric cultural composers of the nineteenth century certainly read enough genuine literature on the Middle Ages and collected enough genuine artifacts that the tradition they sought to preserve was not totally fabricated. It was rather, as Boulton says, a set of values in Medieval literature.[75]

Whatever their personal views on Medieval chivalry and the effort to revive it, it was advantageous during the eighteenth and nineteenth centuries for anyone in the business of founding or fashioning state honours to adjust their rhetoric to it, and to go along with the indisputable popularity of chivalric romance in the population. The significance of the bourgeoisie in the expansion and democratization of state honours lies, in no small measure, in the favourable attitude of many members of the bourgeois reading public toward chivalric ideals. Book sales provide some indication of this sentiment. Scott's *The Lay of the Last Minstrel,* a chivalric romance poem published in 1805, went through six editions in the first three years, with sales approximating 27,000 copies.[76]

In less than two weeks, the first printing of 12,000 copies of his *Ivanhoe* were sold despite a relatively high purchase price.[77] In France, romantic novels were published in numbers averaging 2,611 per edition in 1834, well above the average for works published in that year.[78] The popularity of Dumas is difficult to measure in book sales since most of his works were serialized in magazines or newspapers, but we know that his readership drove him to write at a pace that is truly hard to comprehend. A tabulation made in 1902 identified sixty-seven works of drama, ninety-two works of fiction, fifty-three historical works, thirty-nine books of travel, and thirty-one poems, plus seven "hypothetical works" for which he was given credit.[79]

The popularity of chivalric romance should not be exaggerated. For every enthusiast there was an equal or greater number who had scant interest in chivalric ideals. Many laughed at the fantasy and pomposity of it all. It was certainly not a major driving force in the expansion of state honours. The Romantic, Gothic, and chivalric movements of the late eighteenth and nineteenth centuries post-dated the creation of important state honours in the seventeenth and eighteenth centuries.

Yet there is no denying the passion of those who loved chivalry and romance. In taking a relatively instrumentalist approach to the cultural and institutional collections adopted for state honours, I have not claimed that interest in these cultures was insincere. On the contrary, my argument very much rests on the fact that large numbers of people were passionately interested in romance and chivalry. Nor would I deny that many of those who created and administered state honours were themselves passionate in their sentiments toward this culture. In the case of the Order of the Bath, it is evident that the main architect, John Anstis, garter king of arms, was passionate about Medieval imitation, while the prime minister, Robert Walpole, could not have cared less.

HERALDRY

Closely related to orders of knighthood and chivalry were heraldic arms. European heraldry emerged in the eleventh and twelfth centuries. Certain designs became hereditary and were jealously guarded by descendants, though not always successfully. Eventually, the duty of recording arms and other types of heraldic emblem was assigned to royal heralds, who in some cases were also given the right to confer them and to restrict and regulate their use. During the Early Modern period, considerable differences in heraldic institutions evolved among European countries. The use of heraldic signs was more regulated in Britain during the seventeenth and eighteenth centuries, though even in Britain the control exercised by heraldic authorities was far weaker than they would have liked.

At any rate, a number of scholars agree that the heraldic cultural and institutional collection provided a framework for the social construction of much of Early Modern English society.[80] And the use of heraldic emblems as a practice has survived in the Modern era, indeed has spread well beyond its geographical origins. During the nineteenth and twentieth centuries, many of the state officials who were consulted when a state honour was created were specialists in coats of arms, and there was typically an institutional connection between those who managed or designed state honours and official heraldic authorities. Not surprisingly, many of the symbols selected for state honours were heraldic, though they might not have originated in heraldry. These include banners, flags or pennants, and stars. These symbols did not have a standard symbolic meaning. In fact, armorial motifs had traditionally been designed primarily to represent symbolically the institution or family who possessed the arms, usually by the selection of some distinctive feature they possessed. Heraldry was no more and no less than a cultural and institutional collection from which state-honours distributors could select.

ROYALTY

Many European state honours have been imbued with royal or imperial symbolism. It was mentioned in Chapter 2 that monarchical institutions were closely associated with state honours. Along with the observations made there, I can point to the many state honours named after a monarch and badges or medals that often bore an effigy of a monarch or emperor. The effigy on the insignia of the Legion of Honour was initially that of Napoleon. Under the Restoration, he was replaced by the first Bourbon monarch, Henry IV. This design was preserved under the July Monarchy, was altered again under the Second Republic, and was changed yet again during the Second Empire, when Napoleon was returned to his former place.[81] In monarchies, whatever the design, a royal crown frequently surmounted the badge or medal, as in the case of the Order of the British Empire and the Order of Leopold.

If practicable, state honours were handed out by the sovereign in person, with much royal pomp and circumstance. Practices obviously varied. The stiff and socially awkward Dutch king, William I, did not like ceremony, with the result that the efforts of ceremony-enthusiasts in the Netherlands were relatively frustrated. Only for the military order did they institutionalize an ordination at which new members swore an oath.[82] In addition, and more practically speaking, it was impossible that all presentations of state honours be accompanied by great pomp. Indeed, most took place with minimal ceremony or without any ceremony at all.

Yet for many of those who controlled state honours, the ideal was to make presentations majestic occasions for royal symbolism. In 1805, the royal splendour of the installation of knights in the Order of the Garter was pumped up. The visit of George IV to Ireland in 1821 was the occasion for the installation of nine new knights in the Order of Saint Patrick in a ceremony that has been characterized by Peter Galloway as the closest Ireland ever came to a royal coronation.[83] The first presentation of the Victoria Cross was made by Victoria herself, accompanied by members of the royal family, at a review in Hyde Park designed to accommodate a large public. In her words:

June 26 1857 Buckingham Palace
A thick, heavy morning. – Full agitation for the coming great event of the day, viz: the distribution of the "Victoria Cross" … The whole was conducted in full state. Several interesting circumstance combined to make this day, an important one. It was, in the 1st place, the solemn inauguration of the new and honourable order of valour, – also the day of Albert's new title [prince consort] becoming known & the 1st time I had ever ridden on horse-back, at a great Review in London, the 1st time our 2 Boys rode at a great State Review; the 1st time dear little Leopold appeared in public, & lastly the first time Fritz [Crown Prince Frederick of Prussia] appeared in public with us, as our future son-in-law. I rode between him and my beloved Albert. It was a beautiful sight, & every thing admirably arranged. All the Royal Family, including little Leopold, followed in carriages … Constant cheering, & noises of every kind … The sight in Hyde Park was very fine, – the tribunes & stands, full of spectators, the Royal one being in the centre.[84]

In 1906 a special installation service for a small number of GCMGs (knights grand cross in the Order of Saint Michael and Saint George, the highest grade) was held in Saint Paul's Cathedral, in space newly acquired by this order. For the first time, the GCMGs were assembled together as a corporate body, wearing their mantles and collars. This display brought such gratification that it put to shame the more senior Order of the Bath. When George V became king he decided to revive the old ceremony for the Bath. The first show took place on 22 July 1913, with numerous royal personages in attendance. A large procession wended its way from the House of Lords to Westminster Abbey, members decked out in crimson and gold plumes.[85]

THE HISTORICAL EVOLUTION OF HONOURS

The earliest honorific rewards of which we have reliable knowledge are those of Ancient Egypt. Subsequently, for a number of centuries at least, evidence is scarce that similar practices were adopted in other societies, even in the Mediterranean and Middle Eastern region. In Classical and Macedonian Greece, however, we know that honorific rewards were bestowed in a way that matched the practices of Egyptian kings. Like Egyptian awards, these Greek awards included body decorations. The literature does not tell us with any confidence why Greeks in the Classical period made this selection. In contrast, it is clear that the Macedonian Greeks selected and adapted honorific practices primarily from Classical Greek culture, and that the Romans had the precedents of both Classical and Macedonian Greece from which to choose. The Roman system of military honours, known as *dona militaria* (literally, military gifts), exceeded all earlier honorific recognition systems for the military. Some of the cultural objects they adopted were similar to those of the Greeks, specifically wreaths and crowns.

After the decline of the Roman Empire, no comparable honours system emerged in Europe until the Early Modern period. The Medieval monarchical orders, though they certainly could raise a man's status, were not seen primarily as honours by their members. Over time, however, they gradually became less a method of binding powerful men to a ruler and more a status reward. Additional orders were founded in the Early Modern period, which imitated one another, and were further imitated in the nineteenth century. The statutes of the Order of Maria Theresa were adopted by the Russian

Order of Saint George and later by the Military Order of William, founded in the Netherlands in 1815, which was also inspired by the Legion of Honour.[86] Variations in the design of badges worn by different grades in European honours also influenced one another, with the result that a common pattern coalesced by the nineteenth century.[87] By the late nineteenth and early twentieth centuries, the architects of state honours had a large variety of cultural and institutional precedents from which to choose.

This is not to say that making these choices was easy. Artistic creativity was difficult. By the time the Order of the British Empire was being established, it was hard to come up with anything new. Ponsonby recorded that the medallist who was commissioned to design its insignia complained that "every conceivable form has already been used and that it is practically impossible to design a Star which does not form part of an existing Order in Europe."[88] When her designs were sent to an heraldic official for an opinion, he complained about the wreath she had incorporated because it "has always been reserved in British orders for military services, and is therefore not applicable to civilians." He also objected to the Royal crest, which "had already been made use of in the Victoria Cross," and to the lion she had adopted, which he asserted was "meaningless from an heraldic point of view." In the end, however, the lion was expunged for what would seem the opposite reason, because it represented Scotland in the royal arms.[89]

MERIT

I have argued that the cultural lineage of merit evolved from aristocratic culture in the Middle Ages and the Early Modern period. In addition, beginning in the late eighteenth century, the idiom of merit was employed in status and political competition. Members of the professions, particularly in Britain, where professional positions were not venal, were explicitly or implicitly laying claim to status in terms of merit.[90] During the French Revolution, "birth" was the issue on which all those opposed to the existing order could agree and on which they believed the nobility was most vulnerable. In the *cahiers des doléances* (the list of grievances drawn up in 1789), there were no demands for the abolition of either the nobility or decorations, but merely the demand that state honours should be distributed as a recompense to those who have distinguished themselves by their merits and talents.[91] Napoleon adopted the idiom of merit

because he believed it would have a positive effect on his officials
and soldiers, and because he could use it to rally to his side the
state bureaucracy and the socio-economic groups from which this
bureaucracy was drawn.[92]

The battle over merit was nowhere greater than in the bureaucracies of European states. J.A. Armstrong was one of the first to examine in detail the contention in nineteenth-century Europe over the
kind of merit that was most appropriate for civil service. Aristocrats sought to define the administrative role as an undifferentiated
exercise of authority, for which integrity and character were more
important than specific qualifications, while members of the bourgeoisie sought to legitimize their claim to state offices by defining
the role as a specialized, technical activity.[93] Those in opposition to
entrenched political elites typically blamed birth for everything that
was wrong and seized upon merit as one of the standards by which
the state needed to be reorganized. In Germany, Baron von Stein
and his allies claimed to be creating a new society in which heredity
was not the basis of status, but instead talent and resources would
establish the place people occupied in society.[94] Many French historians and sociologists have taken the view that the state bureaucracy
in France was built on the myth of merit, helping the state elite to
legitimate its power and its monopoly of state offices, which became
the preserve of a self-recruiting Parisian state elite. French bureaucrats did all they could to convince themselves and others that they
succeeded as a consequence of their individual merit.[95]

Of course, members of the bourgeoisie were not the only ones
who sought to harness the idiom of merit to their advantage. Aristocrats continued to do so. When the Second Marquess of Westminster castigated Lord John Russell and trumpeted the principle
of merit, it was not because he believed in reward for merit more
than Lord John Russell did. It was because the idiom of merit served
a useful political purpose in his effort to disparage Whig peerage
appointments.

All the same, the aristocracy, in its defence of its claim to higher
merit and in its resistance to the demands of non-aristocrats for
power and status, was increasingly led to stress merit in the blood
and to place more emphasis on pedigree. The French Revolution
and the Napoleonic reconstruction only strengthened this inclina-
tion. The notorious caste-like European nobility anxiously closing
its doors to upstarts – the nobility that we have learned to scorn – is

more a nineteenth-century phenomenon than something of the Old Regime.

It all played into the hands of those challenging aristocratic power, who were effectively undermining the belief that merit could be measured by birth. In its place was gradually substituted the idea that merit had to be and could be measured by other criteria – years of training, examination, credentials, career service and advancement, and graduation from elite schools. As a result of this political struggle and the course it took, few people today in Western Europe would think of merit and birth as anything but opposites.

Culture and Social Change

The European expansion of state honours was not the result of a paradigm shift from aristocratic culture to bourgeois culture, nor conversely of the persistence of the former into the nineteenth and twentieth centuries. In making this statement, I do not want to be misunderstood. First, I am not claiming that no cultural and institutional change occurred. Rather, I am claiming that this cultural and institutional change is best described as the appropriation and adaptation of earlier and existing cultural beliefs, values, and practices for new purposes. Initially, monarchs carried out this appropriation and adaptation, but eventually those who did so were drawn primarily from non-aristocratic social groups. Among them were the status distributors who created and awarded the honours of states.

Second, I am not saying that important social changes are never the consequence of cultural paradigm shifts. Understanding culture as a paradigm and identifying major transformations in such paradigms can be the way in which one needs to understand a particular social change, or at least can be part of that understanding. We cannot comprehend the social, political, and cultural evolution of Western Europe without paying attention to significant cultural transformations. Indeed, I have just acknowledged that there was a noteworthy shift in the criteria that were employed for judging merit in the Early Modern period. In Chapter 6, we shall be looking at several other major cultural changes, most notably the development of a culture of improvement and reform in the Early Modern period. For the most part, however, a selectionist approach to the questions raised in this book proves more useful. Certainly, if we want to understand the effect of the rise of the bourgeoisie and the

role played by aristocratic and bourgeois cultures in the expansion
of state honours, we need to see how a variety of cultural and institutional items can be selected and utilized as a source of power that
people use in power struggles.

For a long time, in cultural studies, the predilection was to focus
on the use of culture for non-instrumental purposes. Even in literature on social movements, the renaissance in the study of culture
that began in sociology in the 1980s led to a greater emphasis, or at
least a call for greater emphasis, on the non-instrumental rewards
and goals of social movements, especially of the so-called "new social
movements." Yet more recently, cultural studies have moved in a
direction that gives greater attention to the instrumental goals of
human action. Those promoting the study of culture in the 1980s
were quite rightly unhappy with earlier sociological writing on culture, which treated culture as merely a reflection of the positions
people occupy in society and the interests we would expect them to
have given those positions. Culture, they knew, was more important
than such assumptions were allowing. This does not mean, however,
that there is no relationship between political and economic structures, on the one hand, and culture on the other. Not only can culture reflect the positions people occupy in society and the interests
that correspond to those positions, but, in addition, as I have suggested in this chapter, culture can be an instrument in the pursuit
of other kinds of power. During the eighteenth, nineteenth, and
early twentieth centuries, state honours acquired significant cultural
power from the aristocratic and bourgeois cultures on which they
were built. In the remainder of this book, I examine how state honours, and the cultural power with which they had become invested,
were used to generate and maintain collective, disciplinary, and
status power.

PART II

State, War, and Collective Power

The second explanation for the evolution of state honours outlined in the Introduction is that state honours have evolved as a method of population management. Parts II and III examine two ways in which honours can perform this function. Part II looks at the mobilization and organization of collective action. Part III looks at the relationship between different social structures and social control.

In Part II, the contention is that the European proliferation of state honours is explained in large part by changing conditions from the late Medieval period through into the Modern period for mobilizing and organizing collective action.

We begin with several preliminary discussions. It is useful for the reader to be aware of the theoretical issues that have shaped this project. Thus, Chapter 4 provides a theoretical discussion of two bodies of literature in the social sciences: socio-cultural evolutionary theory and the theory of collective action. In the subsequent chapters, I discuss the processes that altered conditions for collective action in Early Modern and Modern Western Europe. The changing conditions for collective action created what evolutionists call selection pressures, that is, pressures that lead to adaptive selection.

4

Theoretical Considerations

Just as students of biological evolution now believe that what is critical is the reproduction or disappearance of a gene, rather than a species or even an organism, it is now generally accepted among cultural evolutionists that they need to understand social change in terms of the reproduction or demise of a belief, piece of information, value, pattern of human behaviour, practice, role, or social institution – sometimes called a "meme" – rather than in terms of the survival of a society or of a social system. To be sure, the survival of a meme depends on its adaptive consequences, and these adaptive consequences, like the adaptive consequences of a gene, are with respect to the unit that "carries" the gene or meme. Thus, the fate of the "social carrier" is critical in the same way that the survival of the organism that carries a gene is critical; but the survival of this carrier is not, in itself, what is fundamental for the theory. Indeed, with respect to social change, it is not easy to lay down as a rule what the carrier will be; it may be a society, kinship group, community, elite, social movement, religious sect, state, political regime, economic organization, et cetera. But whatever it is, it is merely the carrier of the social phenomenon in which we are interested.

This cultural evolutionary theory has been critiqued not just by those who reject any kind of evolutionary theory but even by many evolutionists. Some of the latter claim that to adopt the principles of Darwinian theory to explain cultural evolution is nothing more than making an analogy. A social carrier is not an organism. It is not distinct from other carriers. It does not live or die in the way that an organism does. Unlike an organism, when a social carrier disappears, not all of its components disappear. Even if a society is conquered by some other society (Anglo-Saxon England by the Normans, for example), most individuals survive, and in varying degrees, much of their culture does as well. And social carriers select memes, whereas organisms inherit genes.

This difficulty is all the more serious when one is interested in those cultural and institutional items that cannot be seen as critical to the survival of the carriers, but may still contribute to it. Such is the case with state honours. As I have stressed, they were merely one among many innovations adopted in response to the problems that rulers and state officials faced in Early Modern and Modern Europe. No state collapsed, no army lost a war because it did not have enough honours. Socio-cultural Darwinism has not given sufficient attention to this analytical problem, to innovations of this kind, and to the need to develop methods to include them in socio-cultural evolutionary theory.

A closely related difficulty comes from the fact that cultural and institutional items can be both adaptive and maladaptive. Given the complexity of societies and the contradictory forces and interests operating within them, it would be surprising if this were not the case. Emile Durkheim contended that crime, which in most ways is maladaptive, also performs important functions for social solidarity. Free trade is functional in some ways for a Modern society but dysfunctional in other ways. When Marx wrote that religion is the opiate of the masses, he meant that it is functional for the capitalist system, certainly not for the masses. And when Bourdieu developed the thesis that language can serve to reproduce inequality, he was obviously not suggesting that language performs this function for society as a whole.

Jonathan Turner has made a useful distinction between Darwinian selection and Spencerian selection. The driving force of Darwinian selection is competition and the elimination of societies or carriers as a result of competition, whereas the driving force of Spencerian selection is the effort people make in order to cope with new challenges and to come up with innovations in order to do so.[1] Turner emphasizes how societal changes such as population growth generate selection pressures, which force people to find solutions to the problems posed by these pressures and to come up with new ways of doing things.[2] Competition among human groups often intensifies selection pressures, but is not necessary. In Early Modern and Modern Europe, we find that international and national competition contributed to the pressures faced by governments, but that other forces also put pressures on these governments to innovate.

It helps to recognize that no one is claiming that the need to meet selection pressures brings forth the means of doing so, in this case the means to mobilize and organize collective action. Rather, the argument is that, to the extent that the pressures making a particular kind of collective action and organization difficult are not successfully met, this kind of collective action and organization will diminish, will not develop, or will be weaker and less effective. Conversely, to the extent that these pressures are overcome, this kind of collective action and organization will prevail. Thus we would expect the character of collective action and organization to be different in one time period than in another, or in one society versus another, according to variations in selection pressures on collective action and organization and the way they can be met.

This line of thinking suggests how we can link problems caused by selection pressures to an innovation when we cannot assert that the society or the carrier would have disappeared without it. This is not easy. Even Turner has recourse to assertions that if certain challenges are not met, societies will "disintegrate," "collapse," or be "torn apart."[3] Looking for this kind of evidence may be possible in the study of hunter-gatherers and perhaps even horticultural societies, but not in the study of agrarian or industrial societies.

Instead, we need to examine how an innovation contributes to the development and survival not of a society or a carrier but of a certain level of success in meeting a challenge, in the present study a certain kind of collective action. To do so, we have to establish an empirical connection between the problems that are faced and the innovations that we hypothesize were developed to meet these problems. This is relatively straightforward if we can find evidence that the innovations were introduced consciously and intentionally for this purpose. However, social challenges usually result in a plethora of trials and errors, often in imitation of earlier or existing practices; and institutions typically evolve as a result of the cumulative decisions and practices of individuals and the accumulation of precedents. Even when we can identify an initial "mutation" for an innovation, which is not often the case, the evolution of the institution depends on a great number of subsequent decisions that it is impossible to examine in any comprehensive manner. Moreover, people can be motivated in selections they make by certain cognitive processes that are sometimes referred to as "sub-intentional,"

which in this context means that the selection is the result of preferences, attitudes, and perceptions of which an actor may not be fully
conscious, or at least not aware of how they are influencing his or
her decisions. And finally, the investigation is complicated by the
fact that people often have more than one intention in adopting
a practice.

Not surprisingly, the obstacles a researcher faces in trying to
explain innovations as adaptive selections are especially difficult in
historical research. We cannot interview those who may have played
a role, and the documentary material is always limited. We can sometimes find explicit statements by state officials (accurately or inaccurately) providing reasons why practices were adopted. I have made
an effort to find empirical evidence of this kind.

Otherwise, we are left with more indirect ways of determining
adaptive selection. In general terms, we have to demonstrate what
we might call an adaptive affinity between problems and an innovation. This requires a careful investigation of the problems – in this
case, collective-action problems – and the innovation – in this case,
state honours – to evaluate logically whether the latter could help
overcome the former. What kinds of collective action were states
trying to organize? What was difficult about organizing such collective action? How were these collective-action problems different
from those in earlier periods? What would be needed to overcome
these problems? What were the various adaptive characteristics of
state honours? How did state honours in Early Modern and Modern
Western Europe compare to those in earlier periods, and do these
comparisons indicate a change in the function of state honours?
What other practices were being adopted that were similar in function to state honours, and what can they tell us about the challenges
that state officials and other organizers of collective action faced
and the ways they thought about meeting those challenges?

We need to begin with the collective-action problems.

COLLECTIVE-ACTION PROBLEMS

During the past three or four decades a large number of social
scientists in more than one discipline have been concerned with
"collective-action problems," that is, the challenges faced in the
mobilization and organization of collective action and the ways in
which these difficulties are overcome. The collective-action problems that have received the most attention are: (1) legitimation, (2)

motivation, and (3) communication. I will say a few words about each separately, though empirically they can be difficult to distinguish. As we will see, the identification of these problems helps us to determine how the function of honours changed from the Medieval period to the Modern period.

Legitimation

I am using the term "legitimation" in a broad sense to refer to processes by which something is made to seem right, normal, beneficial, and/or necessary. This is usually done by interpreting culture in ways that justify what one seeks to legitimate, while simultaneously shaping the latter in ways that are consistent with elements in a culture.

Legitimation in this sense embraces two other concepts that have become popular in recent decades. First, it includes part of what Bourdieu and his followers mean by "symbolic power." I indicated in the Introduction that they use this term in two different ways. One is the meaning I gave there: the power that a person is able to exert by virtue of his or her prestige and by institutional recognitions of that prestige; it is roughly the same as what I mean by status, that is, the power to command respect. The other meaning of symbolic power in the Bourdieu lexicon is the capacity to legitimate social constructions and make what exists seem natural; it corresponds to what I mean by legitimation.

The second concept is "frame." In a general way, it refers to schemata of interpretation, definitions of reality, and cognitive maps in which social constructions take place. A frame determines how people perceive their social and even physical environment. In a more specific sense, which coincides with what I am calling legitimation, the term refers to the characterization of a social structure, situation, institution, social movement, et cetera according to prevailing values, beliefs, and social constructions, and the adjustment of the latter to suit whatever needs to be legitimated.

In power struggles, these cultural adoptions and adaptations can serve to legitimate the power that different regimes or political factions possess, as well as the efforts by these regimes or factions to augment their power, oppose their enemies, win wars, et cetera. Few social scientists would insist that legitimation is a strict requirement for the mobilization and organization of collective action – people can obviously be compelled against their will – but the majority would agree that it is more effective if those engaging in it believe in the legitimacy of what they are doing.

Motivation

In the social-science literature that we are reviewing, motivation for performance in collective action has been explained chiefly in terms of the presence or absence of rewards. Many social scientists have been interested in one particular motivation problem known as "rational egoism": if a large number of people can benefit from a collective effort, the most rational behaviour for a self-interested individual is to abstain from participation and let others do the work. Rational egoism creates what is usually referred to as the "free-rider" problem. Why should I go on strike and walk the picket line if I can get the same increase in salary as my fellow workers without losing any income? Almost any collective effort in which fates are shared will be subject to this problem. A soldier in battle should engage the enemy as little as possible, leaving it to other soldiers to take the risks.

Closely related to the free-rider problem is the "efficacy problem": the single action of one individual (one person recycling his or her garbage, one soldier risking his life) may be so small in the collective effort that it is not rational for this individual to take this action, no matter how much she or he is committed to the cause. Rarely is a state election determined by one vote, the success of an environmental cleanup by one volunteer, or victory in war by one soldier. Obviously, the larger the active collectivity, the less convinced each participant is that his or her contribution will make a critical difference to the outcome.[4]

Nonetheless, despite rational egoism and the efficacy problem, the mobilization and organization of collective action occurs daily in all parts of the world. Employees work hard. Citizens vote. Young men enlist. And soldiers risk their lives. We can witness many social movements throughout history that mobilized great numbers of people. Hence, a good body of academic literature, some of it in game theory, has sought to explain why and by what means the mobilization and organization of collective action is so prevalent despite the free-rider and efficacy problems.[5]

Again, coercion could help overcome the problem. Unmotivated people may be compelled in one way or another to engage in collective action. However, most writers interested in this issue do not believe that authority or coercion is generally capable of sufficiently overcoming the free-rider and efficacy problems. Military authority is usually insufficient to get soldiers to risk their lives. Even bureaucratic collective action requires more than command to motivate active participation. And neither coercion nor authority can account for participation in social movements.

So we need to find additional reasons to explain motivation for performance in collective action. Writers have identified reciprocity and past co-operation, group identity, personal bonds, and mutual trust among the conditions making it likelier that rational people will engage in a collective effort rather than choose to free ride. I call these sources of motivation "unrestricted incentives." They are meant to elicit behaviour that meets the normative expectations of social contexts, relations, or roles. Unrestricted incentives provide every person involved in the same kind of relationship or role the same reward for contributing to the collective effort. An example would be the expectation of friends to assist one another in a time of crisis. These incentives work better in small groups rather than in large collectivities because there is usually more agreement on what is expected and because individual actions of members can be directly or indirectly observed by others in the group.[6]

With or without unrestricted incentives, but especially in their absence, collective action and organization is also promoted by what Mancur Olson called "selective incentives."[7] In order to avoid confusion, I have chosen not to use his term because he is referring to a different kind of selection than what is meant in the socio-cultural evolutionary literature. By selective incentive, Olson means that only some people get a reward or punishment. I call this a "restricted incentive."

Whatever term we use, it refers to the extra benefits that are not shared by all members of a social group, and so are not undermined by rational egoism. In principle, they are meant to reward behaviour that exceeds normal expectations, and thus justifies the restricted reward. Promotions, bonuses, commissions, individual increases in pay, special praise, and honorific awards are the most common restricted rewards that are utilized to motivate people in Modern society. Restricted rewards can also mitigate the effect of perceived inefficacy – though not the perception itself – by providing rewards for individual efforts.

Communication

Collective action and organization require effective communication among members or potential members of an active collectivity. Achieving effective communication can pose serious challenges for both leaders and participants.

COMMUNICATION PROBLEMS

The first challenge is the communication of expectations. Potential participants need to know what they are expected to do, and how they are expected to behave. Most of the campaigning or advertising that leaders of social movements engage in is intended to tell people what they can do to support the cause. Bureaucrats with an interest in better performance by subordinates will provide them with job descriptions and instructions about how to perform their job well, and will issue circulars informing all employees what good workers do.

The second function of communication is coordination. Effective communication facilitates coordination of various kinds, but one specific coordination problem is the most relevant to our subject. Even if people are motivated to participate, and even if they know what they are expected to do, their contribution to a collective effort might still be less effective if they are uncertain that other people will contribute as well. This coordination problem can be overcome relatively easily in small groups or tightly controlled bureaucratic organizations, but it is a major obstacle to large-scale collective action and organization. I may be perfectly willing to bear the personal cost of assisting a wildlife-protection society; I may be well aware that supporters are expected to make a sizeable monetary donation; but I may still be hesitant to do so out of concern that few others will support the society and that it will collapse, with the result that my money will be largely wasted. In military collective action, this kind of dilemma can emerge when soldiers or units know how to attack the enemy and are willing to do so, but only if they think that other soldiers or other units will do what they are expected to do at the same time.

In the social-scientific literature on various kinds of collective action, much more attention has been given to legitimation, motivation, and the communication of expectations than to coordination.

Those writers who have paid attention to it and have sought to explain why large-scale collective action and organization occurs despite this coordination problem argue that humans have developed a number of instruments that they use to coordinate their activities. Mechanical or material coordination instruments include clocks, traffic lights, and battle standards – all of which work because we know that others besides ourselves can see them.

Human practices can also serve as instruments of coordination. In *Rational Ritual*, Michael Chwe proposes that rituals are used to generate "common knowledge." Unfortunately, his thesis requires some awkward wording to convey: if we know that a number of people have seen the same public activity, and if we know that they know that we and others have seen it, then we are more likely to engage in whatever action the public activity encourages. His thesis helps to explain why many social movements hold demonstrations or marches. When I attend a large demonstration, or observe a march making its way through a city, I know that others have seen or will see it. I also know that they know that they are not the only ones who have seen it.

In a similar vein, it has been suggested that high-status people can be used as instruments of coordination. We are more likely to think that other people will engage in a certain action if a high-status person promotes it. This is true for a number of reasons, one of which is that we know that high-status people are more prominent; they are observed by a larger number of people than are low- or medium-status persons.[8] It is why those trying to organize a collective effort often ask celebrities to promote it. It is also one of the reasons that successful field commanders and naval officers have traditionally made themselves visible to their men, and why conspicuous actions in war are more likely to be regarded as "heroic."

SPACE, TIME, AND NUMBER

Modes of communication vary in the magnitude and nature of their communication power, and this variation determines their capacity to solve the above communication problems under different circumstances.

Some years ago, H.A. Innis distinguished between media that are biased toward communication over space versus those that are biased toward communication over time. The former are lighter and easier to transport or transmit, while the latter are heavier, but survive longer.[9] He gave considerable attention to the difference between papyrus and paper on the one hand, and parchment on the other hand; the former are biased over space, while the latter is biased over time. It is a relative distinction; even media that possess both types of power can be biased one way or the other, with significant consequences. Whether one agrees with the consequences that Innis contemplated – and they have been the subject of debate – his identification of the functions performed by different media can be useful.

An overlapping variable is the number of persons reached by a particular means of communication.[10] Some media of communication can reach great numbers of people, while others cannot, or can do so only at considerable cost. Printing increased the numerical communication power of paper, and moveable type greatly increased the numerical communication power of printing.

GROUP SIZE

Generally speaking, for both motivation and communication, it is clear that, without offsetting mechanisms, collective action and organization become more difficult as group size expands. Larger groups (1) reduce the perceived harm to the group caused by the defection of a single individual, (2) render it more difficult to influence the behaviour of others, (3) make it easier to defect anonymously, (4) make communication in general and coordination in particular more difficult, and (5) exacerbate the efficacy problem. The larger the group, the harder it is for participants to reward or sanction one another interpersonally. People in small groups can adopt comparatively direct instruments of coordination, talk to one another, and observe one another's behaviour. By necessity, in larger collectivities, other kinds of instruments of coordination, such as public demonstrations, become more important.

THE FUNCTION OF HONOURS

How might honours help overcome these collective-action problems? For the most part, I believe that answers to this question must be historically specific: state honours have served different purposes in different ways under different historical conditions. That said, I will make a few observations that are not specific to Western Europe before I proceed with the historical analysis of this region. My remarks are limited to the collective-action problems discussed above.

State honours could be used to legitimate collective action and organization. In Part I, our concern was with the way in which honours were created, shaped, and legitimated by prevailing cultural beliefs, values, and practices. Now the concern is with the other side of the coin: how state leaders may have used state honours to help legitimate the collective efforts they were seeking to organize. These processes are well understood in the historical literature, where honours are often seen as a means of legitimating regimes. It has been shown that in Imperial China, for example, honorific rewards distributed by the emperor were an integral part of a complex of rituals and symbols that were used to legitimate Imperial rule.[11] The *Mingjiang* and *Jiaolao* of the Qing dynasty – when the emperor rode out of the capital city to welcome and congratulate returning commanders and then honoured them with rewards and feasts – were performed within a larger strategy of celebrating war, militarizing culture, and integrating military and civilian practices, in order to strengthen and legitimate Qing rule.[12] The legitimation function of state honours has also been stressed in some relatively recent sociological literature, which asserts that honours are deemed useful in preserving the legitimacy of states that cannot be legitimated by absolute rule or divine right.[13]

Honours can certainly serve as restricted incentives. This is especially evident in the Roman system of military honours, the *dona*, the majority of which were designed to encourage specific acts of war. These include the naval crown (for being the first to lead an assault on an enemy ship), the wall crown (for being the first to lead an assault on the wall of a besieged city), and the fortification crown (for being the first to lead an assault on a hostile camp).

In the copious literature published today on how businesses and other organizations can utilize awards and prizes, the major function is to provide motivational incentives. This literature was mentioned in the opening pages of this book, where I indicated its limitations for helping us explain the evolution of state honours. Here I want to emphasize that this literature does not sufficiently recognize the variation in honorific rewards that exists historically: in the way in which honours provide restricted rewards, in the relative utility of

honours as restricted rewards, and in alternative restricted rewards
that can be available. Nor does this literature identify the motivational problems that led to the evolution of the honorific rewards
that we have today.

State honours can also communicate expectations. Awards are
almost always accompanied by some statement of what the person
has done to be worthy of the award. In this way, state officials justify their choice of a recipient and, at the same time, indicate what
kind of behaviour is to be expected of an admirable soldier, state
employee, citizen, et cetera. Biographical sketches are sometimes
printed in state bulletins, in newspaper reports, and/or in books
written for the general public. Not surprisingly, many books have
been published on recipients of the Victoria Cross.

And state honours can serve as instruments of coordination. They
not only convey knowledge of what is expected but also tell people that it is common knowledge. When we learn that a person has
received an honour, we know that other people know about it as
well, and that they know that others like ourselves know about it.
And we all know that most people will be told for what action or
actions this award has been given. Receiving an honour also raises a
person's status in his or her social world, thus increasing his or her
visibility, and hence utility as a coordination device.

5

Conditions for Collective Action
in Medieval Europe

An explanation of the evolution of state honours in Western Europe requires an understanding of how collective action was mobilized in Medieval Europe and the function that honours may then have performed. It is difficult here to delve fully into the complexity and diversity of society and institutions during the Medieval period, but some general observations can be made.

Mobilizing large numbers of people in collective action and organization was not easy. Travel was slow and arduous. Although geographical mobility was greater than has generally been appreciated by later writers, people were certainly tied to particular locations more than would be the case in later centuries. Until the Early Modern period, social organization in Western Europe was based primarily on ties of lordship, kinship, community, and religion. These institutions provided legitimation, norms of co-operation, restricted rewards and punishments, and expectation/coordination signals.

To understand Medieval state honours, it is lordship that needs the most attention. In Chapter 3, I indicated that the essence of lordship was contract. A higher-status person, the lord (seigneur), was owed deference, loyalty, and services. The best-known form is feudalism, in which a lord leased land to a subordinate in return for loyalty and services. Feudalism, however, was only one variant of lordship. Retaining contracts (the French *alliance*, Scottish bonds of manrent, and in England so-called bastard feudalism) were, in some respects, the opposite: a subordinate attached himself to a lord in return for protection, maintenance, and/or payments. Whatever the contractual arrangement, the mutual obligations of lordship were often institutionalized in laws or customary norms. Ties of kinship, community, or religion could reinforce bonds of lordship, and vice versa. But the major source of motivation for lordship was the contractual relationship between two persons based on conventions of reciprocity. Although it could vary radically from one region to another, the strength of lordship everywhere lay in the personal and affective solidarity in which the relationship of the parties was socially constructed.

Medieval lordship is often seen as inherently decentralizing. Yet one could argue that the feudal bond was the one political force that held Medieval society together when most other forces were pulling it apart. One of the few sources of power that the French king had over the Duke of Normandy or the Count of Flanders was that they were his vassals. Norman England was very much a feudal society. It was also one where lordship was relatively centralized and closely connected with land.

Nevertheless, whether feudalism contributed to decentralization or offset it or both, there is no denying that most of Western Europe in the eleventh and twelfth centuries was politically decentralized, with power in the hands of a dispersed variety of "lords" that included bishops, abbots, priors, castellans, and knights.[1] Although bonds of lordship provided one of the means by which kings and magnates could raise armies, in reality, few powerful men took to the field if they did not think they had something to gain from it, or to lose if they did not do so. And pulling anyone away from their kinship and communal bonds to serve the king, even in the name of their lord, was no easy matter. Men raised by seigneurial levy were frequently unreliable and lacked discipline. The most reliable were members of a lord's household. Otherwise, armies were recruited in a variety of ways, depending on whether operations were defensive or offensive. For defensive collective action – if people were persuaded that their lives or property were at risk – rulers could draw on volunteers, militia, and civic levies. For offensive ventures, kings and magnates were repeatedly obliged to use coercion or the threat of it to recruit fighters. Or they employed adventurers, soldiers of fortune, or mercenaries. They increasingly resorted to the latter in the twelfth and thirteen centuries.

GIFTS

If we were to seek the primordial origins of state honours in the world, we would want to look at gift-giving practices in hunting and gathering societies, in horticultural societies, and especially in agrarian societies, and how some of the earliest honorific rewards distributed by rulers evolved from gift practices. The honorific rewards distributed in Ancient Egypt were mostly ornaments of one kind or another and could be difficult to distinguish from the royal practice of giving away jewellery. Often honorific rewards were socially constructed as gifts. In Ancient China, even ranks of merit awarded to peasants were seen as gifts.[2] The term for Roman military honours – *dona militaria* – also signifies the association between gifts and honorific rewards. In Medieval and Early Modern Europe, monarchs used gifts to create and maintain social bonds and alliances. It has to be acknowledged that they did not do so as lavishly as many rulers in other parts of the world, but gifts were employed in Europe in ways that were similar. They were used to facilitate relations among rulers. They were frequently given to military officers as rewards for loyal service or military accomplishment.[3] And they were routine in royal administrations.

Gifts were critical in activating and maintaining ties of kinship, community, and lordship. Lordship was laced with gifts. They were bestowed by royals or lords on their tenants and retainers, but they were also exchanged between peasants and their lords.[4] Gifts symbolized both the reciprocity and the asymmetry of such relations; norms often mandated what kinds of gifts were appropriate for lords to give subordinates and vice versa. There were also general conventions that indicated the most appropriate dates for gifts (for example, quarter day, New Year's Day, or May Day). Gifts might also be regularly given to commemorate births or battles, or to celebrate coronations, marriages, or visits. A lord who wanted to appear generous, or who saw gifts as an effective tool of governing, might be in for a large annual expenditure. Philip the Bold, duke of Burgundy, usually gave forty to fifty costly gifts just on New Year's Day.[5]

Gifts could even signify subjugation. This point was made especially well by R.R. Davies, who emphasized the exchange of a variety of gifts (furs, saddles, robes, falcons, and hounds) when royals and seigneurs visited one another, but also gifts given by Anglo-Norman kings to Welsh and Irish magnates in order to cloak the capitulation of the latter to the former.[6]

STATUS ELEVATION

The power of the Crown to elevate a man to nobility was limited by the fact that families could become noble without royal elevation by adopting a noble lifestyle, becoming accepted by the local nobility, and acquiring land or engaging in military service. This limitation on royal power was even greater with respect to the landed gentry in the British Isles.

On the other hand, kings and magnates could use elevation in title or rank to mobilize and organize collective action. The titles of "duke" and "count" were military offices in the Roman regime that became administrative offices under Visigothic and Frankish kings, to which the latter added "march counts" and "vice-counts." All four statuses were appointed by kings, the first three acting as governors and the fourth as deputies of counts. With the decline in royal authority during the ninth and tenth centuries, French royal governors and their heirs became hereditary lords or princes. In the thirteenth century, however, French kings began to regain control and continued to do so gradually over the following centuries. They were able to confer lordly dignities by promoting principalities and baronies in rank, a largely honorific practice, but one that was valued by recipients because it gave them hereditary status elevation. This practice reached its peak during the seventeenth century and became part of the French honours system.

In England, the pre-Conquest status of *ealdorman* became earl in the eleventh century. He was technically a removable officer, but his son usually expected to inherit the status. In the twelfth and thirteenth centuries, these earls, along with dukes, marquesses, viscounts, and barons, became the core of the magnates who were summoned to parliaments held by English kings when they needed to consult or gain the support of the most powerful men in the kingdom. With some differences, the same institutional evolution eventually took place in Ireland and Scotland. The result was the evolution of "peerages" that enjoyed political power and eventually the right to attend one of the three parliaments, along with a status that became the most prestigious in each of the kingdoms. Elevation to a peerage could be used by the Crown as a reward, though less so in the Middle Ages than later.

A king had the most control over status elevation when he created and selected members to a monarchical order of knighthood. He could use these orders for a number of purposes. First, a monarchical order of knighthood could help him legitimate his reign and locate what he was doing in an accepted set of beliefs. Almost always one of the reasons for instituting an order of knighthood was to enhance the glory of a ruler by placing him at the apex of an illustrious body. Monarchical orders of knighthood were invariably intended to associate a ruler with prevailing definitions of what was considered virtuous, principally from the perspective of Christendom and "chivalry." Often there was an explicit attempt to associate a ruler with fictional orders, in particular those belonging to the Arthurian romances.[7] In the fourteenth and fifteenth centuries, many rulers were trying to advance their authority by establishing grand courts with refined codes of conduct and etiquette. An order of knighthood could form a significant part of this cultural program. Orders were also founded to strengthen the legitimacy of specific collective action in which a ruler was or would be engaged, most often war. One of the reasons Edward III established the Order of the Garter was to dignify his war with France – to make it look like a magnificent cause pursued by a glorious company of knights against an ignoble adversary.[8]

Second, monarchical orders of knighthood provided restricted rewards to persuade powerful men to support a ruler and his enterprises. The major reward was status, but appointment to an order also brought concrete benefits, such as financial assistance, tax exemptions, commemoration in state chronicles and registers, precedence at ceremonies, easy access to the monarch, and support of the monarch against the dangers faced by a member.[9] Monarchical orders of knighthood were imbued with the contractual reciprocity of lordship. Stress was placed on service and loyalty to the prince, which the order was usually meant to symbolize. [10]

Monarchical orders of knighthood were also imbued with the spirit of gift giving. The Order of the Golden Tree is revealing in these terms. It was founded on 1 January 1403 when Philip the Bold gave an elaborate clasp to powerful lords in France and the Low Countries. The purpose was to bind these lords to resist the designs of the Duke of Orléans against him and his stake in the royal succession. The Golden Tree was not just a gift. It was organized for a specific purpose; Philip clearly wanted to draw these men into a union to an extent greater than was the case with most other gifts he gave. But it did not have a formal organization and it was bestowed at the same time that Philip was distributing other gifts. [11]

Status elevation could also communicate expectations and create common knowledge – to signal what kind of achievement was required by those who served the king and more generally to promote "chivalric" ideals among the elite. Status elevation was usually designed to be widely observed. The dubbing of knights took place on the battlefield or before audiences. Admission to an order of knighthood was typically enacted with much ceremony. Members of orders were provided with elaborate dress and insignia, further to enhance their conspicuity. The statutes of some orders required knights to wear their badges at regular intervals.[12] The hastiludes – where warriors competed and were celebrated – were perhaps the most distinctively Medieval expectation and coordination signals. Warriors not only saw how they were expected to perform but also saw that large numbers of others were watching the same demonstration.

The communication function of monarchical orders of knighthood in this period should not, however, be exaggerated. Few people could imagine themselves doing what a knight did at a hastilude; even fewer thought that they were expected to do what nobles or members of royal orders of knighthood were expected to do. And for the audiences that kings and lords were trying to reach, communication was not a major obstacle to collective action and organization since the Medieval aristocracy in any region was not very large. There was enough social interaction among those who fought together, or might fight together, to communicate what was expected and to coordinate their activities if they wanted to act in concert. The legitimation and motivation functions of royal status elevation were manifestly more critical in the Middle Ages than the communication function.

6

Conditions for Collective Action in Early Modern and Modern Europe

This chapter examines demographic and structural changes, changes in within-state and inter-state competition, and changes in warfare in Western Europe during the period in which state honours evolved. These forces had two consequences relevant to our inquiry. First, they gave rise to the selection pressures in which we are interested. Second, these changes placed constraints on the choices that people could make in meeting selection pressures and in achieving their preferences. I then examine changes in thought and practice that can help us understand the kinds of solutions that were sought in order to deal with these pressures.

Since all the territorial states in this study ultimately developed major honours systems within the time period we are covering, we cannot use societal differences to explain this outcome. There were, however, sharp differences in the chronology of the evolution of state honours. I have mentioned these differences in passing, but will summarize them now.

France was the earliest to bestow honours in large numbers. The Order of Saint Louis (1692) and the Legion of Honour (1802) were the most significant in this regard. The first widely distributed honour in Britain was the Order of the Bath (1725), though it was awarded in much smaller numbers than the Order of Saint Louis and the Legion of Honour. The United Provinces created only a few honours, but when the Kingdom of the Netherlands was established in 1815, the Dutch took up state honorific practices much as other states in Europe did during the nineteenth century. Until 1830, most of the Southern Low Countries did not have independent control over their honours system. When they acquired it, they very quickly created a major honorific order, the Order of Leopold, and subsequently a large number of smaller honours. Finally, the

British undertook the greatest expansion in their honours system during the late nineteenth century and the first quarter of the twentieth century.

DEMOGRAPHIC AND STRUCTURAL CHANGES

I can do no more than highlight the various demographic and structural changes occurring in Early Modern and Modern Western Europe that played a role in the evolution of state honours.

Population Size and Density

There has long been a large body of literature that attaches considerable importance to the effects of increases in population size and density. Best known is the "principle of population" espoused by Thomas Malthus. Karl Marx rejected this principle, but had his own theory of the effects of greater social density, though he did not use that term. It was one of his basic convictions that higher demographic concentrations of the working class would transform their collective action, something that could be either a blessing or a curse for members of the ruling elite; Marx, of course, hoped it would be a curse. Subsequently, the consequences of increases in population size or density have been elaborated in a robust tradition in sociology, building on the work of Spencer and Emile Durkheim. It is a decisive variable in cultural evolutionary theory, where it is seen as increasing competition and the need for greater coordination and control.

Toward the end of the Middle Ages, profound demographic changes began throughout Eurasia. Populations gradually multiplied to unprecedented levels.[1] Figures 6.1 to 6.6 give us the growth in the European population from 1300 to 1900 CE. These are obviously rough estimates, over which there is considerable disagreement among authorities, but for our purposes they suffice. Figure 6.1 shows that the period of rising European population coincides with what we know was the major period in the evolution of state honours. Figure 6.2 indicates that Early Modern France had a far larger population than England and Wales at that time, indeed far larger than the population of the British Isles as a whole; France also experienced a greater increase in population until the middle of the eighteenth century. It was only subsequently that the population in the British Isles expanded at a higher rate and ultimately surpassed that of France.

Figure 6.1
Growth in population of Europe, fourteenth to nineteenth centuries

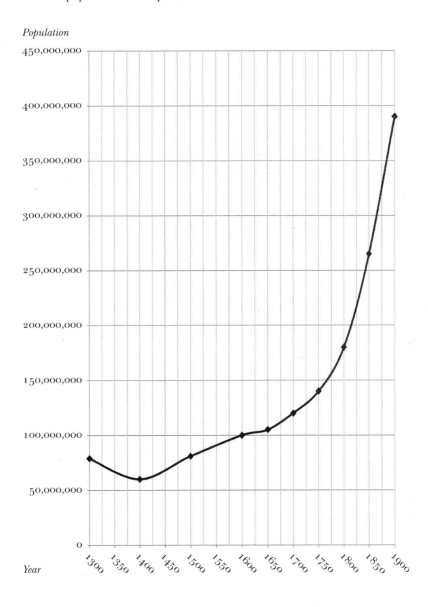

Population

Figure 6.2
Growth in population of the British Isles and France, fourteenth to nineteenth
centuries

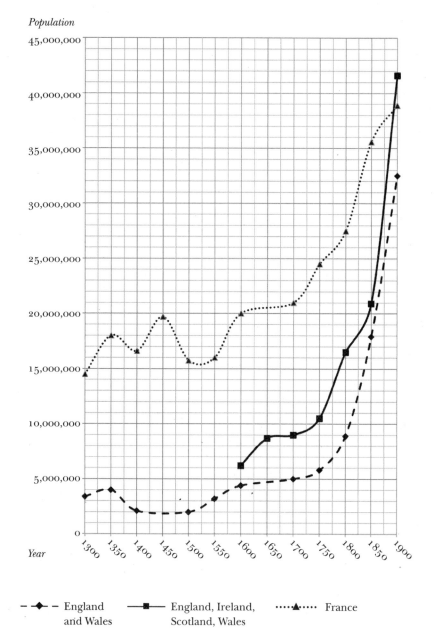

Population

45,000,000

40,000,000

35,000,000

30,000,000

25,000,000

20,000,000

15,000,000

10,000,000

5,000,000

0

Year 1300 1350 1400 1450 1500 1550 1600 1650 1700 1750 1800 1850 1900

- - ◆ - - England
and Wales

——■—— England, Ireland,
Scotland, Wales

·····▲····· France

Figure 6.3
Growth in population of London and Paris, fourteenth to nineteenth centuries

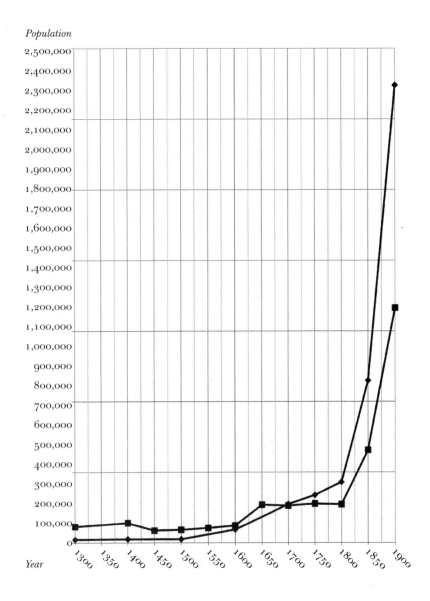

Population

Year

 London   Paris

Figure 6.4
Growth in population of selected European cities, fourteenth to nineteenth centuries

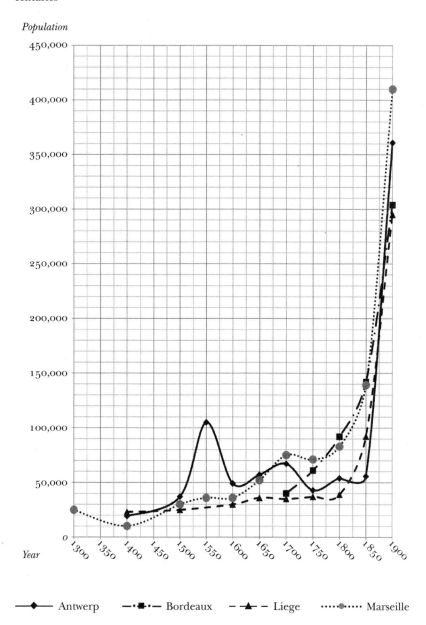

Population

Year

——◆—— Antwerp   —■—— Bordeaux   — ▲ — Liege   ⋯●⋯ Marseille

Figure 6.5
Growth in population of selected European cities, fourteenth to nineteenth centuries

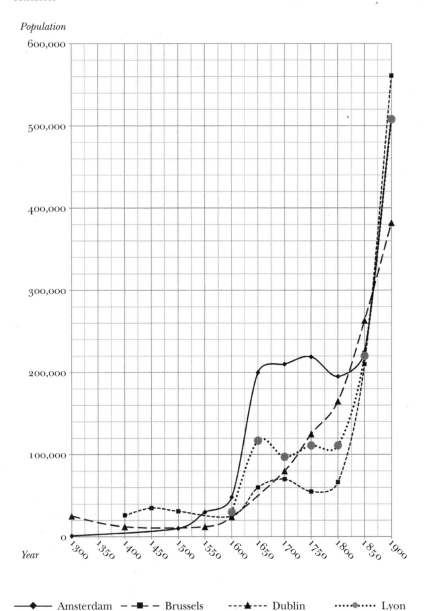

Population

600,000

500,000

400,000

300,000

200,000

100,000

0

Year   1300 1350 1400 1450 1500 1550 1600 1650 1700 1750 1800 1850 1900

◆ Amsterdam   ■ Brussels   ▲ Dublin   ● Lyon

Figure 6.6
Growth in population of selected European cities, fourteenth to nineteenth centuries

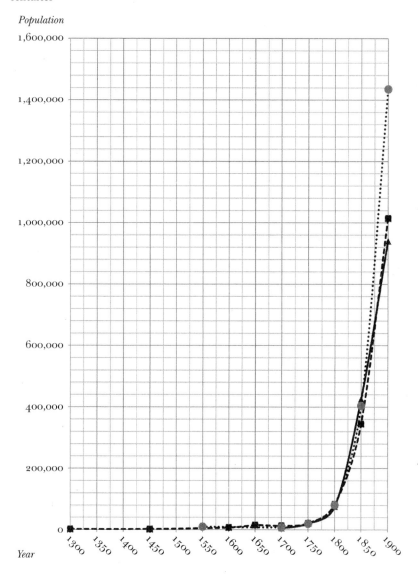

Population

- -■- - Glasgow   ──▲── Liverpool   ⋯●⋯ Manchester

Urban expansion was equally dramatic. It resulted partly from the overall growth in population, but also from rural-urban migration. Since this migration varied regionally, so too did urban growth. In any given period, cities and towns progressed in size in some regions while in others they did not, or even declined. Nevertheless, the Early Modern and Modern periods saw a general increase in the Western-European urban population. Figures 6.3 to 6.6 depict the estimated expansion in the population of several European cities. The Continental cities were larger than comparable cities in the British Isles during the Medieval period and for most of the Early Modern period, and built up earlier than did the British cities. The major exception was London; from the beginning of the eighteenth century, it became larger and grew faster than Paris. A partial exception was Dublin, which advanced sharply in population from the beginning of the seventeenth century, much earlier than did Glasgow, Manchester, or Liverpool. Then, in the nineteenth century, the latter cities expanded astronomically in association with well-known economic changes.

Social Mobilization

The term social mobilization refers to a process in which people become separated from old commitments and available for new patterns of behaviour. Social mobilization occurs when the social relationships, obligations, cultural beliefs, and economic necessities that bind people to existing social patterns and commitments become weakened.

Major economic, political, or cultural transformations can increase social mobilization, but the quantifiable change most closely related to it, as both cause and effect, is geographical mobility. Measuring geographical mobility in earlier centuries is difficult. Here and there we have data on the number of persons living where they were not born and raised, but it is not until the nineteenth century that we are able to determine how far they have moved. Before that, the best measure of the growth in geographical mobility is probably growth in the size of cities.

We should be cautious in our assessment of the effects of social mobilization. It would be inaccurate to describe it as "social breakdown." Social mobilization does not cause people to fall into an atomistic abyss. Yet it is also important not to understate the changes that social mobilization brings about. Karl Deutsch emphasized two consequences: (1) the size of the politically relevant population that must be taken into account by political leaders increases and (2) elites that are able to draw support from socially mobilized populations acquire greater power.[2] Our interest is specifically in the way in which it transforms collective action: mobilizers find it easier, relatively speaking, to draw people away from collective action in which they have been participating and organize them into alternative collective action. Thus, social mobilization represents a political challenge to those elites that have traditionally organized collective action and organization. For those trying to mobilize people into new kinds of collective action and organization, it represents an opportunity – but only an opportunity. They must compete with both traditional mobilizers and other would-be mobilizers. In addition, though drawing people from one kind of collective action to another becomes easier, organizing collective action as such becomes more difficult. The heterogeneity and relative looseness of the populations that mobilizers are seeking to organize are greater than in societies in which less social mobilization has occurred.

Political Centralization

In general terms, we can identify two processes of centralization in Europe: monarchical and parliamentary. All the states on which I have focused in this book have experienced both processes, but one more than the other depending on the time period. These differences in political centralization contribute to the explanation I offer in the next chapter for differences among the honours of the Western-European states. It is, therefore, necessary to outline this process before proceeding further. Readers already familiar with the process of political centralization in Western Europe may want to skip this section.

FRANCE
Medieval French kings were nominal sovereigns of the Regnum francorum, but exercised real power over only a part of this territory, primarily the Île de France. Most of the country was controlled by other powers and administered by provincial assemblies, known as *états*, which emerged as powerful bodies in the thirteenth and fourteenth centuries. During the late Medieval and Early Modern periods, the territory that the French monarchy controlled expanded and royal authority was strengthened, but it was neither a smooth

linear development nor a uniform one. Different provinces were added at different times and with different constitutional arrangements. Medieval kings had sometimes summoned a central assembly known as the États généraux, but political organization at the provincial level was too strong to permit this assembly to have significant power. French kings were inclined to accept these realities and to negotiate with provincial institutions, primarily the *états provinciaux*. The États généraux did not meet from 1614 to 1789. The only centralizing parliamentary institution in the seventeenth and eighteenth centuries was the Parlement de Paris. Although not a small body, its composition was restricted to elite members of the judicial profession. And there were twelve provincial *parlements* that impeded what centralization the Parlement de Paris achieved.

When political centralization eventually did occur, it was carried out by the Crown and its agents. By the sixteenth century, royal administration was based in Paris and French kings were becoming less peripatetic than they had been in former centuries, now spending most of the year in Paris or in nearby palaces. Paradoxically, political centralization in Early Modern France was primarily monarchical as a result of the weakness of the Crown in the Middle Ages and the strength of local institutions. The Crown carried out this centralization by undermining the power of *états provinciaux* – indeed, by means of the disappearance of most of them. The French state was not an "absolute" monarchy, but compared to other Early Modern European monarchies, it was the most powerful. By the eighteenth century, no other European monarchy exercised as much power over as many people as the French monarchy. The Russian and the Habsburg crowns governed larger populations in some periods, but neither exercised as much control over these populations as the French Crown did over its population. The Prussian monarchy came to exercise more direct authority over its population, but that population was smaller than the French. In addition, the French Royal Court surpassed all other royal courts as a cultural and social centre, not just for the French population but for all of Europe.

BRITISH ISLES

A curious difference between the historiography of Britain and France is the greater interest of French historians in political centralization. I say curious because the process of political centralization was crucial in the British Isles as well as in France, though it occurred differently and was less successful.

Under the Norman monarchy, political centralization developed relatively early in England. The comparatively intensive power that William the Conqueror had enjoyed in Normandy was extended to England and gradually expanded to include most of the country. Wales was divided into two regions: one controlled by powerful Norman lords, and a western region over which the Normans exercised little control. There were no provincial assemblies in England or Wales that limited royal sovereignty.

Whereas the weakness of the French monarchy in the Middle Ages undermined parliamentary centralization, the strength of the English monarchy in the Middle Ages led to parliamentary centralization. The English Parliament was a royal creation, initially an extension of the Royal Council. It gave the Crown an institutional means by which to obtain support for collective action that it was trying to organize. The meetings to which English magnates were convened in the twelfth and thirteenth centuries evolved into two parliamentary chambers that drew great lords, "knights of the shire," and burgesses to the centre.

A partially similar process of monarchical and parliamentary centralization evolved in Scotland during the Middle Ages, though large regions – the Highlands and Islands, and even some of the Lowlands – were beyond the authority of the Scottish monarchy. Royal residence and administration were centred in Edinburgh, and by the late fifteenth century, Edinburgh had gradually become the regular site for meetings of the Scottish Parliament. The Union of the Crowns in 1603 removed the Scottish Crown to London, but a certain measure of parliamentary centralization within Scotland persisted until the Union of the Parliaments in 1707. There followed a prolonged period of contentious centralization of political power in London, which was both monarchical and parliamentary, and during which the Highlands and Islands were finally brought within the authority of a central government.

In the twelfth century, Henry II tried to establish English royal sovereignty in Ireland over Gaelic and Norman lords, and made Ireland a separate lordship under his son John, with a royal army, a royal court, and royal officers. Yet beyond Dublin, its authority depended on Norman lords and the personal submission of Gaelic lords. It was during the sixteenth and seventeenth centuries that the English were driven to a conquest of Ireland and a significant displacement of Gaelic and Anglo-Norman elites. Monarchical and parliamentary centralization was institutionalized in the office of the lord lieutenant (the representative of the English Crown) and in the Irish Parliament in Dublin. The eighteenth century was the golden age of this central polity, though the control exercised by the lord lieutenant and the Dublin Parliament was still feeble in some parts of the island. The Act of Union of 1800 eliminated the power of this parliament, after which came a period of contentious monarchical and parliamentary centralization not unlike the political struggles in Scotland during the eighteenth century, but in this case sufficient to destroy the union. For all that, until Irish independence, the amalgamated House of Commons in London – taking representatives from all parts of the British Isles – remained a powerful force of centralization that drew Irish politicians to London, even those in favour of Irish independence.

The nineteenth century was the most politically centralized period in the history of the British Isles, and we know that it was in the last half of nineteenth century and the early twentieth century that British state honours underwent the greatest expansion.

LOW COUNTRIES

While political assemblies can be found in the Low Countries as early as the twelfth century, it was, as in France, primarily during the thirteenth and fourteenth centuries that *états provinciaux* (in Dutch *staten provinciaal*) acquired significant power. The earliest centralization was monarchical, effected by the House of Burgundy. Philip the Good (duke of Burgundy, 1419–67) organized the États généraux (Staten generaal) in 1463, consisting of representatives of the *états provinciaux*. Under Charles V (who inherited the Netherlandish provinces in 1515, Aragon and Castille in 1516, and Germany in 1519), the power of these assemblies greatly weakened and political centralization became mostly monarchical with two centres for the Low Countries: the centre in Brabant of the administration, and the centre in Spain of the administration for all his territories. When Charles' son Philip II inherited the Netherlands in 1556, he sought to acquire more direct management over the people of this region. It was against this Spanish monarchical centralization that leaders in both the Northern and the Southern Low Countries revolted. But it was only the Northern provinces that successfully broke away.

Native monarchical centralization was then established in the Northern Low Countries by William the Silent, prince of Orange, who had been the Habsburg governor (*stadhouder*) of the provinces of Holland, Zeeland, and Utrecht. His assassination, however, resulted in a further increase in provincial autonomy. Efforts to obtain a foreign overlord failed, as did efforts to create a stronger centralized authority by transforming the Council of State into a national administration. William's son, the dour Maurice of Nassau, was *stadhouder* of several provinces, including the most populous province, Holland. On the one hand, he and his successors were politically subservient to the *staten provinciaal*. On the other hand, insofar as any kind of political centralization was evolving in the United Provinces, it owed much to the House of Orange, whose power lay in their *stadhouderschaps* of the provinces, in their military leadership, and in their "royal" court in The Hague.

There was some degree of parliamentary centralization in The Hague. Unlike the French États généraux, the Dutch Staten generaal met regularly. It restricted the power of the *stadhouders* but was, in turn, limited by the *staten provinciaal*, which also met in the Hague. And there was a third source of centralization that was neither monarchical nor parliamentary: the hegemony of Holland, the most populous and wealthiest of the provinces, and its economic centre, Amsterdam.

Still, when further political centralization eventually came, it was initially monarchical. In the mid-eighteenth century, foreign military threats persuaded the provinces to accept an amalgamation of the *stadhouderschaps* as a single hereditary position. During the French Revolutionary period, various efforts at parliamentary centralization were made, but in 1806 centralization that was primarily monarchical was imposed when Napoleon created the Kingdom of the Netherlands and made his brother the king. This political structure was abolished in 1810, and the Netherlands became incorporated into France. When the House of Orange was restored, monarchical centralization was re-established. The Hague remained the royal seat and the centre of the government, while Amsterdam was made the capital city and its old town hall, a royal palace. This was the peak of monarchical centralization in the Northern Netherlands and was also when the major Dutch state honours were created. Subsequently, parliamentary institutions gradually became, as elsewhere, the main institution of political centralization during the nineteenth century.

The success of Spain in maintaining its rule in the southern provinces meant that they had to face the rigours of Philip's absolutism. Philip's determination to increase his direct control waned, however, and he decided that the Southern Low Countries should pass to his daughter Isabella, who would marry the gover- nor general of these provinces, Albert, brother of the archduke of Austria. Together they would be in charge of domestic administra- tion. This period of royal centralization within the Southern Low Countries ended with Albert's death, but the ability of the Spanish to maintain effective control from a distance declined during the seventeenth century, as did the power of Spain in Europe as a whole. Meanwhile, little parliamentary centralization became institutional- ized. In contrast with the United Provinces, the southern provinces had no *états généraux*. The États généraux that had been organized by Philip the Good for all of the Netherlands had little authority after 1585 and did not meet after 1632. Some *états provinciaux* remained powerful and could make demands on the central government in return for co-operating with the latter's need for revenue.

When the Austrians took over the Southern Low Countries in 1714, they were more successful than the Spanish in enforcing a central administration. This centralization culminated in the ambi- tious reforms of Joseph II (Habsburg ruler, 1780–90) in the late eighteenth century, which led to a revolt against Austrian rule. After the French Revolution, the Southern Low Countries became part of the Napoleonic Empire and, after its collapse, into the United King- dom of the Netherlands. When the Southern Low Countries broke away from the Kingdom of the Netherlands in 1830, in spite of cen- turies with little parliamentary centralization, parliamentary central- ization became the much stronger institutional force.

The consequences of these differences in political centralization for state honours are examined in the next chapter, but one obser- vation can be made now. It is evident that monarchical centraliza- tion more than parliamentary centralization led to the expansion in the distribution of state honours that occurred in the seventeenth to early nineteenth centuries. This recalls the connection between monarchies and honours emphasized in the persistence-of-the-old- order thesis. Yet we should not conclude that it was just monarchy and not political centralization that encouraged the creation of state honours during the Early Modern period. Monarchies before then founded orders of knighthood, but did not engage in the mass dis- tribution of honours that began with the Order of Saint Louis. What is most important is the difference between the two modes of centralization. Less parliamentary centralization meant a greater need for alternative instruments of centralization.

State Officialdom

With political centralization came more state personnel. The expansion was uneven and gradual. Yet the changes that occurred in the size and organization of state officialdom in the Early Modern period must be included in any discussion of the emergence of the Western-European state. Rulers expanded state officialdom to weaken the power of local authorities (more bureaucratically in France than in England); they developed instruments for the collection of taxes (more bureaucratically in England than in France); and they organized their armies more bureaucratically (earlier on the Continent than in the British Isles).

During the seventeenth and eighteenth centuries, the French state officialdom expanded in size more rapidly than English and Welsh state officialdom as a result of greater centralization, but also because the French Crown sold offices to raise money. Although the venality of offices can be traced to the thirteenth century, it became more common in the fifteenth and sixteenth centuries. In 1604, the *paulette* or *droit annuel* was introduced, which permitted offices to be inherited on payment of an annual fee, a practice that had been permitted (for a price) in earlier periods, but now became more institutionalized. This resulted in the growth of a vast patrimonial state bureaucracy, many members of which were not full-time state personnel. The abolition of the venality of offices with the fall of the Old Regime effected a decline in state personnel, but it was still large in comparison to other European states.

Data on state employment over time are notoriously problematic. As governments grew, the proportion of state officials who were full time as opposed to part time rose significantly. Since the latter were often not included in the count, the numbers we have may represent both an increase in state officials and an increase in full-time officials. Yet, for our purposes, it is actually this combination of the two that we want to measure. Well aware of these features of the data, Mann has provided estimates of the growth in state personnel in France and Britain from the late eighteenth century. The exact figures are problematic, but they suggest that in the late eighteenth and early nineteenth centuries, the French officialdom was far larger than the British; during the last half of the nineteenth century, however, the latter shot up dramatically and exceeded the size of the French state by the early twentieth century.[3]

A Greater Scale of Competition

The combination of these and other forces led to a greater scale of competition within and between these centralizing states.

DOMESTIC COMPETITION

There was a nationalization of contention in Early Modern Western Europe. Local power holders were undermined and/or drawn into national networks of politics and patronage. And the arenas of contention broadened around national centres. To a considerable degree, this process resulted from the centralization of power. As the autonomy of local power holders was eroded, local conflicts more often became linked to the positions held by local elites in larger social networks. As a number of writers have asserted, however, participants in local power struggles could have their own reasons for connecting these local struggles to less-local political contention.[4]

Obviously, the manner and extent of this nationalization of contention varied with a number of factors: ethnic and linguistic differences, the geographical distance of regions from a centre, the concentration of population in a centre, and the institutional form of political centralization. The earliest nationalization of contention occurred in England and Wales. It expanded to include Scotland and Ireland when their separate parliaments were abolished. The nationalization of contention in Old-Regime France took two forms: (1) struggles within and among those institutions linked with the centre (the Royal Court, the state bureaucracy, and the Parlement de Paris) and (2) between the Crown and provincial institutions, most notably provincial *parlements* and the *états provinciaux*. The French Revolution nationalized contention on an unprecedented scale, as did regime changes and parliamentary politics in France during the nineteenth century.

INTER-STATE COMPETITION

The Early Modern period also saw an increase in the scale of competition among European territorial states, creating pressures on political leaders to improve the effectiveness of their states and the populations over which they ruled. People more often came to believe that the victor in inter-state competition would be the state, economy, and society that operated most efficiently.

Well before the Industrial Revolution, a considerable expansion occurred in the marketing of manufactured goods, agricultural products, and raw materials. Substantial research has been done in the past forty years on the early evolution of capitalism, proto-industry, merchant networks, and regional economic differentiation, particularly between the economies of Western Europe and those of Central and Eastern Europe. These economic developments generated unprecedented concerns among state officials about economic threats posed by other European countries. Far more than is the case today, economic competition among territorial states was then considered zero-sum.

At the same time, military competition among European states intensified. In the seventeenth century, war reached an unprecedented scale. One can get a good sense of the magnitude of warfare in the seventeenth, eighteenth, and early nineteenth centuries by noting the number of protagonists engaged in this military competition. The Thirty Years' War (1618–48) was fought between Sweden, Denmark, Britain, the Dutch Republic, France, and German Protestant princes on the one side, and the Spanish and Austrian Habsburgs, and their Catholic allies, on the other. From the 1650s to the 1680s the British and the Dutch fought five naval wars. The War of the League of Augsburg (1688–97) put France up against a large number of antagonists that included Britain and the United Provinces. The War of the Spanish Succession (1701–14) pitted the Dutch Republic, Britain, Austria, and Portugal against France and Spain. In the War of the Austrian Succession (1740–48), it was Prussia, Spain, and France against Austria, Britain, the Dutch Republic, and Russia. The Seven Years' War (1756–63) set Britain, Prussia, and a number of other German states against France, Austria, Russia, Spain, Sweden, and Saxony. And the French Revolutionary and Napoleonic Wars (1793–1815) engaged France and those forced to fight on its side against the rest of Europe.

Western-European states also became more involved in overseas wars. During the sixteenth, seventeenth, and eighteenth centuries, contacts between Europeans and people in other parts of the world had increased, along with the settlement of Europeans on other continents. Until the Seven Years' War and the American War of Independence, the struggles for power stemming from these contacts and migrations involved primarily naval forces and relatively small land forces. Large wars involving Western-European states were mostly within Europe. Even the immense French Revolutionary and Napoleonic Wars were, for the most part, limited to Europe.

In the nineteenth century, a larger portion of Western-European colonial possessions consisted of colonies of conquest as opposed to the earlier colonies of settlement. In colonies of conquest, Europeans remained a numerical minority, which meant that indigenous populations had to be subdued and ruled. Western-European governments became more involved in power struggles with and among elites and communities outside Western Europe. They were also driven (by a combination of national pride and paranoia over the ambitions of their European rivals) to become increasingly entangled in military conflicts across the world involving rival European states.

CHANGING WARFARE

The social changes discussed above, technological innovations, and the increase in inter-state competition brought about major transformations in the nature of warfare, which in turn imposed selection pressures on those seeking to mobilize military collective action and organization.

In order to judge the magnitude of these transformations, it is necessary to approach the subject from a comparative perspective. Numerically, footmen have predominated over horsemen in the majority of military forces in human history. There have been significant exceptions, however, most notably armies composed mainly of horse archers, which were dominant in the Asian steppes until the eighteenth century. In addition, in the rest of Asia, even in armies with a substantially greater number of infantry, the constant threat from these steppe horse archers impeded the development of an infantry culture.[5] In many armies throughout Eurasia, it was frequently the horsemen who determined the outcome of a battle, enjoyed higher status, were better trained, and were more generously rewarded than infantry. This was true in the elite heavy cavalry of Ancient Persia. It was also true of horsemen who fought in chariots, which were once decisive in battles among Ancient Middle Eastern states, and in Ancient India and China.

In contrast, in Ancient Greece and Rome, infantry was the most critical segment of the armed forces and also carried a prestige that infantries do not usually enjoy. The seminal period was Classical

Greece, when infantry units known as hoplites were formed by Greek states. Hoplite units consisted of phalanxes of tightly packed soldiers with huge shields that created a wall. This wall advanced at a slow pace. Victory went to the side that pushed the opposing force back until it broke. Under the Macedonians, infantry phalanxes were made more flexible and fought alongside horsemen. Alexander the Great achieved his victories over the Persian and Indian armies by fusing the heavy infantry tradition of the Mediterranean with the heavy cavalry tradition of the East.

Roman armies were shaped by these same traditions, but during the first millennium CE, a number of changes led to a greater adoption of cavalry by Romans. The principal sources of innovation came from the nomad horse archery of Central Asia, but the Romans were more directly influenced by the heavily armed cavalry and horse archery of the Parthian and Sasanian armies they fought against.[6] In the eighth century, the advantage of cavalry was elevated further by the introduction of saddles with stirrups. It was in Asia that stirrups first evolved. They were common in China by the fifth century, and were certainly known in Europe by the late sixth century.

This did not mean that Roman infantry forces became less important. Rather, it meant that the advantages of very large infantries decreased relative to smaller infantries fighting alongside cavalry. Consequently, as L.M. Dudley puts it, there were no longer the same economies of scale in military force that there had been during the golden age of Mediterranean infantry.[7] Whether or not this development contributed to the decline of the Roman Empire is a question that is not necessary for us to answer. What is significant for our purposes is that European armies came to be composed of a necessary combination of cavalry and infantry.

The reasons for this were not solely military. The size and composition of Medieval armies were also a function of the political fragmentation of Medieval Europe and the limited resources to which rulers had access. Infantries still outnumbered cavalry. Indeed, the ratio of infantry to cavalry was all the higher if the cavalry consisted of a small number of very heavily armoured horsemen. But a cavalry culture came to prevail in which the role of the horseman was glorified and his contribution celebrated.

Warfare continued to evolve in the first half of the second millennium CE, before the "military revolution" of the sixteenth and seventeenth centuries. It should be acknowledged that the pace of evolution was slower in the Middle Ages than later on. Yet the later innovations were built, both negatively and positively, on earlier Medieval innovations. Military historians believe that the first innovation that undermined Medieval methods of warfare, and more precisely the pre-eminence of cavalry, was the English longbow. Adopted from the Welsh and perfected over several centuries by the English, it became the most effective weapon of warfare in Europe until the sixteenth century. Second, changes in artillery undermined the security of Medieval castles, which were built to resist artillery such as the catapult, but were more vulnerable to newer heavy artillery. Third, in several parts of Europe during the fourteenth century, long pikes had been utilized against infantry and cavalry. During the fifteenth century, the Swiss perfected their use, further undermining the pre-eminence of cavalry and changing the way in which cavalry would be employed.

Meanwhile, explosive devices evolved as the most potent military weapons. It is not known exactly when and where gunpowder was invented, but it was known to the Chinese in the eleventh century, if not earlier, and was adopted in Europe in the fourteenth century. Initially, the most significant consequence was the vulnerability of castles to cannon fire. But lighter weapons were also gradually introduced and improved over the course of the fourteenth, fifteenth, and sixteenth centuries. Many of these changes favoured the employment of not just infantries, but large infantries. Lighter gunpowder weapons enabled foot soldiers to be both very destructive and mobile, thus increasing the economies of scale in their use.[8] The need to reload a musket and the necessities of sieging and garrisoning a greater number of better-built forts also contributed to the pressure for larger infantries. (I should note that the effects of the necessities of sieging and garrisoning forts has been the subject of considerable debate.)

These technological changes enhanced the importance of infantry at the expense of cavalry. Yet infantries had been an important component of Medieval armies.[9] And cavalry continued to be important in Early Modern armies. More significant were: (1) a shift from heavy cavalry to lighter cavalry, (2) a greater emphasis on coordinating this cavalry with infantry, and (3) an enormous increase in the size of armies.

The last-mentioned was facilitated by political centralization and population growth. This does not mean that central states enjoyed an abundance of manpower to draw upon, or that the regions with the densest populations had the largest armies. In general, economically prosperous areas paid for recruits from less prosperous areas.[10] Nonetheless, demographic growth made possible larger armies and pressured rulers into a manpower competition, in which the winner was typically the side that could mobilize the largest numbers.

Estimating the size of armies is extremely difficult. Sources can exaggerate. It is not always clear who is being included. And records are sparse. In some cases, an expeditionary force should be regarded as the size of the army that a ruler could mobilize, while in other cases it should not. And frequently we do not know whether the figures we have refer just to expeditionary forces or to an entire army, to a standing army or to one that was mobilized during a war, to soldiers or to the larger number of persons that often accompanied soldiers on campaign.

Still, the numbers we have enable us to draw some comparative conclusions. Medieval rulers were never able to mobilize entire armed forces of more than 50,000 men, and much fewer usually appeared at a single battle. Armies of this size are common in world history, but they do not match some massive armies that have been mobilized outside Europe, at least according to our historical records. The Persian king Xerxes supposedly mobilized an army of several hundred thousand for his invasion of Greece in the fifth century BCE.[11] The total size of the Ptolemaic army may have been between 200,000 and 300,000 in the third century BCE.[12] In Ancient India, Chandra Gupta (375–415 CE) reportedly assembled an army of 600,000 infantry, 30,000 cavalry, and 9,000 elephants.[13] And an Ottoman army of 200,000 was mobilized to invade Persia in 1514.[14] Even if the above figures are exaggerated, they represent far larger armies than those in Europe until the seventeenth century. The first enormous Western-European army was formed by the Spanish. It was a multinational force generated by Spain's struggle to maintain its possessions in the Low Countries. It had an effective strength of perhaps 150,000, though on paper it had 300,000.[15]

The United Provinces did not have sufficient population to support a big army, but they were able to compensate to some degree by recruiting foreigners. In the late sixteenth century, they had a force of 20,000 to 30,000. They succeeded in expanding the number to something between 55,000 and 65,000 in the 1620s, though several estimates put it much higher. In the 1640s, the number was around 60,000; in the 1670s, some 90,000; and by the end of the century, more than 100,000, a size that was not surpassed during the eighteenth century. In the nineteenth century, it numbered around 60,000.

The Austrians did not maintain a large army in the Southern Low Countries, but they did raise "national regiments." Moderate in size, these regiments nevertheless expanded during the course of the eighteenth century, from close to 8,000 men in 1742 to 9,000 in 1763, 11,000 in 1773, and 17,000 under Joseph II.[16] In the nineteenth century, Belgium was forced to think big in order to maintain its sovereignty during the first decade of its independence. The number prescribed to be on a war footing in 1831 – whatever the new Belgian government could actually have put into the field – was set at 80,000. In each of the years 1833 to 1839, this prescribed number was approximately 110,000; between 1839 and 1870, it was around 80,000; and thereafter, it was approximately 100,000, equivalent to about 35,000 men in peacetime, and enough to create a mobilized army of 72,000 for the Franco-Prussian War. During the Great War, though recruitment was constrained by the fact that the majority of the country was occupied by enemy forces, the troop strength rose from 70,000 in November 1914 to 168,000 in 1917.[17]

Until the Civil War, British armies generally numbered less than 10,000, exceeding that number only during major conflicts. This war brought more than 100,000 troops into combat. When Charles II became king, the size of the royal army was drastically reduced; at the end of his reign, it comprised less than 9,000 men in the English army, 7,500 in the Irish army, and 2,200 in the Scottish army.[18] To resist William of Orange's invasion in 1688, James VII/II (VII of Scotland and II of England and Wales) was able to mobilize a field army of around 30,000, along with an estimated 5,000 troops in garrison, and an estimated 5,000 readying themselves for service.[19] It was under William (now William II of Scotland and William III of England and Wales) that the greatest increase took place. By 1694, the combined armies of the British Isles were roughly five times larger than they had been ten years earlier.[20] In the Seven Years' War, over 200,000 troops, including foreign mercenaries, were in British pay; and the British army was larger per capita than the French.[21] During the Napoleonic Wars, the regular army grew to roughly 250,000 men. And during the Great War it reached 4 million.

It is believed that French armies, in the fifteenth and sixteenth centuries, were 10,000 to 20,000 strong during peacetime, and around 50,000 during wars. These numbers roughly tripled during the Thirty Years' War, reaching 180,000 in 1636. By 1666, the number had fallen to 72,000, but the War of Devolution raised it to 134,000 in 1667–68 and the Franco-Dutch War to a paper strength of 280,000 in 1678. The conclusion of this war led to a sharp reduction in military personnel, but during the War of the League of Augsburg and the War of the Spanish Succession, the numbers may have approached 400,000. During the Revolutionary and Napoleonic Wars, however, numbers ranged from 500,000 to 1 million. Effectives were around 500,000 for the Crimean, Italian, and Franco-Prussian wars. For the Great War, the French mobilized no less than 4 million troops.[22]

At the same time, European armies were coming under more central control. In France, military centralization was led by Michel Le Tellier, marquis de Barbezieux, who was appointed secretary of state for war in 1643, and by his son, François Michel Le Tellier, marquis de Louvois, who succeeded his father as secretary of state for war in 1666. Louvois utilized the *commissaires des guerres*, the *intendants des armées*, and the provincial intendants to exert more direct control over soldiers. In France and other Continental states, the central state intensified its role in commissioning junior officers and in their recruitment.

The most critical was the last mentioned. The limited administrative capacity of states to do their own recruiting had previously forced them to rely on various methods of subcontracting. In the fifteenth and sixteenth centuries, professional contractors of one kind or another raised large numbers of soldiers, who were effectively mercenaries. Whole regiments could be recruited from other European countries, usually under the command of a native of that country. Alternatively or in addition, commissions were given to local magnates or military officers, who would mobilize and take command of regiments. A local lord could mobilize his subordinates by claiming a seigneurial right to do so, by drawing on ties of kinship or clientage, or by virtue of his command over a local militia.

Things began to change during the last half of the seventeenth century. Existing modes of recruitment were insufficient to supply enough soldiers for major wars. Recruitment by means of seigneurial obligation became more difficult. The unsuccessful efforts of Richelieu to raise the *ban* and *arrière ban* (the right of a lord to call up his vassals and their vassals) and of Charles I to use commissions of array (commissions issued by the Crown authorizing lords of manors to muster and array their tenants) discouraged relying on seigneurial recruitment.

The evolution of new methods was gradual. Indeed, the larger armies of the late seventeenth century could not have been built without contracting out. The employment of mercenaries continued, as did enlistment by colonels and captains. But central states increasingly restricted the powers of these officer-entrepreneurs, and the employment of mercenaries was brought under greater administrative control. Regiments could still be raised by local aristocrats in some districts, such as Scotland, during the seventeenth century and even much of the eighteenth century. In fact, recruiting was always easier in a district if carried out in co-operation with a local notable. Nevertheless, during the eighteenth and nineteenth centuries, central control over recruitment significantly increased. The combination of larger armies and more central control meant that, in a relatively short period of time, the number of military personnel that central governments and military commanders had to organize was beyond anything known in Europe since the Roman Empire.

CHANGES IN THOUGHT AND PRACTICE

A number of cultural collections were known to political and military leaders when the above demographic and structural changes were taking place and the nature of warfare was being transformed. These include the cultural collections considered in Part I of this book. In addition, during the Early Modern period, certain beliefs and practices emerged that I call a "culture of improvement and reform."

Contributing Ideational-Institutional Developments

We can begin with a brief mention of three broad ideational-institutional developments that contributed to the culture of improvement and reform.

THE RELIGIOUS REFORMATION

The Protestant Reformation evolved out of a number of Medieval movements that protested against the mercenary practices of the Catholic Church and the worldliness and materialism of the Church hierarchy, problems that became the focus of the Counter-Reformation as well. The elimination of "abuses" was one of the fundamental objectives of these movements. Protestants also rejected certain items of Church doctrine and the claim of the Church hierarchy to final authority over religious thought. I discuss these in Chapter 9. Here, it is the demand for reform to which I want to call attention.

THE DECLINE IN CULTURAL MONOPOLIES

In addition, religious institutions were losing the cultural monopoly they had once enjoyed. During the late Medieval and Early Modern periods, there evolved a greater differentiation of culture, in particular between religious and non-religious cultures. A growing interest in classical learning, the evolution of universities specializing not only in theology but also in law and medicine, a displacement of Latin as the language of state and secular culture, the evolution of princely courts as centres of culture, and the organization of learning outside of universities in academies and various kinds of societies – all of these institutional changes contributed to this process of cultural differentiation. Technological changes also played a part: moveable-type printing helped to undermine earlier literate monopolies and created a reading public.

INSTRUMENTALISM

The above changes were reciprocally linked in a causal relationship with a gradual but significant ideational change that can be referred to as "instrumentalism." People more often came to assume that there are a variety of ways of doing things, some more effective than others; that their environment was alterable; that there are correct and incorrect procedures for studying it; and that deliberate efforts to discover new ways of doing things are beneficial. This kind of thinking gave rise to new intellectual perspectives on the universe and the natural environment, and to the development of a commitment to general claims that are substantiated by recognized methods of investigation in which truth is empirically determined. Those who adopted these methods increasingly restricted the word "science" (which was not a new term in the sixteenth or seventeenth century) to these general claims and methods of investigation, and repeatedly challenged knowledge that they thought had not been "scientifically" substantiated. This ideational evolution was more advanced in relatively urbanized regions, where social mobilization had, to a degree, undermined traditional understandings and where culture was more differentiated. Yet it could be imposed on less urbanized regions.[23]

The Culture of Improvement and Reform

The Early Modern culture of improvement and reform can be detected in a number of spheres. We can see it in the physiocratic belief that the interests of a state and its population depended on its agricultural productivity and that concrete measures should be taken to improve this productivity. We can also see it in the mercantilist belief that exports could be increased and imports reduced through an improvement in the quality of domestically manufactured goods and in the methods by which they were manufactured. For our purposes, evidence of this culture in two institutional settings warrants some discussion.

ASSOCIATIONS FOR IMPROVEMENT AND REFORM

The seventeenth and eighteenth centuries saw an enormous expansion in associational activity in Europe. In Chapter 9, more effort is made to understand the phenomenon. Here, I am specifically interested in those associations that sought to contribute to improvement and reform. I can briefly mention two types.

First are the so-called "useful societies," which were established with the objective of directly trying to improve, by means of their organization and activities, the state and society in which members of these associations lived. These bodies included agricultural societies, societies for the improvement of manufacturing and commerce, life-saving societies, and miscellaneous "patriotic societies" that were founded with the broad purpose of bettering their homeland.

A second category consisted of "learned societies," the members of which were interested in advancing the new science at the expense of "superstition," usually with a view to practical benefits. The earliest of these societies were the Renaissance humanist associations, which often operated under the patronage of a prince and could be linked to the latter's court. Only a minority of these Renaissance associations were interested in science, however, and it was not until the seventeenth and eighteenth centuries that the scientific associations became widespread.

This associational activity was a European-wide phenomenon, but the greatest number of associations, especially learned societies, were found in the British Isles, France, the Low Countries, and northern Italy.[24] Some were officially linked to the state, while others were privately organized; the former were more likely to be called "academies" and the latter "societies," but this was not always the case.[25] Many of these associations were ephemeral, but others, most prominently the Royal Society of London and the French Academy in Paris, have continued to this day. In the nineteenth century, along with the useful, learned, and moral-reform societies, there emerged an increasing number of specialized associations composed of professionals.

STATE IMPROVEMENT AND REFORM

The culture of improvement and reform also spread through state institutions. Although British state administration was plagued by corruption and patronage, its governments were able to construct a comparatively efficient bureaucracy for collecting taxes in the seventeenth and eighteenth centuries. The Crown relied heavily on excise and customs for its revenue, which could be centralized and standardized with less difficulty than other kinds of taxes. The number of tax officials expanded dramatically, tripling from 1690 to 1782. The majority of the additional personnel were full-time employees operating under tighter bureaucratic control than other branches of the state.[26]

In France, state reform was impeded by the venality of offices. However, from the middle of the seventeenth century, the provincial intendants were dispatched to improve the collection of taxes, link local and central governments, introduce reforms, and look after army regiments situated in their jurisdiction. In these and other activities in which provincial intendants were engaged, the documents betray a concern to increase the effectiveness of the state and to make things run more smoothly. In a study of the actions taken by provincial intendants and the instructions they received from the central government from the mid-seventeenth century to the end of the Old Regime, I found that 30 per cent of the instructions were concerned with state finance. No less than 38 per cent of these dealt with problems of equity, with relief and exemption from taxes where necessary, and with improving the financial health of communities.[27]

The more semiotic features of this culture of improvement and reform have been illustrated by Chandra Mukerji in her study of the gardens at Versailles.[28] In her view, the gardens were meant to symbolize the territorial power of the French Crown. What is most relevant to the present concern is her contention that the Crown sought to use the gardens to demonstrate the mastery of the state over land, to express the spatial and technical orderliness of the Bourbon territorial state, and to symbolize its commitment to rationality and symmetry. Her point is not that the operation of the Early Modern French state was greatly improved and reformed – that is a separate issue – but that it functioned in a culture in which this was seen as the best way to insure the survival of the Bourbon regime against its internal and external enemies.

State efforts to improve and reform were more vigorous on the Continent than in Britain. The culture of improvement and reform was most manifest in Germany, where the Reformation contributed significantly. The influence of ideas of religious reform on attitudes toward the reform of state and society has been illuminated particularly well by Philip Gorski for Brandenburg Prussia and the Northern Netherlands.[29] It was also mainly in Germany that there emerged, during the seventeenth and eighteenth centuries, an intellectual and administrative movement known as "cameralism." It claimed to be an administrative science, utilizing statistics and rational theory for the better operation of state and society, for raising state revenue, for the improvement of the welfare of a population, and for competing with other states and societies. Frederick William I/II, king of Prussia and elector of Brandenburg, established chairs of cameralism at the University of Frankfurt an der Oder and the University of Halle in 1727. These chairs were gradually imitated. In 1730, the Swedish king created an endowed chair in Rinteln, and cameralist chairs were subsequently introduced in Leipzig (1742); Vienna (1752); Göttingen (1755); Prague (1763); Freiburg, Innsbruck, and Klagenfurt (1768); and Ingoldstadt (1780).[30]

The preceding discussion does, I have to confess, overstate the strength of the culture of improvement and reform. As those who genuinely believed in it would have been the first to admit, their program was far from hegemonic in the societies in which they lived. Many people celebrated improvement and reform, but displayed limited genuine commitment to it. Most sectors of society were resistant to change. Indeed, Andre Wakefield has taken the position that cameralism was mostly a sham to cover up the corruption and mismanagement of state officials.[31] Yet, all of this does not deny the existence of the culture of improvement and reform. Instead, it helps us appreciate the difficulties faced by those seriously interested in it when they sought to modify collective action and organization.

COLLECTIVE ACTION AND ORGANIZATION

We now turn from basic social, political, military, and cultural changes to the effects of these changes on the character of collective action and organization. Mobilizing collective action on a bigger scale, in a more competitive and denser environment, among people whose participation can be more easily gained or lost, many of whom do not know one another well – mobilizing collective action under these conditions created new opportunities and challenges. Most discernibly, as Mann argues, the sheer power of active collectivities became potentially greater.[32]

Population Maintenance and Extraction

First, and most obviously, as a result of demographic changes and political centralization, state officials in the Early Modern and Modern periods found themselves having to deal with much larger populations than did rulers in the Middle Ages. Urban centres alone constituted a huge management problem for governments. Their growth was the product of little planning, created new demands on governments, and required new methods of social control. Even populations further from centres of government became a resource that could – indeed had – to be used to augment tax revenue and provide rulers with soldiers. Anything that afflicted these populations – disease, civil conflicts, economic crises, food shortage, et cetera – weakened the state. Medieval lords had depended on populations in the same way, but the populations were then more stable and much smaller. Eventually, by the Modern period, governments also came to concern themselves with the skill and educational levels of the populations over which they ruled.

The expanding pressure for population maintenance and extraction forced state officials to adopt new practices and modify old ones. There was a gradual advance in the role of central governments in the regulation of the economy, in rules and regulations governing subjects, in public health and hygiene, in the regulation of the food supply, economic exchange, and in methods of dealing with problematic segments in the population, most notably vagrants and the poor. This regulation was often referred to as "police."[33]

Population maintenance and extraction operated on a much greater scale on the Continent than in the British Isles. As just mentioned, French provincial intendants occupied a good deal of their time with problems of tax relief and exemption, and the general financial soundness of communities in their jurisdiction. They were also active in maintaining public health, in the regulation and improvement of the local economy, and in the regulation of the food supply or price of food. And they had to deal with the management of relations between the army and local populations.[34]

The interest in population maintenance and extraction was closely related to a growing interest in the administration of the physical environment.[35] Both projects drew information and inspiration from the new science and what I call instrumentalism. Population maintenance and extraction went hand in hand with building new roads (often to gain more control over comparatively lawless regions), public works, regulation of waterways, and efforts to prevent the deterioration of agricultural land.

Population maintenance and extraction of this kind required more information about the targeted populations. Population census as we know it today developed in Western Europe during the nineteenth century, but we should not overlook earlier efforts by European governments to collect population information. During the sixteenth and seventeenth centuries, measures were introduced to collect vital statistics in a number of countries. In England, the registration of baptisms, marriages, and burials by the clergy of the Church of England began in 1538.[36] In addition, the English Poor Law meant greater population surveillance in England than was the case in Continental states.[37] On the other hand, Continental states were more often faced with the need to know the numbers of people living in different districts in order to supply food during famines and to raise troops. In all of Europe, population information was also necessary for increasing tax revenue. Frequently, this information collection was carried out by local officials, in most cases not closely administered by the central government, with the notable exception of French provincial intendants, who routinely received orders to collect information on a wide range of subjects.

Efforts were sometimes made to estimate populations by means of multipliers, that is, ratios that were calculated on the basis of careful information collected in a limited number of districts and then extrapolated to much bigger populations. Several possible statistics could be taken as the numerical base. Sébastien Le Prestre de Vauban (Louis XIV's military engineer) estimated the population of

France in the first decade of the eighteenth century using per capita grain production as the numerical base. But it was more common to use vital statistics. Later, Jean-Baptiste Moheau (a French demographer of the late eighteenth century) used births to estimate the population of France in 1715, arriving at a number similar to that of Vauban.[38] Gregory King employed the same method to estimate the population of England and Wales in the late seventeenth century, but we know little about the bases he used for his estimations.

A number of obstacles impeded the implementation of a large-scale national population census. One was public opposition. It is only to be expected, therefore, that the first determined effort to count the entire population in France was made during the French Revolutionary period when such opposition could be dealt with more ruthlessly than under the Old Regime. It began in 1795 and was known as the "Census of the Year IV." It was imposed on people living in France, but also on those living in other territories ruled by the French, including the Southern Low Countries. These endeavours were not altogether successful, but they were followed by the gradual introduction of population censuses in the Low Countries during the first half of the nineteenth century, that is, over the same period that they evolved in France and the British Isles.[39]

Population Mobilization

During the Early Modern period there were noteworthy differences between our two major states in the challenges they faced when trying to mobilize various segments of the population.

ELITE MOBILIZATION

The French state was more powerful than the British state. It had a larger state officialdom and, from the mid-seventeenth century, its provinces were administered by provincial intendants, tightly controlled by the Crown. It also had a much larger army to resist a challenge by force. And it did not have a strong central parliament that could oppose it. However, this also meant that, when it tried to mobilize elites, the French Crown did not have very effective institutional links with most people in the provinces, not even with many members of the provincial nobility. In some provinces, it still had to negotiate with *états provinciaux*, whose primary objective was to protect local interests. The problem was similar, indeed worse, for the Spanish and Austrian monarchies in the Low Countries owing to longer geographical distances between centres and peripheries, linguistic and national differences, and greater dissimilarities in interests between the centres and the peripheries.

The British Crown had its own difficulties in mobilizing elites. It had a much smaller body of officials; in particular, it had no equivalent to France's provincial intendants. It had to bring on side different parliamentary assemblies, which often challenged royal authority, most notably with respect to taxation and war. Not infrequently, the monarchy was prevented from going to war or forced to make peace as a result of the opposition of members of the British Parliament, especially members from outside London. During the reign of Charles II, Parliament gradually established the right to shape foreign policy and determine what wars Britain was going to fight.[40]

Yet, should the British Crown get the support of Parliament, the latter could be used to mobilize resources in a way that the French, Spanish, and Austrian crowns could not. Despite the greater control of foreign affairs acquired by Parliament under Charles II, William II/III was able, for the most part, to obtain what he needed for his Continental wars. Although Parliament sometimes hampered his efforts, it was in fact the support of Parliament that enabled him to mobilize the resources he needed.

These differences between France and Britain had already shaped the major rebellions against the two monarchies in the mid-century. Both the Civil War in Britain and the Fronde in France were challenges to gradual increases in royal power, and more specifically to royal demands for more revenue. And both coincided with social unrest in the general population. The major difference lay in the central institutions that the two monarchies struggled against: the English Parliament, on the one hand, and the Parlement de Paris, on the other. The former was able to unite opposition to the Crown. (Religious interests facilitated this anti-Crown coalition, but it is still remarkable how Parliament was able to bring together diverse groups with different grievances and goals.) In contrast, members of the Parlement de Paris could not – indeed, did not want to – unite factions in the same way. They had quite specific interests, stemming mostly from their positions as state officers. They certainly had little interest in taking advantage of the popular revolts that were erupting in Paris and in the countryside. Nor were they willing and able to unite the aristocracy. The first revolt, known as the Parlementary Fronde, was followed by an aristocratic Fronde, which only further contributed to the inability of anti-monarchical factions to join forces.

MASS MOBILIZATION

With or without the help of elites, central states sought to mobilize resources in the larger population. The relationship between political centralization and mass mobilization by states was reciprocal. Mass mobilization by states facilitated political centralization, but political centralization, as Charles Tilly stressed so much, was a major force in the (frequently violent) state mobilization of populations.[41] Early Modern states increasingly made demands – especially in taxation and manpower – directly on populations, often leading to significant unrest. The British monarchy faced revolts in Ireland and in the Highlands and Western Islands. Peasant revolts also broke out in France both before and during the French Revolution.

The French Revolutionary and Napoleonic Wars led to more state demands on populations, not just for military service but also for higher taxes and economic sacrifices, and not just in France but throughout Europe. In turn, these demands on populations by central states inevitably generated more claims on the state by those segments of the population on which central states came to depend, such as requests from military veterans for benefits in recognition of their services.

Governments were not the only ones trying to mobilize larger numbers of persons. Between the middle of the eighteenth century and the middle of the nineteenth century, as a consequence of the nationalization of contention, political struggles within states broadened in such a way that participation by a large segment of the population in centrally organized collective action and organization became more critical in determining who won power struggles. Greater demands by central states coincided with this increasing domestic conflict. In Britain, popular discontent over state demands intensified at a time when elites – including new radical elites bent on reform – were looking for broader support. This interaction of escalating demands on populations by central states and political mobilization expanded the size of the body politic well before major changes to the electoral franchise.[42]

RECRUITMENT OF SOLDIERS

As central states sought to meet the greater need for military man-power, whom did they recruit? The most accurate answer is a diversity of persons ranging from high status to low status. Officers continued to be drawn from the better-off segments of society; even members of the rank and file could include men with a claim to aristocratic ancestors and relations, usually young men with limited expecta-tions of a decent inheritance. Nonetheless, during the seventeenth and eighteenth centuries, the rank and file in armies were drawn increasingly from the poor, especially the marginalized poor – "gal-lows fruit" or "stews of the earth," as they were sometimes called. In both France and Britain, recruits were frequently picked up at fairs and markets, their enlistment in some cases facilitated by their state of intoxication. Not infrequently, they were kidnapped and held in recruitment depots that resembled prisons. Officially, such tactics were disowned by statesmen of the day, but unofficially, they could be unashamedly acknowledged. "It is a very poor excuse," wrote the remorseless Louvois in 1677, "for a soldier, to justify desertion to say that he was recruited by force. If we admitted reasons of this sort, there would not be a single soldier left in the king's forces, for there is hardly one who does not believe that he has good reason to com-plain of his recruitment."[43]

In the British Isles, impressment was given some scattered measure of legal approval in the eighteenth century. The moral justification for coercive recruitment can be found in the words of several con-temporaries quoted by Nicholas Rogers. These recruits are "idle and reprobate Vermin," said one, while another took it for granted that "those who are of least use at home are the fittest to be employed in the service of their country abroad." Beggars, pickpockets, barrow-men, chimney sweeps, and market people are all "dead weight upon the community."[44] Impressment for naval service could not be as indiscriminate as army recruitment, given the skill required to oper-ate (immensely expensive) sailing vessels. By the same token, how-ever, naval impressment could be merciless and difficult to avoid for those who made their living on the sea.[45]

The French Revolutionary armies were different. Initially, they were composed of volunteers, but in 1793, conscription was intro-duced: first, the *levée des 300.000* in the spring, and then the *levée en masse* in August, which conscripted all bachelors and childless wid-owers. The Revolutionaries were driven to these measures by the serious threat posed by the expansion of the War in March and by the poor performance and unreliability of the existing line army.[46] The *levée des 300.000* was raised by assigning quotas to towns and villages. It is true that these communities were left to decide who was to be sent, and there was a tendency for the burden to fall disproportionately on more marginalized members. It is also true that foreign elements remained prominent in French armies. All the same, the Revolutionary armies were composed of a greater number of less marginalized members of French society than the armies of the Old Regime.

This change in the social composition of the army had notable consequences, two of which I will mention here. First, it meant that the Revolutionary army could not be managed in the way in which pre-Revolutionary armies had been managed. Most officers did not have the social pre-eminence that their predecessors had. Although it is important not to exaggerate the point, these officers would find it more difficult to bully soldiers, who were now more often drawn from the bourgeoisie and better-off members of the working class. The effect of this change in social composition was magnified by the egalitarian ideology of the Revolution. Traditional modes of discipline were incompatible with the cause for which soldiers were now presumably fighting. In 1790, the line army was plagued by a series of mutinies, in part a consequence of the civic rights now asserted by those who served.[47] When Mathieu Dumas, president of the Legislative Assembly and an officer in the French army from 1780, proposed new disciplinary measures in 1792, his ideas were met with considerable opposition from those who, he claimed, "looked upon discipline but as an instrument of despotism."[48] Although he seems to have carried the day, the tension – between traditional methods of discipline and the new patriotic spirit – created challenges for military leadership that had not existed before, or at least not to the same degree.

The second consequence of the change in the social composition of the French army was a transformation in public attitudes toward the common serviceman. To the extent that the army came to be composed, relatively speaking, of husbands, sons, brothers, nephews, and neighbours of the majority of the French population, the negative attitude of the population toward soldiers declined. The French serviceman was now treated, overtly at least, with more respect. He was a volunteer – even if in reality a conscript – supposedly fulfilling his duties of citizenship and serving for noble reasons.[49]

Under the First Empire, the ideology may have shifted to honour, patriotism, and dedication to Napoleon, but the common serviceman was still portrayed as a person of competence, dedication, and loyalty.[50] These social constructions did not reflect what the majority of conscripts actually felt, even in the early 1790s. Before the seizure of power by Napoleon, the ideological commitment of soldiers had further diminished, and under the Consulate and the Empire the French army was professionalized, such that more soldiers came to see military service as a career and were committed not so much to the nation but primarily to the army as an institution.[51]

It is important, however, to distinguish between two meanings of the term "professional," though they certainly overlap. First, the term can refer to the fact that a soldier is highly trained, competent, and skilled for the position he holds. To repeat, changes in the ways in which war was fought during the Early Modern period did not introduce merit into European armed forces – it was there all along – but it did cause a shift in the conception of what was meritorious. Intelligence and foresight, along with knowledge of new technologies of warfare and how to organize large armies, became more significant than devotion, bravery, charisma, or even martial skill. Professionalism of this kind was articulated in the Early Modern military culture and in the growing literature on methods of warfare, both of which were institutionalized in military schools of the Early Modern period. The new military ethos demanded general standards of professional competence, duty, and obedience. It was influenced by what I have called instrumentalism and the culture of improvement and reform.

Although the new culture did not result in a decline in aristocratic participation in the officer corps of European armies in the eighteenth century, the French Revolutionary and Napoleonic Wars did have this effect, at least in France.[52] These wars also changed the way in which people thought about military recruitment and promotion. It should be acknowledged that many of the officers of the Restoration army were returned *émigrés* with little military experience, but the Republican and Imperial periods set the standard for the French army for the remainder of the century – that officers should be selected on the basis of new notions of competence, either from the ranks of *sous-officiers* or from the *grandes écoles*, principally the École Saint-Cyr and the École polytechnique.[53]

The same evolution came later in Britain. Indeed, during the late seventeenth and eighteenth centuries, at a time when the officer corps in Continental armies was increasingly being selected by new criteria (if still almost entirely from the nobility), British battlefield commissions and promotions were being replaced by the purchase of commissions, which undermined the competence of officers and discouraged military education.[54] Nevertheless, professionalization in the British military occurred gradually over the eighteenth and nineteenth centuries. Although the purchase of commissions was not abolished until 1871, the Royal Military Academy was founded as a gunnery school at the Woolwich Arsenal in 1741. And in 1799, Colonel J.G. le Machant (born in France and a descendant of the Huguenot leader Admiral Gaspard de Coligny) and Francis Jarry (an exiled French general) organized an officers' training college, which became the Royal Military College Sandhurst. Admission to these schools eventually came to be based on competitive examinations.

In its second meaning, the term "professional" denotes persons who are engaged in military service full-time, usually for a large part of their lives. European armies had long included professional soldiers in this sense – mercenaries, peasants, and other less-privileged segments of society. The standing armies that were built up during the seventeenth and eighteenth centuries increased this kind of professionalization, but the French Revolutionary and Imperial armies reduced it, at least proportionately, in the so-called "citizen army" or "nation in arms."

Britain was also at this time forced to raise a mass army drawn from a wide segment of the population. Indeed, as a percentage of its population, Britain's mobilization for war in 1800 and 1810 was greater than that of France.[55] As in France, the British armed forces were no longer composed of relatively marginalized members of society. State officials were increasingly forced to adopt a more considerate attitude toward the common serviceman and his family relations. Programs were introduced to provide educational assistance to the children of servicemen, to enable families to petition for the effects of deceased servicemen, and to permit seamen to remit some of their wages to wives or mothers; in addition, an existing provision that allowed sailors to make lump sum payments to their families was expanded and improved.[56] The significance of these measures for the present discussion does not lie in the improvement, if any, that they brought to the lives of soldiers and their families, but rather in the change that these measures suggest in what governments were expected to do for their benefit. There may also have developed a more paternalistic attitude on the part of officers toward their men, perhaps as a result of the exigencies of mass mobilization, perhaps also as a result of other forces in British society altering relations between elites and other segments of the population.[57]

Similar forces led to the demise of naval impressment in Britain. Even before the French Revolutionary and Napoleonic Wars, discontent with naval impressment was pervasive because the press gangs were seizing not just marginalized members of society but also seamen who were well known and integrated in coastal communities. Moreover, in the 1790s, many seamen had some familiarity with the radical ideas that were circulating at that time, ideas that found expression in several mutinies, during which it was evident that the men were rejecting the traditional stigmatization of impressed sailors.[58] The response of the government was draconian, but an effort was also made to include ordinary seamen in the public praise that came with the naval victories in which they participated.[59] After the Napoleonic War, dissatisfaction with the treatment of sailors was widespread, a development exploited by British radicals. Consequently, impressment declined as a means of recruiting for the navy, which came to depend less on the press gang and more on making the occupation more attractive (or at least, less unattractive), along with raising the status of sailors in British society. Although we should not exaggerate how much things changed, it is clear that, as in France, a shift took place in techniques of mobilizing men for war.

However, the British armies did differ in two significant respects from French armies. First, Britain did not conscript, either during the French wars or later in the century. Its armies were composed of two groups: (1) until 1871, officers who purchased their commissions, and (2) non-commissioned officers and private, who continued to be drawn from lower strata in the social order. Second, there was no citizen army in Britain, mythical or otherwise, and so public attitudes toward the army remained less positive than in France, with the result that servicemen could be subjected to harsh discipline well into the nineteenth century. Whereas in France, corporal punishment was formally abolished in 1789 and generally avoided in the nineteenth century, branding was not given up in the British army until 1871 and flogging not until 1881.[60]

Without dismissing the importance of changes that took place in Britain and its armies during the French wars, it can safely be said that, in the British Isles, the greatest transformation in attitudes toward the common soldier occurred during and after the Crimean

War. This was the first war in history during which a medium of communication permitted almost-immediate news to come from the battlefront, specifically in the telegraph reports of William Russell, correspondent for *The Times*. Public opinion was also influenced by the letters of Florence Nightingale and other accounts of conditions at the Selimiye Barracks in Scutari, and by her post-war campaign for improvements in health care for soldiers. In addition, reports of the incompetence of some officers in the Crimean War became symbolically powerful, perhaps as powerful as the mythical citizen army in France. The impact of the Crimean War on British public opinion had two consequences that interest us. First, it increased sympathy for the common soldier. Second, it initiated a long-term undertaking on the part of political elites to reform the officer corps in the British army.

7

Collective-Action Problems and the Honours of States

It is evident that, in varying degrees, the three major collective-action problems discussed in Chapter 4 had changed by the seventeenth and eighteenth centuries as a result of the social and political transformations just discussed. These collective-action problems produced selection pressures on governments, to which they responded in a variety of ways, one of which was to increase modes of honorific recognition.

LEGITIMATION

How collective action and organization came to be culturally situated and legitimated was different in the Early Modern and Modern periods from what it had been in the Medieval period. It is true that the legitimation of collective action and organization in terms of the values, norms, and assumptions of lordship, kinship, community, and religion continued to be important in the Early Modern period. Governments routinely used them to justify domestic and international collective action and organization. This was even true of lordship. Its principles were moulded to legitimate the rule of centralized monarchies. "Subjects" were expected to have the same loyalty and devotion to their king or queen that they would have to a lord. Eventually, however, these earlier cultural frames were insufficient to meet the legitimating needs of centralized states.

Indications of the Legitimation Function of Honours

Monarchies used state honours to associate their regimes with the ideals of "chivalry," and the heritage and symbolism of heraldry

and orders of knighthood. At the same time, both monarchical and
republican governments tried to use state honours to associate their
regimes with meritocratic principles in order to please or appease
the expanding bourgeoisie, whose members claimed that this was
what the bourgeoisie stood for. Other cultural accumulations associated with honours that were thought to fortify the legitimacy of
political regimes included Christianity, classicism, and Romanticism.
Nineteenth-century European states also liked to demonstrate their
commitment to economic development by awarding prizes that recognized economic endeavours. We will turn shortly to the utilization
of these prizes as incentives, but they were also useful because they
linked the state to the culture of capitalist industrialization that was
gradually taking hold in Western Europe and beyond during the
nineteenth century.

Whatever the cultural source, state honours were definitely
employed to perform a legitimation function for states and regimes.
Some examples immediately come to mind. Henry IV of France, in
order to authenticate his conversion to Catholicism, founded the
Order of Our Lady of Mount-Carmel in 1608 and then united it
with the Order of Saint Lazarus of Jerusalem. James VII/II founded
the Order of the Thistle in an effort to bolster the legitimacy of
his fragile regime. The Jacobites in exile awarded British honours
(unrecognized in Britain, of course) in order to legitimize their
claim to the monarchy; these awards were sometimes recognized
by France, Spain, and the Papacy.[1] The smaller German states often
feared for their survival. It was partly in an effort to legitimate their
sovereignty – to behave like sovereign states – that they fashioned
numerous orders, some of them house orders, the majority of them
very exclusive.

In some cases, a legitimation motive is suggested by the timing of
the creation of an order. The Order of the Crown of Rue was established in 1806, a year after Saxony became a kingdom, by Frederick Augustus, the first king. The Order of Saint George was founded
in Hanover in 1839, the third year of the dynastic separation of the
Kingdom of Hanover. In the Netherlands, the Military Order of William and the Order of the Dutch Lion were founded in 1815, the
same year that the international agreement was signed at the Congress of Vienna that brought the United Kingdom of the Netherlands into being. William I was doing all that he could to confirm

the legitimacy of this new state. Unfortunately, it was not enough to prevent a mortal fracture in 1830.

If William had been nervous in 1815, the Belgian state builders had good reason to be even more nervous. To help legitimate the Revolution in the eyes of the Belgian population and to legitimate their state in the eyes of the world, they instituted a number of new state honours during the first few years of independence. This state had never existed before. Its formation was made possible by the support the Belgian Revolutionaries received from other European powers, on whom it now depended for survival. Its existence continued to be contested by the Dutch until 1837. Moreover, the new state was being consolidated on the basis of a new monarchy that had no dynastic roots in the country. Its politicians felt a need to invent a national honour because inventing honours was seen as something that sovereign states do. In particular, the international respectability of the Belgian government required a national decoration comparable to the decorations of neighbouring countries, so that honours could be exchanged with the dignitaries of these countries.[2]

Two additional indications of this concern among Belgian state officials are evident. First, in 1838, a further grade was added to the existing four grades of the Order of Leopold. The new grade was called *grand officier*, and became the second level in the hierarchy. It was introduced to enable the Belgian state to exchange equivalent honours with other countries whose similar decorations had five grades. The difference in number of grades had caused diplomatic embarrassment and diminished the stature of the new state in the eyes of foreigners, or at least so it was believed. "It is contrary to the dignity of the Belgian government," wrote the spokesman of the parliamentary committee reviewing the legislation, "to be forced to confer the grade of *grand cordon* when a State of equal or inferior rank conferred on a Belgian subject only that of *grand officier*."[3]

Second, Belgian governments awarded an extraordinary number of decorations to non-Belgians. I have sampled recipients of three major honours in Western Europe: the Legion of Honour, the Order of Leopold, and the Order of the British Empire. In the sample of members of the Order of Leopold from 1833 to 1887, 40 per cent of civilians were foreigners, even excluding members of royal families (Table B.1 in Appendix B). Indeed, the Belgian government seemed more interested in handsomely rewarding foreigners than its own meritorious citizens; as a rule, the higher the grade, the higher the percentage who were foreigners (Table B.3). Gradually, as concern over the legitimacy of their new state declined, so too did foreign representation. Excluding non-Europeans for the moment, in my 1932 weighted sample, I found that less than 1 per cent of the civilians were foreigners, though it should be noted that in the unweighted sample, half of the *grands cordons* (the highest grade) were foreigners (Tables B.2 and B.4; see Appendix B for an explanation of the weighting of the samples).

Whether or not one of the reasons Napoleon created the Legion of Honour was to help legitimate his regime, it is certain that this was one of the reasons for all the aristocratic trappings discussed in Chapter 2, and also for establishing the Imperial nobility. It can also be recalled that, when the Bourbons were restored to power, though they did not abolish the Legion of Honour, they did seek to reinforce their Old-Regime credentials. They revived a number of Old-Regime orders and replaced the image of Napoleon on the insignia of the Legion of Honour with that of Henry IV. After the Revolution of 1830, the new king, Louis-Philippe, introduced a number of new decorations, two of which – the July Cross and the July Medal – celebrated the July Revolution that brought him to power.

It is well known that Napoleon III sought to legitimate his rule by associating it with that of his uncle, while simultaneously trying to build a broad base of support that was not limited to die-hard Bonapartists. Recent research has challenged the notion that the Second Empire was a strong state, a notion that fails to recognize the struggle over legitimacy that was fought between the Bonapartists and those opposed to them. The Legion of Honour played a significant role in this effort because it was a genuinely First-Empire institution that had survived subsequent regimes and was well integrated into the political and social structure of the country. In 1852, the most important pieces of legislation in the history of the Order were enacted.[4] A Council of the Order was created to replace the former Committee of Consultation, which had ceased to be active. And in 1857, to associate his regime even more to that of his uncle, Napoleon III created the Medal of Saint Helena, to be awarded to those who had fought for France between 1792 and 1815. It is estimated that some 400,000 persons received this medal.[5]

War, Nation, and Empire

As was the case during the Middle Ages, state honours were used to legitimate wars that governments undertook. It has already become clear that the earliest European honours awarded to large numbers of persons were primarily for military personnel. Indeed, it is not unreasonable to take the position that rewarding military personnel was the main driving force in the evolution of state honours in Western Europe. Why was this the case? My answer will put considerable emphasis on the evolution of new conditions for motivating and communicating in Early Modern and Modern military forces, but we should not overlook what is, in some ways, the most obvious explanation. State honours for military personnel helped to glorify the military endeavours in which they were engaged. Honours might even help governments deal with a lack of popular support for a war. The Victoria Cross came about as a consequence of public sympathy for the soldiers who fought in Crimea, but also as an effort by state officials to blunt widespread criticism of this war in Britain.

There is no doubt that state honours were employed during the nineteenth century to legitimate the forging of nations. It is well known that the French Revolutionaries adopted the "nation" and *patrie* as idioms in an effort to mobilize support and distinguish their governments from the monarchy of the Old Regime. They tried to draw a connection between the state honours they created and the French "nation," for example, in the decree of August 1790 on "pensions, bonuses, and other national recompenses," which included "symbols of honour, awarded by the nation."[6] And the motto of the Legion of Honour was *Honneur et Patrie*.

We have to be careful, however, not to exaggerate the importance of state honours in the legitimation of nations. First, the expansion of state honours began before the social and political construction of "nation," at least as it was constructed during the long nineteenth century. Second, joint references to nation and state honours are not as common in the documents as one might think, certainly not as common as I had expected them to be. Although leaders of the French Revolution did award some honours, they did not see state honours as particularly useful for the construction of the French nation. And one could make a case that the word *patrie* had a different history than "nation" and carried a different connotation in the motto of the Legion of Honour. In any case, the Legion of Honour might have had a different motto if it had been created a few years later under the Empire. Finally, the most nationalistic of the states examined in this book, the Irish Free State and the Irish Republic, has largely resisted state honours. In Chapter 10, I propose that the significance of "nation" for understanding state honours lies less in its value for legitimation and nation building and more in its value for social control.

When we are talking about legitimation, we need to keep in mind the association of state honours with the persistence of the old order. This association made state honours more useful for the legitimation of monarchies and empires than nations. Irish nationalists detested state honours because they associated them with British rule and the Anglo-Irish elite, but also because they saw that state honours were being used by European states to legitimate empires, a view that was dramatically reinforced when the Order of the British Empire was created in the year following the Easter Rising (a failed revolt in Dublin in 1916), complete with motto, "For God and the Empire." This imperial legitimation is also evident in the substantial number of orders and medals that were introduced for colonial possessions or for armed forces serving outside Europe. Taking all state honours together, Britain did not lead the way in the great expansion, but Britain was – as the most vigorous imperial state – the most precocious in the creation of honours for military and civilian personnel in overseas colonies or possessions. During the last decade of the eighteenth century and over the course of the nineteenth century, the British government and the East India Company introduced a number of military medals for men who had fought in overseas engagements – the Seringapatam Medal, the Ghuznee Medal, the Medal for the Defence of Kelat-I-Ghilzie, the Candahar Medal, and the Punjab Medal, to mention only a few. These awards were plainly being used to legitimate both British imperialism and these wars.

French governments, for their part, established or encouraged the establishment of orders in their colonies, a number of which subsequently became colonial decorations under the control of the government in Paris. These included the Royal Order of Cambodia (adopted as a French colonial order in 1896), the Order of the Dragon of Annam (founded as a French colonial order in 1886), the Order of Nichan el Anouar (adopted as a French colonial order in 1896), the Order of the Black Star (adopted as a French colonial order in 1896), and the Order of the Star of Anjouan (adopted as a French colonial order in 1892).

The shakier the legitimacy of a particular colonial regime, the more likely honours would be used in this fashion. Most illustrative of this point are decorations created by Leopold II to legitimate his personal claim to sovereignty over the Belgian Congo: the Order of the Star of Africa, the Order of the Lion, and the Order of Leopold II. Dutch colonizers adopted state honours as a way of shoring up the legitimacy of what they were doing in the East Indies. For both financial and ideological-ethical reasons, there was considerable opposition in the Netherlands to this colonial enterprise, and especially to wars with indigenous populations. An effort was made to use honours to undermine this opposition. At the same time, it was hoped that they would strengthen the legitimation of the colonial regime in the East Indies.

State honours were often used to legitimate a colonial regime or administration by raising the status of those linked with it. No possession is too small to benefit from the pomp of a splendid honour. A good illustration is the Order of Saint Michael and Saint George. The Treaty of Vienna transferred sovereignty over the island of Malta to the United Kingdom. It also placed the Ionian Islands under British protection. The administration of both was given to a Scot by the name of Thomas Maitland. He believed that British honours and titles would help dignify his regime. He had been made a knight grand cross of the Order of the Bath in 1815, and was anxious that the insignia be sent as soon as possible in order to impress the elites of Malta and the Ionian Islands.[7] His mindset is starkly revealed in an instruction to have himself cited in the government gazette of the islands as "The Right Honourable Sir Thomas Maitland, Knight Grand Cross of the most Honourable Order of the Bath, Member of the most Honourable Privy Council of His Majesty, Lieutenant General and Commander-in-Chief of the Forces of His Majesty in the Mediterranean, Governor of the Island of Malta and its dependencies, and Lord High Commissioner of His Majesty for the United States of the Ionian Islands."[8] To the same end, he persuaded the British government to create the Order of Saint Michael and Saint George as a way of dignifying his regime. Maitland was installed as grand master in a royal ceremony in a new (rather lavish and very expensive) palace that was built for the Order of Saint Michael and Saint George on the Ionian Islands in a neo-classical style; and in Malta, the Order was set up in the old palace of the grand masters of the Order of Malta, a formerly sovereign power, whose symbols were carefully covered over.[9]

The Limitations of Legitimation by Means of State Honours

The use of state honours to legitimate regimes obviously did not work for everyone, or at least not with equal facility. State honours could threaten the legitimation of republican regimes.

While the solution for Irish nationalists was, for the most part, to reject them, other regimes struggled with the issue, and, consequently, did not always follow a consistent policy. Although the United Provinces introduced very few state honours, they did reward those who served their federation by according them honorific and material gifts (money, silverware, carpets, golden necklaces, and commemorative medals).[10] However, these gratuities did not compare with the honours that were being distributed in neighbouring countries. Moreover, none of these rewards were intended to bolster the federation's sovereignty. Only the so-called "Ambassadors' medal," created in 1628, might have been seen in these terms, at least in part; it was routinely distributed to foreign representatives.[11] Even later, in the Kingdom of the Netherlands, the contradiction between state honours and egalitarian principles has been a source of unease among the Dutch, perhaps intensified by Calvinist and republican traditions.[12]

Most torn were the French Revolutionaries. On the one hand, they worried that state honours would have a negative effect on the legitimacy of their governments, given the association of such honours with the Old Regime. On the other hand, they could not avoid the temptation to glorify their own heroes, celebrate those who participated in the Revolution, and reward soldiers for defending the patrie. Given also the vicissitudes of the course of events in France during the 1790s, it is not surprising that there was a less than consistent direction in the policies adopted by Revolutionaries toward honours. In August 1789, the Commune introduced a gold medal and certificate signed by Lafayette, 104 of which were distributed; and in October, an award was bestowed on so-called *bonnes citoyennes*.[13] In June 1790, on the same day that the Constituent Assembly abolished the French nobility, it also instituted an award for those who had stormed the Bastille.[14] In August, a proposal was made that it would be appropriate to have "marks of honour bestowed by the nation" on those who were working in the interests of the people.[15] In 1791, the Constituent Assembly banned "any kind of order, any corporation, any decoration, any exterior sign that presumes distinctions of birth," thus doing away with all the royal orders, with the exception of the Order of Saint Louis, which was to be accorded to all officers with twenty-four years' service, including Protestants.[16]

In 1792, the Legislative Assembly introduced military awards, consisting of medals, crowns, and rings, for individual officers and soldiers.[17] In September of the same year, however, the National Convention was elected, and it took a much stronger position against honours, its leaders declaring that they undermined the egalitarian principles of the Revolution. Awards that had been instituted since 1789 were abolished, along with the Order of Saint Louis. Yet the leaders of this regime turned around and awarded banners, boot buckles, and crowns to recognize service to the *patrie*; they also awarded retiring soldiers with their weapons.[18] And it was during the French Revolution that the Church of Sainte-Geneviève was secularized and made into a memorial to great Frenchmen. State funerals were used by the leaders of the Revolution to honour its heroes.[19] These practices were maintained by the Directory, with one of its last acts being to codify all the *récompenses nationales*.

Next, it was the turn of the Consuls. In December 1799, they created the Arms of Honour, which was awarded for outstanding services.[20] And in 1802, they launched the Legion of Honour. As we have repeatedly seen, in debates over its creation, considerable conflict emerged between the values and preferences that Napoleon inherited from the Old Regime, on the one hand, and more revolutionary views, on the other. This conflict made the Legion of Honour a mixture of the two cultural collections, which the Revolution and the Napoleonic regime blended together. In Table 7.1, I have summarized some of the items in this mixture as they appeared in the Legion of Honour.

Table 7.1
Old and new features of the Legion of Honour

Old features	New features
Its insignia was similar to the insignia of the Order of Saint Louis, and was seen by many as almost the same.	Unlike the Order of Saint Louis, the insignia of the Legion of Honour was a star rather than a cross.
Royal ceremony was imitated at the first large public distribution of the Legion of Honour at Les Invalides.	The date chosen for the presentation at Les Invalides was intended to coincide with the fifteenth anniversary of the storming of the Bastille. (It was actually held the next day because the 14th fell on a Saturday.)
It was often referred to as an order (and eventually became the National Order of the Legion of Honour).	It was purposively called a legion to separate it from the earlier orders.
A significant number of old nobility (mostly military) were appointed to the Legion of Honour.	The legislation establishing the Legion of Honour required members to combat any enterprise tending to re-establish the "feudal" regime. Every member was required to swear an oath to oppose the return of "feudal" institutions.
The term "grand master" was used to refer to Napoleon as the head of the order.	The grades of the Legion of Honour were different from those of earlier monarchical orders, including the Order of Saint Louis.
Napoleon saw it as part of a package of innovations that would help legitimate his regime in the royal courts and cabinets of the major European powers.	The number of members of the Legion of Honour greatly exceeded Early Modern royal orders, even the Order of Saint Louis, something that could only undermine its legitimacy in the royal courts of Europe.

After the fall of the July Monarchy, under the short-lived Second Republic, the nobility and noble titles were once again abolished and no new state honours were created. As we saw in Chapter 2, the new government was divided over the question of abolishing or maintaining state honours, but those who had no objection to them prevailed and new appointments to the Legion of Honour were made in 1848. When the Second Republic fell victim to the Bonapartists, a less ambiguous attitude came to prevail. I have already reviewed how they sought to use state honours to help legitimate their regime. Clearly, state honours posed little difficulty for them.

But they sure did for the Third Republic. For many of its founders, there was a fundamental contradiction between state honours and the equality of republican citizenship.[21] They ended the awarding of noble status and noble titles. Many of them would have been happy to do the same with the Legion of Honour. A decree of September 1870 suppressed the oath that legionnaires had been obliged to swear. In October, Republican deputy Jules Ferry, a vitriolic critic of the Second Empire (and later a prime minister of France), called for the abolition of the Legion of Honour. Others demanded that it be reserved for the military. An October 28 decree stipulated that the Legion of Honour, with a new insignia, be preserved as a military recompense, but this decree was rescinded in legislation of 1873.[22] However, an April 1872 law did ban deputies from being awarded the Legion of Honour or promoted within it, except for acts of war, a provision that was subsequently extended to senators.[23]

All this surgery was one thing. Abolishing the Legion of Honour or turning it into a military decoration for bravery was another. The basis of the Republic was not solid enough for anything like that. Too many influential people belonged to the Legion of Honour or hoped to belong. And the Republicans could not resist the temptation of using state honours for their own purposes. As Avner Ben-Amos observes, the Third Republic was much like a parvenu who wanted to exhibit his wealth in order to earn respectability; consequently, it held a large number of state funerals.[24]

For the same reason, despite all the rhetoric, it soon began to decorate lavishly. Members of the Mobile Guard and the National Guard were awarded the Military Medal. From 1870 to 1872, the government of National Defence, and subsequently the government of Adolphe Thiers, named 10,000 military legionnaires. The 1873 legislation also introduced significant changes to laws governing the operation of the Legion of Honour, most notably with respect to discipline, a subject we return to in Chapter 10. In addition, the Third Republic created a large number of new decorations. Of the sixty-five state honours held on the eve of the Great War, fifty-one were founded under the Third Republic.[25]

Still, when all is said, the legitimation function performed by state honours provides, at best, a very partial answer to the major questions posed in this book. Medieval regimes needed legitimation as often as did regimes of the seventeenth, eighteenth, and nineteenth centuries; and, as we have seen, orders were then founded or in other ways employed for this purpose. In later periods, the performance of the legitimation function by state honours was more problematic. It was in monarchies (Britain, Belgium, the Kingdom of the Netherlands, as well as Central and Eastern Europe) where honours were most effective as instruments of legitimation. They were also seen as effective for the legitimation of imperial rule overseas. But back home their adaptiveness for the needs of Western-European governments was mixed.

MOTIVATION

The eventual purpose of this section is to determine the function of state honours in motivating people to engage in collective action and organization in Western Europe during the Early Modern and Modern periods, just as the previous section assessed their legitimation function. However, several preliminary discussions are warranted before doing so.

New Rewards

First, it is useful to examine some other motivational rewards that evolved concurrently. Although secondary to the main concern of this book, they illustrate other ideas and practices that were being tried during the Early Modern period owing to selection pressures similar, I would argue, to those that gave rise to state honours. The most relevant rewards are prizes.

Prizes were far from new in the Western cultural tradition. Evidence of prizes has been found in very early Mediterranean and Middle Eastern societies, including the Egyptians, Hittites, and Mycenaeans. The Greeks and Romans went in for them in a big way. Prizes were also awarded in Europe during the Medieval period, often by associational bodies, such as shooting societies and guilds. Yet, their use at that time was limited. Prize competitions were not particularly adaptive in the major institutions on which Medieval society was based – lordship, kinship, community, and religion – all of which had better ways of motivating people than handing out prizes. At best, prizes would supplement the motivations provided by these institutions. However, with the decline in the strength of ties of lordship, kinship, community, and religion, the utility of prizes increased. Indeed, people saw prizes as more effective to the extent that they believed they were independent of these other sources of persuasion.

During the seventeenth and eighteenth centuries, the number of prize competitions in Western Europe expanded as more associations offered more and more prizes. According to Jeremy Caradonna, the number of academic-prize contests in France rose from 48 in 1670–79 to 476 in 1780–89; altogether two thousand distinct prize competitions were organized in France from 1670 to 1789.[26] The institutions that awarded prizes varied greatly in size and resources. Some, most notably the Royal Society and the French Academy, were large and well funded – at least relative to others – but many were small and lasted only a short time. In Germany, the Göttingen Society of the Sciences, which struggled with a number of difficulties, including financial problems, nevertheless sponsored over fifty prizes in its first thirty years.[27] In many regions, those who competed in these contests came from a surprisingly wide range of participants, including marginalized intellectuals, artisans, and even unskilled workers and peasants.[28]

The majority of prizes were offered for one or more of five purposes. First, they were used to promote debate and intellectual exchange. One of the best known is a prize awarded to Jean-Jacques Rousseau. His first major philosophical work, *A Discourse on the Arts and Sciences*, was the winner in an essay competition organized by the Academy of Dijon in 1750.[29] Given the state censorship that operated in Continental countries during this period, the amount of social and political criticism that one finds in submissions is quite remarkable. Most of this debate was philosophical, but no small number of contestants went on to play active roles in the French Revolution.[30]

Second, prize competitions were seen as a way of stimulating achievement and recognizing merit. Shooting societies still gave prizes for marksmanship. Schools and universities awarded prizes for the highest grades, accomplishment in a specific subject, general conduct, and evidence of intelligence or industry. Prizes were also awarded in educational institutions to the winners of competitions for the best essay, poem, oration, answer to a question, et cetera. Art schools and academies naturally gave prizes for works in painting, sculpture, and architecture. In the mid-eighteenth century, C. Ph. De Tubières, count of Caylus, who was an honorary member of the French Royal Academy of Painting and Sculpture, endowed an annual prize for the student who produced the best drawing or modelling of a head with the truest expression of a given passion.[31] Musical societies and other associations interested in promoting culture gave prizes for the best compositions or performances. Beginning in 1784, the Drejers Club in Copenhagen gave a prize for the best speech, cantata, song, or music on the King's birthday.[32] And literary associations, of course, gave prizes for the best literary work.

Third, prize competitions were seen as agents of improvement, instrumental progress, and reform. These prizes were mainly of two types: (1) those for work accomplished, and (2) those for an innovative proposal, the best essay on a designated subject, the best answer to a specific instrumental question, et cetera, or to encourage research on a certain problem.[33] Medical prizes were often awarded for achievements in different branches of medicine, or for the best answer to a medical question. In 1736, an endowment that had earlier been made to the Royal Society by Godfrey Copley was used to establish a prize for "the most important scientific discovery." Even suggestions for the administrative reform of the state were sometimes solicited. Improved methods of farming were commonly sought by means of competitions. Other contests were intended to solve very precise problems, such as finding sources for saltpeter, the improvement of urban lighting, or ways of dealing with public begging, plagues, or floods. Prizes were bestowed by an assortment of institutions for the improvement of manufacturing – the best spinning, weaving, engraving, casting, et cetera. H.J. Erlanger discovered a case where a peasant received a prize for installing a lightning rod on his house.[34] Many prizes were sponsored by state officials, most notably French provincial intendants. In a world without the specialized sciences and technical expertise that we have today, the prize contest became, in Caradonna's words, a "collective problem-solving operation."[35]

Fourth, prizes were employed for political or particularistic purposes. In 1786, the Etruscan Academy presented a prize for the best biography of the Tuscan Amerigo Vespucci that would refute the credit that had been given to the Genoese Christopher Columbus for the discovery of America.[36] Prize contests were used for propaganda purposes, especially by state bodies or academies, often by inviting essays that glorified a particular monarch or something for which he or she was responsible. The most numerous of these were contests to solicit the best essay praising Louis XIV. And prizes were awarded for answers or essays that served the interests of different political factions or competing cultural movements.

Fifth, and closely related to these competitions, were prize contests used to promote particular religious beliefs, moral conformity, or public compliance. Many prizes were given to advance or discredit opposing theological views. The Hague Society for the Defence of the Christian Religion gave a prize for the best refutation of Deism.[37] Other associations sought to reduce domestic or inter-state conflict. An anonymous endowment made possible a French-Academy competition for the best poem on the blessings of peace.[38] The Class of Moral and Political Sciences (instituted by the Thermidorian Convention in 1795 as a branch of the National Institute) organized prize contests for questions on establishing public morality.[39]

To sum up, this little survey of prize contests suggests that during the seventeenth and eighteenth centuries, a large number of organizations and individuals were taking up public prizes as a way of motivating people. Their emergence at this time, and then relative decline during the nineteenth century, suggests that a new era of mobilizing collective endeavours emerged in the Early Modern period using methods that had less often been employed earlier, and for which alternative solutions were generally found in the nineteenth and twentieth centuries. Gradually, prize competitions offered to a large public were replaced by institutional awards or awards given to specialists in different fields. Nevertheless, the former provided one of the lineages that has led to present-day awards in literature, entertainment, and professional associations.

The cultural collections utilized by those who awarded prizes and those who awarded state honours were intermixed. Indeed, we should not draw too sharp a distinction between prizes distributed by non-state associations and awards distributed by states.[40] Not only did governments found academies and distribute prizes but they also encouraged non-state associations to do so, sometimes assisting them in their efforts. Non-government bodies might see little difference between what they were doing and what governments were or should be doing. A case in point is the honour medal initiated in 1795 by the Dutch Society for General Benefit to recognize "noble deeds"; members of the Society clearly believed this was something the government should be doing but was not. [41] There were, however, significant differences between prizes and state honours, one of which was that the distribution of the former faced fewer institutional constraints than the distribution of the latter. As we will see in Part IV, the distribution of state honours was shaped to a greater degree by existing status structures.

Military Rewards

In the Medieval and Early Modern periods, honour and glory were offered as restricted incentives for young men, particularly aristocrats and those who emulated them, to join armies and risk their lives. Indeed, the "chivalric" revival of the fifteenth and sixteenth centuries may have led to an increase in the importance of honour as a military reward, at least for certain segments of the population. Many aristocratic adventurers enlisted because they believed that only a military career would confirm their status as true gentlemen and distinguish them from the expanding commercial, professional, and office-holding bourgeoisie. As late as 1680, a military treatise advised commanders to motivate soldiers by recounting the military accomplishments of their ancestors.[42] The writer was himself, however, a professional soldier; and the growing professionalism of armies during the seventeenth and eighteenth centuries steadily undermined the position of men who claimed to serve for chivalric reasons. The opportunities enjoyed by aristocratic adventurers for promotion from one rank to another declined. Some of these soldiers also chafed under the requirements for conformity in Early Modern armies.[43]

The changes that displeased young men from aristocratic families meant opportunities for those drawn from other socio-economic groups. In most world societies, armies provided opportunities for social advancement, but the extent to which this was the case varied a lot. Such opportunities were becoming more available in Early Modern Europe, with the result that social advancement could serve as an incentive to enter the military and perform exceptionally. For young men in rural areas with little land to inherit, war provided a means of economic survival. Among the Scots, even lords and lairds could be compelled by financial difficulties to join the armies of Denmark, Sweden, the Dutch Republic, France, Spain, or the Holy Roman Empire.[44] Although they sometimes did not get paid, army wages were generally good as compared with the wages of agricultural labourers.

During the nineteenth century, opportunities for men of humble origin to receive promotions further improved. In his fascinating analysis of the letters written home by soldiers in the Napoleonic army, Alan Forrest found striking evidence of the psychological pleasure soldiers derived from promotions, which not only provided material benefits, but also raised their status and self-esteem.[45] Reaching the heights of a general officer was rare, but not impossible, just as it was not impossible in the Middle Ages for the son of a peasant to become a celebrated knight. Reaching the rank of *officier subalterne* or junior officer was more realistic; and it could represent significant upward mobility for young men from peripheral areas, such as Brittany, Ireland, and Scotland. In the Early Modern period, aristocracies worked hard to keep the officer corps to themselves, but the size of armies and the necessities of war were eroding this monopoly even then.

On the other hand, for men who could not realistically aspire to a military promotion, it was not an effective incentive. Indeed, it was not until the Great War that the aristocratic claim to command was really broken, a subject to which I will return in Chapter 13. And while the general improvements in pay, programs to help families of soldiers, and the (slow) decline in harsh punishment certainly improved morale and the willingness of soldiers fight, for the most part, these were unrestricted incentives: they were not limited to select individuals in the ranks.

The most traditional reward in armies, and still effective in Europe during the Early Modern period, was booty. It could be extracted from civilians in towns through which or near which troops passed. Armies often resembled roving bands of thieves and extortionists Reportedly, the booty taken by Spanish troops from Antwerp after it was sacked in 1576 weighed 2,600 tons.[46] Another reward consisted of the property of killed or captured enemy soldiers. From the point of view of a military commander, the search for plunder could divert soldiers from military objectives, but it was an effective incentive insofar as it motivated soldiers to defeat the enemy.

During the Early Modern and Modern periods, however, the booty that European soldiers could expect declined, for several reasons. First, the long sieges and slow-moving armies of the Early Modern period provided less opportunity for plunder. Second, large armies created more competition for the available loot. And third, during the nineteenth century, the nature of war altered the relations between armies and local populations. The size of armies had outstripped the capacity of states to move supplies, with the result that commanders depended on the co-operation of local populations to furnish their troops with necessities; plundering these local populations was not in the best interests of such armies. In the Peninsular War, for example, British commanders maintained a constant and difficult struggle to discourage extortion and to insure that all supplies were properly purchased. "The people of Portugal deserve well of the army," wrote the Adjutant General in a general order of May 1809; "they have in every instance treated the soldiers well; and there was never an army so well supplied, or which had so little excuse for plunder, if any excuse can at any rate exist."[47]

Honours as Rewards

What role did state honours play in this world of changing motivational rewards? As in the Medieval period, rulers in the Early Modern period used orders of knighthood, simple knighthood, ennoblement, and titular promotion as motivational rewards, often proffered to powerful lords to encourage them to co-operate. Louis XIV was explicit about the motivation function of state honours. Referring specifically to the Order of the Spirit, but speaking generally about status awards, Louis XIV told his son:

> No reward costs our people less and none strikes noble hearts more than these distinctions of rank, which are virtually the first motive of all human actions, but particularly of the most noble and the greatest. It is, moreover, one of the clearest manifestations of our power to give infinite value when we please to what in itself is nothing. It is desirable not merely to make whatever use we can of those that our fathers have introduced, but even to invent new ones sometimes, so long as this is done judiciously, selectively, and with dignity.[48]

This motivational purpose of state honours was a major factor in the nineteenth-century expansion. Nicholas Harris Nicolas, the British antiquarian mentioned in Chapter 1, believed that orders of merit on the Continent were organized "so that everyone who had, in any capacity, benefited his Country might, by receiving an honourable testimony of his Prince's favour, be stimulated to greater exertions."[49]

Like honorific rewards in the Middle Ages, these Early Modern honorific rewards could serve to enhance or create a personal bond between ruler and recipients. Such was almost always the case with small orders, but even very large orders could seek to establish or reinforce a bond of this kind. This was manifestly the intention of those who took part in the creation of the Order of Saint Louis, which was conferred by Louis XIV personally to the officers who were chosen. He did so in ceremonies of splendid solemnity, which in itself was a much-appreciated part of the reward.[50] The same was true of the Legion of Honour, with whose members Napoleon sought to create a personal tie. He divided legionnaires into seventeen territorial groups known as "cohorts." This institution is much more important for the subject of Chapter 10, where it is explained more fully. All I want to point out here is that one of the purposes of these cohorts was to institutionalize this tie.[51] Napoleon also conceived of his Imperial nobility as an aristocracy of vassals devoted to him as master.[52] And the Medal of Saint Helena was intended to create a personal tie between Napoleon III and the veterans who received it.

Nevertheless, a significant change that occurred in state honours between the Medieval period and the nineteenth century was the decline of this kind of personal bond between rulers and the recipients of honours. By the early eighteenth century, Louis XIV had ceased to award the Cross of Saint Louis himself; whatever other reason he may have had, there were simply too many recipients. The personal tie between Napoleon and members of the Legion of Honour was fictional – the cohorts did almost nothing for it – and even the pretense lasted only until Napoleon's Empire was destroyed. Under the Restoration and even the July Monarchy, it did not perform this function at all. The Medal of Saint Helena was unusual, reserved as it was for a unique set of men. But even this honour did not create a personal bond equal to that between a prince and members of a Medieval order of knighthood.

Increasingly, the purpose of state honours was to provide less personal restricted rewards. I turn first to political rewards and those for state employees, and then to military rewards.

POLITICAL AND STATE SERVICE REWARDS

State honours became part of the spoils system of Early Modern politics. Beginning in the fourteenth century, many rulers elevated non-military personnel and supporters to knighthood. By the seventeenth century, knight bachelor in England had become mostly a political reward. The same evolution occurred in orders of knighthood. Gradually, over a period of several centuries, these orders became associations composed of military personnel, civilian officials, political supporters of governments, and various kinds of influentials. Even the Garter was used to reward favourites, political supporters, and state officials, albeit mostly very high state officials who had inherited or been awarded peerages.[53] Beginning in 1560, the Order of Saint Michael – though still limited to the nobility – was utilized so often by the French Crown to motivate networks of loyalty and clientele that the prestige of the honour seriously decreased.[54] The Order of the Holy Spirit was created to provide an exclusive and prestigious alternative.[55] But it, too, was politically motivated; Henry III hoped that it would bind Catholic nobles to him in the face of a decline in support for his monarchy.

Although the baronets created by James VI/I raised money for the Crown, they also served to gratify political supporters and state officials. Providing incentives or rewards for political support was also a major reason that his son (Charles I) and his grandson (Charles II) were liberal with honours of all kinds. (Over 1,700 knights bachelor alone were created during their reigns.[56]) James VII/II established the Order of the Thistle not only to add legitimacy to his regime but also to reward Scottish peers who had supported him in his political struggles. The Order of the Bath was launched to secure support for the government among members of the British Parliament; thirty of the thirty-five initial knights were members of Parliament.[57] One of the most quoted observations on any order is Horace Walpole's assertion that his father founded the Bath as "an artful bank of thirty-six Ribbands to supply a fund in lieu of places." Even the emoluments of the great master of this order, as well as the position of officer, became part of the spoils system.[58] Similarly, the Order of Saint Patrick, founded in 1783, was seen as a way of legitimating and uniting two kingdoms, but also as a means of rewarding supporters of the government in the Irish Parliament or men whose support the government sought.[59] The Lord Lieutenant of Ireland was desperate for some measure to control the Irish Parliament. "Pray let me have my Order of Knighthood," he wrote the Home Secretary in 1782, "as it is necessary for our House of Peers."[60]

In the preceding section I used the establishment of the Order of Saint Michael and Saint George to illustrate the legitimation function that could be performed by honours. It also illustrates how honours served as restricted rewards. Maitland governed Malta and the Ionian Islands with a strict hand, complemented by patronage and the distribution of status symbols. Thus, he flattered the president of the Senate of the Islands with the title "His Highness" and other senators with *Prestantissimo* (the most illustrious). He also appointed a "most illustrious regent" in each island. Admission to the Order of Saint Michael and Saint George was not bestowed lavishly. Rather, specific individuals were targeted: those in positions of influence, primarily politicians and members of the pre-British government, who might be persuaded to provide active support for the British administration. But the Order was also utilized to honour those whom Maitland just wanted out of the way, in other words, as a reward to leave Maitland free to rule with minimal interference from local elites. Count Antonio Comuto, the former prince of the Ionian States, had to be given a grand cross. "This I did," wrote Maitland, "though he was of no use to us, to keep him quiet, and to show the respect we entertained for those ... who had formerly been in power."[61] In a justification that we can truthfully characterize as the pot calling the kettle black, Maitland tried to attribute the effectiveness of such practices to the population he was administering. "Title in this country is everything," he claimed, "and the substance comparatively nothing."[62]

Elevation to the British and Irish houses of lords served two purposes. First, appointments were regularly made in order to install government spokesmen in these chambers, or at least to have men there who could be counted on to vote for government measures. When this was the only reason, we would not call it a restricted reward. Yet a peerage was also an honour and a prestigious rank that could be utilized as a restricted reward to induce political loyalty to the Crown or the government. The motivational purpose of these royal graces was pretty mean and base, but the rhetoric was often idealistic, even fanciful. When Robert Walpole criticized the Peerage Bill of 1719 – which would have restricted the royal prerogative in the creation of peers – he pronounced that, if it were passed, "one of the most powerful incentives to virtue would be taken away" from English political life.[63]

Often it was hard to distinguish between the two purposes, and it would be contrary to my argument to contend there was a clear distinction. However, we can sometimes classify a peerage elevation as serving one purpose more than the other. Illustrative are the eighty-nine peerage creations and elevations of Charles II. Of the eighteen titles between 1660 and 1661, half were rewards for parliamentarians who had assisted the Restoration, while the rest were conferred on royalists for past exemplary service. In addition, some former opponents were awarded peerages to try to persuade them not to oppose the restored monarchy. All these were primarily restricted rewards. In the 1670s, on the other hand, several creations were made in order to increase the Catholic contingent in the House of Lords because the government was considering certain measures of toleration for Catholics.[64] These appointments may have also been seen as honorific rewards, but that was not their major purpose.

Ennoblement could serve similar purposes in Old-Regime France. Letters of ennoblement were often distributed in order to shore up royal power, in particular to secure the co-operation of local elites. The study by Cubells of letters of ennoblement in Provence during the eighteenth century found frequent references to services to the Crown, the *patrie*, or the state.[65] Ennoblements were commonly utilized as instruments of political struggle between provincial intendants and local power holders. Of course, the structure of aristocratic status was different in France than in Britain. Old-Regime France had no equivalent to the British and Irish houses of lords, and the British no equivalent to the Continental nobility. Furthermore, the so-called nobility of the robe in France was a state nobility; noble status was derived from office. Since the majority of these ennobling offices were purchased or inherited, their effectiveness as restricted rewards for the Crown was limited.

After the fall of the Old Regime, French governments were in a better position to use honours as restricted rewards. Whatever the effect of the Legion of Honour on the perceived legitimacy of Napoleon's Empire, its main purpose was to operate as a reward for the men who fought for him and, to a lesser extent, for those who served his state in other ways. Napoleon believed that the ideological energy of the Revolution no longer sufficed to motivate the great majority of the French and to stimulate those whose backing and exertions were necessary for his hold on power and the objectives he sought to achieve. He needed to channel the thirst for upward mobility of large numbers of Frenchmen who had supported the Revolution.[66] Even more often quoted than Horace Walpole's "artful bank of thirty-six Ribbands" is Napoleon's alleged retort to those who opposed a national decoration that, if honours are toys, "then it is with toys that one leads men."

The Old-Regime orders that were revived under the Restoration were employed to reward those who had remained loyal to the monarchy. The Bourbons were also lavish with the Legion of Honour in 1814–15 in an effort to win support for the new regime, but they sought to insure that these appointments would serve their interests and not those of their opponents by requiring all legionnaires to swear loyalty to the new monarch in order to have their status confirmed.[67] It is well known that Napoleon III used the Legion of Honour not only to associate his regime symbolically with the First Empire but also to reward those who had helped repress opposition to his seizure of power. As well, he was able to reward people with the Military Medal. All but two of the first forty-eight recipients of this state honour had helped to suppress opposition to his coup.[68]

Yet another example is provided by the new leaders of Belgium. In addition to hatching the Order of Leopold, they created the Iron Medal and the Iron Cross in 1830 to reward those who had performed noteworthy services during their revolution. They also rewarded artists who promoted the new state.[69]

State honours were also used to reward state employees. In Britain, they were spread out among a number of different orders, including the Order of the Bath and the Order of Saint Michael and Saint George. They were appointed to the House of Lords, but not in big numbers, partly because they could be elevated to this body only after they had completed their careers as state employees. A tradition did develop that the permanent secretary of the Foreign Office and later the head of the civil service were offered peerages when they retired.[70] In the peerage creations of 1901–10, however, only 8.6 per cent were former civil servants; the figures were 6.4 per cent for 1911–20, and 7.5 per cent for 1921–30.[71] A higher percentage could be found in the Order of the British Empire, where state employees represented a remarkable 18.9 per cent (combining the higher and middle levels) of male civilians in my weighted sample of members in 1921 (Table B.9), though it needs to be acknowledged that those classified as state employees include some individuals who had not worked for the state before the War.

Larger percentages can be found in the Legion of Honour and the Order of Leopold. As shown in Tables B.7 and B.10, 23.7 per cent of the civilian males in the 1852 sample of the Legion of Honour and 21.3 per cent of the civilian members of the Order of Leopold in the 1833–87 sample were state employees. By the early twentieth century, recognition of state bureaucrats had risen to 30.4 per cent in the Legion of Honour sample and 40.3 per cent in the Order of Leopold sample (Tables B.8 and B.11). Belgian bureaucrats could also aspire to nobility, as could French bureaucrats until the Third Republic. According to Lucien Fourez, no less than 49 per cent of persons ennobled in Belgium between 1830 and 1957 and whose occupation is known were state employees.[72] For French state employees, a number of ministerial orders were also available, such as the Order of Public Health, the Order of Postal Merit, and the Order of Labour Merit. The profusion of these ministerial awards got so out of hand that eventually, with a few exceptions, they were all abolished in the 1960s.

The growth in state personnel corresponded with the timing of the great expansion in Western-European state honours. As the reader knows, the expansion of both came later in Britain than in France. A difference in the character of bureaucracies might also have been a factor. B.S. Silberman has made a distinction between two basic types of bureaucracies that emerged during the nine-teenth century: (1) organizationally oriented bureaucracies, as in France, in which accountability was sought through organizational rules and (2) professionally oriented bureaucracies, as in Britain, in which accountability was sought through professional norms and standards. I would add that the Belgian state bureaucracy is closer to that of the French structure than to the British. In the organization-ally oriented bureaucracies, careers are more predictable and follow a recognized progression. Commitment to this hierarchical progres-sion is obtained by holding out the possibility that it will culminate in a high office and, in France, a state honour.[73]

This difference could explain a number of other differences between the British distribution of honours and that of the French and the Belgians. First, in France the award of honours became more bureaucratized than in Britain in the sense that the distribution of honours involved more procedures, verifications, attestations, refer-ences, and, in general, more paperwork.[74] Second, honours became an integral part of the state bureaucracy in France, one indication of which was the plentiful number of ministerial decorations.

Third, the distribution of awards was different, at least among the honours for which I have data. In my samples, a proportionately larger number of French high-level state employees were rewarded with the Legion of Honour, or their Belgian counterparts with the Order of Leopold, than the number of British high-level state employees with the Order of the British Empire. This difference is, however, found only at the higher level; that is, we do not find a proportionately larger number of medium-level state employees in the Continental orders than in the Order of the British Empire (Tables B.7 to B.11). And higher-level British state employees were not placed in lower grades of the Order of the British Empire more than were their counterparts in the Legion of Honour and the Order of Leopold (Tables B.12 to B.16). It should be noted that a higher-level state employee in Britain could hope for one of a number of other (very prestigious) honours, not just the Order of the Bath or the Order of Saint Michael and Saint George, but perhaps a knighthood, a baronetcy, maybe even a peerage. Yet these awards were small in number.

In sum, the above data suggest that if the organizationally oriented bureaucracy promised more honorific rewards to state employees, the benefit consisted in the proportionate number distributed to those who had worked their way to a high level in a state hierarchy.

In any case, we should not lose sight of the fact that both state administrations became more bureaucratic. Appointments to state offices and promotions came to be regulated by specific rules and procedures, and to depend, ostensibly at least and relatively speaking, on merit and universalistic criteria as opposed to particularistic-ascriptive criteria. Although, as I have repeatedly asserted, the idiom of merit in Western Europe had aristocratic origins, the transformation in criteria for selection of persons to perform tasks and fill positions – in the state bureaucracy as in the military – is also indisputable. As a result, even in Britain, the control exercised by monarchs and their immediate agents over spoils declined. For a considerable time, this did not bring an end to the use of such spoils for particularistic or political purposes; it only transferred control over them to political leaders. However, during the nineteenth century, the ability of politicians and their agents to use patronage and other spoils for their purposes also declined. In Britain, the Northcote–Trevelyan reforms and the Orders in Council of 1870 and 1871 were instrumental in this process.

Potentially, this development could have had two opposite effects on state honours. On the one hand, it is not unreasonable to hypothesize that during a period of history in which governments were supposedly adopting more bureaucratic criteria for distributing government positions, it became more necessary for them to justify state honours in the same way, especially if state honours were perceived, like promotions and salaries, to be part of the reward structure of the state officialdom. This assertion draws partly on the same historical evidence on which the rise-of-the-bourgeoisie thesis depended, except that now this evidence is seen as a manifestation of a general process of bureaucratization that pervaded states rather than a product of a distinctly bourgeois ideology.

On the other hand, in a state that was becoming more bureaucratic, the significance of state honours may not have been so much that they too became more bureaucratically distributed, even if they did, but rather that their importance as a less bureaucratically controlled reward became all the greater. Thus, both the Crown and politicians did all they could to preserve them as a substitute for other spoils. Already in the early nineteenth century, as the British Crown was losing control over many of the spoils that it had used to get its way, it increasingly turned to honours.[75] When the management of state honours fell largely into the hands of prime ministers and associated political leaders, they too made use of them where formerly they would have used government positions. They could employ them to assist or flatter their friends, clients, or immediate subordinates, and also to achieve political objectives by means that were outside formal state structures. Of course, governments continued to use appointments to state positions for such purposes, but it became more difficult for them to do so than it had once been. Using honours was easier, if not without its own hazards.

Moreover, the need to use state honours for political purposes was reinforced by a major change in political reality in the late nineteenth century. The expansion of the electorate and the advancement of party discipline created new financial challenges for central party leaderships. It has been estimated that the annual expenditures of the headquarters of the British Liberal Party rose tenfold from the 1860s to 1912.[76] The party spent £50,000 in the election of 1880, and £100,000 in each of the elections of 1910.[77] The honours scandals in Britain during this period can be traced directly to the use of honours to reward party benefactors.[78] In this light, the sale of honours that was discussed in Chapter 1 appears less a commodification of honours resulting from the rise of a mercenary bourgeoisie than the result of political necessities in Britain in the late nineteenth and early twentieth centuries, necessities that were the result of fundamental changes in the nature of politics and political institutions.

The Continental pattern was broadly similar. In France, of course, parliamentary centralization and the need to procure the co-operation of members of parliamentary institutions did not come until the beginning of the nineteenth century. Subsequently, however, state honours were used to influence members of parliamentary institutions. Although political assemblies under the Consulate and First Empire were there to do Napoleon's bidding, the Tribunate (one of four assemblies under the Consulate) had successfully demanded that, among the merits to be recognized by the Legion of Honour, there would be mention of "legislative services"; and in the following years, a large proportion of the civilian appointments to the Legion of Honour went to members of political assemblies.[79] In addition, excluding the military, no less than 42.7 per cent of the barons and counts of the Imperial nobility were members of political assemblies.[80] Under later regimes, when political assemblies were less overpowered by the executive, it was all the more worthwhile to bribe them with honours. More than half of the members of the Chamber of Deputies in 1837–39 belonged to the Legion of Honour.[81] Despite the law of 1872 against sitting deputies being appointed to the Legion of Honour, state honours were still part of the reward system for politicians of the Third Republic.

Finally, it is worth mentioning that, in addition to the reasons I have already given for offering honours to foreigners, another purpose was to provide restricted rewards for powerful persons in different countries. This practice could be found in the Middle Ages, but became more routine in the orders and other honours of the Early Modern period.[82] European honours were awarded to rulers, their family members, and powerful individuals in other European countries, and even outside Europe. The so-called "Indian peace medals" were awarded in very large numbers to chiefs of aboriginal communities in North America during the eighteenth century, a practice that eventually became almost mandatory for maintaining alliances between Europeans and the native populations. There was a considerable increase in such practices during the nineteenth and early twentieth centuries. The foreigners who were recipients of the highest grade of the Order of Leopold were mostly diplomats or the leading politicians of other countries. They included such people as M.E. Aali-Pacha, the Turkish minister of foreign affairs, who was appointed in 1849; and F.G. Pereira da Silva, minister of justice in Portugal, appointed in 1867.

MILITARY REWARDS

Ennoblement, or elevation from one noble rank to another, served as a reward for military as well as civilian personnel. We have some illustrious examples. John Churchill was made Lord Churchill of Sandridge and Eyemouth in 1682, Earl of Marlborough in 1689, and Duke of Marlborough in 1702. Then there was Arthur Wellesley, who was made Baron Douro of Wellesley and Viscount Wellington of Talavera in 1809, Earl of Wellington and then Marquess of Wellington in 1812, and finally Marquess Douro and Duke of Wellington in 1814. Lesser lights were also elevated to the peerage or ennobled. Between 1750 and 1779, the British armed services accounted for 18.8 per cent of appointments to the British peerage, in the years 1780 to 1801, 48.6 per cent, and in the years 1802 to 1830, 34.8 per cent.[83] In the Cubells' study of ennoblements in Provence, more military personnel were found among the ennobled than persons in any other occupational category.[84] Over two-thirds of those appointed to Napoleon's nobility were military men.[85] Although Belgium did not have a large army or much of a military culture, a significant proportion of ennoblements have done to the military, 15 per cent according to Fourez's calculations.[86]

Yet the effectiveness of ennoblement as a motivational instrument for the military was limited. Even during peak periods, the number of elevations was minuscule relative to the size of the military establishment. The total number of commanders appointed to the British House of Lords for the entire period 1780 to 1830 was a mere thirty-three.[87] In Old-Regime France, the problem was the reverse. Almost all military officers were already nobles. The best that could be done for them would be to raise them from one noble rank to another, something that was possible only for relatively high-ranking commanders. With these exceptions, ennoblement was not a restricted reward for French officers. Nor could making a soldier a knight bachelor serve as a significant reward. Not only were the number of persons awarded this honour in Britain very limited until the late nineteenth century, it was increasingly conferred for non-military service rather than military service.

Admission to a military order was generally regarded as a more effective restricted reward. We have seen that many of the military orders created during the Early Modern period were in central and eastern Europe. These included the Austrian Order of Maria Theresa, the Bavarian Order of Maximilian Joseph, the Saxon Order of Saint Henry, and the Prussian order known as Pour le Mérite, the last-mentioned also open to civilians. No specifically Belgian military order was created in the Early Modern period, but Belgians were eligible for Austrian military orders. And, of course, two military orders were created in France: the Order of Saint Louis and the Order of Military Merit. Nothing of the same magnitude was established in Britain during the Early Modern period. Most of the Bath appointments in the first decade after it was founded went to Whig supporters of the government. The number of military and civilians entering the Bath was roughly equal from the 1740s to the 1770s. Thereafter, elevations were mostly military.[88] But the Bath was much smaller than the Order of Saint Louis.

These differences were a consequence of a number of other Early Modern differences that we have seen among our cases. The one that I would like to bring up again is the continuum of monarchical versus parliamentary centralization. I have suggested that the two types of political structures had different motivational problems. Central governments of territories where the connection to the centre was mostly monarchical and less parliamentary had less effective institutional links with elites, especially those in relatively peripheral locations. In contrast, governments of territories in which centralization was parliamentary as well as monarchical could mobilize resources through central parliamentary institutions.

Thus, it is not surprising that, in contrast with the military orders established by the French and Austrian Habsburg monarchies, during the Early Modern period, the British founded three much smaller and more exclusive orders mainly for political purposes: the Order of the Thistle, the Order of the Bath (at least initially), and the Order of Saint Patrick. For the British Crown, mobilizing support among independently powerful political figures was essential for its survival. And motivating British politicians to support a war effort, most importantly to finance it, was more critical than motivating soldiers to enlist and fight, many of whom came from outside England. The same was true in the United Provinces, and provides another possible reason for the lack of state honours in this federation. Like the British Crown, the *stadhouders* had to motivate politicians more than soldiers. The Dutch army was composed of regiments financed and administered by different provinces; and military appointments and decisions made by the *stadhouder* had to be approved by the Staten generaal. As for the soldiers in these regiments, many of them came from outside the Low Countries.

I do not want to brush aside the political purposes for which the French Crown did found some of its Early Modern orders. I have just noted the political purpose of the Order of Saint Michael and the Order of the Holy Spirit. But the Order of Saint Louis was not a political reward. In the thinking of those responsible for the establishment of the latter, its primary purpose was to motivate nobles to join the French army and to fight energetically for the Crown. There was considerable concern in the Bourbon regime of the late seventeenth century that the nobility was not making the kind of effort required for the military needs of the state. Too many nobles were happy to spend their days on their country estates or to pursue less exacting and less dangerous civilian careers. And those who did enlist lacked the discipline and commitment that the new-age armies required. The Saint Louis was explicitly created to provide a *recompense* for nobles to overcome these motivational problems.[89] In these terms, it was deemed a great success – a "*monnaie d'honneur*," penetrating the whole army; every regiment counted several members.[90] Indeed, this apparent success as a restricted reward created pressure to maintain a good rate of distribution in order to keep up the high level of motivation it was thought to engender.[91]

During the nineteenth century, a few prestigious "military orders" were founded in Western Europe, most notably the Military Order of William in the United Kingdom of the Netherlands (1815) and the Distinguished Service Order in Britain (1886). In addition, the Order of the Bath was increased in size. We also get more civilian honours and honorific orders that were available to both civilians and military, in which the military were usually overrepresented among recipients. The prototype is the Legion of Honour, which essentially sought to provide the same incentive for both officers and the rank-and-file that the Order of Saint Louis had been intended to provide for officers. Whatever the link between the Saint Louis and the Legion of Honour, it is clear that the reception of the former by French soldiers and the role that it came to serve in French armed forces during the eighteenth century was one of the reasons Napoleon created the latter. Indeed, dissatisfaction with the abolition of the Saint Louis convinced Napoleon that a replacement was necessary if he hoped to fulfill his military ambitions.

Of the close to 40,000 men appointed to the Legion of Honour under Napoleon, all but several thousand were in the military.[92] As a result, no civilians showed up in my sample of men appointed under the First Empire who were still alive in 1852 (Table B.17). The military continued to be much-favoured under the Restoration. No less than 82.6 per cent of those appointed during the Restoration were members of the military. Even during the July Monarchy, 65.5 per cent were in the military. Altogether, 74.3 per cent of my

1852 sample were in the military (Table B.21). This is almost the same as the representation of the military in my 1929 sample of members who were appointed before the Great War. It climbed to 92.7 per cent among those appointed during the Great War, but then dropped to 73.6 per cent among those appointed after the War (Table B.18). Altogether 77.2 per cent of those in the 1929 sample were in the military (Table B.22), almost the same as the 74.4 per cent in 1852.

The Order of Leopold was less militaristic than the Legion of Honour. True, in its early years, the military were favoured over civilians. This is what we would expect, given that the honour was originally conceived as a military order. In my weighted sample, 56.8 per cent of Belgians appointed before 12 August 1847 were in the military. Over the remainder of the century, the presence of the military in the Order of Leopold declined, dropping to 43.1 per cent during the period 13 August 1847 to 1 July 1870, 27.4 per cent during the period 2 July 1870 to 1886, and to 7.7 per cent among members still alive in 1932 but appointed before the Great War (Tables B.19 and B.20). Naturally, the military presence increased dramatically during the War, to 65 per cent, dropping to 38.2 per cent after the War. The composition of the Order of the British Empire, though it was created in response to a widespread view that civilian contributions to the Great War were not being sufficiently recognized, was 36.8 per cent military in my weighted sample of males in 1921 (Table B.23).

Ultimately, however, appointment to an "order" did not become the distinctive method of rewarding members of the military. Instead, decorations in the form of metallic badges or medals became their standard honorific reward. This was because there were far too many men deserving of some token of appreciation to be accommodated in orders, even the Legion of Honour and the Order of the British Empire. It was also because, during the critical period in which the great expansion of honours occurred in Western Europe, medals and similar objects performed the communication function more effectively than other methods of rewarding.

COMMUNICATION

An examination of the communication function of state honours in Western Europe is all the more worthwhile because it helps to explain distinctive characteristics of these honours, characteristics that are now also found well beyond Europe.

New Instruments of Communication

Once again, it is necessary to interrupt for a moment the discussion of honours themselves, in this case to look at modes of communication in more general terms during the Early Modern and Modern periods.

THE COMMUNICATION REVOLUTION

The fifteenth to the eighteenth centuries constituted a revolutionary period in European communications. This in itself strongly suggests that new selection pressures were operating in these centuries and that major demographic, social, political, and/or cultural changes were creating these pressures.

This is not to say that these changes directly caused Johannes Gutenberg to build his moveable-type printing press in the mid-fifteenth century. Indeed, Gutenberg's innovation came before most of the changes I have discussed. And printing itself had been well known for several centuries. In Europe, relief printing from wood is thought to have begun in the thirteenth century. Moveable type was known in Eastern Asia by at least the eleventh century. Woodcuts or blocks continued to be preferred there because of the number and variety of signs in the written languages of that region; when moveable type was used, it was without a press.[93] Nonetheless, large-scale printing in moveable type can be found in Korea in the very early fifteenth century, decades before Gutenberg adopted it.[94] Thus, the "invention" of the moveable-type printing press in Europe at this time is better seen as a modification of technology that already existed there and elsewhere. What the demographic, social, political, and cultural changes did – and this over several centuries – was to create pressures that led to the diffusion of the moveable-type printing press and made it revolutionary in the following centuries.

Closely related to printing, as both cause and effect, was the spread of paper. It shaped the ways in which societies operated, and, in particular, the ways in which governments conveyed information and engaged in population management, as has been demonstrated by J.C. Rule and B.S. Trotter in their recent study of the flow of information in French state administration during the late seventeenth and early eighteenth centuries.[95] However, there is a downside to paper. It serves well for communication over space; with printing, it can have considerable numerical communication power; but it is a relatively poor medium for communication over time. Moreover, the replication of these innovations was limited by the low rates of literacy that generally prevailed in these centuries.

Nevertheless, over time, as a result of a number of forces, including moveable-type printing and the availability of paper, rates of literacy rose, so that by the mid-seventeenth century the populations of most European countries could be referred to as "partially literate." By this I mean that there was great variation in literacy rates from one district to another and among different socio-economic and occupational groups. There was also great variation within communities, resulting in the more literate often reading to the less literate. And there were large numbers of people who could read, but not easily, and certainly not every piece of print or writing they came across.

Along with the growth in printing by means of moveable type, printed illustrations also expanded. The latter could occur independently of the former, but they frequently came together. A literate reader could enjoy both and could also help others read the captions included with illustrations. The same is true of the evolution of caricatures. During the sixteenth century, contention-by-caricature became a popular practice, accelerating further during the seventeenth century. The Dutch political climate and the artistic community in the Netherlands, in particular, encouraged political cartoons, the best known of which were caricatures drawn by Romeyn de Hooghe. His illustrations included cartoons mocking Louis XIV, many of which were smuggled into France. By the eighteenth century, significant communities of cartoonists existed in the British Isles, France, and the Netherlands. Most political figures – Robert Walpole, George III, Louis XVI, Napoleon, George IV, even Wellington – incurred the sting of political artists. Serious efforts were made to stamp out this slander. During the nineteenth century, periodicals appeared that were devoted primarily to political cartoons, one of which was *La Caricature*. Its editor, Charles Philipon, was imprisoned for a year and his publication eventually suppressed.[96]

To repeat, these innovations in communication are relevant to our inquiry because they indicate certain selection pressures that were operating in the Early Modern and Modern periods. We will now turn to another innovation in communication resulting from these same pressures: the evolution of badges and medals. Since this heritage became a vital item in the cultural and institutional collection on which European honours distributors drew, a comparative-historical examination of its history is called for.

Table 7.2
Meanings of numismatic and related terms as adopted in this book

Term	Meaning
Badge	An object identifying one's status, group membership, occupation, et cetera, normally worn on one's person, but not necessarily.
Coin	A small metallic piece used in commercial exchange. It is most often but not always in the shape of a disc.
Device	An emblem or motto inscribed on a medal, badge, or coat of arms and usually claimed as reserved for an individual or family.
Insignia	Any distinguishing sign on a medal, badge, coat of arms, et cetera.
Medal	A small metallic piece not used in commercial exchange. It is most often but not always in the shape of a disc. If a disc, it usually has an illustration or inscription on at least one side.
Medallion	A large medal.

Note: It needs to be recognized that terminology varies greatly, especially among the different specialties, that is, the study of coins, heraldry, orders, or military awards. Several usages that differ from the above illustrate this variation: It is common to refer to a medal or badge itself as an "insignia." Sometimes any medal that can be worn is referred to as a "decoration," but "decoration" is also used to distinguish awards for bravery, such as the Victoria Cross, from other military rewards.

BADGES AND MEDALS

The subject of badges and medals requires some agreement on definitions, Table 7.2 summarizes how I am using these and other terms.

Badges have been adopted from early times. During the Egyptian twelfth dynasty, oyster shells, inscribed with the name of the reigning pharaoh, were worn as a military badge. Standard-bearers in the Egyptian army might also be distinguished by a particular badge. Metal discs called *phalerae* were adopted as badges of rank in the Roman equestrian order. During the fourteenth and fifteenth centuries, the Korean government introduced identification cloth badges known as *hopae*. In Ming and Qing China, cloth badges were widely used as symbols of social rank.

Coins evolved out of a variety of objects used as monetary currency in Ancient commercialized societies. These objects included beads, cowrie shells, ingots, bracelets, bean-shaped metallic pieces, tools, and weapons. The development of Modern coinage has taken two routes, though eventually they came to merge: the Far Eastern route, which for the most part means Chinese coinage, and a

Mediterranean and Middle Eastern route, the latter of which led to the coinage of Modern Europe. In the Mediterranean, Middle Eastern, and European tradition, coins developed in a way that encouraged their use as a means of communication much earlier than in the Far Asian tradition; they replaced other objects that had been used as money earlier; and designs became the norm much earlier.

In China, alternatives to coinage, such "spade money" and "knife money," became well established long before coinage appeared. When the Chinese did adopt coins as a medium of exchange, they typically manufactured them by casting rather than striking. They bore inscriptions without designs; instead, they often had a central hole. Since they were used less often as a mode of communication, Chinese coins remained in circulation through different dynasties more frequently than did coins in the Mediterranean, Middle Eastern, and European tradition. Other East Asian countries, including Japan and Korea, selected their monetary currency from Chinese cultural practices; indeed, Chinese coins often circulated in these countries.[97] Finally, it is worth mentioning that paper currency was known and adopted earlier in China than in Europe.

Mediterranean and Middle Eastern coins began to serve a communication purpose with the introduction of designs and inscriptions. Those with crude designs minted in Lydia during the seventh century BCE are frequently cited as the first coinage in the Mediterranean world.[98] Whether or not this is true, the Lydian coins may have marked a significant event in the evolution of coins. In the first millennium BCE, various Mediterranean and Middle Eastern countries, particularly Greece and Persia, selected from one another's cultures different and similar patterns of coinage.

It is not clear when the first portrait coin was introduced. We do know of portrait coins of Persian governors. We have, for instance, Sasanian coins depicting an equestrian king hunting wild animals.[99] Rulers could engage in propaganda by having their image reproduced on coins they issued. It was typical for a ruler to issue new coins – with an image of himself stamped on them – when he assumed power. During the Roman Republic and Empire, the use of coins for specific political purposes became more common. In 49 BCE, Caesar issued a denarius with an engraving that was meant to represent the futility of opposing him.[100] Augustus subsequently institutionalized the overt use of coinage for political purposes. Coins became, and have remained to this day, a symbol of sovereignty.

They also became, in the Mediterranean, Middle Eastern, and European tradition, a form of art in a way that they did not in Eastern Asia until relatively recently.

When a coin was specially issued to commemorate an individual or an event, or to serve a political purpose, the communication function was obviously seen to be critical along with the monetary function. A coin of this kind was sometimes larger than regular coins and the design more artistic. A number of these "medallions" are especially well known. Artistically impressive pieces – glorifying rulers or cities – were manufactured in Sicily by the Greeks in the fifth century BCE.[101] Also impressive are the coins issued by Philip II of Macedonia to celebrate his equestrian victories at Olympia in 352 and 348 BCE.[102] The subject of considerable research has been the "elephant medallions" issued by Alexander the Great, which were likely manufactured to celebrate his victory over Porus, the Indian rajah, whom he defeated near the Hydaspes River in 326 BCE.[103] Other sizable coins with exceptional designs include Roman bronze coins depicting the head of Janus, issued in the third century BCE, and coins of the first century CE with Emperor Nero on the obverse and a triumphal arch on the reverse.[104]

It should be kept in mind, however, that these large communication coins were much fewer in number than smaller coins. It is not correct, as some sources claim, that there were no medals in the Ancient World. The coins mentioned in the preceding paragraph were probably little used for commercial exchange and could well be regarded as medals. Also well known are some gold medallions found near Aboukir, Egypt, that probably date from the third century CE.[105] Another example is provided by Roman "contorniates," as they are called, a distinctive set of medallions of the fourth and fifth centuries CE that were decorated with images of emperors, philosophers, and intellectuals.[106]

With the decline in commerce that occurred as the Roman Empire gradually collapsed, coinage also declined in much of Europe. In later centuries, territorial rulers monopolized the production of coins, but during most of the Medieval period, control over their distribution was highly variable as a result of political instability in many regions. Maintaining a coinage against alternatives was a problem for European rulers at this time. And communication through coinage was generally limited to simple imagery – monograms and other "logos" – designed to make different issues recognizable.[107]

Coins could also bear the image of a ruler, especially when one ruler was displaced by another.

What survived during the Medieval period better than communication coins or medals were badges, seals, and heraldic symbols that were used for identification, usually by portraying an insignia or device. Indeed, relative to other media of communication, badges and seals became more significant in Medieval Europe than they had been in the Ancient World as a result of the fragmentation of sovereignty, which enhanced the utility of marks of identity and loyalty. In addition, a significant proportion of the elite was illiterate or semi-literate. As a result, visual images were popular, and a small industry thrived on the design and production of these images. Elite families (landed and urban) gave careful attention to the design of their coats of arms, and displayed them on a variety of objects (banners, shields, houses, household possessions, carriages, tombs, horse trappings, et cetera).

Seals provided a bridge between the literate and the illiterate world; they were called into play in order to establish a link between written documents and personal or group identity.[108] "Livery" badges were worn by the supporters, followers, retainers, and servants of a lord. They were intended to communicate not only the allegiance of the person wearing the badge but also information about the achievements, beliefs, and objectives of the lord and his family. They could be made of cloth and sewn onto clothing, but were more commonly metal ornaments, often a brooch. The quality of the metal varied with the status of the recipient.

Recognition of these Medieval attitudes and practices makes it easier to comprehend the efflorescence of portrait medals that occurred in the fifteenth and sixteenth centuries. Some of these medals grew out of local or regional cultures, such as German portrait medals, which were influenced by German traditions of goldsmithery.[109] The most influential portrait medals, however, were those made by Italian Renaissance artists, who were inspired by the coins and medallions of Ancient Greece and Rome. They were also clearly influenced by Medieval seals.[110] The artist most frequently cited in the literature on this subject is Antonio Pisano, generally known as Pisanello.[111] Although he did not establish a school of followers, he initiated a significant cultural movement in Italy that sought to promote medals as an artistic medium. His work became the standard of this art in Europe.

The image on the obverse of a portrait medal was usually a profile of the person who commissioned the medal; and the reverse was, most often, an insignia or device linked to this person. For the most part, these medals were used to communicate symbols of personal and familial identity as these individuals and families wanted themselves to be seen. They were frequently bestowed as gifts or exchanged with other families or representatives of other princely courts. They were also used to commemorate family events, such as births and marriages. Although not necessarily the case, the person celebrated was typically of relatively high rank and affluence. As early as the late fifteenth century, the Medici (the banking family that became economically and politically powerful in Italy beginning in the fourteenth century) were using medals as a means of self-promotion. Over the next several hundred years, this became a general practice among rulers. The state institutionalization of this mode of propaganda progressed in France most of all under Louis XIV, for whom the manufacture of image became serious business.[112] Medals of this kind were also produced by artists or others hoping to sell them on the market or seeking royal favour.

Whereas today, we are more familiar with monuments and written texts that have survived from the Ancient World, the Renaissance growth in interest in Antiquity was inspired and informed as much by the discovery of coins and medals as any other kind of relic.[113] This cultural descent was made possible by the durability of Ancient coins and medals, and because they could be easily transported to other parts of Europe. It was also facilitated by the spread in printing. A common practice in the fifteenth and sixteenth centuries was to provide illustrations of medals in books, often depicting Roman emperors. Pictures of the medals were reproduced by means of woodcuts, but they were accompanied by text that was printed using moveable type.[114]

The Renaissance portrait medal represented a significant advance in the gradual evolution of media with effective communication power over both time and space. The numerical communication power of these media is, however, more variable. It depends on how many can be manufactured, which in turn obviously depends on the cost of the metal that is used to make the piece. It also depends on the competence of the manufacturer.

And it depends on the method of reproduction – whether the piece was struck or cast. Struck medals were manufactured by making dies, which were hand engraved until the mid-nineteenth century. This process was more time consuming than modelling wax or clay for casting a medal. And striking was generally inferior from an artistic point of view. On the other hand, striking was less expensive when making a large number of medals because casting had a longer production process and required a lot of hand-finishing. Hence, the larger the population with whom one wanted to communicate, the greater the advantage of striking over casting. Historically, more medals had been cast than struck, while the opposite held for coins.

Virtually all of the portrait medals of the fifteenth and sixteenth centuries, certainly the Italian medals, were cast. This weakened their numerical communication power, but that was of little concern since they were not intended for mass distribution. Both methods were used for producing medals from the fifteenth through the seventeenth centuries, depending on the number wanted and the artistic requirements of the medal. From the late seventeenth century through the mid-nineteenth century, however, medals were predominantly struck.

Thus, the expansion in the number of medals in Early Modern Europe was accomplished primarily by striking rather than casting them. Like moveable-type printing, this innovation was based not on the discovery of a new technique, but on the adaptation of an existing one to a new purpose. Nevertheless, the adoption of striking for the manufacture of medals provided the technological means for a distinctive phase in the history of communication that is now mostly forgotten, except among numismatic specialists.

By the early twentieth century the production of communication medals had declined, at least in relative terms, principally because, for technological reasons, other communication media had developed, but also because the general population of Western Europe had become more literate. Governments today still issue commemorative medals and coins (as well as stamps). However, the number hardly compares with that of communication medals produced per capita from the sixteenth century to the early twentieth century, which we can call the European "age of the communication medal." The largest category were "commemorative medals," but what I am calling communication medals were by no means limited to commemoration. It is difficult today, given the variety of media of communication available to us, to appreciate the use that was once made of this medium.

The evolution was the result of two distinguishable forces. The first is what I have just been discussing – a numismatic cultural tradition that stretches back to the Ancient World, but experienced a surge beginning in the fifteenth and sixteenth centuries. The second consisted of the selection pressures of the Early Modern period, caused primarily by population growth, political centralization, the growth in the size of armies, and the political struggles that were generated by greater political mobilization – all of which intensified the need to communicate to large, partially literate populations.

To a considerable extent, these two forces were operating in two different segments of the population. Most people who could afford a portrait medal, certainly one that was artistically valuable, were literate. Still, the cultural industry of the portrait medal gave medals a status that they would otherwise not have enjoyed and rendered medal making a craft in which increasing numbers of people participated or tried to participate. Although striking does not necessarily produce a medal of inferior quality, the communication medals of this period did vary greatly in their artistic merit, many being of extremely poor quality because their purpose was less to please the eye than to communicate a message. Medals had advantages similar to those of rituals and demonstrations for coordinating collective action and organization: an individual who saw a medal knew that others had seen it and that they also believed that many others had seen it.

The number of communication medals produced in Europe during the age of the communication medal was undoubtedly in the hundreds of thousands, possibly in the millions. Along with coins, they were employed to memorialize military events (campaigns, victories, successful invasions, or resistance to invasion); to symbolize relationships between families, towns, cities, and countries; to celebrate members of a royal family (their achievements, travels, births, marriages, coronations, recovery from illness); and to commemorate significant events in a country's history (independence, drafting of a constitution, enactment of specific laws, et cetera). Governments used them to mark inventions, railway openings, the launching of ships, shipwrecks, balloon travel, exhibitions, and much more.

The communication power of these medals was not, however, monopolized by governments. Whereas, by the Early Modern period, the use of coins had become reserved for those who had the political power to control their production and enforce their value, communication medals could be employed for any communication purpose, utilized by those with little political power, and produced by the least artistic craftsman in the trade, using the cheapest metal he could work with. Many were humorous and/or satirical, what one numismatic historian has referred to as the equivalent of today's humorous birthday cards.[115]

Others were manufactured for more serious purposes: to decry injustices, ridicule elites, or celebrate military defeats. Enough medals were struck to commemorate French military defeats during the campaigns of 1708–09 that it was possible to put together a medallic history of these campaigns, which was published in Utrecht in 1711.[116] Medals were also distributed to promote political movements or causes. They were used by both sides in British election campaigns. Famous court convictions or acquittals would often stimulate medal production. In England, medals were manufactured to acclaim the acquittal of Lord George Gordon, celebrate the French Revolution, exalt English radicals, denounce the electoral system, bewail the Peterloo Massacre, and oppose the Corn Laws. William Wilberforce's supporters used medals in their agitation against the slave trade.[117] In 1880, a medal was struck to honour the Ulstermen who went to County Mayo to relieve Charles Boycott.[118] Some of these medals paid tribute to an individual by portraying his or her image. John Wilkes, Daniel O'Connell, and Florence Nightingale were all celebrated on medals.[119]

It was also during the age of the communication medal that various associations began to use medals as prizes. It is significant that this happened gradually and after medals had already become an important medium of communication. Medieval prizes were not generally in the form of medals, but rather some other symbolic object or money. In shooting contests, they could be jewellery, arms, cloth, or animals.[120] It would seem that the earliest prize medals in Europe were distributed during the sixteenth century. They became a commonly awarded object in the eighteenth century, reaching peak distribution during the nineteenth century. When the Modern Olympics were founded in 1896, medals were among the objects given to winners and became the standard in 1904, even though they had not been the usual form of reward in the Ancient Greek games.

I have discussed the communication function of medals because I am going to propose that state honours can be understood in similar terms. However, before I do so, it is necessary to say a little about the military communication pressures that developed during the Early Modern period.

WAR AND COMMUNICATION

All war operations require coordination among those who take part. Yet the nature of coordination problems varies. The daring surprise rush is the most primordial mode of group fighting in human history; it was the most common manner in which hunter-gatherers collectively fought. In Western Europe, it was favoured by many Medieval commanders and fighters, and still preferred by some combatants during the Early Modern period, in particular by Irish and Scottish fighters. It depended for coordination on direct observation and common cues or signals, reciprocity and past co-operation, group identity, and mutual trust.

The major alternative to surprise rushes were pitched battles. They, too, can be found throughout human history, even among hunter-gatherers. In pitched battles, contestants drew on the same instruments of coordination available for surprise rushes, but coordination was more difficult to achieve and, therefore, also depended on certain ritualized coordination instruments. In Medieval European pitched battles, commanders frequently inspired their troops with orations, and then led them into battle, though coordination usually then broke down.[121]

The increase in the size of armies seriously elevated coordination pressures. First, since cavalry still constituted a significant part of any battle force, it had to be coordinated with the larger number of infantry. Second, this bigger infantry itself had to be coordinated, a collective-action problem that was most evident in the massive *tercio* infantry units of the Spanish army. Each of these units numbered as much as several thousand men, consisting of squares with limited manoeuverability. Militarily overpowering as these formations were in the late fifteenth and sixteenth centuries, they became difficult to manage in battle against more mobile, smaller units of five or six hundred men, which the French, Dutch, and Swedes, and also the Spanish themselves, began to organize in the late sixteenth and early seventeenth centuries.

The weaponry they were taking up also generated new challenges in coordination. The increasing use of pikes, and the improvements made to them by Swiss mercenaries in the fifteenth century, created intense coordination pressures. Life and victory depended on pikemen being able to move instantly and in good order. Failure of any number of pikemen to stand their ground or to advance in unison undermined their effectiveness and put them at the mercy of cavalry. As was the case with Greek hoplites, the tight formations in which pikemen fought helped provide the solidarity that was necessary for this coordination. And the organization of Swiss pikemen on the basis of their cantons, and bound by community-sanctioned oaths, further enhanced this solidarity. However, the more the pike was adopted in bigger and more ethnically heterogeneous armies, the less adequate was this communal mode of coordination. For the pike to be replicated as a general weapon of warfare in European armies, new instruments of collective action and organization had to develop.

The coordination challenges of pikes were overtaken in the late sixteenth century by the coordination pressures generated by portable firearms. Indeed, the most effective use of these arms necessitated a level of coordination hitherto unknown. Like archery, firearms were more destructive if an almost continuous volley of fire could be maintained, but for a long time after they were introduced, it took significantly more time for a combatant to reload a firearm than for an archer to reload his bow. The problem, then, was to find some way to minimize the intervals between firearm volleys. A large number of commanders and men with military experience struggled with this problem. A rotation of horsemen shooting pistols, known as the caracole, was taken up during the sixteenth century. It had some similarity with cavalry rotations that had been adopted earlier in some parts of the world, most notably by the Mongols in the thirteenth and fourteenth centuries. However, the Mongols did not face enemies using firearms. In the sixteenth century, the pistol caracole could not achieve the constant and accurate fire necessary to defend the horseman against infantries equipped with firearms.

Rather, it was in these infantries that the necessary level of coordination was achieved. In late fourteenth century China, Ming infantry with firearms were organized in three lines to shoot in volleys. In the mid-sixteenth century, Oda Nobunaga (a Japanese territorial lord who brought about the fall of the Ashikaga shogunate) organized his infantry in lines that rotated with one another to minimize the intervals between volleys. Thomas Digges, an Englishman who had served in the Dutch army, suggested similar manoeuvres in the 1570s. Martin de Eguiluz, a Spanish military officer, described the same technique in a military treatise published in 1595. And these measures were put into practice by several members of the House of Nassau – Maurice of Nassau; his cousin William Louis, count of Nassau and *stadhouder* in Friesland; and the latter's brother, John.[122]

After considerable experimentation, the Dutch cousins arranged troops in long lines of blocks of five or six men per rank, each block separated by a "street" of six feet through which those who had fired would walk to the rear.[123] When soldiers in the front rank fired, they would, according to a contemporary witness, "turn, face about, form and reform, unite and divide," all the while able "to maintain their files and ranks."[124] Solidarity was difficult to maintain in these long lines of soldiers separated by the distance required to rotate and reload a firearm, in marked contrast with the close proximity of pikemen or hoplites to one another. Coordination required standardized drills, which became part of the daily routine of Dutch forces.[125]

A great variety of infantry formations have been adopted in different parts of the world. Even hunter-gathers formed two or more lines of warriors, the second entering the fray when the first line had discharged all their spears. The Nassau cousins were influenced by accounts of rotation – known as "countermarching" – in Ancient Mediterranean armies.[126] Similar coordination was achieved by Aztecs warriors, who synchronized the use of three different kinds of projectiles – arrows, slings, and darts – each one replacing the other depending on the supply of projectiles that the soldiers carried and the distance of the adversary. The Aztecs also coordinated hand-to-hand combat weapons, one of which was a sword fitted with blades known as a *maquabuitl*. It was so heavy that soldiers rotated in shifts of roughly fifteen minutes.[127]

These achievements in coordination should be kept in mind for the cross-societal analysis I undertake in Chapter 14. In these routines, however, the back lines usually served primarily to push, support, join, or relieve the front lines. While this involved a considerable measure of coordination, the coordination required to maintain a constant volley of gunfire in the front lines was much greater. Achieving this degree of coordination was the principal contribution of the Nassau cousins, along with their recognition that it could be accomplished only with months and months of day-long practice so that movements and timing would remain precise even in the chaos and terror of battle. In 1607, John of Nassau supervised the writing of a drill manual for the instruction of soldiers, which was translated into several languages.

During the seventeenth century, knowledge of the "Dutch drill" became widespread in European armies, especially in Continental armies, where the need for it was much greater than in the British Isles. It was frequently modified, but nevertheless followed the same basic principles. During the seventeenth and eighteenth centuries, hundreds of manuals were published that helped spread knowledge of their methods and other techniques by which soldiers should be drilled. Authors prescribed what can only be characterized as military choreography – pages and pages of exact instructions and drawings, along with the cues that all soldiers must learn for each motion. There could be as many as fifty different postures and body movements that had to be drilled into a soldier.

As a result of this print literature, the practices initiated by the Nassau cousins were gradually replicated by other military leaders throughout most of Europe, parts of Asia, and eventually among Europeans in the Americas.[128] This replication was also facilitated by the fact that a good number of soldiers in the Dutch army were foreigners, many of them mercenaries who went on to fight in other armies.

Yet these practices were not adopted in all parts of the world. They were certainly not introduced in relatively untrained, non-standing infantries. Where skilled, fast cavalry were available, the pressure to build large well-trained infantries was weaker. The Mughals, in particular, given the superior cavalry on which they could draw, had little inducement to develop drilled and trained infantry able to operate in open fields.[129] The Early Modern Ottoman armed forces bore the marks of two traditions, that of Asian horsemen and that of Mediterranean infantry. The cavalry was larger than the infantry and – in contrast with Medieval Western-European cavalry – was less well trained and had lower status than the elite Ottoman infantry, known as the Janissaries. The latter was a highly trained and effective professional force, better coordinated on the battlefield than most Asian infantries. Nonetheless, it declined to embrace the infantry practices that were being fashioned in Western Europe at least partly because it would have necessitated changes in the Ottoman military structure, which in turn would have undermined the elevated status of the Janissaries.[130]

In any case, some writers, most notably Geoffrey Parker, have taken the position that these methods of warfare developed by Europeans constituted a major factor in the imposition of European rule outside the West. The assertion has not gone uncontested, but it is undeniable that the evolution of highly coordinated infantries often distinguished Western military forces from the indigenous forces they were fighting against. This is what Kaushik Roy argues in his writings on eighteenth- and nineteenth-century India. Roy emphatically rejects, however, Parker's notion that non-European societies lacked sustained, secular military theories.[131]

European and non-European differences in warfare resulted primarily from differences in the pressures each faced and the methods available to them to meet these pressures. Mongol armies in the fourteenth century were as well coordinated as any Western-European army in the Early Modern period. It was, however, a different kind of coordination. It took place among widely dispersed horse archers. What historians find so remarkable was their ability to plan attacks in advance and communicate with one another in order to outmanoeuvre the enemy.[132] These coordination skills were developed among warriors and future warriors in a hunting routine known as the *nerge,* in which large units of horsemen were spread in circling lines over a hundred kilometres long.[133]

For our purposes, it needs to be understood that the objective of European military drills was not just to acquire skills. The belief developed that drills prepared soldiers psychologically to stand their ground and follow commands, and strengthened morale and taught soldiers that they had to perform as parts of a larger whole. They promoted mechanical standards of performance and inculcated the routine of obedience.[134] Some even claimed that drills promoted moral virtue.[135] Most felt that, at a minimum, drills created common knowledge. Military commanders and specialists obviously did not use this term, but what they were advocating is clearly what Chwe calls common knowledge. The drill was as much a ritual as a skill-development exercise. Soldiers were instructed in large fields, with a great number of men and equipment present. Every soldier needed to know what to do. Equally he needed to know that his fellow soldiers knew what to do. In England, during the seventeenth century, martial spectacles consisting of musters, and, in some cases, the re-enactment of battles were held before large audiences; and drills were sometimes performed for public view.[136]

In the nineteenth century, close-order formations in the field were replaced by open-order formations, but drills persisted as part of military exercise and ceremony. Indeed, in the late nineteenth century, commanders were known to persist with out-of-date weapons, such as muzzle-loading firearms, out of opposition to any change in the arms-drill practices they had been using.

Drills came to be complemented by military parades. The big – often colossal – military processions in which soldiers march in perfect unison have become one of the most remarkable features of armies today. These parades are intended to intimidate the enemy or potential enemy, but they are also meant to demonstrate – to the soldiers themselves as well as to others – the capacity of a military force to achieve a remarkable degree of coordination. The difference between these parades and the representation of combat in the hastiludes of the Medieval period illustrates, very dramatically, the transformation in conditions for military collective action and organization between these two historical periods.

Honours as Instruments of Communication

We begin with a few general statements about the communication functions of different kinds of honorific recognition. Monuments, statues, art depictions, and inscriptions have considerable communication power. Indeed, communication was the major reason for selecting this type of reward. Such rewards are manifestly biased toward time rather than space, while their numerical communication power varies with the number of persons likely to see them. Monuments and statues in large cities have significant communication power over numbers, but even those located in areas of lower population density could have power of this kind. Spread across the countryside of Ancient India were hero stones that had been erected in honour of men who had died in battle.[137]

Body ornaments, which are generally light and transportable, have substantial communication power over space; their temporal and numerical communication power varies depending on their durability and the cost or difficulty of making them. If they are made of precious metals, as were some in Ancient Egypt, they were biased primarily toward time and space as opposed to numbers. (This is consistent with the well-known concern among Egyptians with preservation over time.) In contrast, many Greek rewards were made of vegetable matter and were not meant to survive for long. Only a written or pictorial record of them might do so. The same is true of some of the Roman military honours, including the highest honour, the grass crown (also known as the siege crown).

In Early Modern Europe, as in Medieval Europe, the communication function of orders of knighthood was secondary to the legitimation and motivation functions. We should not, however, overlook the communication functions that these orders did then perform. Orders might be created to celebrate a coronation, a marriage, the birth of a royal heir, or a military success. The founding of the Order of Maria Theresa was meant to celebrate the Austrian victory over Prussia in the Battle of Kolin on 18 June 1757.[138]

Commemorative or not, all orders were designed – if often rather unrealistically – to communicate expectations, although some more than others. The one hundred founding knights of the Order of Saint Lazarus of Jerusalem and of Our Lady of Mount-Carmel undertook to follow a relatively severe religious and hospitaller discipline. It was supposedly to instill a new "knightly" ethos in the nobility that the Order of Saint Andrew and the Order of Saint Alexander Nevsky were created in Russia in the early eighteenth century.[139] The duty of members of the Order of the White Falcon, founded in 1732 by Ernest Augustus, duke of Saxe-Weimar-Eisenach, was "to be true to God; to practice virtue and avoid vice; to promote, as much as lay in their power, his Majesty's glory and interest, and to be ready to sacrifice for the Emperor, life and property, if called upon by circumstances to do so."[140]

Although the Order of Saint Louis was founded primarily as an incentive for the nobility, the great number of recipients meant that it could serve as an expectation and coordination instrument as well, not only for the noble population but also for lower-ranked members of the armed forces. In his history of the Saint Louis, written in the nineteenth century, Alex Mazas characterized it principally as a reward for the nobility, but he also indicated that it had a significant effect on the rank and file. According to Mazas, common soldiers urged that their officers be decorated, and the Order increased enthusiasm among non-officers, even though they were ineligible to receive it. He also claimed that a positive effect was produced when officers who had been elevated to the Saint Louis returned to their homes wearing their "brilliant decoration."[141] Whether or not the badge of the Order actually had this effect on the rank and file, the belief that it did was a substantial element in the legacy of the Order of Saint Louis.

In Medieval Europe, the principal purpose of the badges of orders of knighthood had been to identify members, but to the extent that admission to an order was seen as an honour, the badge of the order signified honour. These badges, often made of cloth, were part of the larger system of livery badges discussed above. In fact, livery badges could be used as rewards; rulers sometimes gave livery badges decorated with their personal device to honoured guests or in gratitude for service.[142]

Badges continued to be employed for identification purposes in Early Modern and Modern orders. Indeed, whereas in the Middle Ages they had been part of a larger ensemble of identification dress and ornamentation, in the Early Modern and Modern periods, badges, now mostly metallic, became the most preferred means of identifying members of orders and symbolizing their status. Badges also became symbols of the orders themselves. Since the badge of the Order of Saint Louis had the shape of a cross, the Order was commonly referred to as "the Cross of Saint Louis," or just "the Cross." It was also possible for the name of an order to correspond to the design of its badge, as in the Order of the African Star, the Order of the Black Star, and the Order of the Anjouan Star, to mention only a few.

Of course, this is all the more true of honours that are not called orders, many of which have been known, not just informally but also formally, by the form of their insignia – in Britain: the Waterloo Medal, Victoria Cross, Distinguished Service Cross, and Military Medal; in Belgium: the Iron Medal, Iron Cross, and Military Cross; and in France: the July Cross, July Medal, Mazagran Medal, Military Medal, and Colonial Medal. In addition, when governments founded an order, they sometimes created an affiliated token or medal. When the Order of Saint Louis was established, a silver medal was created for pilots and sailors as a *recompense* for their services. Tokens were distributed when the Military Order of William was founded. In Britain, the Royal Victorian Order and the Order of the British Empire, had an associated medal to go with them.

Why metallic badges and medals? Other symbolic objects – cloth badges, collars or other kinds of jewellery, special dress, distinctive headwear, robes of honour – could have served the identification and status functions equally well. Indeed, such alternatives were common in other world populations, and European honorific orders usually had distinctive ceremonial dress and headwear for the higher grades.

The best explanation is the communication power (over time, space, and numbers) that medals in general had during the age of the communication medal. They were durable; they could be easily transported long distances; and they could now be manufactured in large numbers relatively cheaply. The first of these was probably the most critical. Cloth or paper would have had a very limited life, perhaps little more than a few years depending on the recipient. For many awards distributors, a long life was considered desirable. When Andrew Carnegie established the Carnegie Hero Fund in 1904, he made provision for a medal to "be given to the hero or widow or next of kin, which will recite the heroic deed it commemorates, that the descendants may know and be proud of their descent."[143]

The adoption of metallic badges and medals for honours during this historical period indicates the importance attached to honours as a means of communication. Because state honours emerged in Europe during this era, today a metallic badge or medal of some kind is regarded as essential for a state honour, even though medals no longer serve the singular communication function they once did. It is true that similar cultural objects were bestowed as honorific rewards in other parts of the world independently of their adoption in Europe. One example is the *canipu* of the Inca Empire; it was a metal plate, worn in various places on the honoree's body as an ornament. In the final chapter, I consider these and similar non-European body ornaments in an effort to assess the relative importance of the conditions that have led to the adoption of such cultural objects as rewards. However, it should be noted at this point that, while the *canipu* had significant communication power for the same reasons that metallic badges and medals did, its communication power over space would have been less because it was relatively large in size.

Again we want to determine the European genealogical descent of the practice. Although in general, as in the specific case of the Greek Olympics, medals were infrequently adopted as prizes in the Ancient World, there is some evidence of medals or similar objects, along with commemorative coins, being awarded by rulers in recognition of achievement or service. The commemorative "elephant medallions" mentioned above are thought to have been distributed by Alexander to some of the men who fought with him at the Hydaspes River.[144] The Roman *phalerae* were distributed as an honorific reward as well as a badge of rank.[145] (The term was also applied to the bosses on helmets and the pendants attached to horse harnesses.) The soldier who received *phalerae* as a military decoration wore them on his chest, usually nine of them strung together by leather straps. The size varied, but those of a set found in Newstead, Scotland, were between 86 millimetres and 115 millimetres in diameter.[146]

It is difficult to say exactly when the distinctive honorific rewards of Modern Europe began. But if one were to insist on doing so, it arguably lay in the expansion, during the fifteenth and sixteenth centuries, of portrait and commemorative medals that also served to recognize someone's achievement by portraying his image. In 1441, Pisanello was commissioned to fashion a portrait medal of Niccolò Piccinino, who commanded the Duke of Milan's forces against Venice.[147] In the same category, we can place a medal that was commissioned by Pope Sixtus IV to celebrate the recapture of Otranto by the Duke of Calabria in 1481, with a portrait of the Duke on the obverse and a portrayal of the conquest on the reverse.[148] In 1589 a medal – known as the Drake medal – was produced commemorating Sir Francis Drake's voyage around the world in 1577–80.[149]

A step closer to the Modern state honour was taken when a commemorative medal was bestowed as a reward without the image of the recipient on the medal. It is sometimes unclear whether a medal is primarily commemorative, primarily a reward, or an equal measure of both. Thus the so-called "Dangers Averted Medals" that Elizabeth I gave to a number of participants after the English victory over the Spanish Armada were intended both to commemorate this victory and to reward these participants. On the other hand, medals bestowed by James VI/I on his most distinguished naval commanders were likely meant primarily as rewards.[150] And the medal given to pilots and sailors when the Order of Saint Louis was founded was primarily a reward.

In the British Isles, we find the sharpest increase in medals as rewards during the Civil War.[151] Both sides in this conflict employed medals to celebrate their forces, seemingly in imitation of one another. Perhaps the first of these rewards for service in the field was a medal conferred by Charles I on men who had been selected for recognition by commanders-in-chief in the royal forces. Medals portraying Cromwell's image were authorized by the House of Commons in September 1650 to be bestowed on officers and soldiers who played a significant role in Cromwell's victory at Dunbar. A medal called the "Medal of Parliament" was awarded, in 1651, to a colonel who refused to surrender a castle. Other medals were awarded to officers and soldiers as honorary badges, some adorned with images of Charles I or great lords who had supported him.

During the second half of the seventeenth century, medals were increasingly awarded to individuals as rewards for service. Members of the Amsterdam Town Guard received a medal commemorating the Four Days' Battle in 1666 (one of the longest naval battles in European history). In 1692, the English Parliament authorized a medal for officers, marines, and seamen in royal service at sea "who shall be found to have done any signal or extraordinary service."[152] Several medals were manufactured to commemorate the Battle of La Hogue in 1692 (which prevented a French invasion of England), at least one of which was conferred on officers and seamen.[153] In 1702, medals were produced to commemorate a successful attack at Vigo Bay, one of which was conferred on Admiral Sir George Rooke and several officers. And in 1703, medals were conferred after a naval battle near Granville in Normandy.

This dual purpose – commemoration and reward – continued to characterize many state honours. The majority of those that the French Revolutionaries permitted themselves to bestow recognized the role that recipients had played in various events that the Revolutionaries wanted to celebrate, such as the storming of the Bastille. The Belgian Iron Medal and Iron Cross commemorated the Belgian Revolution of 1830. And the French July Medal commemorated the French Revolution of 1830.

The functions of commemoration and reward were also served simultaneously by medals bestowed on soldiers in recognition of their participation in specific campaigns or engagements. I have already noted that the British government and the East India Company created a number of military medals for soldiers who had fought in overseas engagements. More generally speaking, the British were ahead of other European states in the distribution of commemorative medals for soldiers, service medals for different campaigns, and long-service and good-conduct medals, which altogether constituted the great majority of the military rewards distributed by the British government and by the East

India Company during the last decade of the eighteenth century and the first half of the nineteenth century. The Second Empire, in imitation of service medals awarded by the British to soldiers who fought in the Crimean War, gave medals to those who participated in French adventures in Italy, China, and Mexico.[154] And in 1893, under the Third Republic, the Colonial Medal was introduced for soldiers engaged in overseas expeditions, with a clip attached to the ribbon to indicate the specific campaign or campaigns in which a soldier participated.[155]

Eventually, a nomenclature evolved consisting of "decorations" (usually for bravery or exceptional performance), "service medals" (awarded to individuals in recognition of service), "campaign medals" (service medals for a specific campaign), and "battle honours" (awarded to regiments). Usage of these terms has not, however, always been consistent.

What was it that medals communicated? Most obviously, they communicated expectations, primarily those that were identified in Chapter 3: courage, loyalty, service, selflessness, and constancy. As I argued there, this does not necessarily mean that those who created and conferred the honours were interested in promoting these values as such. It could simply be that they believed that these values led men and women to behave in ways that state officials wanted them to. In either case, the expectations had to be communicated to those whose behaviour was being organized.

The communication of expectations may, however, have been secondary to the purpose that metallic badges and medals served as instruments of coordination. After all, the expectations associated with these metallic badges and medals were mostly well known and were being communicated in a good number of other ways as well, most of which were less enigmatic and more persuasive than what was portrayed on a metallic badge or medal, which usually consisted of little more than a figure and a short motto, often in Latin. The advantage of metallic badges and medals – like demonstrations, state ceremonies, and military parades – was not that they were especially eloquent, persuasive, or forceful, but rather that they communicated expectations in such a way that those who saw them understood that many others had or would see them as well. Even a soldier or civilian who fully understood and accepted what was expected of him or her needed to know that others understood and accepted it as well. A medal or metallic badge acted as a signal that transformed values, beliefs, and standards into common knowledge for coordination.

The argument that I am making is supported by recent literature on military dress and processions. S.H. Myerly has examined British military spectacle – badges, medals, military dress, drills, and processions – in the nineteenth century. As I have asserted with respect to badges and medals, the purpose of military spectacle is to communicate expectations not by providing explicit statements about what is expected but by creating common knowledge. Of course, ceremonies, drills, parades, and dress do not function as coordination devices in exactly the same way as metallic badges and medals. They differ significantly in their communication power. Dress has marginally more communication power over space and time than ceremonies, drills, or parades, but all four would have far less communication power over space and time than metallic badges and medals. With respect to numbers, the differences among these media are a bit complicated. Within their space and time limits, ceremonies, drills, and parades can have impressive power over numbers. The communication power of dress – in particular details of dress – is greatest in small populations, but it has considerable communication power over numbers when it is combined with ceremonies, drills, or parades. Myerly suggests that ceremonies, drills, parades, and dress have an advantage over more durable modes of communication, such as monuments, because they represent living men and exhibit the strength of a military machine.[156]

For any of these media to perform this coordination function, it was critical that as many members of the target population as possible shared the same meaning of the signal. The utility of a state honour as a coordination instrument depended on getting signals right, and consequently much effort was usually invested in doing so.

ENHANCING THE COMMUNICATION POWER OF HONOURS

The communication potential of metallic badges and medals is greater the more frequently those who possess them show them to others. In contrast to badges, medals were not originally considered as something that should be worn by the recipient. It has only been in the nineteenth and twentieth centuries that wearing military medals on one's chest has become the extravagant exhibition that it is today. Not surprisingly, there was resistance in some contexts to it. In France, article 20 of the Report of the Committee of

Public Instruction decreed in January 1792 that marks of honour conferred by the Legislative Assembly should be worn only at national festivals.[157] This sentiment persisted in some quarters through the nineteenth century. When the Orléanists took power in 1830, they were keen to discard not just the Old-Regime orders that had been revived under the Restoration but also the pretentious ceremonies that went with them. Many people had no patience for the fancy display characteristic of the royal orders. They sneered at portraits painted of eminent persons with their chests decorated with the badges of orders to which they belonged. They objected to the award of state honours at public ceremonies because it was associated in people's minds with the Old Regime. There was also a practical reason to reject them: it was becoming increasingly expensive to present state honours in grand ceremonies.

Nevertheless, the purposes that honours performed made it unlikely that these ceremonies would disappear. The Convention permitted the presentation of honorific military rewards at ceremonies before the army.[158] Napoleon, always one to appropriate Old-Regime practices that he thought were useful for his purposes, staged grand ceremonies for the award of the badge of the Legion of Honour.[159] The award ceremony in Boulogne in August 1804 was described by Mathieu Dumas as "the most splendid military spectacle I ever witnessed."[160]

Recent research has devoted considerable attention to French commemorative ceremonies of all kinds during the nineteenth century, which Sudhir Hazareesingh has referred to as the zenith of commemorative activity in France. He cautions against the assumption that state officials were in control of all these commemorative practices. Ceremonies were, instead, modes of contention over collective memory among different political factions. Yet state officials were provided with a means of enhancing the communication power of state honours by associating them with "civic festivities" held for generating common knowledge of various kinds. Hazareesingh has written specifically about the Saint Napoleon festivity. Napoleon had persuaded the Pope to create a new saint, Napoleon, named after an invented Roman martyr, whose memory would be celebrated on Napoleon's birthday, 15 August, replacing the Feast of the Assumption. The Saint Napoleon festival was not celebrated under the Restoration and the July Monarchy, but was revived under the Second Empire. More to the point, the day of this festival was used to honour veterans who had been awarded the Saint Helena Medal.[161] In France, awards have also been made on Bastille Day or during other similar celebrations.[162] Along with civic festivities, the presentation of awards could also be organized to target a certain audience, such as soldiers, state employees, or factory workers. Under the Third Republic, *médailles du travail* were frequently distributed in factories. Even the Legion of Honour could be bestowed in factories or offices.[163]

Like annual commemorative ceremonies, some of these award ceremonies have been repeated yearly. This repetition, the communication power of metallic badges and medals, and the links that were drawn between the founding of a state honour and major national events have made honours part of the collective memory of states, dynasties, and political regimes. Those who created new state honours imitated earlier honours not only in order to take advantage of prevalent cultural symbols but also because these earlier honours, or at least some of them, demonstrated the long-term benefits that honours could have. This purpose – shaping the larger national memory – is well apparent in the historical connection between the Order of Saint Louis, the Legion of Honour, and the Medal of Saint Helena. Napoleon was influenced by his familiarity with the place that the Saint Louis came to occupy in the collective memory of the French military, and Napoleon III by the contribution of the Legion of Honour to the Napoleonic cult.

It is easier in nineteenth-century sources than in those from earlier periods to find explicit recognition of the importance of honours in generating common knowledge of exemplary behaviour. For Nicholas Harris Nicolas, the British government was coming to this appreciation only in the first half of the nineteenth century. In his view, it was a mistake to award military medals when men are discharged because

the true object of rewards, as of punishments, is that they may act as an example to others; and the effect of those Medals must be much greater when they are conspicuously worn among a soldier's comrades, or a sailor's shipmates, than when those on whom they are intended to act as an incentive, see them only for a moment just before the man departs, perhaps for ever, from among them. Honorary Distinctions should be given to the faithful Soldier or Seaman while the Country can have the advantages which they are likely to produce upon himself, as well as upon others. They should be conferred in the most public manner, on parade, or before the whole crew on the quarter-deck, attended by some forms of solemnity.[164]

Some of the privileges enjoyed by those holding an honour were clearly designed to enhance the visibility of the anointed. Military personnel belonging to the Legion of Honour had the right of a salute from servicemen of the same or lower rank who did not belong to the Legion; when they attended public ceremonies, they occupied special places; and when they died, a specified proportion of the garrison had to attend their funeral.[165] The pressure to generate common knowledge of exemplary behaviour was also one of the reasons for codes of conduct imposed on those who received them. It was in these terms that Léon Aucoc (from 1852 to 1879, a member of the French Council of State, the supreme court for administrative justice) defended the need for a code of conduct for members of the Legion of Honour. "The more this distinction raises them above their fellow citizens," he argued, "the more they are obliged to give in their conduct the example of *correction*, of *droiture*, of *loyauté*, the more it means that members unworthy by a *défaillance* to wear the sign of honour be removed from the corporation."[166]

Yet Aucoc's words are about more than the function of honours in collective action and organization, which has been the subject of this and the preceding chapters. In addition to the legitimation, incentives, and communication that rulers and state officials need for the collective action they are trying to organize, they also require a consensus in the population that is being governed on what is virtuous, responsible, and honourable versus what is shameful, disreputable, irresponsible, and inglorious. They also require a disposition in this population to try to meet those standards. Rulers and state officials are also interested in the general conduct of the population they are governing and in maintaining order in this population. In short, in the language that is currently favoured in the social sciences, rulers and state officials want a "disciplined" population.

PART III

Social Structures
and Disciplinary Power

We can begin with a few general observations about disciplinary techniques. They can be external or internal. In the former case, they are imposed on a person by other persons. In the latter, discipline is imposed, directly at least, on a person by herself or himself; in other words, it is self-discipline. Self-discipline may or may not accord with the interests of the actor, but whatever the consequences, the actor is persuaded to behave in certain ways on her or his own initiative.

Disciplinary techniques are linked to the social structures in which they are embedded. The term "social structure" is generally employed in the social sciences to refer to relatively stable patterns of social relationships. It will be useful for us to begin by identifying several of the ways in which patterns of social relationships vary. The variations that have the most relevance to the present inquiry are: (1) personal versus impersonal, (2) diffuse versus specific, (3) communal versus associational, (4) collectivist versus individualized, and (5) hierarchical versus egalitarian. Some of these are self-evident, but several may need clarification. Diffuse relationships are those that involve several roles that a person plays and more than one aspect of his or her personality, competence, et cetera; specific relationships are those that bear on only one role a person plays (for example, a clearly defined occupation) and on only a part of his or her personality, skills, et cetera. Communal relationships are characterized by frequent interaction; associational relationships by common interests. Collectivist relationships are relatively embedded in a social group; people relate to others as members (or not) of the group;

and people are expected to take the interests of the group into account.

The five variations listed do not exist independently of one another. In general, social relationships that are personal are also more diffuse, communal, and collectivist. I shall refer to this combination of four as "communitarian" relationships, with no other connotation intended. (This word is employed in a number of ways, so it is essential to be precise about how I am using it.) Hierarchical relationships may or may not be found together with communitarian relationships.

We often try to make general claims about cross-societal dissimilarities on these variables – that, for example, in some societies social structures are more personal or hierarchical than in others. These are the sorts of contrasts we will want to draw in order to understand the transformation in the disciplinary functions performed by state honours in Western Europe from the Middle Ages to the Modern period. Yet these dissimilarities exist within societies or periods of time as well as between them. And in all societies, there are dialectics among these types of relationships, by which I mean that the opposition between them is interactive. Indeed, the nature of these dialectics is just as important as the overall variation in social structures. It will become clear in the following chapters that the dialectic that requires the most attention for understanding the disciplinary function of state honours is the collectivist–individualist interaction.

It goes without saying that the extent to which social relationships are hierarchical, discipline is based on differences in power and authority. To the extent that they are communitarian (personal, diffuse, communal, and collectivist), discipline is based on the sentiments, emotions, and solidarities of the social groups formed by these relationships; and the principal disciplinary sanction is exclusion, in whole or in part, from these communitarian relationships and/or the benefits that go with them. This kind of discipline is usually referred to as "corporate discipline," though it should be acknowledged that in the academic literature disagreement is rife on the characteristics of groups exercising corporate discipline. The opposite is individualized discipline, where punishment does not entail a significant rupture in communitarian relationships but rather the loss or attenuation of some relatively individualized reward. This

Table III.1
Four basic types of disciplinary practices

Characteristics of disciplinary practices	External to the actor	Internal to the actor
Corporate	Inclusion or exclusion as a restricted reward or punishment	Self-shaming
Individualized	Other restricted rewards or punishments	Individualization

is often because there are no communitarian relationships or they are very weak, but individualized rewards and punishments can also be utilized in communitarian groups, most obviously in families.

Both corporate discipline and individualized discipline may be either external or internal. As shown in Table III.1, by cross-tabulating these two distinctions, we can identify four types of discipline according to the nature of their sanctions. All external discipline operates by means of restricted rewards and punishments. Exclusion is a restricted punishment, but one of a specific kind – the loss of the benefits of membership in a group. I am using the term "self-shame" to refer to the way that people feel inside for letting down other members of a corporate group. I am using the term "individualization" as one can find it being used in the literature on discipline. The basic idea is that, through a process of "normalization," a standard of judgment is established against which we can differentiate what is normal from what is abnormal or pathological. Individualization refers to placing oneself and being placed in such a system of classification. In societies in which people are controlled through individualization, they are infinitely classified and induced, rather than coerced, into submission. These techniques of power show us what we are, but also what we are not but could have been or could become. Normalization and individualization are modes of discipline internal to individuals, but other people obviously contribute to the processes.

8

The Middle Ages

SOCIAL STRUCTURES AND DISCIPLINARY REGIMES

In the Middle Ages, discipline was mainly corporate and depended heavily on communitarian structures. It could be internal or external. Forfeiture of the privileges of membership in one's kinship group or community was a serious punishment as a result of the material losses that such a sanction might entail, but equally because it would isolate a person from the social bonds that were critical to her or his psychological health and identity. Even lordship could be communitarian in nature, the bond between lord and subordinate being personal, diffuse, and communal, as well as instrumental.

In these terms, we can understand the pervasive use of banishment from villages, towns, manorial territories, or royal courts as a mode of punishment in the Middle Ages. Naturally, surviving records tell us the most about banishments from royal courts. They were usually politically motivated, but the choice of banishment as a method of dealing with opponents and politically troublesome individuals reflects the underlying social structures of the society. To take one illustration among many that could be given, during the reign of Charles VII of France, Arthur de Richemont engineered the dismissal of Jean Louvet, along with his followers, from the Royal Court and assisted the ascendancy of Georges de la Trémoille. Subsequently, Arthur de Richemont was banished from the Court as a result of a dispute with Trémoille that Charles himself may have promoted.[1] Banishments could be morally or emotionally charged, even if politically motivated. One of the best-known cases is the accusation of homosexuality made against Piers Gaveston, which forced

Edward II to banish him from court, though Edward's persistent support of his friend eventually pushed Gaveston's enemies into murdering the favourite.

For all that, labelling Medieval society, or even any one of its institutions, as simply corporate is an oversimplification. Corporate discipline was typically enjoined with other kinds of control. Most of these relationships were hierarchical. The patriarch of a family, the master of a guild, the head of a confraternity – people in such positions had relatively greater corporate power over other members of the group, and less reason to fear corporate discipline from these other members. In like manner, a king or lord had more power and less to lose in a relationship with a villein, vassal, retainer, or member of his household than did any of the latter in their relationships with him. It was in the language of personal dependence and submission that these hierarchical relationships were often expressed – of wife on husband, child on father, villein or slave on his master, subject on his king, man on God. Nevertheless, hierarchical and egalitarian norms could be in tension. In some groups, efforts were routinely made to disguise them, and to pretend that a relationship was more egalitarian than it actually was.

Similarly, impersonal and personal relationships were not mutually exclusive, and the interaction between the two was ubiquitous. Efforts to make impersonal contacts personal, or to pretend that they were personal, was so common that people were usually not conscious of them. Communal and associational relations also interacted. Typically, the political or economic basis of social relationships gave rise to, and was shaped by, communal interaction among the parties. The distinctive Medieval mixture of the hierarchical and the egalitarian, the personal and the impersonal, and the communal and the associational gave social relationships in this historical period their particular character, though one that varied from one region to another and from one century to another.

There is no doubting the collectivism of social relations in Medieval society. It is evidenced, as Walter Ullmann pointed out some years ago, in collective punishments, the anonymity of writers, the sameness of handwriting, and the general absence of majority voting procedures.[2] It is also evidenced in the strength of kinship networks and the great variety of corps that were then common. These corps included religious orders, lay confraternities, fraternal brotherhoods, sworn alliances, and the monarchical orders of knighthood. It also included guilds and other types of occupational associations and co-operatives. And it included provincial and municipal governing bodies.

At the same time, strong individualist tendencies could be found, even within organizations that were, for the most part, corporate. According to Brigitte Bedos-Rezak, charters represented individuals as autonomous, voluntary, and empirically present agents.[3] Paradoxically – but significantly – the communitarian nature of social relationships in Medieval society also gave people a measure of individuality. Precisely because they had close and frequent interaction with one another, and were aware of the many aspects of one another's personalities, they had relatively differentiated understandings of one another. Lords, priests, and patriarchs were expected to know individually those over whom they exercised power. Michel Foucault and his followers have referred to this sort of personalized power relationship as "pastoral," which they see as typified by the power exercised by a pastor over his parishioners. Pastors and parishioners form a corporate group, but the pastor influences their behaviour through individualized kindness, the individualized knowledge he has of them, and the careful watch that he performs over them.[4]

Kings could endeavour to expand their pastoral power – enlarge their flock, so to speak – by increasing the direct relationships they had with members of the population over which they claimed to rule. This happened on both sides of the English Channel, but Anglo-Norman and English kings were more successful than French kings in forming direct relationships with their "subjects." William I and his successors required all feudal tenants to recognize the king as their primary lord, whereas in France, the king had no authority over the vassals of his vassals until the early fourteenth century. Later, the Angevins sought to undermine the early Medieval notion of unfreedom as a total submission of a villein to the control of a lord.[5] P.R. Coss, in his analysis of the relationship between the monarchy and the landed elite in the twelfth century, examines the way in which the English Crown asserted the right to call upon or favour whomever it wished as individuals.[6]

My point is that these efforts by the English Crown should not be seen as contrary to the prevailing social structures. The relations that William established with his tenants-in-chief in England were essentially the relations he had with lords in Normandy. All these relations were grounded in the pastoral power of Medieval lordship. At the core of the relationship were individual rights and responsibilities.

Naturally, even as rulers encouraged more individualized social relationships in these and other ways, they also sought to use the fiction of the organic unity of their kingdom to bolster their authority. Royal advocates repeatedly spoke of the kingdom as a family, whose members were the king's children; and they proclaimed the duty of all the king's subjects to perform their allotted role for the integrated whole.[7] In reality, none of the kingdoms of Europe were organic wholes. They were too culturally and linguistically heterogeneous, supra-local social interaction was too limited, and power was too fragmented for significant organic solidarity to emerge beyond small geographical regions.

By the same token, the notion of European society as consisting of three orders formed by the clergy, the nobility, and the third estate is misleading. There was no organic unity among members of the third estate, which was divided into thousands of much smaller communal groups. There was more solidarity among the nobility. Many nobles living in different regions of Europe could be acquainted with one another and shared a common culture. They participated in knightly games and expeditions that often brought together noblemen from several different kingdoms. They adopted common heraldic emblems that were indicative of noble ancestry and were regulated by an international corps of heralds, who prepared universal armorials that included the names and arms of the leading lords and knights of many kingdoms.

Still, as a status group, the nobility did not form a corporate order. Not only was it linguistically, culturally, and territorially divided, it was also split into different ranks, attached to different kinship groups, mobilized by different lords and kings, and affiliated with different princely courts. As mentioned in Chapter 5, there was considerable ambiguity over the criteria for membership in the untitled nobility, many people making disputed claims to noble status. What cohesion there was among the nobility was more the result of ties of religion, lordship, and kinship than their common noble status.

Only the Church could be said to form a large community of some kind, at least insofar as it provided a union of religious faith and a normative regulation of behaviour over the Continent. Thus, it is noteworthy that the Crusades represented the broadest mobilization of the nobility in collective action at a supra-local level during the Middle Ages. All the same, most of the Church's supra-local unity was among elites, churchmen, and scholars, and it was greatly undermined by cultural and linguistic differences in European society, serious fractures within the Church, and the limited means of communication available. The solidarity achieved in the Crusades was as much a product of ties of lordship as it was a consequence of the cohesion of Latin Christendom. Unfortunately for the cause, these same ties of lordship, along with regional and communal loyalties, time and again shattered the unity of the Crusades.

KNIGHTS AND ORDERS OF KNIGHTHOOD

We need to be similarly cautious when we examine discipline among knights, between lords and knights, and in orders of knighthood. Most of the information we have comes from normative statements and idealistic portrayals. If nothing else, however, they tell us what these norms and ideals were.

Norms of lordship were fundamental to the discipline to which knights were subject. A knight who engaged in unsavory conduct, or failed to meet his obligations, would face the sanctions that all soldiers face in these circumstances, whatever society they lived in, but, in addition, the seigneurial tie that he enjoyed with his lord would be threatened. This corporate hierarchical discipline was especially evident among those knights who were directly attached to a king or a lord. Often a king or a great lord would retain a contingent of knights as household knights, some of whom were administrators, while others served as royal bodyguards and/or warriors prepared to take the field when called upon. Many knights also belonged to bands of pledged warriors, among whom discipline was relatively corporate in nature.

Corporate discipline was evident as well in the confraternal orders, fraternal brotherhoods, and sworn alliances in which many knights participated. It was also evident in some of the monarchical orders of knighthood, at least in the formal constitutions and statutes that were designed to regulate the daily conduct of members.[8] I indicated in Chapter 5 that loyalty to the prince was given much emphasis in Medieval orders of knighthood. Only slightly less important was loyalty to other members. Of course, these orders varied in how "confraternal" they were. One of the most confraternal was the Order of the Collar, founded by Amadeus VI of Savoy in 1364 not so much to bring his vassals and neighbours into clientship with him but as an instrumental of mutual support.[9] Its original insignia included friendship-knots, which were hung from a collar and meant to symbolize the union of members of the order.[10] Another example is the Order of the Golden Fleece, which was instituted by Philip the Good in 1430 to create man-to-man obligations among a disparate elite brought under his rule by marriages and accidents of inheritance.[11] Members of this order were not supposed to belong to any other organization that might compete for their allegiance, a requirement that was not unusual in Medieval orders. Most members took the honour of the Order seriously.

We have seen, however, that the term "order" could be used rather loosely in the Middle Ages. It might refer to knighthood in general, to groups like the Order of the Golden Tree, or to a category of men possessing a special status among knights, such as the Knights of the Bath. These groups did not constitute formally organized bodies, with statutes or a constitution. As I said in Chapter 3, the Knights of the Bath were distinguished by the bathing ritual that was performed when the status was awarded. Now, this does not mean that corporate discipline was altogether absent in these "orders." After all, the Order of the Golden Tree was a sworn alliance of loyalty to Philip. Discipline in "orders" such as the Knights of the Bath was more diffuse and weaker, but members would still be bound by the loyalty expected by anyone knighted by the king. The Knights of the Bath took an oath that made no mention of loyalty to the order, but stressed – along with fearing God and protecting women, children, and the poor – the obligation of knights to "above all other earthly things love the King the Sovereign Lord, him, and his right defend unto thy power, and before all worldly things put him in worship."[12]

Let us move on to orders that were more manifestly confraternal. They abounded in rules to strengthen norms of mutual obligation. Members were often required to take an oath of loyalty to the order. Another order founded by Amadeus VI, the short-lived Order of the Black Swan, enjoined members to assist one another at their own expense and not to quarrel.[13] The companions of the Order of the Golden Fleece were bound to bear "good and true love" to one another, to inform any of their companions of anything dishonourable that was spoken of them, to aid any of their fellow members against whom an evil act was committed, and to uphold the honour of the Order. It was expected that conflicts among members of the Order would be presented to binding arbitration at the next chapter, that is, the next meeting, of the Order. During chapter, the conduct of every knight of the Golden Fleece was supposed to be scrutinized by his companions; all knights had to declare on oath what they knew or had heard of any companion's words or deeds contrary to the honour of chivalry or the statutes of the Order.[14]

Ideally, conformity would be achieved by instilling values and norms that would make members of the group feel ashamed of themselves if they did not live up to them. Minor infractions were typically sanctioned by a fine and collective disapproval, while serious breaches (such as flight from battle, refusal to accept a judgment of the order, or treason) usually entailed expulsion from the group. Any member of the Order of the Black Swan who failed to submit to the arbitration of other members was expelled and the other members bound to make common cause against him.[15] The statutes of the Order of the Garter did not provide for expulsion, but expulsions did take place, usually on the basis of accusations of treason. The rules for the Order of the Band, the Order of the Star, the Order of the Knot, and the Order of the Ship all dictated expulsion for cowardice in battle. The rules of the Order of the Golden Fleece decreed banishment for heresy, treason, and other offences that the sovereign and companions might decide warranted this penalty.[16] In all of these orders, the concern, in addition to meeting the specific purposes of the order, was to avoid behaviour that would threaten its honour.

Yet to characterize knights and orders of knighthood as purely corporate institutions is another oversimplification. The interaction between collectivism and individualism was nowhere greater than among knights, especially higher-status knights. First, and what will become particularly relevant in later discussions, the status of knight and membership in an order of knighthood was individual in the sense that, unlike noble status, it did not automatically pass from one member of a family to another. Second, as just asserted, the relationship between a lord and his subordinates was, in important ways, governed by what we are calling pastoral power, which is both corporate and individualized. This was doubly so when the subordinate was a knight. In much Medieval literature, the special bond between a lord and a knight was glorified more than any other. Members of the Order of the Collar, along with the support they were supposed to give to other members, were also obliged to provide favour, counsel, aid, and service to the head, and to work to preserve his honour and advantage against all but their own lords, vassals, or close relatives.[17] It was expected that knights of the Order of the Golden Fleece would serve their chief whenever he acted to defend

Egyptian necklace of fly beads, New Kingdom, Dynasty 18, 1550–1295 BCE.
A necklace was one of several forms of jewellery used as status rewards.
(Gold: carnelian. Length without modern chain 10 ½ in. Flies 1.1 to 1.7 cm.
William Stevenson Smith Fund, 1980.167 © 2016 Museum of Fine Arts,
Boston)

Roman Phalera medallion: Jupiter flanked by a male and female deity, second century. (© Trustees of the British Museum, London)

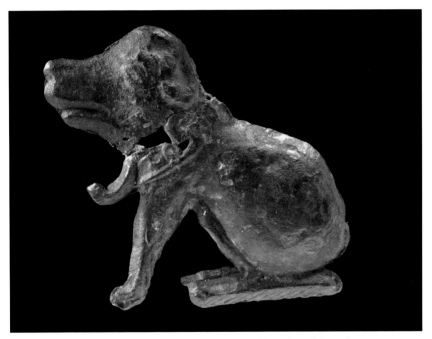

Livery badge of the Talbot family, depicting a talbot dog, fifteenth century. (© Trustees of the British Museum, London)

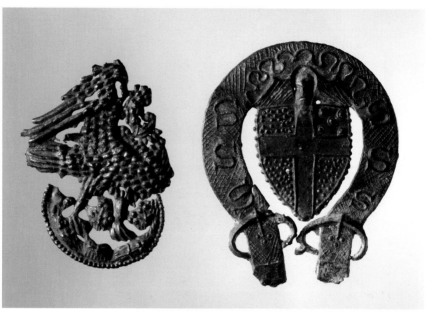

Two livery badges of the House of Lancaster, fifteenth century. The one on the left shows a swan standing in a crescent, the other, a collar surrounding the arms of Saint George. A livery badge was often used as a sign of royal favour.
(© Trustees of the British Museum, London)

Pisanello portrait medal depicting Niccolò
Piccinino in recognition of his military
services to the Duke of Milan, 1438–41.
(© Victoria and Albert Museum, London)

Pisanello portrait medal depicting Cecilia
Gonzaga, daughter of the First Marquis of
Mantua, 1447. (© Trustees of the British
Museum, London)

Medal depicting Martin Luther on the obverse (left) and the theologian scholar Philip Melanchthon on the reverse (right), sixteenth century. From the sixteenth century, medals were often used in religious struggles. (© Trustees of the British Museum, London)

One of the "Dangers Averted Medals" issued to commemorate the defeat of the
Spanish Armada in 1588. Elisabeth on the obverse and a bay tree on an island
protected by Britain on the reverse. (© The Fitzwilliam Museum, Cambridge)

Dutch medal commemorating the Four Days' Battle in 1666 and a favourable
peace concluded with the Bishop of Munster. The obverse depicts a commander
in Roman costume caressing a lion and holding a sceptre to which the shield
of Amsterdam and a laurel wreath are attached. Also on the obverse are two
rhyming sentences of a poem that continues on the reverse and praises valour.
This medal represents an attempt to communicate expectations more than most
medals do. It was awarded to members of the Amsterdam Town Guard.
(© Trustees of the British Museum, London)

Badge of the Order of Saint Louis showing obverse (left) and reverse (right).
(© Musée national de la Légion d'honneur et des ordres de chevalerie, Paris)

Prize medal for the best poem entitled "The Christian Hero," awarded in 1737. The obverse (left) depicts Archbishop John Tillotson, archbishop of Canterbury (1691–94), who was well known for his theological writings, and the reverse (right) depicts James Edward Ogelthorpe, the founder of a colony in North America for persecuted Protestants. (© Trustees of the British Museum, London)

Prize medal awarded in 1793 by the Lycée
des Arts (re-named in 1803 the Athénée de
Paris), a learned society that offered courses
and prize competitions for the public.
(© Trustees of the British Museum, London)

Medal depicting the agitator Lord
George Gordon, late eighteenth century.
The reverse (not shown) represents
Britannia with a Latin inscription.
(© Jewish Museum, London)

Badge of *chevalier* of the Legion of Honour, First Empire.
(© Musée national de la Légion d'honneur et des ordres
de chevalerie, Paris)

Badge of *commandeur* (civil) of the Order of Leopold.
(© Service des ordres, Royaume de Belgique)

French Military Medal, Third Republic.
(© Musée national de la Légion d'honneur et des
ordres de chevalerie, Paris)

Victoria Cross of Sergeant Herman James Good,
1918. (CWM 20130405-001 Tilston Memorial
Collection, © Canadian War Museum)

Badge of commanders of the Order of the British Empire,
1917–37. When worn by ladies it is attached to a ribbon
formed into a bow, as shown here. (Central Chancery of
the Orders of Knighthood © Her Majesty the Queen)

himself, his lands, vassals or subjects, and the Holy Church or the Holy See.[18] The statutes of the Order of Saint Michael made the members virtual retainers of the French king, bound to comply with the "requests, pleasures, and reasonable wishes" of the sovereign of the Order, and "in all sweetness and cordial love, to employ themselves to accomplish [his] good and honest pleasures, without prejudice to their honours and conscience."[19]

In the next chapter, I examine the concept of individualism more carefully, but I want to make an observation now. We need to be careful in what we mean when we refer to the collectivist–individualist dialectic in Medieval knighthood. Although we can, as I have just done, characterize lordship as an individualized as well as a corporate relationship, we cannot refer to the bond as individualist in the sense of individual autonomy. People entered into relationships of lordship in order to limit the autonomy of one another. Rather than a characteristic of lordship, individual autonomy was a threat to it. Thus, there was always a tension between (1) the corporate and pastoral discipline to which knights were normatively subject and (2) the (often fanciful) autonomy they felt they enjoyed by virtue of being knights. Some knights from noble families gloried in self-reliance and their individual right to defend their honour. Kristen Neuschel studied this kind of individualism among nobles in sixteenth-century France, arguing that it explains why nobles formed and broke alliances not infrequently.[20] Individualism was closely connected with the lofty ideals of chivalry. Although these ideals may have been a source of unity among knights – indeed, according to Georges Duby, among the aristocracy in general[21] – we are here talking about a kind of discipline, individualized self-discipline, that was very different from corporate or pastoral discipline, and one that much later becomes the major mode of discipline achieved by state honours.

In the Middle Ages, however, it was primarily a combination of corporate discipline (fear of a breach with their lord or loss of membership in a corporate body) and pastoral discipline (the unique, sometimes emotional, and perhaps paternalistic bond they had or pretended to have with their lord) that controlled the behaviour of knights. Just as the cohesion of Latin Christendom had little impact on the day-to-day lives of people, so the ideal knight was not the major source of inspiration for most European soldiers, who were valuable not so much for their chivalry but for their effectiveness as fighters to defend those who depended on them.

9

Discipline in Early Modern
and Modern Europe

Between the late Middle Ages and the twentieth century, the proportion of social relationships people had that were relatively non-communitarian – impersonal, specific, associational, and individualized – increased. True as this assertion is, the processes to which it refers were complicated and contentious. For an understanding of the evolution of state honours, it is crucial to recognize the continuation of communitarian relationships and corporate discipline, and to examine their interaction with the evolving individualism of Western-European society. This chapter focuses on these interactions, and the next chapter on their impact on the honours of states.

THE PERSISTENCE OF PASTORAL
AND CORPORATE DISCIPLINE

As Western-European society passed from the Middle Ages to the Early Modern period, the pastoral and corporate discipline of kinship groups endured. Indeed, kinship networks remained the most powerful networks in European society throughout the Early Modern period, even in governments, with those of the United Provinces being no exception.[1] Royal pastoral and corporate discipline in some respects actually became stronger. Church pastoral and corporate discipline also persisted in both Catholic and Protestant churches.

Medieval guilds gradually declined in power, though more slowly in some countries than in others. The French Crown tried to assume control over guilds, but succeeded only in strengthening them as part of the state institutional apparatus of industrial regulation, until the Revolution destroyed them. Meanwhile, other kinds of occupational associations emerged. In the long nineteenth century, they underwent considerable organization and reorganization, first among what are referred to in English as the "professions," and then during the nineteenth century among skilled tradesmen, and eventually among unskilled workers. These organizations were "associational," in that they were based on common interests, but as was true of guilds in the Medieval period, they often sought to create communal solidarity and enforce corporate discipline. It was the same for many of the voluntary associations discussed in Chapter 6.

Educational institutions and their pedagogy also strengthened pastoral and corporate discipline, especially during the nineteenth and early twentieth centuries. The discipline promoted by Early Modern Neo-stoicism was also pastoral and corporate insofar as it stressed the duty of obedience to others. Indeed, Gerhard Oestreich went so far as to contrast the collective obligations of Neo-stoicism with the old, regionally secured liberties that people had enjoyed in the Middle Ages.[2] In the late nineteenth century, team sport became a breeding ground for corporate discipline, and it still is today. Pastoral and corporate discipline also survived in the military, though it was significantly transformed. Finally, with the rise of territorial states have come efforts to form the populations living in these territories into large corporate-like nations, into which entry is controlled, and in which members feel a communal solidarity with one another and have specific rights and obligations.

Space does not allow me to say more about all of these, so I shall limit myself to a brief discussion of Protestantism, the voluntary societies, the military, and royal pastoral and corporate discipline in the Early Modern period.

The Reformed Religion

Among Protestant communities, the greatest attention needs to be given to the Reformed churches, and more specifically to those communities that were most influenced by Calvinism. The discipline exercised by the Medieval Church had been largely pastoral and corporate, but it was reinforced by individualized and external restricted rewards. The Reformed churches of the sixteenth century explicitly rejected this system of restricted rewards as a corruption of the true meaning of repentance and as an assumption of the power of God to dispense rewards and punishments to the faithful. Instead, they intensified pastoral and corporate discipline. They did so by taking over existing corporate groups, including institutions of local government and justice, and by turning their churches into corporate communities. The threat of excommunication was commonly used. The deviant could also be forced, or at least encouraged, to leave the community to reside elsewhere.[3] A famous case was that of Jerome Bolsec, a Carmelite turned Protestant, who was banished from Geneva in 1551 for criticizing Calvin's doctrine of predestination.[4] Where Reformed churches had the necessary authority, punishment might include the loss of certain civil rights. In Scotland, during the sixteenth and early seventeenth centuries, the offender could be barred from some offices, from giving witness in law, and from landed income.[5]

Whatever the violation, it was more likely to be sanctioned if it became public knowledge, because it then threatened the moral stature of the Church.[6] Also targeted were those who were self-seeking or acted individualistically, in neglect of their communal obligations.[7] One of the reasons for the condemnation of usury was that it was seen as detrimental to the social bonds among neighbours. The objective must be a corporate community of believers, what Calvin called a "godly commonwealth." Gorski suggests that, among Calvinists, this kind of discipline was regarded as necessary because the presence of an unrepentant sinner at the communion table could provoke God's wrath.[8] Discipline was reinforced with corporate imagery and the rhetoric of mutuality. Communal harmony and submission to the community were essential. In Calvin's own words: "God designs to make us as members of a corps."[9]

At the same time, there was a pastoral aspect to Calvinist discipline. Gorski argues that Calvinist discipline in the Low Countries was not as harsh as the formal powers of the consistory might suggest. The purpose of punishment was not just to purify the community but also to help sinners mend their ways.[10] While excommunication was repeatedly employed as a threat, the actual number carried out was not large. Considerable efforts were made by the clergy and the elders to assist parishioners in difficulty, to reform alcoholics, to rehabilitate the promiscuous, et cetera – all of which required considerable interaction and communication between pastor and delinquent. Often, in their efforts to suppress sexual immorality, pastors or elders would find themselves endeavouring to bring together married couples, reform abusive husbands, or locate missing fathers.[11]

We do not want to exaggerate discipline in the Reformed churches. It was not equally enforced in all communities across Western Europe, but most of all in those regions – southwestern France, the Netherlands, Switzerland, Scotland, and Scandinavia – that were relatively distant from the Hapsburg, French, and English centres of political and military power. In general, the rigour of disciplinary practices was less than what it was in Geneva during the mid-sixteenth century.[12] Regional variation could also be found in the types of offences that were targeted and in how they were punished. (Most notably, punishments varied between those that were relatively penitential and those that were relatively punitive.[13]) Another difference among European regions was the respective role of clergy and non-clergy in the administration of punishment, an issue that led to conflict in many communities.[14]

Voluntary Societies

From Chapter 6 we already know something about the associations that appeared in the seventeenth and eighteenth centuries that were directly or indirectly concerned with improvement and reform: the so-called patriotic, useful, and learned societies. In that period and in the nineteenth century, one can also find a variety of other types of voluntary associations, such as agricultural co-operatives, trade unions, secret or semi-secret societies, occupational associations, mutual assistance societies, institutions for the improvement of morals, and temperance societies.

Not new were secret societies. However, with the development of centralized states in the Early Modern and Modern periods, the active presence of such societies assumed an even more conspiratorial and subversive nature. French and Irish revolutionary societies in the eighteenth and nineteenth centuries, the Carbonari (of Italy, Spain, and France), Jacobite societies in the British Isles, the Communist League (and its precursors the League of Outlaws and the League of the Just), and agrarian secret societies (such as those in Ireland during the eighteenth century and the first half of the nineteenth) – all were secretive because they would otherwise have been repressed.

On the other hand, not every secret society was subversive and their members were not necessarily marginalized in their communities. Their social composition varied and not infrequently included persons of relatively high socio-economic status. In 1718, for example, a number of nobles in Brittany formed a secret society to defend provincial rights against the Crown.[15] In fact, secrecy became something of an aristocratic and bourgeois fashion in the eighteenth century. Peter Clark has suggested that many open and very public British associations made a pretense of secrecy in order to increase club solidarity and incite interest in the community about what went on behind closed doors.[16] The Good Cousins, an association with branches in a number of towns in Franche-Comté during the nineteenth century, was banned by the government. Carol Harrison has suggested that government officials could not understand the value placed on secrecy in provincial sociability and that much of the secrecy was just for fun.[17]

Many secret clubs were casual in nature, and the corporate discipline moderate, but the more radical societies enforced uncompromising discipline. They were collectivist in the extreme. Members were expected to devote themselves to the society at the expense of their own interests; they could even be required to relinquish their identity to a symbol of their membership. Relationships among members were diffuse rather than specific in the sense that, to quote nineteenth-century sociologist Georg Simmel, secret societies "demand the whole man."[18] They typically used oaths and penalties to impose conformity, generate commitment, and maintain secrecy, the ultimate penalty being, of course, exclusion or death.

The evolution of patriotic, learned, and useful societies obviously represented a growth in associational relationships. These organizations were created to serve a purpose in which members were interested – and the prizes that some offered to achieve their goals were individualized rewards. Yet in many ways, these associations relied on communitarian social relations, and they tried to control members through corporate discipline. Most were social clubs as well as instrumental bodies. Their meetings often featured considerable leisure interaction as well as the business that defined the society. They usually met in taverns or in the homes of members. Harmony and conviviality were typically stressed. Regulations of most clubs required that members treat one another amicably.

Several of these associations illustrate the point. The rules of the Aberdeen Philosophical Society stipulated that, after the presentation of a discourse, observations should be made by members "in a free but candid and friendly manner."[19] Reading societies were formed in order to make access to books easier for members, but the "conviviality" of these clubs and their meetings was equally the purpose, which was sometimes reflected in their name, as in the Lancaster Amicable Society.[20] In the early nineteenth century, one of the statutes of the Reading Society of Antwerp stated that "in the assemblies and meetings, each member promises to be motivated by the desire that there reign the genuine friendship and the honest sincerity that make the societies pleasurable."[21] Not unusual was the claim of the president of the Royal Society of Literature (founded in 1820 by George IV to promote literary achievement) that firm morals and religion were requirements for participation in this association.[22] Whether or not these goals were reached is, of course, a different question. Both the importance of amicability and the frequent failure to achieve it were reflected in the humour directed at them. In a late eighteenth-century poem written about one fictitious reading club, the author declared that its members met "to dispute, to fight, to plead, to smoke, to drink – do anything but read."[23]

There was considerable consensus in the associational culture about what association rules were appropriate. Indeed, it is evident that many newly formed clubs copied, almost word for word, the rules of other associations.[24] The organization and strength of these societies varied, however, and so did their discipline. Many had few rules and extremely weak enforcement. For others, regulation seemed to be their raison-d'être. The obligation of members to attend regularly, give presentations, not to leave meetings early, et cetera could be spelled out in great detail, and fines could be imposed on those who failed to meet them. The rules of the Aberdeen Philosophical Society levied a fine of half a crown for the failure of a member "to give his Discourse or send it in Writing at the time appointed, without a reasonable excuse."[25] The rules of late eighteenth- and early nineteenth-century societies in Antwerp included elaborate systems of fines and prohibitions. With or without fines, members who did not live up to the standards of an association would find themselves, to varying degrees, marginalized. And in almost all, if a member did not pay his fine without good reason, he was expelled.

This duality is even more apparent in societies formed, mainly in the nineteenth century, to provide mutual assistance to members in times of hardship. By 1915, there were reportedly 1,235 such societies in Ireland, 2,361 in Scotland and 26,651 in England, with a total membership in the British Isles of over five million.[26] Four and a half million men and women belonged to a French "mutual society" in 1914; it was the leading social movement in the country, well ahead of trade unions and co-operatives.[27] The usual name given to these bodies by the British – "friendly societies" – reflects this duality. Elites and government authorities encouraged them because they were seen as beneficial for the economic security they provided, but also because it was thought that they could serve to raise public morality. They were consequently subject to more government interference than most other associations. Since French governments were, in general, more active in assisting or impeding voluntary association than were British governments, control was more intensive in France than in Britain. Napoleon III was greatly in favour of them, and his government reorganized the mutual societies in France, creating a new category called the "approved societies." They enjoyed certain financial advantages, but were then subject to the administrative oversight of notables, for the most part, landowners, lawyers, physicians, and businessmen. It was their mission to make sure that the society's funds were properly managed, but, in addition, to use the society to promote morality in the working class.[28]

Efforts to raise the moral level of national populations through Early Modern and Modern associations were not unique to France. Those specifically organized for this purpose were typically led by persons with a pastoral attitude toward the working class.[29] Clark highlights the case of the Philanthropic Society founded in London in 1788, which was critical of the indiscriminate charity of other organizations and claimed to be "formed rather on principles of police than of charity." They adopted the practice of sequestering pauper children from the corrupting influence of their families.[30]

The Military

The discipline and coordination problems faced by the commanders of Early Modern armies were discussed in Chapters 6 and 7. It was evident then that some of these coordination problems resulted from a lack of discipline inherited from earlier periods. Many aristocratic soldiers saw battles as a multitude of engagements between warriors. The chivalric revival of the fifteenth and sixteenth centuries did nothing to undermine this egoistic culture. In a practice known as "pickering," English and French gentlemen fighters broke formation, rode to the front line, and fired pistols at one another.[31] For different reasons, mercenary units were also difficult to discipline, as were any soldiers more interested in the loot they could collect than in defeating the enemy.

The lack of discipline among troops was a constant complaint in the copious Early Modern literature on military subjects. One of the major objectives of Neo-stoicism and much of this military literature was to overcome this lack of discipline in armies by means of strict obedience. The general view was that the measures I discussed in Chapter 7 to achieve coordination in battle should be put into practice by means of strict discipline in army units, enabling them to work together as a corps.

At the same time, institutions that survived from previous centuries could provide a measure of pastoral and corporate discipline, especially among those who came from the same geographical area or were mobilized by a local magnate with whom they had ties of kinship or lordship. On at least one occasion, Louis XIV accepted that he could not appoint a new commander to a regiment because all its current officers were either relatives or clients of the incumbent commander.[32] Until the military reforms carried out by Louvois, Breton nobility did not serve in the king's armies but in regiments of which the owners were their former barons.[33] Members of mercenary units, while difficult for outside army commanders to discipline, exerted their own corporate discipline over one another.

Central states gradually eroded these ties of kinship and lordship, and tried to create new bonds of solidarity in regiments. J.E. Cookson has asserted that, in the British army during the late eighteenth and early nineteenth centuries, regimental dress, music, and colours became more institutionalized, the solidarity of regiments was strengthened, their reputation and history became more important to soldiers, and regiments competed with one another for favourable inspections and recognition of their performance on the battlefield.

Concurrently, the relationship between regiment commanders and those under them became, he argues, more paternalistic. Close-order warfare required that men be managed rather than bullied. The ideal, if not the reality, was now that of the brave and kind officer.[34] A similar view is taken by Myerly. Although he recognizes that some commanders cheated and bullied their men, he also suggests that in the nineteenth century, regiments were regarded as families – for some soldiers the best family they had ever known – overseen

by a colonel as a paternal figure.[35] During the same years in which
the significance of status differences between officers and men was
being eroded in France (though certainly not eliminated), British
regiments operated more like a patriarchal family. Cookson notes
the concern of some commanders with the negative effects of flogging. Yet the persistence of harsh discipline until the last half of the
nineteenth century in British armies does not undermine his argument, especially in this period when harsh discipline was the norm
in patriarchal families. Indeed, the increase in regimental solidarity and pride made harsh discipline all the more effective, an even
greater humiliation for those subjected to it, if carried out by an officer who was regarded, on the whole, as considerate of his men.

Royal Courts

The political centralization that occurred in Western Europe during
the Early Modern period initially increased pastoral and corporate
discipline at the centre. Although Norbert Elias's thesis – that inter-
personal discipline hardly existed in the twelfth century and has
evolved since then within a civilizing process – is problematic, his
argument that royal courts provided one of the groups in which
Modern discipline developed has considerable merit. Elias argued
that Early Modern monarchs and great lords sought to tame other
lords not just by monopolizing force but also by drawing the nobility into their courts and cultivating a courtly culture that was hyper-
polite. In this manner, former warlords who had fought against one
another were turned into courtiers. And their actions came under
the disciplinary control of monarchs.[36] Simultaneously, courts
became more concentrated; that is, many illustrious courts of earlier
periods, such as the Court of Burgundy, disappeared, leaving the
royal courts in London and Paris as the major centres for courtly culture. The French Court emerged as the most influential; it became a
centre of society to an extent that no court had ever been before.[37]

   The power of royal courts was both political and social. In addition to the prestige they conferred on those who came to court, they
provided (1) access to the Crown and to those in the royal household who had daily contact with the monarch, (2) a way to keep on
the monarch's good side, (3) a means of acquiring or controlling
royal patronage and largesse, and (4) a place where people went to
meet other people and to exchange information.[38]

As in the Middle Ages, during the Early Modern period banishment from a royal court was a common sanction imposed by monarchs. Mary Boleyn was banished from the court of Henry VIII at the instigation of her own family – in particular her sister, the Queen – for marrying William Stafford, the second son in a minor gentry family. The Second Earl of Essex, a year before he was executed in 1601, was banished from the Royal Court for making a truce with Tyrone, the Ulster chieftain whom he had been sent to defeat. Louis XIV, as he came under the influence of Françoise d'Aubigné (whom he made Marquise de Maintenon), required more sober dress and manners in his court; and when he moved the Court to Versailles, he banished a large number of his brother's homosexual entourage. In 1717, George Augustus, prince of Wales, was expelled from St James's by his father, King George I, who was becoming concerned about the Prince's popularity. In 1737, George Augustus himself (now King George II) expelled his son, Frederick Louis, from his court for what the King believed was outrageous behaviour.

Royal courts continued to be social and political battlefields, where rival factions contended. So we often find factions trying to get members of opposing factions dismissed from a court. Notorious was the struggle between the Whigs and Tories to have their respective female partisans, Sarah Churchill and Abigail Masham, dismissed from the Court of Queen Anne; efforts included encouraging slanderous publications that Masham had a sexual relationship with the Queen.[39]

Royal Pastoral Power

Oestreich vigorously asserted that the evolution of what he called "social discipline" was a cardinal feature of Early Modern "absolute monarchies."[40] The concept of absolute monarchies has (quite rightly) gone out of usage. More to the point, a belief in the need for greater discipline was not limited to any particular set of monarchies in Early Modern Europe. What is true is that the capacity of a state to enforce this discipline was greater in societies where populations had less power to resist it. It is also true that in these states, royal discipline was relatively pastoral and corporate. As in the Middle Ages, French kings were often portrayed as paternal figures, concerned with the welfare of the "family" they governed. According to some philosophers of the sixteenth, seventeenth, and eighteenth centuries, this paternalism was an essential characteristic of royal governance. As N.O. Keohane points out, Jean Bodin (a sixteenth-century French judge and legal author) believed that authority in the state should imitate authority in the family, and vice versa. The family was like a little state, and the state a larger family. At the same time, families were components of a larger corporate structure that Bodin called the "commonwealth."[41]

Monarchs and courtiers, especially in Early Modern France, pretended that the former knew the latter individually and was concerned with their individual wants and needs. This pretense could be expanded numerically by allowing members of the most powerful social groups and those holding positions in state institutions to claim a personal relationship with the Crown. Although not a new idea among French historians, this personalism has recently been stressed by a number of scholars, most notably J.M. Smith.[42] Smith also asserts that, through the "royal gaze," the king was supposed to know what his officials were doing, that nothing should escape his view. Since nobles and state officials craved royal attention and approval, the putative omnipresence of the king would, it was thought, encourage them to strive to serve him to the best of their abilities. For their part, state officials thought that their relationship with the king entitled them to royal favours and special consideration.

The Limitations of Pastoral and Corporate Discipline

In order to understand the Modern relationship between different types of discipline, we need to recognize some limitations on the pastoral and corporate discipline that I have just been discussing, and the reasons for these limitations. They resulted from both structural and ideational changes.

STRUCTURAL CHANGES

A major factor has been the process of social mobilization discussed in Chapter 6 and, more precisely, an increase in non-particularistic ties relative to particularistic ties. To repeat what I said then, my assertion is not that people were left adrift with no social ties. When they entered new social environments, they often preserved earlier ties that integrated their families in strong social networks;

they also established new integrative networks. People did, however, find themselves more often interacting with and being drawn into collective activities with people whom they did not know very well. In these environments, pastoral and corporate discipline was weaker. Indeed, many of the above voluntary associations were trying to compensate for this attenuation of pastoral and corporate disciplinary power.

One such shift that is important for the subject matter of this book is the gradual disappearance of particularistic methods of recruiting soldiers, including not only lordship but also kinship and other communal solidarities. We do not need to exaggerate the earlier strength of these traditional social relationships to recognize a significant decrease in man-to-man obligations in armies. This transformation was a result of political centralization as well as social mobilization, but we should note that it took place both in states with relatively powerful monarchs, like the French monarchy, and those with the weakest monarchy in Early Modern Western Europe, the Dutch *stadhouders*.

Royal pastoral and corporate discipline was also undermined by the decline in royal courts. The waning of the British Royal Court began in the late seventeenth century, much earlier than that of the French Court. Part of the problem was financial, but some contingencies also affected the outcome. First, the revolutions of the seventeenth century broke up the continuity of the Court. Second, James VII/II, William II/III, and Anne were not as inclined as Charles II had been toward Court pleasures. Third, William II/III and George I were foreigners, with not a lot of ties in the British aristocracy. Fourth, Anne suffered from a lack of social skills and poor health. And fifth, the British Royal Court became only tenuously linked to the rising elites of the eighteenth century.[43] Parliament and the London economy provided alternative centres of power. Gradually, the right to attend the Court became less and less valuable. Royal control over patronage became a major source of struggle between the Crown and political leaders in Britain through the eighteenth and nineteenth centuries, until the royal prerogative was largely eliminated in the late nineteenth century, except in the royal household.

The same was true of French royal courts in the long nineteenth century. Personal royal control over spoils during the Early Modern period was interrupted by the Revolution. It was re-established by

Napoleon, but state bounty became a source of struggle in France between politicians and the Crown during the Restoration, the July Monarchy, and the Second Empire. There was no royal centre of power during the Third Republic, when anything like a pastoral distribution of spoils ceased to exist.

The decline in the pastoral and corporate power of monarchs also resulted from growth in the number of persons it became necessary to manage. I have indicated that during the Medieval period, monarchs could try to assert the right to rule their "subjects" directly rather than via the intermediation of lesser lords. During the Early Modern period, this displacement continued to the point that, by the eighteenth century, it was largely complete. The last regional lords to be dislodged in Western Europe were the clan chiefs of the Scottish Highlands and Western Islands. Western-European monarchs also established more direct control over guilds, over most provincial institutions, and over the inhabitants of villages, towns, and cities.

The effectiveness of this royal governance varied. It was observed in Chapter 6 that, whereas during the Middle Ages, the English Crown exercised more control over its subjects in England than did the French Crown over its subjects in France, by the end of the seventeenth century, the French Crown had established direct control over its subjects in all parts of France that was greater than the control exercised by the British Crown over the British Isles. Even so, the British Crown claimed sovereignty over its "subjects" in all parts of the Isles. Members of the Gaelic population in seventeenth-century Ireland were considered subjects of the Crown, albeit recalcitrant subjects much in need of "improvement."[44]

As a result of this whole process, there evolved large territorial-state populations defined in common terms, possessed (in principle) of the same rights, subject (in principle) to the same authority, and governed (in principle) by the same rewards and punishments. This governance had a corporate element to it. Even banishment could still be found as a mode of discipline. Members of the *menu peuple* could find themselves transported to other parts of the world if convicted of a crime. The rich and famous could find themselves banished from Court or city. Enlightenment scholar Madame de Staël was expelled from Paris by Napoleon for more than ten years. The Twentieth Earl of Shrewsbury and his wife were banished from

Victoria's Court. She had left her husband and eloped with the much-younger Shrewsbury in 1882.

An exclusion of this kind, however, did not have the cost that banishment from a royal court once had. The Earl and the Countess separated in the 1890s, but continued to be accepted in many social circles, though she much less so than he.[45] In any case, it was obviously impossible to discipline great numbers of subjects by banishing them from a court, city, or country. The transportation of criminals did not last beyond the nineteenth century. Corporate discipline was not effective on this scale.

Moreover, the very concept of "subject," and the obligations associated with it, were undermined by ideological changes during the eighteenth and nineteenth centuries, and by the emergence of major republics in France and America, as well as struggles to create republics, as in Ireland. These transformations all operated to the detriment of royal pastoral and corporate power, even in countries where monarchies survived.

This decline in pastoral and corporate discipline resulting from the expansion in the number and territorial spread of royal subjects was not offset by the status that has replaced it, that is, citizenship. As a legal status, citizenship has been effectively used to regulate access to membership in territorial states and the rights that go with it, though not without conflicts. In contrast, as a mechanism of discipline, citizenship has been largely ineffective. Personal loss of citizenship is not a major mode of punishment in Modern territorial states, even for the most heinous crimes. Imprisonment certainly represents a loss of the benefits of citizenship, but not the legal status of citizenship itself. For the most part, people think of their citizenship as a source of rights and benefits, not as a source of obligations. Military conscription has been the only major obligation, but it is not borne by all citizens, and is now no longer the principal method of recruiting armies in Western-European states.

The nature of discipline in Modern armies has been dramatically affected by the increase in the size of military forces. Pastoral and corporate solidarity is difficult to maintain in large armies taken as a whole. The increase in army size has also increased their diversity – ethnically, linguistically, and in the geographical origin of soldiers. The corporate solidarity in the regiments that Cookson talks about has developed further since the Napoleonic Wars and has maintained, even strengthened, pastoral and corporate discipline at the regimental level or lower. But pastoral and corporate discipline has been much less effective on a larger scale.

IDEATIONAL CHANGE

The ideational change that undermined pastoral and corporate discipline the most was the growth of individualism. The study of individualism has suffered from a linear perspective, in which it is assumed that the Modern Western world is the most individualist society in history, and that what we need to research are the beginnings, the historical origins, the evolution, and the spread of Western individualism. In very general terms, these assumptions are not altogether mistaken, but they gloss over a complex reality. There are actually two interrelated elements in what we call individualism: (1) individualism as a value and (2) individualism as a construction of social reality. To value individualism is to believe that people have the right to a considerable measure of individual autonomy – the right to advance their self-interests, to be relatively free of ideological and political authority, to be able to pursue their personal development and self-realization, to have the right to do as they please with the property they own, et cetera.

Distinct from individualism as a value is what we can call an individualist or atomistic social construction: the perception that society is an aggregation of individuals, that individuals are distinct, that they have an inner self, and that they have the capacity for individual autonomy, whether or not they take advantage of it or are permitted to do so. Social psychologists have found that people in non-Western cultures are more likely to define themselves and to understand both their own behaviour and that of others contextually than is the case among people in Western cultures; in Western cultures, people usually explain human behaviour, particularly human failings, by reference to characteristics of the individual.[46] In Asia, notions of the self are inseparable from the notion people have of themselves as members of their family. Their self is what has been referred to as a "familial self" or "we-self," the essence of which lies in the interdependence between themselves and members of their family.[47] This can be contrasted with the idea of self that has emerged in the West, which is an individualized "I-self."

Western individualism as a value has deep historical roots. A belief in the dignity of man was present in ancient Greek and Roman cultures. Christianity has been concerned with the salvation of the individual soul. Catholicism was, on the whole, collectivist, but in Medieval writing there were many ways of thinking that were consistent with individualism. Saint Thomas Aquinas is credited with advancing the principle of individual autonomy in the moral sphere. And, as explained in the preceding chapter, Medieval chivalry was in certain respects a highly individualist ideology. Locke's promotion of the human right to life, liberty, and property was based on a central belief in the dignity of man. We associate with the Enlightenment a belief in human dignity, and individual autonomy. Individualism is usually regarded as a fundamental principle of French Revolutionary thinking, Romanticism, and liberalism.

Whether or not people were more individualist in their day-to-day behaviour during the nineteenth century than in earlier centuries, it is clear that in this era individualism as a value, and opposition to it, were more explicit than they had been in earlier centuries. Comparing the countries that are the main focus of this book, the majority of writers would agree that the most pronounced individualism emerged in Britain, followed by Belgium, and then by France. This is not to say that the French did not have their individualists, but merely that there was also intense criticism of individualism in France, where the word had a negative connotation, much more than was the case in Britain or Belgium.[48] Although a more positive attitude toward individualism emerged in France after the middle of the nineteenth century,[49] the differences among these three countries are still with us today. Survey data have revealed that, on average, the British are more individualist than the Belgians, the Belgians more individualist than the French, and all three relatively individualist by world standards.[50]

The preceding two paragraphs have been about individualism as a value. An individualist social construction is also evident in European political, religious, and philosophical thinking during the period that interests us. The Renaissance is regarded by many as a major contributor to the evolution of the Western individualist social construction. It allegedly broke with the organic conception of society. At the same time, Early Modern noble culture contained important individualist elements.[51] And Protestantism, though I have called attention to its pastoral and corporate discipline, is given credit for promoting an individualist social construction by rejecting the need for an intermediary between the individual and God.

An impressive quantity of interdisciplinary literature has developed on the historical evolution in Europe of the notion of "self."

By this is meant the belief held by many people that there exists in themselves and others an inner individuality and psychological depth, which form the basis for their individual identity.[52] On the whole, this literature suggests that, whereas individualism as a value was stronger among the British than it was among the French in the nineteenth century, this was not true of the individualist social construction.[53] Unfortunately, works on the construction of the self in Europe are based almost entirely on literary sources. So we need to be cautious in the generalizations we make. Nevertheless, in those populations where literacy rates were relatively high, the social range of self-analysis could be wide, as M.R.M Towsey has shown to be the case among readers in Scotland during the last half of the eighteenth century and the early years of the nineteenth.[54]

There is debate among scholars over when the European notion of self became a matter of great interest. Few would place it before the Renaissance, while few would insist that it did not emerge until the nineteenth century. Significant for our purposes is that (1) a noticeable interest in the inner self predated any major change in the value placed on individual autonomy and (2) it emerged in Early Modern Europe initially within corporate structures.[55]

A variety of French political philosophers in the seventeenth century were advancing an "individualist" perspective that differentiated the person from the polity and from the demands of state sovereignty.[56] For Hobbes, the individual was the basic social unit on which society was built. For natural-law theorists, the fundamental social unit was the individual, society merely an aggregate of individuals.[57] We associate with the Enlightenment the idea that, as Turgot wrote in Diderot's *Encyclopedia*, "citizens exist independently of society; they form its necessary elements; and they only enter into it in order to put themselves, with all their rights, under the protection of those very laws to which they sacrifice their liberty."[58] For Immanuel Kant, man is the subjective source of knowledge. For Johann Fichte, the world is dependent on the subjective experience of the individual. These and other German writers influenced Madame de Staël, who promoted the idea that there is an inner self not modified by one's environment. An individualist social construction also underlay utilitarianism and positivism, not to the extent that these perspectives denied the influence of society on individuals, but to the extent that they assumed that individuals were distinct entities. Romanticism was more individualist in this sense than in the sense of individual autonomy. Its contribution to the development of individualism lay especially in its interest in self-understanding, an understanding that distinguished the individual as a separate entity. Indeed, a concern with the self was a major preoccupation of French literature throughout the nineteenth century.[59]

MODERN DISCIPLINARY TECHNIQUES

As traditional pastoral and corporate discipline has weakened, two major alternative modes of discipline have evolved in Early Modern and Modern Europe: bureaucracy and individualized self-discipline. The latter is more important for our purposes. It did not displace pastoral and corporate discipline, but transformed it. First, however, a few words about bureaucracy. It reveals very clearly the fundamental contradiction of Modern disciplinary regimes.

Bureaucracy

Bureaucratic rules, norms, and procedures are now the basis for the operation of most economic and political organizations, and pervade social relationships. The entire populations of Modern territorial states are organized bureaucratically.

Bureaucratic practices are usually created intentionally on the basis of a claim to better efficiency and effectiveness. Theoretically, members of bureaucracies relate to one another in terms of the differentiated authority and duties attached to the positions they hold. Theoretically, bureaucracies consist of social relations that are relatively hierarchical and non-communitarian. And theoretically, discipline depends primarily on individualized rewards and punishments; those who are dismissed from a bureaucracy are distressed primarily by the loss of individualized rewards, and only secondarily by the loss of communitarian ties. Rewards for performance and for obeying the rules are generally relatively specific, the most important being (1) monetary rewards and (2) promotion in the clearly defined bureaucratic hierarchy.

In reality, we are talking about a continuum rather than a dichotomy. Most organizations are, to some degree at least, bureaucratic, while even the most bureaucratic structures will not be one hundred per cent bureaucratic. One reason is that the formal bureaucracy is, in some respects, dysfunctional as an organizational structure. A bureaucracy can be alienating to people who work in or have dealings with it. The strict power hierarchy, the rationalization, the clearly defined rules, and the impersonalism of bureaucracy can be emotionally destructive. Thus we often see evidence that the strict rules and sanctions by which bureaucracies operate are ignored in favour of constructing effective personal relations. Employees may deviate from the rules they are expected to follow in the pursuit of their own interests, but they may also do so in order to cope with the alienation and powerlessness they feel by virtue of the subordination of the position they hold. In his analysis of the persistence of codes of honour in nineteenth-century France, William Reddy examines how middle-level state employees responded both to their alienation and to public criticism by pursuing an honour code that was selected from the Old Regime, but was now available to all men in a free competition for reputation. Sadly for them, this response simply generated more disparagement of civil servants and ridicule of their pomposity and sense of self-importance.[60]

Closely related to this dysfunction is the view that bureaucracies suppress individualism. The assertion is often made that the control a bureaucracy exercises over individuals constitutes a major limitation on their autonomy to pursue not just their own interests but also the goals of the organization. It has been frequently argued that bureaucracies constrain individual creativity and initiative, a problem that has been a concern in a large body of literature in Europe and North America. Obviously, the perception of this contradiction is only to be expected given the concomitant evolution of individualism as a value in Western thought. It has been one of the major dialectical issues in Modern organizations and the study of these organizations. The most influential work in the twentieth century was *The Organization Man*, by W.H. Whyte, which led to a large number of commentaries and treatises in the decades following its publication in 1956. In much of this literature, there was a recognition that individuals do not allow themselves to be wholly dominated by the bureaucratic relations in which they are embedded, often adapting the rules to allow the pursuit of their own ideas of what they should be doing for the organization.

Individualized Self-Discipline

The second major mode of Modern discipline is individualized self-discipline, what we are calling individualization. A large literature has developed on the increasing predilection to hold individuals responsible for what happens to them and to place the moral onus for their behaviour on themselves. Many writers regard this disciplinary process as relatively recent, a feature of "late modernity."[61] But it is not. Individualization can be found in the Ancient Mediterranean World and even in Medieval Europe. It developed further during the Renaissance and later the Enlightenment.

These cultural movements, it must be said, were not primarily about discipline. In contrast, the Protestant movement was mostly about discipline. And whereas the contribution of Protestantism to corporate discipline moderated in later periods – depending on the Protestant denomination – the Reformed Church made a lasting contribution to individualized self-discipline, initially through its doctrine of individual predestination but primarily through its promotion of an individualist social construction. To this day, Protestantism is criticized for its emphasis on individual redemption and salvation, and for individualizing human suffering.[62]

The relationship between individualization and individualism as a value is not a simple one. In general terms, an individualist or atomistic social construction is a necessary condition for individualization, while individualism as a value is not. Nevertheless, individualism as a value can indirectly contribute to the effectiveness of individualization as a disciplinary technique. A social environment in which individualism as a value is relatively strong facilitates individualization as a disciplinary process. It creates a preference for a world in which people are free to determine their life course and accept responsibility for what happens to them, thus obscuring the means by which they are being governed.

One piece of evidence that individualized self-discipline became a significant mode of discipline during the Early Modern and Modern periods is the growth in interest in self-fashioning and self-improvement. Although this trend was not separate from more collectivist efforts by pastoral and corporate groups to get people to improve, these collectivist efforts would not have gotten very far if they had not coincided with a greater compulsion among many people to improve themselves. Calvinists were particularly likely to self-discipline by seeking to make themselves better persons in the eyes of God or to persuade themselves that they belonged to the elect. One reason for the enthusiasm for reading in the eighteenth and early nineteenth centuries is that people sought to use it for personal improvement, or for the improvement of those with whom they were close.[63] And many of those who wrote books in the eighteenth and early nineteenth centuries did so with the objective of improving the behaviour and morals of their readers.[64] As Maza points out, self-improvement was closely linked to the use of the idiom of merit by advocates for the bourgeoisie.[65]

We can distinguish between two types of individualization, which I shall call positive and negative. Positive individualization refers to the characterization of an individual as having relatively favourable qualities in a system of classification, while negative individualization refers to the attribution of negative characteristics in such a system. This distinction is similar to the distinction that Foucault drew between "ascending" and "descending" individualization, but it is not the same. His ascending individualization is the individualization of people with relatively more power or privilege, while descending individualization is the individualization of those with less power.[66]

In the literature on discipline, negative individualization receives by far the most attention, in spite of the fact that in Modern societies people are disciplined by positive individualization more than by negative individualization. The process by which these two types of individualization operate differs. Negative individualization makes people compare the normal with the pathological or inferior, while positive individualization gets them to compare the normal with the superior. And people are induced not to fear that they are abnormal but rather to fear that they are normal, that they are not exceptional. In order to achieve this, they must be confronted with the exceptional, and this exceptionalism must be celebrated.

In Early Modern literature, positive individualization can be seen in the great number and variety of stylized hagiographies of the period, of saints and other religious heroes, and of military families and military heroes. It was, however, the long nineteenth century that was the true era of the hero. We witness it in both fictional and philosophical literature. Heroes were central to the Gothic and chivalric tales of the period. Don Quixote was recast as a person to be admired. We know from Chapter 3 that some 12,000 copies of the first edition of Scott's *Ivanhoe* were sold. No less than 110,000 copies of the 1872 Chapman and Hall edition of Carlyle's *On Heroes, Hero-Worship and the Heroic in History* were printed from 1872 to

1895. The National Maritime Museum in Britain holds 163 naval biographies published between 1830 and 1914, twenty-eight of which are biographies of Nelson.[67] Hero cults were also promoted by funerals. State funerals were not numerous (in France an average of 1.8 annually during the Second Empire, and 1.1 annually during the Third Republic down to 1920[68]), but they could be spectacular and potentially touch vast numbers of people.

In his *La figure du sauveteur*, Frédéric Caille has shown that in France, during the nineteenth and early twentieth centuries, the "rescuer" was socially constructed as a particular kind of hero. In contrast with the military hero, the rescuer is a moral hero, a modest person who has performed a purely selfless deed. Carnegie was prompted to create the Carnegie Hero Fund by a case of heroism during a mine disaster in Pennsylvania. His immediate objective was to insure that people who engaged in self-sacrificing acts of heroism would not suffer financially for their acts. Carnegie hero funds were established for Great Britain in 1908 and for France in 1909, followed by the Netherlands, Belgium, Germany, Norway, Sweden, Switzerland, Denmark, and Italy. Heroism, many believed, was representative of the superiority of the society in which they lived. "We live in an heroic age," declared Carnegie.[69]

The hero is one of the prime instruments of individualized self-discipline. As Orrin Klapp suggested some years ago, heroic types serve as norms of self-judgment.[70] Heroes are not what we are but what we could be, or more stingingly, what we might have been. Whereas corporate discipline works by making a person feel a part of a group to whose standards he or she must conform, heroes tell us how we are both similar to and different from the hero. We can identify with the hero, especially with his or her life before becoming a hero, but we usually have trouble imagining ourselves engaging in the exceptional behaviour that makes the hero. Dumas's d'Artagnan (in *The Three Musketeers*) is unreflecting, in harmony with himself by means of instinctive self-knowledge – an imaginary character far removed from the experience of Dumas's readers.[71]

The nineteenth century also gave birth to the most individualizing sports phenomenon in recent history, the Modern Olympics. It is well recognized that the fundamental purpose of the games has been to honour the individual champion, to glorify the individual.[72] At the first competition in 1896, no team sports were contested. In Paris in 1900, there were more team sports, a half dozen or so, but in St Louis in 1904, there were fewer team sports, only basketball, football, and lacrosse. The founder of the Modern Olympics, Pierre de Frédy, baron de Coubertin, was influenced by Charles Darwin and Herbert Spencer. He clearly believed that sports provided a civilized version of the survival of the fittest, and that the Olympic Games would contribute to a "noble and generous outlet for those age-old instincts for battle that lie within us all."[73] George Trevor, a writer for *The New York Sun*, wrote an article just before the summer games of 1928 – an article that received considerable publicity – in which he asked: "Why not take the Olympic Games for what they really are, spirited athletic competitions ... to measure the respective merits of a few superstars?"[74]

Again, however, we see the duality of individualization, on the one hand, and pastoralism and corporatism, on the other. Both were present in Protestantism and in Neo-stoic philosophy. The latter called for pastoral obedience, but Oestreich credits Lipsius with going beyond the traditional "iron discipline" of the military by complementing obedience with self-discipline, because there is no lasting obedience without it. Lipsius's ideal citizen was one who acts according to reason, controls his emotions, and is willing to fight, but is also answerable to himself. The praiseworthy ruler, according to Lipsius, is a "superman," who sees as his principal obligation to preserve peace and tranquillity, not in conquest but at home.[75] And communitarianism is plainly reflected in the celebration of the sacrifice that a rescuer makes for his or her fellow humans. Carnegie, it is worth mentioning, stipulated that a grant for a hero should not "be continued unless it be soberly and properly used and the recipients remained respectable, well behaved members of the community."[76] Heroes may be individualized, but they are rarely free and independent.

Indeed, the emulation of heroes has often served to strengthen corporate collectives – cultural or ethnic groups, nationalities, the citizenry of a state, et cetera. The religious hagiography of the Early Modern period was generated by the solidarities of religious collectives, and the military hagiography by the solidarities promoted by centralizing states. Although Avner Ben-Amos argues that French state funerals separated the hero from his fellow citizen – often made him out to be a Christ-like martyr – he also asserts that the goal of these funerals, indeed of all French commemorations, was to develop a new and meritorious citizenry through emulation of the great man.[77] Coubertin was influenced not only by prevailing notions of individualism and the survival of the fittest but also by the evolving corporate spirit of national solidarity. His belief that nations should contest on the athletic field reflects a corporate way of thinking. So does his dream of improving the mental and physical health of the French nation through sport. Coubertin was greatly influenced by Thomas Arnold (the educational reformer and head-master of Rugby School from 1828 to 1841), who encouraged boys to form groups that imposed their own discipline. Over the course of the twentieth century, more team sports were introduced in the Olympics, and the Games themselves became a major instrument of national competition and rivalry.

Disciplinary Functions
of State Honours

It now falls to this chapter to explain the disciplinary functions that
state honours could perform in the Early Modern and Modern periods. We can begin with an examination of the corporate discipline
enforced by these honours, after which we shall turn to individualized self-discipline.

CORPORATE DISCIPLINE IN MODERN STATE HONOURS

The pastoral and corporate discipline of Modern state honours
resulted from the cultural lineages inherited from earlier periods,
but it performed important functions in the Modern period and was
more than a cultural residue.

In the Tradition of Royal Orders of Knighthood

Since many honorific orders of the nineteenth century styled themselves, in varying degrees, on Medieval orders of knighthood, there
persisted the notion of admission and membership in a community.
This community usually had a staff to serve it. The Order of the Garter had three officers when it was founded, to which two were added
in the sixteenth century. The Order of the Bath had seven officers
when it was created.[1] And the Order of Saint Patrick was equipped
with no less than thirteen: a prelate, chancellor, registrar, secretary,
genealogist, king of arms, usher, two heralds, and four pursuivants –
almost as many as the initial number of members, which consisted of
the Grand Master and fifteen knights.[2] A major purpose of all these

offices was to provide the government with patronage appointments that were distributed for political purposes but financed through fees paid by members of the Order rather than the public purse. Yet the idea that these orders were corporate bodies requiring officers helped the government to get away with it, albeit not without criticism.

It was considered appropriate to "install" members in these orders, not just "award" the honour. Regular meetings and dinners were also considered part of the tradition of an order of knighthood, though the expense of such dinners meant that they often had to be forgone. The first installation of the Order of the Bath at Westminster in 1725 was particularly festive. After the installation ceremonies at Westminster Abbey, a lavish dinner was held at the Court of Requests in Westminster Hall, followed by a ball.[3] Regular dinners to bring together members of the Bath fell into desuetude in the following decades, but were revived by William III/IV when he came to the throne in 1830.[4] Members of the military division of the Bath usually knew one another and formed something of a select club. This was even more the case for members of the Order of Saint Michael and Saint George.

Orders of knighthood with Medieval ancestry typically inherited statutes that set down offenses and punishments, while later orders that were modelled on Medieval orders frequently copied these statutes. Although there was no provision for degradation in the original statutes of the Order of Saint Michael and Saint George, a clause was subsequently introduced providing for degradation in the case of treason, cowardice, felony, or "any grave Misdemeanour derogatory to his Honour as a Knight and a Gentleman."[5] Essentially the same provision was added to the statutes of the Order of Saint Patrick in 1905.[6] The legislation that established the Dutch Military Order of William in 1815 stipulated that members would be expelled for a dishonourable conviction in a court of law; this provision was subsequently extended to include dishonourable discharge from the military.[7] In 1814, Thomas Cochrane, later tenth earl of Dundonald, was degraded from the Order of the Bath after he was convicted of involvement in a stock-market scam. Cochrane had in all likelihood been wrongly convicted, and he was eventually restored to the Bath. (The interest of certain individuals in prosecuting and degrading him was encouraged by his fierce, flamboyant, and irreverent political opposition to the Tory establishment.[8])

In 1816, Sir Charles Coote was expelled from the Bath for indecent conduct.[9] These expulsions were by command of the King, but the royal warrants justified them in characteristically corporate terms: "We ... being firmly resolved to maintain, support, and preserve the Honour and Dignity of Our Said Order ..."[10]

Anything that undermined the respect with which an order was regarded could lead to an expulsion. The illustrious were not necessarily protected. Public pressure during the Great War forced George V to command the expulsion of enemy sovereigns and princes from the Order of the Garter in 1915.[11] No such action was taken with respect to other decorations until the Royal Family gave up its German titles and became the House of Windsor in 1917. Then enemy nationals were expelled from the Royal Victorian Order. The announcement came in June of that year when Andrew Bonar Law, chancellor of the exchequer and leader of the House, stated, in answer to a question, that instructions had been given "that henceforth all alien enemies shall cease to be members of any British Order of Chivalry to which they belonged before the outbreak of the war."[12]

The corporatist spirit of royal orders of knighthood was also apparent in honours that were less manifestly in this tradition and did not have the constitutional structure of such orders. In 1910, a police official in India was expelled from the force for what was considered immoral conduct. It was decided that he should forfeit the Royal Victorian Medal that he had previously been awarded, but it was discovered that this could not be legally done because the statutes of the Order made no reference to forfeitures. So the statutes were revised.[13] When Bonar Law announced that alien enemies would cease to be members of any British order of chivalry, it was unclear even to the Royal Household whether this included recipients of the Royal Victorian Chain – and the issue remained unresolved long afterwards. In 1930, when a list was drawn up of those who had received the Chain, not only had the names of five Germans been removed but even that of Abbas Hilmi, the last khedive of Egypt, who was deposed by the British in 1914. The decision to drop the names was regarded as tentative, but they have never been restored.[14] In 1940, George VI gave orders to remove the names of all persons of German or Italian nationality from the lists of honorary members of British orders of chivalry and from the lists of foreign holders of British decorations and medals; in 1942, memberships that had been granted to citizens of Bulgaria, Finland, Hungary, Japan, Romania, and Siam were terminated.[15]

Corporate Discipline in the Legion of Honour

The greatest effort to establish corporate discipline in a large Modern state honour was made in the Legion of Honour. Napoleon had great plans for the organization of members of his order. Legionnaires were divided into seventeen territorial groups known as "cohorts." Each cohort was endowed with land taken from *biens nationaux* (property confiscated during the Revolution) to be exploited for commercial purposes, the returns to be used to finance the operations of cohorts and to enable them to pay the stipends that had been granted to members and provide hospice for those who were disabled. Napoleon wanted prestigious buildings to serve as the local centres of these cohorts, where members could routinely get together. Each cohort was administered by a council, which was to meet on the first and the fifth of each month, as well as hold an annual assembly to install new members and receive their oaths. Each cohort had a disciplinary council to hear complaints against its members.[16]

Discipline in the Legion of Honour was originally governed by a decree of 15 March 1804, which invested disciplinary power at the national level in the Grand Council of the Legion. It was to be advised by an auxiliary committee, which became known as the Committee of Consultation. When its functions were taken over by the Council of the Order, discipline was made more independent of the government.[17]

Three types of punishment were put into place: censure, suspension of rights, and loss of membership.[18] Censure was merely a caution by the grand chancellor, calling on the member to be more circumspect in the future and not to compromise the sign of honour that he wore. Suspension deprived the member of all or some of the privileges he enjoyed from membership in the Legion of Honour (the right to wear his decoration, his stipend if he received one, ceremonial precedence, et cetera), but held out the possibility of rejoining the corporation if he could overcome the error that had led to his suspension. During a suspension a member was still subject to the disciplinary regime of the Legion. The third type of punishment – expulsion – entailed a permanent loss of these rights, as well as the status and fraternity of membership in the Legion. A member was degraded by being told: "You have been lacking in honour; I declare, in the name of the Legion, that you have ceased to be a member."[19]

Once a person was a member, what was important was not exceptional conduct but meeting his or her duties in the Legion. The status of the Order was paramount from the very beginning. It was explicit in the decrees that established the Legion of Honour and has been repeatedly echoed by later legal commentators. According to one such commentator, Octave Le Vavasseur de Précourt (a legal authority for the Council of State), the founders of the Legion of Honour recognized the importance of the disciplinary provisions for maintaining its integrity. The Order's "disciplinary power," he wrote in the 1870s, "was indispensable in order to preserve the prestige" of the Order and to maintain its "purity" in the public mind against its critics.[20] At the end of Chapter 7, I quoted Léon Aucoc on the necessity of the exhibition of correct conduct by men wearing the badge of the Legion of Honour. Aucoc also believed that legionnaires who were unworthy of the honour must "be removed from the corporation whose prestige they have compromised."[21]

In 1900, Joseph Durieux, an official at the Grand Chancellery of the Legion of Honour, published his doctoral thesis on discipline in the Legion. The language of this treatise often personifies the Order, as though it were a person whose moral integrity was at stake. According to Durieux, its disciplinary regime was concerned with those transgressions that "independently of social disorder and damage to individuals … can undermine the honour of a corps."[22] Included are all those acts "that bring the corporation into disrepute."[23] Durieux likened the disciplinary regime of the Legion of Honour to that of other corps, such as the magistracy, the civil service, lawyers, notaries, and bailiffs.[24] He cited a decree of June 1813 that made bailiffs liable to disciplinary punishment by virtue not only of circumstances concerning their profession but even of those concerning their private life that are of a nature as to undermine the status they enjoy.[25] The scope of the disciplinary regime of the Legion of Honour was a contentious issue from the very early years of its history. There emerged a feeling among some of those associated with it that the disciplinary regime then existing was not sufficiently protecting its honour. Consequently, in 1816, it was decreed that special legislation would specify punishments for legionnaires who had committed acts that could not be or were not covered by penal law but undermined the honour of the Order. There was much opposition to this measure from those who believed that it would grant too much disciplinary power to the Legion and to the government.[26] The Grand Chancellor of the Legion of Honour was accused of trying to establish a "private police."[27] Consequently, no special legislation was enacted, and in the following years legionnaires were, for the most part, disciplined only for acts for which they were convicted in the judicial courts. When the statutes of the Legion of Honour were revised in the 1850s, the provision of 1816 was not reintroduced; however, a provision was inserted that authorized suspension or loss of membership in the Legion for military officers discharged for habitual misconduct or for loss of honour (*faute contre l'honneur*),[28] a measure notably similar to the stipulation for ejectment from the Dutch Military Order of William. Disciplinary action could ensue from military degradation, committal (of a soldier) to a disciplinary unit, or suspension (of a sailor) to a correctional ship.[29]

Discipline of non-military members of the Legion of Honour was broadened in a similar way by the civilian legislation of 1873.[30] Disciplinary action could ensue from dishonourable acts not covered by penal law, such as contracting debts that one had no means of repaying, abuse of confidence, false declaration of title, marriage with a prostitute, keeping a public gaming house, selling one's declaration, disciplinary punishments by other corporations, or appearing in the streets or in public places in a state of dishonesty or drunkenness. Disciplinary action could also result from bankruptcy (but not compulsory liquidation), failure to appear before a court, or any judgment in court condemning a person to ball and chain, public works, or imprisonment, as well as from acts that the penal law covered for which the guilty party had received amnesty or which could not be prosecuted because too much time had elapsed.[31] The extent of this disciplinary power was demonstrated by the expulsion from the Legion of Honour in January 1923 of Victor Margueritte as a result of his authorship of *La Garçonne*, a novel about a young woman who tried to behave like a man.

The Council of the Order did not hesitate to interpret its mandate broadly and was free to arrive at a judgment different from that of the courts.[32] As Aucoc noted, whereas over the course of the nineteenth century the general trend in France was toward the moderation of penalties and toward greater guarantees for those accused of committing crimes, the disciplinary regime of the Legion of Honour moved in the opposite direction: disciplinary justice was broadened and strengthened.[33] It was also extended beyond the Legion to apply to the Military Medal, military commemorative medals, and colonial orders. It was not extended to other decorations, such as the Order of Agricultural Merit, but in some cases, this was because these bodies had their own disciplinary regulations and practices. In addition, since 1834, the set of forfeitures prescribed by "civic degradation" in the penal code has included loss of the right to wear any decoration.[34]

The Legion of Honour possessed a considerable *esprit de corps*, which was galvanized in the 1870s after its headquarters (known as the Palace of the Legion of Honour or Hôtel Salm) was damaged by fire. To raise money for repairs, the Chancellor launched a subscription among legionnaires and holders of the Military Medal that enjoyed appreciable success.[35] Another manifestation of this *esprit de corps* has been the Mutual Aid Society of Members of the Legion of Honour, which was established in 1921 to assist less fortunate legionnaires and, as stated in its statutes, to "re-establish the original cohesion of the members of the Order."[36] In the same period, a subscription was launched to raise money for a museum, though it was successfully inaugurated only with the assistance of several American philanthropists.

The Limitations of Corporate Discipline in Honorific Orders

How general and effective were corporate practices in honorific orders? We should note first that the right of members of orders of knighthood to judge one another was long gone. This privilege of members of the Golden Fleece did not even survive the transfer of the Order to Philip's successor, Charles the Bold.[37] The Irish, Scottish, and English houses of lords, and eventually the British House of Lords, still had jurisdiction over peers and peeresses who were charged with treason, felony, or misprision of treason or felony. In 1856, the British House of Lords had been able to have this competence reaffirmed in the Criminal Justice Act of that year. Yet there was a growing tendency in the eighteenth and nineteenth centuries for the peers to act on the advice of the "law lords," that is, those members of the House who were appointed to serve its prerogative as the highest court of appeal. Gradually, royal justices, whose jurisdiction Medieval peers had sought to evade by means of trial by peers, had become the actual triers of peers.[38]

Not many people were thrown out of honorific orders. Rules for degradation were often copied from other orders without much thought given to them; as a consequence, they were usually rather abstract and vague on the procedures by which forfeitures were to be carried out.[39] The only forfeitures of the Dutch Order of the Oak Crown have been several Frenchmen and one Dutchman.[40] Among the thousands of persons awarded the Order of the British Empire from 1917 to 2012, not many more than a hundred have forfeited it. There have been but eight forfeitures of the Victoria Cross, the last one in 1908. George V had very firm views on the subject. "The King feels so strongly," wrote his private secretary in July 1920, "that, no matter the crime committed by anyone on whom the VC has been conferred, the decoration should not be forfeited. Even were a holder of the VC to be sentenced to be hanged for murder, he should be allowed to wear the VC on the scaffold."[41] Since the Great War, awards for gallantry in Britain have been regarded as irrevocable.

The cohorts organized when the Legion of Honour was founded were short-lived. Abolished in 1809, they became simply a way of classifying legionnaires territorially and not really corporate structures. Several reasons can be given for their demise: (1) the prolongation of the Napoleonic War and the vast increase in the number of members of the Legion of Honour meant that the landed endowments were insufficient to meet the obligations imposed on the cohorts; (2) whether as a result of the War or for other reasons, the local cohort administrations – if there really was a local organization to speak of – were generally ineffective; and (3) under the Empire, the social basis of the Napoleonic regime expanded beyond the military represented in the Legion of Honour.[42] In more general terms, the efforts to promote corporatism in the Legion were rendered extremely difficult as a result of the sheer size of its membership.

In this historical period, it became increasingly evident that Modern orders could no longer claim anything like the corporatism of Medieval orders of knighthood. Even in the seventeenth century, the Order of Saint Louis had marked a significant change in monarchical orders; it lacked the corporatist characteristics of other Early Modern monarchical orders.[43] The personal contacts found in the military division of the Order of the Bath and among members of the Order of Saint Michael and Saint George were unusual for most state honours in the nineteenth and twentieth centuries. The Mutual Aid Society of Members of the Legion of Honour was not typical of state honours. Nor can Modern orders pretend to the lofty ideals of their Medieval predecessors. This was a source of romantic regret for many Europeans, to whose views Abraham Kuyper (Calvinist theologian and prime minister of the Netherlands from 1901 to 1905) sought to appeal. "Only a shadow of what were once the Knights of Saint John and the Knights Templar do we find in today's orders of knighthood," he wrote in 1879. "The ideal of co-operation and union, the social element, is gone."[44]

STATE HONOURS AND INDIVIDUALIZED DISCIPLINE

Individualism as a value has had no direct effect on the discourse of orders and decorations. Neither selfishness nor doing what one pleased with one's property was ever listed as a reason for awarding a person a state honour. On the other hand, individualism as the individualist construction of social reality has provided the basis for individualized self-discipline. It is the foundation on which the disciplinary function of Modern honours rests.

Individualized Self-Discipline

Individualization is about the power that honours exert by persuading individuals – whether or not they have received an honour, whether or not they aspire to an honour – to engage in self-discipline. As already stated, in order for positive individualization to do its disciplinary work, people must be confronted with the exceptional. Insofar as Modern European state honours do this, what is essential is not that recipients fulfill their obligations as members of groups and meet the standards set by groups, but that they demonstrate their singularity and excel beyond group standards, and that they are recognized and admired for doing so.

This orientation is well illustrated in a memorandum sent to enterprises by the selection committee for the award of the first medals to workers and artisans in Belgium in 1847:

The government intends to bestow on artisans and workers who distinguish themselves by extraordinary ability and by irreproachable conduct recompenses of a special order ... As a result we are now requesting that you inform us if, among the workers you employ, there are some whose superiority has contributed in a special manner to giving your products the excellence that distinguishes them. We know that all the workers of a factory work toward the preparation of the products that they provide for consumption, and that consequently each, to the extent of his abilities, furnishes his part in the entire work; but, there are or could be some elite men who, in their speciality, have a very particular merit, and it is these men alone that we want to learn the names; and furthermore, we are requesting their names only if these workers or artisans lead an exemplary life. You understand that a decoration can only have value for those who obtain it, and especially for the mass of workers, on the manifest condition that it is only accorded with justice and restraint. Only in this way will it become an object of noble emulation and contribute to the moralization of the people. You will thus advance the execution of an enlightened philanthropic work, at the foundation of a great and solid institution, by exercising extreme reserve in your submissions. It is better for you and for society to reply in the negative than to yield to the desire to obtain recompenses for the workers in your establishment, if none seem to you to combine the unequivocal qualifications for an high distinction; but also you will deny justice in not signalling out the men who could serve as a model for workers in the circle in which they live.[45]

The difficulties that individualization of this kind could generate are illustrated by an unsuccessful effort in Britain during the Great War. It began in 1915 as an attempt to provide a reward for workers in factories, primarily munitions factories, whose contribution to the war effort, it was felt, was not receiving sufficient notice. The original idea was to give a medal to all munitions workers, but this was abandoned as impractical; instead, it was decided to award it to one in every hundred workers, with recipients chosen by employers. The latter were encouraged to consult with the workers. The preliminary notice of August 1917 stated that the Medal of the Order of the British Empire would "be awarded for services of special merit rendered to the Empire by men and women in manual and other work done for the war. Such service will include acts of great courage, self-sacrifice or of high example; of initiative or perseverance, of skill, resource or invention."[46] A circular letter of October 1917 asked employers to submit names. The distribution encountered difficulty, as evidenced by the following responses:[47]

> Practically impossible to select a certain number for special recommendation without doing an injustice and causing heart-burnings.

> That this meeting of Shop Stewards deprecates the selection of individual men for distinction where all have done their best.

> Our workmen have passed a resolution to the effect that they do not desire to participate in the awards, the reason given being that the men feel that such a distinction would be invidious.

> We are of the opinion that as all have done their best as the opportunity has been given them and ability allowed, we collectively are not able to nominate any particular persons for the honour in question, and to make a distinction as the degree of merit as to the services rendered would only result in bad feeling and jealousy, which does not now exist.

This reaction may well have had political and ideological motives. Nevertheless, it clearly reflected an opposition between the individualization of rewards and collective solidarities in British society. There ensued yet another change in the nature of the medal, but in a way that made it even more individualizing. It became a medal for civilian gallantry; a list of 376 people recognized for "acts of great courage or self-sacrifice" was promulgated in January 1918.[48]

Contradictions resulting from the collective–individualist interaction can also be found in the early history of the Victoria Cross. Initially, it was intended to be an order, known as "the Military Order of Victoria," but Albert, the prince consort, was opposed to this, insisting that it should be a decoration; with the support of the Queen, his will prevailed.[49] Naturally, when conceived as an order, provision was made for the expulsion of members who disgraced it. Yet when it became a decoration, the idea of expulsion was not discarded; indeed, it was amplified. Originally, expulsion would have been occasioned only by desertion or by conviction for a serious offence before a court martial, but this reference to court martial was removed, so that recipients of the Victoria Cross remained vulnerable to expulsion even after they had left the services.[50] The fifteenth provision of the Warrant of 1856 stated:

> In order to make such additional provision as shall effectually preserve pure this most honourable distinction, it is ordained that if any person on whom such distinction shall be conferred, be convicted of Treason, Cowardice, Felony, or of any infamous Crime, or if he be accused of any such offence and doth not after a reasonable time surrender himself to be tried for the same, his name shall forthwith be erased from the Registry of Individuals upon whom the said Decoration shall have been conferred by an especial Warrant under Our Royal Sign Manual, and the pension conferred under Rule Fourteen shall cease and determine from the date of such Warrant.[51]

Under this provision, the Victoria Cross was forfeited during the last half of the nineteenth century for such crimes as bigamy, theft of a cow, and theft of ten bushels of oats.[52]

This corporate discipline differed from the thinking that had framed the introduction of the Victoria Cross. Its creation was justified in the Warrant on the grounds that recognition for individual gallantry was, until then, insufficient for the lower ranks, who were rewarded only "for long service or meritorious conduct, rather than for bravery in Action or distinction before the enemy." When a medal for a particular action or campaign is distributed or a clasp is added to a medal for some special engagement "all share equally in the boon and those who by their valour have particularly signalized themselves remain undistinguished from their comrades."[53] The Victoria Cross was conceived, the Warrant declared, "for the purpose of attaining an end so desirable as that of rewarding individual instances of merit and valour." The sole criterion for the award was to be "conspicuous bravery."[54]

In 1895, T.E. Toomey, a former colour-sergeant 1st Battalion 18th "Royal Irish" Regiment, published a compilation of men who had been awarded the Victoria Cross, with brief accounts of the actions that justified the commendation. In 1904, Philip Aveling Wilkins published a more complete digest of the stories of the 520 men who had received the Cross as of June of that year. Both men drew heavily on the official announcement of awards in the *The London Gazette*, despatches from the front lines, and information received from officers and men. In these two books we can see how recipients of the Cross were individualized for a reading public.

Toomey and Wilkins, and the writers on whom they drew, were torn between a desire to exceptionalize the recipients of the Cross and an unwillingness to deprecate the contribution of men who did not receive the honour. Not always were recipients of the Victoria Cross described as extraordinary among their comrades. For example, according to Wilkins, Lieutenant Joseph Crowe was "merely the first" of his Highland Regiment to storm a redoubt held by the enemy during the Indian Mutiny when all "the gallant Highlanders dashed forward, each man trying to be 'first in.'"[55] Toomey made a point of the fact that Lord William Beresford was the thirteenth winner of the Cross in his regiment and that "no other single regiment in the Service has gained so many."[56] The bravery of Farrier-Major W.J. Hardham was referred to as "typical of the devotion shown by Englishmen to one another in times of peril, and is one of many instances that occurred during the Boer War."[57]

More often, however, those who received the Victoria Cross were said to have uniquely distinguished themselves, or were one of two or three who had done so. During the siege of Delhi in June 1857, Private John McGovern "was a 'marked man' for his bravery."[58] Referring to the seizure of despatches sent by the Emperor of Russia to an island in the Baltic Sea in August 1854 for which Lieutenant John Bythesea received the Victoria Cross, Toomey asserted that "there is hardly another case – in the many acts of bravery for which the Queen's Cross has been awarded – to compare with this."[59] Those who received the Victoria Cross were frequently said to have served as an "example" to their men or to have rallied them and provided leadership.[60] During the Indian Mutiny, Sergeant Cornelius Coghlan "cheered and encouraged a party which showed signs of hesitation."[61] During the 1863 Umbeyla Expedition in India, Lieutenant Henry Pitcher led a charge "in advance of his men, his conduct being the admiration of all present."[62] In the Zulu War, the defence of a post would not have occurred "had it not been for the fine example and excellent behaviour" of Lieutenants John Chard and Gonville Bromhead.[63] In the Boer War, Captain Matthew Meiklejohn's "conspicuous bravery and fearless example" earned him the Victoria Cross.[64] The success of an engagement in Nigeria in 1903 is credited to the "personal example and skilful leadership" of Lieutenant Wallace Wright.[65] Often, indeed very often, those who received the Victoria Cross had volunteered for a dangerous mission. In addition to "brave," or some synonym thereof, the most commonly employed word, as consistent with the Warrant, was "conspicuous."

Men could be commended for doing their "duty," or they could be praised for exceeding it. This difference may reflect divisions in opinion among the military throughout Western Europe at this time. According to M.J. Crook, the old view was that an effective army required restraining and that military decorations were problematic because they encouraged recklessness. He believes that those who created awards for bravery during the nineteenth century rejected this view. They wanted to reward men for exceeding their duty. In fact, strictly speaking, a man could not receive the Victoria Cross if he was merely performing his duty; and during the Crimean War, Lieutenant William Hewitt received the Cross for ignoring a command to retreat.[66]

This policy was affirmed by Edward Lugard, a senior military official in the War Office, in a letter he wrote in 1861 that transmitted the determination of the Secretary of State with respect to one Captain Dartnell, who had received a Victoria Cross recommendation for his role in storming the Taku Forts in China in 1860. "If Captain Dartnell," wrote Lugard, "simply discharged his duty on the occasion in question, however gallantly he may have done so, it appears to the Secretary of State that his claim to this high distinction is not established. An act of duty, bravely performed should not, in the Secretary of State's Opinion, be held of itself as a sufficient qualification for the Victoria Cross."[67]

Admittedly, it proved impossible to adhere strictly to this principle, and so efforts were made to alter the Warrant to cover men who have displayed "marked gallantry in the performance of their duty," but these efforts were unsuccessful, partly owing to Victoria's unwillingness to alter the original Warrant. Although the Warrant of 1881 was often interpreted as authorizing the Victoria Cross for gallant acts performed in the line of duty, this practice was declining in the face of an increasing determination to reward pre-eminent action.

This trend – toward rewarding the exceptional as opposed to doing one's duty – cannot be explained by the changing nature of war. Hotheaded heroism is not especially adaptive in Modern warfare. On the contrary, as we have seen, the transformation in European warfare during the Early Modern and Modern periods undermined the value of the autonomous warrior. Then why, asks William Goode, is it now rewarded more? As he suggests, it is not because military leaders want to encourage extraordinarily gallant acts by the daring few, but rather because they want to instill bravery in each and every soldier so that he will stand firm in the face of the most terrifying threat.[68] While pastoral and corporate discipline is instilled in military units for this purpose – and in the present discussion, we should not lose sight of this – individualizing self-discipline has also become an essential part of the means of Modern warfare. The ordinary soldier is not expected to imitate recipients of the Victoria Cross. He is expected to admire them, to compare himself with them, to judge himself by reference to them, to evaluate his own behaviour in terms of their behaviour. Although it was initially conceived as an order, the Victoria Cross eventually became one of the most individualizing state honours in Western Europe.

THE COLLECTIVIST–INDIVIDUALIST DIALECTIC

The nature of the disciplinary dialectic is also evident in the evolution of noble status from familial to individualized possession, and in the rarity of honorific awards for collectives.

Individualized Possession

The evolution that occurred in the possession of state-recognized noble status should not be seen as black and white. Medieval honours were not all familial. The members of Medieval orders of knighthood were individuals, and with some exceptions, membership did not pass from one family generation to another. The British status of "peer" was also limited to a single individual. True, it was familial in that it was inherited by an offspring, and all members of a peer's family enjoyed prestige and title by virtue of his status. The same was true of the British status of baronet. Yet this familialism was still very different from the familialism found in the earlier nobilities in the British Isles and in Continental countries under the Old Regime, where all members of a family and all descendants in the male line usually enjoyed noble status.

Higher-status members of this Continental nobility had titles, but members of the large lesser nobility were untitled. In contrast, a title was all that Napoleon's Imperial nobles had, and only one individual held it. Although it was hereditary if a *majorat* was created, only the title was inherited, not noble status. And it descended to only one person, not to all members of a family.[69]

After the fall of the First Empire, the French nobility became more collectivist as a result of the restoration of the pre-Revolutionary nobility. It is true that the Imperial nobility remained simply a body of individual titleholders, and that, for some time, it was possible for commoners to be made barons without being first ennobled. However, in 1824, an ordinance decreed that only nobles or persons ennobled would be awarded a hereditary title.[70] The same was true of the French peerages created during the Restoration period: they were individual, but peers had to be members of the nobility.

The legal status of the existing nobility was not affected by the July Revolution, but it did become more individualist again because noble status was no longer conferred, only titles.[71] After the nobility was abolished under the Second Republic, a decree under the Second Empire revived noble titles, but not nobility.[72] Since the beginning of the Third Republic, neither has been awarded.

One of the few exceptions to individualist state honours in Europe has been the Belgian nobility, where four types of ennoblement are granted: (1) noble status *à titre personnel*, (2) a title *à titre personnel*, (2) noble status *héréditaire*, and (4) a title *héréditaire*. All other state honours in Belgium and France are granted to individuals for life. Indeed, almost all the state honours founded in the Early Modern and Modern periods that we have been discussing in this book have been non-inheritable. Today, even British peerages are awarded for life.

The transition that I have just described is usually depicted as one in which birth has been displaced as the principal criterion of state honours. Honours are now awarded for merit, for political reasons, or for reasons of status. Thus it no longer makes sense that they should be inherited. Fair enough, but I want to remind readers of the argument made in Chapter 3 that merit was far from irrelevant in the Middle Ages and the Early Modern period. Then, however, it could be based not only on one's personal achievements but also on the achievements, service, loyalty, et cetera of one's ancestral family. What has happened in the past several centuries is that merit has been individualized as a criterion for state honours. It is no longer considered appropriate to receive or hold a state honour because one's ancestral family did great things.

Awards to Collectives

There is a long history in Western Europe of distributing honorific rewards to collectives as well as individuals. From the seventeenth through the twentieth centuries, battle honours have been awarded to regiments that had engaged in a particular battle, and campaign medals to those who had participated in a specific campaign. In some cases, a regiment might be recognized as having acted exceptionally. In 1918, the Belgian government established the Fourragère Medal to be awarded to particular regiments, battalions, or other units that had engaged in an *action d'éclat* during the Great War.[73]

The French Revolutionaries, despite the individualism in their ideology (and also despite the opposition to state honours among many of them), recognized the contributions of regiments and also of towns, the first being Lille, which received a "well merited" mention by the *patrie* in 1792.[74] Napoleon honoured regiments in a number of ways, as did his brother, Louis Bonaparte, king of Holland. In one well-known case, Louis commanded that the Third Dutch Hussar Regiment wear the letter *L* in place of their regiment number in recognition of their distinguished service in Spain.[75] Napoleon granted the Legion of Honour to large numbers of soldiers simultaneously, but every recipient became an individual member of the Legion. When he returned from Elba, however, he bestowed the Legion of Honour on three towns – Chalon-sur-Saône, Tournus, and Saint-Jean-de-Losne – to convey, as stated in the Imperial decree of May 1815, his "satisfaction" with the "conduct they demonstrated during the Campaign of 1814."[76]

No collective awards of the Legion of Honour were made under the Restoration and the July Monarchy, not even to regiments, though the latter were honoured in other ways. Napoleon III awarded the Legion of Honour to several regiments for service in Italy and Mexico. He also authorized the town of Roanne to add the insignia of the Legion to its coat of arms in recognition of its contribution to the Bonapartist cause in 1814.[77] In Belgium, several towns and communes that had contributed to the success of the Revolution of 1830 were awarded "flags of honour" in 1831.[78] The Third Republic awarded the Legion of Honour to seven towns for their role in the Franco-Prussian War. Four other towns were similarly decorated before the Great War, and no less than twenty-five for their role in this war.[79] Several schools have also been awarded the Legion of Honour, as well as a few other organizations, such as the Red Cross and the French national railway.

Not too much should be made of all this. The number of collective recipients represented a small percentage of the total membership of the Legion of Honour, and awards of this kind have been discontinued since 1962. In the Kingdom of the Netherlands, though a unit that distinguished itself could have its standard decorated with the insignia of the Military Order of William, until the Second World War only three such awards were made, in 1849, 1877, and 1930 – all for actions in Indonesia.[80] In the United Kingdom, the number of collective awards was smaller still. The award of the George Cross to the people of Malta in 1942 (in recognition of their resistance to Axis efforts to seize the island) and to the Royal Ulster Constabulary in 1999 are regarded as exceptional.

On the other hand, and in contradiction to its individualization of recipients, there have been some collective awards of the Victoria Cross. Clause 13 of the Warrant of 1856 stipulated as follows:

It is ordained that in the event of a gallant and daring act having been performed by a Squadron Ship's Company a detached body of Seamen and Marines not under fifty in number or by a Brigade Regiment Troop or Company in which the Admiral General or other Officer Commanding Such Forces may deem that all are equally brave and distinguished and that no special selection can be made of them, Then [*sic*] in such case the Admiral General or Other Officer Commanding may direct that for any such body of Seamen and Marines or for every Troop or Company of Soldiers one Officer shall be selected by the Officers engaged for the Decoration; and in like manner one Petty Officer or Non-commissioned Officer shall be selected by the Petty Officers and Non-Commissioned Officers engaged; and two Seamen or Private Soldiers or Marines shall be selected by the Seamen or Private Soldiers or Marines engaged respectively for the Decoration; and the names of those selected shall be transmitted by the Senior Officer in Command of the Naval Force Brigade Regiment Troop or Company to the Admiral or General Officer Commanding who shall in due manner confer the Decoration as if the acts were done under his own eye.[81]

The idea that members of a unit should decide collectively who received an honour is corporatist, but the insistence that only one person receive it, even though an entire unit had been meritorious, is individualizing. Yet it was not individualizing enough in the mindset of those who administered the Victoria Cross. Only forty-six awards by ballot have been made; only seventeen of them since the Indian Mutiny of 1857.[82] Thereafter, the authorities were not favourably disposed toward selection by ballot. One reason was that, once Clause 13 had been invoked and the election carried out, it became difficult to consider claims for individual merit in the engagement. Such a restriction was at odds with the discourse I have just discussed that led to the founding of the Victoria Cross and with its operating principles that recognized the right of individuals to extra distinction.[83] Later, it was suggested that whenever the Victoria Cross was awarded by ballot, the battery should be granted a badge or that an emblem of the Cross be added to its colours or be worn by the staff sergeants and sergeants. But these suggestions were rejected on the grounds that the Victoria Cross was an individual decoration.[84] Similarly, a proposal in 1920 that the new warrant of that year should contain a stipulation that men who participated in a ballot should have a notice to that effect in their records came to nought, though such notices were in fact placed in files by the Admiralty.[85]

Issues of this kind reveal the operation of the dialectic between the individual and the collective in the distribution of Modern honours. When all is considered, the significance of the collective in Modern honours is not represented by the number of awards going to towns, military regiments, or other collectives. Rather, it is the interaction that we have just seen between the valorization of collectives versus that of individuals. Another example of this dialectic involving the Victoria Cross ensued from an ambush of the Q Battery, Royal Horse Artillery, at Korn Spruit in South Africa during March 1900. Subsequently, four men were collectively awarded the Victoria Cross under the terms of Clause 13, but Field Marshal Lord Roberts recommended three additional Crosses to other men who took part in the engagement. Since these men were members of a different unit, the additional awards should not have posed a problem under Clause 13, but they were rejected because the collective award had already been decided upon and because the affair at Korn Spruit, taken as a whole, was not something the Army could boast about. Thus, the collective prevailed in this instance, or at least would have if the sister of one of the unsuccessful nominees, Lieutenant Francis Aylmer Maxwell, had not written a letter to a woman who was in a position to have it seen by the Queen. From the Queen's private secretary came a communication that stressed the particular merits of Maxwell and his family:

> The Queen is greatly interested in the family of Maxwell's splendid record of six sons in the Army and five fighting at the front. Miss Maxwell's letter was read to Her Majesty who is much struck at the fact that one brother Frank has been twice recommended for the VC and HM cannot help thinking that if this really is the case his claim to the coveted honour is a strong one. Of course Her Majesty does not wish to issue any special orders on the subject but if the Commander in Chief was subsequently able to recommend this officer for the VC she would gladly approve.[86]

Helped by the fact that Lord Roberts was commander-in-chief by this time, Maxwell received his Cross, but the other two who had been recommended did not.[87]

The Struggle over Individualism

Individualism as a value came under enormous criticism in the nineteenth century. Its fault-finders argued that one person's freedom was often at the expense of another person's welfare, and that, in a wholly individualist society, the powerful would take advantage of the less powerful, man would exploit man, cutthroat competition would turn everyone against one another, workers would become increasingly alienated, conflict would ensue, et cetera – views held in both England and France.[88] Many observers saw European politicians and writers in the nineteenth century as divided into two opposed factions: the individualists on the one side, the collectivists on the other.

   Yet, in many ways, it was impossible in the nineteenth century for the collectivists to deny many of the arguments of the individualists and vice versa. Some years ago, Harold Perkin went so far as to argue that in Britain, the nineteenth-century debate between individualists and collectivists was mostly a false one. British collectivists wanted to protect individual freedom against abuse by other individuals. They shared with individualists a common value of individual

freedom so long as it did not impair that of others. Most individualists, for their part, did not believe that individuals had the right to
pursue their self-interest without limits at the expense of others.[89]
In their writings, if not in their personal behaviour, individualists
found it hard to make selfishness a virtue. In March 1873, Herbert
Spencer – an individualist if there ever was one – wrote a letter to
economist J.E. Cairnes in which he indicated that for him laissez-
faire does not mean unbridled self-interest, but rather forcing people to accept responsibility for their actions:

> I do not think that laissez-faire is to be regarded simply as a polit-
> ico-economical principle only, but as a much wider principle –
> the principle of letting all citizens take the benefits and evils of
> their own acts: not only such as are consequent on their indus-
> trial conduct, but such as are consequent upon their conduct in
> general. And while laissez-faire, as I understand it, forbids the
> stepping between these private acts and their consequences, it is
> quite consistent with the doctrine that a government should, far
> more effectively and minutely than at present, save such individ-
> ual [sic] from suffering evils or claiming benefits due to the acts
> of others.[90]

By the nineteenth century, most collectivists as well as individualists in Western Europe accepted the individualist social construction. Collectivism as a value – the view that an individual should
serve the interests of a collective – often coexisted with an individualist social construction. Thus, members of orders, secret societies,
or other kinds of associations that required them to sacrifice their
own interests for the corporate group could still have thought in
terms of individuals as distinct entities. And social movements or
states can recognize individuals as distinct entities, while at the same
time demand that they make sacrifices for the proletariat, for a religious denomination, or for the nation.

Many of the Romantics were both individualists and organicists,
particularly the German Romantics, but the English Romantics as
well, such as Coleridge and Shelley. Romantic nationalism and liberalism combined an individualist social construction with support for
national struggles, in which the liberty of the individual was equated
with the liberty of the nation. This interaction between nationalism and individualism was particularly manifest in Belgium, where

bourgeois audiences enjoyed applauding scenes in plays in which the word "liberty" was heard and where – allegedly – the 1830 revolt against Dutch rule was sparked by the singing of a patriotic and revolutionary song in Daniel Auber's *La Muette de Portici*. On the other side of the ideological divide, the Catholic revival in France in the late nineteenth century sought individuality – through trial and suffering – in the service of a corporate body and in a collective identity.[91]

The world is not divided into individualist societies and collectivist societies. All societies have elements of both in their cultures, and all people have elements of both in their minds. Humans are ambivalent and torn between the two, at conscious and unconscious levels. Moreover, the self is not holistic or fixed; it has inner contradictions and can shift slowly or at times dramatically. Even in Medieval Europe, in addition to the evidence of individualism reported in the preceding chapter, we find evidence of a notion of interiority, notable in the works of Bernard of Clairvaux, Peter Abelard, and Aelred of Rievaulx.[92]

We should not carry this line of thinking to the point of denying the difference between collectivist and individualist orientations. A belief in an inner individuality naturally clashed with the generalized view in Medieval Europe and many other parts of the world that personal identity was based on similarity with others – with members of the same community, kinship group, ethnicity, religion, et cetera. Yet, as I have tried to make clear, I think it is a mistake to suppose that Medieval collectivism in Europe was simply displaced in Early Modern and Modern Europe by individualism and the individualist construction of social reality. Their combination was not so much a synthesis or compromise as interactive.

In Service of a Larger Collective

So, if collectivism was not displaced and there was a dialectic between individualism and collectivism in both the Middle Ages and later periods, what changed? The answer is: the nature of the dialectic. I suggest that it changed for two reasons. First, though an individualist construction of society was by no means absent in Medieval Europe, this way of thinking became more consciously articulated in Western Europe during the Early Modern and Modern periods. Second, the nature of the collectives with which individualism interacts has altered. For state honours, the collective whose welfare a hero is most often praised for serving has become the "nation" to which he or she belongs. I explained in Chapter 7 that honours have been used to legitimate nations, but no more than they have been used to legitimate other state forms. The greater significance of nations and national sentiments is that they have provided a major reference group for individualization.

Nations are very different from other collectives in which disciplinary regimes operate. They require and foster a very different dialectic. Unlike the many smaller corporate groups we have discussed in this and the preceding chapters, large states require more than exclusion and punishment to get people to make personal sacrifices in its interests. To repeat, loss of citizenship has not been a major disciplinary technique in Modern states. Nevertheless, citizenship has come to play a critical role in the operation of individualized self-discipline in these states. As Bruce Curtis has argued, we cannot take as natural the collectives in which discipline is organized. Collective citizenry is not a natural given. It is constructed.[93] The individualized internal discipline that state honours promote has contributed both to this construction and to the management of the large populations organized in this construction. Men and women are honoured with decorations for serving their nation in a great variety of ways, but most obviously for contributing to their nation's interest in foreign competition. The celebration of those who advance and protect the interests of national populations in military struggles has evolved from earlier celebrations of those who fight in a variety of contexts. In the twentieth century, disciplinary pressures have been put on many people to perform in an international context, most obviously on athletes to win international tournaments and Olympic medals.

It needs to be made clear that the historical evolution of nations, and the large body of (contentious) literature on this subject, are not our concern here. Our concern is with discipline in large collectives, whatever their exact nature and historical origins. Moreover, being a social construction in more than one language, the collective that I have been discussing has been designated by a number of terms in addition to "nation." Those seeking to mobilize workers in Britain employed both "nation" and "people" as the collective.[94] Sometimes the word "citizenry" or "national citizenry" is used to represent the collective. As noted in Chapter 7, during the

French Revolution, the sacred collective was the "*patrie*" as well as the "nation." In the legislation establishing the Legion of Honour, members were required to swear that they would devote themselves to the "Republic,"[95] but it was given the motto: *Honneur et Patrie.* The collective welfare of the "*pays*" was often invoked in France and Belgium during the nineteenth century. In the Third, Fourth, and Fifth Republics, the construction that has resounded in nationalist literature, in public documents, and in political discourse is the "Republic." Thus, members of the Legion of Honour still swear that they will devote themselves to the "Republic."[96]

This dialectic can be further illustrated by Caille's analysis of the imagery of the rescuer as it evolved in nineteenth-century France. Much stress was placed on the individualist nature of the act of risking one's life to save another. It was not seen as the result of collective pressure nor as a consequence of the efforts of an individual to meet a standard of the social groups to which she or he belonged. Rather, it was seen as a sudden individual decision to rescue, in most cases, one person. In the voluminous literature that praised rescuers and recounted their bravery, a contrast was often drawn between the behaviour of the individual rescuer and the bravery of soldiers, policemen, and firemen. People often explained the sacrifice of the latter, but not the former, by reference to collective pressures, norms of performance, et cetera. Nevertheless, as Caille shows, great efforts were made to collectivize the social construction of rescuing and the benefits the rescuer provided. The rescuer became a symbol of the Third Republic and the willingness of French men and women to make sacrifices for fellow members of this collective. Similarly, members of the many associations formed to assist and celebrate the rescuer believed that they were contributing to the construction of a coherent and universalized civic for the nation, far beyond their small association.[97]

The interaction between individualism and collectivism is especially evident in the bestowal of honours on rescuers. But all decorations awarded during the Third Republic were based on an underlying belief that singling out individuals for celebration not only motivated people to engage in the kind of behaviour that was being celebrated but also had a beneficial effect on the moral integrity and health of the "Republic."

Yet underlying it all was the contradiction inherent in the collectivist–individualist interaction. No small number of people rejected the idea that individualized rewards and service to a collective were compatible. Inevitably, there were those who regarded honours as mostly the stuff of vanities, and believed that there is nothing virtuous in acts for which people become entitled to an honorific reward. Camille Mélinand claimed, in an article on "Sanction" in *La Grande Encyclopédie,* that rewards and punishments suppress morality because they lead people to act "with the reward in mind or out of fear of punishment"; in contrast, virtue correlates with unselfishness – "the more unselfishness, the more virtue."[98] In fact, theoretically, individualized internal rewards should make individualized external rewards unnecessary, even counterproductive. The individual should be motivated to serve the collective without the flattery of an award. Only the rescuer, many believed, escapes the hypocrisy of honorific awards because she or he acts instinctively without any thought of reward.

Status Structures and Status Power

We now turn to the relationship of state honours to status structures and status struggles in Early Modern and Modern Western Europe. The underlying argument is that status is driven by power struggles. Although cultural forces have shaped many of the structures and changes in structures that we shall discuss, status struggles have their own dynamic and often lead to consequences to which the cultural has to adapt.

By way of reminder, there are two types of status power: (1) the possession of an effective claim to esteem, as Weber defined it, and (2) "status-distribution power." In all societies, people struggle over both. Most obviously, they engage in these struggles because they want prestige for themselves, their kinsmen, and their friends. Pursuits of this kind can be advanced not only by according status directly to oneself or one's fellows but also by developing institutions, values, and norms that lead to higher status for those social groups or categories in the population to which one belongs. People can also use status and status-distribution power to undermine the political or economic power of others. And people seek status-distribution power because they want status distributed according to their tastes, standards, beliefs, values, and preferences.

When people struggle over status-distribution power and the entitlements of status, they utilize whatever resources are available to them. Relatively more powerful individuals or groups, possessing more resources of any kind, are generally more successful in these struggles than are less powerful individuals or groups. Nevertheless, the latter often resist the former's ascendancy, try to undermine or evade it, and/or seek to change the rules of status distribution. Economic power can play a major role in the appropriation of status power, but in the distribution of state honours it does so only indirectly and to a limited extent. Indeed, for many people that is the advantage of state honours: they can be utilized by those groups that have more political than economic power.

A theoretically based analysis of status has not been a major concern of sociologists. The respect or disrespect in which certain groups are held – racial minorities, women, celebrities, the elderly, et cetera – has received attention, but these social categories are rarely studied using the conceptual and theoretical tools that have been developed for understanding status.[1]

Marxists have generally regarded status as an epiphenomenon of class. Weber provided the foundation for the conceptualization of status that is used by most sociologists who focus on it. Yet he unwittingly contributed to its neglect by implying that status is of decreasing significance in market societies compared to less commercialized societies. This view has encouraged the notion in sociology that status is no longer important to study.

Admittedly, the neglect of status is surprising given Bourdieu's interest in it. As noted in the Introduction, part of the difficulty is that Bourdieu and his followers do not use the term "status" much, at least not in the Weberian sense. Instead, they employ two concepts that refer to other things as well. The first is "symbolic power," which includes two types of power that really should be distinguished: (1) status in the sense of a claim to social esteem and (2) legitimation. The second concept is "cultural capital," which includes cultural knowledge and skills but also the status one enjoys by virtue of possessing cultural assets, such as credentials from a prestigious educational institution, the ability to speak a language in a manner that is deemed correct, and the possession of high-status cultural objects.

Bourdieu and his followers are primarily interested in the effect that status inequality has in generating and maintaining other kinds of inequality, primarily economic inequality. They are not alone. Even those sociologists who explicitly research and write about status do so primarily in order to understand other kinds of inequality. Cecilia Ridgeway, who certainly recognizes status as an independent force and believes that status processes should be analysed in their own right, nevertheless felt compelled in her 2013 presidential address to the American Sociological Association to make a plea for the study of status by calling attention to its role in generating and maintaining other kinds of inequality.[2]

My position is that status inequality is indeed interdependent with other kinds of inequality, but that status differences in themselves are enormously important to people. In fact, their interest in their economic well-being is often as much about status as it is about basic material welfare. For people to have higher (or lower) status than others with whom they interact, in their employment and social circles, gives them influence (or makes them victims of influence), enjoyment (or torment), and daily pleasures (or displeasures). Their status position can entangle them in jealousies, ego battles, and other vulgarities of status competition that seriously affect how they behave and how they can (or cannot) co-operate with those with whom they work and live. This status competition sometimes involves awards and prizes, but, whether or not it does, status awards and prizes enable us to see very clearly the operation of status dynamics and the consequences they can have.

11

Honours and Existing Status Structures

THE STATE INSTITUTIONALIZATION
OF SUPERIOR STATUS

A major process that has occurred in Europe over the past 600 years has been the greater institutionalization of status by the state. It has not been a linear process; it has not institutionalized all statuses; and it certainly has not institutionalized them all in the same way. Nonetheless, the lives of people today are shaped, to a considerable degree, by how the state has institutionalized different statuses. State border control, citizenship and residency statuses, civil rights, penal incarceration, mass education, credentialism, electoral laws – all these are ways in which states now institutionalize status.

Our interest is specifically in the institutionalization of what we can call "superior status," that is, the evolution of stable norms and values that (1) designate some people as better, more qualified, or more worthy in some way; (2) specify their rights and obligations; and (3) prescribe how one should interact with them. Organizational hierarchies, promotion in these hierarchies, status symbols, and status awards have institutionalized superior status in nongovernmental and governmental organizations. In addition, governments institutionalize superior status in the recognition they give to professional statuses and credentials, and in their distribution of state honours.

The state institutionalization of aristocratic status in Western Europe has been discussed on several occasions in earlier chapters. It is useful to summarize the process here. It increased slowly from the late Medieval period until the end of the Early Modern period, after which it was gradually replaced by the state honours that are the subject of this book, though vestiges of state-recognized aristocratic statuses have survived to this day. Understanding this earlier way in which Western-European states institutionalized superior status is essential for understanding the dynamics of the overall process.

The Middle Ages and the Early Modern Period[1]

In the Middle Ages, superior status was institutionalized less by the state than by the norms and values of local communities, by royal law, and by local customary law, which decided who was a noble and who was a commoner, who was a lord and who was a vassal, who was a freeman and who was a serf, and what the rights and duties were of each. The concept of nobility could be imprecise, more so in some periods of time or regions than in others. Indeed, noble status was defined differently from one region to another. Even when and where it became a legal status, it was impossible to enforce owing to the fragmentation of political power. Noble status was often acquired by prescription. And there were many disputes over who was and who was not a noble. Rules governing coats of arms were recognized, but little strict control was exercised over which status groups were permitted to have coats of arms.

In the eleventh and twelfth centuries, words that we translate as knight were employed to refer to heavy-cavalry men, but beginning in the twelfth century – probably in the later twelfth century – the status of knight was adopted by members of the nobility in many localities as a claim to distinction, one that passed from generation to generation in a ritual known in English as "dubbing." From the early thirteenth century, the status of knight became increasingly restricted to those who enjoyed noble status, resulting in a decline over time in the number of those who could claim it.[2] The status slowly became honorific.

In the late Middle Ages and in the Early Modern period, centralized states progressively institutionalized this status. They gradually acquired a monopoly over the dubbing of knights.[3] In Britain, the title of knight became reserved for higher grades in royal orders and for the relatively prestigious title of knight bachelor. In France, in contrast, the status of *chevalier* was used to refer to the lowest grade in the Order of Saint Louis, a designation that was adopted for other orders as well, including the Legion of Honour and the Order of Leopold.

The Continent and the British Isles also went in different directions in the regulation of aristocratic status. Although heraldry became more institutionalized in the British Isles during the late Middle Ages and the Early Modern period, the institutionalization of aristocratic status was much greater on the Continent, where governments legislated on noble privilege and even tried, though not altogether successfully, to certify who was and who was not a noble. The French government created commissions – known as *recherches* or *reformations* – to examine noble credentials. The first of such commissions were empowered in the fifteenth century. They were ordered on numerous occasions in the sixteenth century, were quite common in the seventeenth, and then almost disappeared in the eighteenth. The "proofs" they expected noble families to produce were exacting and the proportion of families whose legitimacy was rejected was as high as 30 or 40 per cent in some districts.[4]

This Early Modern institutionalization of aristocratic status in Continental countries was in unison with a program to regulate noble privilege. Governments sought to improve their fiscal position by expanding their control over noble status and limiting the number of persons who could claim noble tax exemptions. This meant trying to control noble membership. In addition, Continental governments sought to regulate titles, duelling, heraldry, court etiquette, and ceremony. Ennobling offices and royal grants of nobility also increased the state institutionalization of noble status.

In the Spanish/Austrian Low Countries there were no noble *recherches*, nor as many ennobling offices as in France. On the other hand, comprehensive statutes to regulate aristocratic status were enacted by the Habsburgs in 1595, 1616, and 1754. And an effort was made to codify and modify customary law in order to standardize the rules for superior status. The general evolution was toward a situation where, in order to be accepted as a noble, it was considered necessary to have official accreditation, even if it was not altogether uniform, consistent, or free from corruption.

In the British Isles, the Medieval nobility did not get the kind of recognition that it did on the Continent and became less and less institutionalized, to the point that by the Early Modern period, the term "noble" was more often reserved for lords of parliament. At the same time, a lesser nobility, usually referred to as the "landed gentry," gradually took shape as a status group. It was institutionalized not by the state but rather by communal recognition and cooptation based primarily on landed wealth, a prestigious genealogy, and possession of a coat of arms. Coats of arms were subject to a greater measure of control by state institutions in the British Isles, especially in Scotland, than they were in Continental countries, but, as in the Middle Ages, they did not demarcate who was and who was not a member of the landed gentry. What did become institutionalized by the state was a titled aristocracy of knights, peers, and, from the early seventeenth century, baronets.

The Modern Period

The long nineteenth century began in France and the Low Countries with a massive de-institutionalization of superior status on the part of the state. In June 1790, the nobility, noble titles, and coats of arms were abolished in France; and in July, French royal orders of knighthood met the same fate. These proscriptions were extended to the Southern Netherlands in 1795.[5] In the Northern Netherlands, what legal status the nobility had enjoyed was brought to an end along with the abolition of orders of knighthood.

Still, the pre-Revolutionary institutionalization of superior status in Continental countries had long-term consequences. By formally abolishing the nobility and other distinctions of rank that had existed under the Old Regime, the French Revolutionaries acknowledged the legal basis on which these statuses had rested, thus validating the supposition that those status distinctions authorized by the state are the most authentic. This made possible the legal alterations that were made to the status of nobles in the Low Countries when the Kingdom of the Netherlands was put together after the Napoleonic Wars and when the Kingdom of Belgium was formed in 1830. It also led to the significant alterations to the status of French nobles with every regime change in France over the course of the nineteenth century.

It is an irony of the aristocratic experience in Early Modern and Modern Europe that the status of the landed gentry in Britain was better protected against anti-aristocratic aggression than was the status of the Continental nobility because it had no legal status that could be abolished. The titled aristocracy in the British Isles did have legal status and, therefore, could have been legally abolished. In fact, the status of Scottish peers was legally altered by the union of the Scottish and British parliaments in 1707, and the status of Irish peers by the union of the Irish and British parliaments in 1801. In the past several decades, the House of Lords has been significantly altered and is now a very different institution than it once was. However, for the periods in which we are interested, the British House of Lords constituted a politically powerful faction, whose elimination would have given rise to a political crisis that no government would have taken on. Only Ireland had the sort of revolution that was needed to overthrow this kind of status. Otherwise, in the British Isles, the legally recognized superior statuses continued to be legally recognized, while the landed gentry – which constituted the great majority of those with aristocratic pretensions – persisted as a status group without much legal recognition. This stability contrasted markedly with the vicissitudes of superior statuses in Continental countries during the nineteenth century.

The greater institutionalization of superior status on the Continent during the Early Modern period had an effect on other honours as well. For one thing, it contributed to the earlier expansion of state honours on the Continent. Of course, there were other reasons for this difference between the British Isles and the Continent, reasons that earlier chapters in this book have sought to illuminate. But the institutional reasons should not be ignored. The Legion of Honour and the Imperial nobility were regarded as all the more necessary by the Napoleonic administration because the members of institutionalized superior statuses of the Old Regime – its honorific orders and the nobility – still believed themselves to be legitimate holders of these statuses. The restoration of the old nobility and Old-Regime honours when the Bourbons returned to power after the fall of Napoleon was intended to serve a similar purpose – this time to prevent the Napoleonic institutionalization of superior status from limiting the control of the new regime over superior status. They would have preferred to abolish the Legion of Honour altogether, but, as was later the case under the Third Republic, the number of members was simply too large for them to dare doing so. So the Bourbons renamed it an "order" and instituted other changes that they hoped would mean it would no longer be seen as "Napoleon's legion." I provide a few more details about this in the next chapter.

Similarly, the transformation of state honours in the Low Countries after the defeat of Napoleon – the establishment of new honours in the United Kingdom of the Netherlands, the partial restoration of the old nobility in this kingdom at the same time, official recognition of this restoration in the Kingdom of Belgium, and the founding of the Order of Leopold – were all clearly driven, at least in part, by the need to replace or incorporate older state-institutionalized statuses in order to make state honours dependent on the new regimes.

In contrast, in the British Isles, just as there was no numerically large state-institutionalized nobility, there was also no numerically large Early Modern state honour – like the Order of Saint Louis – that might have led new governments to institutionalize superior statuses differently from the ways in which they were already institutionalized. Furthermore, of course, the fact that no radical regime change took place in Britain meant that there were no pressing political reasons for increasing state control over superior status, other than the impulsion to gratify supporters of one faction or another with honours.

An additional long-term consequence of the greater institutionalization of superior status on the Continent during the Early Modern period brings us back to an observation made in Chapter 7. I indicated there that the distribution of honours was more bureaucratized in France than in Britain, and I ventured that this was a result not only of the greater bureaucratization of the French state in general during the eighteenth and early nineteenth centuries but also of what Silberman calls an organizationally oriented bureaucracy. Yet the greater bureaucratization of the distribution of honours in France was also a consequence of the history of status institutionalization in France. Bureaucratic procedures had already been introduced in France for the verification of noble status and for appointments to the Order of Saint Louis and the Order of Military Merit. Although the Revolution disrupted the continuity of this institutionalization, it was not long before it was re-established. During the nineteenth century, nominations to the Legion of Honour produced large dossiers profiling applicants, outlining their wonders, providing testimonials to support claims made in the nominations, and leaving historians with a plenitude of archival data. A large jurisprudence also came into being, which specified not just rules for the moral conduct of members of the honorific orders (the discipline we discussed in Chapter 10) but also rules relating to the wearing of decorations, ceremonial precedence, relations with the honours of other countries, false claims to a decoration, foreign decorations, and stipends. No small measure of corruption and negligence could be found in this administration, of course. Usually, however, the effect of scandals has been an increase in rules and procedures, and a greater concern on the part of state bureaucrats that everything be done by the book. Not surprisingly, the cost of this administration has been considerable.[6]

While the bureaucratization of status distribution may have been greater in France than in most other European countries, the reality was that, whenever and wherever state honours have expanded – even in Britain – a bureaucracy of some kind has emerged to manage them. Personnel are required to establish the nomenclature of awards and grades, to design and coordinate the manufacture of badges, to arrange the nomination and selection of recipients, to announce these selections, and to organize their presentation. Everywhere, the practices of the status distributors could come under scrutiny and criticism. Indeed, the lower level of institutionalization in the United Kingdom seems to have led to more such questions about how things were being done, often requiring government ministers to take time to deal with them.

As a result of the pervasive institutionalization of the distribution of marks of superior status in Modern society, state and non-state institutions have committees and staffs, procedures for nomination and adjudication, ceremonies and symbolic tokens, and all the other institutional requirements of a world of status awards. As Ihl has asserted, the effect of this institutionalization has been to objectify merit, to establish official criteria – in the language of Bourdieu and his followers, to legitimate certain standards of judgment – of what is meritorious. This does not mean, however, that we now have a greater consensus in society as a whole on what is meritorious. On the contrary, the great variety of status awards in the public and private sectors testifies to a lack of such a consensus, and further contributes to it.

CONSTRAINTS IMPOSED BY
EXISTING STATUS STRUCTURES

Some general remarks on the nature of status interactions will place the following discussion in a larger intellectual framework. Status in the sense of esteem or prestige is inexpansible; its distribution is zero-sum.[7] Whereas the total wealth of a social group can be increased, if the status of one person in a group is raised, that of someone else in the group is lowered. Thus, every time a state honour is granted, the status of others around the recipient is altered. If low-status people are given status awards that place them above or even equal to a person whose status has been high within an existing status structure, then the existing status structure is disrupted, potentially causing insult, uncertainty, resentment, embarrassment, decline in morale, et cetera. Even the status of a recipient can be negatively affected by a state honour: receiving an honour that would be considered below one's rank in society can lower one's status. When the numbers are small, these kinds of disruptions do not cause much notice. They appear only in personal, and often private, indignation; letters of complaint; and attacks on the character of those who are getting honours. When the numbers are large, however, the effect can be dramatic. Every new distinction that is created has the potential – or is seen by contemporaries to have the potential – to disrupt the existing distribution of status.

Thus, those with status-distribution power frequently face a difficult choice: they often want to raise the status of some people without lowering that of others. Their reluctance to do the latter could be due to their belief in the value of the existing structure of status. Almost invariably, however, their reluctance also arises from a sensitivity to the conflicts and discontent that can be caused by disturbing the existing structure of status.

Constraints Imposed by the Existing Structure of State Honours

Status structures are often threatened by "status inflation," that is, by an increase in the number of persons possessing a status of some kind – a university degree, a high-status occupation, or the possession of a certain article of consumption – resulting in an alteration in the relative status power of those who have the status.

This status process is nowhere more evident than in the "inflation of honours" that occurs when the numbers receiving one or more decorations dramatically increases. Well known to historians is the inflation of honours in Britain in the late sixteenth and early seventeenth centuries.[8]

Many regarded the expansion of honours during the eighteenth and nineteenth centuries as a debasement of the honours system. This was more true in the United Kingdom than on the Continent, even though honours expanded much more in the latter than in the former until the twentieth century. In several earlier chapters, I specifically called attention to the aristocratic critique of the proliferation of honours in England in the late nineteenth century. Similar disgust had, of course, been felt among French aristocrats during and after the French Revolution, but at that time, the inflation of honours was the least of their problems. When the Bourbons were restored to power, efforts were made to put matters right. Now, the shoe was on the other foot. It was members of the Legion of Honour who complained, most of them indignant over the revival of the Order of Saint Louis, the Order of Saint Michael, and the Order of the Holy Spirit.[9]

The creation of a new honour, whether or not it reduced the value of existing honours, could beget status turbulence. Even Napoleon caused members of his precious Legion of Honour grief when he established the Order of Reunion in 1811. In February 1812, the grand chancellor of the Legion of Honour, Etienne de Laville, count of Lacépède, expressed this disquiet to the Emperor in the first of several letters:

My lord, Your Imperial and Royal Majesty deigned to speak to me yesterday morning about the new order that you have just established. It is my duty to have the honour to inform you of the effect this creation has already produced, relative to the Legion in public opinion and particularly in the opinion of several members of the Legion. They fear that the establishment of a new order diminishes the benevolence with which Your Majesty has until now honoured his Legion of Honour ... The Legion of Honour consists of five grades and there are only three decorations. It is the only order that does not have a decoration for each grade. The *grand officiers* and the *commandants* have the same decoration as the *officiers* ... The new Order of the Reunion has only three grades and three decorations. As a result the *commandeurs* of the Reunion are equated not only with the *officiers* and the *commandants* of the Legion but also with the *grand officiers*, who do not have any other decoration than that of the *officiers* and the *commandants*, and the grade of *grand officier*, so coveted until now, will necessarily lose its value.[10]

It was no fun having to face discontents and disputes over state honours. One of the many whose job it was to do so was Frederick Ponsonby, the son of Queen Victoria's private secretary. Recall from Chapter 2 that he wanted to broaden the social range of state recognition, in particular through establishment of the Order of the British Empire. Easier said than done. The difficulties did not emanate from members of the British population with economic and political power. The difficulties were created by the structure of British state honours itself.

First was the reaction of many people who already held a British decoration, and who saw the Order of the British Empire as undermining the prestige of British decorations, a subject I mentioned in Chapter 1. Previously, the commonly held view in Britain was that Continental honours were less respected than British honours because they were distributed more freely. Now, the British government was about to do the same thing.

Second, there arose a problem of precedence, not unlike the one that affected the Legion of Honour a little over a hundred years earlier. The issue was the ranking of different grades of the Order of the British Empire relative to the grades of other orders. Those in the highest grade of the new honorific order would naturally have precedence over those in the second grade of other orders, including the prestigious Order of the Bath. In the discussions that led up to the creation of the Order of the British Empire, it was first suggested that no knighthood would be attached to membership because many potential recipients were, for ideological reasons or otherwise, opposed to receiving a title. However, this would mean that there would be people in the first grade of the Order of the British Empire who were not knights but who would have precedence over those in the second grade of other orders who were knights – an unacceptable situation to the latter.

It needs to be stressed that the trouble did not arise because Ponsonby had internalized the British status structure as part of what

Bourdieu and his followers would call his "habitus." The attitude toward honours of his father, Henry Ponsonby, while positive, was not lacking in cynicism, a feeling that was even greater in the world view of Mary Ponsonby, Frederick's mother. In any event, Frederick shared his parents' somewhat irreverent attitudes toward royal and aristocratic pomp.[11] In the case at hand, he thought the issues being raised about precedence were absurd. Yet the existing status structure of British honours had to be taken into account when a new honour was created. In a letter of October 1916, he complained about the "hideous problems of precedence which seemed to me quite inane."[12] Douglas Dawson, secretary of the Central Chancery of the Orders of Knighthood, was aware of the same reality. In his opinion, "any attempt to place Members of the Order of the British Empire, without Knighthood, in the same precedence as that accorded to those of other Orders would cause an outcry." The indignation would come "not only from Knights Commanders of other Orders, but from the whole community of Knights Bachelors." The result would be "endless confusion in assigning precedence at Functions, and give rise to bickering and annoyance."[13]

In the end, it was decided to confer knighthood with the first two grades of the Order of the British Empire, and to create a second honorific order, originally called the National Service Order, but later the Order of the Companions of Honour, which would carry neither knighthood nor precedence. It could be awarded to those who did not want a title.

What we can see here is that the status power of persons already holding the title of knight prevented those who were administering the Order of the British Empire from disrupting the existing structure of status. This occurred without their taking any concrete action. The fear that altering their position in the status hierarchy would create conflicts and embarrassments was enough to constrain the behaviour of those, like Ponsonby and Dawson, who were engaged in distributing status awards.

Not infrequently, status troubles arose because the sort of care that Ponsonby and Dawson took was absent. An example is the failure of the statutes of the Order of Merit to specify ceremonial precedence. The King (Edward VII) indicated that members of the Order were personally not entitled to precedence. The Order itself would have a precedence, which it was eventually agreed would be after the Order of the Bath but before the Order of the Star of India. The precedence of individual members at ceremonies and social events, however, was another matter, and was left open to different interpretations. Confusion reigned, along with arrogance and acrimony. On 3 May 1914, the ever-so-sensitive musical composer Edward Elgar explained to a friend why he did not dine at the Royal Academy of Arts: "I went in, found they had *omitted* my O.M. & put me with a crowd of nobodies in the lowest place of all – the bottom table – I see no reason why I should *endure* insults."[14]

Constraints Imposed by Other Status Structures

Early Modern orders of knighthood were largely restricted to aristocrats. To restate a point made in an earlier chapter, one of the reasons rulers created these orders was to help them deal with the political and military power of the aristocracy. Yet aristocrats were favoured also because rulers were operating in an existing status structure. Selection of a commoner for membership in a French royal order of knighthood would have created embarrassment and dissatisfaction, felt especially by nobles who were being overlooked. It was something that rulers were prepared to accept only if there was some good reason for it. And, in such cases, monarchs usually elevated the commoner to aristocratic status before or at the same time as his admission into the order. In the British Isles, the same consideration was afforded to titled aristocrats and members of their families, and to higher-status members of the landed gentry. Even elevation to a British peerage favoured members of the extended families of peers. Some years ago, John Cannon demonstrated that the great majority of persons awarded a peerage in the eighteenth century were connected to a peerage family.[15] Those who were not related to the peerage were almost always large landowners.

Similarly, it was generally believed that state honours granted to military men in the Early Modern period should conform to military ranks. Almost all the prestigious Early Modern military honours were restricted to officers. Some war medals of the seventeenth century were awarded to common soldiers as well as to officers, but the military orders established throughout Europe in the seventeenth and eighteenth centuries, including the Order of Saint Louis, the Order of Maria Theresa, and the (French) Order of Merit, were restricted to officers. British titles were awarded to military personnel according to their military status; that is, there was a correspondence between the status of the title (duke, et cetera) and military rank.

This does not mean that conformity to existing status structures was contentedly accepted. I will say more about this in the next chapter but would like to share one example now. In October 1798, when news arrived in England of Horatio Nelson's victory on the Nile – in which the French Mediterranean fleet was destroyed without the loss of a British ship – the government was immediately faced with the question of what honour should be granted to Nelson in recognition of this enormous achievement. The King believed that, given Nelson's social position, he should receive a good pension, but not a peerage. It was also pointed out that Nelson was not the commander-in-chief of the Mediterranean fleet; John Jervis held that position, and he had been made an earl in reward for the British success at the Battle of St Vincent in February 1797. Under these circumstances, the government decided that a barony was the best they could do for Nelson.

The decision was denounced in many quarters. "The argument that he commanded only a Detachment was absurd," declared General George Walpole in the House of Commons. "It was the same as to say, that in the distinction of reward, more attention should be paid to rank than to merit," to which the prime minister, Pitt the Younger, replied: "Attention to the difference of rank in the distribution of Honours was not absurd … not a question for the consideration of the House … reserved entirely for the determination of the Crown … In no instance within his recollection where the merits of achievement were equal, had an inferior Officer been distinguished by the same honour as an Officer of higher rank."[16]

Throughout the nineteenth century, and to the present day, honours distributors have had to tread carefully in the context of these and other status hierarchies in European society. Although there were countless cases of inconsistency, incompetence, carelessness, and favouritism, most distributing authorities were cautious in order to avoid anything that would invite criticism.[17] Many well-meaning suggestions or recommendations had to be rejected for fear of what was euphemistically called "social confusion." In the 1890s, in Groningen, the director of an institution for the deaf was appointed a knight in the Order of Orange-Nassau. Emma, widow of William III and regent to the young Queen Wilhelmina, had the bright idea that the medical officer of the same institution, who was also a local councillor, be appointed a knight in the Order of the Dutch Lion or an officer in the Order of Orange-Nassau, both of which were higher in status than a knight in the Order of Orange-Nassau. The minister of the interior, Johannes Tak van Poortvliet, pointed out that an appointment for the medical officer that was higher than what had been given to the director of the institution would not be seemly. As a consequence, the medical officer was given the same grade as the director, knight in the Order of Orange-Nassau.[18]

As the number of rewards and recipients increased, they became more differentiated so that they conformed to existing hierarchies. Traditionally, monarchical orders of knighthood – in contrast with religious orders of knighthood – had only one grade. Different grades were introduced for monarchical orders in France in the late sixteenth century when Henry III founded the Order of the Holy Spirit and included separate clerical and serving classes.[19] However, it was not until the Order of Saint Louis was founded in the late seventeenth century that we see a status hierarchy of members of the kind that has since characterized most orders.[20] Stratification by grade has enabled status distributors to be more "egalitarian" by permitting a broad range of people to be recognized. Yet, it has also facilitated conformity to the existing social hierarchy by permitting the assignment of people to different grades depending on their social position. These practices were sometimes justified on the grounds that higher honours should go to those whose position carried a higher level of responsibility. We can allow some truth to this claim, but it is clear that the status of the prospective recipient was a more general factor than the responsibility of their position. Countless examples can be given of persons who received higher grades because their status in society was high, even though they did not bear a heavier responsibility in whatever it was that they did. Higher grades were invariably given to members of European royal and princely families as well as members of British peerage families.

1 2

Status Struggles

It often seemed that no matter how hard honours distributors tried to avoid ruffling feathers, it was impossible for them to escape criticism for one reason or another. Indeed, depending on the circumstances, conformity to existing status structures could itself generate acrimony and opposition. Just as the increasing autonomy of cultural fields has led to struggles over what is the "best" art or literature, the evolution of "merit" as the supreme criteriŏn of worth has led to struggles in Modern Europe over what is most meritorious. The reality is that status, as a form of power, is not fixed. Nor are status structures. They should not be imagined as buildings, which are stable and into which humans fit. They are instead structures of power relations, consisting of human interaction, which frequently becomes contentious. Different actors, sectors, and organizations vie with one another to promote their criteria of worth and merit. In these contests, status awards constitute one of many weapons. Even within the state officialdom, diverging forces pull at one another in power struggles over the distribution of status awards. It is to these struggles – internal and external to the state – that we now turn.

STATUS COMPETITION

The increase in status competition in Modern societies has led – indeed, has often forced – individuals and groups to use status awards in this competition. Implicitly or explicitly, many of the awards or prizes offered by scientific societies or other kinds of associations in the eighteenth and nineteenth centuries were designed to raise the status of some group or activity – science or a particular branch of science, medicine or a particular branch of medicine, and so forth. Governments, politicians, and other state officials could, for one reason or another, do the same in order to raise the status of a certain vocation, sphere of government, or social group.

Since one reason for the creation of the Legion of Honour was Napoleon's wish to shape the status hierarchy of French society so that it would not align mainly with wealth, he used the Legion to raise the status of those who served the state, particularly the military.[1] In the legislative debates over the project, Lucien Bonaparte (Napoleon's more revolutionary brother) insisted that those who had been awarded with their Arms of Honour were lost in the crowd and their achievements not recognized. A new state honour was necessary that would give them the visibility they deserved.[2] During the July Monarchy, many prominent politicians tried to use the Legion of Honour to raise the status of the "middle class" relative to the old aristocracy. During the Third Republic, the person mainly responsible for the French *médailles de travail* was Édouard Lockroy, minister of commerce and industry. He had strong trade-union sympathies; he and some of his colleagues wanted to raise the status of workers and incorporate them into French society as equal citizens.[3] Others in the Third Republic wanted to raise the status of schoolteachers, whom they regarded as critical to their cause. In 1892, the Minister of Public Instruction decried the lack of nominations of schoolteachers to the Legion of Honour.[4]

People could seek honours as a means of enhancing their own status. They could do so by private solicitation or by taking advantage of connections they enjoyed with honours distributors. Alternatively, status seekers could behave in ways or engage in activities that promised state laurels. The medals that were established in France to encourage men with social standing to take on the leadership of mutual societies were much sought after by members of local elites as a means by which to raise their public stature.[5] Or status seekers could entreat government officials to recognize persons in a category to which they belonged.

British army surgeons provide an example. During the first half of the nineteenth century, medical officers in the army felt growing discontent over their low status: they were looked down upon by other army officers; they were not promoted at the same rate; and their courage, they believed, was insufficiently recognized. They complained that they were excluded from the honours that other officers received, in contrast with French army surgeons, a number of whom had been decorated since the days of Napoleon. Their demands for recognition met strong resistance in the military, but eventually they and their supporters achieved their objective, beginning with several appointments to the Order of the Bath in 1850.[6]

The struggle faced by the British medical officers was one engagement in a much larger struggle between military and civilian personnel over state honours. Given that the earliest honours recognizing large numbers of persons were awarded to members of the military, the latter generally insisted that they had more entitlement. In Britain, military officers were unhappy when a civil division of the Order of the Bath was inaugurated in 1815; they considered it an inferior status. The soldiers who fought for Napoleon believed that the Legion of Honour was a military decoration and were against the idea of sharing it with civilians. Sentries often declined to present arms to civilian members of the Legion of Honour, who were derisively referred to as *les pékins*.[7] (The origin of this term is debated. Among the possibilities: it could be a play on words equating the Chinese city of Canton with civilian administrative districts in France or a reference to Chinese silk cloth fashionable at that time in the leisure classes.)

The same kind of struggle emerged when the new Belgian state came into being in 1830. Since the Order of Leopold was first conceived as a military order, suggestions that it should include civilians met considerable resistance. A motion was proposed in the Chamber of Representatives that the new honorific order should be referred to as a "military order" rather than a "national order." Ironically, the outcome of this motion was the opposite of what its authors had intended. It was narrowly defeated, enabling the King to install civilians in the Order.[8]

As a result of status competition, rulers and their ministers had always been faced with demands for honours and with complaints from those who did not receive them. The creation of new honours only encouraged the practice and intensified the vicious cycle. It was not long after the Order of the Bath was founded in 1725 that it generated a thirst for inclusion that was impossible to satisfy. Galloway provides a colourful example. In 1764, Major-General Sir William Draper was promised the Bath by a member of George Grenville's government, but the next vacancy was given to Major-General Robert Clive (first baron Clive) to enhance his stature as he departed for India to serve as governor of Bengal. Draper was offended personally; he also believed that men like himself were being ignored in favour of political appointments.[9] "It is not a little mortifying," he complained, "that we, who serve government from principle and affection, should be so often sacrificed to these new converts to administration, who serve it only from self-interest and convenience." He was no longer going to sacrifice himself. "Whenever I am employed again, I will be a most dirty dog, rob and pillage wherever I can, deserve to be hanged, and then carry every point for myself and my associates."[10] After Grenville was dismissed in July 1765, Draper got his Bath, but the challenge that governments faced in trying to meet the demand for this honour only became worse for subsequent administrations.

Pitt the Younger's peerage creations were driven by the same dynamic. With every appointment came a score of military or diplomatic self-assertors and status competitors who declared that their services were greater than those who had just been favoured.[11] At the turn of the century, the Duke of York supported bestowing a peerage on the heir of the (less than illustrious) General James Abercrombie because he (the Duke of York) believed that the army was not getting its share of peerages relative to the navy. Yet, in 1812, naval officer Sidney Smith argued that it was the navy that was being slighted, without whose support, the army "would not have accomplished any one of the objects for which its distinguished officers are so deservedly rewarded."[12]

Over the course of the nineteenth century, European governments continued to face snowballing pressure from organizations and individuals for more honours, pressure that was difficult to meet without undermining the value of honours and without encouraging still more demands. By the middle of the nineteenth century, if not earlier, Modern honours had developed their own momentum that would lead, over the next hundred years, to an ever-growing number of awards and recipients.

STRUGGLES OVER STATUS DISTRIBUTION

That status is a kind of power is evident not only in struggles to use state honours to raise the status of particular individuals and social groups but also in the role played by state honours in political and ideological power struggles that were being waged in the larger polity and society.

Political Struggles

It would be repetitious to recount the many political struggles in which Western-European state honours became entangled, but a few general observations can be made.

New honours introduced by a government were generally regarded skeptically by its their political adversaries or by those who feared that these honours would serve purposes to which they were opposed. Even the Legion of Honour could be denigrated for this reason; no small number of persons refused it in order to indicate their opposition to a particular regime. In the debates that took place in Belgium when the Order of Leopold was being established, three different factions were opposed to it. First, Orange supporters of the previous kingdom were against anything that legitimated the new regime and were, in particular, displeased with early appointments; second, liberals worried that it would increase the power of the crown vis-à-vis the legislature; and third, egalitarians believed that it was unconstitutional and that all citizens were equal before the law.[13] Similarly, in France, republicans and socialists were more critical of honours than Bonapartists and conservatives. And then there were the Irish revolutionaries, for whom British rule and state honours were indistinguishable.

The conjunctures of politics frequently determined the position that different factions took. Consequently, honours distributors were subject to differing, changing, and often contradictory pressures. The extent of politicization also varied. Some honours, such as the Order of the British Empire, were relatively less politicized. At the other extreme was the British House of Lords, for which it is impossible to separate the status power and the political power of its members. We have also observed the role of the Legion of Honour in French politics, and in the political struggles that brought about or followed the replacement of one regime by another.

When a new government came to power, it typically sought to manipulate the honours system to strengthen its position at the expense of its opponents. After the fall of Napoleon, the Bourbons, in addition to restoring Old-Regime honours, appointed conservatives to the Legion of Honour, and altered the rules of precedence to the disadvantage of members of the Legion by putting each of its grades – with the exception of *grand croix* – below the level of its equivalent grade in the Order of Saint Louis.[14] The July

Monarchy was no less willing to use the Legion of Honour for its own purposes. Its manipulative practices gave rise to considerable contention between the government and the legislature over honours. The deputies objected to King Louis Philippe's liberal use of what were called appointments *à titre exceptionnels*.[15] (The ordinance of 1816 allowed exceptional service as a justification for appointment to the Legion of Honour at the discretion of the king and the government.) The dispute led to a proposal for a complete reform of the Legion of Honour in 1839. Several deputies unsuccessfully demanded the creation of a consultative council that would guarantee the credibility of admissions to the Legion. Later in the century, in the early years of the Third Republic, the Legion of Honour was used shamelessly to reward republicans and raise their status. Again, demands for an independent council were made, but the Republican government was not willing to give up its control any more than were previous regimes.[16]

Public Attitudes

As we have repeatedly observed, public skepticism about honours was pervasive in Western Europe during the Early Modern and Modern periods. Honours were often ridiculed – by those who regarded them as fundamentally pernicious, by those who thought the institution was being abused or poorly administrated, and by those who just thought they were silly.

There were several reasons why honours might be regarded as fundamentally pernicious. First, as suggested at the end of Chapter 10, honours were vulnerable to the criticism that they rewarded people for engaging in what was alleged to be unselfish behaviour. Many writers argued that honours were thus hypocritical, superficial, artificial, and contrived.[17] Honours were often denounced for promoting and rewarding vanity. Alexis de Tocqueville made fun of Modern honours as a democratic fashion, a pale imitation of aristocratic mores. For Jules Barni, a republican and Protestant historian in France, they represented the most visible of vanities. He saw the Legion of Honour as the emblem of a new court society, which "ruined what still remained, I would not say just of a republican spirit, but also of civic virtue, in giving the head of State the means to entice and attach through the distinctions that he controls as master, not only the soldiers of the army, but the civil servants of his government or his administration, and more generally, the citizens of the entire country."[18] And we can recollect the position that Kuyper took on Dutch honorific orders. For him and other members of his Christian party, they were devoid of the Christian virtues of the great orders of knighthood of the past.

Whether or not honours were seen as fundamentally pernicious, criticisms of the way in which they were being distributed were common and could be deeply felt. Many critics asserted that honours were established for political reasons and/or that the wrong people were receiving them – not of the right cloth, not meritorious, not the kind to maintain respect for the decoration, et cetera. A recipient could be exposed to some unpleasant publicity. Gérard Legrelle, one of the first civilians to receive the Order of Leopold, was ridiculed in a Belgian newspaper where it was reported that "it seems that a decoration has gotten lost in the neighbourhood of the chest of M.G. Legrelle. A fair reward will be paid to anyone who can put it back in its right place."[19]

It needs to be recognized that disdain toward recipients was not new. Lord Stanhope, fourth earl of Chesterfield, characterized the Order of the Bath as "one of the Toys, Bob [Walpole] gave to his boys."[20] Appointments to it irritated him enough that he wrote several mock pieces for publication. The final two stanzas of one, which poked fun at a recipient whose badge had been stolen, were:

Rouse up ye true Knights-Errant,
N'er give this Catiff Quarter
    Ye Knights of the Toast,
    Or Knights of the Post,
Or T[histle], B[ath], or G[arte]r.

Learn hence, ye courtly lordlings,
Who hear his fatal story,
    On how slight strings
    Depend those things
Whereon ye hang your glory.[21]

Either overgenerous distribution or conformity to existing status structures could elicit disapproval in the larger public. The latter was especially scorned. We have already heard of General George Walpole denouncing the government for offering Nelson only a barony. Such contempt has only increased over the years. In 1986, almost two hundred years later, John Walker, an ardent and irreverent critic of British honours, wrote:

> There lies, buried in Whitehall, a series of formulae which are rigorously applied to the honours list twice yearly – the same number and rank of honours goes to the same categories of people in each list. And there is a pecking order. No man (or woman) must be allowed to rise above his or her station – the gong you get depends not on the goodness of your deed, but on your position in society. Knighthoods for the nobs and BEMs for the bums; it would never do, would it, for the Head of the Home Civil Service to receive an MBE when a clerk in the Social Security office in Newcastle received a peerage?[22]

Accusations of this kind did not come just from political dissidents. When John Major was trying to reform the British honours system in the early 1990s, he coined the term "automaticity" to refer to the practice of routinely bestowing honorific rewards to persons who had occupied certain positions, regardless of any special merit. More generally, he wanted to reduce the proportion of honours that went to the public sector and to generate a greater emphasis on merit. He did not make a lot of progress, at least not in the eyes of most observers. Automaticity and conformity to bureaucratic hierarchy were still the subject of much criticism in testimony before the House of Commons Committee of 2003–04.[23] The hard truth of the matter was that, when it came to selecting people for status awards, it was extremely difficult to avoid "automaticity."

And, of course, there has been intense criticism of "corruption" in the distribution of honours – favouritism, patronage, awards to the seemingly undeserving, or the exchange of honours for money. Throughout the nineteenth century, "abuses" in the distribution of status awards were denounced in France. The most serious incident was the so-called "Wilson affair" in 1887. In the United Kingdom, alleged sales of honours during the late nineteenth and early twentieth centuries were repeatedly denounced in the House of Commons and in the British public. I say more about both of these in the next chapter.

Finally, it is clear from several previous discussions that some people routinely criticized state honours as contrary to their egalitarian beliefs. The attitude persisted among many members of the European public throughout the nineteenth century. Those who saw

themselves as challenging the existing social and political structure
often refused honours. The ostentatiously unselfish Giuseppe Garibaldi and the ostentatiously independent Gustave Courbet wanted
nothing to do with them. Anti-aristocratic British reformer Richard
Cobden declared that accepting any such tribute would threaten
his political independence. However, it was not necessary to be a
Garibaldi, a Courbet, or a Cobden to take this position. Herbert
Spencer declined all honours because he believed that they disad-
vantaged those who did not receive them, especially men early in
their careers, who, "already at a disadvantage, are artificially dis-
advantaged still more; while those who have already surmounted
their difficulties have their progress artificially facilitated."[24] English
painter Francis Bacon refused all honours. Although he insisted that
he had no opinion on the honours system, he reportedly explained
that "he came into this world with no advantages and that's how I
want to go out."[25]

Not surprisingly, criticisms of honours could lead to calls for their
abolition. Some members of Kuyper's party drew this conclusion.
Later, Dutch Social Democrats tried to have honorific orders abolished when the Dutch Constitution was under revision.[26] The greatest number of demands for abolition came from France, but calls for
the abolition of titles could surface even in Britain.[27] It goes without
saying that the significance of these demands is not that they have
led to a decline of honours. On the contrary, most of this ruckus
indicates that honours have been taken seriously by many people in
Western Europe, in spite of the mockery that has sometimes been
directed at them.

Monarchs

State honours frequently became the object of contention between
the heads of state and politicians or state bureaucrats. This was more
true in monarchies than in republics. In French Republican periods, state honours were legally under the control of the president,
and so it was more difficult for others to challenge his practices.
French presidents were elected officials vested with the most political authority in the state apparatus. The president had the right of
final decision on appointments to state honours, and the right to
suspend or terminate the membership of a legionnaire. Obviously,
French presidents were subject to political forces that constrained

or enabled them, but by the time of the Third Republic, there was no ambiguity over their formal authority.

Between monarchs and their governments, on the other hand, there was much ambiguity and considerable room for contestation. Royals usually regarded honours as one domain over which they still had control when most other domains were being taken from them. With some justification, they claimed a traditional prerogative over honours. In the Middle Ages, whereas sovereigns had limited control over most superior statuses, their control over membership in royal orders of knighthood was almost total. The increasing state institutionalization of superior status from the late Medieval period, along with a growth in the centralization of political power over the Early Modern period, brought royal power over honours to a pinnacle in the seventeenth and eighteenth centuries. Subsequently, a transformation in the power structures of these monarchies gradually forced royals to share this power with bureaucrats and later with politicians. Eventually, during the nineteenth century, monarchs came to lose most of their authority in the distribution of state honours. All this did not happen, however, without struggles, which varied depending on the power that different monarchs possessed in different years during the century.

In 1815, the situation was in some ways ideal for the re-organized monarchy of the Low Countries. Europe had been in a state of war for most of the preceding twenty-five years and had become heavily militarized. The Dutch knew that the great powers expected the House of Orange to provide a strong united government that would act as a buttress against France. William I was relatively free of earlier political traditions that had constrained the House of Orange. He played a considerable role in establishing the new decorations and in the (sometimes contentious) drafting of their statutes.[28] Originally, the selection of recipients was to be administered by members sitting in chapter, but William managed to put an end to the chapter and thus turn the honours into personal grants of the king.[29] His personality – forceful, patriarchal, calculating, and resourceful – made him perhaps the most imperious post-Napoleonic ruler in Europe.[30]

Yet it was not an especially strong monarchy. From 1815 to 1830, it ruled over two distinguishable populations, Northern Netherlanders and Southern Netherlanders, that had not shared state institutions since the sixteenth century and were different economically and religiously. William's autocratic style prevented him from overcoming these divisions. The breakup of the Union left the monarchy with a more homogeneous population to rule, but with greatly diminished prestige both internationally and domestically. William's high-handed methods (and his decision to marry a Roman Catholic after the death of his first wife) made him increasingly unpopular. This unpopularity, along with revisions to the Dutch constitution to which he was strongly opposed, led him to abdicate in 1840. There then commenced a period during which Crown and Parliament struggled over constitutional reform until, in 1848, fearing revolution, William II agreed to significant constitutional revision that reinforced the requirement for ministerial countersignature for all decorations.[31]

Notwithstanding these royal concessions, when William III inherited the throne in 1849, one might not know that anything had changed. In his first year as king, he suggested to the Russian ambassador in The Hague that he would provide Russian Tsar Nicholas I, William's uncle, with decorations for the most deserving Russian army officers. The Russian army had recently assisted the Austrians in repressing a rebellion in Hungary, a rebellion with which many Dutch people were sympathetic. The minister whose authority it was to countersign decorations yielded, but he wrote a letter to the King complaining that he felt ambushed by the King's offer, did not support it, but countersigned it to spare the King embarrassment.[32]

William III continued to make appointments on his own and to infuriate government ministers in doing so.[33] In 1850, his ministers made it clear that under the new constitution he was required to consult with them on matters of decoration – but he did his best to ignore this.[34] During the remainder of the reign, politicians and the King battled with one another over the procedures and regulations governing nominations to state honorific orders, and irritated one another over appointments that were made. The contestation was all the more difficult because William III used decorations for political purposes; for example, he rewarded a general in the army who shared his hardline views of the role of the military, and overlooked a general who did not share his views.[35] Finally, after the death of William III, the role of the Crown in status distribution became more restricted. But Emma, his widow, did not shy away from participating in the process, as we have seen in the case of the medical officer whom she wanted to make a knight in the Order of the Dutch Lion.

When Leopold of Saxe-Coburg ascended the throne of Belgium, his situation was very different from that of William I. When the latter became king of the United Kingdom of the Netherlands, he was the descendent of a long line of Dutch *stadhouders*. Leopold, in contrast, was the non-inheriting son of a German ducal family, who had sought employment in the Russian army and was still in service when he won the heart of Princess Charlotte of Wales. All the same, his presumptions were such that he was most displeased with the constitutional structure in which he found himself. He thought the Belgian Constitution gave too much power to Belgians and was much disappointed at the restrictions it imposed on him. Needless to say, he believed that decorations were at his pleasure as much as they had been for the Dutch monarchy. He freely conferred the Order of Leopold without consulting his ministers, without obtaining an *arrêté royal*, and sometimes without even informing the government. Albert-Joseph Goblet, the minister theoretically in charge of decorations, occasionally had to turn to the press to learn about awards that had been made.[36] Although few of the laurels Leopold handed out were inappropriate, they were often spur-of-the-moment favours, or justified on the basis of the personal relationship he had or the personal obligation he felt toward the recipient.

He was able to do this because he came to power at a time when the control of monarchs over decorations was greater than it would be later, but also because he shared an advantage with William I: he was the first monarch of a newly created kingdom. A totally new government was being formed in Brussels, with few precedents to follow and a lot more important things to worry about than the King dispensing decorations. Over the course of the 1830s, however, a functioning government was gradually put in place, and by the 1840s, the King's control over the distribution of decorations had waned. The government was able to establish procedures for the conferral of honours, and the number of appointments the King made on his own declined markedly. This change was facilitated by the unpopularity of decorations among some people in the general public, and especially by public discontent with the power the Crown had over them.[37] That said, Leopold could still, in the 1840s and '50s, secretly get his way with the government in specific cases.[38]

No British monarch during the nineteenth century was ever in a position comparable to that of William I and Leopold I as sovereigns of newly created kingdoms. Constitutional understandings of the relational power of the British monarchy and the government were relatively well institutionalized. In the first half of the century, though it was expected that state honours were to serve the interests of the country and the government, they were still seen as a royal prerogative.

During Victoria's formative period, when Melbourne was prime minister, the relative power of the Crown was weaker than it had been in preceding reigns. After Victoria married Albert, however, the influence of the Crown over honours increased. Albert took a great interest in appointments and played an active role in the reform and reorganization of the honours system. He had strong views, and was protective of the rights of the Crown to dispense honours. One example will illustrate the stance that the Queen took when Albert was at her side. The parliamentary commission established in the United Kingdom to inquire into the mishandling of the Crimean War was disparaging of a number of commanders who had been awarded the Bath, a circumstance that led to public criticism of the Order and to unfavourable discussions in the House of Commons. When it was moved that Parliament be provided with a complete list of all recent awards, Victoria expressed her indignation to Lord Palmerston (Henry John Temple, third viscount Palmerston), who was then prime minister: "The Queen hopes the Government will not allow the House of Commons so much further trespass upon the prerogatives of the Crown as virtually to take also control over the distribution of honours and rewards into their own hands."[39]

Actually, Albert's interventions did not usually generate much conflict, given his genuine interest in improving the honours system. This was especially true of the Order of the Bath, of which he became great master, though he did exceed the privileges of this office by trying to persuade ministers to send nominations to him before they went to the Queen.[40] When Albert was alive, the royal couple also resisted awarding the Order of the Garter or the Order of the Bath to non-Christians.[41] After the death of Albert, Victoria withdrew from the public arena and tried to avoid ceremony. Although ministers typically found this withdrawal frustrating, it contributed to an appropriation by politicians and others of the task of adapting the monarchy to the changes taking place in British society. The development of ceremonial practices on the part of the British monarchy in the late nineteenth and early twentieth centuries was, it may be remembered, largely the work of politicians.

Victoria was most interested in decorations for members of royal families or German princes. Flattering these sorts was not new for her. During her marriage with Albert, she had made her cousin, Count Alexander Mensdorff-Pouilly, a civil KCB (knight commander, second highest grade in the Bath) and her brother-in-law, Ernst, prince of Hohenlohe Langenburg, an honorary civil GCB (knight grand cross, highest grade in the Bath).[42] After Albert died, Prince Christian of Denmark was made a civil GCB in 1863, and Prince Leiningen, the son of her half-brother, a civil KCB in the same year and a civil GCB in 1866. There followed a series of appointments to the Order of the Bath of minor German princes related to the Queen.[43]

Governments went along with Victoria's fancies, but not always. Palmerston rejected her wish that a KCB be awarded to Major-General Robert Bruce, who had taken on the job of trying to bring the Prince of Wales into line. For Palmerston, this man's services "were of a private character which it would be inappropriate to recognize with a public distinction." The Queen's reply – that the Order of the Bath was established to recognize services to the monarchy – failed to change his view.[44] Later, Victoria wanted a state funeral for Napoleon III's son, whose mother had become a friend of hers. When Benjamin Disraeli rejected this, Henry Ponsonby proposed that a badge of GCB be laid on the young man's coffin; this too was rejected by the government.[45] These refusals were not easy. When the Queen took an interest, she could be forceful, using language that made it clear she would not be happy if her request was denied.[46]

Appointments to the House of Lords provided a significant source of conflict during Victoria's reign. As the Queen became personally more conservative, she more often resisted democratization of the upper house. Given her poor relationship with Gladstone, she was especially opposed to attempts on the part of the Liberals to strengthen their position in the House of Lords, but she was also against any significant change to the social character of its membership. When Gladstone recommended ten new peers in 1869, she objected to two Catholics among them. She professed to be concerned that the creation of these peerages for Catholics came too soon after the enactment of Irish Disestablishment (the separation

of the Anglican Church in Ireland from the state). "The govt &
many people in this country," she complained, "seem to be totally
blind to the alarming encroachments & increase of the R. Catholics in England & indeed all over the world. The Pope was never so
powerful & the Queen is quite determined to do *all* in her power
to prevent this."[47] Eventually she accepted these Catholic appointments, but she was more stubborn when it came to Jews. She refused
to accede to the prime minister's proposal to elevate Lionel Rothschild to the House of Lords. Gladstone sought to revive the idea in
1873, but was rebuffed once again. Only in 1885 was a Jew, Lionel's
son, elevated to the peerage, followed by a number of other Jews.
The Queen had again resisted, but Gladstone returned his original
list and she acquiesced.[48]

This attitude toward Jews makes Disraeli's ability to manage Victoria all the more impressive. Although he had converted to Christianity and was a member of the Anglican Church, Disraeli suffered
more from anti-Semitism than did the Rothschilds.[49] It was also Disraeli who was able to persuade Victoria, in 1878, to allow all state
honours to be channelled through the prime minister's office, a
change that dramatically undermined the influence of the Crown
over their distribution. Since then, the control of the monarchy over
honours has steadily waned in Britain, a loss often felt most bitterly
by monarchs when they have been forced to accept decisions with
which they did not agree. It is an understatement to say that David
Lloyd George's honours lists gave George V much pain.[50]

In addition to trying to resist the loss of their authority over the
distribution of state honours in their kingdoms, monarchs also created new honours over which they claimed exclusive jurisdiction.
These royal honours were usually, though not always, for members
of the royal family or household. As a rule, governments went along
with them as a means of facilitating the transfer in power over other
state honours. Of course, honours of this kind were far from new.
What was new was that these favours became one of the last sources
of royal status largesse. As politicians gained more control over state
honours during the nineteenth century, monarchs relied increasingly on these personal handouts to distribute status.

No one was better at this game than William III of the Netherlands. When the Kingdom of the Netherlands was dismembered in
1830, the Great Powers had allotted the German-speaking part of
the Duchy of Luxembourg to the Dutch Crown. In 1841, William II

created the Luxembourg royal order, the Order of the Oak Crown, which was beyond the constitutional power of his Dutch ministers. He awarded a relatively small number of these little trophies, but William III distributed hundreds. In conjunction with the Duke of Nassau, William III also created the Order of the Golden Lion of Nassau, which he used as he pleased with no interference from his ministers.

In Belgium, though Leopold I did issue gold medals in a personal and private capacity, he otherwise did not create his own house decorations, not even for the royal family.[51] He was content handing out the Order of Leopold. In 1833, however, his older brother, Ernest, duke of Saxe-Coburg-Gotha, revived a Medieval Saxian order, calling it the Order of the Ernestine Branch of Saxe. The Belgian King first made use of this honorific order in 1836, and took more and more advantage of it as his freedom to use the Order of Leopold declined.[52]

Leopold II did not make as many appointments to the Saxian order as did his father, and eventually, he could not give anyone this gem because the ties between the two houses were severed in 1880. As an alternative, he created other decorations over which he had personal control. In 1889, he invented a medal for employees of the households of members of the royal family, another for employees in foreign courts, and a third for particularly meritorious acts in his household or in the households of other members of the royal family.[53] After acquiring personal sovereignty over Congo, he created four honorific orders of his own – the Order of the African Star, the Order of the Crown, the Order of Leopold II, and the Order of the Lion – which he could distribute without referring to the Belgian government. In the end, his boldness and ingenuity did not triumph. As a result of the brutal exploitation of the Congolese population (resulting in an enormous humanitarian disaster in which as many as 10 million may have died), the sovereignty over Congo was transferred to the state of Belgium in 1908, and the exclusive rights of the Crown with respect to these honorific orders was relinquished.[54]

Several of the British honorific orders founded in the late nineteenth and early twentieth centuries were the personal prerogative of the monarch: the Order of the Crown of India, the Royal Victorian Order, the Royal Victorian Chain, the Royal Victorian Medal, and the Order of Merit. Nevertheless, in 1907, Edward VII was unhappily pushed into giving the Order of Merit to Florence Nightingale.[55] Although the general trend in the twentieth century has been for control over British honours to pass from the Crown to the government, in 1946, Clement Attlee and Winston Churchill agreed that members of the Garter and the Thistle would be selected by the sovereign without any previous formal submission from the prime minister.

The possible consequences of these struggles with heads of state for the distribution of status are examined shortly, but a few remarks are in order now. First, it is clear that the reason that the expansion of state honours in Britain was chronologically later than their expansion in Continental countries was not that British rulers had more control over their distribution. Kings in the Low Countries had as much power as British monarchs in the last half of the nineteenth century and, if anything, more power earlier in the century. Second, we should recognize that, in spite of these struggles, considerable interdependence existed between monarchies and their governments in the use each made of honours, a point already made in Chapter 2. In some ways, this became even more the case in the late nineteenth century as the role of monarchies became less political and more ceremonial. Kings and queens needed honours to enhance the royal ceremonial project, but by the same token, governments in the monarchical countries used royalty to give lustre to the state honours they were distributing. We also need to keep in mind that, in the end, the role of monarchies and the struggles they had with governments and legislatures did not make a great difference. Ultimately, the honours systems in the different European countries on which this study is based became remarkably similar.

Resistance to State Institutionalization

The expansion of honours also gave rise to power struggles between the state and those who did not accept its status-distribution authority. Foremost among these opponents were people who sincerely or otherwise believed that they enjoyed noble status even though it was not recognized by the state. Admittedly, this sort of struggle was found only on the Continent. In the United Kingdom, no significant number of persons claimed to be peers, baronets, or knights without state recognition. On the Continent, in contrast, opposition to the right of the state to make nobles had a long history. Royal ennoblements in the late Medieval and Early Modern periods were much resented among those who claimed a long lineage of noble status, many of whom believed that monarchs could recognize nobility but not create it. The same sort of attitude could be found in the nineteenth century, especially in France, as a result of the repeated revisions of noble status, which led to a situation in which a good number of persons claimed to be of noble descent but did not have state accreditation.

Although a significant number of old nobility were elevated into the Imperial nobility of the First Empire, they represented only a small percentage of the old nobility. Since those who were not chosen still believed they were nobles, they regarded Napoleon's Imperial nobility as the illegitimate one. Under the Bourbon Restoration, there should not have been such problems because, in principle, all Old-Regime nobles, as well as members of Napoleon's Imperial nobility, were recognized. Still, uncertainties and resentments arose as a result of the absence of a definitive list of old nobility. Under subsequent French regimes, descendants of the Old-Regime nobility have not been officially recognized by the state, but they can legally claim noble descent. Personal names, which can include a particle (like the "de" in "de Tocqueville"), can have legal status; some people use this to establish a claim to nobility. This presumption was reinforced by a decree of 1859, which gave the sovereign the power to confer honorary particles. Yet, most French nobles deny that a particle is evidence of noble status. If all this were not enough to create "social confusion," it is possible in France to have a hereditary title verified by the state. Doing so is not required for a title to be legal, but the demands for proof are actually more exacting than they had been under the Old Regime. (A French sovereign must have conferred the title during the period of time in which he ruled and it must have legitimately descended to the applicant.) Needless to say, no small number of persons still lay claim to a title even though they have not been able to produce the necessary documentation.

With varying degrees of concern, European governments have struggled with usurpation. In France, the Penal Code of 1810 included a proscription against the usurpation of Imperial titles, which was changed to royal titles in 1816 under the Bourbons. During the July Monarchy, this interdiction was rescinded, but it was re-established in 1858 when it again became criminal to usurp titles. This remains the case today in France insofar as it is illegal to assume a name or accessory to a name that is not recognized in the civil registry.

In Belgium, the Penal Code strictly forbids the attribution to oneself of titles of nobility that one does not possess. Although it had been argued by some Belgians that this provision in the Code was unnecessary, since public ridicule would suffice to deter pretensions of this kind, the determination to protect the monopoly of the state over noble status was enough to persuade legislators to leave nothing to social pressure and to make usurpation a criminal offense.[56] Be that as it may, we can find persons in Belgium today who claim noble status, or at least noble descent, and reject the right of the state to tell them otherwise. In France, where – unlike in Belgium – nobility is not a state-accorded honour, the number of unofficial nobles is much larger. Indeed, in France, noble status really depends on informal recognition of one's claim by the community of families whose members agree that they have noble descent.

13

Status Consequences of State Honours

What were the effects of these power struggles on the status structures of Western Europe? More generally speaking, what were the
status consequences of the great expansion of state honours in Western Europe? To what extent did they reinforce, or undermine, the
existing distribution of status?

SOCIAL POSITIONS

Let us first consider several specific social positions in Western
Europe whose status was affected by the Modern honours phenomenon. There are marked differences among groups in these effects,
much of which we would expect, but some of which are not obvious
and are worthy of our notice.

The Military

We have already seen in Chapter 7 that the military were well represented in the major honours that I have sampled. Not surprisingly,
there is a strong correlation between military rank and the honour
grade in which an individual was placed. As can be seen in Table
B.28 in Appendix B, when it came to making a man a GBE (highest grade in the Order of the British Empire), only general officers
would do; not even field officers were numerous enough to show up
in my sample. To be a KBE (second-highest grade), it was evidently
necessary to have held the military rank of either general officer or
field officer; the exceptions were a small number of junior officers
and persons with a civilian occupation. Even OBES (second-lowest

grade) were predominantly field officers. It was only MBES (lowest grade) who were predominantly junior officers, along with a few NCOS. Those lower in rank were not sufficiently numerous for even one to turn up in my sample.

The same kind of correlation was found in my samples of the Legion of Honour and the Order of Leopold. As shown in Tables B.26–B.27 and B.29–B.30, with the exception of men with civilian occupations, virtually all the military personnel who were anointed *grands croix* and *grands officiers* (two highest grades in these orders) were general officers; most of the *commandeurs* and *officiers* (third and fourth grades) were either general officers or superior officers; and the majority of *chevaliers* (lowest grade) were *officiers subalternes* or *sous-officiers*. Service and campaign medals usually had only one grade and were distributed without regard to rank. In contrast, awards for performance, if they did not have different grades, were usually targeted at certain ranks in the military. As we have seen, this was true of the Order of the Bath until 1815. The Distinguished Service Order, founded in 1886 and awarded for meritorious service in combat, was specifically for those who were officers but not of sufficient rank to be conceded membership in the Bath. Officially, it had only one grade, though it was treated as a military fourth class of the Bath. Similarly, the Conspicuous Service Cross (founded in 1901 and renamed the Distinguished Service Cross in 1914) and the Military Cross (created in 1914) were designed for warrant and junior officers. They had only one grade, but were considered third-level decorations below the Bath.

Alternatively, alterations could be made to a decoration to reflect military statuses. Sometimes medals were made of different materials for different military ranks. The Seringapatam Medal, for example, was manufactured as follows: gold for the highest-ranking commanders; silver, silver-gilt, or bronze for lower-ranked officers; and tin for the lowest ranks. In 1795, the Naval Gold Medal was introduced for British seamen – a larger version of the medal for admirals and a smaller one for lesser officers. The Army Gold Medal was created in 1810 with a similar distinction. The *chevrons de front* instituted in Belgium in 1916 were in gold for officers, and wool for *sous-officiers*, corporals, and soldiers.[1]

Needless to say, this kind of conformity to rank easily led to automaticity, or at least the perception of it. In a series of letters to the

Queen in 1854, the Duke of Newcastle (Henry Pelham-Clinton, fifth duke of Newcastle-under-Lyme), then secretary of state for war, expressed his dissatisfaction with some nominations he had just received. In the first letter, he conveys his disagreement with the rec- ommendation of Lord Raglan (FitzRoy Somerset, first baron Rag- lan, master general of ordnance and former secretary to the Duke of Wellington) that nearly every officer of a certain rank and class be decorated. Newcastle feared that "if decorations are given to all who are named in a dispatch some who have done little to deserve such reward will receive them whilst many who have borne the bur- den and heat of the day will feel slighted."[2] In a letter written sev- eral weeks later, Newcastle reported that Commander-in-Chief Lord Hardinge (Henry Hardinge, first viscount Hardinge) agreed with Raglan. "He maintains that no principle can be properly adopted but that of giving to all officers according to their rank the various degrees of the order without distinction of whether they took part in the action or not." Newcastle indicated that he was not convinced by Hardinge's argument, believing "that the Bath would then become little more than an appendage to certain rank in the Army provided only the officer served in the field." Newcastle knew that he was up against a widespread view represented in Ragan's "great aversion to making what he would consider invidious distinctions."[3]

The fact of the matter was that these opposing views reflected a dilemma in the distribution of state honours that made it impossible for either view to prevail over the other. Consequently, in spite of the pressure to conform to the existing military status hierarchy, Mod- ern state honours have not simply reinforced the status quo in armed forces. The status range of Modern military honours has gradually broadened over the past several centuries. Even in 1693, though the Order of Saint Louis was restricted to officers, this included the great number of junior officers in the French army. Recall that an estimated 2,000 men received this honour under Louis XIV. The Legion of Honour was not limited to officers. According to a calcu- lation made in 1810, 45 per cent of the members of the Legion were *sous-officiers* or simple soldiers.[4] Under the Bourbon Restoration and the July Monarchy, the number from these ranks declined propor- tionately, but in my 1852 sample of the military, *sous-officiers* and sim- ple soldiers were still a good 32.4 per cent of military members of the Legion of Honour.

The Military Medal of the Second Republic was intended to increase the ways in which soldiers below officer ranks could be recognized. We need to acknowledge that the effect of creating it was less than satisfactory from the point of view of these lower-ranked soldiers: it came to be seen as the appropriate reward for lower ranks, while the Legion of Honour was more appropriate for officers. Whether for this or other reasons, the percentage of the military in the Legion represented by *sous-officiers* fell sharply between my 1852 sample and my 1929 sample (Tables B.31 and B.32), while *officiers subalternes* (junior officers) rose as a percentage between the two samples. Even so, the Military Medal became a prestigious award with a similar insignia to that of the Legion of Honour, and subject to the same discipline and regulations. Other French decorations that significantly raised the status of lesser ranks included the Saint Helena Medal and later the War Cross, which was created in 1915 for heroism in combat. Similarly, the Belgian War Cross is open to lower ranks.

On the other side of the English Channel, a widespread feeling had also developed in the mid-nineteenth century that lower-ranked soldiers were not being given sufficient recognition for their contributions to the nation. The inconsistency between the lack of rewards for these soldiers and the appointment to the Bath of a significant number of high-ranking officers contributed to the outrage referred to in the preceding chapter, which in turn led to the Distinguished Conduct Medal and the Victoria Cross. The former was created in 1854 to honour privates, NCOs, and warrant officers in any branch of the service in recognition of distinguished conduct in battle. Two years later, the Victoria Cross was established more specifically for bravery and was available to all ranks. As shown in Table B.39, between 1856 and 1920 the Victoria Cross was awarded mostly to junior officers, NCOs, and privates. Later decorations that elevated the status of lower-ranked British military personnel have included the Distinguished Service Medal of 1914 (not to be confused with the Distinguished Service Order and the Distinguished Service Cross) and the Military Medal of 1916.

We should also note that the recipient of a military honour was accorded higher respect if the award departed from the well-understood status conformity that we have just witnessed. For example, the great majority of military personnel in the second-highest grade in my 1921 sample of the Order of the British Empire (KBE) were general officers or field officers, but a small percentage were junior officers (Table B.28). Most observers at the time would assume that the latter were placed in that grade in recognition of quite exceptional performance.

Moreover, irrespective of the rank or socio-economic position of those who received them, awards for bravery became the most esteemed of all state honours. Those in the middle and lower military ranks of armed forces are not just eligible for such awards but are far more likely to be in a combat role and thus able to display gallantry.

On the whole, the greatest beneficiaries of the increase in military state honours have been junior officers. From as early as the seventeenth century, when Louis XIV founded the Order of Saint Louis, they were included in status awards that excluded lower ranks. When honorific rewards became open to the lower ranks, junior officers still benefitted greatly, along with field officers and NCOs, especially if we take into account the number of field officers, junior officers, and NCOs in the armed forces compared to lower ranks (Tables B.31–B.35 and B.39).

The Civilian Public Sector

Two of the structural changes that I have argued led to the evolution of state honours are the growth in the size of the state and political centralization. In the Early Modern period it was especially monarchical centralization that encouraged the expansion of state honorific recognition. In the nineteenth and twentieth centuries, it has been primarily the evolution of centralized parliaments. Not surprisingly, state employees and politicians have been major beneficiaries of these rewards.

STATE EMPLOYEES
During the formative stage in the making of Modern European honours, the only group to whom the civilian public sector had to take second place was the military. The Legion of Honour, created primarily to reward Napoleon's soldiers, nevertheless recognized a large number of state officials. The civil division of the Order of the Bath was intended for politicians and high-ranking state officials. The Order of Saint Michael and Saint George was transformed over the course of the nineteenth century into an order for state officers. And we saw in Chapter 7 that state employees were well represented

not only in the Legion of Honour but in all three of the major state honours I have sampled.

Distributing honours to state officials was truly formidable. State bureaucracies formed complex hierarchies with less consensus than we find in the military about what was appropriate for different positions. If there has been a "formula," as Walker claimed, it has not been a simple and fixed one. Nevertheless, we can see the pressures to conform to the bureaucratic hierarchy by comparing honours conferred on different levels of state employees. As shown in Tables B.7–B.8 and B.10–B.11, in my samples of members of the Legion of Honour and the Order of Leopold, the percentage of awards bestowed on higher-level state employees exceeded the percentage bestowed on middle-level state employees, even though there were obviously much fewer of them. This was not the case for the Order of the British Empire in 1921 – perhaps evidence of the special purpose of this order at that time and the objective of recognizing "humble people," as David Lindsay called them (Table B.9).

There were also substantial differences in the grades into which the two groups were put. In my sample of the Legion of Honour in 1852, higher-level state employees could be found in the two highest grades and did best in the third and fourth grades, while middle-level state employees were expected to be happy with the fourth and fifth grades (Table B.12). In the twentieth-century sample of the Legion of Honour, the higher-level state employees were found in all grades, but, on the whole, had higher percentages in the more elevated grades, while the middle-level civil servants were confined to the two lowest grades (Table B.13).

In the Order of Leopold sample of 1833–87, higher-level state employees were spread out, but were proportionately fewest in the highest grade and the lowest grade, while middle-level state employees were proportionately concentrated in the third grade and in the lowest grade (Table B.15). In the sample of 1932, higher-level state employees were even more spread out than they had been in the earlier sample, while the middle-level state employees were even more concentrated in the lowest grade (Table B.16). A willingness to bestow lofty state honours on higher-level state employees in Belgium is also seen in the numbers that were raised to the Belgian nobility. The reader can recall from Chapter 7 that, according to one calculation, roughly half of those ennobled in Belgium between 1830 and 1957 and whose social position is known were state officials.

Similar differences in grades between higher-level state employees and middle-level state employees could be found in the Order of the British Empire in 1921 (Table B.14). While the purpose of this order may have been to recognize a broad segment of the population by means of a large numerical distribution, this was not – indeed, could not be – taken to the point of giving "humble people" the same grade as those with claims to greater distinction.

In addition to conforming to the bureaucratic hierarchy, governments were under pressure to support the status of state officials in the public mind. Honours were seen as useful for the prestige that was necessary for different positions. There was nothing like a flashy decoration to enhance the lustre of a colonial official. Remember the anguish of William Draper, whose spot in the Bath went to Lord Clive because Clive was being appointed governor of Bengal. Promotion in the Order of Saint Michael and Saint George during the nineteenth and early twentieth centuries usually coincided with promotion in the Imperial service.[5]

On the other hand, British status distributors felt the need to be cautious in making status awards to officials permanently in the colonies. Although a few exceptions might be justified, they did not want these officials getting prestigious British awards for services that were of "lesser importance" than those performed by officials in England. As Lord Stanley (Edward George Geoffrey Smith-Stanley, fourteenth earl of Derby) put it in 1844 when he was secretary of state for war and the colonies, the Order of the Bath should not be downgraded by the admission of persons performing services that were "so purely colonial in character, and bearing so exclusively on local affairs, as hardly to be fit subjects for the distinction of an Imperial Order." It would be much better to create local honorific orders, "which would be, though in a less degree, objects of local ambition, and which, being dispensed by the Crown, would add, not inconsiderably, to the influence of the local executive, and tend to connect the colonies with the mother country."[6]

POLITICIANS

Politicians benefited from the expansion of honours in relatively early periods. Although the Order of the Bath was founded as a military order, it was initially used to please politicians. Politicians were also visible in Napoleon's Imperial nobility. Natalie Petiteau found that 14 per cent of the titleholders listed in the *Armorial du Premier Empire* played a role in local or national politics.[7]

Unfortunately, it is difficult to determine the representation of politicians in the major state honours that I sampled. In the source I used for the Legion of Honour (the *Annuaires* of the Legion of Honour), the social position recorded could be either their political office or their longer-term occupation. National politicians were more often designated by the former, local politicians by the latter. In my samples, the percentage of civilians who were recorded as politicians in 1852 was 11.4 per cent; in 1929, it was 6.7 per cent (Tables B.7 and B.8). These figures can be compared with the findings of Bruno Dumons for Saône-et-Loire and Var. He took his data from nomination files, which gave him both occupations. He found that, from the 1870s to 1930s, half of those nominated for the Legion of Honour in Saône-et-Loire and a third of those nominated in Var had held a political mandate for at least some period of time, almost half of them as mayor.[8]

The percentages we have for politicians were higher in the Order of Leopold sample. For the years 1833 to 1887, excluding foreigners, 21.0 per cent of the civilians in the Order were identified as politicians (Table B.10). Their representation was lower in the early twentieth-century sample, where only 7.9 per cent of civilians were listed as politicians (Table B.11). In my 1921 sample of the Order of the British Empire, only 3.7 per cent of the male civilians were recorded as politicians (Table B.9). Here again, however, we cannot assume that others in the sample did not engage in politics during their lifetime.

We face similar methodological problems with our data on the grades of politicians in these honorific orders. Since local politicians were (1) more likely than nationalist politicians to be listed in the *Annuaires* by some other occupation and (2) more likely to be put in lower grades than national politicians, my samples may underestimate the number of politicians in lower grades. This distortion cannot, however, account for the very high grades in which some politicians were placed. In the Legion of Honour list of 1852, the grades to which politicians were appointed in proportionately the largest numbers were the highest grades (Table B.12).

Indeed, politicians largely monopolized the civilian *grands croix* in the Legion of Honour, and were almost as predominant among the *grands officiers*.[9]

Belgian politicians were not so highly situated in the Order of Leopold, but they were the vast majority among civilians (again, excluding foreigners) in the uppermost grade (*grand cordon*) for the years 1833–87, and the largest in the second grade (*grand officier*) (Table B.15). In 1932, the majority of the civilian *grands cordons* and *grands officiers* were again politicians (Table B.16). In addition, prominent Belgian politicians could dream of becoming members of the Belgian nobility. According to Fourez, about a fifth of those ennobled in Belgium from 1830 to 1957 were politicians.[10]

British politicians also had more than one honour to which they could aspire: the Order of the Thistle, the Order of Saint Patrick, and the Order of the Bath. During most of the eighteenth century, civilians outnumbered military men in elevations to the House of Lords. In the last quarter of the century, peerage prizes for politicians declined in the face of a sharp increase in military elevations as a result of the French wars.[11] During the nineteenth century, as the reasons for elevations became even more political, politicians became the most common source of new peers and the principal beneficiaries of the growth in the size of the House of Lords. Between 1885 and 1914, roughly two-thirds of appointments to the House of Lords went to men who had sat in the House of Commons.[12] This does not mean that those elevated were all career politicians, but it is clear that most new peers had been active in politics in one way or another.

Possibly as a consequence of available alternatives, but no doubt also as a result of the special purpose of the Order of the British Empire in its earliest years, the presence of politicians in this order was modest in 1921 (Table B.9). They were, however, well represented in the highest grade as shown in Table B.14. Eventually, politicians were installed in the Order of the Companions of Honour in substantial numbers. Churchill used it to recognize the war services of members of the Coalition Cabinet during the Second World War. In contrast, between 1917 and 1939, few politicians were to be found in the Order of the Companions of Honour, one of the few being Churchill himself, who was in Lloyd George's resignation honours list.[13]

Professions

The experience of professional occupations in the world of Modern state honours is highly varied. Most important are differences between the judicial professions and other professions, but there is also noteworthy variation within each group.

JUDICIAL PROFESSIONS

If military leaders, state officials, and politicians were going to be flattered with honours, it was impossible not to reward the higher judiciary. They had inherited distinction from previous centuries. The highest court in France, the Parlement de Paris, had its origin in the Curia regis. It became a separate court in 1307. Provincial *parlements* were added in the following centuries.[14] Eighteenth-century France has often been referred to as a country of laws, lawyers, and judges, what David Bell has called a "judiciary society."[15] The status of the *parlementaires* was derived not only from their exalted position and enormous legal power but also from the wealth they acquired from fees, inheritance, and marriage alliances with wealthy families.[16] In addition, high court positions were ennobling.

The highest judicial status in the British Isles was likewise prestigious, all the more because the court of final appeal was the committee of the House of Lords composed of the law lords. But other high courts had a distinguished heritage, descended as they were from Medieval common-law courts. The rights of English high-court judges were strengthened by law in the eighteenth century; the dismissal of a judge required a petition from both houses of Parliament or impeachment for a criminal offence.[17]

The socio-economic position of lawyers obviously varied much more than that of the higher judiciary, but we can still consider law the most prestigious among the professions in Western Europe during the Early Modern period. It is true that, like all the professions, law was regarded negatively in the prevailing military culture, but it was becoming a chosen occupation for some members of aristocratic families. Law could also be a source of entrants into the landed elite, most notably in the British Isles during the first half of the eighteenth century.[18] Throughout Western Europe, significant aristocratic links to law persisted in two ways: (1) many lawyers were drawn from aristocratic families and (2) lawyers had more social ties with members of the aristocracy than did those in other social positions.

At the same time, connections between relatively successful lawyers and the political arena also increased in Western Europe during the Early Modern and Modern periods. Members of the judicial professions not only served the state in their capacity as lawyers but were also numerous, proportionately speaking, in local government and in national legislatures. Lawyers were influential in the Belgian political world during the nineteenth century for an additional reason: some had played a significant role in the Belgian Revolution and in the creation of the new Belgian state.[19]

Whatever the reason, the judicial professions could not complain about their share of state honours. There had to be enough legal men in the British House of Lords to provide the requisite law lords. It is true that, until the late nineteenth century, the number of lawyers being made peers or baronets was limited by the necessity for those holding either of these two dignities to have sufficient wealth, preferably landed wealth, to sustain a hereditary title. Only a small percentage of lawyers qualified. Eventually, however, lawyers became an overrepresented source of peerage appointments. No less than 18.6 per cent of the persons elevated to the peerage in 1901–10 were from the judiciary, 13.8 per cent in 1911–20, and 17.2 per cent in 1921–30.[20]

The judicial professions had a strong presence in the major orders I sampled, at least relative to their representation in the total work force. Dumons found that a significant number of local nominations to the Legion of Honour were made for lawyers.[21] Judicial professionals constituted 15.8 per cent of my 1852 civilian sample of the Legion of Honour, 12.1 per cent of the 1833-87 civilian sample of the Order of Leopold, 8.3 per cent of males in the 1921 civilian sample of the Order of the British Empire, 10.4 per cent of the 1929 civilian sample of the Legion of Honour, and 6.7 per cent of the 1932 civilian sample of the Order of Leopold (Tables B.7–B.11). If we turn our attention to the grades into which they were deposited, we find that in most cases, judicial occupations did not do as well as politicians or higher-level state employees. Relative to their percentage in each order, they were the most over-represented in one of the two highest grades in the 1833-87 sample of the Order of Leopold, the 1921 sample of the Order of the British Empire, and the 1929 sample of the Legion of Honour (Tables B.12–B.16). Finally, it can be observed that, though considerable differences existed in the organization and autonomy of judicial occupations, among my sample countries, they do not seem to have created major differences in the award of state honours.

OTHER PROFESSIONS

In the eighteenth century, the prestige of members of other professional pursuits was even more varied than that of judicial occupations. On the whole, the standing of other professional positions was lower, but there was regional variation. A significant difference between the British Isles and France in this period was that, in the former, members of the professions could lay claim to the status of "gentleman," whereas French professionals, even lawyers, could not lay claim to "noble" status unless they had inherited it, were granted noble status by letters patent, or acquired it through an ennobling office.[22]

The respect enjoyed by members of the professions, as a group, was dragged down by irregulars. Even lawyers did not escape this threat to their prestige.[23] But it was much more of a problem for physicians and academics. While some physicians, especially those with a wealthy and powerful clientele, enjoyed distinction, most in the Early Modern period were poorly trained, with dubious credentials. Although the status of physicians and academics rose over the course of the eighteenth century, they were still quite consciously engaged in a struggle to raise their status, one manifestation of which – forming associations and offering of prizes – we have examined in several preceding chapters. The distinct status of the professions was based on their claim to unique knowledge, but knowledge was only one source of power in Early Modern society – and it was subject to no small degree of public skepticism and ridicule.[24] The knowledge claimed by most professions was not as firmly based as the knowledge that the judiciary could claim as their expertise.

Greater progress was made in the nineteenth century in the institutionalization of the status of professionals. It is during this period that the most significant differences between the British Isles and Continental countries developed, beginning with the Napoleonic period. In France and the Low Countries, state control over the professions greatly increased. In addition, the control exercised by members of the French professions over themselves became more centralized vis-à-vis Paris than among British professions vis-à-vis London.[25] While this state control and centralization restricted the autonomy of professionals, it did mean that some professional positions enjoyed a more solid monopoly over the provision of their services than was the case in the British Isles. Standardization eventually served to raise the status of the professions on both sides of the English Channel, but it did so earlier in France and the Southern Low Countries, a difference that was especially beneficial to lower-status professionals, such as notaries.[26]

In any case, members of professions were well recognized by state honours during the nineteenth and twentieth centuries. Some status awards were specifically intended for one or more professional pursuits. The longest living of these niche awards in the countries we are looking at is the Order of the Academic Palms. Instituted by Napoleon for personnel at the University of Paris, it was extended beyond the university community under Napoleon III, who made eligible anyone contributing to French education or culture. This modification resulted in its bestowal on writers and artists, such as painter Louis Dewis and sculptor Pierre Louis Rouillard. In the Netherlands, artists, scientists, and physicians were among the intended recipients of a medal established by William I in 1817 to reward contributions to the well-being of the population of his kingdom.[27] Professionals could be found among the recipients of several other Dutch decorations, including the Order of the Dutch Lion. The Order of Merit was created in Britain in 1902 for the purpose of rewarding outstanding individuals in science, art, and music, though it was not restricted to such persons. Members of the professions have also been awarded baronetcies, peerages, and knighthoods in the United Kingdom.

In addition, people in the professions were eligible for the major state honours I have sampled. Tables B.7–B.11 give the percentages for what I have called the professions (see Appendix B for a list of included occupations). With some exceptions, professionals were granted these rewards in greater numbers than those in any other civilian social position. The same is true among the Companions of Honour. Even if we exclude the clergy, they constituted the largest social group among members for the period 1917 to 1939 (Table B.40).

Yet the prestige of the status awards that professionals received was mixed. In the Netherlands, teachers could be found among those given "honour medals" or "brother medals," which were lower-status awards.[28] (I explain these shortly.) In Britain, they were appointed only rarely to the House of Lords. It was not until 1897 that a physician was blessed with a peerage[29] – and this elevation was not the beginning of a large number. Professionals constituted only 2 per cent of elevations to the House of Lords in the years 1901–10, 3 per cent in 1911–20, and 2 per cent in 1921–30.[30] In my sample of members of the Legion of Honour in 1852, professionals were primarily in the two lowest grades (Table B.12). They did better in the Order of Leopold. In the 1833–87 sample, they were spread through all grades, except the highest, the *grand cordon*. Still, they were most over-represented (relative to their percentage in this order) in the third and fourth grades (Table B.15). In my sample of the Order of the British Empire in 1921, professionals were most over-represented in the second-lowest grade (OBE) (Table B.14).

On the other hand, celebrated professionals could receive high honours. In addition to the small number in the House of Lords, some British professionals were knighted. As shown in Table B.14, professionals had good representation among the KBE recipients (second-highest grade in the Order of the British Empire). In my 1929 sample of the Legion of Honour, professionals provided 16.7 per cent of the *grands croix* and 38.7 per cent of the *grands officiers* (Table B.13). And it would seem that 14 per cent of those enno-bled in Belgium from 1830 to 1957 were professionals of one kind or another.[31]

It is worth pausing for a moment to take a brief look at a few of the professionals who received relatively high honours. Those who were made *grand officier* in the 1833–87 sample of the Order of Leopold consisted of two academics, two artists, and a writer; in the 1932 sample, professionals among the *grands officiers* were all academics, though one of them, Albert J. Carnoy, was also an important pol-itician. In the 1852 sample of the Legion of Honour, there were no professionals among the *grands croix* and the *grands officiers*. The *grands croix* of 1929 included Fulgence Marie Auguste Bienvenüe, who designed the Paris Metro, and three academics: mathemati-cian Paul Émile Appell and two medical scientists. My 1929 sample of *grands officiers* in the Legion of Honour included three univer-sity academics, two architects, a medical inspector and author, and three playwrights.

All of these samples differ sharply from my sample of members of the Order of the British Empire in 1921 because the initial appointments to this order went largely to persons who had made some significant contribution to the war effort. One of the GBEs (highest grade), for example, was Harry Livesey, a civil engineer. During the Great War, he was the deputy director of Inland Waterways and Docks at the War Office and then director of contracts at the Admiralty. Those with the grade of KBE (second highest) included physicians who managed military health facilities, a writer who spent the War helping with the propaganda campaign in the United States, and a number of accountants. Arthur Cornelius Roberts, one of those accountants, was awarded a KBE in recognition of the managerial and auditing positions he held in a number of departments during the War.

Non-Landed Ownership and Top Management

I remarked earlier that state honours were used by those with political power to raise their status relative to those who are economically powerful. Thus, during the formative period of these status awards, the representation of businessmen was not impressive when compared with the representation of military personnel, politicians, and state officials. They received hardly any recognition during the first half of the nineteenth century. No more than a dozen businessmen were admitted to the Legion of Honour under Napoleon; they were manufacturers of products that were in short supply as a result of the Continental blockade.[32] *Négociants* and manufacturers constituted only 1.6 per cent of those inducted into the Imperial nobility (though it must be acknowledged that this representation was no worse than that of other non-state social positions).[33] The number of businessmen appointed to the Legion of Honour was greater during the July Monarchy.[34] Still, the presence of non-landed owners and top managers in my sample of the Legion of Honour in 1852 was negligible, and those who were chosen had to be content with the grade of *officier* (Table B.12). The number of businessmen in the Legion of Honour rose over the course of the nineteenth century. Dumons's research tells us that local businessmen were well recognized. He found that a very large number of them were nominated for the Legion in Saône-et-Loire and Var from the 1870s to the 1930s.[35] In my national sample of members in 1929, in contrast, non-landed owners and top managers represented only 6.7 per cent of civilians (Table B.8). And from the beginning they have been scarce among the *grands croix.*

Businessmen were slightly better represented in the Order of Leopold. Non-landed owners and top managers constituted a tenth of the civilians in the 1833–87 sample (Table B.10). Their representation rose marginally in the late nineteenth and early twentieth centuries. Even after the Great War, they were still a bit better represented than they had been in 1833–87 (Table B.11). In the same years, an increase also occurred in the number of businessmen raised to the Belgian nobility.[36] The source that I used for the social composition of the Belgian nobility suggests that about a quarter of those ennobled in Belgium from 1830 to 1957 were industrialists or financiers.[37] Yet their share of membership in the Order of Leopold in 1932, according to my sample, was far less than that of professionals or higher-level state employees, roughly the same as middle-level state employees (Table B.11). More remarkable still, with the exception of one *grand croix*, the only grade in which they were over-represented (relative to their percentage in this order) was the lowest: *chevalier* (Table B.16).

Businessmen were no more numerous in the Order of the British Empire in 1921 than their counterparts were in the Legion of Honour in 1929 or the Order of Leopold in 1932, but they were placed in relatively higher grades. Perhaps more significantly, there was a sharp increase in the number of businessmen receiving British peerages in the late nineteenth and early twentieth centuries. The expansion began under the Conservative administration of 1886–92, continued under the Unionist administration of 1895–1905, and again under the Liberal administration of 1905–15.[38] In the years, 1901–10, no less than 28 per cent of new peers were in business; in 1911–20, the figure was 32 per cent; and in 1921–30, it was 36 per cent.[39] They were generally either bankers/financiers or the heads of industrial enterprises.[40]

When a non-landed owner or manager received a state honour, it was typically for one or more of four reasons: (1) payments to individuals distributing the awards or persons connected to these distributors, (2) political support, (3) philanthropy, and (4) politics or public service.

What is known as the Wilson affair in France falls into the first of these categories. Various parties tried to traffic in the Legion of Honour, making use of letters of Daniel Wilson, former undersecretary of state, an influential deputy, and son-in-law of President Jules Grévy, who, as a result of the scandal, was eventually forced to resign in 1887.[41] Similarly, during a later period, accusations were made in Britain that members of ruling parties were personally accepting payments for facilitating awards of honours to wealthy patrons.

Less objectionable perhaps were honours awarded in return for supporting governments in power, usually in the form of financial donations to political parties or favourable coverage in communications media controlled by businessmen. In Britain, the practice of rewarding political donations with honours became more apparent in the 1880s. It was a scattered practice of both the Liberals and the Conservatives in the 1890s. In 1892, the Liberal Unionist Party used its alliance with the Conservatives to raise funds for the party in return for honours.[42] In the mid-1890s, the first British honours scandal broke out when it became known that a bargain had been struck by the Liberals with two men who were to be awarded peerages in return for large donations to the Party.[43] However, this exposure did not bring an end to honours for donations in British politics. In the years 1899 to 1905, Herbert Gladstone (William Gladstone's son), who was the Liberal Chief Whip, raised £275,000 from twenty-seven people, eighteen of them businessmen; seventeen of the twenty-seven eventually obtained a peerage or a baronetcy from the Liberal government.[44]

A cynical attitude among some politicians toward state honours could encourage bargains of this kind. Kuyper's unflattering comparison of Modern orders of knighthood with the great orders of knighthood of the Middle Ages may partially explain his recommendation in 1903 of a decoration for an Amsterdam businessman in return for a political donation to his party.[45] There is no doubt that Lloyd George's cynical attitude toward honours played a part in such exchanges. Indeed, the "market" in British honours reached its peak under his coalition government, when sales were so blatant that a royal commission was established to examine the practice and to propose ways to curb it.[46] The scandal led to widespread disgust with the trafficking of honours. A scrutiny committee was instituted to vet nominations, and legislation was enacted in 1925 – known as the Honours (Prevention of Abuses) Act – which prohibited the sale of peerages or any other honours.

Since then, the direct exchange of honours for political donations has not been much in evidence, but honours have certainly been granted to persons who have supported political parties in various ways, including the provision of financial assistance. The reconstitution of the House of Lords under the Labour government of 1997–2010, which required political parties to nominate persons to the House of Lords, created a new potential for abuse. In 2006, the nomination of persons for peerages in return for loans to the Labour Party came to light, but no charges were laid.

Philanthropy was a more respectable route to honours. The late nineteenth and early twentieth centuries stand as one of the great eras of philanthropy. The Cadbury family, Andrew Carnegie, the Rothschilds, John D. Rockefeller, the Guinnesses, and Henry Ford are some of the best-known philanthropists of this period. Benjamin Guinness and his sons, Arthur and Edward, were all three philanthropists in the late nineteenth and early twentieth centuries. Benjamin and Arthur served as Conservative members of the House of Commons, but Edward focussed his energies almost entirely on managing the Guinness company, of which he became sole proprietor, and on his philanthropy, which, as the wealthiest man in Ireland, he could well afford on a lavish scale. He was made a knight in the Order of Saint Patrick in 1895, a viscount in the Peerage of the United Kingdom in 1905, a knight grand cross in the Royal Victorian Order in 1910, and an earl in the Peerage of the United Kingdom in 1919.

It was unusual for wealthy people to solicit an honour explicitly as a reward for philanthropy, but it certainly did happen. Donations to museums and art galleries were sometimes openly exchanged for honours in the Netherlands. Indeed, some wealthy Dutch were known to demand an assurance from the government that a certain honour would be forthcoming before they were willing to commit themselves to a donation.[47] David Cannadine provides examples of similar practices in Britain.[48]

Finally, with or without great wealth, a businessman could qualify for a state honour by engaging in politics or public service. Most of the businessmen that Dumons found in the nomination files for the Legion of Honour had been mayors in their localities. A Belgian by the name of Lucien Beauduin was a managing director of a large sugar refinery and an international figure associated with the sugar industry in a number of different countries. He was also, at various times, a *bourgmestre* of Lubeek, a member of the Belgian Senate, and an ambassador to Turkey. In 1932, he was made a *grand officier* (second-highest grade) of the Order of Leopold. Another Belgian, Félicien Cattier, originally an academic, became a managing director of the Banque d'Outre-Mer and then director of the major colonial holdings of the Société Générale (a large Belgian investment bank founded in 1822). He was one of the founders of the Fonds national de la recherche scientifique and served as its president. He had earlier vigorously opposed public exhibitions of Africans, spectacles that had become popular in Western Europe during the late nineteenth century; he was especially outraged over an exhibition of Africans at the Universal Exhibition in Belgium in 1897. He also helped lead the campaign against the abuses that occurred in Congo in that period, which he wrote about in *Etude sur la situation de l'Etat indépendant du Congo*. He was made a *commandeur* (third-highest grade) in the Order of Leopold in 1922.

Businessmen who were honoured for public service were, like professionals, particularly numerous in the Order of the British Empire in 1921 and in the Order of the Companions of Honour. The Great War offered businessmen a greater opportunity to assist than had any previous war in European history. Much of this assistance was financially beneficial to them, but not always. No small number of businessmen lent a hand by serving on boards and committees; some even accepted administrative positions on a short-term basis. They typically took full or partial leave from their enterprises to do so. Two examples will have to suffice. Leonard Wilkinson Llewelyn was the director of several coal, iron, and steel companies. He served as controller of materials of munitions supply during the Great War. He was made a KBE (second-highest grade in the Order of the British Empire). Percy Bates was the director of a number of shipping lines. During the War he served as head of the Commercial Branch Transport Department of the Admiralty and director of Commercial Services, Ministry of Shipping. He, too, was made a KBE.

It is necessary, however, to keep the larger picture in mind. Businessmen who were not conspicuous in political donations, philanthropy, or politics and public service rarely received a state honour, with the result that, taken as a whole, the non-landed ownership and managerial category was not a large one in the major honorific orders that I sampled. Governments did not expand the honours they distributed during the Early Modern and Modern periods in order to serve the business community.

When businessmen began to receive a significant share of honours, their reception could be less than gracious. The increase in the number of businessmen receiving honours in the later decades of the nineteenth century created much displeasure, most noticeably in the United Kingdom. The honours bestowed on shipbuilder W.J. Pirrie were resented in many quarters. His elevation to the peerage in 1906, in return for helping finance the Liberal campaign in Ulster, was not well received in the House of Lords. His admission to the Order of Saint Patrick in 1909 was so resented by his fellow knights that they refused to take part in the investiture.[49]

Queen Victoria's opposition to the appointment of Lionel Rothschild to the House of Lords reflects aristocratic disdain for business as well as contemporary anti-Semitism. Men like Albert Grant only served to reinforce such sentiments. In 1875, Lord Stanley (Edward Henry Stanley, fifteenth earl of Derby) reacted to the prospect of awarding a state honour to this crooked financier. Grant (né Abraham Gottheimer) had just purchased *The Echo* (a half-penny evening newspaper published in London) and was going to turn it into a Conservative paper. He had also developed Leicester Square, and made a gift of it to the city of London. In 1874, he had been removed (for improper spending) from a seat he had won as a Conservative in the General Election of that year. In June 1875, when Stanley was foreign secretary and still a member of the Conservative Party, he wrote in his diary that "the position which Albert Grant is making for himself and us will be difficult. He has done too many dirty acts to be whitewashed: and too many that are useful to be neglected. Probably some day he will ask for a baronetcy."[50] In 1868, Grant had been made a hereditary baron by Victor Emmanuel II of Italy, and in 1872, he was made a commander of the Portuguese Order of Christ; in both cases, it was claimed that he had purchased the titles. He was never made a British baronet.

Not surprisingly, there was also much displeasure with the award of the Order of the British Empire to some of the businessmen whose companies supplied munitions for the Great War. The money they had made was widely regarded as compensation enough for their "contribution" to the war effort.[51] And the honours scandals in both Britain and France added to a negative public attitude toward businessmen insofar as they were among those who used money to obtain status awards.

Petite Bourgeoisie, Working Class, and Peasantry

If one were to limit one's research to state honours in France during the first half of the nineteenth century, one might conclude that the expansion of honours significantly benefited persons in lower socio-economic groups. Napoleon, to achieve what he sought by creating the Legion of Honour, did not hesitate to enrol sons of peasants and workers. We do not have data on the social origins of military personnel in the Legion – the *Annuaires* provided only their military rank – but we have seen that a large percentage of the military in the Legion of Honour in 1852 were *sous-officiers* (NCOs).

Members of the petite bourgeoisie and working class represented 12.6 per cent of the civilian members of my sample of the Legion of Honour still alive in 1852; and the peasantry represented another 1.6 per cent (Table B.7). In contrast, over the next fifty to seventy years, the representation of these lower socio-economic positions in the Legion of Honour declined (as did the representation of *sous-officiers*). In my sample for 1929, the representation of the petite bourgeoisie and working class was only 5.9 per cent and no one classified as belonging to the peasantry was in the sample (Table B.8). The petite bourgeoisie and working class made up only 2.7 per cent of my nineteenth-century sample of the Order of Leopold, with no one who would be considered a peasant (Table B.10). No one in any of these social positions was to be found in the 1932 sample of the Order of Leopold (Table B.11). Furthermore, when members of these social positions were chosen for a status award, they were invariably put in the lower grades (Tables B.12–B.16).

As in the case of soldiers, by the twentieth century, part of the reason for the declining presence of lower socio-economic groups in the major orders is that, over the preceding period, other honours were created that were open to the working class, some specifically designated for the working class. As just noted, in the Kingdom of the Netherlands "honour medals" or "brother medals" were introduced specifically for those whose status did not seem to fit with a major national honour. Kees Bruin recounts the experiences of several midwives in the Netherlands who had to be satisfied with one of these medals.[52]

When a state honour was awarded to a member of the petite bourgeoisie or working class, it was usually for one or more of the following reasons. The first was the hope that awards and prizes could be used to improve the morals, manners, prudence, and sobriety of the working classes. A second, closely related, reason was to encourage loyalty toward "superiors." In particular, the loyalty of police officers or national guardsmen to a political faction or regime could bring recognition. The instability of political regimes in France during the first half of the nineteenth century may have contributed to the relatively large representation of the petite bourgeoisie and working class in the Legion of Honour sample of 1852. Over half of these two groups in the sample were *gardes* of different kinds. Their presence may also reflect what Charle calls the "old paternalism," which still prevailed in France during the first half of the nineteenth century.[53] Yet efforts continued to be made to instill loyalty in workers even as relations between them and their employers became more contentious during the second half of the century. The *medaille de travail* was bestowed on workers with "thirty years of consecutive service in the same industrial or commercial establishment within the territory of the French Republic."[54] Beginning in 1895, the honour medal attached to the Order of Orange-Nassau was awarded to employees in the private sector for long service; and later it came to be conferred on domestics for years of service.[55] Most countries eventually created long-service rewards for state employees.

Third, occasions could arise in which members of lower socio-economic positions were seen to be making extraordinary contributions. Rescue awards often went to persons in lower socio-economic groups. To repeat an earlier observation, military rewards for battlefield performance usually went to lower ranks in the military, though not necessarily the lowest. I also made the point that soldiers were sometimes given rewards normally reserved for higher ranks as a way of acknowledging exceptional behaviour on their part. Indeed, any individual who was among a small number of persons in a lower socio-economic position receiving a high-status reward or grade in an order – and such people can be found in Tables B.7–B.11 – was obviously regarded as exceptional. In particular, this was one of the reasons for appointing members of lower-ranked social strata to the Order of the British Empire. Although no members of the working class were to be seen in my 1921 sample, there were a significant number of members of what I have called the lower bourgeoisie (mostly clerks, secretaries, or supervisors). Almost all members of the lower bourgeoisie appointed by 1921 were being recognized for exceptional work in a civilian organization associated with the war effort.

Fourth, members of the working class could be recognized for their craftsmanship. The practice of awarding prizes to craftsmen during the seventeenth and eighteenth centuries for work of superior quality continued in the nineteenth century and became more institutionalized with the growth in commercial and industrial exhibitions. These exhibitions expanded significantly in Western Europe during the first half of the nineteenth century, and led to an increase in the number of prizes available to members of the working class. In addition, special honorific rewards were created for craftsmen over the course of the nineteenth century. In 1847 the Belgian government created the Belgian Industrial and Agricultural Decoration for superior workmanship in manufacturing.[56] (I mentioned it in Chapter 10 to illustrate individualization in awards of this kind.) In 1878, it was broadened to include persons who had contributed to the formation of worker co-operatives. It has evolved into the present-day Labour Decoration.[57]

MAJOR STATUS GROUPS

We now move from specific social positions to major status groups. What effect did the expansion of state honours have on larger status structures? How were state honours distributed among larger status groups? Did this distribution change over the long nineteenth century?

The Aristocracy

Proportionate to their representation in the population, Western-European aristocrats fared well in the new honours of the eighteenth and nineteenth centuries. This was less true in France and the Low Countries, but even there aristocrats could still be favoured in appointments to state honours. Bruin found that, on one occasion, well into the twentieth century, nobles nominated for decorations awarded by the Dutch Ministry of Work were disproportionately successful.[58] In the same period, he found that members of the nobility had been given relatively high-status distinctions, even when there were doubts about their merits.[59]

In the British Isles, the view persisted in the nineteenth century that those elevated to the British peerage should have links to existing peerage families or own large landed estates. In the first fifty years of the reign of Queen Victoria, only 10 per cent of new peers did not have an aristocratic or gentry background.[60] In addition to political considerations, one of the constraints operating on the government was the view that those receiving a hereditary honour should have sufficient wealth to maintain the status in later generations. A feeling also prevailed that men with no claim to aristocratic status would not "fit" in the House of Lords, would not have the right social connections, would not possess the sense of public duty thought to be characteristic of the British aristocracy, and so forth. Appointments of peers in the British Isles had always been limited by the institutional requirements of the three parliaments, but also by norms of social exclusion. In the nineteenth century, there continued to be resistance in the British elite to any change in the nature of appointments to the House of Lords that would allow peerages to be awarded more liberally.

The reasons became exceedingly clear when, in 1856, the Palmerston government had the Queen confer a life peerage on Sir James Parke, who was to become Baron Wensleydale.[61] Palmerston's goal was to find a way to overcome the shortage of law lords in the House of Lords without creating nobles whose families could not afford the cost of maintaining the dignity of a peer in later generations. The House of Lords Committee for Privileges rejected the appointment, and the Crown's prerogative was never again used to create life peers. (In restricted numbers, life peerages for law lords were eventually made possible by virtue of the Appellate Jurisdiction Act of 1876.)

It was the view of the lords in 1856 that the real goal of the government was to establish a precedent for the appointment in the future of peers of modest means. The law lords themselves were much opposed, fearing that it would make it less likely that future candidates for their position would receive a hereditary peerage. It was certainly the case that the government was trying to introduce life peerages as an institutional innovation. Parke could easily have been appointed as a hereditary peer without fear that it would pass to any descendants, since he was seventy-four years of age and had no children. It was even thought by some that Palmerston's move was the first step in Prince Albert's plan to use the House of Lords to recognize literary and scientific men, or that it was the enactment of schemes of radicals to reform the House of Lords. This is doubtful. Palmerston strongly believed that the most important criterion for membership in the House of Lords was landed wealth, and he was not keen on using peerages to recognize eminent authors or professionals.[62] Whatever Palmerston's objective, by preventing the Wensleydale peerage creation, the lords insured that landed wealth would remain a necessary condition for elevation to the House of Lords for some time to come.

British governments sometimes awarded aristocrats a state honour in order to raise its standing. This was most overtly the case in early appointments to the Order of the British Empire; the 1921 list of GBE (highest grade) was well stocked with royals, peers, baronets, and wives of peers or baronets. In addition, the continued prominence of British aristocrats in politics and the state bureaucracy meant that they garnered a disproportionate share of the high-status state honours that went to these sectors.

The same can be said of military honours in both Britain and Continental countries. The aristocracy was greatly over-represented in the officer corps of European armies until after the Great War. Since senior military officers were disproportionately awarded higher-status state honours, this would add to the aristocratic over-representation in these honours. Aristocratic predominance among officers is well known for British military forces, but it was characteristic of the French army as well. It was a result of two conditions: (1) militarism in traditional European aristocratic culture and (2) the proportionately greater number of aristocrats with the education that had become necessary for a military career. Indeed, as indicated in Chapter 7, a growing number of officers in France came from *grandes écoles*, primarily Saint-Cyr and the Polytechnique, during the later part of the nineteenth century. After 1880, recruitment of officers from the ranks of *sous-officiers* declined in favour of recruitment from the *grandes écoles*. This shift reversed the decline in the aristocratic composition of the officer corps, which became more meritocratic, but also better educated, and more Catholic and aristocratic.[63] Charle shows that 10 to 20 per cent of the generals in 1901 were nobles, a remarkably high percentage, given that there had been little addition to the French noble population since the Bourbon Restoration. Moreover, nearly half of the generals came from families that would have been described as belonging to *anciennes fractions* (large proprietors, high civil servants of regimes preceding the Third Republic, or the *bourgeoisie de robe*).[64]

In the United Kingdom, the aristocracy remained greatly over-represented in the officer corps for most of the nineteenth century, especially in the army. In 1875, no less than 18 per cent of officers in the home army were from peerage families, and another 32 per cent were from the landed gentry; as late as 1912, an astounding 30 per cent of the generals and 24 per cent of the major-generals and above were still from peerage families, while an additional 22 per cent of the generals and 40 per cent of the major generals and above were from the landed gentry.[65] This persistence of the aristocracy in high-ranking military positions seriously delayed the extent to which the evolution of state honours could alter the existing status structure in Western-European armies.

Nevertheless, Modern state honours did reflect and contribute to the rise in status power of non-aristocrats. First of all, the erosion in the political power of the aristocracy, which was discussed in Chapter 1, had a considerable effect by reducing their status-distributive power; that is to say, aristocrats were less often in a position to determine who was to be recognized. In the case of the British House of Lords, the pressure for political appointments also served to reduce the percentage of new peers coming from aristocratic families. More precisely, as the composition of the House of Commons became less aristocratic, the number of men linked to aristocratic families who were raised from the lower house to the peerage diminished. This also meant that not a few of those I am referring to above as aristocrats were new aristocrats. The peers and baronets in the GBE grade of the Order of the British Empire included some whose peerage or baronetcy was of relatively recent origin, such as Herbert Gladstone.

All this reflects the larger reality that aristocrats, over-represented as they continued to be, were more and more out-numbered in the pool of potential recipients. Among the 200 individuals who obtained peerages in the years 1886–1914, roughly fifty had aristocratic connections, but this represented only a quarter of the elevations in those years.[66] Similarly, too many men were being made baronets during the late nineteenth and early twentieth centuries for aristocratic kinship groups to monopolize the status. And the vast majority of the thousands of people appointed to the Order of the British Empire in the twentieth century were obviously non-aristocrats. Even in the higher grades their strength was limited. Although, as just indicated, the aristocracy was greatly over-represented, they could not predominate as a percentage of those honoured. If 18.5 per cent of the knights grand cross in the 1921 sample were sons of peers, this means that over 80 per cent were not.

We can also assume that the number of aristocrats receiving high honours for military service fell after the Great War, since the representation of aristocrats in the officer corps of the British army was falling, though they were still over-represented in the higher ranks.[67] The abolition of purchase contributed to this change, but much of it was also demographic. The Great War required more officers than any previous war in British history, and the aristocratic soldiers who fought in that war died in large numbers, leaving the aristocracy unable to meet the officer needs of the British army of the twentieth century in the way that it had done during the nineteenth century.

In France, those claiming noble status became numerically inconsequential in the population, certainly if we do not count those of questionable authenticity. Among the eighty-one *grands croix* (highest grade) in the Legion of Honour in 1929, only three could be identified as sons of nobles. In Belgium, only one of the eighteen *grands cordons* (highest grade) in the Order of Leopold in 1932 was descended from the old nobility. This was Charles de Broqueville, actually of French extraction though he was born in Belgium, who was prime minister of Belgium from 1911 to 1918 and from 1932 to 1934.

As can be seen from Tables B.7–B.11, no recipients in my samples of members of the Legion of Honour or of the Order of Leopold were designated as landowners. The same was true of the Companions of Honours from 1917 to 1939 (Table B.40). And only a very small percentage of members of the Order of the British Empire were so designated in 1921. (There was only one landowner in my sample, a number that was reduced to zero when the sample was weighted. See Tables B.9 and B.14.) This does not mean that no one receiving these honours owned significant assets in land; rather, it means some other designation was given as their social position. Many aristocrats and their sons, besides owning land, had always pursued other endeavours, and they did so increasingly in the nineteenth and early twentieth centuries. Now, however, if worthy of a state honour, they had to share the limelight with large numbers of persons having no claim to an aristocratic ancestry.

Non-Europeans

Needless to say, if state honours had to show some respect for the existing aristocratic hierarchy, the existing racial hierarchy was an even more ingrained status structure to which state honours had to conform. The general expectation in Western Europe was that persons with non-European ancestry should not be recipients of European honours. In 1818, when the Military Order of William was first awarded in the Dutch Indies, only Europeans were acceptable. The Legion of Honour was awarded to persons with non-European ancestry in the nineteenth century, but the numbers were small. *Chevrons de blessure*, instituted in Belgium in 1918, were open to soldiers in the colonial army, but only European soldiers.[68] Officially, the Victoria Cross could be awarded to persons of non-European descent, but only three non-whites received the it before 1911. The first black recipient was a Nova Scotian, William Hall, in 1857, for his participation in the defence of Lucknow during the Indian Mutiny. Suggestions that natives serving in the British Indian services be made eligible were repeatedly rejected.

A number of reasons can be offered for these expectations and practices. Obviously, a major reason was the belief in European racial superiority. Yet it is important to understand that the people who were handing out honours were motivated less by a belief in this racial superiority – whether or not they personally held this belief – than by their perception that it was held by others. It was certainly not that state officials could not imagine non-Europeans performing deeds of valour or acting as competently and as zealously as Europeans, nor that they did not think non-Europeans should be recognized for doing so. If anything, state officials seem to have been all the more impressed if a person with non-European ancestry risked his life or worked tirelessly for a European administration. The problem was that conferring European honours on people with non-European ancestry would unsettle the existing hierarchy in the colonies. The appointment would be controversial and create a reaction that might undermine the colonial administration.

In 1851, the Governor General of the Dutch East Indies wrote to the Minister of the Colonies expressing his concern about the consequences of awarding a star along with knighthood in the Order of the Oak Crown to the Susuhunan (emperor) of Surakarta. "I do not doubt that the award will be received with pleasure," he acknowledged. Still, he wondered if the minister would "consider giving the Susuhunan a rank lower than the knighthood with star." He was worried that "otherwise Susuhunan would have a decoration equal or even higher than mine, the Dutch Lion. Your excellence I trust knows me sufficiently to believe that I do not see any objection in this for myself but I am not sure if it would be a good stance during my visits to the King's lands that my decoration was equal to or lesser than that of the Susuhunan."[69] It is likely that the Minister took more of an interest in his own status than he was pretending, but his apprehension that this award to the Susuhunan could undermine Dutch authority in the colony was no doubt genuine.

J.F.W. van Nes, the vice-president of the Council of Indonesia, was even more concerned that the elevation of the Susuhunan would disrupt the existing hierarchy, and expressed his views in terms that were more clearly racist. He did not approve of "natives" getting Dutch decorations. "How high a Javan may climb up in civilization," he declared, "he must never be equivalent to the Dutchman and even less may he be honoured above the Dutchman ... If we want to maintain law and order, then there must remain a strict division between the two nations."[70]

For the most part, the problem was handled by segregating them. The best thing, according to the Vice-President, was that "the natives have their own decorations, their own nobles," which they keep, "just as we the Dutch have our own and should keep ours."[71] He recommended a colonial civil medal for natives, which was eventually established in 1871 and explicitly named the "Medal for the Civil Services of Natives," though this was changed in 1893 to the "Star for Loyalty and Service."[72] In 1839, the Dutch government created a separate military honour for colonial indigenous populations. The idea of bestowing an ornate kris (a Malaysian dagger) on worthy non-Europeans had been proposed earlier, but the 1839 decoration was a medal in the shape of a window inscribed with the words "For Bravery and Loyalty."[73]

Some of the late eighteenth-century service medals conferred by the British government and the East India Company were open to both European and native soldiers, but the Monghyr Medal (for the suppression of a mutiny at Monghyr in 1766), the Deccan

Medal (for service in two wars in India from 1778 to 1784), and the Mysore Medal (for service in the Mysore Campaign of 1791–92) were specifically for natives.

In 1837, the British government had established a separate military order for India known as the Order of Merit. An official in the Indian government, writing in 1834, explained that the objective was "to increase the respectability and improve the prospects of the Native Commissioned Officers, by placing within their reach honours, distinctions and superior emoluments, without imparting to them such additional power and influence over the Native Soldiery as might be injurious to the authority, which, in consideration of the composition of the Indian Army, it has hitherto been deemed necessary to vest exclusively in European Officers."[74]

When the Victoria Cross was created, native Indian troops were ineligible because they already had this award. In 1907, another decoration, the Indian Distinguished Service Medal, was established for Indian armed forces and police. It was not until 1911 that the exclusion of Indians from the Victoria Cross was lifted. When the very prestigious Order of Merit was established in 1902 to recognize British accomplishment in science, art, and music, the earlier Indian order of this name was quickly renamed the Indian Order of Merit.

Other racially segregated British honours included the Kaiser-I-Hind (Empress of India) Medal, which was instituted in 1900 and was awarded mostly to Indians. Similarly, the Belgians introduced a large number of special state honours or grades for the native population of Congo.[75] Such segregation of honours enabled the authorities to recognize the outstanding achievements of non-Europeans without undermining the larger status hierarchy.

It also yielded blatant inconsistencies. Natives witnessed the award of European honours to Europeans whose contributions were no greater, and often less, than their own. Many Europeans also recognized these inconsistencies. Particularly in the Netherlands, considerable opposition to the exclusion of persons with non-European ancestry emerged. In 1864, it seemed ridiculous to a parliamentary committee that the Military Order of William could not be awarded to a person with non-European ancestry when it was "not only accessible to Netherlanders, but also to aliens serving in the lowest ranks of the army and navy, as long as they are Europeans."[76] They pointed out that non-Europeans were well aware of the incompetence of many Europeans in the imperial officialdom and military forces. As early as 1826, the Dutch Minister of the Colonies wrote a letter to the King in which he requested approval for the appointment of the Prince of Solo, Adipati Mangko Negoro, to the Military Order of William. Speaking more generally, he raised doubts about the principle of rewarding and punishing natives and Dutch persons differently in the Indies:

> One wants to make believe that the European is somehow a being of higher character than the native; one wants the latter to treat the former with respect and reverence but the native witnesses daily himself the immorality that reigns amongst many Europeans and the harsh sentences that are meted out publicly and often it is the native who lends his hands to execute the pronounced sentences on the guilty Europeans. One proclaims that all, natives as well as Europeans, have the same protections under the law and they are equal subjects of His Majesty but there is a whole other criminal code that natives are sentenced under – they are put to forced labour and other services that the European is never subjected to.[77]

Honours distributors were caught in a dilemma. Although awarding non-Europeans with honours that were equal to or above those awarded to European colonial officials could undermine the authority of the latter, the exclusion of people with non-European ancestry from European honours could in its own way also undermine the overseas power of a European state. Many of the non-Europeans who sought European honours were important for international relations or colonial administration. Indeed, many colonial administrators saw honours as a means of gaining the support and loyalty of powerful locals. Giving them a European decoration could be extremely beneficial; rejecting them, or giving them less than they expected, could not be done without cost. And high-status members of native populations were sufficiently in tune with the hierarchy and rules of precedence of European honours to know when they were being slighted. To make matters worse, as more and more people were given awards created specifically for non-Europeans, the prestige of these honours declined. Powerful natives became offended that the only recognition they received was the same as persons whom they regarded as their inferiors. If European officials had a status hierarchy to 'which they had to conform, so too did the indigenous populations.

Moreover, as Cannadine has argued, no small number of European colonial administrators had considerable respect for local status hierarchies. In *Ornamentalism*, he suggests that Europeans who lamented the decline of the traditional social hierarchy in Western Europe were often (even if they themselves were not highly placed in this hierarchy) favourably disposed toward the traditional hierarchies they found in the colonies, and were willing to use European power to help support them. Awarding European honours to members of native elites was one way of doing so.

Whatever the reason, European honours were sometimes bestowed on persons of non-European descent. Although there were a few even in the early nineteenth century – Adipati Mangko Negoro was admitted to the Military Order of William in 1826 – it was not until the late nineteenth century that the number of non-Europeans to benefit from European honours became noticeable, and they were limited mostly to persons of political importance. In 1891 Abbas Hilmi of Egypt received the first of his four British honours, a knight grand cross of the Order of Saint Michael and Saint George.[78] Among the 69 knights grand cross (highest grade) in the 1921 list of members of the Order of the British Empire were 7 persons of non-European descent. Among the 484 knights commander (second-highest grade), 5 did not have European descent. They were all members of Indian princely families.

A larger number of heads of state or high officials with non-European descent received the Order of Leopold in the early twentieth century. Not included in my sample of 1932 were fifty persons of non-European descent who were made *grands cordons* and *grands officiers* (two highest grades), among them Reza Khan Pahlavi (shah of Persia), Yoshihito (emperor of Japan), Amanoullah Khan (king of Afghanistan), and Haile Selassie (emperor of Ethiopia).[79]

Some non-Europeans could accumulate an impressive number of eminent memberships. During the years 1885 to 1902, Japanese statesman Ito Hirobumi was made a grand cross of no less than nine European orders: the Swedish Order of Vasa, the Austro-Hungarian Order of the Iron Crown, the Prussian Order of the Red Eagle, the Russian Order of Saint Alexander Nevsky, the Spanish Order of Charles III, the Belgian Order of Leopold, the French Legion of Honour, the Italian Order of the Annunciation, and the British

Order of the Bath. Pridi Banomyong, a left-wing Thai politician who strongly opposed Thai militarism and Japanese influence on Thailand, was awarded high grades in five European honours: grand cross of the Legion of Honour, grand cordon of the Order of Leopold, grand cross of the Order of Saint Michael and Saint George, commander grand cross of the Swedish Order of Vasa, and grand cross of the Order of the German Eagle.

Women

From a twenty-first-century perspective, the exclusion of women from the major honours of states in the long nineteenth century is shocking. No woman received the Legion of Honour until 1851. And this event did not herald a large number of female appointments; in total, there were only seven under the Second Empire.[80] It was not until the Great War that the number of women named to the Legion of Honour became substantial. The Order of the British Empire and the Order of the Companions of Honour were the first major British honorific rewards that were bestowed on a large number of women. In 1855, Palmerston had wanted to confer an honour on Florence Nightingale, but he recognized that he could not admit her to the Order of the Bath because she was a woman.[81] Over half a century after she had become a national public figure, she was given the Order of Merit. It was not too little, but it was too late. Nightingale, then eighty-seven, was not mentally capable of understanding what she was receiving.[82] Women were not eligible for the Victoria Cross until 1920; and the inclusion of them in the warrant of that year faced considerable opposition, including the misgivings of George V.[83] When honours were being handed out in such vast numbers to men, how could women have been almost totally excluded?

There are a number of answers, no one of which by itself is sufficient. First, we can certainly argue that women were perceived as inferior and therefore unworthy of state honours. The problem with this explanation is that much anecdotal evidence suggests that, as was the case with people of non-European ancestry, insofar as women were regarded as inferior, this was, in the view of many, all the more reason to give status awards to the few whose actions were undeniably exceptional. Many people believed, as did Palmerston, that Nightingale was exceptional. A wide public held the same attitude toward Juliette Dodu, a French woman who allegedly forwarded Prussian communications to the French military during the Franco-Prussian War. She did not have to wait a half-century for a state honour. She was awarded both the Military Medal and the Legion of Honour. It is possible that the whole story of her heroism was concocted to raise French spirits in the wake of the military defeat of 1871. In any case, people believed it and supported her celebration.

Second, it was not regarded as desirable to motivate women to do the sorts of things that bring status awards. Thus, the awards to women went almost entirely to those in domains of activity deemed appropriate for women. In 1871, King Charles I of Württemberg created the Order of Olga (named after his wife), which was open to both men and women, but specifically in recognition of charitable works.[84] The Order of Maria Anna (Saxony) was founded in 1906 to be awarded to ladies for charitable work in the line of welfare and nursing.[85] Most of the early appointments of women to the Legion of Honour went to the directors of charities or hospitals and to nurses, especially nuns.[86] The majority of women in my sample of the Order of the British Empire in 1921 were designated as engaged in "charitable work," and most of the others were in nursing or hospital administration. Seven of the fifteen women appointed to the Order of the Companions of Honour from 1917 to 1939 were in charity or volunteer work. This pattern can be explained at least partly by the widespread view that these were the proper spheres for women.

It can also be explained by the fact that, at this time, a relatively large number of women in the public sphere were to be found in these domains. Thus a third reason for the exclusion of women from state honours is that they were, voluntarily or involuntarily, not doing the things for which people were most often given honours: fighting wars, managing states, et cetera. Thus, whether or not those distributing state honours believed women were inferior, whether they did or did not want to motivate them to engage in certain enterprises, the probability that a woman would do something outstanding in these activities was statistically low, and so the lists of possible candidates for state honours did not include many women. This was no doubt a factor, but as many single cases revealed, there were enough women engaged in "male" activities – even fighting battles alongside men – that it is difficult to explain the almost total exclusion of women as the result of a lack of worthy candidates.

Indeed, a few of them, like Dodu, were recognized. Another example is a woman who received the Belgian Commemorative Volunteer Cross for having participated in the Revolution of 1830.[87]

Fourth, women lacked status-distributive power. Men created state honours and held the offices or sat on the committees that decided who would receive them. Yet again, this can be only a part of the explanation. There were certainly enough powerful men who were willing to confer a state honour on women that we should have seen more state honours for women in the nineteenth century than we do. Such men were not small in number, and were not limited to radicals. Palmerston was an old, crusty aristocrat.

Moreover, we have to be careful not to underestimate the power of women in nineteenth-century society. Many women could find ways to influence those who had status-distribution power. There is little evidence, however, that when they enjoyed influence, they used it to get more women decorated. Napoleon III's wife, the independent-minded Empress Eugénie, did make such an effort. In 1865, when she was regent in her husband's absence, she appointed a female artist, the very unusual Rosa Bonheur, to the Legion of Honour. Yet there was no general pattern of women promoting their gender whenever they got the chance. Victoria was adamantly opposed to major decorations going to women. There is also considerable anecdotal evidence that women used what influence they possessed to secure decorations not for women but for men, usually a husband, brother, son, or nephew. Women had long been known to lobby for peerages for their husbands or sons. James Ferguson provides a number of examples of women lobbying for the selection of their husband or son to be anointed as one of the sixteen peers of Scotland.[88] In Chapter 10, we saw the role played by several women in obtaining the Victoria Cross for Lieutenant Francis Aylmer Maxwell. The belief by some contemporaries that women were more interested in state honours for their husbands than were the husbands themselves provides the amusement in Arnold Bennett's *The Title*. While this notion greatly understates the vanity of men, it does reflect a certain reality in which many women felt that decorations for other women would threaten the status of the men with whom they were connected.

This brings us to the fifth reason for the exclusion of women. As the reader can expect me to assert, women were excluded because giving them honours would affect the existing status structure in ways that would cause embarrassment, discontent, and resentment. Giving a woman a state honour meant elevating her not only above all the men in her country who had never received any state honour but also above those men who were awarded a lower-status decoration in the great pecking order of state honours. Although women broke into the Legion of Honour earlier than they did into other decorations, it was not until 1931 that a woman attained the rank of *commandeur* (third-highest grade), and not until 1953 that a woman was named a *grand officier* (second-highest grade).[89] The British were not as slow to put women in higher grades of their orders; the highest grade in the Order of the British Empire had a significant number of women. As I have already mentioned, however, many were the wives of peers and baronets. And the percentage represented by women in other grades was greatest in the lowest grade, the MBEs (Table B.38).

As was the case for people with non-European ancestry, the solution was segregation. A significant number of state honorific rewards for women were created during the nineteenth century. It is true that there were some decorations for which both sexes were eligible. Many were royal house orders; others were religious orders, such as the revived Order of the Hospital of Saint John of Jerusalem. (Three years before Nightingale was conceded the Order of Merit, she had been made a Lady of Grace of the Order of Saint John of Jerusalem.[90]) Nevertheless, the majority of women who were decorated in Europe during the nineteenth century were given honours designed specially for them. The exception was France, where no honour was introduced specifically for women until the Family Medal of 1920, though Empress Eugénie had tried to introduce a separate honorific order for women before she pushed for their appointment to the Legion of Honour.[91] Some of the female orders had Old-Regime origins, such as the very prestigious and exclusive Habsburg Order of the Star-Cross, but most were established during the nineteenth century. In 1814, Frederick William III of Prussia founded the Order of Louisa, "to do honour to the female sex" for their care of the sick and wounded, and for "cheerfully" yielding their husbands and sons for the war effort.[92] In the United Kingdom, the Royal Order of Victoria and Albert was instituted in 1862 for the sovereign and forty-five ladies, subsequently expanding to include women who belonged to European royal families or the

British aristocracy. (No appointments were made after the death of Victoria.) The Imperial Order of the Crown of India was founded in 1878 for the wives and other female relatives of high personnages in India. A military order for nurses, the Royal Red Cross, was created in the United Kingdom in 1883. I earlier referred to the Order of Maria Anna (Saxony), which was for women only. In Belgium, the Medal of Queen Elizabeth was awarded to women who helped civilians or soldiers during the Great War.

It is clear, therefore, that the main obstacle to honouring women was not that status distributors never wanted to recognize deserving women. They just did not want them competing with men. We do not know what most of them personally thought of the existing gender structure. For what it is worth, Frederick Ponsonby's mother was (by the standards of the time) a feminist. All we know for certain is that, until the twentieth century, the distribution of state honours in Europe did not deviate significantly from the existing gender structure. And insofar as they conformed to that status structure, those with status-distribution power intentionally or unintentionally reinforced it. By seeking to avoid the trouble caused by granting a woman an honour that would have placed her above men, they made it all the more difficult for themselves and other status distributors to recognize the accomplishments of women.

Nonetheless, as was the case with non-Europeans, the segregation of women that prevailed until the twentieth century could generate criticism. In France, their exclusion was especially difficult to justify, given the enormous number of men who had been decorated by the state since the seventeenth century. During the nineteenth century, it was commonly believed that several women had been awarded the Legion of Honour by Napoleon, but Claude Ducourtial (curator of the National Museum of the Legion of Honour, 1964–84) did not think so. His view was that the women in question were given special awards of some kind, probably medals on which Napoleon's likeness had been engraved.[93] Be that as it may, the myth that some women had been admitted indicates that during the nineteenth century, many French people thought it appropriate that women should receive state honours. It was one such individual, Marie Duchemin, who, in 1851, became the first woman we know for certain to be admitted to the Legion of Honour. Remarkable stories of devotion and courage had been attributed to her; at the age of sixty-one, she had become a popular figure of veneration. Public opinion also played a role in the award of the Military Medal and the Legion of Honour to Juliette Dodu.

Meanwhile in Britain, women were still confined almost entirely to female decorations. In the 1840s, when a medal was struck for those who had participated in the Battle of Trafalgar, a woman, Jane Townshend, was listed for the award because *The Gazette* indicated that all who were present in this action should have a medal without restriction as to sex. However, on further consideration, her nomination was tossed out because a large number of other women had been on board ships during naval action between 1793 and 1840 and they might all demand some kind of status recognition.[94] Male prerogative triumphed, but the whole business was embarrassing to the authorities. The same was true in 1870 when a nun in Mauritius was nominated for the Order of Saint Michael and Saint George by seventy-two high-society women and her candidacy was supported by the Governor. Although the "noble conduct" of the woman was recognized by the Colonial Office, the nomination was rejected. Admitting that "there was no expressed exclusion" of women from the Order, it was nevertheless asserted that "the word knight to a certain extent shows that it was not intended that women should be admitted."[95]

The inconsistency became increasingly difficult to sustain as movements for women's rights grew in strength during the last half of the nineteenth century and the early decades of the twentieth. Although the electoral franchise was of much greater concern to feminists than honours – which most feminists regarded as a lot of male pomposity – the two injustices had similarities. Just like the vote was being given to men who were much less educated and informed than large numbers of women who were still denied it, great numbers of men were being given state honours for doing less than what a good number of women were known to have done.

The exclusion of women from the Order of the British Empire would have been just too much. If awarded only to men, it would have contradicted the very rationale for it, that is, correcting the inconsistency between the number of honorific awards becoming available for the military, while little was available to recognize the substantial contributions many civilians were making to the war effort. This blatant discrimination would not have been easy for authorities to manage, especially given the enormous number of women who were making such a contribution. All this did not mean that as many women as men were to be recognized. In my 1921 weighted sample, women represented only 26.2 per cent of civilian members and only 18.3 per cent of the total if we include the military.

Obviously, changing attitudes toward the role of women in Western societies provided a critical force in breaking down barriers to the admission of women into "male" orders. Yet it was clearly not the only factor. If we ask ourselves why the French began to accept women into mostly male state honours (admittedly in small numbers) a half a century before status distributors in the United Kingdom began to do so, the answer is not that the French had more advanced attitudes toward women or that women were more politically or economically powerful or that the feminist movement was stronger there. None of this was the case. In fact, in the United Kingdom, the electoral franchise was extended to women over thirty years of age in 1918 and to all women over twenty-one years of age in 1928. In France, it was not granted to all women over twenty-one years of age until 1945. The delay in France has a rather complex explanation.[96] Suffice it to say, we should not quickly jump to the conclusion that attitudes toward women changed much earlier in the United Kingdom than France. The point is simply that it is impossible to explain the earlier admission of women into mostly male state honours in France as a result of a difference in attitudes toward women. Rather, I would argue, the explanation is that the great expansion in honours began in France much earlier than in Britain, and so the status processes we have been examining in these chapters led to an earlier recognition of women. Honours systems have their own institutional dynamic, and their own normative constraints and enablements.

THE OVERALL EFFECT

What overall effect did the expansion of state honours and the power struggles that it entailed have on the distribution of power in Modern Europe?

We begin with one possible consequence that state honours generally did not have. They had relatively little direct effect on the existing economic structure of Western-European society. The extent to which people have been able to use state honours to increase their individual economic capital has been minimal. Scientific awards have occasionally provided commercial value for recipients, but usually do not. Military awards have had little economic return; recipients of the Victoria Cross, perhaps the highest status award there is today, do not get rich as a consequence. In this respect, state honours contrast sharply with literary, entertainment, and athletic awards, which can be used to increase individual economic capital. To repeat a point made earlier, however, most of these awards came relatively late in the evolution of Modern status awards and their commodification took place mostly after the great expansion of state honours.

Honours have affected political structures. Earlier chapters have shown how they have been utilized to maintain the existing distribution of power or to organize collective action that challenged the existing distribution of power. My contention, however, was not that state honorific recognition was a critical element in these processes. It was, rather, that the imperatives of these processes encouraged the adoption of state honours. In almost all societies, political power is determined primarily by larger political and economic forces. Political power and the fluctuation of political power among different groups in society have a far greater effect on the distribution of status by states than the other way around.

The major effect of state honours on power in Modern Europe has been on status power. Indeed, in my view, this is one of the main reasons for studying them. The question we need to answer, then, is whether state honours have reinforced existing status structures or undermined them. Unfortunately, I cannot provide a straightforward answer. In reviewing what we have learned in the preceding pages, it is clear that there have been a number of effects, not all in the same direction.

Effects on Existing Status Structures

The pressure to conform to existing status structures meant that the status of many recipients of state honours was already relatively high when they collected a state honour. This was more true in the United Kingdom than in the Low Countries or in France. For many British aristocrats, there was less to gain from a state honour, with the exception of a peerage if they did not already have one. For a long time, even many non-aristocratic recipients of state honours came from families already possessing relatively high status. Again, one can take

Herbert Gladstone as an example. He was not a member of the old aristocracy – he did not even inherit a title from his father – but he certainly enjoyed high status that was independent of the state decorations he eventually received. He was educated at Eton and University College Oxford, married the daughter of a baronet, and became a prominent politician, as a result of which he was awarded a knight grand cross of the Order of the Bath, a knight grand cross of the Order of Saint Michael and Saint George, a knight grand cross of the Order of the British Empire, and a peerage. Belgian writer Maurice Maeterlinck, who was made a *grand cordon* (highest grade) of the Order of Leopold and a count in the Belgian nobility, was from a wealthy family in Ghent. A number of examples in more local status structures in France are provided by Dumons. For instance, one Philippe Druard, descendant of a family of *notables* in the Department of Saône-et-Loire, was a candidate for the Legion of Honour in 1890, and his nephew Maxime Druard, a banker, who succeeded him as mayor, was a candidate in 1925.[97]

We can also find examples of individuals who were born into families of relatively low status but were later in life recipients of state honours, occasionally top honours. This was most common in France. Émile François Loubet and Gaston Doumergue, both farmers' sons who became presidents of the Third Republic, were made *grands croix* (highest grade) of the Legion of Honour. Alexandre Millerand, son of a cloth merchant, was also a president of the Republic; he was made a *grand croix* in 1920. Personal trajectories of this kind were less numerous in Belgium, but we can cite the case of Louis Bertrand, a socialist Belgian politician and founder of the Belgian Workers Party, who began his working life as a mason; he was made a *grand cordon* (highest grade) of the Order of Leopold in 1926.

The British political arena in the nineteenth and early twentieth centuries had proportionately the fewest number of careers of this kind. Among prime ministers, there were none until Lloyd George. He grew up in northwest Wales in straitened circumstances; he was raised to the peerage shortly before he died in 1945. Ramsay MacDonald was born in a small coastal village on the northeast coast of Scotland, the illegitimate son of a farm servant and ploughman. He was eventually offered the Order of the Thistle, but declined it.

Of course, as the above examples demonstrate, even if an individual rose from a relatively modest background, the state honour that he or she received was not responsible for their upward mobility. The state honour usually came afterwards. The same is true in cases of people who became known and celebrated for a significant achievement, and then received an honorific reward. To this extent, these honours had a limited effect on the existing distribution of status.

Nevertheless, a state honour did create a distinction over and above what would have been derived from a successful career or a significant accomplishment. Even a person placed in the lowest grade in an honorific order could benefit relative to others living in his or her social circle and locality. This was the case for most of the people studied by Dumons in Saône-et-Loire and Var. A state honour would provide state confirmation of the person's status, something all the more valuable to an individual who had risen from a comparatively low status. Awards for rescuers usually helped to bring distinction to persons who had formerly lived very private lives. Military awards, especially for courage, have had a significant impact on the respect in which many individuals are held. These and other elevations or confirmations of status could be beneficial not only to individuals but also to the social groups to which they belonged.

Insofar as state honours have altered existing status structures, a number of forces have been operating to bring this about. There is insufficient space to discuss most of them – economic and political transformations, political contests and necessities, egalitarian ideologies, and so forth. Rather, I will examine two forces that were internal to the status processes themselves.

First is the pressure for consistency to which I have repeatedly alluded, that is, consistency in the rationale for bestowing awards and determining eligibility. One of the earliest, though least problematic, of these consistency pressures was between military honorific rewards and those for other state employees, a pressure that we have seen in the eighteenth century and most visibly during the early years of the Legion of Honour. Over the course of the nineteenth century, this consistency pressure was relieved by increasing the number of honorific rewards bestowed on non-military personnel, particularly higher-level state employees. The latter are one of the principal groups that has benefited from the evolution of Modern state honours in Western Europe.

More problematic were pressures for consistency among military personnel. Napoleon met this pressure by distributing the Legion of

Honour up and down the military hierarchy. Subsequently, however, the Legion of Honour became less egalitarian, creating pressures that led to the Military Medal and a number of other honorific rewards intended to recognize lower ranks. In the British Isles, a growing perception of inequity from the early and mid-nineteenth century forced honours distributors to give more recognition to lower-ranked soldiers, most of whom appeared to the public to be more meritorious than the generals who had been collecting most of the honours. Ultimately, military honours and changing public attitudes toward soldiers have interactively transformed their status.

Even more problematic were the inconsistencies we have noted in colonial settings. Over time, it became more and more difficult to justify the presentation of European state decorations in colonies to Europeans whose contributions to the imperial state were manifestly less than the contributions of many people with non-European ancestry. Similarly, the inconsistency between the honours available to men and those available to women was one of the forces that led to the erosion of the barrier to the latter's admission. Although the number of persons in these two groups who were admitted during the period covered by this book was not impressive, the experiences of these non-Europeans and women in Modern European state honours illustrate the pressures for consistency that honours distributors came to face. For reasons that the chapters in this section have tried to demonstrate, the distributors usually reacted hesitantly to pressures, but the pressures toward consistency were pervasive, and their cumulative effect over time has been considerable.

Jews provide another illustration. During most of the nineteenth century, they were conspicuous for receiving few if any honours in spite of accomplishments or contributions that would clearly have yielded honours for non-Jewish candidates. In his efforts to persuade Victoria to grant a peerage to Lionel de Rothschild in 1869, Gladstone asserted that Rothschild was exceptional among "commercial men" and that it was difficult to find a comparable member of the business world, a world that Gladstone felt was important not to leave unrecognized. "It would not be possible ...," Gladstone insisted, "to find any satisfactory substitute for his name. And if his religion were to operate permanently as a bar, it appears that this would be to revive by prerogative the disability which formerly existed by statute."[98] Victoria claimed that it was not just a matter of his religion; she did not think a man whose money had been amassed by speculations on the stock market and by making loans to foreign governments was worthy of a peerage. Yet it was hard for her to persuade Gladstone that the issue was not primarily Rothschild being a Jew, especially given that she ultimately allowed almost all the other recommendations made by Gladstone at the same time, which she had initially resisted.

As more and more businessmen received honours in Western Europe in the late nineteenth century, the exclusion of Jews from the British peerage became increasingly untenable. Indeed, the Rothschilds enjoyed considerable admiration and respect in British society during the last half of the nineteenth century, even on the part of Victoria, despite the reasons she gave for resisting a "Jew peer."[99] The inconsistency here stemmed from contradictions in the expectation that the distribution of honours should conform to the existing status structure. The Rothschilds enjoyed a position in society that should have entitled them to high honours, while belonging to a minority group that entitled them to no high honours.

However, the underlying source of inconsistency pressure in the distribution of state honours in Western Europe during the late nineteenth and early twentieth centuries was the justification of honours on the basis of merit. Much in the way that the aristocracy's culture of merit and their claim to superiority in merit over the bourgeoisie contributed to their own destruction, so the idiom of merit created a leaven in the status structure, and in the honours system in particular, that had considerable transformative capacity.

Let me propose that this dynamic was one of the reasons that members of the professions received a relatively large number of state honours. It cannot be denied that political elites are interested in promoting science, medicine, art, and literature, but it is difficult to maintain that the desire to do so has been the only reason for the bestowal of honours on the professions. An additional reason is that it strengthens the perception that the honours system is based on merit. More precisely, it makes it easier to claim that the status awards given to politicians, state officials, and military personnel are also based on merit. Certainly, this objective was constrained by the need to avoid elevating professionals above prominent politicians, higher-level state officials, or higher-ranking military men. Hence, many professionals were placed in relatively lower grades. Nevertheless, the gradual long-term effect in the twentieth century has been to increase the merit coefficient, so to speak, and thus to increase the potential for honorific rewards to alter existing status structures.

Therefore, we should pay special attention to female professionals in honorific orders. In the Order of the Companions of Honour, of the fifteen women appointed from 1917 to 1939, six were professionals (specifically: two physicians, two theatre entrepreneurs, a teacher, and a writer). It was the best-represented social position for women outside of charitable work. Similarly, except for charitable work, professions constituted the most numerous social position in my sample of women in the Order of the British Empire in 1921. Their representation was 18.7 per cent, far above the next largest, which was 7.4 per cent for what I have called the lower bourgeoisie (Table B.37). Also noteworthy were the grades that female professionals received in the Order of the British Empire. If we exclude royals or wives of peers or baronets as well as those engaged in charitable work, all the dames grand cross and dames commanders were in the professions (Table B.36). The first woman to be awarded a grade higher than *chevalier* in the Legion of Honour was Bonheur, who was raised to *officier* (second-lowest grade) in 1895. The first to be promoted to the grade of *commandeur* were six women in 1931, five of whom were writers or intellectuals.

In the three major honours I have sampled, the most elitist female recipients were the dames grand cross of the Order of the British Empire. Yet amongst all these "grand ladies" were some women of a less exalted background who had built their own careers in nursing and hospital administration. Sarah Swift, daughter of a substantial farmer in Lincolnshire, trained as a nurse, became a hospital matron and organizer of nurses as a profession, and during the Great War was matron-in-chief of the joint war committee of the Saint John Ambulance Association and the British Red Cross Society. Another woman, Maud McCarthy, was the daughter of an Australian solicitor, who died when she was twenty-two. After helping her mother raise her siblings for ten years, she began her career as a probationer at London Hospital, Whitechapel in 1891. With the outbreak of war in South Africa, she was selected by Princess Alexandra to go to South Africa as one of her "military" nurses. In 1903, McCarthy was appointed a matron of Queen Alexandra's Imperial Military Nursing Service. In 1910, she became principal matron of the War Office and during the Great War was matron-in-chief of

the British Expeditionary Force in France, the only BEF department
head to hold the same post for the duration of the War. Both of
these women found their names on the same short list of dames
grand cross as two daughters of Queen Victoria and twenty daughters of peers, all married to peers. By means of merit that could not
be denied, women such as Swift and McCarthy, along with soldiers
who won military decorations for bravery, paved the way for the men
and women today whose lives have been relatively obscure until they
were awarded an honour of state.

The Intensification of Status Competition

There is another force – one that I suspect readers will find less
pleasing – that causes honours to alter the existing status structure.
An intensification of status competition during the eighteenth and
nineteenth centuries was clearly one cause of the great expansion of
state honours. Equally, however, intensified status competition has
been a consequence of the expansion. A significant segment of the
population who cared more about many other things than awards,
prizes, or state honours were drawn into competition for such trophies as a result of their bestowal on acquaintances, relatives, or
fellow workers. During the long nineteenth century, successive generations became more interested in these kinds of rewards than had
earlier generations.

There is no doubt that the number of persons in nineteenth-
and twentieth-century Europe who were pleased with an honour
they received was greatly exceeded by the number who resented
not receiving an honour or who believed that the honour they had
been awarded was less than what they deserved. In 1879, French
artist Gustave Doré complained to sculptor and writer Lord Ronald
Gower that he had not received any award for his works at an exhibition of that year. Doré had earlier been made a *chevalier* in the
Legion of Honour, and subsequently was elevated to a higher grade,
but he believed, and Gower agreed, that the civil distribution of the
Legion of Honour "does an immense amount of harm and causes
endless ill-feeling among the French."[100] The Order of the British
Empire, which was designed to bring pleasure to a much larger segment of the population than any previous British decoration, also
created much discontent among those who thought they deserved a
higher-status state honour.[101]

Groups as well as individuals in the population could be offended. There was much bitterness in the United Kingdom of the Netherlands when those who had belonged to the Order of Union (which had been created earlier by Louis Bonaparte when he was king of Holland) or the Order of Reunion (which Napoleon had created in 1811) were not included in the Military Order of William when it was set up in 1815.[102] When the British established the Waterloo medal for those who had fought at the Battle of Ligny, the Battle of Quatre Bras, and the Battle of Waterloo, considerable discontent emerged among the veterans of other campaigns in the French wars. And bitterness caused by the Order of the British Empire in its early years emerged among a number of occupational groups and localities. The private secretary of King George received a letter from a lord lieutenant in 1918 indicating that anger was widespread in his county over the number of appointments to the Order they had received relative to other counties.[103]

The response of those offended could be petty. French politician and romantic writer François-René, vicomte de Chateaubriand, was awarded the Order of Saint Louis in 1814 and the Legion of Honour in 1821. Although royal orders had precedence over the Legion of Honour during the Restoration, in a portrait painted in 1828, Chateaubriand wore the badge of the Legion of Honour above the Cross of Saint Louis, because, it was said, he had been offended that his political enemy Jean-Baptiste de Villèle had been admitted to another royal order, the Holy Ghost, before Chateaubriand's admission in 1824.[104] One would have thought that Nelson would be above this sort of behaviour, but when he received only a barony for his Nile victory, he wore his foreign honours – including a magnificent aigrette bestowed by the sultan of Turkey – to diminish the honour of the barony.[105] One of the undecorated and bitter British veterans of the French Wars observed that Wellington had been promoted to field marshal and duke as rewards for his contribution, while he (the veteran) received "not a vestige of a medal, cross, or ribbon," and suggested that he might hammer flat two musket balls he had received and suspend them from coloured ribbons on his chest.[106]

In addition to those given in the preceding chapter, a not-uncommon reason why an award was declined was that it was not high enough in status. Chesterfield's mockery of the recipient of an honour whose badge was stolen was characteristically hypocritical. He was not indifferent to the fashionable world of honours or uninterested in them for himself. He could be fastidious about the etiquette of honours, and advised his son to be familiar with all the Continental sovereign orders of his day in case they came up in conversation.[107] When offered the Bath, he turned it down. He wanted a knight of the Order of the Garter, which he obtained in 1730. A more recent example is provided by Charles Cowper, premier of New South Wales. In 1870, he accepted the award of Companion in the Order of Saint Michael and Saint George but then refused it because he believed he deserved the Bath.[108]

The Order of the British Empire was faced with a large number of refusals in its early years, partly because it was offered to many individuals who were not interested in honours, but primarily because of this sort of discontent. Kenneth Walker, an officer in the Royal Army Medical Corps, was angry when he was given an OBE (second-lowest grade in the Order of the British Empire) in 1919. He had been recommended for the higher-status Distinguished Service Order for having worked in trenches in an effort to understand the shock suffered by wounded men. He wrote to Churchill, then secretary of state for war, pointing out that music-hall artist George Robey had been appointed a CBE (next higher grade) for raising money for the War. He asked that his name be removed from the roll of the Order. He later wrote "that he would be ashamed to be found in a ditch with it."[109] Refusals could be a headache for governments. On 24 January 1876, Lord Stanley (Edward Henry) received a visit from L.G.N. Starkie, a Conservative member of Parliament. According to Stanley, Starkie announced that "he had refused the offer of a baronetcy from Disraeli, not thinking it worth his acceptance: he wanted a peerage: and asked my support to obtain one."[110] Starkie's request presented Stanley with a classic dilemma. "He is a large land-owner, rich, active in the service of his party, and has political influence: but rather stupid and loutish ... I could not think him exactly of the stuff from which peers should be made: but many peers are made from the same sort of material."[111] Stanley's attitude toward honours distribution, as reflected in the two entries in his diary that I have quoted, is not unusual. Politicians and state officials often expressed concern, annoyance, sometimes disgust, at the awards they were pressured to make. The historical records include large numbers of documents in which officials worried that decisions they were making would cause offence.

The birthday honours list of June 1892 announced the award of a baronetcy to Henry Wiggin, a Birmingham businessman. It came in return for his funding contributions to the Liberal Unionist Party. This created considerable embarrassment for John Jaffray, owner of *The Birmingham Daily Post* and *The Birmingham Mail*, who had aspired to the same award but whose name was not on the list. According to a Unionist party member in Birmingham, the editor of the *Post* was most "anxious that Jaffray's name shd. go forward for the honour which he covets. Jaffray, it seems, has to meet the enquiries of his friends, who constantly ask him why Wiggin shd. be chosen and he neglected, and his life is miserable."[112] Party officials were sufficiently worried about the impact on the political position taken by Jaffray's newspapers, which had been supporting the Liberal Unionist Party, that they persuaded the prime minister, Lord Salisbury, to include Jaffray for a baronetcy, even though he had not been on the original birthday list.

As honours led to more honours, and the award of honours led to more demands for honours, they became more and more of a headache for governments. In 1888, Salisbury was talking up the idea of an order of merit for science and art but gave it up after a conversation with the president of the Royal Academy, Sir Frederic Leighton, who was worried about the "heartburnings" that the selections would cause among scientists and artists.[113] Salisbury himself thought that demands for honours revealed "the baser side of human nature," and detested having to deal with it; the wicked, he thought, "should be condemned eternally to the task of distributing two honours among a hundred people so as to satisfy them all."[114]

We should not allow these complaints to divert our attention from the power that an honours system gave government officials – a power clearly enjoyed by some monarchs and politicians. Yet exercising it entailed considerable costs of both an emotional and practical nature. H.H. Asquith (British prime minister from 1908 to 1916) considered putting together an honours list to be a task "as uncongenial and even hateful, as can fall to a man."[115]

The acrimony generated by honours should not surprise us. A number of writers have contended that the past several centuries have seen an increase in status anxiety in Western societies.[116] Honorific awards in both the public and private sectors have contributed to this process. They have intensified status competition, sometimes even generating it where it hardly existed before. Most refusals were not the result of inflated vanity. To accept a certain honour and the grade in which one had been placed – to let it be publicized, to acknowledge it, to wear the badge – was to validate the status one had been assigned by the award distributors relative to the status they had assigned others. It was often a difficult decision for an individual to make. Should one be delighted with the prize and wear it proudly? Should one accept it and hide one's disappointment? Or would it be better to refuse it? Cowper's letter refusing the Order of Saint Michael and Saint George testifies to this anguish. "Numbers of my fellow colonists during several years past have several dignities of higher degrees conferred on them: while I who am one of the oldest and most prominent among our public men am proposed to be placed in a position inferior to any."[117]

At the same time, as I have argued in Chapter 10, honorific rewards in the Modern period have become an instrument of "individualization." Together, these two processes – individualization and status competition – have contributed to a social environment where people are constantly put in the position of judging themselves, comparing themselves with others, and taking personal responsibility for their position in a status hierarchy.

Of course, those who believe in status awards claim that they boost morale by instilling a desire to serve whatever cause the award is meant to promote. The general assumption in Modern Western society is that status awards and status inequality produce higher levels of performance. This view focuses attention on the high performers – actually, on those deemed to be high performers by the status distributors – ignoring the impact of status awards on the morale and level of performance of others engaged in the same activity, individually or taken as whole. Honorific rewards may increase the motivation of those who receive one or think they might receive one. Whether they increase the motivation of those who do not receive them is another matter.

STATE HONOURS IN
COMPARATIVE PERSPECTIVE

A Global Analysis

The principal methodology of this book has been to examine social and political conditions in Medieval, Early Modern, and Modern Western Europe, identifying causal processes and mechanisms that accounted for the evolution of state honours.

In-depth causal-process analysis of one country or region has, however, its limitations. It restricts the geographical scope of a research project, something that is especially problematic when the geographical region is Western Europe given the tendency of most scholars – until recently – to use Western Europe as a standard by which to understand other parts of the world. More broadly speaking, a single case obviously limits the extent to which one can generalize.

Many historians would insist that this is not a problem because they are not interested in generalization. In truth, they often generalize or assume generalizations implicitly or explicitly because historical explanation requires a minimum level of generalization about causal connections. Any explanation an historian provides implies generalization since, if we do not find a general relationship between a social or political condition and an outcome, we cannot be very confident in the causal argument that has been put forward about such a relationship in a single case. In the present study, it would be hard for me – or anyone – to convince the reader that the evolution of honorific rewards in Western Europe was the result of population growth, political centralization, or certain methods of warfare if there are no general relationships between honorific rewards and these conditions among other societies.

The goal of this chapter is to determine whether or not we find such generalizations in a more global comparative analysis. To begin, it is useful to provide a survey of rewards bestowed in different parts of the world. Although unavoidably cursory, it will serve as the database for a more systematic cross-cultural analysis.

A VERY BRIEF GLOBAL SURVEY OF HONORIFIC REWARDS

Rewards by leaders or rulers for performance have been universal in human history, but they have varied greatly. They can be more or less numerous, more or less valuable, and more or less honorific as opposed to material. Until relatively recently, the most universal military reward was permission to collect and retain booty. In addition, an impressive variety of honorific rewards for both military and non-military service can be found.

Asia

The most widely employed honorific reward has been elevation in office, title, or rank. This has been especially true in Asia. Titles could be entirely honorific or, in varying degrees, both honorific and material/powerful/privileging. The Mughal *mansabdar* system provides one of the best-known illustrations of the combination. It was established by Jalal-ud-Din Muhammad Akbar, the third Mughal emperor. Officials and military officers were given a rank having a numerical value, which could be raised or lowered by the emperor with or without a change in the state position that an official or military officer held. Raising or lowering an individual's *mansab* status was determined by the merit of his services, including victory or defeat in battle, and by the number of cavalry he maintained for the emperor.[1]

Other widespread status rewards in Asia included ceremonial celebration, dress and regalia, land, gifts, privileges, and monuments of various kinds. Mughal rulers awarded standards, kettledrums, horns, weapons (often jewelled), gold coins, ornaments and precious medals, and bonuses.[2] The honorary name "hero" could be awarded by the Mughal emperor for military accomplishments; a soldier who carried the head of a feared enemy to the Court would be awarded with this "hero" appellation.[3] In some Asian societies, rulers bestowed a family name or a "gift name" as a reward. I want to call particular attention to an honorific reward in Ancient India known as the *prasadapatta*, which was a head band made of gold awarded to state officials and soldiers.[4]

An expansion in military honorific rewards was effected in Ancient China by Shang Yang (390–38 BCE), an influential Qin official during the Warring States Period. He instituted a system of seventeen ranks, with soldiers in the general population eligible for eight of them. A soldier was accorded one degree of rank for the capture of one enemy head and two degrees for two heads. Officers were elevated on the basis of the number of heads collected by their subordinates.[5] (Third-century BCE Chinese Legalist philosopher Han Fei argued that calculating the bravery of a soldier by the number of heads he had cut off, though rather crude, had the advantage of providing an objective standard of merit.[6]) Over time, the seventeen ranks evolved into a structure of twenty ranks to which a person could be elevated. These ranks were extended throughout the population; indeed, title was the major honorific reward that common people could receive.[7] By the late Han period, a nine-rank hierarchy had also evolved for state employees.[8] Something similar was instituted for Court officers in both Japan and Korea.

There also developed in China a status known as "meritorious official," which was, in principle at least, a nobility of merit to which people were appointed in recognition of achievements, especially military achievement.[9] Status rewards in Ancient China also included special doors and stairways, carriages and clothing, musical instruments, and other status symbols. Grand ceremonies for victorious armies on their departure or return were also common in Asia.

Cloth was a prevalent honorific reward in Asia. Chinese emperors were especially well known for it. A particular form of cloth widely selected as a status reward was the so-called "robe of honour," a piece of cloth or item of clothing normally placed over the shoulders of the recipient that signalled an appreciation on the part of the bestower for something that the recipient had done. It is important to understand that robes were adopted to denote rank and type of office and were presented just as gifts. But they also functioned as honorific rewards.

Although bestowing cloth or clothing has a very ancient history in the Middle East, robes of honour as such became more institutionalized during the eighth and ninth centuries CE and were adopted during the next five hundred years in an area that stretched from

Spain to China, but principally in Central and Southern Asia.[10] The majority of the countries that took up robes as an honorific reward were Muslim. The Mughals used them extensively. Yet non-Muslim populations, such as the Mongols and Byzantines, also adopted them. Although Hindu rulers were slow to make use of robes of honour, by the eighteenth century they could be found in much of India.[11] Most of the recipients were persons of high status, often members of a royal or princely court, but it was not unusual for robes of honour to be awarded to lower-status members of the population. Rulers might hand them out in large numbers, occasionally in the thousands.[12] Needless to say, robes conferred on higher-status recipients were made of superior materials in comparison with those conferred on lower-status persons.

For comparative purposes, we should also take note of other kinds of dress utilized to signify honorable recognition in Asia. These included special head wear, shoes, and belts. In Early Modern China, the right to wear peacock feathers was awarded for exemplary service; feathers were classified into one-eyed, two-eyed, and three-eyed ranks.[13]

The Americas

There was no shortage of status rewards in late Medieval and Early Modern Meso-America. They included appointment to powerful positions, privileges, status elevation, land, celebration in art, gifts, hair style, special dress and insignia, and honorific titles. Warriors were often granted rights to parts of the bodies of defeated warriors (scalps, heads, bones, and flayed flesh), which could be worn as decoration. Diego de Landa, a sixteenth-century Spanish bishop, testified that the bones of killed captives were worn as ornaments.[14] Lip plugs, frequently made of precious metal, were also a status symbol in Meso-American societies. They were generally restricted to very high-status groups, but the right to wear a lip plug could be granted to soldiers as a status reward. Among the Aztecs, a warrior had the right to wear an increasingly elaborate costume depending on the number of captives he had taken.[15] The most accomplished Aztec warriors were appointed to one of two elite military statuses known as Jaguars and Eagles. They were allowed to wear a special mask and robe. The Aztecs also had what we would call a nobility.

Individuals could be rewarded by elevation to this status, though in limited numbers.

Inca rewards included land, gifts, privileges, a share of booty, special clothing, tunics, and titles. I called the reader's attention to the *canipu* in Chapter 7 because of its similarity to medals and metallic badges. Some sources suggest that it was a mark of noble status, but it was also employed as an honorific reward for soldiers; the metal used to make a *canipu* signified the warrior's prowess, copper being the lowest, then silver, and gold the highest.[16]

Honorific rewards among native North Americans in the eighteenth and nineteenth centuries had similarities with those of the Meso-Americans and the Inca. Some communities, such as those on the Pacific Coast, had nobilities of sorts. Otherwise, North American status rewards were less institutionalized than those of the Mayans, Aztecs, and Incas. The status of an accomplished warrior was often raised by oral praise, ceremonial honours, body painting, decoration of his domicile, special clothing, weapons, and rights to parts of the bodies of defeated warriors, again typically scalps or heads. Superior warriors were usually allowed to decorate their homes with scalps or heads they had taken.

That said, in North American communities, live captives were generally preferred to scalps or heads, and military achievement was often measured by the number of captives brought back from a battle. In some aboriginal populations of the Great Lakes, marks might be put on captives to indicate who had taken them or on a warrior to indicate the number of enemy he had captured.[17] Common on the Plains was the adoption of feathers as a body decoration, typically as a headdress. It was meant as a symbol of status and power, but feathers usually had to be earned by means of bravery or accomplishment in battle.[18] In addition, many North American communities signalled accomplishments by decorating their bodies with tattoos. And war shirts were used to raise the status of accomplished warriors. Like Asian robes of honour, these shirts could be ornamentally decorated.

The Inuit had few special tangible rewards for outstanding performance. Distinctive facial tattoos represented at least one kind of reward that was symbolic of military feats. Enemy warriors, or more commonly their women and children, might be taken captive and incorporated into a community. However, the information we have suggests that this practice was less common among the Inuit than among their enemies. The Lowland Cree typically killed Inuit adult males and the elderly, and then took young women and children home.[19] In any case, taking captives did not have the symbolic significance among the Inuit that it had among other North Americans.

Ancient Mediterranean and Middle East

Again, status elevation in title or rank was widespread. In addition, material objects were often employed as symbols of recognition. In the Egyptian twelfth dynasty (twentieth to nineteenth centuries bce), staffs, daggers, and bows were handed out by rulers.[20] In the New Kingdom (sixteenth to eleventh centuries BCE), state officials, members of royal courts, and military personnel were rewarded with body ornaments, titles, privileges, land, gifts, tomb inscriptions, and weapons. Ornaments were sometimes in the form of a lion or fly that was fixed to arm clasps, bracelets, or necklaces and often made of gold. The term "Gold of Honour" is commonly applied to them, but strictly speaking, Gold of Honour refers to a rare status reward symbolizing that the recipient was known to the king; although usually given to high-ranking officials, this was not necessarily the case.[21]

I have already noted that robes of honour had a long history in the Middle East. We know that rulers in Ancient Persia bestowed robes to indicate favour or to serve as a special reward for services.[22] It is also known that in Ancient Persia records were kept of those who fought particularly well or valiantly in a battle, but we are less informed about how these noteworthy individuals were rewarded. Rulers did grant land, gifts, proximity to their person, other privileges, and (to the very few) honorary diadems.[23] We have a Roman witness to Sasanian soldiers wearing "gold arm rings and necklaces, and especially pearls" after military victories.[24] Officers or members of elite units sported a number of symbolic objects, such as personal armour and weapons, maces, medallions, seals, and body ornaments, such as badges, *torques*, and rings, typically decorated with precious metals. Yet it does not seem that any of these were special rewards for specific actions.

In Classical Greece (500–300 BCE), soldiers could be singled out for praise and receive a status award known as the "prize of valour" or *aristeia*. The material objects that accompanied this award varied (in addition to body ornaments, they could include shields, statues, or chariots), but if conferred after a battle, the objects usually

consisted of a certain share of the booty. A prize of valour was most
often bestowed for military performance but could also be given to
civilians for various kinds of merit. Soldiers and civilians alike were
awarded crowns, usually made of some vegetable matter or, in special cases, of gold.[25]

The Greeks, of course, were keen on honorific rewards for their
athletic competitions. The most common athletic rewards were
wreaths and crowns, usually made from wool or foliage. Other athletic rewards included cauldrons, tripods, dishes, horses and mules,
money, free meals, animals, weapons, and axes as well as banquets,
ceremonial precedence, and seats of honour.[26]

Under Macedonian rulers Philip II and Alexander the Great,
an assortment of rewards, some of which varied with accomplishment, were an essential part of their military organization. These
rewards included material benefits: booty, cash payments, land
grants, rations, gifts, death benefits, and miscellaneous perks such
as assistance to a soldier's family or payment of debts. In addition,
of course, military accomplishment could be rewarded with promotion. And mercenaries and foreign troops might be granted citizenship. Many of the honorific rewards they distributed were similar to
those in Classical Greece. These included prizes of valour and honorary decrees, ceremonial precedence, honorary seats at theatrical
or athletic performances, crowns, monuments, statues, dedications,
and ornaments, such as metal bracelets.[27]

In historical memory, Roman military leaders have acquired a
reputation as exceptionally committed to achieving discipline by
means of rewards and severe punishment. The *dona militaria* have
more similarity with present-day honours than any other rewards
in world history. In addition to the grass crown, there was the civic
crown (the second highest honour after the grass crown), the naval
crown, the wall crown, the fortification crown, and the gold crown.
Other objects used as honorific rewards included *torques* (collars),
vexillae (standards), *hastae* (spears), *armillae* (bracelets), and *patellae*
(dishes). There were also the metal discs known as *phalerae*, mentioned in Chapter 7. The typical practice during the Empire was for
the *phalerae* to be awarded to centurions and soldiers of lower rank,
typically along with other rewards. *Torques*, also awarded mostly to
these lower ranks, were considered a lower-status decoration.[28]

The liberality with which different *dona* were distributed varied.
The siege crown and the wall crown were rarely accorded, while

the fortification crown was, in comparison, widely distributed.[29] Although it is difficult to be certain, the numbers of military who received a *donum* seem large in comparison with honorific rewards in other armies in the Ancient World. Valerie Maxfield has tried to estimate the percentage receiving a *donum*. She has counted the number indicated on lists of the members of particular units that fought in the second century CE. These data have to be treated with caution, particularly when used as estimates of the total number of awards made, but they suggest that, on average, around 10 per cent of the members of a unit received a *donum*.[30] If this percentage is roughly correct, a reasonable guess is that sixteen to seventeen thousand men in the Roman army held a donum at that time.

COMPARATIVE METHODOLOGY

In the past two or three decades, a large body of literature has emerged in several disciplines in social science on the appropriate methodologies for comparative-historical research. In the following pages, I outline several methodological practices and indicate which one I have adopted and why.

The most common method has been the "big-case–small-N" comparison, in which a small number of cases are broadly compared. This means one compares not only the phenomena one is trying to explain but also a large number of social and political conditions thought to be related to them. Often the cases are geographically close to one another and the time periods being compared coincide. In other studies, the cases are wide apart geographically and/ or the periods of time are different. These works tend to be case-specific, designed primarily to explain what happened in the countries being studied.

This approach has yielded a large number of solid comparative studies.[31] Yet the number of cases being examined remains small. This problem is compounded in the present study by the fact that the outcome in which we are interested was largely similar in the European cases that I have examined. What differed was the timing – when the evolution of Modern state honours reached a certain size and acquired certain characteristics. I have used these differences to support some of my causal arguments. I have suggested that the early evolution of state honours in France coincided chronologically with population expansion, the growth in the size of armies, political centralization, and the institutionalization of a large state officialdom. Still, the fact remains that the evolution of state honours in Western Europe was an encompassing process not a number of separate processes.

In big-case–small-N comparisons, a researcher will often try to classify cases into major societal types, such as "patrimonial states," "empires" (perhaps "bureaucratic empires"), "agrarian societies," "oriental despotism," "industrial societies," "capitalist societies," or "modern societies." Depending on the question one is asking, these and other typologies may be useful.[32] In particular, they can help to organize differences among states and societies.

Societal typologies are, however, open to criticism for a number of reasons. First, the meanings of the types in a typology can vary. Much of the academic debate in the 1970s about the rise of capitalism in Europe was the result of differences in what various writers meant by "capitalism." Second, typologies usually obscure degrees of difference. Third, they can lead a researcher to overlook variations that are not represented in the typologies.

And fourth, typologies can become overloaded concepts. Recently, Mourina Charrad and Julia Adams have called attention to the diversity of characteristics that have been attributed to "patrimonial states."[33] Further to their point, one can find this term being used to refer to states in which (1) administration is decentralized, (2) rule is autocratic, (3) there is comparatively less differentiation between the private and the public sphere (many state positions are privately owned in some sense), and (4) certain kinship groups hold the most powerful state positions (a ruler or major power holder typically appoints members of his family to these positions, and succession is based on kin lineage). These characteristics often go together, but not always. The French state could be said to have had all of them to some degree during the sixteenth century. On the other hand, during the seventeenth and eighteenth centuries, it was patrimonial in one sense but less in another. The king's advisers were no longer mostly members of his family and state administration was less controlled by powerful kinship groups; at the same time, many state positions were still privately owned and the differentiation between the private and public sphere was less than it would become later in the nineteenth and twentieth centuries.

Finally, serious problems arise when typologies are used not just as descriptive concepts but also as explanatory tools. Explanatory typologies can sometimes be justified when they are derived from and meant to contribute to a robust theory.[34] Unfortunately, more often we find writers treating a typology itself as a theoretical explanation, often attributing an essence to a particular type. This essentialism reifies what is actually simply a concept.

The alternative to typologies is to examine variations that are relevant to a particular study and to compare societies on these variations. These variations may include characteristics that some writers have incorporated into typologies, such as political centralization, bureaucratization, or rational-legal thinking, but they are now treated as different variations. Which ones go together and which ones do not will be determined by the empirical associations we find rather than by preconceived typologies. This approach helps specify what it is about different types of societies that is important for a given research project.

Social scientists make a distinction between two ways of studying these variations, which are usually described as qualitative versus quantitative but should be referred to as non-statistical versus statistical since both methods can be quantitative. Non-statistical quantitative comparative analysis is usually carried out by coding cases on different variables and then using logic to establish causality, a logic that is often (implicitly or explicitly) built around "set theory" and necessary versus sufficient conditions.[35] Although very different from the typological approach as just described, non-statistical quantitative comparative analysis does seek to identify empirically "configurations of conditions" that affect an outcome.

At the present time, a well-respected non-statistical method of comparison is known as Qualitative Comparative Analysis (QCA), originally developed by Charles Ragin. By this method, each case is given a value on the explanatory variables and a value on the variable that one wants to explain. By placing these values side-by-side and using Boolean logic, we are able to see which combinations of the former are associated with the latter. In doing so, we are able to distinguish between necessary and sufficient conditions.[36]

Like other non-statistical methods, QCA is case oriented; that is, for the most part it tries to explain particular cases, and often to do so for all the cases that are being studied. Those who adopt this method do not take samples but instead select a set of cases that are appropriate for a particular investigation. The fundamental logic of this method is based on a dichotomous classification of variations, or, in the language that is frequently employed, cases are classified according to their "membership" in binary categories, such as "democratic" versus "non-democratic," "agrarian" versus "industrial," "empire" versus "nation-state."

Criticisms of this dichotomous construction of variables persuaded Ragin to modify QCA by allowing for "fuzzy sets," that is, degrees of membership.[37] Whereas, with dichotomous variables, cases are given a value of 0 or 1 on each variable, in fuzzy-set analysis, cases are given a value on a continuous range between 0 and 1 on each variable. In this way one seeks to quantify proximity to a pure example of a concept.[38] The analysis of fuzzy sets is more statistical than earlier QCA, but the objective still remains the identification of necessary and sufficient conditions.[39] Unlike the original QCA, however, fuzzy-set QCA seeks to determine degrees of necessity and sufficiency by means of (actually rather complex) calculations.[40]

In statistical analysis – in contrast with these "qualitative" methods – there is not the same interest in explaining the characteristics of each case. Instead, the cases studied represent a sample of a larger "population" of cases. One is not trying to establish necessary and sufficient conditions but instead trying to predict how much certain conditions contribute to an outcome by estimating how many units of a dependent variable change with a one-unit change in an explanatory variable. Correlation coefficients are calculated to determine this estimate. In multiple-regression analysis, a statistical equation is constructed showing how the typical value of the dependent variable changes when an explanatory condition is varied while other explanatory variables are held fixed.

The great advantage of multiple-regression analysis is that we are controlling some explanatory variables to determine the independent effect of others and can thereby establish which explanatory variables make the greatest contribution to the outcome and whether some correlations are spurious. The major constraint is that controlling for variables requires a large number of cases, and the more variables being controlled, the larger the required sample. My sample would have to be far larger than is possible in order to control the number of explanatory variables I want to control. A common expectation in regression analysis is a sample size of at least ten cases per variable. Thus, even a relatively small model with one dependent variable, one explanatory variable, and four control variables would require at least sixty cases. In the following analysis, quite a few more than four variables would need to be controlled for a respectable regression analysis.

The method I chose is ordinal correlation analysis. Like regression analysis, it is carried out by computing a statistical coefficient, but the coefficient I use is much simpler to calculate and understand than either fuzzy-set QCA calculations or regression coefficients. Unlike regression analysis, ordinal correlation analysis does not enable us to predict increases or decreases in a dependent variable but simply helps to measure the strength of an association between two variables by calculating how similar or different is the ranking of cases on these variables.

As would be true if I were doing a regression analysis, the following cross-cultural analysis is based on a sample. Its purpose is to evaluate the case-specific explanations I provided for Western Europe by going beyond them. I am not interested in explaining the individual cases in the cross-cultural sample for their own sake. This contrasts with QCA and other case-oriented approaches.

Admittedly, it is difficult to control variables using ordinal correlation analysis. It can be done only on a small scale by dividing the sample into several groups. For our purposes, however, the difficulty in controlling variables is not a huge handicap. A number of the explanatory variables in the following analysis are highly correlated with one another. Under these circumstances, to try to determine which one or two is the core explanatory variable could be misleading; small differences in which variables are controlled can lead to wild swings in the coefficients in a regression equation.

The principal measures of rank-order correlation used in social sciences are the Spearman *rho*, the Kendal *tau*, and the Goodman-Kruskal *gamma*. Which of these is the most suitable for the following analysis has been determined by another characteristic of our data. We do not have sufficient information to rank all the cases in a precise order for each variable. Instead, the cases are sorted into ordinal categories. This enables us to present them in tabular form, which gives us a visual representation of the data. It means that, in statistical terms, we have many cases that are being treated as ties. The *gamma*, rather than the Spearman *rho* or Kendal *tau*, is the appropriate correlation coefficient when there are ties among cases. A *gamma* coefficient ranges from 1.0 (perfect positive correlation) to -1.0 (perfect negative correlation), with 0.0 indicating no correlation.

The ordinal categories that I have constructed are not ideal types. Nonetheless, I employ typological language descriptively to refer to some of the formations in the sample. Not surprisingly, for example, hunter-gatherers and simple horticulturalists are quite different from bureaucratic empires with respect to some of the variations that concern us. But I do not essentialize these classifications. Nor do I employ them as discrete categories. Rather, they reflect empirical degrees of difference.

Another divergence between the methodology in the preceding chapters and this cross-cultural investigation is the distinction often made between diachronic analysis and synchronic analysis. In the former, one compares cases over relatively long periods of time; in the latter, one examines each case for a limited time period. Causal-process analysis is diachronic if the processes are long-term or synchronic if the processes are short term. Big-case–small-N studies are usually diachronic but can be synchronic. In contrast, QCA and the statistical methods discussed above are generally synchronic in that they are used to compare social or political conditions in limited periods of time. The time periods for synchronic comparison can be contemporaneous (for instance, a statistical analysis of poverty and social unrest in different countries in the same time period) or they can be non-contemporaneous (for instance, a comparative analysis of murder rates in different countries, some in the nineteenth century, others in the early twentieth century, still others in the late twentieth century). Comparing non-contemporaneous cases poses difficulties and must be done with care, but major studies in comparative history, such as Moore's *Social Origins of Dictatorship and Democracy* and Skocpol's *States and Social Revolutions*, compare non-contemporaneous cases.

THE CROSS-CULTURAL ANALYSIS

The analysis is based on a comparative reading of the twenty states and societies listed in Table 14.1. They have been selected mostly from the societies discussed above in the global survey. An effort has been made to include cases differing in social and political structures, in global location, and in the nature of their honorific rewards. Otherwise, the selection was random.

The size of the sample was limited for two reasons. First, it was not possible to obtain all the information needed on many states and societies that might have been included. Second, an effort was made to maintain reasonable case independence by not including any society that was significantly influenced by another society in the

Table 14.1
Cross-cultural sample of twenty states and societies

Name used in tables	Socio-political formation and period sampled
Egypt	New Kingdom of Egypt (sixteenth to eleventh centuries BCE)
Athenians	Classical Athens (fifth to fourth centuries BCE)
Han	Western Han Empire of China (second century BCE to early first century CE)
Romans	Roman Empire (first century BCE to fifth century CE)
Gupta	Gupta Empire of India (fourth to sixth centuries CE)
Byzantium	Early Byzantine Empire (fifth to eleventh centuries CE)
Sasanians	Second Golden Age of Sasanian Empire (fifth to seventh century CE)
Russia	Kievan Rus' (ninth to thirteenth centuries CE)
Mongols	Mongol Empire (1227 to 1259 CE)
Ashikaga	Ashikaga/Muromachi shogunate of Japan (fourteenth to sixteenth centuries CE)
Aztecs	Aztec Empire (fifteenth to sixteenth centuries CE)
Inca	Inca Empire (fifteenth to sixteenth centuries CE)
Choson	Early Choson dynasty of Korea (fifteenth to eighteenth centuries CE)
Mughals	Mughal Empire (sixteenth to eighteenth centuries CE)
Ottomans	Ottoman Empire (seventeenth to eighteenth centuries CE)
Iroquois	Iroquois Confederacy (seventeenth to eighteenth centuries CE)
Qing	Qing (Manchu) Empire of China (seventeenth to eighteenth centuries CE)
Iñupiaq	Iñupiaq Inuit of Northwest Alaska (first half of the nineteenth century CE)
Aborigines	Australian aborigines (nineteenth century CE)
Zulus	Zulu Kingdom (nineteenth century CE)

sample. Thus, though I would have liked to include both Classical and Macedonian Greece, I could not because they are clearly not independent cases. Some might argue that the same could be said of the Roman Empire, the early Byzantine Empire, and the Ottoman Empire. The early Byzantine Empire, also known as the Eastern Roman Empire, evolved directly out of the Roman Empire. I have, however, included both in the sample because there was a significant difference in their honorific rewards. And I felt that the Ottoman conquest of Constantinople represented a sufficient break in the cultural and institutional evolution of this centre to permit both cases to be included in the sample. Still, it is necessary to recognize that there remain some regional contextual effects in the sample. An effort will be made to control for these by dividing the sample into three regional groups.

The time periods sampled varied in length for a number of reasons. Sometimes the information available was insufficient to establish short chronological boundaries. A case in point is the period sampled for Egypt: it is longer than others because the exact years and even centuries in which events or developments took place can be unclear in the sources on which Egyptologists rely. In contrast, limited information and the diversity of the Inuit population led me to select a particular group and period of Inuit history that has been studied relatively carefully – the Iñupiaq of Northwest Alaska in the first half of the nineteenth century.[41] In still other cases, the period sampled was determined by the life span of the state formation. This was true for Kievan Rus', which existed only from the late ninth to the mid-thirteenth centuries. The Mongol Empire was the most problematic. Mongol state and society were very different from the states and societies over which the Mongols came to rule. The geographical area selected for the following analysis was that covered by the Empire in 1227, when Ghenghis Khan died. The chronological period I chose was from 1227 to the end of the reign of Möngke Khan in 1259 CE. The coding for this area and time period is very different from what it would be for the entire Empire at its peak.

Until the current chapter, this book has been about long diachronic processes in Western Europe: cultural lineages, the expansion of state honours, population growth, political centralization, the transformation of warfare, and so forth. In contrast, the following data analysis is synchronic. The sample is mostly non-contemporaneous; included are states in the Ancient World, in the Middle Ages, and in the Early Modern period. Unlike the analysis of Western Europe, this analysis does not take into consideration the causes of the conditions we are comparing (any more than a researcher who finds a statistical association between socio-economic status and voting would be compelled to determine the different ways in which the subjects in the study acquired their socio-economic status).

The social and political conditions that I have argued in earlier chapters shaped the evolution of state honours in Western Europe can be divided into two categories: (1) selection pressures and (2) cultural and institutional innovations or developments. The latter emerged either as a response to these selection pressures or independently of them but had an effect on how selection pressures were or were not met. To illustrate, whether or not a large administrative officialdom developed as a result of demographic selection pressures, large-scale administration certainly affected the way in which demographic pressures were met.

It should also be made clear that the cultural and institutional innovations or developments themselves also created selection pressures that were met (or not met) by other cultural and institutional innovations or developments. They were also met (or not met) by the state population-management practices that I have asserted have to be taken into account not because these practices have a causal effect on state honours but rather because they provide, according to my argument, evidence of actions that were being taken for reasons similar to those for which state honours were adopted. Table 14.2 provides a summary of the processes discussed earlier in this book.

Needless to say, it is very difficult to rank twenty states and societies on these variations. Even the demographic data in this analysis are rough estimates. However, since we are simply ranking them in three or four ordinal categories, demographic estimates are sufficient. The same is true for the size of armies. All the other variables had to be coded subjectively on the basis of intensive reading on each state and society

There is really no way in which to rank cases on social mobilization as such. Thus, the size of the largest population concentration had to suffice as a measure of both population density and social mobilization.

For political centralization, I took into account both the size of the territory that a state claimed to rule and the effectiveness of this rule. To take Classical Athens as an example, though the city exercised very effective control over Attica, this region was small in comparison with most other territories sampled in this study, so it scored low on this variable. The score for the Mongol Empire is not as high as one might expect for the opposite reason. The territory controlled was large, but the control exercised over this territory – though in some respects impressive – did not match the control that the two Chinese centres in the sample (the Han and the Qing) exercised over their territories, though it should be kept in mind that none of the cases in the sample were as politically centralized as Modern states.

Table 14.2
Social and political processes associated with the evolution of state honours
in Western Europe

Selection pressures	Cultural and institutional innovations and developments	State management of populations
Population size and density	Large officialdom	Maintenance and extraction
Social mobilization	Religious Reformation	Mobilization
Political centralization	Decline in cultural monopolies	Individualization
Greater scale of competition	Instrumentalism	
Changes in warfare	Culture of improvement and reform	
	Militarism	
	Changes in criteria for merit	

It proved impossible to come up with a way to rank the cases on domestic competition. I tried to use frequency of war to measure inter-state competition, but war was so endemic that the effort had to be abandoned. I did not code changes in warfare as one variable. Rather, I coded size of armies, importance of infantry as opposed to cavalry (or chariotry), coordinated army, and coordinated infantry. The importance of infantry refers to the contribution that an infantry made to winning (or losing) battles.

Coordinated infantry takes into consideration the size of an infantry, the extent to which it was important for winning (or losing) battles, and how well coordinated it was. A high score on this variable can be achieved only if a society has a minimally large infantry, it depends heavily on this infantry, and this infantry is well coordinated. Thus, though coordination in the Aztec and Inca infantries was not superior to coordination in the Byzantine or Sasanian infantries, the former obtained higher scores on this variable because their infantries were more important relative to horsemen – of which they had none – than were the Byzantine or Sasanian infantries. The states and societies with the lowest scores on this variable were the Mongols,

Gupta, Inuit, and Australians, but for different reasons: the Mongols because their infantries were much less important than their cavalry; the Gupta because their infantries – though more important than Mongol infantries – were less important than most others in the sample and not especially well coordinated; and the other two because their infantries were poorly coordinated. Inversely, the Romans have higher scores than do the Athenians not because they had better coordinated infantries or relied on infantry more than the Athenians but because Athenian infantries were much smaller.

Among the cultural and institutional variables, it is possible to rank the size of the state officialdom, merit, and militarism. State officialdom refers to the number of positions that are filled by full-time employees. This is not a simple matter, but I was able to sort my cases on this variation if defined in this way.

Although merit itself was impossible to code with any confidence, I was able to rank the cases on whether important positions were inherited. In all the cases in the sample, many important positions were hereditary, but there were enough non-hereditary positions in some states and societies to construct this variable. It is true that non-hereditary selection often took place within upper social strata in which membership was mostly hereditary. My coding rule was that if a position was filled non-hereditarily (by examination, for example) from a social group such as a nobility that was hereditary, it was coded as non-hereditary. On the other hand, if appointments were filled by tanistry or a similar institution in which the worthiest individual is selected from within a specified set of kin, it was deemed to be hereditary. Of course, just because a position was not hereditary does not mean that the appointment was based on merit. The appointment could be political or personal. Nevertheless, ranking societies according to non-hereditary appointments provides the best approximation of how they would be ranked if we had more information available.

What I am calling militarism also needs to be explained. As just said, all the populations in the sample were engaged in war most of the time. And invariably, political leaders had to control military forces either directly or indirectly to stay in power. None of this varied much. I ranked the cases in the sample according to (1) the relative hegemony of their military culture; (2) differentiation between military and non-military elites, in particular, the extent to which there existed in a society a significant non-military elite and how much political and cultural power it had; and (3) the extent to which war was the principal occupation of leaders.

What is meant by size of army is the number of soldiers that our sources indicate were permanently in service or mobilized during wars. It would include conscripts and men whose primary occupation was something else, so long as our sources indicate that they were in fact sometimes mobilized. The number engaged in a particular battle would obviously be less.

Religious reform, cultural monopolies, instrumentalism, and a culture of improvement and reform – all proved impossible to code. For population maintenance and extraction, the only variation that I could code was population-information collection, which generally meant population census or tax registers.

With the exception of population-information collection, the above variables are all treated as explanatory variables. The dependent variables correspond to the main features that have characterized the Western-European honours system: (1) the number of different honorific rewards, (2) the number of different metallic body ornaments bestowed as honorific rewards, and (3) the number of different honorific rewards eligible to a wide social range of recipients.

Since medals and metallic badges as such were rare outside the lineages I described in Chapter 7, I correlated my dependent variables with honorific metallic body ornaments as the most similar to medals and metallic badges. This included what we would call jewellery, but only if it was granted as a reward and had an honorific value greater than its material value. When I coded social range, I took into account the size of the population. A wide social range in a very small society is not the same as a wide social range in a society of hundreds of thousands or millions of people. This variable is, however, distinct from population size. In spite of the way in which it was constructed, it actually has a relatively weak correlation with total population.

In all studies of this kind, coding errors and disagreements are inevitable. This is all the more true in this analysis for several reasons: (1) I encountered considerable within-case variation, which had to be averaged out; (2) the sources from which I gathered evidence are limited; and (3) most of my measures are subjective. Still, so long as the errors and disagreements are random, they make it more difficult not easier to find correlations that support the causal arguments I have made earlier in the book.

Table 14.3
Gamma coefficients between selected variables and honorific rewards

	Dependent variables		
Selected variables	Number of honorific rewards	Metallic body ornaments as honorific rewards	Social range of honorific rewards
SELECTION PRESSURES	Coefficients with dependent variables		
Total population	0.76	0.32	0.40
Largest population concentration	0.98	0.52	0.82
Political centralization	0.79	0.30	0.45
Army size	0.80	0.37	0.50
Importance of infantry	-0.36	-0.13	-0.01
Coordinated army	0.71	0.25	0.56
Coordinated infantry	0.64	0.70	0.71
CULTURAL AND INSTITUTIONAL CONDITIONS			
Size of state officialdom	0.83	0.32	0.52
Non-inherited positions	0.79	0.57	0.80
Militarism	-0.22	0.07	-0.15
POPULATION MANAGEMENT			
Population-information collection	0.82	0.28	0.54

It should also be stated that only state rewards are included in the analysis unless the society does not have what we would call a state; then any honorific reward is included.

Results

Table 14.3 gives us the *gamma* coefficients between the explanatory variables and the three dependent variables. Most of them are high by the standards of social-science research. Tables C.1–C.10 in Appendix C provide cross-tabulations of some of these associations. I have divided the sample into three global regional groups: (1) Asia, (2) the Mediterranean and Middle East, and (3) a residual category consisting of those in other regions. Superscripts in the tables indicate into which group a case falls.

A table with a diagonal relationship from the top-left cell to the bottom-right cell indicates a statistically strong and positive linear correlation (as, for example, in Table C.2). A table with a diagonal from bottom left to top right indicates a negative linear correlation. (Table C.5 provides an example, though it is a weak correlation.) Cases that fall well off a diagonal are outliers (the Gupta Empire in Table C.8 for example); they weaken any linear correlation whether positive or negative.

SELECTION PRESSURES

We begin with the two measurements of population pressure: the total population claimed to be governed and the size of the largest population concentration. As shown in Table 14.3, the highest *gamma* coefficients for these variables are between total population and number of honorific rewards (.76) and between largest population concentration and both number of rewards (.98) and social range (.82). They are all positive.

The cross-tabulation of total population and number of honorific rewards is given in Table C.1. Those states that most writers would call large bureaucratic empires are relatively close to the lower-right end of the diagonal (high scores on both variables), but not equally so. The Han, Mughals, Qing, and Romans have the highest scores on both variables (the Qing with a population of over 400 million), while other large bureaucratic empires (Gupta, Sasanians, and Byzantines) have lower scores on both variables, though still toward the lower-right end of the diagonal. The societies at the upper-left end of the diagonal (lowest scores on both variables) are the hunter-gatherers or horticulturalists. Athens is an outlier. It has been given a relatively low score on population because this score is based on the population of Attica. It could be argued that Athens controlled a larger population. However, if we were to put the Athenians in the over-a-million category, it would result in a higher *gamma* coefficient (.80) than what is shown in Tables 14.3 and C.1.

The cross-tabulation of the size of the largest population concentration and the number of honorific rewards is in Table C.2. It is similar to Table C.1, but there are a number of differences, one of which is that Athens is no longer an outlier. And the *gamma* coefficient is much higher (.98). The Qing and the Romans are at the extreme lower-right end of the diagonal (highest scores on both variables). The population of Beijing may have reached over a million by 1800 and that of Rome a million by the second century CE.[43] The Mongols eventually ruled over populous urban centres, but in the area and period of time I have sampled, cities were not large, not even the Mongolian capital, Karakorum, which was likely never much more than 10,000 persons. In other parts of the Empire it was characteristic of Mongol rulers to prefer living in tents.[44] Even the khan could follow a nomadic lifestyle outside the capital for much of the year.[45]

Table 14.3 indicates a strong relationship (.82) between size of largest population concentration and the social range of honorific rewards. Table C.3 gives us the cross-tabulation. Since the coding on social range took into account not just the equality of honours distribution but also the numbers involved, the hunter-gatherers and horticulturalists were given low scores. Although the distribution of rewards was relatively egalitarian in these societies, the number of persons who benefited was in absolute terms small. In contrast, the wide social range of honours by states relatively close to the lower-right end of the diagonal, such as the Han, the New Kingdom, et cetera, benefited a large number of persons.

As can be seen in Table 14.3, relative to other coefficients, army size has a strong association with the number of honorific rewards (.80), a moderate association with social range (.50), and a weak association with metallic body ornaments (.37). Table C.4 gives us the cross-tabulation for number of rewards. Mobilized armies, like cities, involve concentrations of populations. The Gupta and Ottoman empires are slight outliers. They do not have an especially large number of honorific rewards, but as mentioned in Chapter 6, they had very large armies. The states in the sample at the lower-right end of the diagonal (highest scores on both variables) are the Han, Mughals, Qing, and Romans. Their rulers could put together armies in the hundreds of thousands. A Han army of 300,000 men, for instance, was mobilized in 133 BCE for an expedition against the Hsiung-nu, a nomadic people in Mongolia.[46] If up to strength, the Roman army could be as large as 300,000, maybe more, but its size varied sharply as a result of mobilizations and de-mobilizations.[47] It was rarely less than 100,000 to 200,000 spread over its vast territories. In 1707, Mughal emperor Bahadur Shah reportedly mobilized an army of 300,000 against his brother.[48] In 1748, the Qing Emperor mobilized an army of more than 200,000 troops in an expedition against aggrandizing chieftains in Western China.[49]

One explanation for the strength of these correlations is simply demographic: more people, more potential recipients, more honours. In societies of less than 10 million with population concentrations of less than 100,000 or with armies of less than 20,000, the demand for honours would have been weaker, and so a smaller number of rewards would have been needed. However, since size of largest population concentration has higher coefficients on all three dependent variables than does total population, it could be that the number of honorific rewards is determined less by the number of potential recipients than by something more associated with population concentration.

Let me carry this suggestion further and propose that the significance of total population lies less in its direct relationship with honorific rewards than in its relationship with other variables with which it is highly correlated and which have even stronger correlations with the number of rewards. As just noted, for largest population concentration, the difference in the strength of the coefficients is large (.76 versus .98). For another four, the differences are not large, but they are consistent. Political centralization, army size, the size of state officialdom, and population-information collection all have higher coefficients with number of rewards than does total population. Given the limits of our data and methodology, it seems best to treat these as a set of highly interrelated variables for which we are not going to try to determine which is the most important or what caused what. It can be referred to as the population-state set.

As shown in Table 14.3, importance of infantry (as opposed to cavalry or chariotry) has negative correlations with all three dependent variables, especially with the number of honorific rewards. Regional differences may partially account for these negative relationships. Table C.5 indicates that in four states in Asia and in the Mediterranean and Middle East – the Qing, Mughals, Byzantium, and the New Kingdom – infantry was less important but a relatively large number of honorific rewards were distributed. In four societies outside these regions – the Aborigines, Iñupiaq, Iroquois, and Zulus – infantry was all-important (no cavalry), but there were relatively small numbers of honours. If we exclude the second group, the relationship becomes a small positive one of .06 (not shown). Positive or negative, the point is that there is no real tendency for countries that rely more on infantry to have more state honours.

These findings contrast with the positive *gamma* coefficients between coordinated armies and number of rewards (.71) and between coordinated infantry and all three dependent variables (.64, .70, and .71). The *gamma* coefficients between selection pressures, on the one hand, and metallic body ornaments and the social range of honorific rewards, on the other, are lower than those between selection pressures and the number of honours, with one important exception. Coordinated infantry has higher coefficients on body ornaments and social range than it does on the number of honorific rewards. It could be argued that the Romans employed body ornaments – most notably crowns – as honorific rewards because they were influenced directly or indirectly by the Athenians. However, if we exclude the Romans from the sample, we still get a *gamma* coefficient of .65 (not shown) between coordinated infantry and metallic body ornaments.

CULTURAL AND INSTITUTIONAL INNOVATIONS AND DEVELOPMENTS

Table 14.3 reveals a negative correlation between militarism and number of honorific rewards. This is a rather surprising finding, worthy of a more careful look at the cases. The cross-tabulation is shown in Table C.10. The early Byzantine Empire and early Choson Korea were ranked as the least militaristic. In the former, considerable power was enjoyed by the large and complex civilian bureaucracy and considerable prestige by cultural elites, both of which were represented in the Byzantine nobility. Similarly, in Early Choson Korea, power was divided between the civilian and the military segments of the state nobility, known as the *yangban*. The civilian segment consisted of scholarly officials who maintained their position by (at least one member in a generation) passing the examinations required for access to office.

The largest group of cases in Table C.10 is in Column 2. These states and societies were certainly militaristic, but they also had significant non-military elites. Most of the Iroquois confederates, for example, had two kinds of chiefs, non-military chiefs and "war chiefs."[50] The Gupta conquered all of northern India to establish their empire, mobilized enormous armies, and fought numerous wars but were also influenced and limited by a vigorous anti-militaristic culture that had existed for centuries in Ancient Indian society.[51]

As these observations suggest, the lack of a strong positive correlation between militarism and the number of honorific rewards could be the result of the universality of militarism. The early Byzantine Empire and Choson Korea, while less militaristic than the other cases in the sample, cannot really be described as non-militaristic.

The Early Byzantine Empire was almost constantly at war and its leaders were no less interested in its armed forces than those of other states, both then or later. They have left us one of the best-known military manuals of the Ancient Mediterranean and Middle East, the so-called *Strategikon*, usually attributed to Emperor Maurice, who ruled from 582 to 603 CE. The founder of the Choson dynasty, Yi Sŏng-gye, was an army general who, with his son and successor Yi Banggwa, achieved power militarily. The centralization of military command was essential for Korean rulers to undermine traditional military power, a process that was thwarted for a time by the persistence of private armies.[52]

Non-inherited positions has a relatively strong positive correlation with number of honorific rewards (.79) and social range (.80). We might think that it should be included in the population-state set, but, in fact, it is not highly correlated with the variables in the set, with the exception of population-information collection, with which it has a *gamma* of .72, and city size, with which it has a *gamma* of .83 (neither shown).

STATE POPULATION MANAGEMENT

Table 14.3 indicates that, relative to other coefficients, the association of population-information with metallic body ornaments is weak (.28) and with social range, moderate (.54) but with number of honorific rewards, relatively strong (.82).

This makes sense. To repeat, population-information collection is not seen as a causal variable in this analysis but rather another instrument of population management, which, in my view, was caused by the same selection pressures as state honours. Thus, there is no reason why it should be associated with ornaments, a broad range of distribution, or any other particular characteristic that honours can have. But the correlation with the number of honours does support my thesis that population-information collection is found together with honorific rewards of some kind.

Caveats

It is necessary to acknowledge the limitations of the above analysis. I have already called attention to some coding issues and difficulties that should be considered in the interpretation of the results. It was owing to such difficulties that many variables could not be included in the cross-cultural analysis, most notably domestic competition and cultures of improvement and reform.

Another issue that I have mentioned is the possibility that some correlations we have found could be a result of the contextual effects of different locations; that is, two variables could correlate because high (or low) scores on these variables are both found in the same region and so have been influenced by similar cultural collections and have been involved in common events and processes. This issue has already been raised with regard to the cultural influence of Athenians on Romans.

We can try to assess whether regional contextual effects are responsible for some of our correlations by examining the correlations between our variables within major global regions. The regions that make the most sense for our subject and sample are those indicated by superscripts in the tables, that is, Asia, the Mediterranean and Middle East, and the residual Other category. There can be little regional effect among the cases in the residual category because they are geographically too dispersed. Yet there is another reason for separating them from the rest of the sample. These societies include all the hunter-gatherers and horticulturalists in the sample, and they score relatively low on most of the explanatory and dependent variables. By separating them out we are able to see what associations we get in the two remaining regions.

Regrettably, the number of cases within each region is too small for calculating *gamma* coefficients, and there are far too many tables for me to present. But it is possible to assess regional contextual effects by visually examining the tables in Appendix C. Looking carefully at each region separately, one perceives that the associations found in the entire sample remain sufficiently strong in all three regions or become stronger in two of the regions and weaker in one. None of the conclusions of the preceding analysis is undermined by the regional sub-analysis.

CONCLUSION

Toward an Explanation of Modern State Honours

In the opening pages of this book I indicated that, though the questions I am trying to answer are fairly simple – principally how do we explain the evolution of state honours in Western Europe? – the answers are not so simple. Nevertheless, if pushed to answer it in a few pages, I would suggest what follows. Although this answer is specific to Western Europe, where possible I indicate whether the explanation I give for Western Europe is supported by the comparative analysis of the preceding chapter.

Historically, it is clear that the evolution of state honours in Western Europe resulted from a number of cultural lineages that gave Early Modern and Modern governments several cultural collections that could be adopted for their purposes. The lineage that contributed the most consisted of earlier honorific rewards: (1) those of the Ancient World of the Mediterranean and the Middle East; (2) the Medieval and post-Medieval monarchical orders and knights bachelor; and (3) the major orders that were created from the late seventeenth century, most notably the Order of Saint Louis, the Order of Maria Theresa, and the Legion of Honour. In addition and closely related to this lineage were the aristocratic, heraldic, and chivalric cultural collections that developed in the Middle Ages and were revived and imitated in the Early Modern and Modern periods. Finally, the evolution of coins and medals in the Middle East and Europe has yielded one of the most distinctive characteristics of Modern European honours.

A number of ideational changes occurring during the Early Modern and Modern periods also contributed to the evolution of honorific rewards in state and non-state institutions. These changes include what I have referred to as a culture of improvement and reform, manifested in a number of ways, most notably in (1) various associations devoted to progress of one kind or another and (2) the introduction of new approaches to governing. There also emerged new understandings of the human self and more individualist conceptions of society.

Recognition of these cultural and institutional forces is necessary for any understanding of the evolution of Western-European honours, but taken alone it is plainly insufficient. Cultural and institutional practices do not persist on their own. There was nothing inevitable about the influence of Egyptian, Greek, and Roman honorific rewards, Medieval orders of knighthood, or Mediterranean and Middle Eastern coinage. The same is true of European aristocratic culture, heraldry, and romantic chivalry. These cultural and institutional traditions had an influence because they were for some reason favoured not only by those who originated them but also by those who picked them up and adapted them in their efforts to meet social and political challenges. The culture of improvement and reform would not have developed as it did without the selection pressures that made it adaptive. And the consequences of new ideas about the self and society would have been limited, for the most part, to the ruminations of cultural elites if they had not coincided with certain social and political changes. Thus we need to include these social and political changes in our explanation of the evolution of Modern Western European honours. This has been the major purpose of most of this book. I can now outline what I think this research has demonstrated.

As it became necessary for Western-European states to manage larger populations and armies and as these states became more politically centralized and the size of the state officialdom increased, like other states with these challenges, they selected a large number of instruments to meet them, one of which was to expand their honours system. Once again we can point to the fact that the expansion of state honours in Western Europe was led by France during the seventeenth, eighteenth, and early nineteenth centuries when its population size and state centralization were greater than in the British Isles. The cross-cultural correlations with the population-state set of variables are consistent with this explanation. The growth of large cities may have posed particular challenges. In the cross-cultural survey, the variable that has the strongest relationship with the number of honours is population concentration, which suggests that it creates an additional pressure over and above that of total population. For Western Europe, I ventured that the reason for this was the pressure to manage denser, more socially mobilized populations and to compete for power in these populations. At all events, it is clear that the weight I have given to population pressures is supported by the cross-cultural analysis.

In addition to these pressures, Early Modern Europe experienced remarkable changes in the nature of warfare, which have formed an important part of my explanation for the evolution of state honours. This argument is supported in the cross-cultural analysis by the strong correlations for the warfare variables, with the notable exception of the importance of infantry. However, this difference – in the *gamma* coefficients for the importance of infantry as compared with the other warfare variables – does go along with the idea that the shift in the relative utility of Western European cavalry and infantry was not, in itself, as crucial as the increase in the size of armies and the ways in which they fought.

The strong positive relationship in the cross-cultural sample between non-inherited positions and honours is a significant finding given the role that merit is thought to have played in the evolution of state honours in Western Europe. I proposed that the distribution of state honours according to merit emerged in Western Europe as a consequence of several forces: (1) an aristocratic tradition of merit, (2) the manipulation of the idiom of merit in the social and political struggles between the aristocracy and the bourgeoisie, and (3) the dynamics of status competition.

The most common explanation for the evolution of meritocratic standards in Western Europe is that they are a consequence of more rational ways of thinking and norms of rationality. It is true that state bureaucracies have institutionalized norms of merit and these norms have had some effect on the distribution of state honours, but to posit that they constituted a major factor is problematic for several reasons. First, these bureaucratic norms played little role in the formation of state honours during the seventeenth, eighteenth, and early nineteenth centuries. Second, in significant ways, modern state bureaucracies have undermined the meritorious distribution of state honours by forcing status distributors to conform to bureaucratic hierarchies.

Despite the negative coefficient between militarism and honours, we should be careful before deciding that militarism did not contribute to the evolution of state honours in Early Modern Europe. There was a correlation within Europe between militarism and the chronology of the expansion of honours. France was the most militaristic and the most engaged in honorific rewarding in Western Europe during the seventeenth and eighteenth centuries. Nevertheless, the negative association in the cross-cultural sample does suggest that we should not put too much stress on militarism – as opposed to other military factors – in our efforts to explain the Western European experience. Certainly, Europeans were no more militaristic than many other societies in world history.

Yet Western European honorific practices were not identical to those adopted or created by other centralized, bureaucratic states when faced by the same challenges. Most of all, they bore the stamp of the lineages outlined above and other features of Western European culture and institutions. The adoption of metallic badges and medals is to be explained by the distinctive history of coins and medals in Europe, but also, I have asserted, by the advantages they possessed as a mode of communication, enabling them to function effectively as coordination devices. The exposure of large numbers of Europeans to these symbolic signals created common knowledge – or more accurately, common knowledges – of expected behaviour. Military decorations helped to instill among soldiers the attitude required to form an effective combined force on the battlefield. Drills and what Myerly calls "military spectacle" performed the same function.

If metallic body ornaments can be used as a substitute for medals and metallic badges, the correlations found in the cross-cultural analysis between infantry coordination and such ornaments lend some support to my thesis. Admittedly, with a few exceptions, none of the infantries in my sample were impelled by the need to reload firearms while maintaining a constant volley. Pre-Modern states that achieved a relatively high level of coordination had other reasons for doing so and were no doubt conducting manoeuvres that were different from those the Nassau cousins sought to instill. But coordination signals of some kind would have played a part in the development of the mentality that enabled Roman soldiers and relatively well-coordinated soldiers in other armies in world history to form effective units. We should remember that the inspiration for countermarching in Early Modern Western Europe came from countermarching in the Ancient Mediterranean world.

In general, Modern societies require more coordination than most pre-Modern societies. People today are coordinated by daily routines, schedules, calendars, measures of time, and devices such as traffic lights and signs. Obviously, honorific rewards do not function directly to achieve this sort of coordination, but it could be argued that they help to create the mentality in the general population that leads people to accept this regulation of their lives.

I have not sought to make such an argument, but I have sought to persuade the reader that state honours function as a mode of discipline in our lives. Early Modern and Modern Europe saw a significant transformation in the way in which people came to be disciplined as a result of individualist conceptions of society and the evolution of new collectives that interacted with these individualist conceptions. This interaction has enabled honours to function as instruments of individualized self-discipline in Western society. Whether or not this is the case for other awards and prizes and for non-Western regions is for others to determine, but I do have a little more to say about individualization outside Europe in the Epilogue.

Finally, like most status processes, Western European honours were driven forward by status competition – among states, among political factions, among social groups, and among individuals. These were power struggles over two kinds of status power: the power to command respect (what Weber defined as an "effective claim to social esteem"), and what I have called status-distribution power. In societies with very stable status structures, status is less distributable, and hence, the ability of those with status-distribution power to alter significantly the existing status structure is relatively weak; even the power of a king to do so is limited. On the other hand, in societies where status structures are relatively unstable, status-distribution power becomes more useful, and hence more valuable, to those who are able to acquire and hold it, whether on a grand societal scale, on a meso scale, or in micro social interactions.

The formative period in the evolution of state honours was determined primarily by the different functions state honours could serve for evolving states in the Early Modern and Modern periods. But status processes have played an additional and increasing role in the expansion of state honours, another subject on which I have a little more to say in the Epilogue.

The Endless Spiral of Honours

BEYOND EUROPE

Although it is not possible in the present study to examine the various paths that non-European countries have taken in the evolution of their honours systems, it is possible to trace the influence of European honours on some of these paths. This influence can be seen as a continuation of the historical lineages that shaped European state honours.

The process began with the distribution of European honours to people of European descent who were representing or were employed by European states in places outside Europe. To illustrate, the Order of Saint Louis was awarded to many officers in the French army who lived in French colonies. On a smaller scale, in 1818, the Military Order of William was first awarded in Indonesia to Dutch naval commander A.A. Buyskes for his role in suppressing a rebellion in the Moluccas; this elevation was followed by several more Dutch honorific rewards to expatriates of European descent.[1] Individuals in colonies who were of European descent could even be awarded a noble title. In the late seventeenth century, Charles Le Moyne, seigneur of Longueuil, New France, was made Baron de Longueuil in recognition of service to the French Crown.[2] Guy Carleton, who served as governor of Quebec twice and then as governor of British North America, was made a knight companion of the Order of the Bath in 1776 and raised to the British peerage as Baron Dorchester in 1786. Several Canadians of European descent were awarded the Victoria Cross before Confederation in 1867. Four Australians won the Victoria Cross the year before the Commonwealth of Australia came into being in 1901. Two New Zealanders received it before New Zealand became a dominion in 1907.

It may be recalled that the Order of Saint Michael and Saint George evolved during the nineteenth century from its original purpose as a reward for persons connected with Malta or the Ionian Islands to a reward primarily for British foreign and colonial officials.[3] The number of recipients not connected to the Islands rose steadily after 1830, requiring periodic revisions to the statutory limits on the size of the Order's membership.

Although Belgium was a late colonial power, it brought honours to a good number of Europeans working outside Europe, particularly in Congo. In addition to the members of the three orders created by Leopold II for his colony, not a few colonial officials who served in Congo were elevated to the Order of Leopold, two of them as *grands officiers*, two as *commandeurs*, and twenty-six as *officiers*.[4]

The distribution of European state honours to persons of European descent living outside Europe continued after colonies became independent states. Two founding fathers of Canadian Confederation, John A. Macdonald and George-Étienne Cartier, were beneficiaries of British state honours, a knight commander of the Order of the Bath for the former and a baronetcy for the latter.[5] The first Canadian to be elevated to the British peerage was George Stephen, who was born in Scotland and retired in England but lived most of his life in Canada, where he organized the financing of the Canadian Pacific Railway. He was made a baronet in 1886 and a baron in 1891. A knight grand cross or a knight commander of the Bath (the two highest of three grades) was given to 11 Canadians from 1867 to 1935; no less than 166 Canadians have become companions (the lowest of the three grades) in the Bath since Confederation.[6] Even more numerous were Canadians appointed to the Order of Saint Michael and Saint George: fourteen grand cross (the highest of three grades) and 382 companions (the lowest of three grades).[7]

Obviously, awards of the Victoria Cross varied with fluctuations in the mobilization of men for war. After the early appointments of Canadians before Confederation, there were no awards of the Victoria Cross to Canadians until 1900. Subsequently, ninety Canadians received this honour, mostly for service in the Great War. The Victoria Cross has been awarded to eighteen New Zealanders of European descent after New Zealand became a dominion. It was awarded to ninety-two Australians of European descent after the creation of the Commonwealth of Australia.

The distribution outside Europe of European state honours to persons of European descent was not limited to the colonies or former colonies of the country bestowing them. The Legion of Honour has been awarded to citizens of a large number of countries, including Australia, Brazil, Mexico, New Zealand, the United States, and Canada. To take one remarkable illustration, José Paranhos, a nineteenth-century Brazilian politician, prime minister, and a major player in the abolition of slavery in Brazil, had the right to call himself a grand cross not only of two Portuguese orders (the Order of the Rose and the Order of the Immaculate Conception of Vila Viçosa) but also of the Spanish Order of Charles III, the Italian Order of Saints Maurice and Lazarus, the French Legion of Honour, the Russian Order of the White Eagle, the Russian Order of Saint Anna, and the Austrian Order of Leopold.

The second process leading to the expansion of state honours outside Europe was the distribution of European honours to persons of non-European descent. This practice came up for discussion in Chapter 13, where I indicated the difficulties it created for both European and native status structures in the nineteenth century. As then said, those honoured were mostly high-ranking individuals – emperors, kings, princes, and prominent politicians – but there were exceptions, such as William Hall, the Nova Scotian who won the Victoria Cross.

And finally, non-European countries, both former colonies and countries that were never colonized, founded their own state honours or took over honours that had been established by European governments. The general dissemination and influence of European institutions, the introduction of European honours in colonies, and the prestige that these European honours enjoyed led governments outside Europe to select cultural items from European honours, most visibly in the structures and vocabulary that they adopted.

In Japan, a European-style state honours system was initiated shortly after the Meiji Restoration. The Imperial Council established the Order of the Rising Sun in 1875. It was followed by the Order of the Chrysanthemum in 1876 and three others in 1888 (the Order of the Paulownia Flowers, the Order of the Sacred Treasure, and the Order of the Sacred Crown).[8] Japanese "medals of honour" were also introduced in this time period. And additional orders and medals were created in the twentieth century.

The Chinese followed a similar path, inventing a number of European-style state honours during the nineteenth and early twentieth centuries, including the Order of the Double Dragon, instituted in 1882 for exceptional service to the emperor. Several orders were founded in 1912 along with a medal, the Merit Medal of the Republic, which was awarded to officers by the Sun Yat-sen government. Another ten or more orders or medals were founded from 1911 to 1933, mostly for the military. Finally, the People's Republic of China has had no qualms about adopting European-style state honours, creating several dozen major military awards, many in the decade after the formation of the new state.

As a result of its close ties to Britain, the establishment of a Canadian state honours system came late. The appointment of Canadians to British honours served as a substitute until the 1967. In that year, the Order of Canada was instituted, and Canadians subsequently made up for lost time with an explosion of state honours at the national, provincial, and municipal levels, including a national Order of Military Merit and a significant number of other military decorations.[9] In 1993, a separate Canadian Victoria Cross came into existence. In 1991 a separate Australian Victoria Cross had been established, and in 1999 a separate New Zealand Victoria Cross was created.

The cultural and institutional lineages that contributed to the formation of present-day honours systems in non-European countries would have had limited impact without certain conditions and forces operating in these non-European states and societies, including some of the conditions that we have been able to measure in the cross-cultural analysis. Through the nineteenth and twentieth centuries, the size of the populations that non-European governments had to manage expanded, the percentage of people living in large urban centres rose dramatically, effective political rule became more centralized, and the average size of state officialdom and military forces grew. All of these processes would have to be taken into account by anyone interested in tracing the evolution of honours in a non-European country.

Individualization, in the sense of individualized self-discipline, may also have become a factor in the non-European world. Academic literature on individualism and individualized social relations in non-European countries has grown during the past decade. Some scholars have asserted that individualism and individualized social relations in relatively traditional societies or in earlier periods of non-European history have been underestimated, while other writers have stressed the relative recency of increasing individualism and individualized social relations in various parts of the world.[10] I have proposed that the determinant of Western-European individualization as a mode of discipline lay in the changing collectivist-individualist dialectic. Paramount was the development of larger collectives that individuals were expected to serve and for which corporate and pastoral discipline were inadequate. For Western-European state honours, the social construction in Europe of nation as the collective was critical.

However, in the past hundred years or so, the construction of nations has been undertaken in other parts of the world. It has often been difficult, in no small part because European political constructions have been imposed on these regions and also because different constructions of nations have emerged in opposition to one another. Yet these struggles have simply increased and exacerbated the interaction between individuals or their families, on the one hand, and larger collectives, on the other. Nation-building governments have found it necessary to disembed people from their communities and families, all of which can contribute to individualization. It has been put forth that even Communist China, despite its explicit rejection of individualism as a value, has promoted individualized social relations in a number of ways. Initially, it was by attacking traditional values, including familism, thus weakening the control of families and communities over individuals and re-embedding these individuals into a much larger collective represented by the party-state.[11]

NON-STATE HONORIFIC REWARDS

Status rewards have also evolved in non-state institutions and organizations. Although they warrant a separate historical explanation, I will conclude with a few remarks on this subject.

The early formation of the Western-European non-state path was introduced in Chapter 7, where I talked about the variety of prizes offered by associations in the seventeenth and eighteen centuries. The direction of this path has been determined by certain conditions, some of which correspond to the conditions that shaped the growth of state honours, others of which do not. And some conditions have been more important for non-state awards than for state awards. These include cultural differentiation, economic transformations, and the development of a more competitive economic environment.

Literary prizes exemplify several noteworthy status processes and mechanisms in the evolution of non-state status awards. Like other prizes, literary prizes began during the Early Modern period as a result of the formation of academies and literary societies. In the nineteenth century, the sway that these bodies exercised over literary legitimation led to the founding of new literary societies – such as the Société des Lettres formed in 1838 in France – to assist writers and to nominate some of them to the Legion of Honour; prizes were also established to compete with the prizes of the French Academy, though they remained few in number and less respected.[12] Eventually, aristocratic domination of the Academy provoked the creation of the Goncourt Prize, which was first conferred in 1903. It significantly raised the status of (some) less well-known writers, but the exclusion of women from its jury provoked the founding of the Femina Prize, whose jury was, and still is today, comprised entirely of women. Literary status competition is also driven by commercial interests, most obviously the interests of publishers, a phenomenon that has led to much criticism of such prizes, several scandals, and accusations of commercialization being directed at the whole project. Still, literary prizes have played a significant role in raising the status of writers. In France, the announcement and bestowal of these prizes has become a national celebration of French literature.[13]

In addition, competition among national states has driven the process. Governments and literary groups have been motivated to introduce new prizes in response to international respect for the prizes of other countries. In an effort to keep up with the French, the British have created a number of literary prizes, though it was not until 1920 that they really got started and not until 1969 that the Booker Prize was founded in explicit imitation of the Goncourt.[14] The growth in literary prizes in the United States began at the end of the nineteenth century and rose precipitously thereafter. James English has estimated that the number of prizes per thousand new titles grew tenfold in the United States from the beginning to the end of the twentieth century, when it reached a hundred prizes per thousand, well above the thirty or so prizes per thousand in the United Kingdom at the end of the twentieth century.[15] Smaller countries could not expect to challenge this onslaught of literary awards offered in the larger countries, but most have introduced their own awards to try and help overcome the obscurity that their native writers face, even in their own countries.

The effects of status dynamics can also be seen in the growth of honours awarded by voluntary societies, interest groups, occupational associations, businesses, et cetera. Status rewards have multiplied as a result of status competition among such organizations, each one reacting to the introduction of honours by other organizations and occupations and motivated by a desire to raise or maintain their status relative to these other organizations or occupations. The evolution of new organizations and occupations has intensified the spread of what could be described, not unfairly, as a recognition epidemic. The consequence is a perpetual multiplication of honorific rewards. Few professional associations do not have an awards system. The American Sociological Association has nine major awards, but honours are also distributed by the large number of sub-societies, or "sections" as they are called, such as the "Global and Transnational Sociology Section" or the "Organizations, Occupations, and Work Section." Almost every year over the past three or four decades, new sections have been created. Whenever one is formed, it sets up its own slate of awards because new sections need to establish their legitimacy and make a claim to status relative to existing sections. At the present time, there are over fifty sections offering in total almost 200 annual awards.

Visual-entertainment status rewards have proliferated in the same manner but on a much larger scale and for an additional reason. As in the case of other non-state awards, the growth has been propelled by an increase in the number of organizations whose members feel the need to distribute prizes. It has also, however, been driven by technological changes that have led to new media. At the present time, there are so many prizes offered for visual entertainment in the United States that it is impossible to draw up a complete list. I was able to find 1,672 different awards created in the United States between 1920 and 2009. The only ones on my list that were founded in the 1920s were the Academy Awards, of which there were 11 at that time. I identified 20 awards that were founded in the 1930s, 34 in the 1940s, 97 in the 1950s, 59 in the 1960s, 220 in the 1970s, 321 in the 1980s, 420 in the 1990s, and 490 from 2000 to 2009. The honorific reward is one of the most pervasive features of the societies in which we live. We need to understand it and ask what it tells us about these societies.

APPENDICES

Was There a Rise of the Bourgeoisie or Middle Class?

Few issues in European history have generated more debate than that of the rise of the bourgeoisie or middle class. Unfortunately, much of the debate arises from different and vague conceptualization. There is not the space here to examine much of the literature, but it is important for me to make my position clear.

It has often been pointed out that the middle class was too heterogeneous to be a class. First, and most obviously, there was a large social cleavage between the business and non-business bourgeoisie. In Western Europe, but especially in France, the bourgeoisie that gained political power at the expense of the aristocracy was not so much the business bourgeoisie as the professional and administrative bourgeoisie. Yet it has been insisted that even the business bourgeoisie was too heterogeneous to be considered in these terms, and certainly too heterogeneous to engage in collective action. Although Marx seemed to believe that the bourgeoisie would engage in collective action on its own behalf, there is little in his writings on capitalist society to lead us to expect it to be able to do so. This contrasts with his analysis of proletarians that provides a number of reasons to expect them to acquire a capacity for collective action – physical concentration, common relations to the means of production, and shared impoverishment and alienation. The very ideology of the business bourgeoisie is not one that encourages collective approaches to problems.

The business segment of the French bourgeoisie was deeply divided along sectoral, geographical, and cultural lines; only toward the end of the century did French businessmen seek to organize themselves to overcome these impediments.[1] It is true that some

businessmen entered politics, but it is likely that in most of Western
Europe, as Henry Peiter has shown for France, organized pressure
groups representing business evolved as a result of efforts by business leaders to improve their relations with politicians and bureaucrats, who had far more political power.[2]

Cultural historians like to analyze social categories as social constructions.[3] From this perspective, in both France and Britain, the
notion of the bourgeoisie or middle class was less the designation of
a real group engaging in collective action than a social representation used by a variety of people for political purposes. There is some
disagreement over whether this representation was more powerful
in Britain or in France, but there is general agreement that it did
not evolve as a result of long-term economic and social changes but
instead was the product of political struggles.

While I concur with the basic objectives of this literature and with
the claim that the idea of a middle class emerged from political
struggles, I think it goes too far in its dismissal of the literature on
the bourgeoisie or middle class in nineteenth-century Europe. The
problem is both conceptual and empirical. Marxists and Weberians
alike define class economically – Marxists in terms of relations to
the means of production, Weberians in terms of "market situation."
Both believe that classes may or may not be conscious, organized,
cohesive, capable of collective action, and/or recognized by people
in a society. Marxists refer to a class that is conscious as a "class for
itself" and one that is not as a "class in itself." Most Marxists believe
that the nineteenth-century bourgeoisie was a class for itself. The
above literature attacking the bourgeois thesis has taken the Marxist
version as representative of the thesis and assumed that all one has
to do is undercut this version and the bourgeois thesis is discredited.
In other words, critics have assumed that if they can demonstrate
that in most periods the bourgeoisie or middle class was not conscious, cohesive, organized, and so forth, then it was little more than
a "myth" or "idiom."[4]

The problem is that, for most social scientists, class is not just
a social construction but also a social-scientific concept used to
describe certain patterns of social relations – relations of power,
authority, inequality, social distance, and, for many scholars, exploitation. These patterns are a social reality and they can exist whether
or not anyone recognizes them. To insist, as Maza does, that "classes

exist only if they are aware of their own existence"[5] is to hold that a society where no one is aware of classes is a classless society and that classes come into existence when people begin to think that they exist and disappear when people do not think they exist.

Much of the debate over the rise of the bourgeoisie or middle class has been about the extent to which the bourgeoisie or middle class was group conscious, and it is not an unworthy debate. We do need to understand where, when, and why the bourgeoisie became more or less conscious, organized, and collectively active. It is equally important to understand where, when, and why people thought there was such a social phenomenon. Yet this is not all that needs to be done. We also need to study classes objectively, that is, examine those relations of power, authority, and so forth that we find useful to call class relations. In both Marxist and non-Marxist literature, the capitalist bourgeoisie exerts its force on history not as an organized or recognized class, not as a collective actor, but as independent owners of the means of production, as individuals engaged in class relations.

To accept that the middle class could still be a class even if it was not group conscious would not, however, end the debate. There remains the assertion that it was not a class even in an objective sense because it was economically too diverse. Certainly, the "middle class" as conceived by Jürgen Kocka is diverse, including as it does merchants, manufacturers, bankers, capitalists, entrepreneurs, business managers, rentiers, doctors, lawyers, ministers, scientists, professionals, university professors, secondary schoolteachers, men and women of letters, and officials in public and private bureaucracies.[6] We would have to remove the role that people played in the economy from our definition of class in order to include most of these – much less all of them – in what we mean by the "middle class."

A much better conceptualization, in my view, is to treat the nineteenth-century "middle class" as what Weber called a *Stand*. In Weber's work, this term is generally translated into English as "status group." I am sure this translation annoys German historians, but from a sociological point of view, it is actually an appropriate translation because Weber did not really mean what most historians would understand by the term *Stand*. In this context, he used it to refer to a collectivity that enjoyed a similar claim to social esteem. In contrast with a class, which Weber defined in terms of the role people play in the economy, a *Stand* or status group is defined by the prestige and respect members of a group enjoy in a society and by their level and patterns of consumption.

This has always been, I submit, the central core of what is meant by European historians when they refer to the "middle class." I just do not think it is useful to call it a class, and for this reason, I do not employ the term in most of this book. Instead, I prefer the term "bourgeoisie," and I use it to refer to those who could not claim to belong to the aristocracy but had a relatively respected occupation and sufficient resources to live comfortably. In defining the bourgeoisie in this way, I depart from the original meaning of the word; it was once used to refer to the privileged members of a town, a status group that no longer exists. I am also not using it in the Marxist sense of capitalist owners of the means of production. Some readers may think that we should try to invent a new term that has not been used in such a variety of ways, but I actually believe that, in France at least, it has been implicitly used since the early nineteenth century in the sense that I am proposing. Although I do not agree with the Weberian assumption that status groups are always demarcated by consumption, I do believe that this is true in the case of the European bourgeoisie. Of course, drawing precise boundaries between the different groups in a society and placing every person in one or another group is impossible. However, this does not undermine the utility of such concepts. I am simply arguing that we will understand the rise of what has been called the "middle class" in Western Europe in the eighteenth and nineteenth centuries much better if we define it as a status group rather than a class.

When all is said on the subject, there can be no doubt that over the course of the nineteenth and twentieth centuries there was a "rise of the bourgeoisie" in the sense that (1) this status group became proportionately larger in society and (2) political power, economic power, and eventually cultural and status power shifted from the aristocracy to this group.

Characteristics of Members of the Legion of Honour, the Order of Leopold, and the Order of the British Empire

SAMPLING

The following tables are based on samples of members of the three orders. They were sampled by grade. If I had sampled the entire list, my sample would have included only a small number of members in the higher grades since they were awarded in relatively small numbers. Indeed, members of the highest grades could easily have not made it into the sample at all. By sampling different proportions within each grade, I was able to obtain a sufficient number of members in each grade for analysis. The only qualification I need to mention is that the grand crosses in the Legion of Honour, 1852 and 1929, the knights grand cross and dames grand cross of the Order of the British Empire, 1921, and the grand cordons of the Order of Leopold, 1933, had numbers so small that I did not take a sample but used the entire population.

This method is optimal for an analysis of the distribution within grades but is erroneous for analysis in which grades are combined. For example, if we want to know what percentage of the members of an order were generals in the armed forces, we cannot simply take the number in my sample and divide it by the total sample, since generals are usually found in the higher grades and I have sampled different proportions of each grade. In order to analyze representations in the population as a whole, or any segment in the population that includes all grades, I had to weight the sample by adjusting the frequencies according to the percentage that a grade has in the entire population.

CODING OF SOCIAL POSITIONS

Most of the social positions are self-explanatory, but a few need a little elaboration. "Middle bourgeoisie" consisted mostly of small business owners, school headmasters, auctioneers, railway superintendents, engineers, and various kinds of inspectors. The "judicial professions" consisted of judges, lawyers, and notaries. The "professions" included academics, architects, writers, physicians, teachers, artists, civil engineers, and musicians. "Lower bourgeoisie" and "petite bourgeoisie" refer to occupations such as clerks, supervisors, salespersons, artisans, skilled manual workers, small shopkeepers, mechanics, members of the national guard, et cetera. "Civilian social position" in the military tables refers to those who were in the military but performed what we would consider a civilian occupation, such as physician or engineer; their military rank varied.

SOURCES

Annuaire de l'Ordre Impérial de la Légion d'Honneur, 1852. Paris: Imprimerie impériale, 1853; *L'Ordre de Léopold: Liste de tous les dignitaries depuis la fondation de l'Ordre jusqu'au 31 décembre 1886.* Brussels: Hochsteyn, 1887; *Burke's Handbook to the Most Excellent Order of the British Empire.* London: Burke, 1921; *Annuaire official de tous les membres de l'Ordre de la Légion d'Honneur au 1er Avril 1929.* Paris: Quillet, 1929; *Mémorial du centenaire de l'Ordre de Léopold, 1832–1932.* Brussels: Maison d'Éditions "J. Rozez," 1933.

Table B.1
Belgian and foreign civilians in the Order of Leopold 1833–87 (weighted sample)

	Frequency	*Percentage*
Belgians	405	59.6
Foreigners	274	40.4
Total	679	100.0

Table B.2
Belgian and foreign civilians in the Order of Leopold, 1932 (weighted sample)

	Frequency	*Percentage*
Belgians	262	99.6
Foreigners	1	.4
Total	263	100.0

Table B.3
Belgian and foreign civilians in the Order of Leopold, 1833–87, distinguished according to grade in the Order (sampled by grade)

	Percentage of members by grade				
	Grand Cordon *n=145*	*Grand Officier* *n=124*	*Commandeur* *n=150*	*Officier* *n=139*	*Chevalier* *n=191*
Belgians	9.7	20.2	21.3	51.1	73.3
Foreigners	90.3	79.8	78.7	48.9	26.7
Total	100.0	100.0	100.0	100.0	100.0

Table B.4
Belgian and foreign civilians in the Order of Leopold, 1932, distinguished according to grade in the Order (sampled by grade)

	Percentage of members by grade				
	Grand Cordon *n=14*	*Grand Officier* *n=56*	*Commandeur* *n=66*	*Officier* *n=63*	*Chevalier* *n=67*
Belgians	50.0	98.2	95.5	98.4	100.0
Foreigners	50.0	1.8	4.5	1.6	0.0
Total	100.0	100.0	100.0	100.0	100.0

Table B.5
Belgian and foreign civilians in the Order of Leopold, 1833–87, distinguished according to period of appointment (weighted sample)

	Percentage of members by period of appointment		
	1830 to 2 August 1847 *n=93*	*13 August 1847 to* *1 July 1870* *n=212*	*2 July 1870 to 1886* *n=346*
Belgians	34.4	50.5	71.1
Foreigners	65.6	49.5	28.9
Total	100.0	100.0	100.0

Note: Members of the sample whose period of appointment is unknown have been excluded.

Table B.6
Belgian and foreign civilians in the Order of Leopold, 1932, distinguished according to period of appointment (weighted sample)

	Percentage of members by period of appointment		
	Before the Great War *n=12*	*During the Great War* *n=6*	*After the Great War* *n=244*
Belgians	100.0	100.0	99.6
Foreigners	0.0	0.0	0.4
Total	100.0	100.0	100.0

Note: Members of the sample whose period of appointment is unknown have been excluded.

Table B.7
Civilians in the Legion of Honour, 1852, distinguished according to social position
(weighted sample)

Social position	Frequency	Percentage
Landowner	0	0.0
Non-landed ownership and top managerial	0	0.0
Higher-level state employee	26	13.7
Politician	22	11.6
Middle bourgeoisie	15	7.9
Judicial professions	30	15.8
Professions	51	26.8
Middle-level state employee	19	10.0
Petite bourgeoisie or working class	24	12.6
Peasantry	3	1.6
Total	190	100.0

Table B.8
Civilians in the Legion of Honour, 1929, distinguished according to social position
(weighted sample)

Social position	Frequency	Percentage
Landowner	0	0.0
Non-landed ownership and top managerial	9	6.7
Higher-level state employee	27	20.0
Politician	9	6.7
Middle bourgeoisie	31	22.9
Judicial professions	14	10.4
Professions	23	17.0
Middle-level state employee	14	10.4
Petite bourgeoisie or working class	8	5.9
Peasantry	0	0.0
Total	135	100.0

Note: Members of the sample whose social position is unknown have been excluded.

Table B.9
Civilians in the Order of the British Empire 1921, distinguished according to social
position, males only (weighted sample)

Social position	Frequency	Percentage
Landowner	0	0.0
Non-landed ownership and top managerial	19	8.8
Higher-level state employee	10	4.6
Politician	8	3.7
Middle bourgeoisie	50	23.0
Judicial professions	18	8.3
Professions	55	25.3
Middle-level state employee	31	14.3
Lower bourgeoisie	19	8.8
Working class	1	0.5
Rural worker	0	0.0
Charitable worker	6	2.8
Total	217	100.0

Note: Members of the sample whose social position is unknown have been excluded.

Table B.10
Civilians in the Order of Leopold, 1833–87, distinguished according to social
position (weighted sample)

Social position	Frequency	Percentage
Landowner	0	0.0
Non-landed ownership and top managerial	41	10.2
Higher-level state employee	60	14.9
Politician	85	21.0
Middle bourgeoisie	43	10.7
Judicial professions	49	12.1
Professions	89	22.0
Middle-level state employee	26	6.4
Petite bourgeoisie or working class	11	2.7
Peasantry	0	0.0
Total	404	100.0

Note: Foreigners and members of the sample whose social position is unknown have
been excluded.

Table B.11
Civilians in the Order of Leopold, 1932, distinguished according to social position
(weighted sample)

Social position	Frequency	Percentage
Landowner	0	0.0
Non-landed ownership and top managerial	32	12.7
Higher-level state employee	68	26.9
Politician	20	7.9
Middle bourgeoisie	13	5.1
Judicial professions	17	6.7
Professions	69	27.3
Middle-level state employee	34	13.4
Petty bourgeoisie or working class	0	0.0
Peasantry	0	0.0
Total	253	100.0

Note: Foreigners and members of the sample whose social position is unknown have
been excluded.

Table B.12
Civilians in the Legion of Honour, 1852, distinguished according to social position
and grade in the Order (sampled by grade)

	Percentage of members by grade				
Social position	Grand Croix $n=41$	Grand Officier $n=75$	Commandeur $n=40$	Officier $n=38$	Chevalier $n=39$
Landowner	0.0	0.0	0.0	0.0	0.0
Non-landed ownership and top managerial	0.0	1.3	0.0	2.6	0.0
Higher-level state employee	12.2	13.	32.5	26.3	12.2
Politician	87.8	77.3	50.0	28.9	8.2
Middle bourgeoisie	0.0	1.3	0.0	5.3	8.2
Judicial professions	0.0	6.7	10.0	13.2	16.3
Professions	0.0	0.0	7.5	13.2	28.6
Middle-level state employee	0.0	0.0	0.0	10.5	10.2
Petite bourgeoisie or working class	0.0	0.0	0.0	0.0	14.3
Peasantry	0.0	0.0	0.0	0.0	2.0
Total	100.0	100.0	100.0	100.0	100.0

Table B.13
Civilians in the Legion of Honour, 1929, distinguished according to social position
and grade in the Order (sampled by grade)

	Percentage of members by grade				
Social position	Grand Croix n=24	Grand Officier n=31	Commandeur n=28	Officier n=34	Chevalier n=30
Landowner	0.0	0.0	0.0	0.0	0.0
Non-landed ownership and top managerial	4.1	6.4	3.6	8.8	6.6
Higher-level state employee	54.2	32.3	35.7	20.6	20.0
Politician	25.0	6.5	28.6	8.8	6.7
Middle bourgeoisie	0.0	0.0	0.0	20.6	23.3
Judicial professions	0.0	16.1	7.1	11.8	10.0
Professions	16.7	38.7	21.4	17.6	16.7
Middle-level state employee	0.0	0.0	0.0	11.8	10.0
Petite bourgeoisie or working class	0.0	0.0	3.6	0.0	6.7
Peasantry	0.0	0.0	0.0	0.0	0.0
Total	100.0	100.0	100.0	100.0	100.0

Note: Members of the sample whose social position is unknown have been excluded.

Table B.14
Civilians in the Order of the British Empire, 1921, distinguished according to
social position and grade in the Order, males only (sampled by grade)

	Percentage of members by grade				
Social position	Knight Grand Cross (GBE) n=44	Knight Commander (KBE) n=99	Commander (CBE) n=60	Officer (OBE) n=48	Member (MBE) n=45
Landowner	0.0	1.0	0.0	0.0	0.0
Non-landed ownership and top managerial	27.2	37.4	23.3	8.2	0.0
Higher-level state employee	15.9	14.1	15.0	2.1	2.2
Politician	25.0	6.1	5.0	6.3	0.0
Middle bourgeoisie	0.0	2.0	10.0	25.0	28.9
Judicial professions	18.2	9.1	16.7	4.1	8.9
Professions	11.4	28.3	18.3	31.3	22.2
Middle-level state employee	0.0	1.0	8.3	16.7	15.6
Lower bourgeoisie	0.0	1.0	1.7	4.2	17.8
Working class	0.0	0.0	1.7	0.0	0.0
Rural worker	0.0	0.0	0.0	0.0	0.0
Charitable worker	2.3	0.0	0.0	2.1	4.4
Total	100.0	100.0	100.0	100.0	100.0

Note: Members of the sample whose social position is unknown have been excluded.

Table B.15

Civilians in the Order of Leopold, 1833–87, distinguished according to social
position and grade in the Order (sampled by grade)

	Percentage of members by grade				
Social position	Grand Cordon $n=14$	Grand Officier $n=24$	Commandeur $n=31$	Officier $n=71$	Chevalier $n=140$
Landowner	0.0	0.0	0.0	0.0	0.0
Non-landed ownership and top managerial	0.0	4.1	3.2	12.7	9.9
Higher-level state employee	7.1	16.7	22.6	23.9	12.9
Politician	78.6	29.2	16.1	19.7	20.7
Middle bourgeoisie	0.0	4.2	0.0	2.8	12.9
Judicial professions	7.1	25.0	22.6	12.7	11.4
Professions	7.2	20.8	25.8	28.2	20.7
Middle-level state employee	0.0	0.0	9.7	0.0	7.9
Petite bourgeoisie or working class	0.0	0.0	0.0	0.0	3.6
Peasantry	0.0	0.0	0.0	0.0	0.0
Total	100.0	100.0	100.0	100.0	100.0

Note: Foreigners and members of the sample whose social position is unknown have
been excluded.

Table B.16

Civilians in the Order of Leopold, 1932, distinguished according to social position and grade in the Order (sampled by grade)

	Percentage of members by grade				
Social position	*Grand Cordon* n=6	*Grand Officier* n=54	*Commandeur* n=62	*Officier* n=61	*Chevalier* n=64
Landowner	0.0	0.0	0.0	0.0	0.0
Non-landed ownership and top managerial	16.6	1.8	4.8	3.3	14.6
Higher-level state employee	16.7	24.1	32.3	32.8	24.5
Politician	66.7	51.9	27.4	14.8	4.7
Middle bourgeoisie	0.0	0.0	0.0	1.6	6.2
Judicial professions	0.0	11.1	12.9	18.0	3.1
Professions	0.0	11.1	22.6	26.2	27.1
Middle-level state employee	0.0	0.0	0.0	3.3	16.2
Petite bourgeoisie or working class	0.0	0.0	0.0	0.0	3.6
Peasantry	0.0	0.0	0.0	0.0	0.0
Total	100.0	100.0	100.0	100.0	100.0

Note: Foreigners and members of the sample whose social position is unknown have been excluded.

Table B.17
Military and civilians in the Legion of Honour, 1852, distinguished according to
period of appointment (weighted sample)

	Percentage of members by period of appointment				
	Empire $n=127$	Restoration $n=132$	July Monarchy $n=357$	Republic, pre-coup $n=99$	Republic, post-coup $n=29$
Military	100.0	82.6	65.5	64.6	69.0
Civilians	0.0	17.4	34.5	35.4	31.0
Total	100.0	100.0	100.0	100.0	100.0

Table B.18
Military and civilians in the Legion of Honour, 1929, distinguished according to
period of appointment (weighted sample)

	Percentage of members by period of appointment		
	Before the Great War $n=76$	During the Great War $n=109$	After the Great War $n=406$
Military	75.0	92.7	73.6
Civilians	25.0	7.3	26.4
Total	100.0	100.0	100.0

Note: Members of the sample whose period of appointment is unknown have been
excluded.

Table B.19
Military and civilians in the Order of Leopold, 1833–87, distinguished according
to period of appointment (weighted sample)

	Percentage of members by period of appointment		
	1830 to 2 August 1847 $n=74$	13 August 1847 to 1 July 1870 $n=188$	2 July 1870 to 1886 $n=339$
Military	56.8	43.1	27.4
Civilians	43.2	56.9	72.6
Total	100.0	100.0	100.0

Note: Foreigners and members of the sample whose period of appointment is unknown
have been excluded.

Table B.20
Military and civilians in the Order of Leopold, 1932, distinguished according to
period of appointment (weighted sample)

	Percentage of members by period of appointment		
	Before the Great War n=13	*During the Great War* n=20	*After the Great War* n=393
Military	7.7	65.0	38.2
Civilians	92.3	35.0	61.8
Total	100.0	100.0	100.0

Note: Foreigners and members of the sample whose period of appointment is unknown
have been excluded.

Table B.21
Military and civilians in the Legion of Honour, 1852 (weighted sample)

	Frequency	*Percentage*
Military	553	74.3
Civilians	191	25.7
Total	744	100.0

Table B.22
Military and civilians in the Legion of Honour, 1929 (weighted sample)

	Frequency	*Percentage*
Military	457	77.2
Civilians	135	22.8
Total	592	100.0

Table B.23
Military and civilians in the Order of the British Empire, 1921, males only
(weighted sample)

	Frequency	Percentage
Military	315	36.8
Civilians	542	63.2
Total	857	100.0

Table B.24
Military and civilians in the Order of Leopold, 1833–87 (weighted sample)

	Frequency	Percentage
Military	223	35.5
Civilians	405	64.5
Total	628	100.0

Note: Foreigners have been excluded.

Table B.25
Military and civilians in the Order of Leopold, 1932 (weighted sample)

	Frequency	Percentage
Military	165	38.6
Civilians	262	61.4
Total	42	100.0

Note: Foreigners have been excluded.

Table B.26
Military in the Legion of Honour, 1852, distinguished according to military rank
and grade in the Order (sampled by grade)

	Percentage of members by grade				
	Grand Croix $n=16$	*Grand Officier* $n=85$	*Commandeur* $n=132$	*Officier* $n=127$	*Chevalier* $n=141$
MILITARY RANK					
Officier general	100.0	98.8	44.7	1.6	0.0
Officier supérieur	0.0	0.0	52.3	73.2	8.5
Officier subaltern	0.0	0.0	0.0	12.6	49.6
Sous-officier	0.0	0.0	0.0	5.5	29.1
Soldat/matelot	0.0	0.0	0.0	0.8	7.1
CIVILIAN SOCIAL POSITION	0.0	1.2	3.0	6.3	5.7
Total	100.0	100.0	100.0	100.0	100.0

Table B.27
Military in the Legion of Honour, 1929, distinguished according to military rank
and grade in the Order (sampled by grade)

	Percentage of members by grade				
	Grand Croix $n=57$	*Grand Officier* $n=95$	*Commandeur* $n=70$	*Officier* $n=117$	*Chevalier* $n=102$
MILITARY RANK					
Officier general	96.5	84.2	32.9	3.4	0.0
Officier supérieur	0.0	2.1	51.4	6	2.9
Officier subaltern	0.0	0.0	0.0	15.4	65.7
Sous-officier	0.0	0.0	0.0	0.0	5.9
Soldat/matelot	0.0	0.0	0.0	0.0	6.9
CIVILIAN SOCIAL POSITION	3.5	13.7	15.7	15.4	18.6
Total	100.0	100.0	100.0	100.0	100.0

Table B.28

Military in the Order of the British Empire, 1921, distinguished according to
military rank and grade in the Order, males only (sampled by grade)

	Percentage of members by grade				
	Knight Grand Cross (GBE) n=7	Knight Commander (KBE) n=41	Commander (CBE) n=96	Officer (OBE) n=94	Member (MBE) n=46
MILITARY RANK					
General officer	100.0	26.8	11.5	0.0	0.0
Field officer	0.0	53.6	79.2	71.2	6.5
Junior officer	0.0	9.8	3.1	24.5	91.3
NCO	0.0	0.0	0.0	0.0	2.2
Private	0.0	0.0	0.0	0.0	0.0
CIVILIAN SOCIAL POSITION	0.0	9.8	6.2	4.3	0.0
Total	100.0	100.0	100.0	100.0	100.0

Table B.29

Military in the Order of Leopold, 1833–87, distinguished according to military
rank and grade in the Order (sampled by grade)

	Percentage of members by grade				
	Grand Cordon n=1	Grand Officier n=21	Commandeur n=17	Officier n=35	Chevalier n=79
MILITARY RANK					
Officier general	100.0	95.2	88.2	22.9	1.3
Officier supérieur	0.0	0.0	11.8	57.1	13.9
Officier subaltern	0.0	0.0	0.0	2.9	40.5
Sous-officier	0.0	0.0	0.0	11.4	35.5
Soldat/matelot	0.0	0.0	0.0	0.0	2.5
CIVILIAN SOCIAL POSITION	0.0	4.8	0.0	5.7	6.3
Total	100.0	100.0	100.0	100.0	100.0

Note: Foreigners have been excluded.

Table B.30
Military in the Order of Leopold, 1932, distinguished according to military rank
and grade in the Order (sampled by grade)

	Percentage of members by grade				
	Grand Cordon $n=11$	Grand Officier $n=28$	Commandeur $n=39$	Officier $n=44$	Chevalier $n=41$
MILITARY RANK					
Officier general	100.0	96.4	82.1	6.8	0.0
Officier supérieur	0.0	0.0	5.1	43.2	2.4
Officier subaltern	0.0	0.0	0.0	2.3	83.0
Sous-officier	0.0	0.0	0.0	38.6	0.0
Soldat/matelot	0.0	0.0	0.0	0.0	0.0
CIVILIAN SOCIAL POSITION	0.0	3.6	12.8	9.1	14.6
Total	100.0	100.0	100.0	100.0	100.0

Note: Foreigners have been excluded.

Table B.31
Military in the Legion of Honour, 1852, distinguished according to military rank
(weighted sample)

	Frequency	Percentage
MILITARY RANK		
Officier general	8	1.5
Officier supérieur	87	15.7
Officier subaltern	248	44.9
Sous-officier	144	26.0
Soldat/matelot	35	6.3
CIVILIAN SOCIAL POSITION	31	5.6
Total	553	100.0

Table B.32
Military in the Legion of Honour, 1929, distinguished according to military rank
(weighted sample)

	Frequency	Percentage
MILITARY RANK		
Officier general	4	0.9
Officier supérieur	55	12.0
Officier subaltern	266	58.1
Sous-officier	23	5.0
Soldat/matelot	27	5.9
CIVILIAN SOCIAL POSITION	83	18.1
Total	458	100.0

Table B.33
Military in the Order of the British Empire, 1921, distinguished according to
military rank, males only (weighted sample)

	Frequency	Percentage
MILITARY RANK		
General officer	8	2.6
Field officer	172	54.6
Junior officer	122	38.7
NCO	2	0.6
Private	0	0.0
CIVILIAN SOCIAL POSITION	11	3.5
Total	315	100.0

Table B.34
Military in the Order of Leopold, 1833–87, distinguished according to military rank (weighted sample)

	Frequency	*Percentage*
MILITARY RANK		
Officier general	19	8.5
Officier supérieur	44	19.7
Officier subaltern	74	33.2
Sous-officier	68	30.5
Soldat/matelot	5	2.3
CIVILIAN SOCIAL POSITION	13	5.8
Total	223	100.0

Note: Foreigners have been excluded.

Table B.35
Military in the Order of Leopold, 1932, distinguished according to military rank (weighted sample)

	Frequency	*Percentage*
MILITARY RANK		
Officier general	9	5.5
Officier supérieur	19	11.5
Officier subaltern	101	61.2
Sous-officier	14	8.5
Soldat/matelot	0	0.0
CIVILIAN SOCIAL POSITION	22	13.3
Total	165	100.0

Note: Foreigners have been excluded.

Table B.36
Women in the Order of the British Empire, 1921, distinguished according to social
position and grade in the Order (sampled by grade)

| | Percentage of female members by grade | | | | |
Social position	Dame Grand Cross (GBE) n=10	Dame Commander (KBE) n=12	Commander (CBE) n=9	Officer (OBE) n=8	Member (MBE) n=29
Landowner	0.0	0.0	0.0	0.0	0.0
Non-landed ownership and top managerial	0.0	0.0	0.0	0.0	0.0
Higher-level state employee	0.0	0.0	0.0	12.5	0.0
Politician	0.0	8.3	0.0	0.0	0.0
Middle bourgeoisie	0.0	8.3	11.1	0.0	3.4
Judicial professions	0.0	0.0	0.0	0.0	0.0
Professions	40.0	25.1	11.1	0.0	24.2
Middle-level state employee	0.0	0.0	0.0	0.0	6.9
Lower bourgeoisie	0.0	0.0	0.0	0.0	10.3
Working class	0.0	0.0	0.0	0.0	0.0
Rural worker	0.0	0.0	0.0	0.0	0.0
Charitable worker	60.0	58.3	77.8	87.5	55.2
Total	100.0	100.0	100.0	100.0	100.0

Note: Members of the sample whose social position is unknown have been excluded.
The data for the dames grand cross are not based on a sample but on the full list of
members for which an occupation is provided in the source.

Table B.37
Gender in the Order of the British Empire, 1921, distinguished according to social
position, civilians only (weighted sample)

| | *Percentage of civilian members by gender* | |
| | Male | Female |
Social position	*n=217*	*n=75*
Landowner	0.0	0.0
Non-landed ownership and top managerial	8.9	0.0
Higher-level state employee	4.8	2.4
Politician	3.8	0.1
Middle bourgeoisie	22.9	3.4
Judicial professions	8.3	0.0
Professions	25.4	18.7
Middle-level state employee	14.1	5.0
Lower bourgeoisie	8.9	7.4
Working class	0.3	0.0
Rural worker	0.0	0.0
Charitable worker	2.6	63.0
Total	100.0	100.0

Note: Members of the sample whose social position is unknown have been excluded.

Table B.38
Gender in the Order of the British Empire, 1921, distinguished according to grade
in the Order, military and civilians (sampled by grade)

| | *Percentage of military and civilian members by grade* | | | | |
Gender	*Knight/Dame Grand Cross (GBE) n=94*	*Knight/Dame Commander (KBE) n=180*	*Commander (CBE) n=200*	*Officer (OBE) n=234*	*Member (MBE) n=262*
Male	68.1	88.3	94.0	90.6	71.0
Female	31.9	11.7	6.0	9.4	29.0
Total	100.0	100.0	100.0	100.0	100.0

Table B.39
Ranks of recipients of the Victoria Cross, 1856–1920, by military engagement

	Percentage of recipients by military engagement						
	Crimea $n=109$	Indian Mutiny $n=160$	Misc. 1856– 1881 $n=133$	Misc. 1882– 1920 $n=13$	Boer War $n=78$	The Great War $n=632$	Total $n=1125$
MILITARY RANK							
General officer	0. 0	0.0	0.0	0.0	0.0	0.3	0.2
Field officer	10.1	3.1	9.0	0.0	5.2	10.3	8.6
Junior officer	33.0	35.6	48.9	92.3	43.6	34.5	37.5
NCO	23.9	23.8	12.8	7.7	25.6	31.7	26.9
Private	33.0	32.5	25.6	0.0	25.6	22.9	25.5
CIVILIAN SOCIAL POSITION	0.0	5.0	3.7	0.0	0.0	0.3	1.3
Total	100.0	100.0	100.0	100.0	100.0	100.0	100.0

Source: *Register of the Victoria Cross* and Wilkins, *History of the Victoria Cross*.

Table B.40
Members of the Companions of Honour, distinguished according to social position and father's social position (recipients June 1917–August 1939)

Social position	Percentage of members $n=77$	Percentage of members' fathers $n=48$
Landowner	0.0	0.0
Business proprietor	6.5	25.0
Charity, volunteer work	11.7	0.0
State employee	11.7	0.0
Manager	3.9	6.2
Professions and the arts	35.0	12.5
Clergy	19.5	22.9
Union official	11.7	0.0
Agent, clerk	0.0	4.2
Farmer	0.0	4.2
Working class	0.0	25.0
Total	100.0	100.0

Note: For twenty-nine members, father's social position was not provided.
Source: Galloway, *Companions of Honour*.

Cross-Tabulations of Characteristics of Honours and Social-political Characteristics of States and Societies Sampled in the Comparative Analysis

Numbers from 1 to 5 in the furthest left column or the top horizontal row in the tables refer to the categorized ordinal ranks of states and societies on the variables coded subjectively, with 1 representing the lowest category and 5 the highest category. Within each cell, states and societies are grouped in three global regions. See Table 14.1 for a more precise designation of each of the states and societies, including their chronological period. An explanation of how variables were coded is also provided in Chapter 14.

Table C.1
Cross-tabulation of total population and number of honorific rewards

Number of honorific rewards	Total population					
	Under 100,000	100,000–1 million	1 million–10 million	10 million–50 million	More than 50 million	Total
1	Aborigines O Iñupiaq O Iroquois O		Russia O			4
2		Zulus O				1
3			Ashikaga A Choson A	Gupta A Mongols A Sasanians M Inca O	Ottomans M	7
4		Athenians M	Egypt M	Byzantium M Aztecs O		4
5					Han A Mughals A Qing A Romans M	4
Total	3	2	4	6	5	20

Gamma = .76

Note: A = Asia, M = Mediterranean and Middle East, O = Other

Table C.2

Cross-tabulation of largest population concentration and number of honorific rewards

Number of honorific rewards	*Largest population concentration*					
	Less than 2,000	*2,000– 10,000*	*10,000– 100,000*	*100,000– 1 million*	*More than 1 million*	*Total*
1	Aborigines ^O Iñupiaq ^O Iroquois ^O		Russia ^O			4
2		Zulus ^O				1
3			Mongols ^A Inca ^O	Ashikaga ^A Choson ^A Gupta ^A Ottomans ^M Sasanians ^M		7
4				Athenians ^M Byzantium ^M Egypt ^M Aztecs ^O		4
5				Han ^A Mughals ^A	Qing ^A Romans ^M	4
Total	3	1	3	11	2	20

Gamma = .98

Note: ^{A} = Asia, ^{M} = Mediterranean and Middle East, ^{O} = Other

Table C.3
Cross-tabulation of largest population concentration and social range of honorific rewards

Social range of honorific rewards	Largest population concentration					
	Less than 2,000	2,000– 10,000	10,000– 100,000	100,000– 1 million	More than 1 million	Total
1	Aborigines O Iñupiaq O		Russia O			3
2	Iroquois O		Mongols A Inca O	Choson A Gupta A Ottomans M Sasanians M		7
3		Zulus O		Ashikaga A Han A Mughals A Byzantium M Egypt M Aztecs O	Qing A	8
4				Athenians M	Romans M	2
Total	3	1	3	11	2	20

Gamma = .82

Note: A = Asia, M = Mediterranean and Middle East, O = Other

Table C.4
Cross-tabulation of size of army and number of honorific rewards

Number of honorific rewards	Less than 5,000	5,000– 20,000	20,000– 100,000	More than 100,000	Total
		Size of army			
1	Aborigines [O] Iñupiaq [O] Iroquois [O]	Russia [O]			4
2		Zulus [O]			1
3			Ashikaga [A] Choson [A] Mongols [A] Sasanians [M] Inca [O]	Gupta [A] Ottomans [M]	7
4			Athenians [M] Byzantium [M] Egypt [M] Aztecs [O]		4
5				Han [A] Mughals [A] Qing [A] Romans [M]	4
Total	3	2	9	6	20

Gamma = .80

Note: [A] = Asia, [M] = Mediterranean and Middle East, [O] = Other

Appendix C

Table C.5
Cross-tabulation of importance of infantry and number of honorific rewards

Number of honorific rewards	Importance of infantry				
	1	*2*	*3*	*4*	*Total*
1		Russia ᴼ		Aborigines ᴼ Iñupiaq ᴼ Iroquois ᴼ	4
2				Zulus ᴼ	1
3	Mongols ᴬ	Gupta ᴬ Sasanians ᴹ	Ashikaga ᴬ Choson ᴬ Ottomans ᴹ	Inca ᴼ	7
4		Byzantium ᴹ Egypt ᴹ		Athenians ᴹ Aztecs ᴼ	4
5	Qing ᴬ	Mughals ᴬ	Han ᴬ Romans ᴹ		4
Total	2	6	5	7	20

Gamma = -.36

Note: ᴬ = Asia, ᴹ = Mediterranean and Middle East, ᴼ = Other

Table C.6
Cross-tabulation of coordinated army and number of honorific rewards

Number of honorific rewards	Coordinated army				
	1	*2*	*3*	*4*	*Total*
1	Aborigines ^O Iñupiaq ^O	Iroquois ^O Russia ^O			4
2		Zulus ^O			1
3	Gupta ^A	Ashikaga ^A Choson ^A	Ottomans ^M Sasanians ^M Inca ^O	Mongols ^A	7
4		Egypt ^M Aztecs ^O	Athenians ^M Byzantium ^M		4
5			Han ^A Mughals ^A Qing ^A	Romans ^M	4
Total	3	7	8	2	20

Gamma = .71
Note: ^A = Asia, ^M = Mediterranean and Middle East, ^O = Other

Table C.7
Cross-tabulation of coordinated infantry and number of honorific rewards

Number of honorific rewards	Coordinated infantry				
	1	*2*	*3*	*4*	*Total*
1	Aborigines [O] Iñupiaq [O]	Russia [O] Iroquois [O]			4
2		Zulus [O]			1
3	Gupta [A] Mongols [A]	Ashikaga [A] Choson [A] Sasanians [M]	Ottomans [M] Inca [O]		7
4		Byzantium [M] Egypt [M]	Athenians [M] Aztecs [O]		4
5		Mughals [A] Qing [A]	Han [A]	Rome [M]	4
Total	4	10	5	1	20

Gamma = .64

Note: [A] = Asia, [M] = Mediterranean and Middle East, [O] = Other

Table C.8
Cross-tabulation of coordinated infantry and metallic body ornaments as honorific rewards

Metallic body ornaments	Coordinated infantry				
	1	*2*	*3*	*4*	*Total*
1	Mongols [A] Aborigines [O] Iñupiaq [O]	Ashikaga [A] Choson [A] Iroquois [O] Russia [O]			7
2		Mughals [A] Qing [A] Byzantium [M] Sasanians [M]	Han [A] Ottomans [M]		6
3	Gupta [A]	Egypt [M] Zulus [O]	Athenians [M] Aztecs [O] Inca [O]	Romans [M]	7
Total	4	10	5	1	20

Gamma = .70

Note: [A] = Asia, [M] = Mediterranean and Middle East, [O] = Other

Table C.9
Cross-tabulation of coordinated infantry and social range of honorific rewards

Number of honorific rewards	Coordinated infantry				
	1	*2*	*3*	*4*	*Total*
1	Aborigines [O] Iñupiaq [O]	Russia [O]			3
2	Gupta [A] Mongols [A]	Choson [A] Sasanians [M] Iroquois [O]	Ottomans [M] Inca [O]		7
3		Ashikaga [A] Mughals [A] Qing [A] Byzantium [M] Egypt [M] Zulus [O]	Han [A] Aztecs [O]		8
4			Athenians [M]	Romans [M]	2
Total	4	10	5	1	20

Gamma = .71

Note: [A] = Asia, [M] = Mediterranean and Middle East, [O] = Other

Table C.10

Cross-tabulation of militarism and number of honorific rewards

Number of honorific rewards	Militarism				
	1	*2*	*3*	*4*	*Total*
1		Iroquois [O]	Aborigines [O] Iñupiaq [O] Russia [O]		4
2				Zulus [O]	1
3	Choson [A]	Gupta [A] Ottomans [M] Sasanians [M]	Ashikaga [A] Inca [O]	Mongols [A]	7
4	Byzantium [M]	Athenians [M] Egypt [M]		Aztecs [O]	4
5		Han [A] Romans [M]	Qing [A] Mughals [O]		4
Total	2	8	7	3	20

Gamma = -.22

Note: [A] = Asia, [M] = Mediterranean and Middle East, [O] = Other

Notes

INTRODUCTION

1 See, just as examples, Berger, Rosenholtz, and Zelditch, "Status organizing processes"; Ridgeway and Walker, "Status structures"; Ridgeway, Boyle, Kuipers, and Robinson, "How do status beliefs develop?"

2 Mayer, *Persistence of the Old Regime*.

3 The idea can be traced to George Homans's proposition that esteem is accorded in exchange for the performance of services to the human group. See his *Social Behavior*, Chapter 8. It was developed further by William Goode in his *Celebration of Heroes*. See also Taylor, "Celebration of heroes under communism."

4 This argument is most clearly stated by Ihl in *Mérite et la République*, "Emulation," and "Gouverner par les honneurs." Others have included this idea along with other explanations. See Caille, *Figure du sauveteur*, and his "Une citoyenneté superieuré"; Dumons, "*Saints de la République*"; Dumons and Pollet, eds., *Fabrique de l'honneur*; Hazareesingh, *Saint-Napoleon*, and his "Médailles de Sainte-Hélène." These French scholars have done some of the best work on the evolution of state honorific rewards.

5 Caille, "Société de la distinction."

6 Elias, *Civilizing Process and Court Society*; Foucault, *Discipline and Punish*; Gorski, "Protestant ethic re-visited," "Protestant ethic and the spirit of bureaucracy," and *Disciplinary Revolution*.

7 Frank and Cook, Winner-Take-All Society; Crane, *Fashion and Its Social Agendas*; De Botton, *Status Anxiety*. The classic work is Veblen, *Theory of the Leisure Class*.

8 This summary is based primarily on Bourdieu, *Cultural Production*, especially 37; Bourdieu, *State Nobility*, especially 264–5; Swartz, *Culture and Power*, especially 77; English, *Economy of Prestige*; Do, "Aux prises avec les prix," especially 23–4.

9 As a sample of this large literature, see Blute, "Socio-cultural evolutionism"; Langton, "Darwinism and the behavioral theory of sociocultural evolution"; Boyd and Richerson, *Culture and the Evolutionary Process*; Durham, *Coevolution*; Burns and Dietz, "Cultural Evolution"; Runciman, "Heritable variation and competitive selection," "Selectionist paradigm," *Social Animal*, *Theory of Cultural and Social Selection*; Sanderson, *Evolution of Human Sociality*; Turner, *Human Institutions*; Blute, *Darwinian Sociocultural Evolution*; Hopcroft, *Sociology*. On the utility of Darwinian theory for the study of history, see especially Blute, "History versus science: The evolutionary solution."

10 Weber, *Economy and Society*, vol. 1, 305.

CHAPTER ONE

1 Clark, "Nobility, bourgeoisie and the industrial revolution in Belgium," 154–7.

2 McCahill, "Peerage creations," particularly 269–70.

3 Guttsman, *British Political Elite*, 41.

4 Ibid., 37.

5 Cannadine, *Decline and Fall of the British Aristocracy*, 188–9.

6 Coninckx, "Sociaal-politieke samenstelling van de Belgische Kamer"; Clark, "Nobility, bourgeoisie and the industrial revolution in Belgium," 158–68.

7 Bartier, "Partis politiques et classes sociales en Belgique," 49, 93; and sources he cites.

8 Coninckx, "Sociaal-politieke samenstelling van de Belgische Kamer," 355.

9 For the effect of the Belgian Revolution of 1830 on lawyers, see François, "Intellectuelen en revolutionaire bedrijvigheid."

10 Coninckx, "Sociaal-politieke samenstelling van de Belgische Kamer," 359.

11 Hobsbawm, *Age of Capital*, 275; Perkin, *Origins of Modern English Society*.

12 Habermas, *Structural Transformation of the Public Sphere*, 13.

13 O'Boyle, "Middle class," 835.

14 Kocka, "European pattern and the German case," 5–6, 9; and his "Middle classes," 785–7. See also his *Industrial Culture and Bourgeois Society.*

15 Perkin, *Origins of Modern English Society,* 221–2.

16 Corfield, *Power and the Professions,* and her "Rivals."

17 Mann, *Rise of Classes and Nation-States,* 241.

18 Blake, *Conservative Party,* 17. See also Thompson, *English Landed Society.*

19 Charle, *Social History of France,* 28.

20 Kocka, "Middle classes," 785–7, 789–90. Again see also his *Industrial Culture and Bourgeois Society.*

21 For the Northern Low Countries, see Bruin, *Kroon op Het Werk,* 89–91; and Van Zelm van Eldik, *Moed en deugd,* 423–4.

22 The most stimulating work on this subject is Caille, *Figure du sauveteur.*

23 Galloway, *Order of the British Empire,* 43.

24 A recent work making this point is Matikkala, *Orders of Knighthood,* 109–29.

25 Neville, *Orders of Imperial Germany and Austria,* 76.

26 Ducourtial and Bonneville de Marsangy, *Légion d'Honneur,* 153, 199.

27 Caille, "Une citoyenneté supérieure."

28 Ducourtial and Bonneville de Marsangy, *Légion d'Honneur,* 203–6.

29 *L'Ordre de Léopold: Liste de tous les dignitaries depuis la fondation de l'Ordre jusqu'au 31 décembre; Mémorial du centenaire de l'Ordre de Léopold, 1832–1932.*

30 Galloway, *Order of the Bath,* 152, 193, 289.

31 These data come from Hanham, "Sale of honours," 278–9n4.

32 Beckett, *Aristocracy in England,* 486–7.

33 Borné, *Distinctions honorifiques de la Belgique,* 113–14, 130, 185, 257–9.

34 Van Zelm van Eldik, *Moed en deugd,* 462.

35 Ducourtial and Bonneville de Marsangy, *Légion d'Honneur,* 177.

36 Tartié, "Décorations dans la France révolutionnaire," 26.

37 Ihl, *Mérite et la République,* 14.

38 Petiteau, "De la Légion d'honneur à la noblesse d'Empire," 114–15.

39 *Archives parlementaires de 1787 à 1860,* 685.

40 Nicolas, *Orders of Knighthood,* vol. 1, xi.

41 Blum, *End of the Old Order,* 421.

42 Lee, "Nicolas"; Risk, *History of the Order of the Bath,* 45; Galloway, *Order of the Bath,* 149.

43 Bruin, *Kroon op het werk*, 210; Cannadine, *Decline and Fall of the British Aristocracy*, 299–307.

44 Pumphrey, "Creation of peerages," 24.

45 Cardoza, *Aristocrats in Bourgeois Italy*, 19.

46 This extract from Carrion de Nisas's speech, including the alleged quotation from Vildepatour, can be found in an insert in *Annuaire de la Légion d'Honneur, 1852*.

CHAPTER TWO

1 Kristol and Beloff, "Of lords, sirs, and plain misters," 69.

2 Frey, "Knight fever," 13.

3 This is a rather complex subject, which is nicely elucidated in McCreery, *Order of Canada*, 24–48.

4 Ibid., 34.

5 Mayer, *Persistence of the Old Regime*, 83.

6 Anderson, "Origins of the present crisis," 39.

7 Thompson, "Honours uneven," 199, 201.

8 Cecil, "Creation of nobles in Prussia," 791–5.

9 Kaudelka-Hanisch, "Titled businessman."

10 Neville, *Orders of Imperial Germany and Austria*, 14.

11 On the French nobility see, for example, Higgs, "Politics and land-ownership among the French nobility"; Daumard, "Evolution des structures sociales"; Tudesq, "Survivances de l'Ancien Régime"; Bécarud, "Noblesse et représentation parlementaire"; Vidalenc, "Société française sous la Monarchie constitutionelle"; Guillemin, "Patrimonie foncier et pouvoir nobiliaire"; Bergeron, *Capitalistes en France*, 17–23, 30–3; Bergeron, *France under Napoleon*, 125–30; Denis, "Stratégies de la noblesse"; Estèbe, *Ministres de la République*, 28–9. See also Charle, *Social History of France*, 74 and sources he cites. On the Belgian nobility, see Coninckx, "Sociaal-politieke samenstel-ling van de Belgische Kamer"; Janssens, "Politieke invloed van de adel," and his "Het lot van de Belgische adel in de revolutiejaren"; and Clark,"Nobility, bourgeoisie and the industrial revolution in Belgium."

12 Maza, *Myth of the French Bourgeoisie*, 22, 25.

13 Ibid., 58.

14 Ibid., 182–92.

15 Van Zelm van Eldik, *Moed en deugd*, 200.

16 Petiteau, *Noblesse d'Empire*, 34–5.

17　Ducourtial and Bonneville de Marsangy, *Légion d'Honneur*, 55;
　　Aulard, *Études et leçons*, 295–6; Ducourtial, *Ordres et décorations*, 60.
18　Sutherland, *France 1789–1815*, 367.
19　Van Zelm van Eldik, *Moed en deugd*, 200.
20　Ibid., 177–84, 200.
21　Cannadine, "Context, performance and meaning of ritual."
22　Caille, *Figure du sauveteur*, 77–91; Caradonna, "Monarchy of virtue"
　　and his *Enlightment in Practice.*
23　Galloway, *Order of the British Empire*, 2.
24　Galloway, *Most Illustrious Order of St Patrick*, 54–80.
25　Ducourtial and Bonneville de Marsangy, *Légion d'Honneur*, 173.
26　Vidal, "Symbolique et héraldique."
27　This view is held by de Ghellinck Vaernewyck, "Titres de l'empire
　　français," 73; and Hamoir, *Qualité princière et dignités nobiliaires*, 7.
28　Bergeron, *France under Napoleon*, 69–70.
29　Petiteau, *Noblesse d'Empire*, 26–7.
30　This interpretation of the recasting of the British monarchy has been
　　promoted especially by Kuhn, *Democratic Royalism*, but it is consistent
　　with Hayden, *Symbol and Privilege* and Cannadine, "Context, perform-
　　ance and meaning of ritual."
31　Adams, *Familial State*, especially 71–2, 83, 97, 160–3.
32　Laureyssens, "Société Générale"; Witte, *Politieke machtsstrijd*, 75–6;
　　Laureyssens, "Willem I, de Société Générale."

CHAPTER THREE

1　Dewald makes this point in *Aristocratic Experience*, 70.
2　Lieven, *Aristocracy in Europe*, 190–1, 199.
3　Kerautret, "*Ordres et décorations* de la Prusse," 17.
4　Mericka, *Orden und Ehrenzeichen*, 50.
5　Text of the bill can be found in Ducourtial and Bonneville de Mar-
　　sangy, *Légion d'Honneur*, 52.
6　Blaufarb, "*Ancien régime* origins of the Napoleonic social
　　reconstruction."
7　Mosse, "Bureaucracy and nobility in Russia," 609.
8　Pumphrey, "Creation of peerages," 1, and Walpole, *Life of Lord John
　　Russell*, i, 457.
9　Searle, *Corruption in British Politics*, 114.
10　On this culture of achievement in the Medieval and Early Modern
　　periods, see Jouanna, "Honneur perdu," 57, and her "Perception et

appreciation de l'anoblissement"; Keen, *Chivalry*, 2, 9, 151; Dewald, *Aristocratic Experience*; Caron, *Noblesse et pouvoir royal en France*, 36; Clark, *State and Status*, 337–8; Smith, *Culture of Merit*, Chapters 1 and 2.

11 Keen, *Chivalry*, 2, 156–9.

12 Jouanna, "Honneur perdu," 58–9.

13 Schalk, *Valor to Pedigree*, especially xiv–xv and Chapter 1.

14 Caron, Noblesse et pouvoir royal en France, 14–15.

15 Keen, *Chivalry*, 9, 151.

16 Jouanna, "Honneur perdu," 58–9.

17 Smith, *Culture of Merit*, Chapters 1 and 2.

18 This view was developed by Georges Duby in a number of articles collected in his *Chivalrous Society*.

19 Spiegel, "Genealogy," 51.

20 Keen, *Chivalry*, 152.

21 Ibid., 156–7.

22 See the example provided by Dewald in *Aristocratic Experience*, 50–1.

23 Manning, *War and Peace*, Chapter 4.

24 Dewald, "Social groups and cultural practices," 56.

25 Manning, *War and Peace*, Chapter 5, and his "Justifications and explanations of war."

26 Manning, "Justifications and explanations of war."

27 Oestreich, *Neostoicism*, 52.

28 Manning, *Apprenticeship in Arms*, 25.

29 See, for example, Béchu, "Noblesse d'épée et tradition militaire."

30 Smith, *Culture of Merit*, 83–4, 88–9.

31 Fox, *History in Geographic Perspective*, and his "The argument: some refinements and projections"; see also Clark, *State and Status*, 105–12.

32 Clark, *State and Status*, 285; Manning, *Swordsmen*, 17–19.

33 Manning, *Swordsmen, and his Apprenticeship in Arms*.

34 Rogers, *Press Gang*, 104.

35 There is more literature than I can cite on this subject, but see Petiteau, *Lendemains d'empire*, and Hazareesingh, *Saint-Napoleon*.

36 Jouanna, "Honneur perdu"; Smith, *Culture of Merit*, especially Chapters 2–3.

37 Cubells, "Politique d'anoblissement."

38 O'Brien, "Traditional virtues."

39 Smith, *Culture of Merit*, especially Chapters 5 and 6.

40 Hudemann-Simon, *Noblesse luxembourgeoise*, 48–9.

41 Schalk, *Valor to Pedigree*, especially xiv–xv and Chapter 1; Smith, *Culture of Merit*, especially 57–61.

42 Smith, *Culture of Merit*, 73.

43 Wagner, *Heralds of England*, 205–7; Wagner, *English Genealogy*, 358; Williams, *Recovery, Reorientation and Reformation*, 98.

44 Durye, *Généalogie*, 12–14; Smith, *Culture of Merit*, 78–91.

45 Adams, *Familial State*, especially Chapter 3.

46 This subject is discussed at length in Wagner, *English Genealogy*.

47 For Britain, see Corfield, *Power and the Professions*, and her "Rivals."

48 Lieven, *Aristocracy in Europe*, 2–3.

49 Bien, "Réaction aristocratique."

50 Smith, *Nobility Reimagined*.

51 Hofstede, *Culture's Consequences*, especially 2–4.

52 Bourdieu, *State Nobility*, 1–2.

53 This approach to culture has been explicitly developed by Ann Swidler, who coined the metaphor of "tool kit"; see her "Culture in action," "Cultural power," and *Talk of Love*. Other writers have developed the notion of cultural repertoires of collective action from which people are able to choose. See Tilly, *Popular Contention*.

54 Augustine, *Patricians and Parvenus*, 243.

55 Frevert, "Honour and middle-class culture."

56 Schopp, *Alexandre Dumas*, 280.

57 Wahrman, *Imagining the Middle Class*.

58 Smith, *Nobility Reimagined*, 8, 30–1.

59 Louis XIV, *Mémoires for the Instruction of the Dauphin*, 80.

60 Wodey, "L'honneur: signe et insigne," 291.

61 Boulton, "Crusading orders," 132–3.

62 Ibid., 132–3.

63 Among the many works on this subject, see Galvin, *History of the Order of Malta ss*; Beltjens, *Aux origines de l'ordre de Malte*; Riley-Smith, *Hospitallers*; Boulton, "Crusading orders," 4–5

64 Beltjens, *Aux origines de l'ordre de Malte*, 197–8.

65 Von Hammer-Purgstall, *History of the Assassins*, 56–7.

66 Boulton, *Knights of the Crown*, xvii–xxi.

67 Ibid., 451–2.

68 On this cultural and institutional collection, see Boulton, "Influence of religious orders" and "Curial orders."

69 Galloway, *Order of the Thistle*, Chapter 1.

70 Again see Galloway, *Order of the Bath*, Chapter 1.

71 Matikkala, *Orders of Knighthood*, 1 and *passim*.

72 The best read on this subject is Girouard, *Return to Camelot*.

73 On this point, see Garside, "Scott, the romantic past and the nineteenth century," 153.

74 The above is based mostly on Duff, *Romance and Revolution*.
75 Boulton, "Notion of 'chivalry.'"
76 Stafford, *Reading Romantic Poetry*, 196.
77 Lang, "Editor's introduction to *Ivanhoe*," xiii.
78 Allen, *Popular French Romanticism*, 100.
79 Davidson, *Alexandre Dumas*, 385–413.
80 Matikkala, *Orders of Knighthood*, 11–12; Sharp, "Edward Waterhouse,"
     39, 43; Hunter, *Elias Ashmole*, 11–12.
81 Ducourtial and Bonneville de Marsangy, *Légion d'Honneur*, 130–2,
     157, 174.
82 Van Zelm van Eldik, *Moed en deugd*, 192.
83 Galloway, *Order of St Patrick, 1783–1983*, 24.
84 Crook, *Evolution of the Victoria Cross*, 51.
85 The preceding is based on Risk, *History of the Order of the Bath*, 89–92;
     Galloway, *Order of the Bath*, 319–25.
86 Matikkala, *Orders of Knighthood*, 251n379; Van Zelm van Eldik, *Moed
     en deugd*, 192, 198.
87 Boulton, "Influence of religious orders," 23–9.
88 Galloway, *Order of the British Empire*, 84.
89 This exchange is narrated in Galloway, *Order of the British Empire*,
     84–5.
90 Corfield, *Power and the Professions*, especially 188, 194, 210, 213, 237.
91 Aulard, *Etudes et leçons*, 267.
92 Petiteau, "De la Légion d'honneur à la noblesse d'Empire," 111–13.
93 Armstrong, *European Administrative Elite*, 78–9.
94 Gray, *Prussia in Transition*, 89, 130.
95 Charle, *Haute fonctionnaires*, 29–31, 216.

CHAPTER FOUR

1 Turner, *Human Institutions*, 24. The distinction is made in a number
    of his works. For a short statement of it, see his review of Runciman,
    Theory of Cultural and Social Selection.
2 Turner, *Human Institutions*, especially 39, 53, 79, 89–90, 142–3,
    184–5, 223, 258.
3 Ibid., 28–9, 54, 77, 79.
4 On this particular point, see Vasi and Macy, "Mobilizer's dilemma," 4;
    Kollock, "Social dilemmas," 200–1.
5 As further examples, see Macy, "Learning to cooperate"; Macy and
    Flache, "Beyond rationality in models of choice"; Ostrom, *Governing*

the Commons, and her "Collective action and the evolution of social norms."

6 Olson, *Logic of Collective Action*, 45, 62–5.
7 Ibid., 51.
8 Clark, Clark, and Polborn, "Co-ordination and status influence"; Ermakoff, *Ruling Oneself Out*; Simpson et al. "Status hierarchies and the organization of collective action."
9 Innis, "Bias of communication." See also his *Empire and Communications.*
10 Dudley, "Space, time, number: Harold A. Innis."
11 Wechsler, *Offerings of Jade and Silk*, especially Chapter 1.
12 On this subject, see Waley-Cohen, *Culture of War in China*, especially Chapter 4.
13 Taylor, "Celebration of heroes under communism"; Clark and Clark, "Patrons, publishers, and prizes."

CHAPTER FIVE

1 Bisson, "Medieval lordship," 751.
2 Lewis, *Early Chinese Empires*, 62. See also his "Gift circulation."
3 Davis, *Gift in Sixteenth-Century France*, 51.
4 Ibid., Chapter 3.
5 Chattaway, *Order of the Golden Tree*, 63.
6 Davies, *Domination and Conquest*, 54–6.
7 Boulton, *Knights of the Crown*, 22–4.
8 Keen, *Chivalry*, 184.
9 Boulton, *Knights of the Crown*, 470–1.
10 Ibid., 491–2.
11 The essential work on this order is Chattaway, *Order of the Golden Tree.*
12 Keen, *Chivalry*, 185, Boulton, *Knights of the Crown*, 478.

CHAPTER SIX

1 Chase-Dunn and Hall, *Rise and Demise*, 214–21.
2 Deutsch, "Social mobilization and political development."
3 Mann, *Rise of Classes and Nation-States*, 390–2, 806–7.
4 See, for example, Bearman, *Relations into Rhetorics*, 43.
5 Roy, "Military synthesis in South Asia," 667.
6 Fagan and Trundle, "Introduction," 12.
7 Dudley, *Word and the Sword*, 94–7.
8 Ibid., 116–18.

9 DeVries, *Infantry Warfare in the Early Fourteenth Century*.

10 On the manpower problems faced by states, see Manning, *Apprenticeship in Arms*.

11 Santosuosso, *Soldiers, Citizens and the Symbols of War*, 40–1, and sources he cites.

12 Eckstein, *Mediterranean Anarchy*, 82.

13 Neiberg, *Warfare in World History*, 13.

14 Roy, *Military Transition in Early Modern Asia*, 44.

15 Nimwegen, *Dutch Army*, 293.

16 Ruwet, *Soldats des régiments nationaux*, 20–4.

17 *Geschiedenis van het Belgisch leger*, 87, 147, 176, 182, 342.

18 Childs, *The Army, James II, and the Glorious Revolution*, 1–2.

19 Ibid., 3–4.

20 Manning, *Apprenticeship in Arms*, 400.

21 Clark, *State and Status*, 48.

22 These are mostly Lynn's numbers. See his "Growth of the French army" and "Pattern of army growth."

23 For rural Ireland, see Carroll, *Science, Culture, and Modern State Formation*, especially Chapter 2.

24 McClellan, *Science Reorganized*, 6–7.

25 Ibid., 13–14.

26 Brewer, *Sinews of Power*, especially Chapters 2–4.

27 Clark, "Human intentionality in the functionalist theory of social change," 237.

28 Mukerji, *Territorial Ambitions and the Gardens of Versailles*.

29 Gorski, "Protestant ethic re-visited," "Protestant ethic and the spirit of bureaucracy," and *Disciplinary Revolution*.

30 Forrester, "Rational administration," 290–1.

31 Wakefield, *Disordered Police State*.

32 This is a major thesis of Mann in his *History of Power from the Beginning* and his *Rise of Classes and Nation-States*.

33 Oestreich provides an outline of "police" in his *Neostoicism*, especially Chapter 9.

34 Clark, "Human intentionality in the functionalist theory of social change," 238–9.

35 For Ireland, again see Carroll, *Science, Culture, and Modern State Formation*.

36 Higgs, *Information State in England*, 31.

37 Ibid., 40–1.

38 Rohrbasser, "Counting the population."

39 Van Waelvelde, "Evolution of population census in Belgium"; Oomens and den Bakker, "Dutch historical statistics."

40 Lachs, "Advise and consent: Parliament and foreign policy under the later Stuarts."

41 This has been a theme in much of Tilly's writings. See, for example, *Contentious French*; *Coercion, Capital, and European States*, 103–7; *Popular Contention*; and "Why worry about citizenship?"

42 This is a large literature, but see, for example, Colley, *Britons*, especially Chapters 7–8; Tilly, *Popular Contention*; Steinberg, "'The great end of all government …'"; Howell, *Rural Poor*; Rogers, *Press Gang*, especially 106–9; Morrison, "Channeling the 'Restless spirit of innovation.'"

43 Anderson, *War and Society*, 124.

44 Rogers, *Press Gang*, 10.

45 Ibid.; Barnett, *Britain and Her Army*, 140–2.

46 Forrest, "*Patrie en danger*," 11–12, and sources he cites.

47 Ibid., 11–12, and sources he cites.

48 Dumas, *Memoirs of His Own Time*, 297.

49 Forrest, "*Patrie en danger*," 13, and *Napoleon's Men*, 53.

50 See Forrest, *Napoleon's Men*, Chapter 3.

51 Forrest, *Conscripts and Deserters*; *Napoleon's Men*, 9, 19, and 93; and "Patrie en danger," 29–30.

52 Forrest, *Napoleon's Men*, 14, and "*Patrie en danger*," 29–30.

53 Strieter, "French officers commissioned from the ranks."

54 Manning, *Apprenticeship in Arms*, 430, 432.

55 Mann, *Rise of Classes and Nation-States*, 393.

56 Lin, "Caring for the nation's families."

57 Cookson, "Regimental worlds."

58 Rogers, *Press Gang*, 106–9.

59 Ibid., 110–11.

60 Burroughs, "Crime and punishment in the British army"; Skelley, *Victorian Army at Home*.

CHAPTER SEVEN

1 Matikkala, *Orders of Knighthood*, 211–28.

2 Veldekens, *Livre d'or de l'Ordre de Léopold*, 137–8, 140–1.

3 Ibid., 141.

4 Durieux, *Action disciplinaire de la Légion d'Honneur*, 46–7.

5 Hazareesingh, "Médailles de Sainte-Hélène." See also his *Saint-Napoleon*.

6 Caille, "Une citoyenneté supérieure," 9.

7 Galloway, *Order of St Michael and St George*, 16.

8 Ibid., 12–13.

9 Ibid., 22–5.

10 Bruin, *Kroon op Het Werk*, 20.

11 Ibid., 19–20.

12 Ibid., particularly 209. See also his "Distinction and democratization."

13 Caille, "Une citoyenneté supérieure," 9.

14 Aulard, *Etudes et leçons*, 268.

15 Ibid., 268–9.

16 Ibid., 269.

17 Caille, "Une citoyenneté supérieure," 10.

18 Ducourtial, *Ordres et décorations*, 53–4.

19 Ben-Amos, *Funerals, Politics, and Memory*, Chapter 1.

20 Ibid., 53–5.

21 Caille, "Une citoyenneté supérieure," 13.

22 Ducourtial and Bonneville de Marsangy, *Légion d'Honneur*, 193–4.

23 Ibid., 195.

24 Ben-Amos, *Funerals, Politics, and Memory*, 285.

25 Caille, "Une citoyenneté supérieure."

26 Caradonna, *Enlightenment in Practice*, 44–5.

27 McClellan, *Science Reorganized*, 115–16, and sources he cites.

28 Caradonna, *Enlightenment in Practice*, Chapters, 1–4, especially 23, 41, 94, 117.

29 Kelly, *Rousseau as Author*, 18. For a critical review of the literature on this see Caradonna, especially the Introduction and Chapter 4.

30 Caradonna, *Enlightenment in Practice*, 2–5.

31 Erlanger, *Prize Medal*, 79.

32 Ibid., 186.

33 McClellan, *Science Reorganized*, 11; Weisz, *Medical Mandarins*, particularly 98–9.

34 Erlanger, *Prize Medal*, 144.

35 Caradonna, *Enlightenment in Practice*, 149–50.

36 Erlanger, *Prize Medal*, 139.

37 Ibid., 187.

38 Ibid., 114.

39 Straum, "Institute prize contests."

40 Caradonna examines them jointly.

41 Bruin, *Kroon op Het Werk*, 23.

42 Manning, *Apprenticeship in Arms*, 276.

43 On the experiences of British soldiers with an aristocratic background, see Manning, *Swordsmen*, Part I, Chapter 2.

44 Manning, *Swordsmen*, 26.

45 Forrest, *Napoleon's Men*, 95–6.

46 Parker, *Military Revolution*, 58–9, and sources he cites.

47 *General Orders 1809*, 43.

48 Louis XIV, *Mémoires for the Instruction of the Dauphin*, 80.

49 Nicolas, *Orders of Knighthood*, vol. 1, li.

50 Mazas, *Ordre de Saint-Louis*, 55.

51 Ducourtial and Bonneville de Marsangy, *Légion d'Honneur*, 37.

52 Petiteau, *Noblesse d'Empire*, 47.

53 Again on this subject see Matikkala, *Orders of Knighthood*, 109–29.

54 Chagniot, "Ordres royaux de chevalrie," 17.

55 Boulton, "Curial orders," 324–5.

56 Manning, *Swordsmen*, 95–6.

57 Risk, *History of the Order of the Bath*, 1–3, 15–16.

58 Ibid., 13.

59 Galloway, *Order of St Patrick and its Knights*, Chapter 1.

60 Ibid., 16.

61 Galloway, *Order of St Michael and St George*, 21. On this subject, see Chapters 1 and 2.

62 Ibid., 12.

63 Matikkala, *Orders of Knighthood*, 29.

64 On Charles II's peerage appointments, see Swatland, *House of Lords in the Reign of Charles II*, 30.

65 Cubells, "Politique d'anoblissement."

66 Petiteau, "De la Légion d'honneur à la noblesse d'Empire," 111.

67 Ibid., 122–4, 132–3.

68 Massian, *Médaille militaire*, 18.

69 Borné, *Distinctions honorifiques de la Belgique*, 91, 98–9; Tamse and Witte, "Inleiding," 47.

70 Guttsman, *British Political Elite*, 123

71 Ibid., 122.

72 Fourez, "Nécessité d'anoblissement," 25.

73 Silberman, *Cages of Reason*, especially 153–4.

74 On this subject, see Ihl, *Mérite et la République*, particularly 14–15.

75 Foord, "The waning of 'the influence of the Crown,'" 493–4; Thompson, *English Landed Society*, 9–10.

76 Hanham, "Sale of honours," 282.

77 Searle, *Corruption in British Politics*, 85.
78 Ibid., 85–6.
79 Ducourtial and Bonneville de Marsangy, *Légion d'Honneur*, 68, 195.
80 Petiteau, *Noblesse d'Empire*, 457.
81 Girard, *Chambre des Députés en 1837–1839*, 21.
82 Boulton, *Knights of the Crown*, 464–5.
83 McCahill, "Peerage creations," 271.
84 Cubells, "Politique d'anoblissement," 179.
85 Petiteau, *Noblesse d'Empire*, 458.
86 Fourez, "Nécessité d'anoblissement," 25.
87 McCahill, "Peerage creations," 271.
88 Galloway, *Order of the Bath*, 39–40.
89 Mazas, *Ordre de Saint-Louis*, Chapter 1.
90 Ibid., 185–6.
91 Ibid., 176–7, 274.
92 Ducourtial, *Ordres et décorations*, 62.
93 Gernet, *History of Chinese Civilization*, 335–6.
94 Ibid., 335; Eckert et al., *Korea Old and New*, 128.
95 Rule and Trotter, *World of Paper*.
96 Goldstein, "Fighting French censorship," 790.
97 Overviews of the history of coinage can be found in Carson, *Coins*, and Grierson, *Numismatics*.
98 Carson, *Coins*, x. But see also Thompson, "The 'invention' of coinage."
99 Harper, *Cultural Identity: Monuments and Artifacts of the Sasanian Near East*, 120–1.
100 Nousek, "Caesar's elephant denarius."
101 Holt, *Elephant Medallions*, 125.
102 Kyle, *Sport and Spectacle in the Ancient World*, 232–3.
103 For a critical summary of this literature, see Holt, *Elephant Medallions*.
104 Carson, *Coins*, 110, 131.
105 Koester, "Gold medals of Abukir"; Dahmen, "Alexander in gold and silver."
106 Dahmen, "Alexander in gold and silver," 513.
107 For more on this subject, see Stahl, "Coinage and money in the Latin Empire of Constantinople."
108 Bedos-Rezak, "Medieval identity: A sign and a concept," 1514–15.
109 Hill, *Medals of the Renaissance*, 102.
110 Scher, "Renaissance portrait medal," 4–5.
111 For Pisanello's life and work, see Syson, *Pisanello*, 1.
112 More on this subject can be found in Burke, *Fabrication of Louis XIV*.

113 Cunnally, "Numismatics, prestation, and the genesis of visual literacy."

114 Ibid.; Stahl, "Numismatics in the Renaissance."

115 Adams, *Medals Concerning John Law*, 29.

116 Burke, *Fabrication of Louis XIV*, 142.

117 Whiting, *Commemorative Medals*, 162–3.

118 Ibid., 178–80.

119 Ibid., 181.

120 Erlanger, *Prize Medal*, 10–11.

121 DeVries, *Infantry Warfare in the Early Fourteenth Century*, 196–7.

122 The main sources that I have drawn on for this discussion are Tallet, *War and Society in Early-Modern Europe*, 24–6; Parker, "Battle of Nieuwpoort"; González de León, *Road to Rocroi*, 129; Nimwegen, *Dutch Army*, 105–12; Roy, *Military Transition in Early Modern Asia*, 21, 77–8, and sources he cites.

123 Nimwegen, *Dutch Army*, 108–10.

124 Parker, "Battle of Nieuwpoort," 343–4.

125 Tallet, *War and Society in Early-Modern Europe*, 25.

126 Parker, "Battle of Nieuwpoort," 337–43.

127 Aguilar-Moreno, *Handbook to Life in the Aztec World*, 111–17, 120–4.

128 Parker, "Battle of Nieuwpoort," 358–66.

129 Gommans, "Warhorse and gunpowder," 116, cited in Roy, *Military Transition in Early Modern Asia*, 71.

130 Levy, "Military reform and the problem of centralization in the Ottoman Empire," 230.

131 Roy, "Conventional war," "Military synthesis in South Asia," *War, Culture and Society in Early Modern South Asia*, especially Chapter 2, and *Military Transition in Early Modern Asia*, 76.

132 For accounts of this kind of coordination, see Weatherford, *Genghis Khan*, especially 61–2, 94–6.

133 Lane, *Daily Life in the Mongol Empire*, 107–9; May, Mongol Art of War, 46.

134 Roy, *Military Transition in Early Modern Asia*, 61, and sources he cites.

135 Manning, *Apprenticeship in Arms*, 147.

136 Ibid., 149, 347.

137 Roy, *Historical Dictionary of Ancient India*, 127.

138 Szabo, *Seven Years War*, 65.

139 Hughes, *Russia in the Age of Peter the Great*, 179.

140 Neville, *Orders of Imperial Germany and Austria*, 34–5.

141 Mazas, *Ordre de Saint-Louis*, 143–4, 171, 320.

142 Chattaway, *Order of the Golden Tree*, 31–2, and sources she cites.

143 "Carnegie founds fund for heroes," *Chicago Daily Tribune.*
144 Holt, *Elephant Medallions,* 147.
145 Maxfield, *Military Decorations of the Roman Army,* 91.
146 Ibid., 95.
147 Hill, *Medals of the Renaissance,* 37–80.
148 Ibid., 68.
149 Wallis, "Cartography of Drake's voyage," 149–50.
150 Nicolas, *Orders of Knighthood,* vol. 4, 4–5.
151 References to the following examples of British medals in the six-teenth and seventeenth centuries can be found in Ibid., vol. 4, 8–14; Hill, *Medals of the Renaissance,* 159–60; and Wyllie, *Orders, Decorations and Insignia,* 2.
152 Nicolas, *Orders of Knighthood,* vol. 4, 12.
153 Ibid., 12.
154 Boniface, "Décorer les militaires," 104.
155 Ibid., 105.
156 Myerly, *British Military Spectacle,* 48–9.
157 Caille, "Une citoyenneté supérieure," 10.
158 Ibid., 10.
159 Ducourtial and Bonneville de Marsangy, *Légion d'Honneur,* 65.
160 Dumas, *Memoirs of His Own Time,* 216.
161 Hazareesingh, *Saint-Napoleon,* Chapter 4.
162 Ducourtial and Bonneville de Marsangy, *Légion d'Honneur,* 200; Dumons and Pollet, "Médailles du travail," 77.
163 Dumons and Pollet, "Médailles du travail," 79; Ducourtial and Bonneville de Marsangy, *Légion d'Honneur,* 200.
164 Nicolas, *Orders of Knighthood,* vol. 4, 55.
165 Durieux, *Action disciplinaire de la Légion d'Honneur,* 69–71.
166 Aucoc, "Discipline de la Légion d'Honneur," 3–4.

CHAPTER EIGHT

1 Vale, *Charles VII,* 37–40.
2 Ullmann, *Individual and Society in the Middle Ages,* 31–4.
3 Bedos-Rezak, "Medieval identity: A sign and a concept," 1509.
4 Foucault, "The subject and power" and "Politics and reason"; Dean, *Governmentality,* Chapter 4.
5 Hyams, *Lords and Peasants in Medieval England,* 152–5.
6 Coss, "Formation of the English gentry," 61–2.
7 Ullmann, *Individual and Society in the Middle Ages,* 18–20.

8 Boulton, *Knights of the Crown*, xvii–xviii.

9 Ibid., 266–7.

10 Cox, *Green Count of Savoy*, 181; Boulton, *Knights of the Crown*, 259.

11 Vale, *War and Chivalry*, 40; Jones, "Order of the Golden Fleece,"
33; Keen, *Chivalry*, 184. On this important order, see also Boulton,
Knights of the Crown, Chapter 13, and Baelde, "De Orde van het Gulden Vlies."

12 Upton, *De Studio Militari*, cited in Perkins, *Most Honourable Order of the
Bath*, 40.

13 Cox, *Green Count of Savoy*, 78.

14 On these and other obligations of members of the Order of the
Golden Fleece, see Boulton, *Knights of the Crown*, 381–2.

15 Ibid., 78.

16 For all of these orders, see Boulton, *Knights of the Crown*, 377.

17 Ibid., 266.

18 Jones, "Order of the Golden Fleece," 33; Boulton, *Knights of the
Crown*, 380.

19 Boulton, *Knights of the Crown*, 440.

20 Neuschel, *Word of Honor*, especially 1–16, 23–5, 196–8, 205–6.

21 Duby, *Chivalrous Society*, 181.

CHAPTER NINE

1 Adams, *Familial State*.

2 Oestreich, *Neostocism*, 242.

3 Valeri, "Religion, discipline, and economy in Calvin's Geneva," 132.

4 Benedict, *Christ's Churches Purely Reformed*, 103–4.

5 Smout, *History of the Scottish People*, 74.

6 Gorski, "Protestant ethic re-visited," 279.

7 Valeri, "Religion, discipline, and economy in Calvin's Geneva," 125,
128, 137.

8 Gorski, *Disciplinary Revolution*, 124–5.

9 On this subject see Valeri, "Religion, discipline, and economy in Calvin's Geneva," 133–8.

10 Gorski, *Disciplinary Revolution*, 56–7; Benedict, *Christ's Churches Purely
Reformed*, 97.

11 Gorski, *Disciplinary Revolution*, 56–8; Benedict, *Christ's Churches Purely
Reformed*, 479–80.

12 Benedict, *Christ's Churches Purely Reformed*, 467–70.

13 Ibid., 463.

14 Ibid., 39–40, 86–7, 97–8, 462–3.

15 Frotier de la Messelière, *Noblesse en Bretagne*, 4–5.

16 Clark, *British Clubs and Societies*, 223, 262.

17 Harrison, *Bourgeois Citizen in Nineteenth-Century France*, 38–43.

18 Simmel, "Sociology of secrecy and of secret societies," 481.

19 *Minutes of the Aberdeen Philosophical Society*, 77.

20 Allan, *Nation of Readers*, 62.

21 Greefs, "Ondernemers en de genootschappen," 27.

22 Williams, "Royal Society of Literature," 244–5.

23 Shillito, *Country Book-Club*, 32.

24 For British reading societies, see Allan, *Nation of Readers*, 41.

25 *Minutes of the Aberdeen Philosophical Society*, 77.

26 Cormier and Coulton, "Civil society, mobilization, and communal violence," 497.

27 Dreyfus, "Médailles mutualistes," 166.

28 Ibid., 163.

29 On this subject see Clark, *British Clubs and Societies*, 64–6, 95, 106.

30 Ibid., 106.

31 Manning, *Apprenticeship in Arms*, 407–8.

32 Collins, *State in Early Modern France*, 94.

33 Frotier de la Messelière, *Noblesse en Bretagne*, 38.

34 Cookson, "Regimental worlds."

35 Myerly, *British Military Spectacle*, 7–8.

36 Elias, *Court Society* and *Civilizing Process* are both worth reading on this evolution.

37 See Clark, *State and Status*, 346–51 for a more detailed account of different courts in this period.

38 Bucholz's classic work, *Augustan Court*, demonstrates how these processes operated, or sometimes did not operate.

39 Clark, *Scandal*, 13.

40 Oestreich, *Neostoicism*, especially Chapter 15.

41 Keohane, *Philosophy and the State in France*, 68–9.

42 Smith, "'Our sovereign's gaze'" and *Culture of Merit*.

43 Bucholz, *Augustan Court*, 23–5, 30, 113–14, 153–4, 244–6.

44 Leerssen, "Wildness, wilderness, and Ireland," 33; Carroll, *Science, Culture, and Modern State Formation*, 143–5.

45 Perkin, *Women and Marriage in Nineteenth-Century England*, 111.

46 Smith and Bond, *Social Psychology across Cultures*, 104–7, 113–14; Miller, "Culture and the development of everyday social explanations."

47 Roland, *In Search of Self in India and Japan*, especially 6–10, 326–31.

48 Lukes, *Individualism*, Chapter 1; Swart, "Individualism."

49 Swart, "Individualism," 85.

50 Hofstede, *Culture's Consequences*, 215; Van den Broek and Heunks, "Political culture: Patterns of political orientations and behaviour," 75–6, 255. In the Van den Broek and Heunks study, the three countries' rank on economic individualism: Great Britain the most individualist, followed by Belgium, followed by France. On cultural individualism, they were almost the reverse. However, what Van den Broek and Heunks call cultural individualism is actually disrespect for authority not cultural individualism. Unsurprisingly, the French have less respect for authority than the British. On the other hand, what Van den Broek and Heunks call economic individualism is indeed a legitimate measure of individualism.

51 Clark, *State and Status*, 343–4.

52 Martin, "Discovery of the individual in Renaissance Europe," 1334.

53 Dror Wahrman claims that the modern "self" emerged first in England, but he examines only a short period in the late eighteenth century. See his *Making of the Modern Self*.

54 Towsey, *Reading the Scottish Enlightenment*, Chapter 6.

55 Baldwin, "Individual and self in the late Renaissance," 364; Parker, "Introduction," 8–9.

56 Keohane, *Philosophy and the State in France*, especially 451.

57 Lukes, *Individualism*, 73–4.

58 Ibid., 77.

59 Robinson, *French Literature*, Chapter 3.

60 Reddy, *Invisible Code*, xi–xiii, 10–11, 129–36; on public criticism of the bureaucracy in nineteenth-century France, see Chapter 4.

61 Beck, *Risk Society*; Beck and Beck-Gernsheim, *Individualization*.

62 Snyder, *Protestant Ethic and the Spirit of Punishment*, especially Chapter 3.

63 Again see Towsey, *Reading the Scottish Enlightenment*; Allan, *Nation of Readers*.

64 See, as an example, the Third Earl of Shaftesbury in ibid., 217–18.

65 Maza, *Myth of the French Bourgeoisie*, 148–9.

66 Foucault, *Discipline and Punish*, 192–3.

67 Hamilton, "Naval hagiography and the Victorian hero," 382.

68 Ben-Amos, *Funerals, Politics, and Memory*, 391–3.

69 "Carnegie founds fund for heroes," *Chicago Daily Tribune*.

70 Klapp, "Heroes, villains and fools," 61.

71 Robinson, *French Literature*, 26–7.

72 Lucas, "Baron Pierre de Coubertin," 149, 153.

73 Ibid., 135.

74 Ibid., 136–7n27.

75 Oestreich, *Neostoicism*, 30, 50, 53–4.

76 "Carnegie founds fund for heroes," *Chicago Daily Tribune.*

77 Ben-Amos, *Funerals, Politics, and Memory*, 22, 25–6, 267–8.

CHAPTER TEN

1 Galloway, *Order of the Bath*, 13.

2 Galloway, *Order of Saint Patrick and its Knights*, 27.

3 Galloway, *Order of the Bath*, 30.

4 Ibid., 145.

5 Galloway, *Order of St Michael and St George*, 34.

6 Galloway, *Order of St Patrick and its Knights*, 78.

7 Van Zelm van Eldik, *Moed en deugd*, 192.

8 Lloyd, *Lord Cochrane*, part II.

9 Stephen and Lee, *Dictionary of National Biography*, vol. 4, 1087.

10 Nicolas, *Orders of Knighthood*, vol. 3, 214.

11 Martin, "Royal Victorian Chain," 94.

12 Ibid., 94.

13 Stanley, "Royal Victorian medal," 80.

14 Martin, "Royal Victorian Chain," 94–5.

15 Galloway, "Royal Victorian Order," 34.

16 On the cohorts, see Blandin, "Cohortes"; see also Durieux, *Action disciplinaire de la Légion d'Honneur*, 39, and Echappé, "Légion d'honneur: ses statuts, son statut," 276–7.

17 Wodey, *Guide de recherches*, 55.

18 Durieux, *Action disciplinaire de la Légion d'Honneur*, 149–50.

19 Ibid., 37.

20 Le Vavasseur de Précourt, "Legion d'Honneur," 305–6.

21 Aucoc, "Discipline de la Légion d'Honneur," 3–4.

22 Durieux, *Action disciplinaire de la Légion d'Honneur*, 2.

23 Ibid., 6.

24 Ibid., 5, 8.

25 Ibid., 8–9.

26 Ibid., 40–1; Aucoc, "Discipline de la Légion d'Honneur," 13–14.

27 Durieux, *Action disciplinaire de la Légion d'Honneur*, 41–2.

28 Ibid., 47; Aucoc, "Discipline de la Légion d'Honneur," 14.

29 Durieux, *Action disciplinaire de la Légion d'Honneur*, 47, 125–6.

30 Ibid., 49–50, 135; Aucoc, "Discipline de la Légion d'Honneur."

31 Aucoc, "Discipline de la Légion d'Honneur," 10, 17; Durieux, *Action disciplinaire de la Légion d'Honneur*, 46–7, 118–19, 123–6, 136–7.

32 Aucoc, "Discipline de la Légion d'Honneur," 17–19.

33 Ibid., 4.

34 Falcimaige, *Discipline de la Légion d'Honneur*, 48.

35 Wodey, *Guide de recherches*, 63–4.

36 Ibid., 64.

37 Boulton, *Knights of the Crown*, 383.

38 On this subject, see Lovell, "The trial of peers in Great Britain."

39 This point is made by Van Zelm van Eldik with respect to the Military Order of William. See *Moed en deugd*, 191.

40 Ibid., 507.

41 Crook, *Evolution of the Victoria Cross*, 64.

42 Blandin, "Cohortes," 179–85; Echappé, "Légion d'honneur: ses statuts, son statut," 277.

43 On this, see Herman, "Knights and kings in early modern France."

44 Van Zelm van Eldik, *Moed en deugd*, 616.

45 Borné, *Distinctions honorifiques de la Belgique*, 113–14.

46 Galloway, *Order of the British Empire*, 104–5.

47 Ibid., 106.

48 Ibid., 106.

49 Crook, *Evolution of the Victoria Cross*, 23–5.

50 Ibid., 58.

51 Ibid., 282.

52 Ibid., 66–7.

53 Ibid., 280.

54 Ibid., 280.

55 Wilkins, *History of the Victoria Cross*, 99.

56 Toomey, *Heroes of the Victoria Cross*, 234.

57 Wilkins, *History of the Victoria Cross*, 352.

58 Toomey, *Heroes of the Victoria Cross*, 98.

59 Ibid., 28.

60 Ibid., 4, 9, 24, 58.

61 Wilkins, *History of the Victoria Cross*, 67.

62 Ibid., 199.

63 Ibid., 244.
64 Ibid., 305.
65 Ibid., 379.
66 Ibid., 17.
67 Crook, *Evolution of the Victoria Cross*, 158.
68 Goode, *Celebration of Heroes*, 170–1.
69 Cusas, *Statut de la noblesse en France et en Belgique*, 99–100.
70 Ibid., 117.
71 Ibid., 82.
72 Ibid., 83, 125.
73 Borné, *Distinctions honorifiques de la Belgique*, 339.
74 Ducourtial and Bonneville de Marsangy, *Légion d'Honneur*, 233–4, 235.
75 Van Zelm van Eldik, *Moed en deugd*, 249.
76 Ducourtial and Bonneville de Marsangy, *Légion d'Honneur*, 240.
77 Ibid., 241–2, 273–5.
78 Tripnaux, *Origine de l'Ordre de Léopold*, 25, 95.
79 Ducourtial and Bonneville de Marsangy, *Légion d'Honneur*, 242–60.
80 Van Zelm van Eldik, *Moed en deugd*, 249-52.
81 Crook, *Evolution of the Victoria Cross*, 281–2.
82 Ibid., 100.
83 Ibid., 105.
84 Ibid., 108.
85 Ibid., 116.
86 Ibid., 107–8.
87 Ibid., 108.
88 Swart, "Individualism," 80–1.
89 Perkins, "Individualism versus collectivism." See also David Harris's earlier article, "European liberalism," 508–9.
90 Herbert Spencer to J.E. Cairnes, 21 March 1873, in Spencer, *Life and Letters*, 161.
91 Robinson, *French Literature*, Chapter 4.
92 Martin, "Discovery of the individual in Renaissance Europe," 1322.
93 For the role of population counting in that construction, see Curtis, *Politics of Population*.
94 Colley, *Britons*, 5–6.
95 Ducourtial and Bonneville de Marsangy, *Légion d'Honneur*, 52.
96 Ibid.
97 Caille, *Figure du sauveteur*, especially 16–18, 51–4, 60–1, 131.
98 Ihl, "Gouverner par les honneurs," 16.

PART FOUR

1 The conceptual and theoretical development of this literature has been built on Weber, and more recently on Homans, *Human Group* and *Social Behavior*, Goode, *Celebration of Heroes*, Jasso, "Studying status," and Milner, *Status and Sacredness*, with the last mentioned providing the most comprehensive theory of status. In the Introduction, I referred to the large body of literature on status interaction in small groups. Among Bourdieu's major works, the most concerned with status as such is *Distinction*, but he discusses it explicitly or implicitly in many of his writings. Also important is Frank, *Choosing the Right Pond*. Literature on "status attainment" is not using the term "status" in the way it is used in the above literature and in this book.

2 Ridgeway, "Why status matters for inequality." A recent call for the study of status has also been made by Kurzman et al. in "Celebrity status."

CHAPTER ELEVEN

1 For a fuller treatment of this subject, see Clark, *State and Status*, Chapter 5.

2 Boulton, "The notion of 'chivalry,'" 21–3.

3 See Clark, *State and Status*, 167–8. A good summary of these processes is found in Boulton, "Curial orders," 35–8.

4 Clark, *State and Status*, 172.

5 On this subject, see Janssens, "Het lot van de Belgische adel in de revolutiejaren."

6 An insightful work on the bureaucratization of honours in France is Ihl, *Mérite et la République*.

7 This is a major proposition of Murray Milner's theory of status. See *Status and Sacredness*, 34–5.

8 Stone, "Inflation of honours" and *Crisis of the Aristocracy*.

9 Ducourtial and Bonneville de Marsangy, *Légion d'Honneur*, 144.

10 Ibid., 116–17.

11 Kuhn, *Henry and Mary Ponsonby*, 186, 212.

12 Galloway, *Order of the British Empire*, 8.

13 Ibid., 10.

14 Kennedy, *Portrait of Elgar*, 218.

15 Cannon, *Aristocratic Century*, 20–31.

16 Vincent, *Nelson*, 270–1.

17 Bruin, *Kroon op Het Werk*, 112–13.
18 Van Zelm van Eldik, *Moed en deugd*, 565.
19 Boulton, "Influence of religious orders," 27–8.
20 Ibid., 29–30.

CHAPTER TWELVE

1 Bertaud, "Napoleon's officers."
2 Wodey, "L'honneur: signe et insigne," 271.
3 Dumons and Pollet. "Médailles du travail."
4 Caille, "Mémoire fragmenteé," 226.
5 Dreyfus, "Médailles mutualistes."
6 Blanco, "Prestige of British army surgeons."
7 Blaufarb, "*Ancien régime* origins of the Napoleonic social reconstruction," 415.
8 L'Hoist, *De la Toison d'Or à l'Ordre de Léopold II*, 62.
9 Galloway, *Order of the Bath*, 46–9.
10 Ibid., 49.
11 McCahill, "Peerage creations," 272.
12 Ibid., 272–3.
13 L'Hoist, *De la Toison d'Or à l'Ordre de Léopold II*, 62.
14 Ducourtial and Bonneville de Marsangy, *Légion d'Honneur*, 141.
15 Ibid., 153.
16 Ihl, *Mérite et la République*, 245–6.
17 Ibid. Although not carefully researched, this work is worth reading on this contradiction and the polemics to which it gave rise in both the Early Modern and Modern periods.
18 Ibid., 267.
19 Tripnaux, *Origine de l'Ordre de Léopold*, 114.
20 Matikkala, *Orders of Knighthood*, 176.
21 Galloway, *Order of the Bath*, 28–9. A "catiff" is a worthless, despicable person, and "post" in this context refers to a person who would lie before a law court in return for payment.
22 Walker, *The Queen Has Been Pleased*, 4–5.
23 *Matter of Honour*, 17.
24 Herbert Spencer to J.D. Hooker, 28 March 1874, in Spencer, *Life and Letters*, 168.
25 Stanley Martin provides this information from a personal source. See his *Order of Merit*, 485–6.
26 Van Zelm van Eldik, *Moed en deugd*, 593–8.

27 Searle, *Corruption in British Politics*, 368–9.

28 Van Zelm van Eldik, *Moed en deugd*, 414.

29 Bruin, *Kroon op Het Werk*, 64; Van Zelm van Eldik, *Moed en deugd*, 436.

30 On this subject, see Van Sas, "Grote nederlands van Willem I," and other articles in Tamse and Witte, eds., *Staats- en natievorming in Willem I's koninkrijk.*

31 Van Zelm van Eldik, *Moed en deugd*, 431.

32 Ibid., 431–2.

33 Ibid., 443–7.

34 Bruin, *Kroon op Het Werk*, 76.

35 Ibid., 77.

36 Tripnaux, *Origine de l'Ordre de Léopold*, 120.

37 Ibid., 133–93.

38 Ibid., 181–2.

39 Risk, *History of the Order of the Bath*, 69.

40 Galloway, *Order of the Bath*, 184–6.

41 Ibid., 209–11.

42 Ibid., 233.

43 Ibid., 233–8.

44 Lee, *King Edward VII*, vol. 1, 111.

45 Galloway, *Order of the Bath*, 238.

46 Ibid., 241.

47 Pumphrey, "Creation of peerages," 102.

48 On this subject, see ibid., 98–105; Ferguson, *House of Rothschild*, 252–6, 520n47.

49 Davis, "Disraeli, the Rothschilds, and anti-Semitism."

50 Searle, *Corruption in British Politics*, 363–4.

51 Borné, *Distinctions honorifiques de la Belgique*, 210.

52 Tripnaux, *Origine de l'Ordre de Léopold*, 177–8.

53 Borné, *Distinctions honorifiques de la Belgique*, 211.

54 Ibid., 192, 199.

55 Hibbert, *Edward VII*, 283.

56 On all this legislation, the best source is Cusas, *Statut de la noblesse en France et en Belgique*. See especially, 126–8, 178, 258.

CHAPTER THIRTEEN

1 Borné, *Distinctions honorifiques de la Belgique*, 322.

2 Crook, *Evolution of the Victoria Cross*, 5–6.

3 Ibid., 6. See also Galloway, *Order of the Bath*, 202–3.

4 Blaufarb, "*Ancien régime* origins of the Napoleonic social reconstruction," 415.

5 Cannadine, *Ornamentalism*, 87.

6 Galloway, *Order of the Bath*, 170.

7 Petiteau, *Noblesse d'Empire*, 73.

8 Dumons, "*Saints de la République*," 112–13, 478–80.

9 A biographical list of all the *grand croix* is provided in Wattel and Wattel, *Grand'Croix*.

10 Fourez, "Nécessité d'anoblissement," 25.

11 McCahill, "Peerage creations," 271.

12 Cannadine, *Decline and Fall of the British Aristocracy*, 196.

13 Galloway, *Companions of Honour*, 68.

14 Barbiche, *Institutions de la monarchie française*, 106.

15 Bell, "'Public Sphere,'" 933.

16 Dewald, "Social groups and cultural practices," 46.

17 Corfield, *Power and the Professions*, 93.

18 Stone and Stone, *Open Elite?* 199–201, Table 6.2.

19 Witte, "Wijzigingen in de Belgische elite in 1830"; François, "Intellectuelen and revolutionaire bedrijvigheid."

20 Guttsman, *British Political Elite*, 122.

21 Dumons, "Saints de la République," 478–9.

22 On the status of "gentleman" in the eighteenth century, see Corfield, "Rivals."

23 Corfield, *Power and the Professions*, 77.

24 On respect and disrespect for professional knowledge in Britain, see ibid., especially Chapters 2, 3, and 10.

25 Charle, *Intellectuels en Europe*, 46.

26 For the Southern Low Countries, see Stevens, *Revolutie en notariaat*, 324.

27 Van Zelm van Eldik, *Moed en deugd*, 395–9.

28 Ibid., 753.

29 Corfield, *Power and the Professions*, 236.

30 Guttsman, *British Political Elite*, 122.

31 Fourez, "Nécessité d'anoblissement," 25.

32 Ducourtial and Bonneville de Marsangy, *Légion d'Honneur*, 68–9.

33 Petiteau, *Noblesse d'Empire*, 458.

34 Ducourtial and Bonneville de Marsangy, *Légion d'Honneur*, 151–2.

35 Dumons, "Saints de la République," 478–9.

36 De Belder, "Adel en burgerij, 1840–1914," 82; Janssens, "Chefs d'entreprise et aristocrates belges."

37 Fourez, "Nécessité d'anoblissement," 25.

38 Pumphrey, "The introduction of industrialists into the British peerage," 9; see also Searle, *Corruption in British Politics*, 157; Cannadine, *Decline and Fall of the British Aristocracy*, 199–202.

39 Guttsman, *British Political Elite*, 122.

40 Ibid., 124.

41 Dansette, *Affaire Wilson*.

42 Jenkins, "Liberal Unionist Party and the honours system," 921–3.

43 Hanham, "Sale of honours," 283–5; Searle, *Corruption in British Politics*, 85–6.

44 Cannadine, *Decline and Fall of the British Aristocracy*, 309–10. ·

45 Bruin, *Kroon op Het Werk*, 69.

46 Cannadine, *Decline and Fall of the British Aristocracy*, 314–25; Searle, *Corruption in British Politics*, Chapter 15.

47 Bruin, *Kroon op Het Werk*, 81; Van Zelm van Eldik, *Moed en deugd*, 659.

48 Cannadine, *Decline and Fall of the British Aristocracy*, 308–9.

49 Galloway, *Order of St Patrick*, 1783–1983, 47.

50 Stanley, *Diaries of Edward Henry Stanley*, 227.

51 Galloway, *Order of the British Empire*, 41.

52 Bruin, *Kroon op Het Werk*, 111–12.

53 Charle, *Social History of France*, 242–4.

54 Dumons and Pollet. "Médailles du travail," 69.

55 Van Zelm van Eldik, *Moed en deugd*, 663–4.

56 Borné, *Distinctions honorifiques de la Belgique*, 113–14.

57 Ibid., 222.

58 Bruin, *Kroon op Het Werk*, 113.

59 Ibid., 113–15.

60 Guttsman, *British Political Elite*, 117.

61 See Anderson, "Wensleydale peerage case."

62 Ridley, *Lord Palmerston*, 504–5.

63 Strieter, "An army in evolution"; Charle, *Social History of France*, 163–4.

64 Charle, "Recrutement des hauts fonctionnaires," 387.

65 Razzell, "Social origins of officers," 253.

66 Cannadine, *Decline and Fall of the British Aristocracy*, 196.

67 Razzell, "Social origins of officers," 253.

68 Borné, *Distinctions honorifiques de la Belgique*, 120.

69 Bruin, *Kroon op Het Werk*, 60–1.

70 Ibid., 61–2.

71 Ibid., 61–2.

72 Ibid., 63.

73 Ibid., 58–9; Van Zelm van Eldik, *Moed en deugd*, 313.

74 Crook, *Evolution of the Victoria Cross*, 118.

75 Borné, *Distinctions honorifiques de la Belgique*, 204, 240–1, 248–9, 297, 328.

76 Van Zelm van Eldik, *Moed en deugd*, 334.

77 Ibid., 309.

78 Galloway, *Order of St Michael and St George*, 94.

79 *Mémorial du centenaire de l'Ordre de Léopold*, 482, 494–7.

80 Ducourtial and Bonneville de Marsangy, *Légion d'Honneur*, 217–19.

81 Ridley, *Lord Palmerston*, 479–80.

82 Cook, *Life of Florence Nightingale*, 418.

83 Crook, *Evolution of the Victoria Cross*, 171–8.

84 Neville, *Orders of Imperial Germany and Austria*, 37.

85 Ibid., 72

86 Ducourtial and Bonneville de Marsangy, *Légion d'Honneur*, 224.

87 Borné, *Distinctions honorifiques de la Belgique*, 183.

88 Fergusson, *Sixteen Peers of Scotland*, 89–90.

89 Ducourtial and Bonneville de Marsangy, *Légion d'Honneur*, 229–30.

90 Tooley, *Life of Florence Nightingale*, 343.

91 Seward, *Eugénie*, 135.

92 Hudson, *Life and Times of Louisa, Queen of Prussia*, vol. 2, 414.

93 Ducourtial and Bonneville de Marsangy, *Légion d'Honneur*, 16.

94 Dorling, *Ribbons and Medals*, 93.

95 Galloway, *Order of St Michael and St George*, 72.

96 On this subject, see Read, *Republic of Men*.

97 Dumons, "Saints de la République," 96.

98 Pumphrey, "Creation of peerages," 104.

99 Davis, "Disraeli, the Rothschilds, and anti-Semitism," 10–11.

100 Gower, *My Reminiscences*, 428.

101 Galloway, *Order of the British Empire*, 39–41.

102 Van Zelm van Eldik, *Moed en deugd*, 197.

103 Galloway, *Order of the British Empire*, 39–40.

104 Damien, "La Légion d'honneur face aux nouvelles décorations," 96.

105 Jordan and Rogers, "Admirals as heroes," 219.

106 Myerly, *British Military Spectacle*, 93.

107 Stanhope, *Letters to his Son*; Matikkala, *Orders of Knighthood*, 23, 247.

108 Galloway, *Order of St Michael and St George*, 71.

109 Galloway, *Order of the British Empire*, 40–1. See also Walker, *I Talk of Dreams*, 205–7.

110 Stanley, *Diaries of Edward Henry Stanley*, 273.

111 Ibid., 273.
112 Jenkins, "Liberal Unionist Party and the honours system," 921–2.
113 Martin, *Order of Merit*, 19–20.
114 Taylor, *Lord Salisbury*, 147.
115 Rose, *King George V*, 246.
116 A much-read book on this subject is De Botton, *Status Anxiety*.
117 Galloway, *Order of St Michael and St George*, 71.

STATE HONOURS IN COMPARATIVE PERSPECTIVE

1   A good body of literature can be found on this subject. See Ali, *Apparatus of Empire*; Moosvi, "Evolution of the 'mansab' system"; or for a short description, Richards, *Mughal Empire*, 24–5.
2   For military rewards, see Irvine, *Army of the Indian Moghuls*, 29–35.
3   Schimmel, *Empire of the Great Mughals*, 69.
4   Joshi, *Defence Administration in India*, vol. 1, 211.
5   Yates, "Law and the military in early China," 32.
6   Gernet, *History of Chinese Civilization*, 91.
7   Lewis, *Early Chinese Empires*, 32, 110, 234.
8   Hucker, *Dictionary of Official Titles*, 4–5.
9   Ch'ü, *Han Social Structure*, 83–4.
10 Gordon, "Robes of honour," 225–7.
11 Ibid., 237.
12 Schimmel, *Empire of the Great Mughals*, 28.
13 Garrett, *Chinese Dress*, 25, 73.
14 Landa, *Relación de las Cosas de Yucatan*, 123.
15 Vaillant, *Aztecs of Mexico*, 114, 137.
16 Rowe, "Inca culture," 123; McEwan, *Incas*, 129.
17 This was common among Lowland Cree. Kinietz, *Indians of the Western Great Lakes*, 260–1; Bishop and Lytwyn, "Barbarism and ardour," 39.
18 "Trophies, war" in *Encyclopedia of Native American Wars and Warfare*, 323.
19 Lytwyn, *Original People of the Great Swampy Land*, 60.
20 Aldred, *Jewels of the Pharaohs*, 18.
21 Binder, *Gold of Honour*, 26, 257, 261–3.
22 Llewellyn-Jones, *King and Court in Ancient Persia*, 65.
23 Canepa, "Technologies of memory in early Sasanian Iran," 571.
24 Drijvers, "Roman image of the 'Barbarian' Sasanians," 70.
25 On this subject, see Jordan, "Honors for Themistocles"; Hanson, *Hoplites*, 143; Hamel, *Athenian Generals*, 64–70; Thériault, "Les 'prix de la valeur.'"

26 Kyle, *Sport and Spectacle in the Ancient World*, 58, 62–4, 81, 91.
27 All of these are discussed in Chaniotis, *War in the Hellenistic World*.
28 A good account of the *dona* is provided by Maxfield, *Military Decorations of the Roman Army*.
29 Ibid., 68, 78–90.
30 Ibid., 137.
31 To name only some of them: Moore, *Social Origins of Dictatorship and Democracy*; Skocpol, *States and Social Revolutions*; Downing, *Military Revolution and Political Change*; Orloff, *Politics of Pension*; Clark, *State and Status*; Ertman, *Birth of the Leviathan*; Lachman, *Capitalists in Spite of Themselves*; Mahoney, *Legacies of Liberalism*; Charrad, *States and Women's Rights*; Boone, *Political Topographies of the African State*; Steinmetz, *Devil's Handwriting*.
32 Bailey, *Typologies and Taxonomies*; Elman, "Explanatory typologies"; and Collier et al., "Putting typologies to work."
33 Charrad and Adams, "Patrimonialism."
34 Elman, "Explanatory typologies."
35 Goertz and Mahony, *Tale of Two Cultures*, 2, 11.
36 For an illustration, see Ragin, *Comparative Method*, 155.
37 Ragin, *Fuzzy-Set Social Science and Redesigning Social Inquiry*; and Rihoux and Ragin, *Configurational Comparative Methods*.
38 Goertz and Mahoney, *Tale of Two Cultures*, 133.
39 Ibid., 25–9.
40 Ragin, *Fuzzy-Set Social Science*, 272–3, 295–7.
41 The source is E.S. Burch's study of this population. See his *Alliance and Conflict*.
42 On Roman cavalry, see Dixon and Southern, *Roman Cavalry*.
43 Modelski, *World Cities*, 49, 63.
44 Morgan, *Mongols*, 142.
45 Allsen, "Reign of the Grand *Qan* Möngke," 506.
46 Gernet, *History of Chinese Civilization*, 118.
47 Mullen, "How big was the Roman army?"
48 Richards, *Mughal Empire*, 253–4.
49 Lococo, "Qing Empire," 131.
50 Richter, *Ordeal of the Longhouse*, 45; Fenton, *Great Law*, 11.
51 For references to this culture in Ancient India, see Wolpert, *New History of India*; Chaurasia, *History of Ancient India*, 126; Kulshrestha, *Culture India*; Rosen, *Societies and Military Power*, 75.
52 Eckert et al., *Korea Old and New*, 107–13.

EPILOGUE

1 Van Zelm van Eldik, *Moed en deugd*, 305–6.
2 McCreery, *Canadian Honours System*, 21.
3 Galloway, *Order of St Michael and St George*, 71–2, 78.
4 *Mémorial du centenaire de l'Ordre de Léopold*, 400.
5 McCreery, *Canadian Honours System*, 25.
6 Ibid., 26.
7 Ibid., 26–7.
8 Kinokuniya, *Decorations of Japan*.
9 See McCreery's appendices in *Canadian Honours System*.
10 Popkin, *Rational Peasant*; Shatzmiller, "Early Islamic world"; Moon and Koo, "Global citizenship and human rights"; Suzuki et al., "Individualizing Japan"; Kim, "Female individualization?"; Dupret, *Standing Trial*; Kipnis, ed., *Chinese Modernity*.
11 Yan, "Chinese path to individualization," especially 491–4, 507–9. See also his *Individualization of Chinese Society*.
12 Clark and Clark, "Patrons, publishers, and prizes," 214–15.
13 Ibid., 220.
14 English, *Economy of Prestige*, 66, 324.
15 Ibid., 324.

APPENDIX A

1 Peiter, "Consolidation of the business community," 510, 513, 517–18.
2 Ibid., 510.
3 Bonnell and Hunt, "Introduction."
4 The best representatives of this line of thinking are Wahrman, *Imagining the Middle Class* and Maza, *Myth of the French Bourgeoisie*.
5 Maza, *Myth of the French Bourgeoisie*, 6.
6 Kocka, "Middle classes," 784.

References

PRINTED PRIMARY SOURCES

Annuaire de l'Ordre Impérial de la Légion d'Honneur, 1852. Paris: Imprimerie imperial, 1853.

Annuaire official de tous les membres de l'Ordre de la Légion d'Honneur au 1er Avril 1929. Paris: Quillet, 1929.

Archives parlementaires de 1787 à 1860: Recueil complet des débats législatifs et politiques des Chambres françaises. Paris: Assemblée Nationale, 1864.

Awards, Honors and Prizes. Detroit: Gale Research Company, 1969–.

Burke's Handbook to the Most Excellent Order of the British Empire. London: Burke, 1921.

"Carnegie founds fund for heroes." *Chicago Daily Tribune,* 16 April 1904.

Dumas, Mathieu. *Memoirs of His Own Time; including The Revolution, The Empire, and The Restoration.* 2 vols. London: Bentley, 1839.

General Orders. Spain and Portugal, April 27th to December 28th, 1809, vol. 1. London: Egerton, 1811.

Louis XIV. *Mémoires for the Instruction of the Dauphin,* translated by Paul Sonnino. New York: Free Press, 1970.

A Matter of Honour: Reforming the Honours System, Public Administration Select Committee, Fifth Report of Session 2003–4, vol. 1: *Report, Together with Formal Minutes and Annex,* H.C. 2004 (212-1).

Mémorial du centenaire de l'Ordre de Léopold, 1832–1932. Brussels: Maison d'Éditions "J. Rozez" 1933.

The Minutes of the Aberdeen Philosophical Society, 1758–1773, edited by H.L. Ulman. Aberdeen: Aberdeen University Press 1990.

L'Ordre de Léopold: Liste de tous les dignitaries depuis la fondation de l'Ordre jusqu'au 31 décembre 1886. Brussels: Hochsteyn 1887.

Register of the Victoria Cross. Cheltenham: This England, 1988.

Shillito, Charles. *The Country Book-Club: A Poem.* Dublin: printed by Zachariah Jackson, for Richard White, 1790.

Spencer, Herbert. *The Life and Letters of Herbert Spencer*, edited by David Duncan. London: Williams and Norgate, 1911.

Stanley, E.H. *A Selection from the Diaries of Edward Henry Stanley, 15th Earl of Derby (1826–93) between September 1869 and March 1878*, edited by John Vincent. Camden Fifth Series, vol. 4. London: Royal Historical Society, 1994.

SECONDARY SOURCES

Adams, J.W. *The Medals Concerning John Law and the Mississippi System.* New York: The American Numismatic Society, 2005.

Adams, Julia. *The Familial State: Ruling Families and Merchant Capitalism in Early Modern Europe.* Ithaca: Cornell University Press, 2005.

Aguilar-Moreno, Manuel. *Handbook to Life in the Aztec World.* New York: Oxford University Press, 2007.

Aldred, Cyril. *Jewels of the Pharaohs: Egyptian Jewellery of the Dynastic Period.* London: Thames and Hudson, 1971.

Ali, M. Athar. *The Apparatus of Empire: Awards of Ranks, Offices, and Titles to the Mughal Nobility, 1574–1658.* Delhi: Oxford University Press, 1985.

Allan, David. *A Nation of Readers: The Lending Library in Georgian England.* London: British Library, 2008.

Allen, J.S. *Popular French Romanticism: Authors, Readers, and Books in the 19th Century.* Syracuse: Syracuse University Press, 1981.

Allsen, T.T. "Guard and government in the reign of the Grand *Qan* Möngke, 1251–59." *Harvard Journal of Asiatic Studies* 46/2 (1986).

Anderson, M.S. *War and Society in Europe of the Old Regime, 1618–1789.* London: Fontana, 1988.

Anderson, Olive. "The Wensleydale peerage case and the position of the House of Lords in the mid-nineteenth century." *English Historical Review* 82 (1967).

Anderson, Perry. "Origins of the present crisis." *New Left Review* no. 23 (1964).

Armstrong, J.A. *The European Administrative Elite.* Princeton: Princeton University Press, 1973.

Aucoc, Léon. "La discipline de la Légion d'Honneur." *Revue politique et parlementaire* (August 1895).

Augustine, Dolores L. *Patricians and Parvenus: Wealth and High Society in Wilhelmine Germany.* Providence: Berg, 1994.

Aulard, Alphonse. *Etudes et leçons sur la Revolution française.* Paris: Alcan, 1908.

Baelde, M.E.J. "De Orde van het Gulden Vlies." *Spiegel historiael* 19 (1984).

Bailey, K.D. *Typologies and Taxonomies: An Introduction to Classification Techniques.* Thousand Oaks: Sage, 1994.

Baldwin, Geoff. "Individual and self in the late Renaissance." *Historical Journal* 44 (2001).

Barbiche, Bernard. *Les institutions de la monarchie française a l'époque moderne: XVIe–XVIIe siècle.* Paris: Presses universitaires de France, 1999.

Barnett, Correlli. *Britain and Her Army, 1509–1970: A Military, Political and Social Survey.* Harmondsworth: Penguin, [1970] 1974.

Bartier, Jean. "Partis politiques et classes sociales en Belgique." *Res publica* 10 (1968).

Bearman, P.S. *Relations into Rhetorics: Local Elite Social Structure in Norfolk, England, 1540–1640.* New Brunswick: Rutgers University Press, 1993.

Bécarud, Jean. "Noblesse et représentation parlementaire: les députés nobles de 1871 à 1968." *Revue française de science politique* 23 (1973).

Béchu, Philippe. "Noblesse d'épée et tradition militaire au XVIIIème siècle." *Histoire, économie et société* 2 (1983).

Beck, Ulrich. *Risk Society: Towards a New Modernity,* translated by Mark Ritter. London: Sage, 1992.

Beck, Ulrich, and Elisabeth Beck-Gernsheim. *Individualization: Institutionalized Individualism and its Social and Political Consequences.* London: Sage, 2002.

Beckett, J.V. *The Aristocracy in England, 1660–1914.* Oxford: Basil Blackwell, 1986.

Bedos-Rezak, Brigitte Miriam. "Medieval identity: a sign and a concept." *American Historical Review* 105/5 (2000).

Bell, D.A. "The 'Public Sphere,' the state, and the world of law in eighteenth-century France." *French Historical Studies* 17 (1992).

Beltjens, Alain. *Aux origines de l'ordre de Malte: de la fondation de l'hôpital de Jérusalem à sa transformation en ordre militaire.* Brussels: Alain Beltjens. 1995.

Ben-Amos, Avner. *Funerals, Politics, and Memory in Modern France, 1789–1996.* Oxford: Oxford University Press, 2000.

Benedict, Philip. *Christ's Churches Purely Reformed: A Social History of Calvinism.* New Haven: Yale University Press, 2002.

Berger, Joseph, Susan J. Rosenholtz, and Morris Zelditch Jr, "Status organizing processes." *Annual Review of Sociology* 6 (1980).

Bergeron, Louis. *Les capitalistes en France (1780–1914).* Paris: Gallimard, 1978.

– *France Under Napoleon*, translated by R.R. Palmer. Princeton: Princeton University Press, [1972] 1981.

Bergier, J.F. "The industrial bourgeoisie and the rise of the working class, 1700–1914." In *The Fontana Economic History of Europe: The Industrial Revolution*, edited by C.M. Cipolla. Glasgow: Collins, 1973.

Bertaud, Jean-Paul. "Napoleon's officers." *Past and Present* no. 112 (August 1986).

Bien, D.D. "La réaction aristocratique avant 1789: l'exemple de l'armée." *Annales: Economies, Sociétés, Civilisations* 29 (1974).

Binder, Susanne. *The Gold of Honour in New Kingdom Egypt*. Oxford: Aris and Phillips, 2008.

Bishop, C.A., and V.P. Lytwyn. "Barbarism and ardour of war from the tenderest years." In *North American Indigenous Warfare and Ritual Violence*, edited by R.J. Chacon and R.G. Mendoza. Tucson: University of Arizona Press, 2007.

Bisson, T.N. "Medieval lordship." *Speculum* 70 (1995).

Blake, Robert. *The Conservative Party from Peel to Churchill*. London: Collins, 1970.

Blanco, R.L. "The prestige of British army surgeons, 1789–1850." *Societas* 2 (1972).

Blandin, Laetitia. "Les cohortes." *Revue européene d'histoire des ordres et décorations: la Phalère* no. 1 *Napoléon et la Légion d'honneur* (2000).

Blaufarb, Rafe. "The *ancien régime* origins of the Napoleonic social reconstruction." *French History* 14/4 (2000).

Blum, Jerome. *End of the Old Order in Rural Europe*. Princeton: Princeton University Press, 1978.

Blute, Marion. *Darwinian Sociocultural Evolution: Solutions to Dilemmas in Cultural and Social Theory*. New York: Cambridge University Press, 2010.

– "History versus science: The evolutionary solution." *Canadian Journal of Sociology* 22 (1997).

– "Socio-cultural evolutionism: an untried theory." *Behavioral Science* 24 (1979).

Boatwright, Mary. *A Brief History of the Romans*. New York: Oxford University Press, 2006.

Boniface, Xavier. "Décorer les militaires (xixe–xxe siècles)." In *La fabrique de l'honneur: les médailles et les décorations en France, xixe–xxe siècles*, edited by Bruno Dumons and Gilles Pollet. Rennes: Presses Universitaires de Rennes, 2009.

Bonnell, Victoria E., and Lynn Hunt. "Introduction." In *Beyond the Cultural Turn: New Directions in the Study of Society and Cutlure*, edited by

Victoria E. Bonnell and Lynn Hunt. Berkeley: University of California Press, 1999.

Boone, Catherine. *Political Topographies of the African State: Territorial Authority and Institutional Choice.* Cambridge: Cambridge University Press, 2003.

Borné, André-Charles. *Distinctions honorifiques de la Belgique, 1830–1985.* Brussels: private, 1985.

Boulton, D'A.J.D. "Crusading orders." Published in part in *Knights in History and in Legend,* edited by Constance Bouchard. Richmond Hill: Firefly Books, 2009.

– "The curial orders of knighthood of the confraternal type: Their changing forms, functions, and values in the eyes of contemporaries, 1325–2005." In *World Orders of Knighthood and Merit,* edited by Guy Stair Sainty and Rafal Heydel-Mankoo. Buckingham: Burke's Peerage & Gentry, 2006.

– "The influence of religious orders on the monarchical orders of knighthood: Ranks, titles and insignia, 1325–1918." *Heraldry in Canada* 32–3 (1998–9).

– *The Knights of the Crown: The Monarchical Orders of Knighthood in Later Medieval Europe, 1325–1520.* Woodbridge: Boydell, 1987.

– "The notion of 'chivalry' as the social code of the later Medieval nobilities: A modern construct and why it should be abandoned." Forthcoming.

Bourdieu, Pierre. *Distinction: A Social Critique of the Judgement of Taste,* translated by Richard Nice. Cambridge: Harvard University Press, 1984.

– *The State Nobility: Elite Schools in the Field of Power,* translated by L.C. Clough. Stanford: Stanford University Press, [1989] 1996.

Boyd, Robert, and P.J. Richerson, *Culture and the Evolutionary Process.* Chicago: University of Chicago Press, 1985.

Brewer, John. *The Sinews of Power: War, Money and the English State, 1688–1783.* Cambridge: Harvard University Press, 1990.

Bruin, Kees. "Distinction and democratization: Royal decorations in the Netherlands." *Sociologia Neerlandica* 23 (1987).

– *Kroon op Het Werk: Onderscheiden in het Koninkrijk der Nederlanden.* Amsterdam: Boom Meppel, 1989.

Bucholz, R.O. *The Augustan Court: Queen Anne and the Decline of Court Culture.* Stanford: Stanford University Press, 1993.

Burch, E.S. *Alliance and Conflict: The World System of the Iñupiaq Eskimos.* Calgary: University of Calgary Press, 2005.

Burke, Peter. *The Fabrication of Louis XIV*. London and Haven: Yale University Press, 1992.

Burns, T.R., and Thomas Dietz, "Cultural evolution: Social rule systems, selection and human agency." *International Sociology* 7 (1992).

Burroughs, Peter. "Crime and punishment in the British army, 1815–1870." *English Historical Review* 100 (1985).

Caille, Frédéric. "Une citoyenneté supérieure; l'improbable 'fonction' des membres de la Légion d'Honneur dans la République." *Revue française de science politique* 47 (1997).

– *La figure du sauveteur: naissance du citoyen secoureur en France 1780–1914*. Rennes: Presses universitaires de Rennes, 2006.

– "Une mémoire fragmenteé: gouvernement collectitif et governement de soi par les décorations (XIXe–XXe siècles)." In *La fabrique de l'honneur: les médailles et les décorations en France, XIXe–XXe siècles*, edited by Bruno Dumons and Gilles Pollet. Rennes: Presses Universitaires de Rennes, 2009.

– "Une société de la distinction: politiques de l'honneur." In *Dictionnaire critique de la République*, edited by Vincent Duclerct and Christophe Prochasson. Forthcoming.

Canepa, M.P. "Technologies of memory in early Sasanian Iran: Achaemenid sites and Sasanian identity." *American Journal of Archaeology* 114 (2010).

Cannadine, David. "The context, performance and meaning of ritual: the British monarchy and the 'invention of tradition,' c. 1820–1977." In *The Invention of Tradition*, edited by Eric Hobsbawm and Terence Ranger. Cambridge: Cambridge University Press, 1983.

– *The Decline and Fall of the British Aristocracy*. London: Picador, 1990.

– *Ornamentalism: How the British Saw Their Empire*. New York: Oxford University Press, 2001.

Cannon, John. *Aristocratic Century: The Peerage of Eighteenth Century England*. Cambridge: Cambridge University Press, 1984.

Caradonna, J.L. *The Enlightenment in Practice: Academic Prize Contests and Intellectual Culture in France, 1670–1794*. Ithaca: Cornell University Press, 2012.

– "The monarchy of virtue: The *prix de vertu* and the economy of emulation in France, 1777–91." *Eighteenth-Century Studies* 41 (2008).

Cardoza, A.L. *Aristocrats in Bourgeois Italy: The Piedmontese Nobility, 1861–1930*. Cambridge: Cambridge University Press, 1997.

Caron, Marie-Thérèse. *Noblesse et pouvoir royal en France: XIIIe–XVIe siècle*. Paris: Arman Colin, 1994.

Carroll, Patrick. *Science, Culture, and Modern State Formation*. Berkeley: University of California Press, 2006.

Carson, R.A.G. *Coins: Ancient, Mediaevel, and Modern.* London: Hutchinson, 1970.

Cecil, Lamar. "The creation of nobles in Prussia, 1871–1918." *American Historical Review* 75 (1970).

Chagniot, Jean. "Les ordres royaux de chevalrie avant la Révolution." *Revue européenne d'histoire des ordres et décorations: la Phalère* no. 1 (2000).

Chaniotis, Angelos. *War in the Hellenistic World.* Oxford: Blackwell, 2005.

Charle, Christophe. *Les haute fonctionnaires en France au XIXe siècle.* Paris: Gallimard/Julliard, 1980.

– *Les intellectuels en Europe au XIXe siècle.* Paris: Seuil, 1996.

– "Le recrutement des hauts fonctionnaires en 1901." *Annales: Economies, Sociétés, Civilisations* no. 2 (March–April 1980).

– *A Social History of France in the Nineteenth Century,* translated by Miriam Kochan. Oxford: Berg, 1994.

Charrad, Mounira. *States and Women's Rights: The Making of Postcolonial Tunisia, Algeria, and Morocco.* Berkeley: University of California Press, 2001.

Charrad, Mounira, and Julia Adams. "Patrimonialism, past and present." *Annals of the Academy of Political and Social Science* 636 (2011).

Chase-Dunn, Christopher, and T.D. Hall. *Rise and Demise: Comparing World-Systems.* Boulder: Westview, 1997.

Chattaway, Carol M. *The Order of the Golden Tree: The Gift-Giving Objectives of Duke Philip the Bold of Burgundy.* Turnhout: Brepols, 2006.

Chaurasia, Radley. *History of Ancient India.* New Delhi: Atlantic, 2008.

Childs, John. *The Army, James II, and the Glorious Revolution.* New York: St Martin's Press, 1980.

Ch'ü, T'ung-tsu, *Han Social Structure,* edited by J.L. Dull. Seattle: University of Washington Press, 1972.

Chwe, Michael Suk-Young. *Rational Ritual: Culture, Coordination, and Common Knowledge.* Princeton: Princeton University Press, 2001.

Clark, Anna. *Scandal: The Sexual Politics of the British Constitution.* Princeton: Princeton University Press 2004.

Clark, C. Robert, Samuel Clark, and Mattias Polborn. "Co-ordination and status influence." *Rationality and Society* 18 (2006).

Clark, Peter. *British Clubs and Societies, 1580–1800: The Origins of an Associational World.* New York: Oxford University Press, 2000.

Clark, Priscilla P., and T.N. Clark. "Patrons, publishers, and prizes: The writer's estate in France." In *Culture and Its Creators: Essays in Honor of Edward Shils.* Chicago: University of Chicago Press, 1975.

Clark, Samuel. "Human intentionality in the functionalist theory of social change: The role of French provincial intendants in state-society differentiation." *Archives européenes de sociologie/ European Journal of Sociology/ Europäisches archiv für soziologie* 46 (2005).

– "Nobility, bourgeoisie and the industrial revolution in Belgium." *Past and Present* no. 105 (1984).

– *State and Status: The Rise of the State and Aristocratic Power in Western Europe.* Montreal and Kingston: McGill-Queen's University Press, 1995.

Colley, Linda. *Britons: Forging the Nation.* New Haven: Yale University Press, 1992.

Collier, David, Jody LaPorte, and Jason Seawright. "Putting typologies to work: Concept formation, measurement, and analytic rigor." *Political Research Quarterly* 65 (2012).

Collins, J.B. *The State in Early Modern France.* Cambridge: Cambridge University Press, 1995.

Coninckx, J.L. "De sociaal-politieke samenstelling van de Belgische Kamer van Volksvertegenwoordigers (8 augustus 1870–15 mei 1880)." *Revue belge d'histoire contemporaine* 17 (1986).

Cook, E.T. *The Life of Florence Nightingale.* London: Macmillan, 1913.

Cookson, J.E. "Regimental worlds: Interpreting the experience of British soldiers during the Napoleonic Wars." In *Soldiers, Citizens and Civilians: Experiences and Perceptions of the Revolutionary and Napoleonic Wars, 1790–1820*, edited by Alan Forrest, Karen Hagemann, and Jane Rendall. Houndmills: Palgrave, 2009.

Corfield, Penelope J. *Power and the Professions in Britain, 1700–1850.* London: Routledge, 1995.

– "The rivals: Landed and other gentlemen." In *Land and Society in Britain, 1700–1914: Essays in Honour of F.M.L. Thompson,* edited by Negley Harte and Roland Quinault. Manchester: Manchester University Press, 1996.

Cormier, Jeffery, and Phillipe Couton. "Civil society, mobilization, and communal violence: Quebec and Ireland, 1890–1920." *Sociological Quarterly* 45 (2004).

Coss, P.R. "The formation of the English gentry." *Past and Present* no. 147 (1995).

Cox, E.L. *The Green Count of Savoy: Amadeus VI and Transalpine Savoy in the Fourteenth Century.* Princeton: Princeton University Press, 1967.

Crane, Diana. *Fashion and Its Social Agendas: Class, Gender, and Identity in Clothing.* Chicago: University of Chicago Press, 2000.

Crook, M.J. *The Evolution of the Victoria Cross: A Study in Administrative History.* Tunbridge Wells: Midas, 1975.

Cubells, Monique. "La politique d'anoblissement de la monarchie en Provence de 1715 à 1789." *Annales du Midi* 94 (1982).

Cunnally, John. "Of Mauss and (Renaissance) men: Numismatics, prestation, and the genesis of visual literacy." In *The Rebirth of Antiquity: Numismatics, Archeology, and Classical Studies in the Culture of the Renaissance*, edited by A.M. Stahl. Princeton: Princeton University Library, 2009.

Curtis, Bruce. *The Politics of Population: State Formation, Statistics, and the Census of Canada, 1840–1875.* Toronto: University of Toronto Press, 2001.

Cusas, Eric. *Le statut de la noblesse en France et en Belgique: précis de législation nobiliaire et héraldique.* Brussels: Bruylant, 1997.

Dahmen, Karsten. "Alexander in gold and silver." *American Journal of Numismatics* 30 (2008).

Damien, André. "La Légion d'honneur face aux nouvelles décorations des XIXe et XXe siècles." In *La Légion d'honneur: deux siècles d'histoire*, edited by Jean Tulard, François Monnier, and Olivier Echappé. Paris: Perrin, 2004.

Dansette, Adrien. *L'affaire Wilson et la chute du Président Grévy.* Paris: Perrin, 1936.

– "L'évolution des structures sociales en France à l'époque de l'industrialisation (1815–1914)." *Revue historique* 167 (1972).

Davidson, Arthur F. *Alexandre Dumas (pere): His Life and Works.* Westminster: Archibald Constable & Co., 1902.

Davies, R.R. *Domination and Conquest: The Experience of Ireland, Scotland, and Wales 1100–1300.* Cambridge: Cambridge University Press, 1990.

Davis, Natalie Z. *The Gift in Sixteenth-Century France.* Madison: University of Wisconsin Press, 2000.

Davis, R.W. "Disraeli, the Rothschilds, and anti-Semitism." *Jewish History* 10 (1996).

Dean, Mitchell. *Governmentality: Power and Rule in Modern Society.* London: Sage, 1999.

De Botton, Alain. *Status Anxiety.* Toronto: Viking, 2004.

De Belder, Joseph. "Adel en burgerij, 1840–1914." In *Algemene geschiedenis der Nederlanden*, vol. 12. Haarlem: Fibula-Van Dishoeck, 1977.

de Ghellinck Vaernewyck, Xavier. "Les titres de l'empire français au point de vue nobiliaire belge." *Recueil de l'office généalogique et héraldique de Belgique* 2 (1952).

Denis, Michel. "Reconquête ou défensive: les stratégies de la noblesse de l'ouest au XIXe siècle." In *Noblesse française: noblesse hongroise, XVIe–XIXe siècles.* Paris: CNRS, 1981.

Deutsch, K.W. "Social mobilization and political development." *American Political Science Review* 55 (1971).

DeVries, Kelly. *Infantry Warfare in the Early Fourteenth Century: Discipline, Tactics, and Technology*. Woodbridge: Boydell, 1996.

Dewald, Jonathan, *Aristocratic Experience and the Origins of Modern Culture: France, 1570–1715*. Berkeley: University of California, 1993.

– "Social groups and cultural practices." In *Renaissance and Reformation France, 1500–1648*, edited by M.P. Holt. Oxford: Oxford University Press, 2002.

Dixon, Karen, and Pat Southern. *Roman Cavalry: From the First to the Third Century AD*. London: Batsford, 1992.

Do, Phuong-Thao. "Aux prises avec les prix: les du Femina." PhD dissertation, University of Western Ontario, 1998.

Dorling, H.T. *Ribbons and Medals: The World's Military and Civil Awards*, edited by F.K. Mason. Garden City: Doubleday, 1974.

Downing, B.M. *The Military Revolution and Political Change: Origins of Democracy and Autocracy in Early Modern Europe*. Princeton: Princeton University Press, 1992.

Dreyfus, Michel. "Médailles mutualistes." In *La fabrique de l'honneur: les médailles et les décorations en France, XIXe–XXe siècles*. Rennes: Presses Universitaires de Rennes, 2009.

Drijvers, Jan Willem. "A Roman image of the 'Barbarian' Sasanians." In *Romans, Barbarians, and the Transformation of the Roman World: Cultural Interaction and the Creation of Identity in Late Antiquity*, edited by R.W. Mathisen and Danuta R. Shanzer. Burlington: Ashgate, 1998.

Duby, Georges. *The Chivalrous Society*. Berkeley: University of California Press, 1977.

Ducourtial, Claude. *Ordres et décorations*. Paris: PUF, 1957.

Ducourtial, Claude, and Louis Bonneville de Marsangy. *La Légion d'Honneur*. Paris: Charles-Lavauzelle, 1982.

Dudley, L.M. "Space, time, number: Harold A. Innis as evolutionary theorist." *Canadian Journal of Economics* 28/4a (1995).

– *The Word and the Sword: How Techniques of Information and Violence Have Shaped Our World*. Cambridge, MA: Basil Blackwell, 1991.

Duff, David. *Romance and Revolution: Shelley and the Politics of a Genre*. Cambridge: Cambridge University Press, 1994.

Dumons, Bruno. *Les "Saints de la République": les décorés de la Légion d'honneur (1870–1940)*. Paris: Boutique d'histoire, 2009.

Dumons, Bruno, and Gilles Pollet. "Une distinction républicaine: les médailles du travail au tournant des XIXe et XXe siècles: éclairage sur le modèle républicain de la citoyenneté." In *Cultures et folklores républicains*, edited by Maurice Agulhon. Paris: CTHS, 1995.

Dumons, Bruno, and Gilles Pollet, eds. *La fabrique de l'honneur: les médailles et les décorations en France, XIXe–XXe siècles*. Rennes: Presses Universitaires de Rennes, 2009.

Dupret, Baudouin, ed. *Standing Trial: Law and the Person in the Modern Middle East*. London: Tauris, 2004.

Durham, W.H. *Coevolution: Genes, Culture, and Human Diversity*. Stanford: Stanford University Press, 1991.

Durieux, Joseph. *Etude sur l'action disciplinaire de la Légion d'Honneur*. Paris: A. Rousseau, 1900.

Durye, Pierre. *La généalogie*. Paris: PUF, 1963

Echappé, Olivier. "La légion d'honneur: ses statuts, son statut." In *La Légion d'honneur: deux siècles d'histoire*. Paris: Perrin, 2004.

Eckert, C.J., Ki-baik Lee, Y.I. Lew, Michael Robinson, and E.W. Wagner. *Korea Old and New: A History*. Seoul: Ilchokak, 1990.

Eckstein, A.M. *Mediterranean Anarchy, Interstate War, and the Rise of Rome*. Berkeley: University of California Press, 2006.

Elias, Norbert. *The Civilizing Process: Sociogenetic and Psychogenetic Investigations*, translated by Edmund Jephcott. Revised edition edited by Eric Dunning, Johan Goudsblom, and Stephen Mennell. Oxford: Blackwell Publishers, [1939] 2000.

– *The Court Society*, translated by Edmund Jephcott. Oxford: Basil Blackwell, 1983.

Elman, Colin. "Explanatory typologies in qualitative studies of international politics." *International Organization* 59 (2005).

English, J.F. *The Economy of Prestige: Prizes, Awards, and the Circulation of Cultural Value*. Cambridge: Harvard University Press, 2005.

Erlanger, H.J. *Origin and Development of the European Prize Medal to the End of the Eighteenth Century*. Haarlem: Schuyt, 1975.

Ermakoff, Ivan. *Ruling Oneself Out: A Theory of Collective Abdications*. Durham: Duke University Press, 2008.

Ertman, Thomas. *Birth of the Leviathan: Building States and Regimes in Medieval and Early Modern Europe*. New York: Cambridge University Press, 1997.

Estèbe, Jean. *Les ministres de la République, 1871–1914*. Paris: Fondation des sciences Politiques, 1982.

Fagan, G.G., and Matthew Trundle. "Introduction." In *New Perspectives on Ancient Warfare*, edited by G.G. Fagan and Mathew Trundle. Leiden: Brill, 2010.

Falcimaige, Charles. *La Discipline de la Légion d'Honneur*. Paris: Librairie générale de droit de jurisprudence, 1929.

Ferguson, Niall. *The House of Rothschild: The World's Banker, 1849–1999*. New York: Penguin, 1998.

Fergusson, James. *The Sixteen Peers of Scotland: An Account of the Elections of the Representative Peers of Scotland, 1707–1959*. Oxford: Clarendon, 1960.

Foord, A.S. "The waning of 'the influence of the crown.'" *English Historical Review* 62 (1947).

Forrest, Alan. *Conscripts and Deserters: The Army and French Society during the Revolution and Empire*. New York: Oxford University Press, 1989.

– *Napoleon's Men: The Soldiers of the Revolution and Empire*. London: Hambledon and London, 2002.

– "*La patrie en danger*. The French Revolution and the first *Levée en masse*." In *The People in Arms: Military Myth and National Mobilization since the French Revolution*, edited by Daniel Moran and Arthur Waldron. Cambridge: Cambridge University Press, 2003.

Forrester, D.A.R. "Rational administration, finance and control of accounting: The experience of cameralism." *Critical Perspectives on Accounting* 1 (1990).

Foucault, Michel. *Discipline and Punish: The Birth of the Prison*, translated by Alan Sheridan. New York: Vintage, [1975] 1979.

– "Politics and reason." In *Politics, Philosophy, Culture: Interviews and Other Writings, 1977–1984*, translated by Alan Sheridan et al. and edited by L.D. Kritzman. New York: Routledge, 1988.

– "The subject and power." In *Michel Foucault: Beyond Structuralism and Hermeneutics*, edited by H.L. Drefus and Paul Robinow. Chicago: University of Chicago Press, 1982.

Fourez, Lucien. "De la nécessité d'anoblissement pour le maintien d'une noblesse nationale." *Recueil d'Office Génealogique et Héraldique de Belgique* 9 (1959).

Fox, E.W. "The argument: some refinements and projections." In *Geographic Perspectives in History*, edited by E.D. Genovese and L.J. Hochberg. Oxford: Basil Blackwell, 1989.

– *History in Geographic Perspective: The Other France*. New York: Norton, 1971.

François, Luc. "Intellectuelen en revolutionaire bedrijvigheid: een elitewijziging? Casus: de Oostvlaamse advokaten van 1830." *Revue belge d'histoire contemporaine* 12 (1981).

Frank, R.H. *Choosing the Right Pond: Human Behavior and the Quest for Status*. New York: Oxford University Press, 1985.

Frank, R.H., and P.J. Cook. *The Winner-Take-All Society: Why the Few at the Top Get So Much More Than the Rest of Us.* New York: Penguin, 1995.

Frevert, Ute. "Honour and middle-class culture: The history of the duel in England and Germany." In *Bourgeois Society in Nineteenth-Century Europe,* edited by Jürgen Kocka and Allan Mitchell. Oxford: Berg, 1993.

Frey, B.S. "Knight fever: towards an economics of awards." Institute of Empirical Research in Economics, University of Zurich, Working Paper 239 (2005)

Frotier de la Messelière, Henri. *La noblesse en Bretagne avant 1789.* Rennes: Université de Rennes, 1902.

Galloway, Peter. *Companions of Honour.* London: Chancery Publications, 2002.

– *The Most Illustrious Order: The Order of St Patrick and its Knights.* London: Unicorn, 1999.

– *The Most Illustrious Order of St Patrick, 1783–1983.* Chichester: Phillimore, 1983.

– *The Order of the Bath.* Chichester: Phillimore, 2006.

– *The Order of the British Empire.* London: Central Chancery of the Orders of Knighthood, 1996

– *The Order of St Michael and St George.* London: Order of St Michael and St George, 2001.

– *The Order of the Thistle.* London: Spink, 2009.

– "The Royal Victorian Order." In *Royal Service,* vol. 1. London: Victorian Publishing, 1996.

Galvin, John R. *The History of the Order of Malta.* Dublin: Irish Association of the Order of Malta 1977.

Garrett, Valery M. *Chinese Dress: From the Qing Dynasty to the Present.* Tokyo: Tuttle Publishing, 2007.

Garside, P.D. "Scott, the romantic past and the nineteenth century." *Review of English Studies,* new series 23 (1972).

Gernet, Jacques. *A History of Chinese Civilization.* 2nd ed. Cambridge: Cambridge University Press, 1996.

Geschiedenis van het Belgisch leger van 1830 tot heden. Brussels: Centrum voor Historische Dokumentatie van de Krijgsmacht, 1982.

Girard, Louis, et al. *La Chambre des Députés en 1837–1839.* Paris: Sorbonne, 1976.

Girouard, Mark. *The Return to Camelot: Chivalry and the English Gentleman.* London: Yale University Press, 1981.

Goertz, Gary, and James Mahoney. *A Tale of Two Cultures: Qualitative and Quantitative Research in the Social Sciences.* Princeton: Princeton University Press, 2012.

Goldstein, R.J. "Fighting French censorship, 1815–1881." *French Review* 71 (1998).

Gommans, Jos. "Warhorse and gunpowder in India: c. 1000–1850." In *War in the Early Modern World: 1450–1815*, edited by Jeremy Black. London: Routledge, 1999.

González de León, Fernando. *The Road to Rocroi: Class, Culture and Command in the Spanish Army of Flanders, 1567–1659*. Leiden: Brill, 2009.

Goode, William J. *The Celebration of Heroes: Prestige as a Social Control System*. Berkeley: University of California Press, 1978.

Gordon, Stewart. "Robes of honour: a 'transactional' kingly ceremony." *Indian Economic and Social History Review* 33 (1996).

Gorski, P.S. *The Disciplinary Revolution: Calvinism and the Rise of the State in Early Modern Europe*. Chicago: University of Chicago Press, 2003.

– "The Protestant ethic and the spirit of bureaucracy." *American Sociological Review* 60 (1995).

– "The Protestant ethic revisited: disciplinary revolution and state formation in Holland and Prussia." *American Journal of Sociology* 99 (1993).

Gower, Ronald. *My Reminiscences*. New York: Charles Scribner's Sons, 1884.

Gray, Marion W. *Prussia in Transition: Society and Politics under the Stein Reform Ministry of 1808*. Philadelphia: American Philosophical Society, 1986.

Greefs, H. "Ondernemers en de genootschappen: een onderzoek naar het gezelschapsleven te Antwerpen tussen 1796–1830." *Bijdragen tot de geschiedenis bijzonderliyk van het aloude Hertogdam Brabant* 75 (1992).

Grierson, Philip. *Numismatics*. London: Oxford University Press, 1975.

Guillemin, Alain. "Patrimonie foncier et pouvoir nobiliaire: la noblesse de la Manche sous la Monarchie de Juillet." *Etudes Rurales* nos. 63–4 (1976).

Guttsman, W.L. *The British Political Elite*. London: MacGibbon & Kee, 1968.

Habermas, Jürgen. *The Structural Transformation of the Public Sphere: An Inquiry into a Category of Bourgeois Society*. Cambridge: MIT Press, [1962] 1989.

Hamel, Debra. *Athenian Generals: Military Authority in the Classical Period*. Leiden: Brill, 1998.

Hamilton, C.I. "Naval hagiography and the Victorian hero." *Historical Journal* 23 (1980).

Hamoir, *Qualité princière et dignités nobiliaires: essai comparatif sur les distinctions de dignités au sein du second ordre dans divers pays.* Brussels: Librairie Encyclopédique, 1974.

Hanham, H.J. "The sale of honours in late Victorian England." *Victorian Studies* 3 (1960).

Hanson, Victor Davis. *Hoplites: The Classical Greek Battle Experience.* London: Routledge, 1991.

Harper, P.O. *In Search of Cultural Identity: Monuments and Artifacts of the Sasanian Near East, 3rd to 7th Century AD.* New York: Bibliotheca Persia, 2006.

Harris, David. "European liberalism in the nineteenth century." *American Historical Review* 60 (1955).

Harrison, Carol E. *The Bourgeois Citizen in Nineteenth-Century France: Gender, Sociability, and the Uses of Emulation.* New York: Oxford University Press, 1999.

Hayden, Ilse. *Symbol and Privilege: The Ritual Context of British Royalty.* Tucson: University of Arizona Press, 1987.

Hazareesingh, Sudhir. "Une déférence d'état: les médailles de Sainte-Hélène sous le Seconde Empire." *Genèses* 55 (2004).

– *The Saint-Napoleon: Celebrations of Sovereignty in Nineteenth-Century France.* Cambridge: Harvard University Press, 2004.

Herman, C.W. "Knights and kings in early modern France: Royal orders of knighthood, 1469–1715." PhD dissertation, University of Minnesota 1990.

Hibbert, Christopher. *Edward VII: A Portrait.* London: Allen Lane, 1976.

Higgs, David. "Politics and landownership among the French nobility after the Revolution." *European Studies Review* 1 (1971).

Higgs, Edward. *The Information State in England: The Central Collection of Information on Citizens since 1500.* London: Palgrave Macmillan, 2004.

Hill, George. *Medals of the Renaissance,* revised and enlarged by Graham Pollard. London: Colonnade, [1920] 1978.

Hobsbawm, Eric. *The Age of Capital, 1848–1875.* New York: Mentor, 1975.

Hofstede, Geert. *Culture's Consequences: Comparing Values, Behaviors, Institutions, and Organizations Across Nations.* 2nd ed. London: Sage, 2001.

Holt, F.L. *Alexander the Great and the Mystery of the Elephant Medallions.* Berkeley: University of California Press, 2003.

Homans, George. *The Human Group.* New York: Harcourt, Brace, 1950.

– *Social Behavior: Its Elementary Forms.* New York: Harcourt, Brace & World, 1961.

Hopcroft, Rosemary L. *Sociology: A Biosocial Introduction.* Boulder: Paradigm, 2010.

Howell, D.W. *The Rural Poor in Eighteenth-Century Wales.* Cardiff: University of Wales Press, 2000.

Hucker, C.O. *A Dictionary of Official Titles in Imperial China.* Stanford: Stanford University Press, 1985.

Hudemann-Simon, Calixte. *La noblesse Luxembourgeoise au XVIIIe siècle.* L'Institut Grand-Ducal and La Sorbonne, 1985.

Hudson, Elizabeth H. *The Life and Times of Louisa, Queen of Prussia, with an Introductory Sketch of Prussian History,* vol. 2. London: Isbister, 1874.

Hughes, Lindsey. *Russia in the Age of Peter the Great.* New Haven: Yale University Press, 1998.

Hunter, Michael. *Elias Ashmole, 1617–1692: The Founder of the Ashmolean Museum and his World: A Tercentenary Exhibition.* Oxford: Ashmolean Museum, 1983.

Hyams, P.R. *Lords and Peasants in Medieval England: The Common Law of Villeinage in the Twelfth and Thirteenth Centuries.* Oxford: Clarendon Press, 1980.

Ihl, Olivier. "Emulation through decoration: A science of government." In *The Jacobin Legacy in Modern France: Essays in Honour of Vincent Wright,* edited by Sudhir Hazareesingh. Oxford: Oxford University Press, 2002.

– "Gouverner par les honneurs: distinctions honorifiques et économie politique dans l'Europe du début du XIXe siècle." *Genèses* 55 (2004).

– *Le mérite et la République: Essai sur la société des émules.* Paris: Gallimard, 2007.

Innis, H.A. "The bias of communication." *Canadian Journal of Economics and Political Science* 15/4 (1949).

– *Empire and Communications.* Oxford: Clarendon, 1950.

Irvine, William. *The Army of the Indian Moghuls: Its Organization and Administration.* New Delhi: Eurasia, 1962.

Janssens, Paul. "Chefs d'entreprise et aristocrates belges aux XIXe et XXe siècles." In *De lokroep van het bedrijf: handelaars, ondernemers en hun samenleving van de zestiende tot de twintigste eeuw: liber amicorum Roland Baetens,* edited by Greta Devos. Antwerp: *Universitaire Faculteiten Sint-Ignatius Antwerpen,* 2001.

– "Het lot van de Belgische adel in de revolutiejaren 1789–1799." *De achttiende eeuw* 28 (1996).

– "De politieke invloed van de adel in het Koninkrijk der Nederlanden." In *Staats- en natievorming in Willem I's koninkrijk, 1815–1830,* edited by C.A. Tamse and E. Witte. Brussels: VUBPRESS, 1992.

Jasso, Guillermina. "Studying status: an integrated framework." *American Sociological Review* 66 (2001).

Jenkins, T.A. "The funding of the Liberal Unionist Party and the honours system." *English Historical Review* 105/417 (1990).

Jones, G.G. "The Order of the Golden Fleece: Form, function, and evolution, 1430–1555." PhD dissertation, Texas Christian University, 1988.

Jordan, Borimir. "The honors for Themistocles after Salamis." *American Journal of Philology* 109/4 (Winter, 1988).

Jordan, Gerald, and Nicholas Rogers. "Admirals as heroes: Patriotism and liberty in Hanoverian England." *Journal of British Studies* 28 (1989).

Joshi, Hargovind. *Defence Administration in India*, vol. 1: *Ancient India*. New Delhi: Akansha, 2002.

Jouanna, Arlette. "L'honneur perdu de la noblesse." *L'histoire* no. 73 (1984).

– "Perception et appreciation de l'anoblissement dans la France du xvie siècle at du début du xviie siècle." In *L'anoblissement en France xvème–xviiième siècles: Théories et réalités*, edited by Bernard Guillemain. Bordeaux: Université de Bordeaux III 1985.

Kaudelka-Hanisch, Karin. "The titled businessman: Prussian commercial councillors in the Rhineland and Westphalia during the nineteenth century." In *The German Bourgeoisie: Essays on the Social History of the German Middle Class from the late Eighteenth Century to the Early Twentieth Century*, edited by David Blackbourn and R.J. Evans. New York: Routledge, 1991.

Keen, Maurice. *Chivalry*. New Haven: Yale University Press, 1984.

Kelly, Christopher. *Rousseau as Author: Consecrating One's Life to the Truth*. Chicago: University of Chicago Press, 2003.

Kennedy, Michael. *Portrait of Elgar*, 2nd edition. London: Oxford University Press, 1982.

Keohane, N.O. *Philosophy and the State in France: The Renaissance to the Enlightenment*. Princeton: Princeton University Press, 1980.

Kerautret, Michel. "Les ordres et décorations de la Prusse: Aigle noir, Pour le méite et croix de fer." *Revue européenne d'histoire des ordres et décorations: La Phalère* no. 2 (2001).

Kim, Youna. "Female individualization? Transnational mobility and media consumption of Asian women." *Media, Culture & Society* 32 (2010).

Kinietz, W.V. *The Indians of the Western Great Lakes, 1615–1760*. Ann Arbor: University of Michigan, 1965.

Kinokuniya, *Decorations of Japan*. Tokyo: Shōkunkyoku, 1965.

Kipnis, A.B., ed. *Chinese Modernity and the Individual Psyche*. New York: Palgrave, 2012.

Klapp, Orrin E. "Heroes, villains and fools, as agents of social control." *American Sociological Review* 19 (1954).

Kocka, Jürgen. "The European pattern and the German case." In *Bourgeois Society in Nineteenth-Century Europe*, edited by Jürgen Kocka and Allan Mitchell. Oxford: Berg, 1993.

– *Industrial Culture and Bourgeois Society: Business, Labor, and Bureaucracy in Modern Germany, 1800–1918*. New York: Berghahn, 1999.

– "The middle classes in Europe." *Journal of Modern History* 67 (1995).

Koester, A. "The gold medals of Abukir." *Burlington Magazine for Connoisseurs* 11/51 (1907).

Kollock, Peter. "Social dilemmas: the anatomy of cooperation." *Annual Review of Sociology* 24 (1998).

Kristol, Irving, and Max Beloff. "Of lords, sirs, and plain misters: An exchange between Irving Kristol and Max Beloff." *Encounter* 69 (1987).

Kuhn, W.M. *Democratic Royalism: The Transformation of the British Monarchy, 1861–1914*. Houndmills: MacMillan, 1996.

– *Henry and Mary Ponsonby: Life at the Court of Queen Victoria*. London: Duckworth, 2002.

Kulshrestha, Mahendra. *Culture India: Philosophy, Religion, Arts, Literature, Society*. Chichester: Lotus 2007.

Kurzman, Charles, et al. "Celebrity status." *Sociological Theory* 5 (2007).

Kyle, D.G. *Sport and Spectacle in the Ancient World*. Malden: Blackwell, 2007.

Lachman, Richard. *Capitalists in Spite of Themselves: Elite Conflict and Economic Transitions in Early Modern Europe*. New York: Oxford University Press, 2000.

Landa, Diego de. *Papers of the Peabody Museum of American Archaeology and Ethnology, Harvard University*, vol. 28: *Landa's Relación de las Cosas de Yucatan*, edited by A.M. Tozzer. Cambridge: Peabody Museum, 1941.

Lane, George. *Daily Life in the Mongol Empire*. Westport: Greenwoold Press, 2006.

Lang, Andrew. "Editor's introduction to *Ivanhoe*." In *Ivanhoe*, by Walter Scott. London: Macmillan, 1900.

Langton, John. "Darwinism and the behavioral theory of socio-cultural evolution: an analysis." *American Journal of Sociology* 85 (1979).

Laureyssens, Julienne. "De Société Générale." *Spiegel Historiael* 7 (1972).

– "Willem I, de Société Générale en het economisch beleid." In *Staats- en natievorming in Willem I's koninkrijk, 1815–1830*, edited by C.A. Tamse and E. Witte. Brussels: VUBPRESS, 1992.

Lee, Colin. "Nicolas, Sir Nicholas Harris (1799–1848)." In *Oxford Dictionary of National Biography*. Oxford: Oxford University Press, 2004.

Lee, Sidney. *King Edward VII: A Biography*, vol. 1: *From Birth to Accession 9th November 1841 to 22nd January 1901*. London: Macmillan, 1925.

Leerssen, Joep. "Wildness, wilderness, and Ireland: Medieval and Early-Modern patterns in the demarcation of civility." *Journal of the History of Ideas* 56 (1995).

Le Vavasseur de Précourt, Octave. "Legion d'Honneur et Médaille Militaire." *Revue critique de législation et jurisprudence* 6 (1877).

Levy, Avigdor. "Military reform and the problem of centralization in the Ottoman Empire in the eighteenth century." *Middle Eastern Studies* vol. 18/3 (Jul., 1982).

Lewis, M.E. *The Early Chinese Empires: Qin and Han*. Cambridge: Harvard University Press, 2007.

– "Gift circulation and charity in the Han and Roman Empires." In *Rome and China: Comparative Perspectives on Ancient World Empires*, edited by Walter Scheidel. Oxford: Oxford University Press, 2009.

L'Hoist, André. *De la Toison d'Or à l'Ordre de Léopold II*. Brussels: Association de l'Ordre de Léopold, 1939.

Lieven, Dominic. *The Aristocracy in Europe, 1815–1914*. New York: Columbia University Press, 1992.

Lin, Patricia Y.C.E. "Caring for the nation's families: British soldiers' and sailors' families and the state, 1793–1815." In *Soldiers, Citizens and Civilians: Experiences and Perceptions of the Revolutionary and Napoleonic Wars, 1790–1820*, edited by Alan Forrest, Karen Hagemann, and Jane Rendall. Houndmills: Palgrave, 2009.

Llewellyn-Jones, Lloyd. *King and Court in Ancient Persia: 559 to 331 BCE*, Edinburgh: University of Edinburgh Press, 2013.

Lloyd, Christopher. *Lord Cochrane: Seaman-Radical-Liberator*. London: Longmans, Green, 1947.

Lococo, Paul. "The Qing Empire." In *A Military History of China*, edited by D.A. Graff and R.D.S. Higham. Boulder, CO: Westview, 2002.

Lovell, C.R. "The trial of peers in Great Britain." *American Historical Review* 55 (1949).

Lucas, J.A. "Baron Pierre de Coubertin and the formative years of the modern international Olympic movement." Unpublished Doctor of Education thesis, University of Maryland, 1962.

Lukes, Steven. *Individualism*. Oxford: Basil Blackwell, 1973.

Lynn, J.A. "The growth of the French army during the seventeenth century." *Armed Forces and Society* 6 (1980).

– "The pattern of army growth, 1445–1945." In *Tools of War: Instruments, Ideas, and Institutions of Warfare, 1445–1871*, edited by J.A. Lynn. Chicago: University of Illinois Press, 1990.

Lytwyn, V.P. *Muskekowuck Athinuwick: Original People of the Great Swampy Land.* Winnipeg: University of Manitoba Press, 2002.

McCahill, M.W. *Order and Equipose: The Peerage and the House of Lords, 1783–1806.* London: Royal Historical Society, 1978.

– "Peerage creations and the changing character of the British nobility, 1750–1850." *English Historical Review* 96 (1981).

McClellan, J.E. *Science Reorganized: Scientific Societies in the Eighteenth Century.* New York: Columbia University Press, 1985.

McCreery, Christopher. *The Canadian Honours System.* Toronto: Dunburn, 2005.

– *The Order of Canada: Its Origins, History, and Development.* Toronto: University of Toronto Press, 2005.

McEwan, G.F. *The Incas: New Perspectives.* Santa Barbara: ABC-CLIO, 2006.

MacMullen, Ramsay. "How big was the Roman army?" *Klio* 62 (1980).

Macy, M.W. "Learning to cooperate: stochastic and tacit collusion in social exchange." *American Journal of Sociology* 97 (1991).

Macy, M.W., and Andreas Flache. "Beyond rationality in models of choice." *Annual Review of Sociology* 21 (1995).

Mahoney, James. *The Legacies of Liberalism: Path Dependence and Political Regimes in Central America.* Baltimore: Johns Hopkins University Press, 2001.

Mann, Michael. *The Sources of Social Power*, vol. 1: *A History of Power from the Beginning to AD 1760.* Cambridge: Cambridge University Press, 1986.

– *The Sources of Social Power*, vol. 2: *The Rise of Classes and Nation-States.* Cambridge: Cambridge University Press, 1993.

Manning, R.B. *An Apprenticeship in Arms: The Origins of the British Army, 1585–1702.* Oxford: Oxford University Press, 2006.

– "Justifications and explanations of war." Unpublished manuscript.

– *Swordsmen: The Martial Ethos in the Three Kingdoms.* Oxford: Oxford University Press, 2003.

– *War and Peace in the Western Political Imagination from Classical Antiquity to the Age of Reason.* Forthcoming.

Martin, John. "Inventing sincerity, refashioning prudence: the discovery of the individual in Renaissance Europe." *American Historical Review* 102 (1997).

Martin, Stanley. *The Order of Merit: One Hundred Years of Matchless Honour.* London: Taurus, 2007.

– "The Royal Victorian Chain." In *Royal Service*, vol. 1, edited by Peter Galloway et al. London: Victorian Publishing, 1996.

Massian, Michel. *La médaille militaire*. Paris: Charles Lavauzelle, [1976] 1992.

Matikkala, Antti. *The Orders of Knighthood and the Formation of the British Honour System, 1660–1760*. Woodbridge: Boydell, 2008.

Maxfield, Valerie A. *The Military Decorations of the Roman Army*. London: Batsford, 1981.

May, Timothy. *The Mongol Art of War: Chinggis Khan and the Mongol Military System*. Yardley: Westholme, 2007.

Mayer, A.J. *The Persistence of the Old Regime: Europe to the Great War*. New York: Pantheon, 1981.

Maza, Sarah. *The Myth of the French Bourgeoisie*. Cambridge: Harvard University Press, 2003.

Mazas, Alex. *Histoire de l'Ordre royal et militaire de Saint-Louis, depuis son institution en 1695 jusqu'en 1830*, completed by Anne Théodore. 2nd ed. Paris: Firmin Didot, 1860.

Mericka, Václav. *Orden und ehrenzeichen der österreichisch-ungarischen monarchie*. Wien und München: Verlag Anton Schroll & Co., 1974.

Miller, Joan G. "Culture and the development of everyday social explanations." *Journal of Personality and Social Psychology* 46 (1984).

Milner, Murray, Jr. *Status and Sacredness: A General Theory of Status Relations and an Analysis of Indian Culture*. New York: Oxford University Press, 1994.

Modelski, George. *World Cities: -3000 to 2000*. Washington: Faros, 2000.

Moon, Rennie J., and Jeong-Woo Koo. "Global citizenship and human rights: A longitudinal analysis of social studies and ethics textbooks in the Republic of Korea." *Comparative Education Review* 55/4 (2011).

Moore, Barrington. *Social Origins of Dictatorship and Democracy: Lord and Peasant in the Making of the Modern World*. Boston: Beacon, 1966.

Moosvi, Shireen. "The evolution of the 'mansab' system under Akbar until 1596–7." *Journal of the Royal Asiatic Society of Great Britain and Ireland* no. 2 (1981).

Morgan, David. *The Mongols*. Oxford: Blackwell, 1986.

Morrison, Bruce. "Channeling the 'Restless spirit of innovation': Elite concessions and institutional change in the British Reform Act of 1832." *World Politics* 63 (2011).

Mosse, W.E. "Bureaucracy and nobility in Russia at the end of the nineteenth century." *Historical Journal* 24 (1981).

Mukerji, Chandra. *Territorial Ambitions and the Gardens of Versailles.* Cambridge: Cambridge University Press, 1997.

Myerly, S.H. *British Military Spectacle: From the Napoleonic Wars through Crimea.* Cambridge: Harvard University Press, 1996.

Neiberg, Michael. *Warfare in World History.* London: Routledge 2001.

Neuschel, Kristen B. *Word of Honor: Interpreting Noble Culture in Sixteenth-Century France.* Ithaca: Cornell University Press, 1989.

Neville, D.G. *Medal Ribbons & Orders of Imperial Germany and Austria.* St Ives: Balfour, 1974.

Nicolas, Sir Nicholas Harris. *History of the Orders of Knighthood of the British Empire; of the Order of the Guelphs of Hanover; and of the Medals, Clasps, and Crosses, Conferred for Naval and Military Services,* 4 vols. London: Hunter, 1842.

Nimwegen, Olaf van. *The Dutch Army and the Military Revolutions, 1588–1688.* Woodbridge, 2010.

Nousek, Debra L. "Turning points in Roman history: The case of Caesar's elephant denarius." *Phoenix* 62 (2008).

O'Boyle, Lenore. "The middle class in Western Europe, 1815–1848." *American Historical Review* 71 (1966).

O'Brien, D.C. "Traditional virtues, feudal ties and royal guards: The culture of service in the eighteenth-century *maison militaire du roi.*" *French History* 17 (2003).

Oestreich, Gerhard. *Neostoicism and the Early Modern State,* edited by Brigitta Oestreich and H.G. Koenigsberger, translated by David McLintock. Cambridge: Cambridge University Press, 1982.

Olson, Mancur. *The Logic of Collective Action: Public Goods and the Theory of Groups.* Cambridge: Harvard University Press, 1965.

Oomens, C.A., and G.P. den Bakker. "Dutch historical statistics: 19th century population censuses." *Netherlands Official Statistics* 12 (1997).

Orloff, Ann Shola. *The Politics of Pension: A Comparative Analysis of Britain, Canada, and the United States, 1880–1940.* Madison: University of Wisconsin Press, 1993.

Parker, C.H. "Introduction: Individual and community in the Early Modern world." In *Between the Middle Ages and Modernity: Individual and Community in the Early Modern World,* edited by C.H. Parker and J.H. Bentley. New York: Rowman and Littlefield, 2007.

Parker, Geoffrey. "The limits to revolutions in military affairs: Maurice of Nassau, the Battle of Nieuwpoort (1600), and the legacy." *Journal of Military History* 71 (2007).

– *The Military Revolution: Military Innovation and the Rise of the West, 1500–1800.* 2nd ed. Cambridge: Cambridge University Press, 1996.

Peiter, Henry. "Institutions and attitudes: The consolidation of the business community in bourgeois France, 1880–1914." *Journal of Social History* 9 (1976).

Perkin, Harold. "Individualism versus collectivism in nineteenth-century Britain: A false antithesis." *Journal of British Studies* 17 (1977).

– *The Origins of Modern English Society, 1780–1880.* London: Routledge and Kegan Paul, 1969.

Perkin, Joan. *Women and Marriage in Nineteenth-Century England.* London: Routledge, 1989.

Perkins, Jocelyn. *The Most Honourable Order of the Bath: A Descriptive and Historical Account.* 2nd ed. London: Faith Press, [1913] 1920.

Petiteau, Natalie. *Elites et mobilités: la noblesse d'Empire au XIXe siècle: 1808–1914.* Paris: Boutique de l'histoire, 1997.

– *Lendemains d'empire: les soldats de Napoléon dans la France du XIXe siècle.* Paris: La Boutique de l'Histoire, 2003.

– "De la Légion d'honneur à la noblesse d'Empire: la recomposition d'un hiérarchie sociale dans la France révolutionnaire." *Revue européenne d'histoire des ordres et décorations: la Phalère* no. 1 (2000).

Popkin, S.L. *The Rational Peasant: The Political Economy of Rural Society in Vietnam.* Berkeley: University of California Press, 1979.

Pumphrey, R.E. "The creation of peerages in England, 1837–1911." PhD dissertation, Yale University, 1934.

– "The introduction of industrialists into the British peerage: A study in adaptation of a social institution." *American Historical Review* 65 (1959).

Ragin, C.C. *The Comparative Method: Moving Beyond Qualitative and Quantitative Strategies.* Berkeley: University of California Press, 1987.

– *Fuzzy-Set Social Science: An Analytical Approach to Social Theory.* Chicago: University of Chicago Press, 2000.

Razzell, P.E. "Social origins of officers in the Indian and British home army: 1758–1962." In *British Journal of Sociology* 14 (1963).

Read, Geoff. *The Republic of Men: Gender, Race, Women, and the Political Parties in Interwar France.* Baton Rouge: Louisiana State University Press, 2014.

Reddy, W.M. *The Invisible Code: Honor and Sentiment in Postrevolutionary France, 1814–1848.* Berkeley: University of California Press, 1997.

Richards, J.F. *The Mughal Empire.* Cambridge: Cambridge University Press, 1995.

Richter, D.K. *The Ordeal of the Longhouse: The Peoples of the Iroquois League in the Era of European Colonization.* Chapel Hill: University of North Carolina Press, 1992.

Ridgeway, Cecilia L. "Why status matters for inequality." *American Sociological Review* 79 (2014).

Ridgeway, Cecilia, Elizabeth Boyle, Kathy Kuipers, and Dawn Robinson. "How do status beliefs develop? The role of resources and interactional experience." *American Sociological Review* 63 (1998).

Ridgeway, Cecilia L., and H.A. Walker. "Status structures." In *Sociological Perspectives on Social Psychology,* edited by Karen S. Cook, G.A. Fine, and J.S. House. Boston: Allyn and Bacon, 1995.

Ridley, Jasper, *Lord Palmerston.* New York: Dutton, 1971.

Rihoux, Benoit, and C.C. Ragin, eds. *Configurational Comparative Methods: Qualitative Comparative Analysis (QCA) and Related Techniques.* Los Angeles: Sage, 2009.

Riley-Smith, Jonathan. *Hospitallers: The History of the Order of St John.* London: Hambledon, 1999.

Risk, James C. *The History of the Order of the Bath and Its Insignia.* London: Spink, 1972.

Robinson, Christopher. *French Literature in the Nineteenth Century.* London: David and Charles 1978.

Rogers, Nicholas. *The Press Gang: Naval Impressment and its Opponents in Georgian Britain.* London: Continuum, 2007.

Rohrbasser, Jean-Marc. "Counting the population. The multiplier method in the seventeenth and eighteenth centuries." In *Population and Societies* no. 409 (2005).

Roland, Alan. *In Search of Self in India and Japan: Toward and Cross-Cultural Psychology.* Princeton: Princeton University Press, 1988.

Rose, Kenneth. *King George V.* London: Weidenfeld and Nicolson, 1983.

Rosen, S.R. *Societies and Military Power: India and Its Armies.* Ithaca: Cornell University Press, 1996.

Rowe, J.H. "Inca culture at the time of the Spanish conquest." In *Handbook of South American Indians,* vol. 2, edited by J.H. Steward. Washington: Smithsonian Institution, 1946.

Roy, Kaushik. "Conventional war." In *Science, Technology, Imperialism, and War,* edited by J.B. Das Gupta. vol. 15, Part 1. New Delhi: Pearson Longman, 2007.

– "Military synthesis in South Asia: Armies, warfare, and Indian society, c. 1740–1849." *Journal of Military History* 69/3 (2005).

– *Military Transition in Early Modern Asia, 1400–1750: Cavalry, Guns, Government and Ships.* New Delhi: Bloomsbury, 2014.

– *War, Culture and Society in Early Modern South Asia, 1740–1849*. London: Routledge, 2011.

Roy, Kumkum. *Historical Dictionary of Ancient India*. Lanham: Scarecrow, 2009.

Rubinstein, W.D. "The end of 'Old Corruption' in Britain, 1780–1860." *Past and Present* no. 101 (1983).

Rule, J.C., and B.S. Trotter. *A World of Paper: Louis XIV, Colbert de Torcy, and the Information State*. Montreal and Kingston: McGill-Queen's University Press, 2014.

Runciman, W.G. "Heritable variation and competitive selection as the mechanism of sociocultural evolution." *Proceedings of the British Academy* 112 (2002).

– "The selectionist paradigm and its implications for sociology." *Sociology* 32 (1998).

– *The Social Animal*. London: Harper Collins, 1998.

– *The Theory of Cultural and Social Selection*. Cambridge: Cambridge University Press, 2009.

Ruwet, Joseph. *Soldats des régiments nationaux au XVIIIème siècle: Notes et documents*. Brussels: Palais des académies, 1962.

Sanderson, S.K. *The Evolution of Human Sociality: A Darwinian Conflict Perspective*. Lanham: Rowman and Littlefield, 2001.

Santosuosso, Antonio. *Soldiers, Citizens and the Symbols of War: From Classical Greece to Republican Rome, 500–167 BC*. Boulder: Westview, 1997.

Schalk, Ellery. *From Valor to Pedigree: Ideas of Nobility in France in the Sixteenth and Seventeenth Centuries*. Princeton: Princeton University Press, 1986.

Scher, S.K. "An introduction to the Renaissance portrait medal." In *Perspectives on the Renaissance Medal*, edited by S.K. Scher. New York: The American Numismatic Society, 2000.

Schimmel, Annemarie. *The Empire of the Great Mughals: History, Art, and Culture*. London: Reaktion, [2000] 2004.

Schopp, Claude. *Alexandre Dumas: Genius of Life*, translated by A.J. Koch. New York: Franklin Watts, 1988.

Searle, G.R. *Corruption in British Politics, 1895–1930*. Oxford: Clarendon, 1987.

Seward, Desmond. *Eugénie: The Empress and her Empire*. Phoenix Mill: Sutton, 2004.

Sharp, Andrew. "Edward Waterhouse's view of social change in seventeenth-century England." *Past and Present* no. 62 (1974).

Shatzmiller, Maya. "Economic performance and economic growth in the early Islamic world." *Journal of the Economic and Social History of the Orient* 54 (2011).

Silberman, B.S. *Cages of Reason: The Rise of the Rational State in France, Japan, the United States, and Great Britain.* Chicago: University of Chicago Press, 1993.

Simmel, Georg. "The sociology of secrecy and of secret societies." *American Journal of Sociology* 11 (1906).

Simpson, Brent, Robb Willer, and Cecilia L. Ridgeway. "Status hierarchies and the organization of collective action." *Sociological Theory* 30 (2012).

Skelley, A.R. *The Victorian Army at Home: The Recruitment and Terms of the British Regular, 1859–1899.* London: Taylor & Francis, 1977.

Skocpol, Theda. *States and Social Revolutions: A Comparative Analysis of France, Russia, and China.* Cambridge: Cambridge University Press, 1979.

Smith, J.M. *The Culture of Merit: Nobility, Royal Service, and the Making of Absolute Monarchy in France, 1600–1789.* Ann Arbor: University of Michigan Press, 1996.

– *Nobility Reimagined: The Patriotic Nation in Eighteenth-Century France.* Ithaca: Cornell University Press, 2005.

– "'Our sovereign's gaze': Kings, nobles, and state formation in seventeenth-century France." *French Historical Studies* 18 (1993).

Smith, P.B., and M.H. Bond. *Social Psychology Across Cultures.* 2nd ed. London: Prentice Hall Europe, [1993] 1998.

Snyder, T.R. *The Protestant Ethic and the Spirit of Punishment.* Grand Rapids: Eerdmans, 2001.

Spiegel, Gabrielle M. "Genealogy: form and function in medieval historical narrative." *History and Theory* 22/1 (1983).

Stafford, Fiona. *Reading Romantic Poetry.* Hobeken New Jersey: Wiley-Blackwell, 2012.

Stahl, A.M. "Coinage and money in the Latin Empire of Constantinople." *Dumbarton Oaks Papers* 55 (2001).

– "Numismatics in the Renaissance." In *The Rebirth of Antiquity: Numismatics, Archeology, and Classical Studies in the Culture of the Renaissance,* edited by A.M. Stahl. Princeton: Princeton University Library, 2009.

Stanhope, Philip. *Letters to His Son,* edited by James Harding. London: Folio Society [1774] 1973.

Stanley, David. "The Royal Victorian medal." In *Royal Service,* vol. 1, edited by Peter Galloway et al. London: Victorian Publishing, 1996.

Staum, Martin S. "The Enlightenment transformed: The Institute prize contests." *Eighteenth-Century Studies* 19 (1985).

Steinberg, M.W. "'The great end of all government ...': Working people's construction of citizenship claims in early nineteenth-century England and the matter of class." In *Citizenship, Identity and Social History*, edited by Charles Tilly. Cambridge: Cambridge University Press, 1996.

Steinmetz, George. *The Devil's Handwriting: Precoloniality and the German Colonial State in Quingdao, Samoa, and Southwest Africa.* Atlantic Highlands: University of Chicago Press, 2007.

Stephen, Leslie, and Sidney Lee, eds. *The Dictionary of National Biography*, 22 vols. Oxford: Oxford University Press, 1917.

Stevens, Fred. *Revolutie en notariaat: Antwerpen, 1794–1814.* Louvain: Universitaire Pers Leuven, 1994.

Stone, Lawrence. *The Crisis of the Aristocracy, 1558–1641.* Oxford: Clarendon Press, 1965.

– "Inflation of honours." *Past and Present* no. 14 (1958).

Stone, Lawrence, and Jeanne C. Fawtier Stone. *An Open Elite? England 1540–1880.* Oxford: Clarendon, 1984.

Strieter, T.W. "An army in evolution: French officers commissioned from the ranks, 1848–1895." *Military Affairs* 42 (1978).

Sutherland, D.M.G. *France 1789–1815: Revolution and Counterrevolution.* London: Fontana, 1985.

Suzuki, Munenori, Midori Ito, Mitsunori Ishida, Norihiro Nihei, and Masao Maruyama. "Individualizing Japan: Searching for its origin in first modernity." *British Journal of Sociology* 61 (2010).

Swart, K.W. "'Individualism' in the mid-nineteenth century (1826–1860)." *Journal of the History of Ideas* 23 (1962).

Swartz, David. *Culture and Power: The Sociology of Pierre Bourdieu.* Chicago: University of Chicago Press, 1997.

Swatland, Andrew. *The House of Lords in the Reign of Charles II.* Cambridge: Cambridge University Press, 1996.

Swidler, Ann. "Culture in action." *American Sociological Review* 51 (1986).

– "Cultural power and social movements." In *Social Movements and Culture*, edited by Hank Johnston and Bert Klandermans. Minneapolis: University of Minnesota Press, 1995.

– *Talk of Love: How Culture Matters.* Chicago: University of Chicago Press, 2001.

Szabo, F.A.J. *The Seven Years War in Europe, 1756–1763.* Harlow: Pearson, 2008.

Tallet, Frank. *War and Society in Early-Modern Europe: 1495–1715.* New York: Routledge, 1992.

Tamse, C.A., and Els Witte, eds. "Inleiding." In *Staats- en natievorming in Willem I's koninkrijk, 1815–1830*, edited by C.A. Tamse and E. Witte. Brussels: VUBPRESS, 1992.

– *Staats- en natievorming in Willem I's koninkrijk, 1815–1830*, edited by C.A. Tamse and E. Witte. Brussels: VUBPRESS, 1992.

Tartié, Agnès. "Les décorations dans la France révolutionnaire." *Revue européenne d'histoire des ordres et décorations: la Phalère* no. 1 (2000).

Taylor, P.A. "The celebration of heroes under communism: on honors and the reproduction of inequality." *American Sociological Review* 52 (1967).

Taylor, Robert. *Lord Salisbury*. London: Allen Lane, 1975.

Thériault, Gaétan. "Les 'prix de la valeur' (*aristeia*) et l'évolution des honneurs civiques à la basse époque hellénistique et à l'époque romaine: peristance des valeurs et mode de reconnaissance sociale." *Cahiers des études anciennes* 44 (2007).

Thompson Alastair. "Honours uneven: decorations, the state and bourgeois society in Imperial Germany." *Past and Present* no. 144 (1994).

Thompson, Christine M. "Sealed silver in Iron Age Cisjordan and the 'invention' of coinage." *Oxford Journal of Archaeology* 22 (2003).

Thompson, E.P. *The Making of the English Working Class*. Harmonsworth: Pelican, [1963] 1968.

Thompson, F.M.L. *English Landed Society in the Nineteenth Century*. London and Toronto: Routledge and Kegan Paul and University of Toronto Press, 1963.

Tilly, Charles. *Coercion, Capital, and European States, AD 990–1990*. Cambridge: Basil Blackwell 1990.

– *The Contentious French*. Cambridge: Belknap, 1986.

– *Popular Contention in Great Britain: 1758–1834*. Cambridge: Harvard University Press, 1995.

– "Why worry about citizenship?" In *Extending Citizenship, Reconfiguring States*, edited by Michael Hanagan and Charles Tilly. Lanham: Rowman and Littlefield, 1999.

Tooley, Sarah. *The Life of Florence Nightingale*. London: Cassell, 1911.

Toomey, T.E. *Heroes of the Victoria Cross*. London: George Newnes, 1895.

Towsey, M.R.M. *Reading the Scottish Enlightenment: Books and their Readers in Provincial Scotland, 1750–1820*. Leiden: Brill, 2010.

Tripnaux, Eric. *L'origine de l'Ordre de Léopold dans le cadre des 175 ans de l'Ordre, 1832–2007*. Brussels: Société de l'Ordre de Leopold, 2008.

"Trophies, war." In *Encyclopedia of Native American Wars and Warfare*, edited by William B. Kessel and Robert Wooster. New York: Book Builders, 2005.

Tudesq, André-Jean. "Les survivances de l'Ancien Régime: la noblesse dans la société française de la première moitié du XIXe siècle." *Ordres et classes: colloque d'histoire sociale Saint-Cloud 24–25 mai 1967.* Paris: Mouton, 1973.

Turner, J.H. *Human Institutions: A Theory of Societal Evolution.* New York: Rowman and Littlefield, 2003.

– Review of Runciman, *Theory of Cultural and Social Selection* in *Contemporary Sociology* 40 (2011).

Ullmann, Walter. *The Individual and Society in the Middle Ages.* Baltimore: The Johns Hopkins Press, 1966.

Vaillant, G.C. *Aztecs of Mexico: Origin, Rise and Fall of the Aztec Nation.* Garden City: Doubleday, Doran 1941.

Vale, M.G.A. *Charles VII.* Berkeley: University of California Press, 1974.

– *War and Chivalry: Warfare and Aristocratic Culture in England, France and Burgundy at the End of the Middle Ages.* Athens, Georgia: University of Georgia Press, 1981.

Valeri, Mark. "Religion, discipline, and economy in Calvin's Geneva." *Sixteenth Century Journal* 28 (1997).

Van den Broek, Andries, and Felix Heunks, "Political culture: Patterns of political orientations and behaviour." In *The Individualizing Society: Value Change in Europe and North America,* edited by Peter Ester, Loek Halman, and Ruud de Moor. Tilburg: Tilburg University Press, 1994.

Van Sas, N.C.F. "Het Grote nederland van Willem I: een schone slaapster die niet wakker wilde worden." In *Staats- en natievorming in Willem I's koninkrijk, 1815–1830,* edited by C.A. Tamse and E. Witte. Brussels: VUBPRESS, 1992.

Van Waelvelde, W. "The evolution of population census in Belgium." In *National Population Bibliography of Flanders, 1945–1983,* edited by M. Devisch and D. Vanderstappen. Brussels: Centrum voor Bevolkings-en Gezinsstudien, 1990.

Van Zelm van Eldik, J.A. *Moed en deugd: ridderorden in Nederland: de ontwikkeling van een eigen wereld binnen de Nederlandse samenleving,* 2 vols. Zutphen: Walburg, 2003.

Vasi, I.B., and Michael Macy. "The mobilizer's dilemma: Crisis, empowerment, and collective action." *Social Forces* 81 (2003).

Veblen, Thorstein. *The Theory of the Leisure Class: An Economic Study of Institutions.* New York: Modern Library, 1934.

Veldekens, Ferdinand Jean Josse. *Le livre d'or de l'Ordre de Léopold et de la Croix de fer.* Brussels: C. Lelong, 1858.

Vidal, Philippe-Jean. "Symbolique et héraldique ou l'union des inégaux dans le signe de la Légion d'honneur." *Revue européenne d'histoire des ordres et décorations: la Phalère* no. 1 (2000).

Vidalenc, Jean. "La société française sous la Monarchie constitutionelle (1814–1848)." *L'information historique* 37 (1975).

Vincent, Edgar. *Nelson: Love & Fame.* London: Yale University Press, 2003.

Von Hammer-Purgstall, Joseph. *The History of the Assassins,* translated from the German by O.C. Wood. New York: Burt Franklin, 1835.

Wagner, A.R. *English Genealogy.* 2nd ed. Oxford: Clarendon, 1972.

– *Heralds of England: A History of the Office and College of Arms.* London: HMSO, 1967.

Wahrman, Dror. *Imagining the Middle Class: The Political Representation of Class in Britain, c. 1780–1840.* New York: Cambridge University Press, 1995.

– *The Making of the Modern Self: Identity and Culture in Eighteenth-Century England.* New Haven: Yale University Press, 2004.

Wakefield, Andre. *The Disordered Police State: German Cameralism as Science and Practice.* Chicago: University of Chicago, 2009.

Waley-Cohen, Joanna. *The Culture of War in China: Empire and the Military under the Qing Dynasty.* New York: Tauris, 2006.

Walker, John. *The Queen Has Been Pleased: The British Honours System at Work.* London: Secker and Warburg, 1986.

Walker, K.W. *I Talk of Dreams. An Experiment in Autobiography.* London: Cape, 1946.

Wallis, Helen. "The cartography of Drake's voyage." In *Sir Francis Drake and the Famous Voyage, 1577–1580: Essays Commemorating the Quadricentennial of Drake's Circumnavigation of the Earth,* edited by N.J.W. Thrower. Berkeley: University of California Press, 1984.

Walpole, Spencer. *The Life of Lord John Russell,* 2 vols. London: Longmans, Green, 1889.

Wattel, Michel, and Béatrice Wattel. *Les Grand'Croix de la Légion d'Honneur.* Paris: Archives & Culture, 2009.

Weatherford, Jack. *Genghis Khan and the Making of the Modern World.* New York: Crown, 2004.

Weber, Max. *Economy and Society: An Outline of Interpretive Sociology,* 2 vols. Berkeley: University of California, 1978.

Wechsler, H.J. *Offerings of Jade and Silk: Ritual and Symbol in the Legitimation of the T'ang Dynasty.* New Haven: Yale University Press, 1985.

Weisz, George. *The Medical Mandarins: The French Academy of Medicine in the Nineteenth and Early Twentieth Centuries.* New York: Oxford University Press, 1995.

Wells, Colin. *The Roman Empire.* 2nd ed. Hammersmith: Fontana, [1984] 1992.

Whiting, J.R.S. *Commemorative Medals: A Medallic History of Britain, from Tudor Times to the Present Day.* Newton Abbot: David and Charles, 1972.

Whyte, W.H. *The Organization Man.* New York: Simon and Schuster, 1956.

Wilkins, P.A. *The History of the Victoria Cross, Being an Account of the 520 Acts of Bravery for Which the Decoration Has Been Awarded, and Portraits of 392 Recipients.* London: A. Constable, 1904.

Williams, D.G. "The Royal Society of Literature and the patronage of George IV." PhD dissertation, Harvard University, 1945.

Williams, Glanmor. *Recovery, Reorientation and Reformation: Wales, c. 1415–1642.* Oxford: Clarendon Press, 1987.

Witte, Els. *Politieke machtsstrijd in en om de voornaamste Belgische steden, 1830–1848,* vol. 1. Brussels: Pro Civitate, 1973.

– "Wijzigingen in de Belgische elite in 1830: een voorlopige verkenning." *Bijdragen en mededelingen betreffende de geschiedenis der Nederlanden* 94 (1979).

Wodey, Laurence. *Guide de recherches en histoire de la Légion d'Honneur.* Saint-Rémy-en-l'Eau: M. Hayot, 2002.

– "L'honneur: signe et insigne. la céation de l'insigne de la Légion d'honneur (1802–1804)." *Revue européene d'histoire des ordres et décorations: la Phalère* no. 5 *Du sentiment de l'honneur à la Légion d'honneur* (2004).

Wolpert, Stanley. *A New History of India.* 7th ed. New York: Oxford University Press, 2004.

Wyllie, R.E. *Orders, Decorations and Insignia, Military and Civil: With the History and Romance of their Origin and a Full Description of Each.* New York: G.P. Putnam's Sons, 1921.

Yan, Yunxiang. "The Chinese path to individualization." *British Journal of Sociology* 61 (2010).

– *The Individualization of Chinese Society.* New York: Berg, 2009.

Yates, R.D.S. "Law and the military in Early China." In *Military Culture in Imperial China,* edited by Nicola Di Cosmo. Cambridge: Harvard University Press, 2009.

Young, H.P. *Individual Strategy and Social Structure: An Evolutionary Theory of Institutions.* Princeton: Princeton University Press, 1998.

Index

Aali-Pacha, M.E., 163
Abbas II Hilmi Bey, khedive of
  Egypt and Sudan, 232, 322
Abbey of Cîteaux. *See* Cistercians
abbeys. *See* monasteries and
  monastic communities
Abelard, Peter, 251
Abercrombie, James, 275
Aberdeen Philosophical Society,
  210, 211
Académie française. *See* French
  Academy
academies, 122, 123–4, 134, 148–
  52, 377, 378
Academy Awards (Academy of
  Motion Picture Arts and Sciences),
  378
Academy of Dijon, 149
achievement/ascriptive
  orientations, 6–7, 28, 161
Adams, Julia, 349
adaptive affinity, 82. *See also* culture:
  selection; evolutionary theory
adaptive selection. *See* culture:
  selection; evolutionary theory
Adipati Mangko Negoro, prince of
  Solo, 321, 322
Adolphe, grand duke of
  Luxembourg and duke of
  Nassau, 287
Aelred of Rievaulx, 251

age of the communication medal,
  175–7, 186
Akbar, Jalal-ud-Din Muhammad,
  342
Albert, archduke of Austria and
  sovereign of the Netherlands,
  111
Albert of Saxe-Coburg and Gotha,
  prince consort of Great Britain
  and Ireland, 71, 240, 284, 285,
  315
Alexander the Great, 116, 172,
  186–7, 347
Amadeus VI, count of Savoy, 202,
  203
Amanoulloah Khan, king of
  Afghanistan, 322
Ambassadors' Medal, 144
American Sociological Association,
  378
American War of Independence,
  114
Amsterdam, 28, 103, 110, 188
Anne Boleyn, queen of England,
  Ireland, and Wales, 215
Anstis, John, 69
anti-Semitism. *See* Jews
Antwerp, 102, 153, 211
Appell, Paul Émile, 304
Appellate Jurisdiction Act of 1876
  (British), 314

Aquinas, Thomas, 221
archery, 115, 116, 117, 179, 182.
  See also cavalry and infantry;
  military
aristeia, 346
aristocracy: changes, 25, 37, 38,
  40–1, 54–5, 244–6, 315–17;
  childhood, 44; and collective
  action, 96, 166, 184; concept
  and membership, 14, 20, 40–1,
  93, 201, 204, 245, 259–60, 345;
  culture, 23–4, 32, 33–6, 44–6,
  48–50, 59–61, 68, 75–6, 221,
  277, 367, 368; decline, 3, 17–23,
  27–8, 29, 34, 36, 42, 316, 381–4;
  ennoblement and composition,
  25, 26, 29, 31–56 *passim*, 93,
  154, 158, 160, 163–4, 245,
  260, 269, 280, 288–9, 296–306
  passim, 310, 314, 364, 372; and
  honorific rewards, 24, 26, 28,
  33–5, 41–2, 146, 154, 156, 166,
  184, 259, 269, 313–18, 326–
  7, 377; institutionalization and
  legality of status, 55–7, 145, 146–
  7, 245, 258–64, 288–90, 302;
  and military, 44–5, 47, 48, 50–4
  passim, 131, 133, 134, 152, 153,
  164, 212–13, 315–16, 364; and
  monarchy, 128–30, 140, 155, 214,
  216, 217, 269; power of, 19–43
  passim; 57, 75, 76, 163, 210, 214,
  288–90, 364, 384; and other
  social groups, 35–6, 300–1, 310,
  314; status structure, 158, 260–1,
  269. *See also* landed gentry; status:
  inheritance of
Arms of Honour, 40, 145, 273
Armstrong, J.A., 74
Army Gold Medal, 292
art and literature, 9–10, 46–7, 48,
  51, 67, 69, 95, 150, 211, 222,
  226–7, 235, 303, 330. *See also*
  culture; literary prizes

Arthur de Richemont, duke of
  Brittany, 198
Arthurian folklore, 47, 64, 95. *See
  also* art and literature
Ashikaga shogunate. *See* Japan
Asquith, H.H., 339
Assassins, 63
associational activity, 123–4, 148–
  52, 195, 199, 207, 209–12
Athens and people, 354, 356, 361.
  See also Greece and people
Attica, 356, 361
Attlee, Clement, 288
Auber, Daniel, 251
Aucoc, Léon, 193, 234, 235–6
Augier, Émile, 35
Augustine, Dolores, 60
Augustus (Gaius Octavius), 62, 171
Augustus, Ernest, duke of Saxe-
  Weimar-Eisenach, 184
Augustus, Frederick, king of Saxony,
  138
Australia and people, 354, 358, 372,
  373–4, 375
Austria and people, 15, 111, 114,
  119, 129, 165, 184, 282
automaticity, 279, 292–3
Awards, Honors and Prizes. See Gale
  Research Group
Aztecs, 180, 344, 345, 354

Bacon, Francis, 280
badges and medals, 65–6, 70,
  73, 96, 167, 169–78, 185–92
  passim, 264, 292, 345, 346,
  359, 367, 370. *See also* badges
  under names of different
  honours
Bahadur Shah (Muazzam), emperor
  of India, 362
Balzac, Honoré de, 35
banishment, 198–9, 204, 208, 215,
  218–19
Banque de Belgique, 20

Barbezieux, Michel Le Tellier, marquis de, 120
Barni, Jules, 277
baronetcy, 14, 20, 31, 156, 244, 316. *See also* aristocracy
Bastille Day, 192
Bates, Percy, 309
Beauduin, Lucien, 308–9
Bedos-Rezak, Brigitte, 200
Belgian Congo, 143
Bell, David, 300
Beloff, Max, 33
Ben-Amos, Avner, 147, 228
Bennett, Arnold, 325
Bernard of Cairvaux, 251
Bertrand, Louis, 331
Bessborough, Frederick, third earl of, 39
Bienvenüe, Fulgence Marie Auguste, 304
Blake, Robert, 24
Blum, Jerome, 29
Bodin, Jean, 216
body ornaments, 183, 186, 346, 359, 360, 362, 363–4, 365, 370. *See also* honorific rewards
Boer War, 242
Boleyn, Anne. *See* Anne Boleyn
Boleyn, Mary, 215
Bolsec, Jerome, 208
Bonaparte, Louis-Napoleon. *See* Napoleon III
Bonaparte, Lucien, 273
Bonaparte, Napoleon. *See* Napoleon I
Bonaparte, Napoleon Eugene Jean Joseph, prince Imperial of France, 285
Bonapartists, 140, 146, 246, 276. *See also* Napoleon I; Napoleon III
Bonheur, Rosa, 325, 335
Booker Prize, 377
booty. *See* plunder
Boulton, D'Arcy, 46, 68

Bourdieu, Pierre, 9–10, 12, 57–8, 80, 83, 256, 264, 267–8
bourgeoisie: attitudes toward, 35–6; concepts, 14, 381–4; commercial and industrial, 22, 27, 35, 212, 305–11, 334, 381–2; culture, 23–4, 34, 35–6, 39, 42, 43, 48, 59–61, 76, 210, 250–1; and honorific rewards, 17, 25, 27–8, 31, 39, 46, 68, 75–6, 138; power of, 19–43 *passim*; rise of, 7, 17–46 *passim*, 74, 381–4; and self-improvement, 226; and the venality of offices, 49. *See also* lower bourgeoisie; middle bourgeoisie
bourgeoisie de robe, 316. *See also* lawyers and judicial professions
Boycott, Charles, 177
Brabant, 109
Brazil, 374
Brittany, 153, 210
Brontë, Charlotte, 53
Broqueville, Charles de, 317
brother medals, 303–4, 311
Bruce, Robert, 285
Bruin, Kees, 311, 313
bureaucratization, 112–13, 161–2, 263, 369, 370
bureaucrats, 14, 41, 46, 74, 86, 264, 280–1, 382. *See also* state employees
Burke, Edmund, 68
businessmen. *See* bourgeoisie: commercial and industrial
Buyskes, A.A., 372
Byron, George Gordon, sixth baron Byron, 59
Byzantine Empire and people, 344, 354–65 *passim*

Cadbury family, 308
Caesar, Gaius Julius, 171
cahiers des doléances, 73

Caille, Frédéric, 227, 229, 253
Cairnes, J.E., 250
Calvinists, 144, 207–9, 225, 238. *See also* religion
cameralism, 125. *See also* improvement and reform
Canada, 33–4, 372, 373, 374, 375
Candahar Medal, 142
canipu, 186, 345
Cannadine, David, 308, 322
Cannon, John, 269
caracole, 179
Caradonna, Jeremy, 149–51
Carbonari, 209
caricatures, 169
Carleton, Guy, baron of Dorchester, 336
Carlyle, Thomas, 226
Carnegie, Andrew, 186, 227, 228, 308
Carnegie Hero Fund, 227
Carnoy, Albert J., 304
Carrion de Nisas, Henry, 31
Cartier, George-Étienne, 373
Castille, 109
catapult, 117
Cattier, Félicien, 309
cavalry and infantry, 115–18 *passim*, 178–82 *passim*, 259, 342, 357–64 *passim*, 369, 370. *See also* archery; military
Caylus, A. C. Ph. De Tubières, count of, 150
Cecil, Lamar, 34–5
Cecil, Robert. *See* Salisbury
celebrities, 87, 256
census. *See* population management
centralization: and honorific rewards, 8, 64, 111–12, 162–3, 165–6, 281, 295, 341, 348–9, 360, 363, 368–70, 375; and lordship, 92; monarchical/parliamentary, 106–12 *passim*;

political, 8, 11, 54, 64, 92, 106–12, 214, 217, 281, 295, 341, 348–50, 355, 356, 357, 363, 368, 375; and the professions, 302–3; of royal courts, 107, 110, 113, 214, 217
ceremony, 38, 41, 71, 95–6, 183, 189–90, 191–2, 260, 284–5, 288; honours, 33, 71–2, 143–4, 146, 155, 191–3, 231, 233, 264, 268–9, 342–7 *passim*
Chalon-sur-Saône, 246
Chamber of Deputies (French), 22, 163
Chamber of Representatives (Belgian), 22
Chandra Gupta I, king of Gupta Empire, 118
chariotry. *See* cavalry and infantry
Charle, Christophe, 24
Charles Eugene, duke of Württemberg, 30
Charles I, king of Württemberg, 324
Charles I, king of Great Britain and Ireland, 31, 120–1, 156, 187, 188
Charles II, king of Great Britain and Ireland, 119, 129, 156, 158, 217
Charles V, Holy Roman Emperor, 36, 109
Charles VII, king of France, 198
Charlotte, princess of Wales, 38, 283
Charrad, Mourina, 349
Chateaubriand, François-René, vicomte de, 337
Chesterfield, Philip Stanhope, fourth earl of, 278, 337–8
chevrons de blessure, 318
chevrons de front, 292
China, 354; badges, 170; honours, 89, 93, 343–4, 354–5; individualism in, 376; literati, 51; military, 115, 116, 117, 179, 362; money, 170–1; state, 356

chivalry, 11, 36, 46–7, 64, 66–9, 95, 137–8, 152, 226–7, 367, 368; chivalric revivals, 51, 66–8, 152, 212; and individualism, 205, 221

Choson dynasty. *See* Korea and people

Christian IX, king of Denmark, 285

Churchill, John. *See* Marlborough

Churchill, Sarah, 215

Churchill, Winston, 288, 299, 338

Chwe, Michael, 87, 182

Cicero, Marcus Tullius, 51

Cistercians, 62

cities, 10, 21, 22–3, 101–5, 122, 126, 173, 176, 218, 361–2, 368, 375

citizenship, 132, 147, 219, 252, 258

Civil War (War of the Three Kingdoms), 53, 119, 129, 187

Clark, Peter, 210

Class of Moral and Political Sciences, 151

Clive, Robert, first baron Clive, 274–5, 297

Cobden, Richard, 280

Cochrane, Thomas, tenth earl of Dundonald, 231

cohorts (Legion of Honour), 155, 233, 237

coinage. *See* money

Coleridge, S.T., 250

collective action and organization: by classes, 381–2; contentious, 98, 106, 113, 330; effect of group size, 88; effect of population size and density, 98–105, 126–8; effect of social mobilization, 105–6, 126–8; elite mobilization, 128–30; as an explanation of honorific rewards, 4, 8, 77; function of honorific rewards for, 88–90, 176; mass mobilization, 130; in Medieval Europe, 91–6; pressures and

problems, 81–8, 105–6, 126, 130, 381. *See also* legitimation; military; motivation

collective/individualist interaction, 204–5, 206, 212–13, 220–3, 240–7, 250–1. *See also* individualism

Colonial Medal (French), 185, 189

Columbus, Christopher, 151

Commemorative Volunteer Cross (Belgian), 325

Committee of Public Instruction (French), 191–2

communication, 86–8, 167–93, 370. *See also* collective action and organization; coordination; communication function under various honours

Communist League, 209

communitarian/non-communitarian interaction, 195–212 *passim*, 217, 223, 228

Companions of Honour, 268, 299, 303, 309, 317, 323, 324, 335

comparative methodology, 348–53

competition: athletic, 67, 177, 186, 227–9, 252, 330, 347; domestic, 11, 97, 113, 357, 366, 369; in evolutionary theory, 80–1, 98; and individualism, 249; inter-state, 11, 97, 113–15, 229, 252, 357, 371, 377. *See also* prizes; status: competition

Comuto, Antonio, count of, 157

confraternities, 64, 199, 202

Congo. *See* Belgian Congo

Congress of Vienna, 138

Conservative Party (British), 21, 27, 39, 306, 307, 310, 338

Conspicuous Service Cross. *See* Distinguished Service Cross

Constantinople, 354

Constituent Assembly (French), 145

Consulate (French), 133, 145, 163

contorniates, 172
Cookson, J.E., 213
coordination, 86–7, 88, 99, 91, 96, 98, 178–83, 189–90, 213, 357–8, 370–1. *See also* collective action and organization; military; war
Coote, Charles, 232
Copenhagen, 149
Copley, Godfrey, 150
Corfield, Penelope, 23–4
Coss, P.R., 200
Coubertin, Pierre Frédy, baron de, 228, 229
Council of State (Dutch), 110
Council of State (French), 193
Count of Monte Cristo. See Dumas, Alexandre
countermarching, 180, 370. *See also* coordination; military
Counter-Reformation, 121–2. *See also* religion
Courbet, Gustave, 280
Court of Burgundy, 214
Cowper, Charles, 340
credentialism, 258
Crimea and Crimean War, 54, 135–6, 141, 189, 243, 284
Criminal Justice Act. See law lords
Cromwell, Oliver, 188
Crook, M.J., 243
Crusades. *See* religion
Cubells, Monique, 54, 158
cultural monopolies. *See* culture: differentiation of
culture: collections, 11, 58–75, 151–2, 169, 174, 176, 192, 367–8, 374–5; and communication, 168–78; concepts, 57–9, 382; cultural capital, 9–10, 44, 256–7; cultural change, 12, 23–4, 121–6, 225–6, 230, 355–6, 357, 364–5, 367–8; cultural power, 17, 43, 44, 76, 384; differentiation of, 9–10, 272,

357, 376; and honorific rewards, 9–10, 42–3, 61–75, 89, 90, 95; invention of tradition, 66, 68–9; and legitimation, 83–4, 89, 95–6, 137–48; military, 50–5, 61, 89, 115–16, 133, 164, 300, 315, 358–60; and prizes, 148–52; selection, 11–12, 58–61, 77, 79–82; and social change, 75–6, 105, 168; and social structure, 57–8, 59–61, 201–2, 255. *See also* collective/individualist interaction; Renaissance; royal courts
Curtis, Bruce, 252

Dangers Averted Medals, 187
Darwin, Charles, 228
Davies, R.R., 93
Dawson, Douglas, 268
de Hooghe, Romeyn, 169
decentralization. *See* centralization
democratization: and the aristocracy, 24; and honorific rewards, 6, 25, 28, 38–9, 46, 68, 277; political, 17; and Queen Victoria, 285
Denmark, 114, 152, 227
Deutsch, Karl, 105–6
Dewis, Louis, 303
Digges, Thomas, 179–80
Directory (French), 145
discipline: 196–7; bureaucratic, 223–4; collective/individualist interaction, 246–54; concept, 193; and honorific rewards, 140, 147, 230–54; corporate and pastoral, 202–23; in the Legion of Honour, 233–6; Medieval, 198–205; military, 92, 132, 135, 166, 181, 212–14, 370; in orders of knighthood, 202–5, 230–3; religious, 184, 207–9; in royal courts, 214–15;

and social structures, 95–6, 198–202; in voluntary societies, 209–12, 217. *See also* individualization

Discourse on the Arts and Sciences, A. See Rousseau, Jean-Jacques

Disraeli, Benjamin, 285, 286, 338

Distinguished Service Cross, 185, 292, 294

Distinguished Service Medal, 294

Distinguished Service Order, 166, 292, 294, 338

Dodu, Juliette, 324, 328

Don Quixote, 226

dona militaria (Roman), 72, 89, 93, 347–8

Doré, Gustave, 336

Doumergue, Gaston, 331

Drake, Francis, and medal, 187

Draper, William, 274–5, 297

Drejers Club, 150

droit annuel. See paulette

Druard, Philippe and Maxime, 331

Duby, Georges, 205

Duchemin, Marie, 327–8

Ducourtial, Claude, 327

Dudley, L.M., 116

duels, 50, 60, 260

Dumas, Alexandre, 60, 69, 227

Dumas, Mathieu, 132, 191

Dumons, Bruno, 298, 301, 305, 308, 331, 332

Dunbar, 188

Durieux, Joseph, 234

Durkheim, Emile, 80, 98

Dutch drill, 180–2. *See also* collective action and organization; coordination; military; war

Eagles (Aztecs), 344

ealdorman, 94

East India Company, 142, 188–9, 319

Easter Rising (Irish), 142

Eastern Roman Empire. *See* Byzantine Empire and people

Echo, The. See Grant, Albert

École polytechnique, 133, 315

École Saint-Cyr, 133, 315

economy: agriculture, 19, 20, 114, 123, 150; and the bourgeoisie or middle class, 19–20, 382; changes, 19, 105, 114; commercial, 15, 19, 52–3, 170, 256; competition among states, 113–14; and honorific rewards, 33; importance attached to, 24, 127; industrial, 6, 17, 19, 20, 114, 138; of the Low Countries, 20, 42; and military recruitment, 118; and non-state awards, 376; proto-industry, 19, 114; and social mobilization, 105; state regulation of, 126; trade, 19, 80

Edward II, king of England and Wales, 199

Edward III, king of England and Wales, 64, 95

Edward VII, king of Great Britain and Ireland, 268, 285, 287–8

Eguiluz, Martin de, 180

Egypt and people, 62, 72, 93, 148, 170, 183, 232, 322, 346, 354, 355, 368

electoral reform and franchise, 6, 21, 35, 130, 328, 329

Elgar, Edward, 269

Elias, Norbert, 214

Elizabeth I, queen of England, Ireland and Wales, 187

Emma, queen of the Netherlands, 270

English, James, 10, 377

Enlightenment, 23, 28, 221, 222, 225

Erlanger, H.J., 151
Ernest, duke of Saxe-Coburg-Gotha, 287
Ernst I, prince of Hohenlohe Langenburg, 285
Essex, Robert Devereux, second earl of Essex, 51, 215
Essex, Robert Devereux, third earl of Essex, 51
états: généraux,107, 109–10, 165; *provinciaux*, 107, 109–10, 111, 113, 128
Étienne de Laville, count of Lacépède, 266
Eugénie, empress of France, 325, 326
evolutionary theory, 11–12, 79–82, 98. *See also* culture: cultural change, selection
exhibitions, 28, 176, 309, 313

Family Medal, 326
farmers, 21, 22–3, 50, 59, 130, 134, 153, 311
Femina Prize, 377
Ferguson, James, 325
Ferry, Jules, 147
feudalism. *See* lordship
Fichte, Johann, 222
firearms, 117, 179–80, 183, 370
First Empire. *See* Napoleon I; Imperial nobility; Legion of Honour; Order of the Academic Palms; Order of the Reunion; Revolutionary and Napoleonic Wars
Ford, Henry, 308
Forrest, Alan, 153
Foucault, Michel, 200, 226
Four Days' Battle, 188
Fourez, Lucien, 160, 164, 299
Fourragère Medal, 246
frame (cultural), 83. *See also* culture

Franco-Dutch War, 120
Franco-Prussian War, 54, 119, 120, 247, 324
Frederick, prince, and duke of York and Albany, 275
Frederick Augustus, king of Saxony, 138
Frederick I, king of Prussia, 26,
Frederick II, king of Prussia, 30, 45
Frederick III, king of Prussia and German emperor, 71
Frederick William I/II, king of Prussia, 125
Frederick William III, king of Prussia, 30, 326
Freiburg, 125
French Academy (Académie française), 124, 149, 151, 377
Frevert, Ute, 60
Frey, Bruno, 33
friendly societies, 211–12
Fronde, 129–30
fuzzy sets, 351

Gale Research Group, 3
Garibaldi, Giuseppe, 280
Gaveston, Piers, 198–9
genealogy. *See* status: inheritance of
genes, 12, 80
gentleman, status of a, 24, 67, 152, 231, 302
George Cross, 247
George Grenville, 274–5
George I, king of Great Britain and Ireland, 215
George II (Augustus), king of Great Britain and Ireland, 215
George III, king of Great Britain and Ireland, 169
George IV, king of Great Britain and Ireland, 71, 169, 211
George V, king of Great Britain and Ireland, 72, 232, 237, 286, 323

George VI, king of Great Britain and Ireland, 232

Germany and people: aristocracy, 26, 60, 285; associations, 149; and Carnegie hero funds, 227; under Charles V, 109; culture, 23, 60, 222, 250, 285; honours, 34–5, 138, 232; improvement and reform, 74, 125; interest in genealogy, 55; medals, 173; wars, 114

Ghenghis Khan, 355

Ghuznee Medal, 142

Gladstone, Herbert, 307, 316, 330–1

Gladstone, William, 27, 41, 285–6, 307, 333–4

Glasgow, 23, 104, 105

glory: as an incentive, 152

Goblet, Albert-Joseph, 283

Goethe, Johann Wolfgang von, 23

Gold of Honour (Egyptian), 346

Goncourt Prize, 377

Good Cousins, 210

Goode, William, 244

Goodman-Kruskal *gamma. See* ordinal correlation analysis

Gordon, George, 177

Gorski, Philip, 125, 208

Gottheimer, Abraham. See Grant, Albert

Göttingen, 125, 149

Gower, Ronald, 336

grand chancellor (Legion of Honour), 37, 233, 235, 266

Grand Council (Legion of Honour), 37

Grand Council of the First Empire, 233

grandes écoles, 133

Grant, Albert, 310

Great War: armies, 119–20, 153; and businessmen, 309–10; and

honorific rewards, 35, 167, 232, 239, 246, 305, 306, 310, 317, 323, 327, 373; and social or political changes, 7, 34, 35, 153, 167, 306, 315, 317

Greece and people, 354; coinage, 171–2, 173, 186; cultural lineage of, 11, 51, 61–2, 220–1; honorific rewards of, 72, 148, 177, 183–4, 186–7, 346–7, 368; military, 115–17, 179

Grenville, George, 274–5

Groningen, 270

Grosvenor, Richard, second marquess of Westminster, 46

guilds, 64, 148, 199, 200, 206–7, 218

Guinness, Arthur, 308

Guinness, Benjamin, 308

Guinness, Edward, 308

gunpowder. *See* firearms

Gupta Empire, 354, 361, 362, 364

Gutenberg, Johannes, 168

Habermas, Jürgen, 23

habitus, 58, 267–8. *See also* Bourdieu, Pierre

Habsburgs, 107, 111, 114, 165, 260

Hague, The, 110, 282

Hague Society for the Defence of the Christian Religion, 151

Haile Selassie, emperor of Ethiopia, 322

Hall, William, 318, 374

Hammer-Purgstall, Joseph von, 63

Han dynasty, 343, 354

Han Fei, 343

Hanover, 138

Hanoverian dynasty, 53, 66

Hardinge, Henry, first viscount Hardinge, 293

Harrison, Carol, 210

hastiludes, 47, 50, 67, 96, 183

Hazareesingh, Sudhir, 191
Hazlitt, William, 68
Henry Frederick, prince of Wales, 51
Henry II, king of England, 26, 108
Henry III, king of France, 26, 156, 271
Henry IV, king of France, 70, 138, 140
Henry VIII, king of England, Ireland, and Wales, 215
heraldry, 11, 69–70, 73, 137–8, 170, 173, 201, 259, 260, 367–8
History of the Kings of Britain. See Monmouth, Geoffrey
History of the Orders of Knighthood of the British Empire. See Nicolas, Nicholas Harris
Hittites, 148
Hobbes, Thomas, 222
Holland (province), 110
Holland, Kingdom of, 15
Holy Roman Empire, 15, 153
Holy See. *See* papacy
honorific rewards: and collectives, 246–9, 251–4; criticism of or opposition to, 32, 33, 40, 41, 231, 246, 264, 270, 272, 277–80, 284, 288–9, 320–1, 327, 377; functions, 3–6, 88–90; global diffusion, 5, 372–6; inadequacy of current explanations, 4–5; as incentives, 3–4, 89, 156–7, 166, 184, 192; individualized possession, 244–6; inflation of, 46, 266; neglect by social scientists, 3; and non-European populations, 318–23, 333, 374–6; scandals, 27–8, 32, 162, 264, 310–11, 377; utility for understanding status, 5–6
honour medals (Dutch), 152, 304, 311, 312
Honours (Prevention of Abuses) Act (British), 307–8
hopae, 170

hoplites, 115–16, 179, 180
horse archers. *See* archery; cavalry and infantry
horticulturalists. *See* hunter-gatherers and horticulturalists
Hôtel Salm, 236
House of Burgundy, 37, 109
House of Commons (British): composition and elections, 21, 39, 308, 316; criticism of honours, 270, 279, 284; and monarchy, 284; power of, 109; source of elevations to House of Lords, 299
House of Commons (Canadian), 33
House of Commons (English and Welsh), 188
House of Lords (British): composition and elevations, 20, 21, 27, 29–30, 39, 157–8, 159, 164, 285–6, 299, 304, 310, 314–15, 316; constitutional changes, 21, 108–9, 262, 308; as an incentive, 157; power of, 21, 236–7, 262, 276; right to membership, 56, 314–15; size, 31. *See also* landowners; law lords
House of Lords (English and Welsh), 158, 236
House of Lords (Irish), 20, 157, 158, 236, 262
House of Lords (Scottish), 236, 262
House of Peers (French), 29
Hundred Years' War, 52
Hungary, 64, 233, 282
Hunt, Leigh, 68
hunter-gatherers and horticulturalists, 81, 92–3, 352–3, 361, 362, 366
Hydaspes River, Battle of, 172, 187

ideational processes, 121–2, 220–3, 367–8. *See also* culture
Ihl, Oliver, 28, 264
Île de France, 106

Imperial Austrian Order of
  Leopold, 374
Imperial court (Napoleonic), 37
Imperial nobility (Napoleonic), 25,
  28–9, 37, 40–1, 45–6, 140, 155,
  163, 245, 262, 289, 298, 305
Imperial Order of the Crown of
  India, 287, 327
improvement and reform: culture
  of, 75, 123–5, 133, 209, 357, 359,
  368. See also culture
Inca Empire and people, 186, 345,
  354, 357
incentives, 7, 89, 193; honorific
  rewards, 3–4, 89, 156–7, 166, 184,
  192; restricted, 85, 89, 152; social
  mobility, 152–3; unrestricted, 85,
  153. See also prizes
India and people, 354; literati, 51,
  364; and honours, 183, 232, 318,
  319–20, 322, 327, 344
Indian Distinguished Service Medal,
  320
Indian Mutiny, 242, 248, 318
Indian Order of Merit, 320
Indian (American) peace medals,
  163
individualism, 205, 206, 220–3,
  224–5, 229, 238, 246, 249–50,
  251–4, 375–6. See also collective/
  individualist interaction
individualization: concept, 196–
  7, 226; in Early Modern and
  Modern Europe, 224–9; and
  honorific rewards, 238–44.
  See also collective/individualist
  interaction; discipline;
  individualism
Industrial and Agricultural
  Decoration, 313
infantry. See cavalry and infantry;
  military
Ingoldstadt, 125
Innis, H.A., 87–8

Innsbruck, 125
instrumentalism, 122, 127, 133,
  357, 359. See also improvement
  and reform
intendants (French), 52, 120, 124,
  126–7, 128, 129, 158
Inuit, 345–6, 355, 357–8. See also
  Iñupiaq
Iñupiaq, 354, 355, 363
Ionian Islands, 143, 157, 373
Iroquois Confederacy and people,
  354, 363, 364
Isabella Clara Eugenia, 111
Islam. See Muslims
Italy and Italians, 123, 173, 189,
  209, 227, 310
Ito Hirobumi, 322
Ivanhoe. See Scott, Walter

Jacobites, 53, 138, 209
Jaffray, John, 339
Jaguars (Aztec), 344
James VI/I, king of Great Britain
  and Ireland, 31, 51, 156, 187
James VII/II, king of Great Britain
  and Ireland, 119, 138, 156, 217
Janissaries, 181
Japan, 171, 179, 233, 322–3, 343,
  354, 374
Jarry, Francis, 134
Jervis, John, 339
jewellery. See body ornaments
Jews, 286, 310, 333–4
Jiaolao, 89
John of Nassau, 180–1
Joseph II, Holy Roman Emperor
  and Habsburg ruler, 111, 119
Jouanna, Arlette, 49
jousts. See hastiludes
July Cross, 140, 185
July Medal, 140, 185, 188
July Monarchy, 22, 29, 70, 146, 155,
  166–7, 191, 218, 246, 273, 289,
  293, 305

Kaiser-I-Hind Medal, 320
Kant, Immanuel, 222
Karakorum, 362
Kaudelka-Hanisch, Karin, 35
Keen, Maurice, 49
Kendal *tau*. *See* ordinal correlation
    analysis
Keohane, N.O., 216
Kievan Rus', 354, 355
kinship: aristocratic, 52; as a basis
    of social organization, 91, 148–9,
    199, 201, 206, 213, 217, 251, 349,
    358; and collective action, 92, 93,
    120, 137, 201, 213; and discipline,
    198, 206; and Dutch elite, 42;
    familism, 376, tanistry, 358
Klagenfurt, 125
Klapp, Orrin, 227
knight bachelors, 27, 156, 164, 259,
    268, 367
Knights of the Bath, 203
knights of the shire, 108
Knights Templar, 63–4, 238
Kocka, Jürgen, 23, 383
Kolin, Battle of, 184
Korea and people, 51, 168, 170,
    171, 343, 354, 364–5
Korn Spruit, 248
Kristol, Irving, 33
Kuyper, Abraham, 238, 278, 280,
    307

La figure du sauveteur. *See* Caille,
    Frédéric
La Garçonne. *See* Margueritte, Victor
La Hogue, Battle of, 188
La Muette de Portici. *See* Aubur,
    Daniel
La Trémoille, Georges de, 198
Labiche, Eugène, 35
Labour Decoration (Belgian), 313
Labour Party (British), 308
Lafayette, Gilbert Motier, marquis
    de, 145

Lamb, William, second viscount
    Melbourne, 27, 284
Lancaster Amicable Society, 211
Lancelot, 49
Landa, Diego de, 34
landed gentry, 20, 24, 53, 94,
    261–2, 269, 314, 316. *See also*
    aristocracy; landowners
landlords. *See* landowners
landowners, 19–24 *passim*, 212, 269,
    317
Law, Andrew Bonar, 232
law lords, 236–7, 300–1, 314–15. *See
    also* House of Lords (British)
lawyers and judicial professions, 50,
    107, 212, 234, 300–2, 383, 386.
    See also professions
Lay of the Last Minstrel, The. *See* Scott,
    Walter
Le Machant, J.G., 134
Le Moyne, Charles, baron de
    Longueuil, 372
Le Tellier, François Michel. *See*
    Louvois
Le Tellier, Michel. *See* Barbezieux
Le Vavasseur de Précourt, Octave,
    234
League of the Just, 209
League of Outlaws, 209
Legion of Honour: administration,
    140, 233, 235; badge, 24, 40, 70,
    294; ceremony, 146, 191; and the
    collective, 253; communication
    function, 192, 193; composition
    and appointments, 24, 25, 28,
    159–61, 163, 166–7, 263, 273,
    277, 292–329 *passim*, 335, 337,
    374; corporatism, 233–8 *passim*;
    criticism of, 277–9; discipline,
    233–6; founded, 24; grades,
    24–5, 40, 146, 147, 260, 367;
    influences on it, 24–5, 36–7, 40,
    146, 192; its influence, 24, 73,
    192; institutionalization, 147, 262;

legal status, 147; for legitimation, 140, 141–2, 158, 159; and monarchy, 155; name, 25, 36, 146; old/new features, 24–5, 36–7, 40, 45, 62, 145–6; in political and ideological struggles, 40, 45–6, 145–7, 276–7; as a restricted reward, 32, 158–9, 166; size, 24, 26, 97, 146, 237; and status , 266–7, 273, 274, 292–304 *passim*, 317, 332–3, 336, 337, 377

Legislative Assembly (French), 132, 145

legitimation, 63, 74, 83–4, 86, 89, 91, 94, 96, 137–48, 156, 184, 252, 256, 264, 377. *See also* collective action and organization

Legrelle, Gérard, 278

Leighton, Frederic, 339

Leiningen, Ernest Leopold, fourth prince of, 285

Leipzig, 125

Leopold, prince, and duke of Albany, earl of Clarence, and Baron Arklow, 71

Leopold I, king of Belgium, 22, 38, 283, 284, 287

Leopold II, king of Belgium, 22, 143, 287, 373

les pékins, 274

Liberal Party (British), 21, 27, 39, 41, 162, 285, 306, 307, 310

Liberal Unionist Party (British), 306, 307, 339

Liège, 15, 102

Lieven, Dominic, 44

Lindsay, David, twenty-seventh earl of Crawford and tenth early of Balcarres, 25–6, 39

lineages, cultural, 11, 12, 65, 73, 230, 355, 367–8, 370, 372. *See also* culture: collections

Lipsius, Justus, 51, 228

literacy, 169, 222

literary prizes, 10, 376–7. *See also* culture; art and literature

literati, 35, 50–1, 61

Liverpool, 104, 105

livery badges, 173, 185

Livesey, Harry, 305

Llewelyn, Leonard Wilkinson, 309

Lloyd George, David, 286, 299, 307, 331

Locke, John, 221

Lockroy, Édouard, 273

London, 71, 101, 105, 108–9, 214, 217, 303, 310

longbow, 117. *See also* archery

lordship, 35, 47, 54, 91–2, 93, 95, 120, 137, 148–9, 198, 200, 201–2, 205, 213, 217

Loubet, Émile Francois, 331

Louis XIV, king of France, 30, 31, 53, 62, 65, 152, 154, 155, 169, 174, 213, 215, 295

Louis-Philippe, king of France, 40, 140

Louvet, Jean, 198

Louvois, François Michel Le Tellier, marquis de, 120, 131, 213

lower bourgeoisie, 311–13, 335, 386. *See also* bourgeoisie; working class

Lowland Cree, 346

Lugard, Edward, 243

Luxembourg, duchy of, 14, 55, 286–7

Lydia, 171

Macdonald, John A., 373

MacDonald, Ramsay, 331

Maeterlinck, Maurice, 331

Maintenon, Françoise d'Aubigné, marquise de, 215

maison militaire du roi, 54

Maitland, Thomas, 143, 157

Major, John, 279

majorat, 37, 245

Making of the English Working Class, The. See Thompson, E.P.

Malta, 66, 143–4, 157, 247, 373

Maltese Cross, 65

Malthus, Thomas, 98

Manchester, 104, 105

Mann, Michael, 24, 112, 126

Manning, Roger, 53

mansabar, 342

maquabuitl, 180

Margueritte, Victor, 235

Marie Antoinette, queen of France, 68

Marlborough, John Churchill, duke of, 164

Marx, Karl, and Marxism, 80, 98, 256, 381–4 *passim*

Masham, Abigail, 215

Matikkaka, Antti, 67

Maurice, emperor of Byzantium, 365

Maurice of Nassau, prince of Orange, 110, 180–1

Maxfield, Valerie, 348

Maxwell, Francis Aylmer, 325, 249

Mayans, 345

Mayer, Arnold J., 7, 34–5

Maza, Sarah, 35–6, 61, 226, 382–3

Mazas, Alex, 184–5

McCahill, Michael, 20–1

McCarthy, Maud, 335

mechanism: causal, 8, 10–12, 58, 341, 376–7

médailles du travail, 192

Medal for the Civil Services of Natives. *See* Star for Loyalty and Service

Medal for the Defence of Kelat-I-Ghilzie, 142

Medal of the Order of the British Empire, 239–40

Medal of Parliament, 188

Medal of Queen Elizabeth, 327

Medal of Saint Helena: ceremony, 192; communication function, 192; founded, 155; influences on it, 192; legitimation function, 140; and Napoleon III, 155; recipients, 294

medallions, 172, 173, 186–7, 346

medals. *See* badges and medals

Medici family, 174

Mélinand, Camille, 254

memes, 79–80

Mémoires pour l'instruction du Dauphin, 62. *See also* Louis XIV

Mensdorff-Pouilly, Alexander, count of, 285

mercenaries, 92, 119, 120, 121, 134, 178–9, 181, 212–13, 347

merit and meritocracy: and aristocracy, 23, 28–9, 44–57 *passim,* 73, 74–5, 161, 334, 343, 369; and the bourgeoisie, 24, 44, 48, 54, 74, 138, 161, 226, 369; evolution of, 54–7, 73–5, 245–6, 272, 357; and honours, 28–9, 245–6, 334–6, 369; measurement of, 358; in the military, 30, 32, 45, 47–8, 51, 54–6, 133, 343, 345; and the professions, 23–4, 73, 334–6

Merit Medal of the Republic, 374–5

Mexico and people, 189, 246, 374. *See also* Aztecs, Mayans

middle bourgeoisie, 386. *See also* lower bourgeoisie

middle class, 7, 14, 23, 24, 61, 273, 381–4. *See also* bourgeoisie

migration, 10, 105. *See also* social mobilization

militarism, 51, 62–3, 315, 357–9, 360, 364–5, 369–70. *See also* culture: military; military

military: and aristocracy, 23, 35, 44–5, 47, 48, 49, 50, 51–3, 56, 93–4, 153, 213–18 *passim,* 315–16; army size, 10, 51–2, 116, 117–21, 153, 154, 176, 178, 219, 348–9, 357–63 *passim,* 369; attitudes

toward, 52–4, 56, 63, 87, 132–3, 136, 141, 143, 176–7, 226–7, 333; changes in, 11, 54–5, 115–21, 135, 178–83, 219–20, 355, 369; competence and training, 45, 49, 55, 56–7, 115, 133–4, 161, 181; conditions of soldiers, 136, 213–14; demands on populations, 130; and discipline, 135, 207, 212–13, 228, 231, 235–6, 347; dress, 190, 213; heroes, 226–7; legitimation, 89, 95, 141–2; motivation of soldiers, 85, 89, 152–3, 166, 243; power of, 51, 52–3, 120, 129, 165, 358–9, 364–5; professionalization, 133–4; purchase of commissions, 50, 85, 120, 134–5; recruitment and composition of armies, 120–1, 131–5, 165, 219; rewards, 21, 25–6, 30, 45, 72, 80, 89, 93, 142, 144–7 *passim*, 152–4; 156, 163–7, 170, 184–93 *passim*, 231, 240–4, 273, 291–5, 299, 311, 315–17, 328–37 *passim*, 342–8 *passim*, 373, 375; and social mobility, 47, 152–3; and status structures, 269–70, 273–5, 291–5, 311, 312, 315, 333, 342, 344. *See also* coordination; culture: military; militarism; war
Military Cross (Belgian), 65, 185
Military Cross (British), 292
Military Medal (British), 185, 294, 324
Military Medal (French): 25, 147, 159, 185, 236; discipline, 294; founded, 25; insignia, 294; recipients, 25, 294, 328, 333
Military Order of William, badge: 185; composition and appointments, 318, 320–1, 372; discipline, 231, 235; founded, 73; influences on it, 73; legitimation function, 138; and monarchy, 42;

as a restricted reward, 166; and status, 337
milites Christi, 62
Millerand, Alexandre, 331
Ming dynasty, 170, 179
Mingjiang, 89
Mobile Guard (French), 147
modernization: concept, 14; as an explanation of honours, 6–7, 9, 17, 31, 41
Moheau, Jean-Baptiste, 128
monarchical centralization. *See* centralization
monarchical orders. *See* orders of knighthood
monarchy: changes in, 29, 38, 41, 75, 94, 217–19, 281, 284–5, 286, 288; and collective action, 94–6, 128–30, 137–40 *passim*, 214; and communication medals, 176; and gifts, 93, 95–6; and honorific rewards, 20–1, 26, 37–8, 70–2, 93, 111, 137–8, 157, 165–6, 232, 260, 269, 270, 271, 280–8, 315, 326, 339, 372; legitimation, 96, 137–9, 142, 148, 288; and military, 120–1, 217; and motivation, 96, 156–61, 165–6; opposition to, 53, 129–30, 283; political centralization, 64, 106–12, 113, 128–30, 165, 200–1, 295; power of, 21, 41, 42, 53, 64, 93–5, 106–7, 124, 128–9, 137, 157, 200–1, 214–19, 276, 280–8, 289, 339; relations with subjects, 92–3, 155, 200–1, 206, 215–17; revenue of, 112, 124, 129, 156; royal service, 54, 202; and spoils, 156–62, 217–18. *See also* royal courts
monasteries and monastic communities, 62, 63
money, 170–7 *passim*, 186, 342, 347, 367, 368, 370
Monghyr Medal, 319

Möngke Khan, 355
Mongol Empire and Mongols, 179,
182, 344, 354–61 *passim*
Monmouth, Geoffrey, 64
monuments, 174, 183, 190, 342,
347
Moore, Barrington, Jr., 353
motivation, 3–4, 83–96 *passim*, .
148–67 *passim*, 184, 340. *See also*
collective action and organization;
incentives
Mughal Empire and people, 181,
344, 354, 361, 362, 363
Mukerji, Chandra, 124
multiple regression, 351
museums, 9–10
muskets. *See* firearms
Muslims, 62–3, 344
Mycenaeans, 148
Myerly, S.H., 190, 213, 370
Mysore Medal, 320

Napoleon I: attitudes toward
wealth, 37, 45–6, 73; banishment
of Madame de Staël, 218; and
corporatism, 155, 233, 237; and
honours, 24–5, 36–7, 40, 62, 140,
145–6, 158, 164, 166, 191, 246,
262, 266, 273, 303, 311, 327,
332–3, 337; and military, 133,
155, 158, 164, 166, 246; old/new
practices and influences, 40–1,
145–6, 191, 192; and the public,
53–4, 169, 192; reconstruction of
state and society, 137, 158, 273,
311; rule, 22, 30, 110, 163, 218;
social origins of, 24, 45
Napoleon III, 22–3, 140, 155, 159,
192, 212, 246, 303, 325
Nassau cousins, 180–1, 370. *See also*
Maurice of Nassau
National Convention (French), 145
National Guard (French), 40, 147,
312, 386

National Service Order. *See* Order of
the Companions of Honour
Naval Gold Medal, 292
navies, 52–3, 56, 135, 275, 320. *See
also* military
Nelson, Horatio, 53, 227, 270, 278,
337
Neo-stoicism, 51, 207, 213
nerge, 182
Neuschel, Kristen, 205
New York Sun, The. See Trevor,
George
New Zealand and people, 372–5
passim
Newcastle, Henry Pelham-Clinton,
fifth duke of Newcastle-under-
Lyme, 293
Nicholas I, tsar of Russia, 282
Nickle, W.F., 33–4
Nickle resolution. *See* Nickle, W.F.
Nicolas, Nicholas Harris, 29, 154,
192
Nightingale, Florence, 136, 177,
288, 323, 326
Nizari Ismailis, 63–4
nobility. *See* aristocracy
noblesse d'épée, 52,
noblesse de robe, 50, 52
normalization, 197
Northcote-Trevelyan reforms
(British), 162
notability, 22, 24, 36, 212

O'Boyle, Lenore, 23
O'Connell, Daniel, 177
Oda Nobunaga, 179
Oestreich, Gerhard, 51, 207, 215,
228
Olson, Mancur, 85
Olympics: Greek, 186; Modern,
177, 227, 228, 229
*On Heroes, Hero-Worship and the
Heroic in History. See* Carlyle,
Thomas

Order of Andrew, 184

Order of Cambodia, 142

Order of Canada, 34, 375

Order of Charles III, 322, 374

Order of Christ, 310

Order of Generosity. See Pour le Mérite

Order of Labour Merit, 160

Order of Leopold (Austrian). See Imperial Austrian Order of Leopold

Order of Leopold (Belgian): badge, 70–1; composition and appointments, 26, 159–61, 163, 167, 292–329 passim, 331, 373; founded, 38; grades, 139, 260; institutionalization, 263; legitimation function, 139; and monarchy, 38, 283; in politics, 40, 263, 276; as a restricted reward, 159; size, 98; and status, 274, 278, 287, 292, 296, 299, 301–2, 304, 306, 311

Order of Leopold II, 143, 287

Order of Louisa, 326

Order of Malta, 144

Order of Maria Anna, 324, 327

Order of Maria Theresa: commemorative, 184; composition and appointments, 269; founded, 30; its influence, 30, 72–3, 367; and merit, 45; as a restricted reward, 164

Order of Maximilian Joseph, 164

Order of Merit (British): composition and appointments, 303, 323, 326; and the monarchy, 287–8; name, 320; and status, 268–9

Order of Merit (Indian). See Indian Order of Merit

Order of Military Merit (Canadian), 375

Order of Military Merit (French), 165, 263

Order of Military Merit (Prussian). See Pour le Mérite

Order of Military Merit (Württemberg), 30

Order of Nichan el Anouar, 142–3

Order of Olga, 324

Order of Orange-Nassau, 270–1, 312

Order of Our Lady of Mount-Carmel, 138, 184

Order of Postal Merit, 160

Order of Public Health, 160

Order of Saint Alexander Nevsky, 184, 322

Order of Saint Andrew, 184

Order of Saint Anna, 374

Order of Saint George, 73, 138

Order of Saint Henry, 30, 164

Order of Saint Lazarus of Jerusalem, 138, 184

Order of Saint Louis: badge, 40, 146, 184–5, 186; communication function, 184–5; composition and appointments, 164–5, 166, 269, 293, 295, 372; corporatism, 237–8, 239; founded, 36, 184; grades, 24–5, 146, 260; influences on it, 65; its influence, 24, 192, 367; institutionalization, 263; legal status, 145; and the Legion of Honour, 24–5, 36–7, 40, 146, 192; medal of, 187; and monarchy, 155; as a restricted reward, 164–5, 184, 166; significance, 36; size, 30, 97, 111, 146; and status, 266, 271, 278–7, 337

Order of Saint Michael, 156, 205

Order of Saint Michael and Saint George: ceremony, 72, 143–4; composition and appointments, 159–61, 295, 297, 322–3, 328, 331, 338, 373; corporatism, 231, 238; discipline, 231; legitimation,

143–4; as a restricted reward, 157; and status, 338, 340

Order of Saint Patrick, 39, 71, 156, 165, 230, 231, 299, 308, 310

Order of Saints Maurice and Lazarus, 374

Order of the Academic Palms, 25, 303

Order of the African Star, 185, 287

Order of the Anjouan Star, 143, 185

Order of the Annunciation, 322

Order of the Band, 64, 204

Order of the Bath: ceremony, 72, 231; changes to, 29, 31; composition and appointments, 156, 159–61, 165, 284–5, 295, 297–8, 299, 322–3, 331, 372, 373; corporatism, 66, 230–1, 238; criticism of, 54, 284, 294; discipline, 231–2; founded, 26; invention of tradition, 36, 66, 69; and monarchy, 284–5; political function, 156, 165, 278; size, 26–7, 97, 165, 166; status, 267, 268, 274–5, 278, 292–3, 294, 297, 338

Order of the Black Eagle, 26

Order of the Black Star, 143, 185

Order of the Black Swan, 203, 204

Order of the British Empire: badge, 70–1, 73; communication function, 185; composition and appointments, 25, 27, 39, 159–61, 167, 298–324 passim, 331, 335; criticism of, 310–11; discipline, 237; founded, 25; for legitimation, 142; less politicized, 276; size, 31; status, 39, 267–8, 291, 294–5, 296, 297, 301–2, 304, 312–13, 315, 326, 328–9, 336–7, 338

Order of the Burgundian Cross, 36, 37

Order of the Chrysanthemum, 374

Order of the Collar, 202–3, 204

Order of the Companions of Honour, 268, 299, 303, 309, 317, 323, 324, 335

Order of the Crown, 287

Order of the Crown of India, 287, 327

Order of the Crown of Rue, 138

Order of the Double Dragon, 374

Order of the Dragon of Annam, 142

Order of the Dutch Lion, 28, 36, 37, 42, 138, 271, 303, 319

Order of the Ernestine Branch of Saxe, 387

Order of the Garter: composition, 26; discipline, 204; founded, 95; influences on it, 64–5; its influence, 65; and other orders, 39; political, 156

Order of the German Eagle, 323

Order of the Golden Fleece, 204–5, 236

Order of the Golden Lion of the House of Nassau, 287

Order of the Golden Tree, 95, 203

Order of the Holy Spirit, 26, 156, 165, 266, 271

Order of the Hospital of Saint John of Jerusalem, 63–4

Order of the Immaculate Conception of Vila Viçosa, 374

Order of the Iron Crown, 322

Order of the Knot, 204

Order of the Lion, 143, 287

Order of the Oak Crown, 237, 287, 319

Order of the Paulownia Flowers, 374

Order of the Red Eagle, 322

Order of the Reunion, 266–7, 337

Order of the Rising Sun, 374

Order of the Rose, 374

Order of the Sacred Crown, 374
Order of the Sacred Treasure, 374
Order of the Ship, 204
Order of the Star, 204
Order of the Star of Africa, 143
Order of the Star-Cross, 326
Order of the Thistle, 36, 39, 66,
    138, 156, 165, 299, 331
Order of the Three Fleeces, 37
Order of the White Falcon, 184
Order of Vasa, 322–3
Orders in Council of 1870 and
    1871 (British), 162
orders of knighthood: badges
    and dress, 24, 96; composition,
    26, 156, 269, 281; corporatism,
    202–5, 231, 237–8; differences
    among, 24–5, 28, 29, 36, 40–1,
    45, 72, 73, 146, 237–8, 244;
    functions, 95–6, 137–8, 138,
    147–8, 155, 165–6, 184, 185–6,
    269; grades, 25–6, 259–60, 271;
    influences on one another, 36,
    37, 64–5, 72–3; and merit, 28–9,
    50; numbers, 30–1, 35, 40, 111;
    tradition of, 36, 64–6, 67, 68,
    95, 230–1
ordinal correlation analysis, 352
Organization Man, The. See Whyte,
    W.H.
Orléanist monarchy. See July
    Monarchy; Louis-Philippe
Ottoman Empire and people, 118,
    181, 354, 362

Pakubuwono VII, susuhunan of
    Surakarta, 319
Palmerston, Henry John Temple,
    third viscount Palmerston, 284,
    314–15, 323, 325
papacy, 63, 138, 204–5
paper, 88, 168–9, 186
papyrus, 88

Paranhos, José, 374
parchment, 88
Paris and people, 74, 101, 105, 107,
    124, 129–30, 214, 302–3
Parke, James, 314–15
Parker, Geoffrey, 182
parlements (French), 107, 113,
    129, 300
parliamentary centralization. See
    centralization
Parthians, 116
pastoral discipline. See discipline:
    corporate and pastoral
patrimonialism, 349
paulette, 112
Peacock, Thomas Love, 68
peasants. See farmers
Peel, Robert, 29–30, 46
peerage (British) See aristocracy;
    House of Lords
Peerage Bill of 1719 (French), 157
peeresses, 27, 236
Peiter, Henry, 382
Penal Code of 1810 (French), 289
Peninsular War, 154
Pereira da Silva, F.G., 163
Perkin, Harold, 249
Persia and people, 115, 116, 118,
    171, 322, 346
Persistence of the Old Regime. See
    Mayer, Arnold
Peterloo Massacre, 177
petite bourgeoisie. See bourgeoisie;
    lower bourgeoisie
Petiteau, Natalie, 298
phalerae, 170, 187, 347
Philanthropic Society, 212
Philip the Bold, duke of Burgundy,
    95
Philip the Good, duke of Burgundy,
    67, 109, 111, 203
Philip II, king of Macedonia, 172,
    347

Philip II/I, king of Spain and Portugal, and lord of the Netherlands, 109
Philipon, Charles, 169
physicians, 212, 273–4, 302–4
physiocracy, 123
Piccinino, Niccolò, 187
pickering, 212. *See also* coordination; war: methods of warfare
Picts, 66
Piedmont, 31
pikes, 117, 178–9, 180
Pirrie, W.J., 310
Pisanello, Antonio di Puccio Pisano, 173, 187
Pitt, William, the Younger, 27, 270, 275
plunder, 31, 153–4, 342, 345, 347
police, 126, 212
Polytechnique. *See* École polytechnique
Ponsonby, Frederick, 39, 73, 267–8, 327
Ponsonby, Henry, 268, 285
Ponsonby, Mary, 268, 327
Pope Sixtus IV, 187
population (demography), 11, 36, 80, 98, 105–6, 107, 113, 117–18, 126, 127–8, 176
population information collection, 127–8, 359, 360, 363, 365
population maintenance and extraction, 126–8, 357. *See also* population management
population management, 357, 359; global variations, 356, 365; and honorific rewards, 8, 357, 360, 365; and paper, 168
portrait coins and medals, 171, 173–6, 187
Portugal and people, 114, 154, 163, 310, 374

Porus, king of Pauravas, 172
Pour le Mérite, 30, 45, 164
power. *See* collective action; culture: cultural power; discipline; status power; symbolic power; and power of under aristocracy, bourgeoisie, military, and monarchy
Prague, 125
prasadapatta, 342–3
Pridi Banomyong, 323
printing, 88, 122, 168–9, 174, 175
prizes: art and literature, 9–10, 376–7; as incentives, 89, 148–52; individualized, 210, 371; legitimation function, 138; manufacturing, 313; prize medals, 177, 186; and status, 272, 302, 376–8. *See also* honorific rewards
processes: causal, 10–11, 341, 353; encompassing, 348–9
professional and administrative bourgeoisie, 22, 152, 381
professions, 386; attitudes toward, 301; and honours, 300–9 *passim*, 315, 334–6, 378–9; organization and associations, 124, 207, 302–3, 378–9; regulation of, 234; and standards, 160; status of, 24, 56, 73, 258, 302–3, 383
Proust, Marcel, 59
Provence, 54, 158, 164
Prussia and people, 26, 30, 34–5, 44–5, 71, 107, 114, 125, 164, 184, 326
psychological: benefits of honorific rewards, 3–6; benefits of military promotion, 153; effect of honorific rewards, 265; effect of military drills, 182; and individuality, 220; need for social bonds, 198; and self-identity, 222
Ptolemaic army, 118
Punjab Medal, 142

Qing dynasty, 170, 354, 362
Qualitative Comparative Analysis
  (QCA), 350–1, 352, 353

Ragin, Charles, 350–1
Raglan, FitzRoy Somerset, first
  baron Raglan, 293
rational choice, 3–5, 6, 10
rational egoism, 84–5
Rational Ritual. See Chwe, Michael
Reading Society of Antwerp, 211
Red Cross (French), 247
Reddy, William, 224
Reformation. *See* religion: Protestant
  Reformation
Regnum francorum, 106
religion: basis of Medieval social
  organization, 91, 137, 149, 201;
  corporatism, 207–9; Counter-
  Reformation, 121–2; Crusades,
  50, 201–2; decentralization, 92;
  decline in cultural monopoly
  of religious institutions, 122;
  discipline, 80, 207–9, 211, 226,
  228, 250; effect of religious
  reform on state and society, 125;
  European unity in Middle Ages,
  65, 201; and individualism, 221,
  226, 251; and monarchical orders,
  184; monastic communities
  and orders, 62–4; prizes, 151;
  Protestant Reformation, 121–2,
  207–9; religious orders, 199–
  200, 271, 326; secularization, 6,
  23, 145, 182; and the War of the
  Three Kingdoms, 129. *See also*
  Muslims
Renaissance, 50–1, 76, 123, 173–4,
  221, 222, 225
rescuers, 25, 227–9
Restoration (Bourbon): and
  honours, 25, 26, 38, 70, 155,
  159, 166–7, 246, 262, 293, 337;
  and the nobility, 22, 133, 245,
  262, 289; politics, 218; and Saint
  Napoleon festivals, 191
Restoration (Stewart), 158, 188
restricted incentives, 85. *See also*
  honorific rewards; incentives
retaining contracts. *See* lordship
Revolution (Irish), 262
Revolution of 1789 (French): and
  the collective, 141, 145, 252–3;
  consequences, 19, 22, 28, 74,
  113, 130, 132–3, 206–7, 217–
  18, 261, 263; and honorific
  rewards, 40, 62, 141, 144–5,
  188, 246, 263; ideology, 28, 73,
  145, 158, 221, 246; reactions to,
  68, 177, 266; re-organization of
  state and society, 128, 261; and
  Romanticism, 68; war and military,
  131–3
Revolution of 1830 (Belgian), 22,
  28, 139, 159, 188, 246, 301, 325
Revolution of 1830 (French), 22,
  36, 40, 188
Revolution of 1848 (French), 40
revolutionaries: and honorific
  rewards, 39, 40, 261, 273, 276
Revolutionary and Napoleonic
  Wars, 21, 114–15, 119, 120, 130,
  133, 237
revolutions (British), 217
rewards, 3–4, 84–5, 152–4. *See also*
  honorific rewards
Reza Pahlavi, shah of Persia, 322
Richelieu, Armand Jean du Plessis,
  cardinal-duke of, 120
Ridgeway, Cecilia, 256–7
Rinteln, 125
Risk, James C., 29
Roanne, 246
Roberts, Arthur Cornelius, 305
Roberts, F.S., first earl of Kandahar,
  Pretoria, and Waterford, 248–9

Robey, George, 338
Rockefeller, John D., 308
Rœderer, P.L., 29
Rogers, Nicholas, 131
Roman Catholics, 121, 156, 158, 206, 221, 251, 285–6, 315. *See also* religion
Roman Republic, Empire, and people, 354; administration, 94; coins and medals, 170–3; culture and cultural lineage of, 11, 51, 61–2, 173–4, 191, 220, 354, 358, 366, 368, 370; honorific rewards of, 62, 72, 89, 93, 184, 187, 347–8, 361, 362, 364; military, 115–16, 121, 148, 347, 358, 362; size, 361
Romanticism, 11, 64, 66–9, 138, 221, 222, 250, 368
Rooke, George, 188
Rothschild, Lionel Nathan, baron de, 286, 310, 333
Rothschild, Nathan, first baron Rothschild, 286
Rothschild family, 286, 308, 334
Rouillard, Pierre Louis, 303
Rousseau, Jean-Jacques, 149
Roy, Kaushik, 182
Royal Academy of Arts (British), 269, 339
Royal Academy of Painting and Sculpture (French), 150
royal courts: and aristocracy, 22, 217; banishment from, 198–9, 215; benefits, 56, 214, 346; as centres, 107, 110, 214; corporatism, 214–15; courtiers, 47; culture, 214; and military, 51; power of and power struggles, 107, 215, 217–18
Royal Order of Victoria and Albert, 326–7
Royal Society of Literature, 211

Royal Society of London, 124, 149
Royal Ulster Constabulary, 247
Royal Victorian Chain, 232, 287
Royal Victorian Medal, 232, 287
Royal Victorian Order, 185
Rule, J.C., 168
Russell, John, first earl Russell, 46, 74
Russell, William, 136
Russia and people, 30, 46, 72–3, 107, 114, 184, 282, 322, 374, 354. *See also* Kievan Rus'

Saint Andrew, 66
Saint Augustine, 62
Saint-Cyr. *See* École Saint-Cyr
Saint-Jean-de-Losne, 246
Saint Napoleon festivals, 191–2
Sainte-Geneviève Church, 145
Salisbury, Robert Gascoyne-Cecil, third marquess of, 21, 339
salons, 9–10
Saône-et-Loire, 298, 305–6, 331, 332
Sasanian Empire and people, 116, 171, 346, 354, 357, 361
schoolteachers, 273, 383
science, 122–7 *passim*, 150
Scott, Walter, 226
Scutari, 136
Second Empire, 22–3, 70, 140, 189, 191–2, 218, 227, 245, 323
Second Republic, 70, 146, 245, 294
secret societies, 209–10, 250
secularization. *See* religion: secularization
Ségur edict, 56
seigneurialism. *See* lordship
selection pressures, 77, 80–1, 97, 115, 137, 148, 168, 169, 176, 355–6, 357, 360, 361–4, 365, 368
selective incentives. *See* incentives: restricted

self, 220–3. *See also* collective/ individualist interaction; individualism

self-discipline. *See* individualization

Senate (Belgian), 22

Seringapatam Medal, 142, 292

Seven Years' War, 45, 56, 114, 119

Shang Yang, 343

Shelley, Percy Bysshe, 68

Shiites, 63

shooting societies, 148, 150

Shrewsbury, Charles Henry John Chetwynd-Talbot, twentieth earl of, 218–19

Sicily, 172

Sidney, Philip, 51

Silberman, B.S., 160, 263

Simmel, Georg, 210

Skocpol, Theda, 353

Smith, J.M., 54, 56

Smith, Sidney, 275

social confusion. *See* status structure: disruption of

social control, 8, 126, 142. *See also* discipline

Social Democrats (Dutch), 280

social mobility, 6, 9, 47, 56

social mobilization, 105–6, 122, 149, 216–17, 356, 357

social movements, 76, 79, 83–7 *passim*

Social Origins of Dictatorship and Democracy. See Moore, Barrington, Jr.

social regulation, 193, 340, 370. *See also* discipline; social control

Société des Lettres, 377

Société générale, 20, 309

sociétés anonymes, 20

Society for General Benefit, 152

socio-cultural evolution. *See* evolutionary theory

Spain, 15, 41, 109, 110–11, 114, 118, 129, 152, 178, 209

Spearman *rho. See* ordinal correlation analysis

Spencer, Herbert, 80, 98, 228, 250, 280

stadhouders, 31, 109–10, 165, 217, 283

Staël (Madame de), Anne Louise Germaine de Staël-Holstein, 218, 222

Stafford, William, 215

Stand, 383. *See also* Weber, Max

Stanhope, Philip. *See* Chesterfield

Stanislaw II, king of Poland, 30

Stanley, Edward George Geoffrey Smith-Stanley, fourteenth earl of Derby, 297

Stanley, Edward Henry Stanley, fifteenth earl of Derby, 310, 338

Star for Loyalty and Service, 319

Starkie, L.G.N., 338

state employees, 159–60, 161–2, 224, 295–7, 301, 306, 312, 332, 343, 358. *See also* bureaucrats

Staten generaal (Netherlands). *See états: généraux*

staten provinciaal. See états: provinciaux

States and Social Revolutions. See Skocpol, Theda

states. *See* bureaucratization; monarchy; centralization

statistical and non-statistical methods, 350–3

statues, 183, 346, 347

status: competition, 8–10, 12, 224, 257; 272–5, 336–40, 371, 377, 377–8; definitions, 13, 255–6; distribution is zero-sum, 265; and honorific rewards, 5–6; importance to people, 257; inheritance of, 14, 28, 37, 44, 45, 48–50, 55–6, 73–5, 94, 145, 158, 244–5, 261–2, 289,

302; institutionalization of, 13, 55–6, 258–64, 281, 288–90, 302; literature on, 8–10; Marxist treatment of, 256; as a mode of social control, 8; neglect in sociology, 256; and other kinds of inequality, 257; usurpation, 289–90. *See also* status power, status processes, status structures

status awards. *See* honorific rewards

status power, 12; in Bourdieu's conceptualization, 9; relationship with other sources of power, 44, 76, 256–7, 276; status distribution power, 14, 255, 268, 371; types of, 14, 255, 371

status processes, 5–6, 12, 255, 258–9; dynamics of, 65, 257, 275, 329, 332–5, 369, 371, 377–8; elucidated by honorific rewards, 6, 330; in literary prizes, 376–7

status structures, 265–72; disruption of, 265–70, 289, 319; and distribution of honorific rewards, 152; effects of, 258–71, 272, 278–9; effects of honorific rewards on, 291–336; stable/unstable, 371

Stein, Karl, baron von Stein, 74

Stephen, George, 373

stirrups, 116

Strategikon. See Maurice, emperor of Byzantium

Sun Yat-sen, 375

Sunnis, 63

susuhunan of Surakarta. *See* Pakubuwono VII

Sutherland, D.M.G., 37

Sweden and people, 114, 152, 227

Swift, Sarah, 335

Switzerland and people, 55, 117, 178–9, 209, 227

symbolic capital, 9–10

symbolic power, 9–10, 83, 256

Syria and people, 64

Tak van Poortvliet, Johannes, 271

Taku Forts, Battle of, 243

tercio, 178. *See also* military theory: of bureaucracies, 223; collective-action, 82–8; natural law, 222; psychological, 3, 5, 6; rational-choice, 4, 5, 6; set, 350; of status, 256; and typologies, 350. *See also* evolutionary theory

Thermidorian Convention. *See* National Convention (French)

Thiers, Adolphe, 147

Third Republic: ceremony, 227; collective/individualist interaction, 253; distribution of power during, 23, 218, 280–1; honours, 25, 147, 160, 163, 189, 192, 246–7, 262, 273, 277

Thirty Years' War, 114, 119–20

Thompson, Alastair, 34

Thompson, E.P., 59

Three Musketeers, The. See Dumas, Alexandre

Tilly, Charles, 130

Times, The. See Russell, William

Title, The. See Bennett, Arnold

Tocqueville, Alexis de, 277, 289

tool kit. *See* culture: collections

Toomey, T.E., 241–2

tournaments. *See* hastiludes

Tournus, 246

Townshend, Jane, 328

Towsey, M.R.M., 222

Trevor, George, 228

Tribunate (French), 32, 163

Trotter, B.S., 168

Turgot, Anne Robert, 222

Turner, Jonathan, 80–1

typologies, 349–50, 352

Tyrone, Hugh O'Neill, earl of, 215

Ullmann, Walter, 199

Ulstermen, 177

Umbeyla Expedition, 242

Union of British and Irish
Parliaments, 21, 109, 262
Union of British and Scottish
Crowns, 108
Union of British and Scottish
Parliaments, 108, 262
United States of America, 33–4,
374, 377, 378
universalistic criteria, 6, 161
universities, 50, 122, 149
University of Frankfurt an der Oder,
125
University of Halle, 125
University of Paris, 25, 303
unrestricted incentives, 85, 153.
See also collective action and
organization; honorific rewards;
incentives
urbanization. *See* cities
Utrecht, 110, 177

Van Nes, J.F.W., 319
Vauban, Sébastien Le Prestre de,
127–8
venality of offices, 49, 112, 124
Versailles, Palace of, 124, 215
Vespucci, Amerigo, 151
Victor Emmanuel II, king of
Sardinia and Italy, 310
Victoria Cross (Australian), 375
Victoria Cross (British): badge,
65, 73, 185; ceremony, 71;
communication function, 90,
244; discipline, 237, 240–1;
founded, 241, 248; legitimation
function, 142; recipients,
294, 318, 372, 373, 374;
status, 294, 318, 320, 323, 325,
330, 374
Victoria Cross (Canadian), 375
Victoria Cross (New Zealand), 375
Victoria, queen of Great Britain and
Ireland, 41, 71, 240, 249, 284–6,
310

Vienna, 125
Vigo Bay, 188
Villèle, Jean-Baptiste de, 337
Virtuti Militari. *See* War Order of
Virtuti Militari
Visigothic kings, 94
visual-entertainment awards, 378–9
voluntary societies, 209–12, 377–8

Wakefield, Andre, 125
Walker, John, 279, 296
Walker, Kenneth, 338
Wallonia, 19
Walpole, Horace, 156, 158
Walpole, Robert, 69, 157, 169, 278
War of the Austrian Succession, 114
War of Devolution, 120
War of the League of Augsburg, 31,
114, 120
War of the Spanish Succession, 114,
120
War of the Three Kingdoms. *See*
Civil War
War Order of Virtuti Militari, 30
war: magnitude of wars, 114–15,
357; methods of warfare: 86, 135,
178–83, 213, 341, 357, 369, 370.
See also military
water-based powers, 52–3
Weber, Max: conceptualization,
13, 255–6, 382–4; decline in
importance of status, 256
Wellington, Arthur Wellesley, duke
of, 53, 164, 169, 337
Wensleydale. *See* Parke, James
Whyte, W.H., 224
Wiggin, Henry, 339
Wilberforce, William, 177
Wilhelm Meister. See Goethe, Johann
Wolfgang von
Wilhelmina, queen of the
Netherlands, 270
Wilkes, John, 177
Wilkins, Philip Aveling, 241–2

William Louis, count of Nassau-Dillenburg, 180

William the Silent, prince of Orange, 109–10

William I (Conqueror), king of England and duke of Normandy, 108

William II/III, king of Great Britain and Ireland, 119, 129, 217

William III, king of the Netherlands, 270, 282, 286–7

William III/IV, king of Great Britain and Ireland, 231

Wilson affair, 279, 307

women: attitudes toward, 323–4, 327, 329; feminism, 327, 328; and honours, 323–9; literature on, 256; power of, 325; protection of, 203; and the status structure, 326–9

Woolwich Arsenal, 134

working class, 25, 39, 59, 61, 67, 98, 132, 148–9, 211–12, 218, 250, 311–13, 381. *See also* lower bourgeoisie

Wyndham Act (British), 21

Xerxes, king of Persia, 118

yangban, 364

Yi Banggwa, 365

Yi Sŏng-gye, 365

Yoshihito, emperor of Japan, 322

Zeeland, 109–1

Zulu War, 242

Zulus, 354, 363